384.417

00007738

ESRI

DEC - 6 1995

ESRI LIBRARY

D0311927

THE ELECTRONIC AGE
TELECOMMUNICATION IN IRELAND

The Electronic Age

Telecommunication in Ireland

Eamonn G. Hall

B.A., LL.B. (N.U.I.), Ph.D. (Dubl.), Solicitor

WITH A FOREWORD BY

The Hon. Mr Justice Seamus Henchy

OAK TREE PRESS

DUBLIN

The typesetting of this book
was produced by Gilbert Gough Typesetting
for Oak Tree Press, 4 Arran Quay, Dublin 7.

© 1993 Eamonn G. Hall

A catalogue record for this book
is available from the British Library.

ISBN 1-872853-35-8

Printed in Ireland by
Betaprint Ltd

Table of Contents

Foreword

The central and pervasive role of the electronic media in our lives today is such that this pioneering and comprehensive study of the development and regulation of telecommunication in Ireland must be viewed as a work of major importance.

While the juristic basis for the growth and control of telecommunication in this State will be found in provisions of the Constitution, in statutes, regulations, EC laws and international conventions, the author has recognised the importance of social, political and other considerations and has dealt with his subject in the wider context of systems outside of Ireland. As a result, the book should be of interest to all involved in modern methods of telecommunication.

The present era of telecommunication by electronic means has transformed, and will continue to transform, the way people live and work. The interplay of new and rapidly developing technologies opens up a vista of types of telecommunication the implications of which are not yet fully comprehended. This book, as well as reviewing the past and assessing the present by reference to developments both inside and outside Ireland, gives insights into what the future may hold. It is made clear that telecommunication technologies will continue to affect in fundamental degrees the way we live at home and the way we work in offices, factories, government departments, banks, hospitals, universities, libraries etc.

Not the least of the merits of this valuable work is that it deals with legal and technical matters in language that should be comprehensible to the average reader.

Seamus Henchy

(Judge of the Supreme Court 1972-1988;
Chairman of the Independent Radio and
Television Commission 1988-1993.)

Preface

Speech is civilisation itself. The word, even the most con-
tradictory word, preserves contact; it is silence which isolates.

Thomas Mann, *The Magic Mountain*

Electronic communication extends man's senses virtually to the
ends of the universe. This book describes the development and
regulation in Ireland of indispensable components of modern
society, the telephone, broadcasting and other electronic media.

The various divisions of the book (and its limitations) are
described in chapter 1. I hope that the book may be of interest to those
who are participating (and those who wish to participate) in the
current communications revolution, those involved in public service
and private broadcasting and the telecommunication carrier and
computer services (together with their lawyers and advisers). It is
also hoped that those interested in law, commmunications and
journalism, social history and politics — in the sense of the science
and art of government, may also derive some benefit from this book.
Those, whom many of us serve, who use the telephone, listen to the
radio and watch television may gain some insight into the services
that have altered the course of human communications.

Chief Justice William H. Taft, United States Supreme Court (1921-
1930), is reported to have explained his reluctance to review a case
involving radio broadcasting partly because it seemed like "dealing
with something supernatural". He wanted to put it off as long as
possible in the hope that it became "more understandable". I could
sympathise fully with the Chief Justice and now acknowledge a debt
of gratitude to those who have assisted in making the subject matter
of this book more understandable to me and to those who have
assisted in bringing this book to publication.

Professor William Duncan, Trinity College, Dublin, provided
throughtful vision and encouragement at a time when I pursued

certain studies in relation to the subject-matter of this book. The Hon. Mr. Justice Seamus Henchy wrote the Foreword, for which I am grateful. My colleagues, Patrick J.C. McGovern, solicitor, and Séamus Given, solicitor, experts in the law and regulation of tele-communication, read earlier drafts of the book and made many helpful comments and suggestions. Eoin O'Dell, barrister and lecturer in law, Trinity College, Dublin, read the text and I have benefited from his breadth of knowledge and interest in freedom of expression. Others, in a personal capacity, have read individual chapters and have made helpful comments: Gordon Drumm, Louis Garvey, Telecom Éireann; Tom Kenington, Department of Transport, Energy and Communications; Brian Mullane, Department of Arts, Culture and the Gaeltacht; Andraí Ó Broin, Telecom Éireann and Michael O'Keeffe, Chief Executive of the Independent Radio and Television Commission.

The National Archives, Elizabeth Gleeson, Law Librarian, Trinity College, Margaret Byrne and Mary Gaynor of the Law Society's Library, Jonathan Armstrong, King's Inns Library and Lydia Jackson, Librarian of the International Institute of Communications (London) and their respective institutions are thanked for their kindness and courtesy.

Margaret Burns patiently typed the manuscript and put up with an inordinate amount of revisions for which I am most grateful.

The publishers, Oak Tree Press, Gerard O'Connor and David Givens, were always encouraging. Other individuals provided support in various ways; Ron Bolger, Chairman of Telecom Éireann, Peter Charleton, barrister, Brendan Garvan, solicitor, Fergus McGovern, Chief Executive, Telecom Éireann, Gerard Lee, Senior Counsel, Michael Ryan, Company Secretary, Telecom Éireann, the Publications Committee of the Law Society and its chairman, John Buckley.

This book has been written over a period of time when I was in the employment of Telecom Éireann. However, the book has been written completely independently of that company and neither Telecom Éireann nor any of its officers are responsible in any way for the contents therein. Responsibility lies with me alone.

In a book of this size, it is inevitable that the reader and any reviewer will, despite best efforts, find some errors, hopefully only of a typographical nature. I am reminded of the words of the poet and dramatist, John Dryden (1631-1700), who in his Prologue to *All for Love* wrote:

Errors like Straws upon the surface flow;
He who would search for Pearls must dive below.

I am not so presumptuous to assure the reader of any "pearls" in this book. In fact, I am conscious of the judicial caution in *Tomlin v Underhay* (1882) that "mistakes are the inevitable lot of mankind". Accordingly, the reader and any reviewer may draw my attention to any inaccuracy (perhaps privately!) so that someday the matter may be rectified.

Eamonn G. Hall
Dublin

October 1993

Summary of Contents

PART III: THE REGULATION OF
TELECOMMUNICATION IN IRELAND:
DEVELOPMENT AND OVERVIEW

Abbreviations

AC	Law Reports, Appeal Cases (House of Lords and Privy Council) 1890-
affd	affirmed
AG	Attorney General
All ER	All England Reports, England and Wales, 1936-
art	article
BBC	British Broadcasting Corporation
C	Command Paper (UK) (1870-99)
CA	Court of Appeal
Can	Canada
Cd	Command papers (UK) (1900-18)
Ch	Chancery
ch	chapter
Cmd	Command Paper (UK) (1919-56)
Cmnd	Command Paper (UK) (1956-)
Comm/Ent	Hastings (US) Communications and Entertainment Law Journal
CFI	Court of First Instance (EC)
CJ	Chief Justice
CJEC	Court of Justice of the European Communities
COM	EC Commission document
DC	Divisional Court
D/Comm	Department of Communications
DPP	Director of Public Prosecutions
D/T	Department of the Taoiseach
DULJ	Dublin University Law Journal
EC	European Communities
ECJ	European Court of Justice
ed(s)	editor(s)
EEC	European Economic Community
Eur. Court H.R.	European Court of Human Rights
ex rel.	ex relatione
F	Federal

FCC	Federal Communications Commission
HC	High Court
HL	House of Lords
HMSO	Her/His Majesty's Stationery Office
ILRM	Irish Law Reports Monthly
ILT	Irish Law Times
ILTR	Irish Law Times Reports
Interception Act, 1993	Interception of Postal Packets and Telecommunications Messages (Regulation) Act, 1993
IR	Ireland; Irish Reports
IRA	Irish Republican Army
ITI Ltd/plc	Irish Telecommuncations Investments Ltd/plc
ITU	International Telecommunication Union
J JJ	Judge(s) of the High Court and Supreme Court
KB	Court of the King's Bench; also Kings Bench Division of the High Court 1901-1952 (UK)
L Ed	Lawyers' edition of the US Supreme Court Reports
LQR	Law Quarterly Review, 1885-
MLR	Modern Law Review, 1937-
Minister for Arts and Culture	Minister for Arts, Culture and the Gaeltacht
Minister for Communications	Minister for Transport, Energy and Communications
MR	Master of the Rolls
n	note
NI	Northern Ireland; Northern Ireland Reports
ns	new series
OJ	Official Journal of the European Communities
OECD	Organisation for Economic Co-operation and Development
P	President
para	paragraph
PO	Post Office
P & T	Posts and Telegraphs
Pl	Presentation number of a publication presented to the Houses of the Oireachtas of a series subsequent to July 1981
PTS Act, 1983	Postal and Telecommuncations Services Act, 1983
Prl	Presentation number of a publication presented to the Houses of the Oireachtas of a series up to July 1981

QB	Court of Queen's Bench; also Queen's Bench Division, High Court, England and Wales, 1875-1901 and 1952-
R	Rex (the King) or Regina (the Queen)
R & B	Radio and Broadcasting
reg	regulation
RTE	Radio Telefís Éireann
s	section
SC	Supreme Court, Senior Counsel
sgd	signed
SI	Statutory Instrument
S Ct	Supreme Court Reporter (US)
Sess	Session
SLT	Scots Law Times
SLTR	Scots Law Times Reports
S R & O	Statutory Rules and Orders
ss	sections
Telecom Éireann	Bord Telecom Éireann
TD	Teachta Dála (Dáil Deputy)
TS	Treaty Series
UK	United Kingdom of Great Britain and Northern Ireland
UN	United Nations
UNESCO	United Nations Educational, Social and Cultural Organisation
US	United States; United States Reports (US Supreme Court)
USC	United States Code
USCA	United States Code Annotated
V-C	Vice-Chancellor
v	versus, against
vol	volume
WLR	Weekly Law Reports

For Irene and Alan

PART I

Introduction

Stand anywhere in the quiet countryside, away from the crowded cities, ploughed fields or other signs of men's activities. Then your picture may well be the same as that of your forefathers, hundreds or even thousands of years ago. And yet, during the last few decades, a subtle change has occurred, which none of our senses can register. Radio waves, bearing messages in many tongues, flow ceaselessly around us. We can only hear and see them if we convert them to other waves to which our ears and eyes are receptive.

Preface to *From Semaphore to Satellite*, International Telecommunication Union, Geneva, 1965

There came a day when, without the slightest warning, without any previous hints of feebleness, the entire communication system broke down all over the world and the world as they understood it, ended. . . .

E.M. Forster, *The Machine Stops* (1911)

1

The Electronic Age

INTRODUCTION

Only a few lifetimes ago, information moved at the speed of human messengers. For thousands of years and until recent times, talking to others who were unseen and far away occurred only in mythology. Deities and evil spirits talked from the sky across the world—but not man. Today, the human voice can travel at the speed of light to any part of the civilised world. Electronic forces are directly and indirectly shaping our lives. We search for words to describe the phenomenon of change that is transforming civilisation. Some speak of the Information Age, the Global Village and the Space Age. The Electronic Age, the title of this book, is yet another description.

Telecommunication — communication at a distance — encompasses communication via the telephone and related communications services such as mobile telephony, paging services and the transmission of data by wire and microwave. The term "telecommunication" also includes communication by means of radio, television and cable services. Telecommunication systems affect the economic, political and social life of a nation or a state. The telecommunication network is the backbone of the information infrastructure of a country in the same way as a transport system is an integral part of the physical infrastructure of a country.

Every person, no matter how unimportant he or she may consider himself or herself to be, is a living piece of history. The story of how we communicate, how our parents and their parents communicated (which is considered in this book) is not merely of technical interest; it touches upon the social fabric. One way to endeavour to understand a society is to study its messages and communications facilities. The story of how mankind communicates and the restraints imposed upon man in so communicating is part of the story of civilisation.

Eugene O'Neill reminded us, "Man is born broken, he lives by mending, the grace of God is glue." The processes of telecommunication and the telephone, in particular, represent a form of glue. It is via the telecommunication processes that we hear good news and experience occasions of joy. Likewise, of course, we experience sorrow. Communications systems, like the telephone and broadcasting, facilitate the exchange of information and ideas. In this process, man's relationship with man is often profoundly affected.

The telecommunication sector (including computing and broadcasting) accounted in 1993 for an annual world turnover of over 500 billion ECU (IR£402 billion) with an annual turnover of over 300 billion ECU (IR£241 billion) in Europe.[1] It is estimated that by the year 2000 the telecommunication sector will be the third largest in Europe, after food and drink, and chemicals. In Europe, over 50 per cent of employment depends on the use of information and telematic systems. Further, stemming from its RACE programme (Research and Development in Advanced Communications Technologies in Europe), the EC enjoys a lead in the conceptual development of advanced communications networks and services.

This book considers the development and regulation of telecommunication in Ireland and the telephone and broadcasting in particular. Telecommunication is considered in this book as a single corpus; this is apt because of the convergence of relevant technologies. The book is divided into five parts.

Part I considers aspects of telecommunication in the electronic age and introduces the reader to themes which are considered later in the book.

Part II considers the development of telecommunication in Ireland. In effect, this section tells the story of telecommunication from the early days of electrical communication — the telegraph — to the present time.

Part III examines the various phases and influences in the regulation of telecommunication in Ireland. The term "regulation" as used in this book describes any intervention by Government to direct or constrain those involved in telecommunication. Regulation is one of the most difficult of governmental arts and has multi-functional interests in relation to telecommunication serving legal, economic, cultural and political ends. These various ends are intertwined.

Part IV examines the privileges, powers and duties of public and private telecommunication agencies including the Minister for Transport, Energy and Communications and the Minister for Arts, Culture and the Gaeltacht, Telecom Éireann, RTE, the Independent Radio and Television Commission and the Broadcasting Complaints

Commission. The final section, Part V, contains a general analysis and conclusions.

Apart from the Constitution of Ireland, the primary instrument of regulation in relation to telecommunication is statute law together with associated delegated legislation. In addition to relevant legislative codes, the *travaux préparatoires* of legislation are considered. Cabinet papers, files from Government Departments, decisions of the courts and regulatory agencies such as the Department of Communications, the Independent Radio and Television Commission and the Broadcasting Complaints Commission have also been considered. Comparative references have been made to the wealth of regulatory *dicta* in the United States and other jurisdictions. However, certain aspects of law which impinge on telecommunication such as copyright, defamation and contempt of court are outside the scope of this book.

Throughout the book, the reference to the Minister for Communications is to the Minister responsible for telecommunication with the exception of certain matters relating to broadcasting. The formal title of that Minister is, at present, the Minister for Transport, Energy and Communications.[2] The Minister responsible for broadcasting policy is entitled the Minister for Arts, Culture and the Gaeltacht referred to in this book as the Minister for Arts and Culture.[3]

Issues involving telecommunication in Ireland are considered in the context of the wider world. The words of the late Seán MacBride are instructive in the context of an examination of the regulation of telecommunication in Ireland:

> As communication is so central to all social, economic and political activity at community, national and international levels, I would paraphrase H.G. Wells and say human history becomes more and more a race between communication and catastrophe. Full use of communication in all its varied strands is vital to ensure that humanity has more than a history ... that our children are ensured a future.[4]

Seán MacBride was writing in *Many Voices, One World* (1988) which contains the text of the International Commission for the study of Communication Problems, chaired by him. The Commission examined issues relating to communications from the historical, political and sociological perspectives.[5]

Although the primary instruments of regulation in relation to telecommunication are the statute and delegated legislation, there have been other significant modes of regulation. For example, between 1926 and the establishment of the Radio Éireann Authority in 1960 (pursuant to the *Broadcasting Authority Act, 1960*), the national radio service in Ireland (Radio Éireann) operated as part of the Civil Service — as an integral part of the Department of Post and Telegraphs. Accordingly, in relation to broadcasting, the decisions of the Cabinet and Ministers for Posts and Telegraphs (as authorities directly responsible for the operation of broadcasting services), assumed an important significance. The telecommunication carrier service (the telephone) was also directly regulated by the Government and Ministers for Posts and Telegraphs prior to the establishment of Telecom Éireann in 1984. Cabinet papers and files from the Department of Posts and Telegraphs in relation to telecommunication up to 1960 have been made available to the National Archives since 1990. These archives are considered in this book.

There is a considerable body of deliberation in parliamentary debates of the United Kingdom and Ireland (in relation to pre-1922 telecommunication legislation) and of the Dáil and Seanad (in relation to post-1922 telecommunication legislation). There are also Government publications (in Ireland and elsewhere) and court decisions which have shaped the regulation of telecommunication in Ireland from the 1840s to date. These have also been considered. Comparative references have been made, where appropriate, to the wealth of case law of the courts of the United States in relation to the regulation of telecommunication. Where appropriate, the system of regulation in other jurisdictions has also been considered.

While *The Electronic Age* is the title of this book, it must be noted that telecommunication first became possible through the medium of electricity: one is conscious that the word "electronic" implies more than the term "electrical". An electron is the smallest supposed component of matter associated with (or consisting of) an invariable charge of negative electricity. An electron could be described as that invisible and almost infinitesimal bit of electricity. It was Joseph John Thompson, professor of physics in Cambridge, who discovered the electron in 1897. The study of free electrons led subsequently to the radio valve and the television receiver. But the telegraph and the telephone had been using electricity prior to the discovery of the electron. However, it was the science of electronics, defined by Handel as the technique of marshalling free electrons for the transmission of images, the recording and reproduction of sound, the storing and treatment of information and the automatic control of processes, that has become the nerve centre of modern power.[6]

Modern developments in telecommunications are considered in chapter 7.

THE MOST INFLUENTIAL MEDIUM

Cardinal Newman said of Napoleon: "He understood the grammar of gunpowder." In the same sense, many have learned and now understand the grammar of the electronic media of telecommunication. Television is the most powerful medium of communication and has impinged on the use of mankind's time like no other invention of the twentieth century — including the car.

Within a short time, television became a dominating force in Irish culture, re-orientating family life, virtually defining news and influencing politics. Almost all Irish homes possess a television set. Members of the average family spend hours each day in front of the set. In a particular sense, broadcasting represents an electronic extension of man himself. People are electronically projecting images of themselves to the community at large. This explains, for example, the competition to feature on radio and television; it is a struggle for coverage, for attention, whether the battle ground is the form of an election, an industrial dispute, or a church event. This struggle for coverage focuses attention on the editorial decisions of the broadcasters and leads to claims of bias. The statutory duties of objectivity and impartiality are considered in chapter 30.

Many argue that television in Ireland and elsewhere is partly to blame for our social ills. The provocative writer and media philosopher, Marshall McLuhan, in *Understanding Media* (1964), expressed the fears of many:

> Once we have surrendered our senses and nervous systems to the private manipulation of those who would try to benefit from taking a lease on our eyes and ears and nerves, we don't really have any rights left. Leasing our eyes and ears and nerves to commercial interests is like handing over the common speech to a private corporation or like giving the earth's atmosphere to a company as a monopoly.[7]

Marshall McLuhan exaggerated; but there may be an element of truth in his dictum. Senior civil servants and Government Ministers in Ireland displayed a marked antipathy over many decades to the participation of private enterprise in broadcasting in Ireland. This

sense of hostility towards private enterprise and its role in broadcasting is chronicled in chapters 11 and 12. It was not until the
enactment of the *Radio and Television Act, 1988* that private enterprise
was allowed participate effectively in broadcasting in Ireland.

Many have criticised the manner in which television programmes
are presented and allege that harm has been inflicted on Irish family
life. For example, the Irish Family League in a submission in 1981 to
the Joint Oireachtas Committee on RTE alleged:

> RTE is increasingly using its monopoly to disseminate what is
> objectionable ranging from vulgarity to open propaganda
> against the standards of morality and decency of the Catholic
> majority of their audience; and to the almost complete sup-
> pression of the views of those . . . who seek equal opportunity
> to defend these standards. . . .[8]

The Society to Outlaw Pornography claimed:

> It is not enough to charge that RTE is letting the Irish people
> down by not observing the mandatory code of standards. It
> must be arraigned for debasing and corrupting the Irish
> people.[9]

The St. Thomas More Society submitted that there was considerable evidence

> of widespread concern . . . about the moral standards of many
> of the programmes being broadcast by RTE and the failure to
> respect traditional Christian values in its treatment of contro-
> versial moral issues.[10]

Some argue that today the young are brought up by the mass
media instead of parents and that television has become a primary
agent in the socialisation process, replacing the church and parents.
However, few would go as far as Donald Wildman (1990), executive
director of the American Family Association, who stated that secular
television is a "mind-polluting tide seeking to submerge us all . . .
and overthrow our faith and our families".[11]

Senior civil servants responsible for the regulation of broadcasting
in Ireland and León Ó Broin, Secretary of the Department of Posts
and Telegraphs (1948 to 1967) in particular, were conscious of the
good and evil that television could generate. This was the substance

of Papal teaching which influenced the philosophy of those who were responsible for the introduction of the Irish television service. Papal teaching was specifically referred to in the First Supplementary Report of the Television Committee which was submitted to the Government in 1956.[12] The Television Committee, comprised of a group of senior civil servants in the Department of Posts and Telegraphs, quoted in the 1956 Report extracts from an address of His Holiness Pope Pius XII to delegates of the European Broadcasting Union in October 1955. The Pope referred to the good and bad which could come from television broadcasts as being both "incalculable and unforeseeable". He warned that regulators must do their utmost to prevent television from "spreading evil and error and [instead] making it an instrument of information, of formation, of transformation".[13] The Pope noted that apart from its influence on teaching in schools, television must be considered as becoming "a means to ensure the unity of the family around the fireside". He noted that the entertainment offered by television could contribute by uniting the whole family around the set. In fact, one has a vision of family audiences gathering nightly around the television set, much as our cave-dwelling ancestors gathered around the fire, for warmth and a feeling of togetherness. Few might have envisaged the situation in Ireland today where two-TV families are common-place. In some families, there is virtually a television in every bedroom. Now a member of the family can actually withdraw and watch television in complete privacy. The notion of Pope Pius XII of television being a means to ensure the unity of the family around the fireside is now a figment of the past.

Dr. Helena Sheehan in her admirable study, *Irish Television Drama: A Society and its Stories*, observed that in the 1960s, priests, politicians and patriarchs in Ireland wanted to keep the rules of television simple.[14] She noted that nuns and priests featured in early television drama. The existence of God was never doubted; the priest was often a mediator; Catholic church dogma defined what was moral or immoral. Although there was sin in Irish television drama, transgressions were recognised as sin, straying from the true path. These features were evident, for example, in "The Riordans", the serial set in the fictional village of Leestown in the County of Kilkenny which was transmitted on RTE from 1965 to 1979 and in "Tolka Row", the domestic soap opera set in an urban setting, which was transmitted on RTE from 1964 to 1968.

Wesley Burrowes has noted that Irish viewers could accept sex and sadism as long as it was foreign; the strictest standards applied to what RTE produced.[15] An example of this was the Irish television serial called "The Spike" broadcast in 1978. In mid run, a storm of protest followed an infamous nude scene. Brother Vivian Cassells called on RTE to take the serial off the television and to "consign the remaining six [episodes] to the obscurity they deserve".[16] The founder of the League of Decency, Mr. J.B. Murray, was reported to have suffered a heart attack because of the stress caused by the showing of the nude scene on "The Spike" television series. Apparently, in an agitated state, he was telephoning the newspapers to complain about the "filthy play" when he suffered the attack.[17]

There is a natural temptation for RTE to eschew modern issues particularly in terms of political drama. Michael D. Higgins, who in 1993 became Minister responsible for broadcasting, summed up this issue in 1984:

> The gatekeepers of [Irish] television and film feel yesterday is safely within the perimeter of the allowable. Today's structures are without. Nostalgia as a convention prevails. Realism is the realism of the past . . . they make programmes about dead and dying radicals and movements long gone, rather than the messy and dangerous present.[18]

The "Late Late Show" on RTE, more than any other programme, has aired many social issues. The "Late Late Show" hosted by Gay Byrne started in the summer of 1962. Gay Byrne understood, more than most, the grammar of the media. On occasions, the "Late Late Show" aroused fierce passions. No account of the electronic era in the context of broadcasting could omit Gay Byrne or the "Late Late Show". One incident which is printed indelibly in the mind of those who lived through the 1960s was the "Bishop and the Nightie" incident. At one point in a game on the "Late Late Show" on February 12, 1966, a woman was asked the colour of her nightdress on her wedding night. After some hesitation, the lady ventured to suggest she had worn none. There were roars of laughter on the show and there was an extensive round of applause. The Bishop of Clonfert, Dr. Ryan, protested vigorously at the inclusion of such a question and others took up the issue. Next morning the Bishop in his sermon lambasted RTE and the programme:

> I regret having to commence my sermon today with a vigorous protest against the contents of the Late Late Show on Telefís Éireann last night. Many of you, I am sure, will have seen the

programme: the fewer the young people that saw it the better.

I know you will all agree with me when I describe it as most objectionable. I am referring to certain morally — or rather immorally — suggestive parts of the show, which were completely unworthy of Irish television, unworthy of Irish producers, unworthy of Irish audiences for whom the programme was destined, unworthy of a public service which is being maintained by public monies contributed in taxes by Irish people.

Surely Irish television is capable of producing, at least, less debasing and less disgraceful entertainment: surely if we want to look at television, we are entitled to see a programme that is more in keeping with moral standards traditional in our Catholic country.

I have registered my protest, I ask you to do the same, in any manner you think fit, so as to show the producers in Irish television that you, as decent Irish Catholics, will not tolerate programmes of this nature.[19]

The Bishop was a powerful figure. Loughrea Town Commissioners in County Galway congratulated His Lordship over the protest. One speaker noted: "It is a dirty programme that should be abolished altogether."[20] Meath Vocational Education Committee, for example, complained that the show displayed "mediocrity, antinational tone and recently low moral tone".[21] The "Late Late Show" and Gay Byrne have been described by Maurice Earls (1984) as functioning, perhaps unwittingly, "as something of a mid-wife to contemporary Irish liberalism".[22]

Television has been blamed for contributing to violent behaviour.[23] Violence and trauma involving injury and death are more common than the common cold on certain television programmes; yet rarely is pain, suffering, disability or disfigurement featured as a consequence of violence. Many demand proof of a direct causal link between violent behaviour on the screen and off. It is impossible, short of general confessions, to establish definitively such a direct causal relationship. Yet this does not exonerate media violence. The UK Broadcasting Standards Council, in the absence of a definitive answer to desensitisation or imitation in relation to television violence, takes the view "that a society which delights in or encourages cruelty or brutality for its own sake is an ugly society, set on a path of self-destruction".[24] RTE has guidelines in relation to standards of taste and decency in the context of portrayal of violence and sex on radio and television;[25] these guidelines are considered in chapter 19.

There is the view that too much crime is reported on television. Some have suggested, for example, that RTE's Crimeline television programme which re-enacts crime scenes in an effort to jog memories and thus assist in solving crime, indirectly teaches others to engage in crime — the copycat phenomenon. This charge is not new. Anthony Comstock, founder and secretary of the New York Society for the Suppression of Vice (1883) was convinced that sensational news reports of crime and corruption were destroying American youth. He noted:

> They make a pure mind almost impossible. They open the way for the grossest evils. Foul thoughts are the precursors of foul actions.[26]

Certainly, we must endeavour to avoid the situation described by Howard Rosenberg, a Pulitzer Prize-winning television critic for the *Los Angeles Times* (1992) where, "increasingly, violent crime is part of the plot, as TV programs continue to bypass the ordinary and define society by the deviant".[27] Violence should not be hidden, but it should not be over emphasised. Violence in the context of its regulation on radio and television is considered in chapter 19. Many civil cases, where the basic conflicts in our democratic society are determined, are ignored by the electronic media.

We must be careful about blaming the electronic media and television in particular for encouraging crime. In the former USSR, Stalin — the "father of the people" applied the Marxist doctrine of withering away of crime; accordingly, in 1934 he banned the publication of any summary statistics on crime and curtailed the reporting of crime in the media. In power, Khrushchev (1958-1964), although not as severe as Stalin, also prohibited the publication of statistics on crime. Leonid Brezhnev (1964-1982), who displaced Khrushchev, preserved his predecessor's ideological philosophy on the coverage of crime. Sensationalism was permitted only for "political criminals". Under Mikhail Gorbachev, who came to prominence in 1985, crime statistics were made available from 1989. Alexei Izyumov, a columnist for *Newsweek*, reported in 1992 that the number of murders in the former USSR had been approximately equal to that of the United States at a time when the possession of firearms in the former USSR was strictly prohibited.[28] The media, including the electronic media in the former USSR, now fully report crime in "breathtaking disclosures".[29]

On the positive side, television does lead to some talk among siblings. There is also frequent interpretation of television by older siblings for younger ones. Comments by parents like "violence is evil", "we should not sort out problems that way", and other interpretative statements can lead to something positive. Studies also show positive aspects in relation to tactile communication between mother and child which increased during co-viewing of television.[30] Further, siblings viewing the same programme, often share laughter. Television is not always silent. There is often talk about the performance of the actors and the plot; these exchanges should establish parents' knowledge or wisdom. Behaviour on television can act as a model — as a prescription or proscription.

Despite all the gloomy talk, television has not destroyed the family or crippled young viewers in Ireland in an intellectual sense. Undoubtedly, television has influenced views and indeed often in a subtle manner. But television has been an instrument of positive education. Robert Abelman has rightly noted that living in a family has never been easy. One need only read the Bible to discover that marital deceit, sibling rivalry, incest, abusive husbands and parents, and family violence are not inventions of the late twentieth century.[31] Television can be both a positive and negative influence on the family depending on how it is used.

INSTANTANEITY

The electronic media of telecommunication have brought us instantaneity; this may be a blessing in many senses but it brings its own difficulties. The fax machine, electronic mail, electronic pagers and cellular telephones can ensure instant and ubiquitous communication every second of the day. A few short years ago, a request for legal advice would be answered by a call for the relevant papers. That ensured at least a 24 hour respite (and perhaps an opportunity to reflect on the issue); the file had to be marked in and out of the registry and delivered by messenger. Today, the papers arrive by fax within minutes.

The linking of computers with telecommunication networks has delivered a rich harvest of benefits. Instantaneous communication has brought with it many benefits; the cruel waste of those who lost their lives in the Battle of New Orleans (1814), a few lifetimes past, would in the future be avoided. In that battle of the war between Great Britain and the United States, over 2,000 soldiers died.

Unknown to those in the battle, the war had been ended by treaty some two weeks earlier.

Today, however, there is less breathing space; we are being habituated to ever shortening time frames. The lap-top computer, the fax machine, the cellular telephone have become, in the words of a workaholic, "like nirvana". As a consequence, there may be the tendency to treat each other as infinitely accessible machines.

The mass of information and speed with which information passing over telecommunication facilities can take hold can have serious consequences. This is particularly so in the financial services sector. Take Black Monday, for example. On Monday 19, 1987, the New York stock exchange collapsed. The Dow Jones industrial average plunged 508 points and lost 25 per cent of its value. The panic selling of stocks set off computers programmed to respond to such events. Computers placed orders, causing other computers to place other orders. Investors in markets in London and Tokyo were monitoring, responding and contributing to the downward spiral in the United States.[32] Such trading would not have been possible without the links of computers and telecommunication networks. There was little time for Government or business to take meaningful action. Valuable lessons have, it is hoped, been learned.

Instantaneous telecommunication facilitates what *Punch* in 1854 termed the "quick fudge".[33] In fact, *Punch* used the term "quick fudge" when complaining of telegraphic "fibs":

> What horrid fibs by that electric wire
> Are flashed about! What falsehood are its shocks,
> Oh! rather let us have the fact that creeps
> Comparatively by the Post so slow
> Than the quick fudge which like the lightning leaps
> And makes us credit that which is not so.[34]

This was long before the invention and use of the adjective "phoney" or, to coin a new word, the "tellie" — the broadcast equivalent of phoney, a fib told on the broadcasting media.

The "quick fudge", the "phoney" comment, the "tellie", leads to a serious issue. Too much is expected of the interviewee on radio and television; we rely too much in both a legal and moral sense on the instant word voiced on the electronic media. Mary Kelly in *Television and Irish Society* (1985) caught the awesome atmosphere of the broadcasting presenter who interviews persons on radio and television. She mentioned Brian Farrell, one of RTE's most celebrated interviewers, who was then one of the principal interviewers on the current affairs television programme "Today Tonight":

> [Brian Farrell] thus drew on the news-values of immediacy, elite involvement, controversy and conflict, establishing the importance of the item and his own central role in investigating it, while his authority to ask hard questions was authenticated by the established nature and credibility of the programme, ritually maintained and reproduced in the programme music and logo, by the close-ups of the presenter — familiar week in and week out to the viewers, and by his own terse style.[35]

In an instant, the interviewee must answer an often delicate question, the response to which may have damaging repercussions. Within a short space of time, such a person may expound, or be expected to expound, a total philosophy. Reality is infinitely more complex. If such persons are in the public eye, the journalist from the printed media preserves (with the aid of a tape recorder) the interviewee's words on the printed pages and preserves these words for posterity. We treat the written word much more reverently than the spoken word. The case of Fr. Bernard Lynch illustrates these issues. He had agreed to appear on the "Late Late Show" to discuss his work involving AIDS-related illnesses. Pleased with the way the interview was going, Gay Byrne suddenly turned to him and asked, "Are you homosexual, Father?" Fr. Lynch later wrote that he was devastated. He wanted to say he was "gay" — but he said "no". He later wrote that the "no" answer was to his "eternal shame and chagrin" as he had to deny his "own creativeness in God".[36] In law and in terms of morality, more weight should be given to the prepared statement than to the oral comment given in the heat of exchange on the electronic media. We should be more tolerant of, and encourage, those who after an interview may wish to correct something said in oral argument. Words, particularly when used in an ex tempore sense over the instant electronic media, cannot cope easily with the evolution of reality and may not convey precise meanings of our thoughts and realities. T.S. Eliot summed up the problem with words:

> Words strain,
> Crack and sometimes break, under the burden,
> Under the tension, slip, slide, perish,
> Decay with imprecision, will not stay in place,
> Will not stay still.[37]

THE NEW ERA

Telecommunication mirrors the nervous system of man. Man's intellect is being extended by electronics. Man receives and imparts communications over his own central nervous system. The sense of touch, sight, hearing, smell and taste travel and use the same human transmission pathways. Soon all forms of telecommunication, voice, vision and data will travel along the same route and the legal and technical distinctions between telegraphy, telephony and wireless telegraphy — voice, vision and data transmission — will blur.[38]

Broadband digital networks with computers linked to them will enable all forms of telecommunication — voice, vision and data — to travel along the same route. We will move from the analogue signals — essentially a nineteenth century technology which is the medium of existing television signals, video recorders and of many telephone lines — to digital signals, bits and bytes, on/off codes, that can easily be stored, edited and manipulated. Digital signals allow users to escape constraints of time, (with vast storage programs in memory banks), constraints of space (by allowing users to interact with electronic systems, be they electronic newspapers, video systems or simple speech, anywhere in the world which shares similar facilities) and constraints of bandwidth (by compressing the images and sending them in "burst mode"). The age of teleshopping and telemarketing, telelibraries, teleconferencing and telepartying is upon us.

Optical Fibres combined with the microchip will facilitate the new advancing technology. Strands of glass (optical fibres) can transmit quantities of information many hundreds of times more voluminous than copper cable or even satellites of today can carry. The new electronic medium of telecommunication of the next century will incorporate in a single apparatus features of the present telephone, television and computer. This device may well be called "the tellyphone". It will be interactive, functioning as a transmitter as well as a receiver, and have a screen.

The interactive screen of the tellyphone will bring the family to Grandmother in her nursing home in living colour and Grandmother to the family, although they may live many kilometres from each other. Grandmother may very well have a big screen in her nursing home. Films and television programmes will be accessible via the tellyphone from anywhere in the world with the new broadband services. Subscribers will simply dial up the appropriate service using relevant codes.

Soon it may be difficult for a business person to survive without a portable tellyphone or telecomputer.[39] This portable machine will carry voice, data and images, have a printout facility, possess other interactive facilities and contain identification features which will ensure, should the user so wish, that he or she can be located anywhere in the world. The tellyphone may be requested to inform the user at what time exactly did John telephone Alan two months ago. A recording of the communication will be available within seconds. Appointments could be made automatically via electronic mail; a library could be accessed for a copy of a journal. If it is inconvenient for the user to read the on-screen information, an appropriate button would deliver the information via a simulated human voice.

Although the newspaper will still be available in paper format, a version will be available on the tellyphone. Electronic mail may be downloaded to the portable tellyphone. On reading a document, the user may use a pen which is wiped over the segment to be preserved for reference in the tellyphone's electronic memory bank. Cryptograhic techniques will exist to secure telecommunication messages from unauthorised persons.

Increasingly, telephone calls will connect to persons not places; the cord that has confined the telephone for more than a 100 years is being cut. To an increasing degree the telephone is freeing itself from its wires. The technology that produced the cellular telephone, once a curiosity, then a trendy toy and status symbol for the yuppie, now an important tool, will be developed further and become the portable tellyphone. This scenario, however, will not only require capital but also precious space on the frequency spectrum. The current logjam on the frequency spectrum could be compared to a sky full of airplanes with no room to manoeuvre and limited landing strips. Pending further technological developments, technical difficulties could be overcome by housing small base stations to facilitate the transmission and reception of telephone calls over the airwaves in places as universal as where fire hydrants are now.

We will see further developments. The wrist telephone is already the subject of considerable research in various telephone laboratories. The telephone that hears and obeys using voice-recognition technology will recognise voice commands like "call", "dial" and "hang-up". A person in his or her office may hear the telephone speak: "Your washing machine has overflowed." The home-alert telephone system has been programmed to call the office in emergencies. The time will come when instead of the familiar ring, the telephone will call out the name of the person or organisation who is seeking contact. The called party can then decide to answer the telephone directly or let the answering machine deal with it.

The picture-phone, first invented by American Telephone and Telegraph Co. in the 1960s, could not be developed because ordinary telephone lines did not have the capacity for television-like pictures. With the installation of optical-fibre cable, which can transport high-quality sound and high-definition television signals, picture-phones will soon be available.

Telecommunication facilities may assist in car-navigational systems of the future. Having keyed in relevant destinations in advance, the system will guide the driver through, for example, one-way systems: "Turn left at the next junction, then right"; "The N2 is blocked at Junction 202, a diversion is in operation, turn left at Junction 201." A satellite system will continually feed navigational data to the car.

Alvin Toffler in *The Third Wave* (1980) wrote of our movement towards "telecommunity".[40] There is something wasteful in millions of people simultaneously shifting across the landscape morning and evening travelling to and from work. He noted that bonds in the home and in the community could be strengthened by the new telecommunication technologies. The concept of telecommunity with persons working from home is already taking hold. For example, in addition to the telephone, many salesmen have a fax machine at home. Their business vans or cars are parked at home; they receive instructions over the fax from headquarters. They do not commute to the office in the mornings and evenings to receive instructions. They thus have greater opportunities to involve themselves in home life and in the life of the community.

Many people travel home from the office exhausted. Telecommunication facilities that enable a person to work more from home should enable such a person to have more time to enjoy life — go to the theatre, films and local exhibitions. The suburbs should not be like social graveyards. Man should no longer be tied physically to the office; technology can take full advantage of man's mobility.

The idea of the electronic cottage is not as farfetched as we think; the tellyphone with electronic terminals at home will be linked to the office. We should be encouraged by the development in the 1970s and 1980s of flexitime — the arrangement whereby within certain fixed limits persons in employment can choose their own working hours. This concept will be further enhanced by the developing telecommunication technology.

The electronic age is bringing increased leisure time in Ireland; yet many of us are unprepared psychologically for leisure. Leisure and work should take on different meanings. A way must be found for occupying our time in a satisfactory manner.

THE CHALLENGE

Fears are being expressed that the new technologies will dehumanise us; we will be overwhelmed by computers and networks and a myriad of television channels. Electronic media bombard us daily with showers of information, which envelop us in images and affect the way we perceive and act. We echo the refrain of T.S. Eliot:

Where is the life we have lost in living?
Where is the wisdom we have lost in knowledge?
Where is the knowledge we have lost in information?[41]

Some may add: "Where is the information we have lost in data?" But we must maintain a sense of balance. Videoconferencing, for example, will not abolish face to face encounters. Robert W. Lucky, executive director of research at AT&T Bell Laboratories (1991), tells the story of a government minister who spoke to him about video-conferencing: "I need to smell the person I'm dealing with," he said. Lucky wrote that the minister was speaking of smell as a metaphor for human experience — some essence not necessarily conveyed by the electronic medium.[42]

The protection of privacy is a central concern of those regulating electronic communication. The Orwellian nightmare, which warned originally against the evils of a totalitarian state, now has more general application:

There was of course no way of knowing whether you were being watched at any given moment. How often, or on what system, the Thought Police plugged in on any individual wire was guesswork. It is even conceivable that they watched every-body all the time. But at any rate they could plug in your wire whenever they wanted to. You had to live — did live from habit that became instinct — in the assumption that every sound you made was overheard and, except in darkness, every movement scrutinised.[43]

The concept of privacy in the context of the interception of tele-communication is considered in chapter 28.

Competent men have with great regularity demonstrated sub-stantial failures of nerve in relation to new forms of communication. Arthur C. Clarke stated that we were like the early Victorians who saw no value in the electric telegraph; semaphores or flashing lights have always been good enough for those who wanted something faster than the mail coach. Changes in telecommunication will con-tinue to occur; great new discoveries will be made. Such discoveries, and the consequent management of spare time, will require courage, imagination and initiative. In the short term, we will have difficulties in coping with the changes. Machiavelli in *The Prince* (1516) tells us of the difficulties:

> It must be remembered that there is nothing more difficult to plan, more doubtful of success, nor more dangerous to manage than the creation of a new system. For the initiator has the enmity of all who would profit by the preservation of the old institutions and merely lukewarm defenders in those who would gain by the new ones.

Cyberspace, the term for electronic space where telecommuni-cation occurs (coined by the novelist William Gibson),[44] will bring its own difficulties. Cyberspace will cause particular difficulties for lawyers — wedded as we are to tangible things like written docu-mentation. John P. Barlow, co-founder of the Electronic Frontier Foundation (1991), stated that cyberspace

> remains a frontier region, across which roam the few aboriginal technologists and cyberpunks who can tolerate the austerity of its savage computer interfaces, incompatible communications protocols, proprietary barricades, cultural and legal ambi-guities and general lack of useful maps or metaphors.[45]

But this is typical of any new technology. Cyberspace is a boon for hackers. Hacking is a technological scourge; teenage hackers using home computers have already broken into "secure" computer systems at the Pentagon, NASA and NATO; computer fraud is estimated to cost banks in the US and EC two billion pounds every year and some experts estimate that 85 per cent of computer fraud is never reported.[46]

George Gilder in *Life After Television* (1992) stated that telecommunication systems — the central nervous system of mankind — "will continue to twitch spastically in embarrassing ways, as long as bureaucracy and politicians fail to comprehend the nature and promise of [the] new technology".[47] This phenomenon is almost inevitable with any new technology.

The force of microelectronics and telecommunication technologies will wipe away many of the existing constraints in relation to those who can and cannot provide telecommunication services; hierarchical systems and the power grids of our time will be affected.

The new telecommunication technologies of the electronic age may fuel unrealistic expectations, may facilitate unwanted surveillance and, in the context of broadcasting, may lead to cultural domination and uniformity. The new technologies also have the capacity to give us greater productivity, cultural pluralism and enrichment, a greater sense of democratisation, security and personal contentment. Let us never forget that the tools of the new technologies are tools to aid mankind. Therein lies the challenge for all of us.

PART II

The Development of Telecommunication in Ireland

When Queen Victoria came to the throne she had no swifter means of sending messages to the far parts of her Empire than had Julius Caesar, or for that matter, than Moses. . . . The galloping horse and the wind-driven sailing ship remained the swiftest means of transport, as they had been for five thousand years. Not until the scientists of the early nineteenth century started to investigate the curious properties of electricity was a servant discovered which within little more than two lifetimes would change the face of the world and sweep away the ancient barriers of time and distance.

Arthur C. Clarke, *Voice Across the Sea* (1974)

[W]hat we are building now is the nervous system of mankind which will link together the whole human race, for better or worse, in a unity which no earlier age could have imagined.

Arthur C. Clarke

2

The Early Development of Telecommunication: The Telegraph

INTRODUCTION

The purpose of this section is to describe the evolution of the process of telecommunication emphasising the development of telecommunication in Ireland. A description of this evolutionary process coupled with a brief technical introduction to the nature of forms of telecommunication may facilitate a greater understanding of the rationale behind the regulation of telecommunication in Ireland.[1]

EARLY DEVELOPMENTS

For millennia, the speed of communication could be equated with the fastest horse or the swiftest runner. Bonfires and the beating of tom-toms facilitated the transmission of information over distance. For instance, it is recorded that the Scottish Parliament in 1455 used fire signals in that country's military campaign against the English:

> One bale or faggot shall be the notice of the approach of the English in any manner; two bales that they are *coming indeed*; and four bales blazing beside each other, to say that they *are coming in earnest*.[2]

The hope of greater speed of communication was kindled with the discovery of the telescope in 1648. A practical telecommunication system was implemented in France in an atmosphere of a life and death struggle for existence. In 1793, in the early days of the French

Republic, France's borders were threatened with simultaneous invasions. Greater speed than that achieved by man on horseback was necessary for the transmission of intelligence. It was in this period of need that Claude Chappe of Brulon, a young mechanic from Normandy, perfected in 1793 a system of optical telegraphs. Signal stations on high ground six to twelve miles apart equipped with a pole, cross-bar and movable arms were used to send coded signals. Operators used telescopes to read the signals and then relayed the messages to the next station. Claude Chappe was acutely conscious of the possible uses of telecommunication to central government. In an open letter dated Fructidor 22, the sixth year of the Republic (early September 1798), he noted:

> The day will come when the Government will be able to achieve the grandest idea we can possibly have of power, by using the telegraph system in order to spread directly every day, every hour, and simultaneously its influence over the whole republic.[3]

The tools of telecommunication were clearly regarded by Chappe and subsequently by many governments as political instruments — instruments of power.

Other countries soon began using the optical telegraph system: the British Admiralty, the Prussians, and Russians were soon working the new system. However, the system of optical telegraphs was limited in its usefulness: signals could not be sent at night; by day, service was dependent on the weather. It is appropriate here to state that despite the images conjured by the words "invention" and "inventor" of lonely men and women of genius often being blessed with good fortune, Horwitz rightly argues that the technological enterprise is generally more communal, and certainly more derivative, than the popular impression of invention.[4] Accordingly, virtually every person associated with inventing a mode of telecommunication was building upon earlier experiments and upon earlier scientific works of theorists.

The radical improvement in the mode of transmitting intelligence came with the discovery and harnessing of electro-magnetic energy. The science of electro-magnetism was influenced by the work of a Danish Professor, Hans Christian Oersted, who publicised the magnetic effect of an electric current (1819). Electro-magnets followed and magnetic forces were used to influence a magnetised needle and ring a bell.

In 1837, William (later Sir William) Cooke who had studied medicine at Heidelberg and Charles (later Sir Charles) Wheatstone, a physics professor at King's College, London, obtained a patent in England for an electric alarm and telegraph system. Cooke and Wheatstone's five-needle telegraph used electric current to transmit messages over five wires. The electric current could deflect each needle to the right or left and the deflection of a pair of needles could point to one of twenty letters on a grid behind the needles. This early telecommunication system was first used on the railways in England to improve the signalling and timekeeping of trains. In fact, the need for fast communication on the railways in the 1830s provided the catalyst necessary for the early development of telecommunication systems. In 1839 the (English) Paddington to West Drayton railway line, a distance of 13 miles, used the five-needle electric telegraph system for signalling purposes. Soon the public was invited to pay a shilling and send their own telegrams — the first species of modern telecommunication messages. The public telecommunication service had been inaugurated.

Further developments followed: Morse code, the dot and dash language of electrical communication associated with Samuel Finley Breeze Morse, facilitated the permanent recording of telegraphic messages on paper. After years of effort Morse finally obtained $30,000 from the US Congress in 1842 for the construction of a telegraphic line between Washington DC and Baltimore which opened on January 1, 1845. Arthur C. Clarke has noted that the debate in Congress over the allocation did not reflect much credit on the elected representatives of the American people: "Several of them were quite unable to appreciate the difference between magnetism and mesmerism."[5] Soon the transmission of telegraphic messages at up to 60 words per minute became possible together with the sending of several messages simultaneously over the same circuit (multiplexing).

In Britain and Ireland, private enterprise, initially in the form of the railway companies and a short time later in the form of newly-formed telegraph companies,[6] used the railway system at first for the transmission of telegraph messages and later developed other routes. Ireland had to await developments from England: the first international telegraph submarine cable between Dover and Calais had been opened to the public on November 13, 1851, well before any telecommunication system became operational in Ireland. The English and Irish Magnetic Telegraph Company was incorporated in August 1851 to provide telegraph links between England and

Ireland by submarine cable.[7] In the early 1850s submarine telegraph cables linked Portpatrick in Scotland with Donaghadee in Down and Holyhead in Wales with Howth in Dublin. Other submarine cross-channel cables followed linking Blackwater (Wexford) with Fish-guard (Pembroke), Newcastle (Wicklow) with Nevin (Caernarvon) and Whitehead (Antrim) with Knock Bay in Scotland.[8] The sub-marine cables enabled the telegraph companies to expand into Ireland.

THE ERA OF THE TELEGRAPH

A major advance in telecommunication was the laying of a trans-atlantic telegraph cable between Ireland and America. A New York businessman, Cyrus West Field, founded the Atlantic Telegraph Company in 1856 and the Anglo-Irish physicist, William Thompson (later Lord Kelvin), became its scientific director. The first successful transatlantic telegraphic line was laid by the Atlantic Telegraph Company in 1858. Valentia in Kerry was linked up with New-foundland. Earlier in 1857, the Atlantic Telegraph Company with the assistance of the Treasury — described by Arthur C. Clarke as "that graveyard of lost hopes"[9] — and with the aid of the warship Niagara, provided by the United States, and H.M.S. Agamemnon, provided by the British Government, laid a telegraph cable across the Atlantic with the shore end of the cable landing at Valentia Bay on August 5, 1857:

> Valentia Bay was studded with innumerable small craft, decked with the gayest bunting — small boats flitted hither and tither, their occupants cheering enthusiastically as the work successfully progressed. The cable boats were managed by the sailors of the Niagara and Susquehanna, and it was a well-designed compliment and indicative of the future frater-nisation of nations, that the shore-rope was arranged to be presented at this side of the Atlantic to the representative of the Queen, by the officers and men of the United States Navy, and at the other side British officers and sailors would make a similar presentation to the President of the great Republic.
>
> For several hours the Lord Lieutenant of Ireland stood on the beach, surrounded by his staff and the directors of the cable company, watching the arrival of the cable and when at length the American sailors jumped through the surge with the hawser

to which it was attached, his Excellency was among the first to lay hold of it and pull it lustily to shore. . . .[10]

However, the cable soon broke ending this brave endeavour. In 1858, another transoceanic telegraph line between Valentia and Newfoundland facilitated the transmission of a 99-word message of greetings from Queen Victoria to President Buchanan. Europe and the United States had been linked: there was much rejoicing. *The Times* commented euphorically:

> The Atlantic is dried up, and we become in reality as well as in wish, one country. . . . The Atlantic Telegraph has half undone the Declaration of 1776, and has gone far to make us once again, in spite of ourselves, one people. . . .

The first press despatch was sent on the twenty-third day of the inauguration of the new service, August 27, 1858. Newfoundland had signalled: "Pray give some news from New York, they are mad for news." Among the news items despatched was the news that the King of Prussia was too ill to visit Queen Victoria and that the "Emperor of France [had] returned to Paris on Saturday".[11] But Queen Victoria's message to President Buchanan had taken sixteen and a half hours before the transmission was completed. The log of all the messages sent from Newfoundland to Ireland on the whole of the sixth day of service of the transatlantic cable illustrates the difficulties involved in successfully laying 2,350 miles of cables:

> "Repeat, please."
> "Please send slower for the present."
> "How?"
> "How do you receive?"
> "Send slower."
> "Please send slower."
> "How do you receive?"
> "Please say if you can read this?"
> "Can you read this?"
> "Yes."
> "How are signals"?
> "Do you receive?"
> "Please send something."
> "Please send Vs and Bs."
> "How are signals?"[12]

The last message before this cable broke was transmitted at 1.30 p.m. on September 1, 1859. Three hundred and fifty thousand pounds of capital and 2,500 tons of cable had been lost leading to a commission of inquiry.[13] However, the short-lived cable had proved to be of assistance to the Government. Orders had been posted to trans-ship two regiments from Canada to India to assist in the quelling of the Indian mutiny. After the dispatch of the orders, a communication was received to state that peace had been restored in India. The authorities were able to countermand the original instructions resulting in a saving of £50,000. Nevertheless, the loss of the Government's investment in the 1858 transatlantic cable was to remain a bitter memory with the civil servants in the Treasury.

Cable faults and the American Civil War postponed effective transatlantic telegraphic communication until 1866. One year earlier in 1865, 20 states signed the first International Telegraph Convention when agreement was reached on a uniform international telegraph system. For almost a century, transatlantic cables carried only tele-graph signals: the development of submerged repeaters made pos-sible the first transatlantic telephone circuits only in 1956. Human speech is a complex phenomenon compared with the simple language of the telegraph code.

Transatlantic telegraphic messages originally cost 20 pence for a 20-word telegram. Records in Newfoundland indicate that the earliest customers, almost without exception, were bankers.[14] An internal memorandum of October 22, 1866 suggests that the Anglo American Telegraph Company considered charging a percentage for the transmission of money via their cables.[15] No such charges were, however, put into effect. The influence of the press resulted in the lowering of tariffs. Reuter introduced cable code, sold space in his telegrams to merchants who could not afford the cost of their own 20 word message and was a powerful influence behind the drive to establish competition in an effort to reduce tariffs. A French transatlantic cable was laid in 1869 with British and French capital. However, a "joint purse" cable monopoly was established among the competing companies: the Anglo American Company took over the French company and Reuter was co-opted on to the board of directors of the Anglo American Company.

In early 1874, Siemens Brothers of London laid a cable on behalf of the Direct United States Telegraph Company between Ballin-skelligs, County Kerry, to a point at Trinity Bay, Newfoundland. The Anglo American Telegraph Company had secured an exclusive landing licence for 50 years from the Newfoundland authorities and the Supreme Court of Newfoundland upheld the validity of that licence forcing the Direct United States Telegraph Company to land its cable at Tor Bay, Halifax.[16]

Frustrated by delays in the transmission of transatlantic telegraphic communications from Valentia, the German Union Telegraph Company under pressure from the Imperial German Post Office, laid a cable between Emden and Valentia (Kerry) which opened for business in 1882. James Graves, Valentia's first telegraph superintendent, received additional monies for looking after the German interests. Records indicate that the German telegraph station at Foilhommerum, Valentia, was maintained until approximately 1904.[17]

Valentia was to remain a focal point for telegraphic transatlantic traffic for almost a century. In the early years, conditions were unfavorable for the staff. The air was damp which led to the absence of staff from duty due to bronchial ailments. Fred Mackey who worked at the Valentia station in the early part of this century noted:

> When an epidemic of sickness descended on the little colony, the small staff were hard pressed to maintain the round-the-clock service expected of them. Some took advantage of the opportunity to indulge in poteen, which had a great reputation for killing microbes. It sometimes killed the patient as well. . .[18]

James Graves in 1885[19] outlined the extensive recreational facilities available to the telegraphic staff on Valentia. The facilities included a full-size billard table in the staff rest room and a library with approximately 800 books. The library subscribed to six periodicals and *The Times*. There were 13 pianofortes and one harmonium. The telegraph cricket club flourished until the migration of telegraphic operators to the Commercial Cable Company's new station in Waterville in 1885.

John W. Mackay and Gordon Bennett of the New York Herald formed the Commercial Cable Company in 1884 to compete against the "joint purse" cable monopoly and to provide advantageous news rates for the Herald; two cables were laid between Canso and Waterville, 12 miles from Valentia, and the company's telegraph cable station was also located at Waterville. Dr. de Cogan notes that competition "bred an atmosphere of introverted secrecy" with the result that records are uninformative.[20] By 1894 a stable system of communication was established in transatlantic telegraphic transmission when both the Commercial and the Anglo American

Company had "fast" cables installed which greatly facilitated the transmission of stock market information.

The monopoly of the Anglo American Company in relation to cable landings in Newfoundland ended in 1904. The Newfoundland authorities used this opportunity to impose a cable tax of $2,000 per landing.

In 1912, Western Union effected closer legal arrangements with the Anglo American Telegraph Company and the Direct United States Telegraph Company with the result that all were managed from the same premises. Western Union introduced a high level of efficiency and accurate record keeping.

Censorship was introduced on all transatlantic cables during the Great War. The use of any form of codes except for Government traffic was prohibited. During the Great War, nearly 200 persons worked in Knightstown, Valentia, on telegraphic and Government duties. After the Great War the Postmaster-General in London purchased an old Atlantic cable from Western Union which gave the Government two lines, one via the Azores and one from Balinskelligs to Harbour Grace, Newfoundland. This latter cable was removed to Cornwall in 1922-1923 and ultimately became owned by Cable and Wireless Limited.[21]

The introduction of the teleprinter towards the end of the First World War resulted in the skilled operator being made redundant; Valentia soon became virtually a mechanical relaying station. Improvements after the war resulted in the laying of further cables — IHV (Valentia to Le Harve) in 1920, 2 PZ (Valentia to Sennen) in 1923; but the focus of telegraphic communication soon moved to the Azores which was to become the nerve centre of Atlantic communications for the remainder of the telegraph era.[22] The Commercial Cable Company suspended all cable operations on January 15, 1952 and closed down Waterville Telegraph station in 1961. The Western Union Cable Station on Valentia Island closed in February 1966.

By 1867, nationalisation of the land-based telegraph companies and other telecommunication undertakings became almost inevitable. Reasons for this inevitability will be considered in Part III dealing with the early regulation of telecommunication.[23] The *Telegraph Act, 1868*[24] authorised the Post Office to purchase the telegraph companies and the telegraphic business of the railway companies. The Postmaster-General acquired the undertakings of land-based telegraph companies in Ireland — the British and Irish Magnetic Company on May 18, 1869 and the Electric Telegraph Company on

May 25, 1869.[25] The monopoly of the transmission of all forms of telecommunication was vested in the Postmaster-General by the *Telegraph Act, 1869.*[26]

The Post Office in Ireland eagerly set about the business of providing telegraphic services throughout the country. Sanger, the Divisional Engineer for the Post Office in Ireland, reported in 1870[27] that since the transfer of telegraphic undertakings to the Post Office, which had commenced in 1869, the Post Office had renewed 591 miles of telegraphic lines; 2,042 miles of new wires on existing poles on railway lines had been erected and 234 miles of lines on roads in the shape of loops between the railway stations and post offices had been completed. The renewal and re-insulation of the so-called "Anglo-American" telegraph line between Waterford and Valentia made the line, in the opinion of Sanger, the finest in the country. He reported that street wires had been reconstructed and raised. Sanger also reported in 1870 that the following apparatus had been received in Ireland and much of it had been installed: 327 single needle instruments, 68 inkers, 272 sets of acoustic instruments, 24,636 battery cells and 496 items of other apparatus. By 1870 an underground telegraph system for Dublin had been planned to replace the overground wires. Soon telegraphic services were reported to be improving. Crown premises were to be fitted out for telegraphic business by the Board of Works. Special telegraph wires could be rented from the Post Office. On the first Tuesday in September 1870, 9,377 words were sent over the special wires of *The Irish Times.*[28]

The Postmaster-General, who had taken over clerks from the telegraph and railway companies, soon realised that many of these clerks were not familiar with the operation of the same form of telegraph instrument. Telegraph schools were subsequently re-organised in 1870. In Dublin, the departmental school of the Postmaster-General and the telegraph school at the Queen's Institute flourished. Schools of telegraphy also existed in Belfast and Cork. However the Scudamore Report on the *Re-organisation of the Telegraph System of the United Kingdom* (1870) noted that in the Cork school "failure to pass the educational test on the part of numerous candidates [had] somewhat interfered with its productive power".[29] By 1870, 21 wires were in operation between Britain and Ireland with two of these wires allotted by agreement to the American cable companies for the despatch of messages between London and Valentia.[30]

By 1870, at the behest of the Secretary of State for War, personnel from the military forces of the Crown in Britain and Ireland were involved in the construction, maintenance and signalling operations of the Post Office telegraphic system.[31] A report on the re-organisation of the telegraph system in 1871 stated boldly, without elaboration, that "the motive for this arrangement and its desirability will be apparent".[32] The keen interest of Government in the process of telecommunication has not waned with the passage of time.

The acquisition by the Postmaster-General of the telegraphic undertakings of the private companies became a burden on the Exchequer for many years. It was estimated in 1867 that it would cost £200,000 to re-organise the telegraph system and give a "perfect" service to 2,950 places.[33] In fact the Post Office had spent £2.134m on such work by September 1873.[34] The Second Secretary of the Department, Frank Scudamore, who had a passionate interest in the improvement of the telegraphic system, anticipating that Parliament would not grant further funds for the telegraph capital account, misappropriated £812,000 in Savings Bank and other Post Office funds for the use of the telegraph branch of the Department. Censured for such "excess of zeal", the incident led to the strengthening of the powers of the Treasury, the further refining of the duties of accounting officers and the authorisation of the Comptroller and Auditor-General to audit the telegraph capital account.

The arrival of organised labour within the Civil Service for the first time in 1871 when the telegraph clerks at Manchester formed themselves into a trade union, the Telegraphists' Association, resulted in greater pressure on the finances of the telegraph service.[35] Although commercial accounts for the telegraph service of the Postmaster-General were not kept until after 1876, the economist W.S. Jevons estimated in 1875, taking pensions and the ultimate redemption of the debt involved in the nationalisation process into account, that £500,000 was then being lost by the Post Office on the telegraph service on an annual basis.[36] The inland telegram service (a modern version of the telegraph service) continued until July 6, 1987 when it was replaced by a telemessage service operated by Telecom Éireann. Messages are now accepted by telephone, telex or facsimile at a telemessage centre and delivered by post the following day. However, international telegram services are still available from Ireland to certain designated countries overseas.[37]

3

The Telephone and Radio Communication

EARLY DEVELOPMENT OF THE TELEPHONE

Alexander Graham Bell (1847-1922) was the first person to be awarded patent rights for the second generation of tele-communication apparatus, the telephone. Bell, born in Scotland and educated at Edinburgh and London Universities, became professor of vocal physiology at Boston University in 1873. The story is told of how on June 2, 1875, in the course of experiments, one of Bell's electrically vibrated reeds got stuck to its electro-magnet. Having told his assistant, Thomas A. Watson, to pluck the sticking reed, Bell noticed in an adjoining room that the corresponding reed began to vibrate and produced a sound of the same tone. Bell deduced that if a single sound could be transmitted electrically then it should also be possible to transmit complicated human speech and music. Further experiments led on March 10, 1876 to what are hailed as the first words over the telephone — "Mr. Watson come here, I want you."

United States Patent No. 174,465 allowed on March 3, 1876 and issued on March 7, 1876, was to become one of the most valuable patents ever issued. Surprisingly, the patent was entitled "Improvements in Telegraphy" and did not mention the word "telephone" but it did refer to the transmission of "vocal or other sounds". Only hours after Bell's patent application was filed at the Patent Office in Washington, Elisha Gray, co-founder of Western Electric Company, came to the same patent office and filed a "caveat" for a speaking telephone. Litigation ensued but Bell's patent was upheld.

In 1877 the first news despatch was sent by telephone to the Boston Globe. The first telephone switchboard for commercial use was installed in New Haven, Connecticut, in 1878 with 21 subscribers; the public telephone service had been inaugurated. While the Postmaster-General in London awaited a reply from the Treasury in relation to a request for the Treasury's permission to allow the Postmaster-General to supply the telephone, the privately-owned Telephone Company was registered on the June 14, 1878 to acquire and work Bell's patent. Initially, the Post Office was not convinced of the telephone's future: Sir William Preece, the chief engineer of the Post Office testified to a special committee of the House of Commons in 1879 that the telephone had little future in Britain:

> I fancy the descriptions we get of its use in America are a little exaggerated, though there are conditions in America which necessitate the use of such instruments more than here. Here we have a superabundance of messengers, errand boys and things of that kind. . . . The absence of servants has compelled Americans to adopt communication systems for domestic purposes. Few have worked at the telephone much more that I have. I have one in my office, but more for show. If I want to send a message — I use a sounder or employ a boy to take it.[1]

In 1879, a rival to the Telephone Company, the Edison Telephone Company, was formed to acquire and work the patents of Thomas Edison. Following a decision of the High Court in 1880, *Attorney General v Edison Telephone Company*[2] which confirmed that the Postmaster-General enjoyed a monopoly in telecommunication transmission, licences were granted by the Postmaster-General to the private telephone companies to operate telephone services. The Bell and Edison Telephone companies amalgamated in 1880 to become the United Telephone Company.

In Ireland, the first telephone exchange was opened in 1880 by the United Telephone Company on the top floor of the Commercial Buildings in Dame Street, Dublin, with five subscribers.[3] Reports indicate that the boy who was employed to operate the switchboard in Dublin was induced by the silence in the switchboard room to adjourn outside to the court-yard to play marbles which led to his dismissal.[4] The boy was replaced by the first lady operator, Miss Agnes Duggan. Boys had generally been employed in many early telephone exchanges in different countries "but were found to be far too unruly, insulting callers and ringing wrong numbers".[5] In January 1878, when the first commercial switchboard went into operation in New Haven, Connecticut, boys were employed as operators — but did not last long. The boys, it appears, were rude: they talked back to subscribers, played tricks with the wires and in the words of one of the early female operators were "complete and consistent failures".[6] Arthur C. Clarke in his inimitable way describes this phenomenon as illustrating "that curious mathematical law with which all efficiency experts are familiar: One boy equals one boy: two boys equals half a boy; three boys equals no boy at all."[7] Subsequently, female operators were used exclusively for many years for day-time work.

The Telephone Company of Ireland acquired the interests of the United Telephone Company in 1882. However, in 1888 there were only 500 lines and three sub-exchanges in Dublin. A trunk route linking Dublin and Belfast was subsequently completed. Following the enactment of the *Telegraph Act, 1892*, the Postmaster-General purchased the main telephone trunk system leaving the Telephone Company of Ireland to operate telephone stations, junction lines and exchanges. The National Telephone Company of Ireland acquired the interests of the Telephone Company of Ireland in 1893. By then telephone service was available only in Dublin, Belfast, Cork, Limerick, Dundalk, Drogheda and Derry. Overhearing on lines generated many complaints and measures were adopted by the National Telephone Company to provide loops on circuits and to lay an extensive underground cable network to alleviate communication difficulties.

Bureaucrats and others remained sceptical about future prospects for the telephone. Arnold Morley, Postmaster-General from 1892 to 1895, was particularly pessimistic:

> Gas and water were necessities for every inhabitant of the country. Telephones were not and never would be. It was no use trying to persuade ourselves that the use of the telephone could be enjoyed by the large masses of the people in their daily life. . . .[8]

Newspaper journalists, often the catalysts for shaming Governments into providing better telecommunication services, were not easily convinced of the necessity for the telephone. Reacting to complaints about poor telephone service and unnecessarily high rates, *The Times*, noted in 1902:

> When all is said and done the telephone is not an affair of the million. It is a convenience for the well-to-do and a trade appliance for persons who can very well afford to pay for it. For people who use it constantly it is an immense economy, even at the highest rates ever charged by the telephone company. For

those who use it merely to save themselves trouble or add to
the diversions of life it is a luxury. An overwhelming majority
of the population do not use it and are not likely to use it at all,
except perhaps to the extent of an occasional message from a
public station.[9]

These sober words must however be viewed in context: the
telephone may well have been considered a luxury because in the
last decades of the nineteenth century Great Britain and Ireland
possessed one of the finest communication systems in the world —
the telegraph and the postal services. The successful campaign of
Rowland Hill in the 1830s for the Penny Post and the nationalisation
of the telegraph services had improved the efficiency of communication systems. By 1872, there were 22,000 miles of telegraph line
with 83,000 miles of operation, with 5,000 telegraph offices in Great
Britain and Ireland.[10] The number of telegrams sent grew from 33
million in 1884-1885 to 50 million in 1886-1887.[11]

Fiscal rectitude, rather than the development of new technology
in the public interest, was a constant influence on governments and
led to perceptions about the development of the telephone service.
The Chancellor of the Exchequer, Michael Hicks Beach, as late as
1904 continued to believe, however, that "telephonic communication [was] not desired by the rural mind".[12]

The first external telephone contact was achieved when Lord
Kelvin formally opened the telephone link between Belfast and
Glasgow and Carlise via submarine cable on April 5, 1893. By 1900
there were 56 telephone exchanges working in Ireland. In 1900 the
Crown Alley, Dublin, telephone exchange was opened with a
capacity for 1,600 lines. Telephone trunk routes were, with some
exceptions, laid along the railways as the Postmaster-General had
acquired wayleave agreements with the various Irish railway
companies.[13]

In Ireland, the telephone, the new medium of communication, the
infant public utility, soon developed from being considered as a
mere electrical toy to being regarded as a complex instrument
accepted as part of normal life. In James Joyce's *Ulysses*, which
describes life in Dublin on June 16, 1904, the telephone is mentioned
eight times.[14] In *Ulysses* the telephone was not regarded as a curiosity
or as a strange technical invention but as part of the Dublin life at the
time. In fact, Joyce in *Ulysses* personalises the telephone; twice its
ring is described as a petulant "whir"; on another occasion, it rings
"rudely" in a woman's ear. On a further occasion, it is treated as a

potential necessity for the dead:

> Of course, he is dead. Monday he died. They ought to have some law to . . . make sure or an electric clock or telephone in the coffin. . . .

The telephone also became part of a fantasy involving, Leopold Bloom, the guilt-ridden hero of *Ulysses*; Joyce foreshadows the use of the telephone as a source of sexual gratification (the obscene telephone call) and in a sense, a new industry, the 'phone sex business:

> [Leopold Bloom] went through a form of clandestine marriage with at least one woman in the shadow of the Black Church. Unspeakable messages he telephoned mentally to Miss Dunn at an address in D'Olier Street while he presented himself indecently to the instrument in the callbox.

However, John Brooks in an interpretation of Leopold Bloom's fantasy with the telephone suggests that for Bloom on June 16, 1904 the telephone instrument had "developed a real and sternly censorious presence of its own".[15]

Efforts to ensure that the telephone and the operators adopted less of a "censorious presence" led the British and Irish Post Office in 1908 to adopt American standard expressions which the operators were obliged to use: "I'm sorry that line is busy" and other such expressions became commonplace. Concern had been expressed about discourteous service which generated bad language and *The Irish Times* in 1908 welcoming the standard expressions with their liberal requirements of "please and thank you" nevertheless considered that the telephone instrument itself was to blame for generating discourtesy:

> Its function encourages, and even requires a graceless brevity of expression . . . and a man is apt to carry these faults into the less mechanised areas of life.[16]

Influenced by many factors,[17] the Government decided to acquire the interests of the National Telephone Company. In 1905, after considerable negotiations, the Postmaster-General reached agreement with the National Telephone Company under which the State would purchase the company's system when its licence expired in

1911. The cost to the Exchequer for the acquisition of the privately-owned telephone system was £12.5m for Britain and Ireland.[18] On December 31, 1911, the date of the expiry of the National Telephone Company's licence, the Post Office telephone monopoly became a reality in practice as well as in law.

The Postmaster-General's department, the Post Office, was immediately faced with an acute shortage of exchange plant and equipment because of the inaction of the National Telephone Company pending the takeover of its control by the State. The British mainland received priority and the war declared in August 1914 virtually halted further development. At the end of the war in 1918 there were approximately 12,500 subscriber telephone lines in the area subsequently to become Saorstát Éireann. More than half of the available telephone lines were in the Dublin area. There were 212 telephone exchanges with 25 in the Dublin area; there were no telephone exchanges in Mayo, Leitrim or Roscommon and only one telephone exchange in Longford.[19]

TELECOMMUNICATION IN SAORSTÁT ÉIREANN

Saorstát Éireann in 1922 inherited a seriously deficient telecommunication infrastructure. The inadequate and inefficient telephone network transferred by the National Telephone Company to the Postmaster-General in 1912 had not been remedied, partly owing to the war of 1914-1918 which entailed the abandonment or postponement of development schemes. The British Government had continued the practice of the National Telephone Company of merely patching up an already obsolete plant. The Dublin Trunk Telephone Exchange, located in the General Post Office, was destroyed in 1916; telephone equipment throughout the country was destroyed in the period from 1916 to 1922 and particularly in the last two years of that period. International and submarine cables were cut by the Irregulars in 1922.[20] In fact, the Civil War in 1922 and subsequent disturbances resulted in what was described in a memorandum in 1927 to each member of the Executive Council of Saorstát Éireann justifying additional capital expenditure for the telephone system as "wholesale destruction of telephone lines" with the damage to underground and distribution plant, and telephone exchanges being described as "very considerable".[21] The Anglo-Irish and civil wars had wrought havoc to the processes of communication.

During the Civil War, transatlantic cables at Valentia were cut and the telegraph station was severely damaged. Dr. de Cogan has stated that Erskine Childers (who was anti-Treaty in the Civil War) viewed Valentia as a British station and the Waterville telegraph station as being American and he assembled references to the effect that it was Erskine Childers who cut the Valentia cables.[22] Dr. de Cogan argues that the events of the Civil War particularly in relation to the Valentia station had far reaching effects on Ireland's role in transatlantic communications. Following the Civil War the Ballinskelligs cable which had been purchased by the British Post Office from Western Union was diverted to Mousehole in Cornwall and Ballinskelligs was permanently closed down. Dr. de Cogan states that even as late as the 1960s when a route for the TAT-I (the first transatlantic telephone cable) was being considered, the events at Valentia in 1922 specifically caused Ireland to be by-passed. TAT-I was landed at Oban in Scotland.[23]

The energies of the Department of Posts and Telegraphs were almost fully occupied during the years 1922 and 1923 in restoring damaged communication systems; no consideration could be given to the development or improvement of the telephone system until 1924.[24]

The first Irish Postmaster-General and Minister for Posts and Telegraphs, James J. Walsh, was a former telegraphist and a member of the Republican garrison in the General Post Office, Dublin. He had been dismissed from the Civil Service for revolutionary tendencies and has been described by Dr. León Ó Broin, a former Secretary of the Department and historian, as the new Government's "political supremo".[25] The Postmaster-General advised the Dáil in 1924 that the British had left the country "in a rather undeveloped state telephonically".[26] The Minister admitted that, with the exception of the cities and certain important towns, it could reasonably be said that the country "had no telephone system at all, that at most it was only a skeleton system".[27]

The Minister lamented the shortage of technical labour; he commented that when the British withdrew "they were wise enough from their own viewpoint to take with them a great many men who were essential to [the development of the telephone system] and who would be very useful to [the State]. . . ."[28] The Minister had conveniently forgotten he had specifically requested of the British Postmaster-General in the conference on questions concerning the transfer of the Post Office to the Irish Free State in London on February 8, 1922 that facilities should be granted for mutual transfers between Ireland and England even after the appointed day for severance of the service.[29] However, the Minister was determined to "push on with a universal system of telephony".[30] He referred to plans for the development of the telephone system into "areas like Connaught" which had practically "no telephones whatever". The Minister stated that the Dáil could "absolutely rely on it that not a moment [was] being lost . . . in bringing this State to that level of telephonic equipment which [was found] in certain continental countries".[31] Preferential treatment was to be given to co-operative creameries.[32]

In 1922-23, IR£64,500 had been allocated out of the Central Fund for the development of the telephone service. Seventy thousand pounds had been similarly advanced in 1923-1924. In 1924-25, IR£150,000 was allocated for the further development of the telephone service.[33]

For many years, the physical nerve-centre of the administration of telecommunication in the State was the General Post Office in O'Connell Street, Dublin. The General Post Office, designed by Francis Johnston, destroyed in 1916, was the subject in 1922 of a IR£1m claim by the Irish Provisional Government against the British Government,[34] and was finally reconstructed in 1929. The President of the Executive Council, W.T. Cosgrave, performed the opening ceremony on July 11, 1929, eight years later to the day and hour when the truce marking the conclusion of hostilities between Ireland and Great Britain became operative. The President noted that in the century that had elapsed, the world had witnessed many changes but that "in no direction have those changes been more revolutionary than in the matter of communications, the service to which this building was first devoted and to which we now rededicate it".[35] The President was exceedingly conscious of the symbolism attached to the re-opening of the General Post Office and proclaimed that the restoration of the building was "symbolical of the new order". The importance of the General Post Office in the mythology of the nation was emphasised by the elaborate ceremony on July 11, 1929. The Executive Council and Parliamentary Secretaries assembled at Government Buildings and drove to the projecting portico of the General Post Office arriving at 12.00 noon; two companies of troops together with a military band formed the guard of honour and rendered the salute as the President arrived. The protocol instructions for the ceremony directed that the other Ministers were to remain seated in their cars while the salute was being given; after the presentation of the key by the builder, the President was to enter the building followed by his Ministers and Parliamentary Secretaries, purchase a postage stamp, send a telegram to the International Telegraph Bureau in Berne and make the first telephone call from the reconstructed building to His Excellency, the Governor General, offering him greetings on the re-opening of the General Post Office.[36]

The automatic telephone described by its inventor Almon Brown Strowger (1839-1902) as the "girl-less, cuss-less telephone" was another landmark in the development of telecommunication. Strowger, a funeral parlour proprietor from Kansas City, became tired of poor service from his local exchange and so devised an automatic switching system based on a "step by-step" principle. The system, which was patented in 1891 was in use in Ireland until 1989. The "step-by-step" system worked when the caller turned the dial of the telephone, where the finger holes were marked with digits, and this "routed" the connection through several switching stages choosing the exchange, and ultimately the number dialled, while concurrently switching on electric current which operated the bell and the ringing or engaged signal and the time-metering mechanism which registered the time for which the caller paid. Although the Strowger automatic exchange system was installed in 1912 at Epsom in Surrey, the conversion of the central Dublin area to an automatic switching exchange was not completed until 1930.[37]

RADIO COMMUNICATION

The hackneyed word "revolutionary" is often used to describe developments in telecommunication. Each new development was and is today still described as revolutionary but that adjective, in the context of telecommunication, should be reserved at the time of writing for the discovery that electro-magnetic waves could travel through space with the speed of light and with characteristics similar to light. James Clerk Maxwell (1831-1879), a Scottish physicist and one of the great mathematicians of the nineteenth century, in his treatise "Electricity and Magnetism" read as a paper to the Royal Society in 1864, argued that the velocity of electric waves in air should be equal to that of the velocity of light waves, both being the same kind of waves but differing in wave length. Heinrich Hertz (1857-1894), the German physicist is hailed as the first person to detect and measure electro-magnetic waves (wireless waves). Guglielmo Marconi (1874-1937) became aware in 1894 at the age of 20 that electro-magnetic waves might be the basis of a means of communication, when used for signalling with the dots and dashes of the morse alphabet. Marconi, son of an Irish mother, who had relations living in London, was introduced to Sir William Henry Preece (1834-1913), the Engineer-in-Chief of the Post Office. Working with the Postmaster-General's Department, Marconi succeeded in transmitting radio communications over a distance of 14 kilometres on May 18, 1897. However, the Treasury could see no future in the project and subsequently on July 20, 1897 Marconi registered his Wireless Telegraph and Signal Company Limited.

The first record of wireless being used in Ireland was in 1898 when Marconi reported on the Kingstown (now Dún Laoghaire, Dublin) regatta from a ship to a temporary station at Dublin. The first commercial use of radio followed the establishment of two stations at Brow Head near Crookhaven and at Malin Head to communicate with ships on the southern and northern Atlantic routes. J.W. O'Neill records that the stations were taken over by the Postmaster-General in 1910 and replaced by more powerful installations at Valentia and Malin Head.[38]

On December 12, 1901, Marconi at the age of 27, succeeded in transmitting the letter "S" — three dots in the Morse Code — from Poldhu in Cornwall to St. John's in Newfoundland, a distance of 1,800 miles: transatlantic radio communication had become a reality. It was a most significant achievement and many marvelled at its accomplishment. Thomas Alva Edison, the inventor of the incandescent lamp and the phonograph and one of the most distinguished inventors of all time enthused: "I would like to meet that young man who has had the monumental audacity to attempt to succeed in jumping an electric wave across the Atlantic."[39] Radio soon proved its value to mankind particularly on ships at sea; the most dramatic early use of radio was the role it played in the rescue of survivors from the Titanic when it struck an iceberg on April 14, 1912. The wireless log of the Carpathia, one of the rescue ships noted at 11.20pm on April 14, 1912: "Hear Titanic calling SOS and CQD. Titanic says: 'Struck iceberg, come to our assistance at once.'" Carpathia's course was altered and 712 persons were rescued.

Marconi erected an experimental high-power transmitting station at Clifden in 1905 with a corresponding receiving station at Letterfrack; the mile-long receiving aerial ran along the top of the mountain behind Kylemore. The transmitter power was nominally 150kw and steam to work the plant was supplied from turf-fired boilers. Commercial transatlantic radio service was provided for a few years but the stations were closed down in 1916 and the traffic was transferred to a new radio station at Caernarvon.[40]

The new medium of telecommunication, radio (wireless telegraphy), was used in a dramatic fashion during the Easter Rising of 1916. A ship's transmitter of the Irish School of Wireless Telegraphy at the corner of O'Connell Street and Lower Abbey Street, Dublin, which had been put out of action at the start of the World War was repaired on Easter Monday 1916 by the insurgents and an aerial was erected on the roof. On Easter Tuesday the station transmitted communiqués in morse code in the names of Pearse, Connolly and Plunkett that the Irish Republic had been proclaimed in Dublin. On Easter Wednesday, the station came under heavy artillery fire and further transmission became impossible. The transmitter was taken across O'Connell Street to Republican Headquarters in the General Post Office, subsequently to be the home of Irish broadcasting from 1926 to 1960, and presumably perished in the flames that destroyed the building.[41]

The Department of Posts and Telegraphs had hoped as early as 1924 that the new form of communication, radio, might play a vital role in modernising the new State's poor telecommunication services. The Minister for Posts and Telegraphs, James J. Walsh, told the Dáil in 1924 that

> if it did happen that we could utilise directional wireless, the expenses of equipping [premises for telephonic communication] ... would be very little: it would be quite infinitesimal.[42]

In essence, the Minister was anticipating microwave links operating at frequencies much higher than ordinary domestic radio apparatus and capable of carrying thousands of multiplexed voice channels between terminals. Even the Minister's hopes were years ahead of the fast-developing technology.

The electro-magnetic spectrum is an essential element in modern forms of telecommunication. The electro-magnetic spectrum consists of a variety of forms of radiation which all have common properties. The essential properties are: (a) all radiation is propagated in the form of waves and (b) all waves travel at 300 million metres per second (186,000 miles per second). The different forms of radiation are distinguished by the distance between the crests of the waves, called the "wavelength". The number of waves passing a fixed point per second is called the "frequency".[43]

Today, wireless telegraphy or radio communication is effected by generating electro-magnetic energy — generally by means of a transmitter — which conveys information (usually by disturbing the electro-magnetic energy.) This energy is then radiated into the environment essentially by means of an antenna. An antenna in another position intercepts some of this radiated electro-magnetic energy which is then processed by a receiver so that the information, be it sound, pictures or computer data, is extracted. The mere passage of the electro-magnetic energy between transmitter and receiver is used to obtain information as in radar.[44]

The term "radio waves" is ascribed to the range of electro-magnetic waves which can be propagated by a transmitter and broadcast through the atmosphere. Although radio waves travel at the speed of light they are subject to absorption, diffusion, reflection and diffraction. The radio waves which pass through the environment change rapidly in magnetic and electrical polarity at a fixed rate per second. This rate of change is known as the frequency of the wave. The scientific unit of measurement for rate of change is a hertz (named after Heinrich Hertz, the nineteenth century German physicist who laid the theoretical framework for the development of radio) and the basic unit for designating lower radio frequencies is the kilohertz(kHz). When a number of kilohertz is designated, this describes a position on the spectrum. A radio station at 885 kHz on the dial is located at 885 kHz on the spectrum. The number of units of kilohertz extends to millions. One thousand kilohertz (1,000 kHz) is the same as one million hertz or one megahertz (MHz). The term "gigahertz" refers to a 1,000 megahertz. The radio spectrum is so vast in scope that it must be divided into portions for the purpose of regulation. At first, the length of the waves was chosen as the basis for regulation. The early regulators divided the spectrum as they knew it into "long waves", "medium waves" and "short waves". Modern regulators tend to label portions of the spectrum in terms of frequency — yet it is still customary to refer to the first three divisions by the comparative length of the waves; 30 to 300 kHz are designated as "the long waves"; 300 to 3,000 kHz are designated as "the medium waves" (medium frequencies), and 3,000 to 30,000 kHz are designated as the "short waves" (high frequencies).

Subsequently, as greater knowledge about the spectrum beyond 30 MHz became known, it was necessary to continue dividing and labelling portions of the spectrum. The frequencies (hertz) of the waves instead of the length became the standard of measurement. The newly discovered portions of the spectrum consisted of waves with higher frequencies and were designated by words qualifying "high". Thirty to 300 MHz were designated as Very High Frequencies (VHF), 300 to 3,000 MHz were designated as Ultra High Frequencies (UHF), 3,000 to 30,000 MHz were designated as Super High Frequencies (SHF) and 30,000 to 300,000 MHz were designated as Extremely High Frequencies (EHF).

The continuum of frequencies is called the electro-magnetic spectrum and the radio portion is called the radio spectrum. The rest of the electro-magnetic spectrum is divided into infra-red rays, visible light, ultraviolet light, x-rays, gamma rays and cosmic rays.

In the radio spectrum, low frequencies stay close to the ground and travel great distances. Medium frequencies travel along the ground and travel greater distances particularly at night by reflecting off invisible ionised layers of molecules in the ionosphere (100 kilometres or more above ground level). High frequencies — the so called short-wave radio — travel great distances between the ionised layers of molecules and the ground and bounce around the world. The highest frequencies tend to travel in a straight line like light and do not reflect off the ionosphere at all. Most use of radio today is confined to frequencies between 10 kilohertz and 40 gigahertz However, this is constantly changing as higher and higher frequencies come into use. In fact, light communication by lasers is already in operational use between satellites in space.[45]

The "standard" broadcasting service is usually called AM broadcasting ("amplitude modulation"). Sounds are produced by holding the frequencies constant but altering the heights of the waves produced in the transmission. The receiving apparatus decodes these differences in height and reproduces the original sounds that were transmitted. The other radio service is called FM broadcasting ("frequency modulation"). In FM broadcasting the height of the waves is held constant but the frequency of the waves transmitted is varied. FM broadcasting provides higher quality service with less interference than AM broadcasts, but FM waves are in the VHF spectrum, serve smaller areas and do not follow the earth's curvature.

Television utilises both kinds of transmission — amplitude modulation for the picture and frequency modulation for the sound. The signals' range is short because the transmissions are either in the VHF or UHF bands. The amount of information that must be transmitted over television has led to channels that are six MHz wide. Accordingly, each VHF broadcaster uses an amount of spectrum space nearly six times greater than that used by the entire AM spectrum.[46]

4

Telecommunication Carrier Services 1930-1993

PRE-WAR AND WAR YEARS

The Dáil was informed in April 1931 on behalf of Ernest Blythe, the Vice-President of the Executive Council and also Minister for Finance and Posts and Telegraphs, that the quality of the telephone service in Ireland had improved; there were fewer complaints and the value of the telephone as a business asset was more and more appreciated by users.[1] Further, telephone revenue and expenditure broke even for the first time in the years 1930-1931. The Opposition was not impressed. Seán MacEntee, TD, stated that the conditions of the telegraph and telephone service were "exceedingly discreditable".[2] He stated that the telephone service in the city of Dublin would be a disgrace to the village of the "Sleepy Hollow" and opined that business persons were so dissatisfied with delays that they preferred to have telegrams and cablegrams transmitted from London rather than the Irish Post Office.[3]

The Second World War put the entire telecommunication infrastructure of the country under enormous strain. Security and the Government's perceived necessity of securing some form of independent means of telecommunication with the United States dominated policy decisions in relation to telecommunication during the war years. In 1940, the British Government, on security grounds, sought the acquiescence of the Irish Government in the cutting, in deep water, of the telegraph lines of the American Western Union and Commercial Cable companies between Valentia and Waterville, County Kerry, and locations abroad.[4] The telegraph cables were to be connected directly to landing points in Britain. The telegraph cables involved were the Commercial Cable Company's three cables to New York via Newfoundland and Nova Scotia, two cables to the Azores connecting with a cable from the Azores to New York; two cables from Waterville to Le Havre and four cables to Weston-

Super-Mare continued by land line to London. The Western Union Company's telegraph cables included were the four cables to New York via Newfoundland and Nova Scotia and three cables to Senen Cove, Cornwall. The telegraph stations in Valentia and Waterville were almost wholly used for the relaying of telegraphic traffic between Britain (and formerly France) and America in both directions. The telegraph traffic specifically relating to the business of Ireland was relatively small. Although the staff of 16 at Waterville and 20 at Valentia were to be affected and local economic loss seemed inevitable, the Irish Government at its Cabinet meeting on July 5, 1940 agreed to the British proposal. One transatlantic traffic cable was to continue in existence. The Western Union cable from Valentia to New York was to provide an outlet for transatlantic traffic from Ireland;[5] submarine cables on the East Coast were not directly affected as they were owned jointly by the State and Britain.[6]

Many emergency measures had to be adopted during the Second World War to ensure that the Irish Government would be able to communicate both within and outside the State and to ensure that the telecommunication service would not be used in an un-authorised manner. The Government, anxious to have an alternative means of communication with the United States apart from the single transatlantic telegraph, made provision for the use of the Shannon Airport radio installed in Ballygirreen and Urlanmore which operated in conjunction with the meteorological station at Foynes and which had been used for transmitting messages in relation to transatlantic flights. An emergency radio service was established in July 1940 between these stations and stations of the Mackay Radio and Telegraph Company, New York, for the trans-mission of messages on the service of the Irish and United States Governments.[7] Emergency arrangements were devised for the pro-vision of electrical power for telephone services in the event of interruption of the ordinary supply from any cause. The military ensured that it had a system of radio communication independent of the Post Office telecommunication system but calls on the telephone system described as "Defence Priority" or "Garda Priority" were given "right of way" over public telephone traffic on all lines.[8]

A rigorous censorship system was established in the State during the war years. Prior to the outbreak of war, the Department of Finance in a memorandum for the Government estimated that 350 persons would be required for postal censorship purposes "owing to the necessity for the examination of all matter passing through the mails" and that others would be required for telegraph censorship.[9] Although communications of virtually all descriptions including communications "by post, telegraph, hand or pigeons" was suggested in August 1939[10] as coming within the scope of censorship, the Office of the Controller of Censorship in a memorandum for the Government admitted that it was possible by 1941 to avoid censorship altogether by using the telephone service between Great Britain and Ireland. An effective "one hundred per cent censorship control of every cross-channel and trans-border telephone conversation" was ruled out as being "impracticable" because of lack of staff.[11] The Office of the Controller of Censorship recommended a partial restriction of telephonic communications between Britain and Ireland and what was termed as "partial control" as the best method for assisting the censorship process.[12] Telegrams were subject to direct censorship and for periods during the war pursuant to the *Emergency Powers (No. 67) Order, 1941* no person could send any communication relating to any event connected with the war or in relation to the supply of commodities by "post, telegraph, telephone, or any other means whatsoever" to any person outside the State unless first authorised.[13] War-time censorship was abolished at the end of the War with effect from May 11, 1945.[14]

Following the fall of France, the Minister for Posts and Telegraphs was required at short notice and as a matter of absolute urgency to provide telephone lines to 84 lookout posts on headlands around the coasts. New telephone routes had to be provided to places such as Achill Head, Slieve League and Brandon Head. Telephone facilities to the headlands were all completed within the months of June and July 1940.[15]

As the war proceeded, arrangements were made to ensure that local engineering staff of the Department of Posts and Telegraphs would put telegraph and telephone facilities in occupied areas "completely out of commission . . . provided they had reasonable opportunity for doing so".[16] However, no action was to be taken in relation to any destruction of telecommunication facilities except on the instructions of competent military officers.[17] The reserved supply of telephone and telegraph apparatus held in Dublin was split up around the country but was principally located in Cork, Limerick and Waterford.[18]

In the context of telecommunication services, as indeed in other areas, the Irish Administration was, in the words of Dr. León Ó Broin,[19] a former Secretary of the Department of Posts and Telegraphs, "more than fair" during the war period: "[A]djustments [were made] at the outbreak of the war to suit [the British] and during the war to avoid leaks of information or criticism. . . ."[20] Dr. Ó Broin recorded that in February 1945 the British request to establish a radar station on Irish territory for use in detecting German submarine activity was approved.[21] In fact, radar was one of the spectacular advances in telecommunication which were developed during World War II. The word "radar", coined from the letters "ra" for radio, "d" for detection or direction finding, "a" from and, and "r" from ranging, was based on the echo principle; a radio wave striking an object whether an aircraft, ship, building or planet in space bounces back or echoes on the radio receiver. With the aid of an appropriate screen, ships, aircraft and physical objects come into view. The allies during World War II used this latest development in telecommunication with devastating effect. When the Luftwaffe bombed England, the German aircrews met unexpected opposition: radar had enabled the RAF fighter planes to mobilise and to battle with the German planes over the English Channel. Developments in radar continued and on January 10, 1946 a radar signal beamed at the moon from Evans Signal Laboratory in New Jersey echoed back in 2.4 seconds; 478,000 miles had been traversed by the radio signal in a return trip to the moon.

CABINET COMMITTEE ON ECOMONIC PLANNING
1943-1946

A major examination of the telephone service was undertaken in the period 1943-1946. The Cabinet Committee on Economic Planning, conscious of the importance of telecommunication, directed in January 1943 that the Department of Posts and Telegraphs prepare and submit for consideration by the Committee proposals for the extension of telephone facilities and the development of their use in cities, urban and rural areas.[22] Responding in October 1943,[23] the Department stated that plans for the development of the telephone service could only be put into active operation on a post-war return of normal supply conditions. The Department argued that there should be a public telephone call office in every post office and that a plan should be formulated to implement this programme over a number of years. By 1943 there were 1,913 post offices (including sub-post offices) in the country with 991 having public telephone facilities. The Department stressed that any plan for the opening of public telephone facilities in every post office was put forward only as an emergency unemployment relief scheme. Specifically, it was stated that the plan was not based on forecasts of normal telephone development requirements and normal principles of administration of the telephone service from the perspectives of revenue, profit and such related issues.[24]

The Cabinet Committee on Economic Planning in October 1943 urged the Department of Posts and Telegraphs to co-ordinate rural telephone development with the proposals of the Electricity Supply Board in relation to rural electrification. The question of the use of the same poles to carry both communication and power circuits was also raised by the Cabinet Committee on Economic Planning.[25] Engineers from the Department of Posts and Telegraphs considered the issue but concluded that any economic advantages that could be gained would not justify the serious risks of electric shock which could be fatal being sustained by users of telephones working over circuits erected for long distance on the Electricity Supply Board poles carrying high tension wires.[26]

The Cabinet Committee on Economic Planning turned to the issue of the development of the telephone again in April 1944. It directed that the Department of Posts and Telegraphs report on preparatory steps which ought to be taken concerning the revision of telephone charges and publicity designed to popularise the use of the telephone with a view to a considerable extension of the installation of private telephones in the cities and larger towns when conditions permitted. Reporting in November 1944[27] the Department stated that in relation to the administration and development of the telephone service, the Department kept constantly before it the principle that while the service should not seek to earn large profits, it should conduct its business so that losses would be avoided. The Department argued that this principle of being self-supporting must be borne in mind in the context of any proposals for altering rates or any other changes which might lead to the more extensive installation of telephones. The Department stated that its profit for the financial year 1942-43 was IR£242,000 but the profit was to some extent inflated by temporary conditions such as the "abnormal extent" to which the telephone was used by the commercial community and private persons during the Emergency due to general transport difficulties and problems of trade. The Department argued that there would be a reduction in demand following restoration of the normal conditions. However, the Department sensibly noted that the telephone service was in "a relatively undeveloped state" and would certainly continue to expand and that as "all classes of people" had acquired the habit of using the telephone extensively during the Emergency, it may be taken that the telephone service would be "used more and more in the future". The Department in its detailed report accepted that a considerable extension of the installation of private telephones in cities and larger towns should be encouraged when conditions permitted such extension. It considered that the provision and maintenance of the highest possible degree of efficiency in the telephone service was the most potent factor in the expansion of the service but that it was impossible to foresee what the financial position of the telephone service would be in the post-war period and accordingly nothing definite could be stated about reduction of the rates of charge. The Department submitted that the cost of the entire programme of work necessary to overtake arrears of development and maintenance and to provide for appropriate expansion for a 5 year period was estimated at IR£2m.

The Cabinet Committee on Economic Planning again requested in April 1945 that the Department of Posts and Telegraphs prepare a detailed programme to increase the number of subscriber telephone installations from the then existing 31,000 to 100,000 over a period of 5 years.[28] Responding in considerable detail to the Government in October 1946[29] the Department argued that because of the immensity of the building and engineering construction programme which would have to be carried out, it would not be practicable to increase the number of installations to 100,000 within a 5 year period. To achieve such a programme would involve the provision of 350,000 miles of subscriber circuits, the replacement of all but the smallest exchanges by automatic exchanges, the provision of about 50 manual exchanges, the extension of the then 23,000 miles of trunk circuits 6 to 8 fold, the erection of about 130 buildings for automatic exchanges and extensive alterations of post offices. The total capital cost for such a scheme was estimated at £10m. Further, the Department argued that the 69,000 additional subscribers could not be attracted within 5 years. It was argued that the minimum period, even under the most favourable conditions, to achieve such a target would be 10 years. The Department in its submission to the Government stated that it "thought better therefore" to request authority not to proceed with the preparation of plans on the lines suggested.[30]

The Department of Posts and Telegraph did outline its own plan to the Government: the attainment of maximum telephone development then provisionally estimated at 100,000 installations was to be achieved "in the shortest possible time"; all new subscribers should be catered for within 2 to 3 years; the telephone service was to be made as efficient, attractive and as cheap as possible; the telephone should be sold by "the best methods of publicity and canvassing"; continuous service would be given by means of automatic equipment at all but the smallest exchanges; the telephone trunk service would be of "demand" standard, i.e. all trunk calls, save "an occasional one at the busiest traffic period" would be connected without the caller having to leave the telephone; telephone kiosks would be provided generously in cities and towns; various tariff changes likely to attract new customers would be considered but reductions in the tariff rate would depend on the financial state of the telephone service at the appropriate time. In its memorandum for the Government, the Department considered it desirable to estimate the ultimate saturation point of telephone development. Taking the most optimistic view, the Department stated that under the most favourable conditions "with general national prosperity" a figure of 80,000 telephone installations (about 130,000 instruments) would represent saturation of telephone development for all classes except farmers. The Department argued that this development would be equivalent to one telephone to every ten people in the cities, towns and villages. This rate of telephone development

> could be attained only if almost everyone slightly above the artisan class had a residence telephone and if fairly small shops as well as every business supplying labour were to have a business line. To effect such development there would have to be radical change in the outlook of the population towards the telephone which most of them at present, rightly or wrongly, regard as a luxury. It is possible to conceive of this change of outlook being brought about under exceptionally favourable conditions by intensive propaganda and by substantial reduction of rates of charge. But the Department is firmly of opinion that the change could be effected only over a long period. If earnings tended to rise steadily it might be possible to reach the estimated degree of development in as little as ten years, but should there be any spell of relative depression within that period, it would not be reached for very much longer. The Department has no doubt whatever that it would not be reached under any circumstances within a lesser period than ten years.[31]

It was estimated that about 20,000 farmers might take the telephone service within a measurable period. This figure represented
approximately the number of farmers with holdings of 100 acres and
upwards — 5 per cent of all the holdings. The Department was
mindful of the fact that the rural electrification scheme might change
the outlook of the farming community towards what may be
regarded as "urban luxuries".

The Department was very conscious of the profit it was then
making on the telephone service: 1943-44 — IR£247,708; 1944-45 —
IR£267,289, but the Department argued that the provision of
equipment and lines too far in advance of being required as a result
of over-optimistic estimates of expansion of demand, or excessive
reduction of rates of charge, would burden the telephone service
with a heavy and unnecessary loss "which would not be eliminated
for many years, *if ever*"[32] (emphasis added).

The Cabinet at its meeting on October 22, 1946 agreed with the
recommendation of the Minister for Posts and Telegraphs that the
Minister should not proceed with the preparation of the plan sought
by the Cabinet Committee on Economic Planning to increase the
number of telephone subscribers' installations to 100,000 within 5
years. The alternative proposals of the Minister were agreed: the
maximum telephone development estimated at 100,000, which
would involve an increase of 69,000 subscribers, was to be achieved
in the shortest possible period; provision was to be made for continuous service at all but the smallest telephone exchanges (one to
four subscribers); there was to be virtually a "no delay" service on
trunk calls; kiosks were to be erected on a generous scale in towns
and cities; favourable consideration was to be given to reductions of
telephone charges, subject to the maintenance of the principle that
the telephone service should, in the long run, be self-supporting.[33]

The fruits of the various deliberations on the telephone service
between 1943 and 1946 were announced by the Minister for Posts
and Telegraphs, Patrick Little, when he spoke in the Dáil on the
second stage of the *Telephone Capital Bill, 1946*.[34] Public anger at the
poor state of the telephone service was vented in the Dáil and in the
media. Delays on trunk telephone calls immediately after the war
had become inordinate; in virtually all the telephone exchanges there
was serious traffic congestion. Owing to the emergency conditions
and the difficulties in procuring equipment for the telephone service,
little was done during the war period towards meeting the demand
for telephones. In fact, the Department of Posts and Telegraphs
refused virtually all applications for telephones for social use and

for many business purposes during the years 1945 and 1946.[35] Yet
traffic on the telephone network continued to increase: trunk traffic
increased from 3.3 million calls in 1938 to 7.118 million in 1945 and
local calls increased from 30 million to 48 million within the same
period.[36] In the Dáil, James Dillon T.D. referred to "pandemonium"
in the telephone service, the lack of trained personnel and the
"fantastic parsimony of the Department of Posts and Telegraphs".[37]
A leading article in the *Irish Press* on November 8, 1946 described the
service as "hopelessly inadequate". The *Irish Independent*, in its
leading article on November 7, 1946 commenting on the Minister's
plan to have the telephone in every post office in the country within
7 to 10 years noted wryly:

> This Ten-Year Plan certainly does not err on the side of rash-
> ness. If this is the best he can do for his own offices, the prospects
> of seeing telephones in farm-houses need hardly be considered
> this side of the year 2000 A.D.

The Department of Finance in a memorandum for the Government in February 1951 admitted that the programme for the telephone service outlined in 1946 was not reaching its projected targets.
Shortage of engineering staff, difficulties in making progress in
building projects and increased public demand for telephones were
stated to be the causes of the Department's failure to provide as many
provincial automatic telephone exchanges and additional trunk
lines as had been intended. By 1951, cross-channel trunk traffic had
outstripped the available capacity of the route; the 48 circuits were
heavily overloaded.[38] Although telephones were being installed at
almost treble the pre-war period, the waiting list was growing.[39]

CARRIER SERVICES 1951-1993

On March 1, 1951, 700 post offices were still without telephones;
5,300 applicants were waiting for telephone service with 3,000 of
those applicants in Dublin.[40] Erskine Childers, Minister for Posts and
Telegraphs, noted in July 1951: "Young people in the country
particularly are beginning for good or ill to dislike isolation and
communications of every kind are now regarded as essential to
modern civilisation."[41] The notion that telephonic communication
was not "desired by the rural mind" had been finally scotched.[42]

In 1951 another plan was prepared by the Department of Posts and Telegraphs. The five-year plan of 1951 made provision "for meeting in full the public demand for telephones and for raising the standard of trunk service to a satisfactory level".[43] Subsequently, in the early 1950s co-axial carrier cables were laid from Dublin to Cork via Limerick with a branch from Portlaoise to Waterford, and from Dublin via Drogheda and Dundalk to the border where they linked with cable from Belfast.[44] [A co-axial cable bears its name because one conductor runs inside, and is insulated from, a surrounding conductor similar to a larger version of the familiar television aerial lead. To carry information in both directions, two cables are required. It was thus possible to provide 600 circuits on the southern and northern cables.]

Substantial advances in the development of telecommunication service could only be possible if the network service became completely automatised. Automatic dialling — without the intervention of an operator — had been possible in many European countries, in particular Switzerland, the Netherlands and Western Germany, by 1957. An engineer from the Netherlands Post Office, G.J. Kamerbeek, with the assistance of the United Nations Technical Assistance Administration, presented a report on automation to the Minister for Posts and Telegraphs in 1958.[45] The Kamerbeek report was accepted, with certain modifications, as the basis for further planning of the telecommunication carrier service in Ireland.

By 1961 subscriber trunk dialling (STD) facilities had been provided in all the main automatic telephone exchanges[46] — but the universal automation of the telephone service in the country was not to be completed until 1987 when Dr Michael Smurfit, Chairman of Telecom Éireann, presided over a ceremony which witnessed the closing of the the the last Telecom Éireann manual exchange in Mountshannon, County Clare, on May 28, 1987.[47] By May 1987, there were 1,023 automatic telephone exchanges in Ireland.

The facility of using microwave links in Ireland for the transmission of telephone messages, first mooted by the Minister for Posts and Telegraphs in 1924,[48] became a reality in April 1960 when an analogue microwave link between Athlone and Galway with a capacity for 240 circuits was introduced.[49] A circuit involves two channels: one for the "go-path" and one for the "return path". Microwaves are radio waves which are used to transmit signals along waveguides and for point-to-point directional radio links. Unlike telephone current, which is a flow of electrons through a conductor, electro-magnetic waves travel through space at a speed of 300 million metres per second. Microwaves can be focused into a beam by a conclave "dish" or antenna in much the same way as the curved reflection of a torch focuses the light for a bulb placed at the focus. Microwaves travel in straight lines but need relay stations every 40 km or so to amplify and retransmit the signal across the country to follow the earth's curvature. Microwaves can be modulated — can have a speech signal superimposed on them. In 1961 the microwave system was extended to carry Ireland's first black and white television service. In 1985 a digital microwave link was introduced between Dublin and Belfast. This link carries two channels each carrying 1920 simultaneous calls or two colour television programmes. In 1988, the new digital system covering the entire country with a trunk network was completed.

Virtually since the invention of the telephone the demand for telephone service in Ireland outstripped the rate at which new service could be supplied. The long delay which applicants were forced to endure for telephone service continued to be a regular source of complaint. In 1953 there were 6,700 applicants for new service. By 1958 that figure had grown to 10,600 and in 1963 the figure was approximately 16,500.[50] By 1973 the waiting list for telephones had grown to around 34,000.[51] The waiting list for telephones on December 31, 1978 was 63,000.[52] The *Dargan Report* (May 1979)[53] noted that the demand for telephone service had been deliberately discouraged and quoted Mr. Ó Droma, Deputy Secretary of the Department of Posts and Telegraphs in charge of the telecommunication carrier service:

> No effort had been made to "sell" telephones; in fact the Department's practice of insisting on payment, by all new subscribers, of rental covering a year at least in advance was designed to contain the enormous latent demand within manageable limits.[54]

By 1993, in general, telephone service could be provided for customers on demand or within a period of days.

In 1956 the Minister for Posts and Telegraphs posed the question in the Dáil as to why there should be so long a waiting list after the war when so many other shortages had disappeared. The Minister put forward two arguments to explain the delay in providing service. Firstly, there was the fundamental necessity to forecast several years in advance what the likely requirements would be. Secondly, the Department of Posts and Telegraphs had been experiencing difficulty in recruiting and retaining suitably qualified engineering staff.[55] Both these explanations were unsatisfactory. In simple terms, the Department was unable to obtain sufficient capital funds largely because of other services which were clamouring for money such as housing and sanitary services, hospitals and agricultural developments. Dr. León Ó Broin, a former Secretary of the Department of Posts and Telegraphs, who retired in 1967 having served ten Ministers and one Parliamentary Secretary, blamed successive Ministers for Posts and Telegraphs for the shortage of capital for telephone service.[56] Dr. Ó Broin described these Ministers as "modest men who came to the Post Office without much in the way of ideas".[57] He described the Ministers as "essentially juniors".[58] None of the Ministers even among those who did attain some seniority "were able to fight their corner in the cabinet room or with the Minister for Finance who controlled the supply of money".[59] Dr. León Ó Broin lamented that "the Post Office was always down towards the bottom of the list".[60] He concluded that the Department did not count for much politically.[61]

The Minister for Posts and Telegraphs in 1973, Dr. Conor Cruise O'Brien, described the policy of the Department of Posts and Telegraphs in relation to the development of the telephone service as "stop-go". He instanced the severe capital restrictions of 1970 as being a further example of that stop-go policy. He instanced the retrenchment measures of 1970 and 1971 such as the laying-off of construction staff, suspension of certain recruitment, reductions in the purchase of engineering stores and the deferment of the placing of major contracts as examples of unsatisfactory policies.[62] By the end of 1973 Dr. Cruise O'Brien confessed that the capacity of the telephone service needed to be "greatly enlarged".[63] Exchanges had insufficient equipment to take on all the applicants for service. Many exchanges were overloaded particularly during the busy periods. These factors resulted in persons encountering the engaged tone or no tone at all. There was a shortage of subscriber equipment. The trunk system was short of lines and equipment and was causing an abnormal failure rate in the busy hours. Telephone density was the lowest in Europe: there were only 12 telephones per 100 of the population as compared with 19 in France which was then the next lowest.[64]

Conscious of the poor state of the telecommunication carrier service, the Government in 1979 approved an accelerated development programme to raise the quality of telephone, telex and data services to the level enjoyed by the industrialised nations of the European Community. Although by 1979, 90 per cent of the telephone subscribers had access to automatic telephone service, the remaining 10 per cent of subscribers were still connected to some 500 manual telephone exchanges.[65] The state of the telecommunication carrier service generally constituted a crisis.[66] The *Dargan Report* considered that the cause of the shortcomings and inefficiences was primarily structural: the shortcomings were particularly in the areas of "planning, provision of capital, the availability of buildings, plant and equipment, pricing policy, personnel policy, and industrial relations and general organisation".[67] The *Dargan Report* is examined in chapter 9.

By 1979 the network used step-by-step equipment at some of the major trunk exchanges and in certain local exchanges.[68] The automatic switch (invented by Strowger), where a train of pulses corresponded to each digit dialled, facilitated a connection on a step-by-step basis until the caller got through to the number required. This system was refined over the years but remained the general prototype for automatic exchanges in Ireland until the mid 1950s. "Crossbar" systems were also used in certain exchanges. Crossbar switching systems had been installed for the first time in Ireland in Limerick Telephone Exchange in 1957. The successor to the old step-by-step switches, the new crossbar switches had fewer moving parts and were more reliable thus requiring less maintenance. Another major advantage was what was termed a "common control" feature. The digits of the required number were first stored and a check was made to ascertain if the line was engaged before any connection was made; this process facilitated complex interconnections. By early 1989 there were 525 crossbar exchanges in Ireland with only two step-by-step models. The last two step-by-step exchanges, Ship Street and Clontarf in Dublin, were closed in April 1989 and customers were transferred to digital exchanges. It is envisaged that the crossbar exchanges capable of providing a high quality service will remain in commission for some years.

Both the step-by-step and crossbar exchanges handled signals in analogue form. In essence this was a form which continuously mirrored or was analogous with the varying pattern of information. The transmission systems consisted in 1979 of co-axial cables paralleled by analogue microwave radio in the main arteries of the network and audio cable fitted with 30 channel pulse-codemodulation systems in the lower levels.[69] Six hundred and fifty million pounds was estimated at 1979 levels as being necessary to achieve the Government's target of constructing more than 500 buildings, replacing the step-by-step telephone exchanges,

expanding the transmission network and the automatisation programme which would make the manual telephone exchanges
redundant. The decision was then made to opt for digital technology
and to build an integrated digital network as early as possible. The
poor state of the telecommunication carrier infrastructure in 1979
enabled the Department of Posts and Telegraphs and Telecom
Éireann to develop and implement a radical telecommunication
development programme that would have been deferred had the
telecommunication infrastructure not been in such a deteriorated
condition.

The public telex network, the venerable successor to the telegraph
network, had become fully automatic in Ireland in 1964 with
approximately 100 subscribers.[70] A new international telex gateway
exchange came into service in Ireland in 1974. This exchange used a
fully computerised stored programme control (SPC) which was the
first of its kind in Western Europe and the second in the world.[71] The
Time Division Multiplex system is now extensively used in the Irish
network and internationally. Facilities in the telex network include
automatic dialling and clearing, broadcast calls, store and forward
capacity, recorded messages, number changes and call re-direction
and automatic advice of duration.[72] By 1988 the telex service was in
the declining phase of its life cycle. The development of newer text
transmission services such as facsimile (fax) hastened the number of
telex cessations and migration to other services. By 1989, there were
5,371 working telex lines in the State. Telecom Éireann launched a
new service for telex users in 1988 which allowed telex messages to
be sent from a personal computer, word processor or electronic
typewriter. This service was called PACTEX (from Packet Telex).

The arrival of "digitisation" brought many benefits to the Irish
telecommunication service. Digitisation involves the encoding,
transformation and transmission of any information — whether in
the form of voice, data or visual, as binary digits or "bits". The
application of micro-electronics to transmission and switching has
facilitated the replacement of electrical signals in analogue form by
transmission in the form of a stream of bits representing the information content — digitisation. In any telephone system the vocal
cords set up sound waves in the air. When the sound waves enter
the mouthpiece of the telephone, they are transformed by a small
microphone into electrical waves of a matching shape. In analogue
transmission systems, which are so called because the electrical
waves are analogous or similar to the spoken sound waves, the
waves of electricity travel along cables through the exchanges which

direct them to the earpiece of the receiving telephone. A miniature loudspeaker in the receiving telephone converts the electrical waves back into the normal source of the human voice. In a digital transmission system, the voice is changed into an electrical wave as in the analogue system. The height of this wave is then sampled thousands of times a second to yield a series of numbers. These numbers are turned into a stream of electrical pulses — on/off binary digits, or bits which then travel through the telecommunication network. At the receiving end, the information is reconstructed as an analogue signal and turned into sound. Digital signals can operate millions of times per second and leave comparatively long intervals between them. Into these intervals other signals can be interleaved by a process called time division multiplexing. Digital computerised exchanges do not need to make continuous connections but instead open and close electronic circuits repetitively at just the right instant to pass on the appropriate streams of digits along the correct route thus handling many calls simultaneously.

Micro-electronics has allowed the electromechanical control system of telecommunication processes to be replaced by computer systems, known as stored program control (SPC). SPC switches are software controlled and facilitate easy maintenance and reconfigurability in addition to making many enhanced services possible.

Facilities like abbreviated dialling, call transfer and call forward, and conference calls are possible in digital exchanges. Communications in any form, be they voice, text, image or data, can be encoded in digital format. The multi-service telecommunication network ISDN (Integrated Services Digital Network) was shaped in the 1980s. Data processing installations are increasingly connected via telecommunication links into interconnected networks. Herbert Ungerer has noted in this context that "telecommunications networks add the dimension of movement to the localised intelligence of traditional computer centres".[73]

In 1980, contracts for the supply and installation of digital telephone exchanges in Ireland were awarded to L.M. Ericsson Ltd for its AXE 10 system and CIT-Alcatel Ltd for its E 10B system. The first "digital" exchange opened in Roslevin, Athlone in 1981. By 1993, the equipped capacity of digital telephone exchanges comprised approximately 66 per cent of the total capacity of Telecom Éireann exchanges.

The extensive microwave link network which provided radio links connecting all the main switching centres in the country and carrying most of the telecommunication traffic between these centres were in place by 1980. The national digital radio link network was completed in 1988.[74] The digital radio link network linking major centres throughout Ireland was provided primarily for the transmission of multi-channel digital telephony and the transmission of data and television signals.[75]

The public mobile telephone service called Eircell became operational in the Greater Dublin area in December 1985. As explained earlier, the radio frequency spectrum is divided into a number of bands, each of which is sub-divided into radio channels. Prior to the 1980s, mobile telecommunication services were limited by the number of radio frequencies allocated for those services and by technological restraints. Cellular telephone technology has resulted in greater numbers of users being served by the same radio channel. The system in use in Ireland operates in the 890-960 MHz band.[76] To facilitate the public mobile telephone service, areas to be serviced are divided into a number of smaller areas called cells. The cellular system is comprised of three main elements interlinked with each other: (a) a radio base station, (b) mobile radio units and (c) a mobile telephone exchange (MTX). Each cell is served by a radio base station which contains a number of transmitters and receivers which communicate via radio signals with mobile telephones located in each cell. When a telephone call is made to someone with a "cellular" telephone, the signal enters the radio network via a mobile telephone exchange and an appropriate Eircell base station to the relevant receiving telephone. A transmitting and receiving aerial — perhaps on the roof of a car — is used to transmit a reply. Each base station is connected to a mobile telephone exchange which in turn is connected to the main telephone network and to other mobile telephone exchanges in the same cellular network. The transceivers used in the cells are of low power, making it possible to engineer the system so that no two adjacent cells use the same set of channels, but the next nearest cells can re-use them. Thus, the relatively scarce radio spectrum can be re-used repeatedly in the network. As no two adjacent cells use the same radio channels, the transmission system in the cellular telephone automatically changes channel when the user moves from cell to cell during a call.

The first phase of Eircell, which was launched in December 1985, consisted of one mobile telephone exchange located at Adelaide Road, Dublin and one radio base station at Three Rock Mountain, about 10 km south of Dublin. At first, these facilities offered extensive coverage in the Greater Dublin area.[77] However nationwide coverage is now almost available. Developments in relation to the

European GSM digital cellular mobile systems are considered in chapter 7.

An optical fibre telecommunication system, using glass fibre as the transmission medium, was installed in the telecommunication network on a trial basis in 1982 on the following telecommunication routes: Sligo-Ballymote, Waterford — Carrick-on-Suir and Dublin/ Adelaide Road — Palmerstown. In 1983 as a result of satisfactory tests, it was decided to use optical fibre in the network rather than co-axial cable for the provision of high and medium capacity digital cable transmission systems.[78] Optical fibre technology provides generous bandwidths with consequent communication handling capacity and the capability of spanning long distances without repeaters. Apart from economic savings over more traditional transmission systems, fibre optics systems offer the possibility of carrying broadband services such as long-distance video, cable television (CATV), video telephony, integrated services digital networks (ISDN) etc.[79] Telecom Éireann decided in 1984 that optical fibre cables would in general supersede co-axial cables and would be exclusively used for the development of the main trunk network and for high capacity systems in metropolitan junction networks.[80] An optical fibre cable (British Telecom — Telecom Éireann submarine cable system) was laid between Portmarnock (Dublin) and Holyhead (Wales) in 1988.[81] An optical fibre submarine cable named Celtic Cable between Wexford and Land's End, to be completed in 1994, is designed to ensure that sufficient capacity is provided to meet certain carrier demands into the twenty-first century. On completion, the cable will be the longest of its kind in the world. By 1993, optical fibre systems comprised 70 per cent of the transmission network of Telecom Éireann.

A video-conferencing service was inaugurated in Ireland in February 1985.[82] By 1987 video-conferencing facilities were available in Dublin, Cork, Limerick, Galway, Sligo and Waterford. The ISDN services which will be available towards the end of 1993 will allow generally for video-conferencing facilities.

Eirpage — a national paging service — was inaugurated in June 1988 by Eirpage Ltd, a joint venture between Telecom Éireann and Motorola Inc. — a US-based electronics company. The paging service allows a person to receive a full text message, a tone (bleep) or a voice message. Messages can be transmitted via a telephone, personal computer or via the telex service.

PTAT — a private transatlantic telephone cable facility — provides for two high capacity optical fibre cables linking North

America and Europe. The first of these cables is known as PTAT-1. PTAT-1 came into service in 1989 and was brought ashore in Ireland near Ballinspittle, Co. Cork via a spur cable off the main transatlantic route.[83] [Incidentally PTAT-1 was the first transatlantic cable to be landed in Ireland since 1905. Several hundred people were present on the beach where the cable was landed on May 24, 1989, a cold, bright morning, to witness the historic occasion.]

5

Radio and Broadcasting

EARLY DEVELOPMENT OF BROADCASTING IN IRELAND

The discovery of the ability to communicate by means of electro-magnetic energy led to the development of radio broadcasting. Broadcasting began in Ireland when the British Broadcasting Company commenced transmission in Belfast on September 15, 1924.[1] The Dublin *Evening Telegraph* noted:

> The first words spoken from the new broadcasting station in Belfast last night reached Dublin in a very English accent . . . I had just been listening through Glasgow to the sturdy accent of the Clyde, and expected from Belfast the accent of the Lagan. . . . But just at present Belfast is more English than the English themselves, and perhaps the choice of an announcer was motivated by this consideration. Another straw showing the present direction of the Belfast wind was the fact that while the British stations are content to finish their programmes with God Save the King, Belfast began its first programme with what most of its inhabitants regard as that good party tune.[2]

The Irish national broadcasting service was inaugurated by the Department of Posts and Telegraphs on January 1, 1926 when Dublin 2RN — the letters "RN" intended to refer to "ERIN" — transmitted its first programme from a single studio in Little Denmark Street, Dublin.[3] Dr. Douglas Hyde, founder of the Gaelic League and later President of Ireland, who delivered the opening speech, was very conscious of the significance of the new radio station and spoke of a new era in Ireland, "an era in which our nation will take its place among the nations of the world".[4]

At the outset, the new broadcasting service was subject to stringent control by the Department of Posts and Telegraphs which was itself subject to the tightest scrutiny from the Department of

Finance.[5] An official broadcasting station was subsequently opened in Cork on April 25, 1927 with the call-sign of 6CK and a one-kilowatt transmitter.[6] The broadcasting service was operated by employees of the State, a branch of the Department of Posts and Telegraphs. Licence fees and advertising were the principal sources of revenue, supplemented in the early years by import duties on receiving apparatus.

Sponsored programmes commenced in 1930 when individual Irish firms organised a segment of Irish broadcasting time. Government policy was that broadcasting was to be self-supporting; the Parliamentary Secretary to the Minister for Posts and Telegraphs, Michael R. Heffernan, stated in the Dáil in 1931: "[T]he broadcasting service should be considered as a business undertaking and should pay its way without assistance from general taxation."[7]

Subsequently, after the inevitable wrangling over cost and location, Athlone was chosen as the site of the first high-power broadcasting transmitter. The Athlone broadcasting transmitter was to facilitate a nation wide broadcasting service. Radio Athlone was formally opened by the President of the Executive Council, Eamon de Valera, on February 6, 1933. The occasion gave de Valera the opportunity of venting strong nationalistic feelings. In his opening speech, he stated that the Athlone broadcasting station would enable the world "to hear the voice of one of the oldest and, in many respects, one of the greatest of the nations".[8] He referred to Ireland's resistance to invaders which would "inevitably continue until the last sod of Irish soil is finally freed".[9] In grandiloquent style, Eamon de Valera concluded his broadcast speech by "calling modern science to the aid of Ireland's age-long mission" which he aspirated as being "true to her holiest traditions, [that] she may humbly serve the truth and help by truth to save the world".[10]

During the war years of 1939 to 1945, Radio Éireann, on the instructions of the Government, endeavoured to preserve (at least to the public) strict neutrality in its broadcasting. No weather forecasts were issued during the war; sports commentators could not refer to the weather; and un-scripted programmes were reduced to a minimum. Maurice Gorham has noted that news bulletins had to be read over to Frank Gallagher, the head of the Government Information Bureau, before they were broadcast and certain sensitive news broadcasts had to be read over to the Taoiseach, Eamon de Valera.[11]

Transmissions from the existing broadcasting stations including Athlone were, during the war years, constantly under observation by a Department Engineering officer in Athlone who was under instructions to stop the transmission of any broadcast where he had any doubt as to its authenticity.[12] The Government decided on July 23, 1940 that if the Minister for Defence, after consultation with the Minister for Posts and Telegraphs, was satisfied that possession of the Athlone Broadcasting Station and the radio stations at Ballygirreen and Urlanmore would be of military advantage to an invader, arrangements should be made for their destruction so that they would not fall into enemy hands.[13] Subsequently, on December 23, 1940 the Government decided that arrangements need not be made for the destruction of the actual stations; the destruction of the radio valves and essential parts was considered sufficiently effective.[14] Arrangements were made to put other radio stations out of order such as those at Valentia and Malin Head together with the telegraph cables at Valentia and Waterville — should the necessity arise.[15] Alternative broadcasting arrangements were made in the event of the Athlone broadcasting station being put out of action:[16] measures were taken to double the power of the Dublin broadcasting station and to use the Ballygirreen transmitter of the Shannon Airport radio installation for Limerick city and region.[17]

THE DEVELOPMENT OF TELEVISION AND RADIO SERVICES

Many demonstrations of television — the transmission of pictures by wire and radio using the cathode ray tube — took place in several countries in the 1930s including France, Britain, the United States, Germany, Italy, the USSR and Japan. High definition television services were first commenced in Germany and Britain in 1935 and 1936.[18] Broadcasting needed wider (radio) bands in higher frequencies as larger information contents were carried compared with sound radio. Television used the equivalent in bandwidth of nearly a 100,000 voice (telephone) circuits. The problem with these very high frequencies is that they pass through the ionosphere and do not bounce off it. Hence, signals for television are carried over long distances by means of relay stations. However, obstacles on the earth's surface such as mountains, forests and oceans restrict the transmission of such signals.

The rapid development of television throughout the world in the late 1940s and early 1950s prompted the Minister for Posts and Telegraphs to examine the feasibility of the introduction of a television service in Ireland. In April 1950, the Minister for Finance authorised the Minister for Posts and Telegraphs to purchase "an ordinary TV receiving set . . . on the understanding that no further expenditure on TV research [would] be proposed in the immediate future".[19] This decision forced the Minister for Posts and Telegraphs in March 1951 to prepare a memorandum for the Government at Cabinet level requesting permission for an officer from the engineering staff and an officer from the programme grades of the Department to travel abroad to study the regulation of television. The Government would then have expert advice when it was called upon to formulate definite decisions regarding the future of television in Ireland. Subsequently, the Minister for Finance consented to the proposal of the Department of Posts and Telegraphs thus ensuring that a formal decision of the Government would not be taken on the issue.[20] However, the Minister for Posts and Telegraphs brought the matter directly to the attention of the Taoiseach.[21]

Eventually, an Irish television broadcasting service was inaugurated on December 31, 1961. President Eamon de Valera in his address to the nation on the opening of Telefís Éireann stressed the influence of the new medium of telecommunication:

> Never before was there in the hands of men an instrument so powerful to influence the thoughts and actions of the multitude. . . . [A]part from imparting knowledge [broadcasting] can build up the character of the whole people inducing sturdiness and vigour and confidence. On the other hand, it can lead through demoralisation to decadence and disillusion. Sometimes one hears that one must give the people what they want. And the competition unfortunately is in the wrong direction so standards become lower and lower.[22]

A second television channel operated by RTE — RTE 2, subsequently renamed Network 2 — was inaugurated on November 2, 1978.

Radio Telefís Éireann broadcasts its television and radio programmes from transmitters located at Donnybrook, Kippure, Mount Leinster, Mullaghanish, Mahera and Truskmore. A microwave radio network links Donnybrook in Dublin where central programmes are generated to the transmission sites. RTE's local studios at Cork, Galway, Limerick, Athlone, Sligo, Waterford and Dundalk are also connected to Donnybrook via a microwave radio network.

Cable television involves the transmission of electrical signals through wires to television sets in houses and elsewhere. The cable television industry began around 1948 when an entrepreneur from Mahoney City, Pennsylvania, connected some local household television sets to a common antenna, which had been raised to high ground to improve reception. The cable television service is sometimes called community antenna television (CATV) — but is more often now designated simply as cable television. The cable television service involves a studio which is sometimes called the "head-end" and co-axial cables that physically connect the head-end with the television set of every user of the system. Certain cable is capable of carrying signals for 40 or more television channels simultaneously. Two or more cables used in conjunction allow a system to carry up to over 100 channels. Signals may be intended for general reception or may be in scrambled form which requires decoders attached to receiving sets. It is also possible to use systems in an interactive mode: home users can send signals back to the head-end and, for example, vote on a question posed in a programme or order goods or services.

By 1987 community antenna cable television (CATV) networks had been provided by CATV licence holders in conjunction with Telecom Éireann in Dublin, Cork, Limerick, Kilkenny, Clonmel and Shannon. The installation of CATV networks involves the supply of trunk cables, amplifiers, power units and direct underground or overhead leads to individual houses. The broadband technology in local areas will facilitate the introduction of interactive telecommunication services such as videophony, video-library and video-conferencing.[23]

Developments in broadcasting technology include Microwave Multipoint Distribution Services (MMDS) and High Definition Television (HDTV). MMDS is a system which is operated widely in the US using microwave frequencies to transmit television channels within a small geographical area. MMDS is expected to allow eventually 650,000 homes in Ireland to receive 11 television channels within 5 years. For the purposes of MMDS, Ireland is divided into radial areas with central transmitters with ranges of up to 40 miles. The system operates between 2.5 and 2.68 gigahertz in the spectrum which is away from VHF and UHF leaving these frequencies free for existing terrestrial television and other telecommunication purposes. MMDS depends on direct line-of-sight from transmitters to receivers. MMDS is capable of carrying stereo television, radio, teletext and other data services. The first European demonstration of MMDS took place in Limerick in September 1989. The first licences for MMDS systems were granted by the Minister for Communications in October 1989. The advantage of MMDS is that it provides many of the facilities of a cable system without the capital expense of laying cable.

European television systems break down the television picture into 625 lines which determine the maximum resolution that can be achieved. Alternative systems are being developed which would significantly enhance the quality of resolution and allow for quality of reception similar to that of a cinema screen. MAC technology offers a quality between current television resolution and high definition television (HDTV). In Japan, experimental 1125-line HDTV is in operation for certain satellite services within that country. HDTV transmission, however, occupies a greater bandwidth than those conforming to the current television standards and requires special receiving equipment.

The first national radio station operated by parties other than RTE and the State, Century Radio, commenced broadcasting on September 4, 1989. Century Radio ceased broadcasting on November 19, 1991 due to financial difficulties. Atlantic 252 (Radio Tara), a joint venture between RTE and the Luxembourg broadcasting company on long-wave and aimed mainly at British audiences, commenced broadcasting on September 1, 1989. The 900-foot radio mast and stays with associated buildings on a 62-acre site at Clarkstown between Kilcock and Summerhill in County Meath became controversial and was the subject of considerable local opposition (including litigation) based on environmental and planning control grounds.[24]

COASTAL AND AERONAUTICAL RADIO SERVICES

The first coastal radio station in Ireland was established by the Marconi Company at Crookhaven in County Cork. Taken over by the British Post Office in 1909, the station was transferred to Valentia Island (Kerry) in 1914 from where Valentia Coastal Radio Station (EJK) operates today. A second coastal radio station was located at Malin Head in Donegal.[25] The radio station at Valentia operates on a 24-hour basis and forms part of an international network of coastal stations. A continuous radio watch is maintained on the maritime frequencies of 500 kHz (wireless telegraphy), 2182 kHz (radio telephony) and channel 16 VHF (radio telephony) for distress calls such as MAYDAY/SOS, urgent calls (PAN/PAN) and safety calls (TTT).[26]

The weather forecast for the Shannon and Fastnet areas is broadcast from Valentia at regular intervals together with appropriate gale and navigational warnings. Ship personnel can avail of a medical service via the Valentia station. Public telecommunication facilities are also available at Valentia station.

A radio station was opened at Baldonnel Aerodrome in 1936 to facilitate the fledgling air service. Dublin Airport at Collinstown, which opened on January 2, 1940, subsequently acquired its own radio facilities. An extensive radio communication network was also established at Foynes. The main radio station for the aeronautical service was located at Ballygirreen, County Clare, where work commenced in 1936. The communications service there was later to be styled Shanwick Radio. Up to April 1943, the communications service for aeronautical services was operated under the control of the Department of Posts and Telegraphs. On April 1, 1943, communications personnel were assigned to the Department of Industry and Commerce.[27]

The 1946 Chicago Convention on International Civil Aviation, to which Ireland is a party, provided for the establishment of the International Civil Aviation Organisation (ICAO). ICAO established the Aeronautical Fixed Telecommunications Network (AFTN) which is an international network linking more than 150 countries. The European Civil Aviation Conference (ECAC) is essentially the European segment of ICAO.

The British and Irish administrations designated Ballygirreen (Shanwick Radio also known as Shannon Airadio) on January 1, 1961 as the sole airground communications station for the Eastern half of the North-Atlantic.[28] In 1992, Shanwick Radio communicated with 215,456 aircraft (an average of 590 per day); 675,144 air-ground-air messages were handled by Shanwick Radio in 1992.[29]

6

Telecommunication via Satellite

October 4, 1957 will long remain as a date which heralded an outstanding scientific achievement: the Soviet Union launched the first artificial satellite, Sputnik I, which circled the Earth at the speed of 27,000 km per hour. The bleeps of Sputnik 1, the radio signals emitted from outer space, proved that rocket technology could not exist without radio technology. The four functions associated with space technology — tracking, telemetry, command and control — are inseparably intertwined with telecommunication processes. Tracking provides data on the location of the satellite; telemetry is the remote measurement of events and conditions which provide data in the form of coded radio signals; command involves the use of ground transmitters to send coded signals to the satellite to activate certain functions such as the starting of a camera; and control involves the direction of the spacecraft and the co-ordination of the network of ground stations so that the space mission can be completed in an effective manner.

The first effective communications satellite, Echo 1, was launched into orbit on August 12, 1960 by the United States National Aeronautics and Space Administration (NASA).[1] The first successful long-term communications satellite, Telstar 1, was launched by NASA on July 10, 1962. Bell Telephone, the private telecommunication carrier of the United States, had designed, made and paid for the launch of Telstar — the first "celestial switchboard". The satellite was used for the transmission of telephone traffic and television pictures.

Satellites oriented to Earth are utilised chiefly for three purposes: the collection of information (for example, information concerning meteorology, remote sensing and environmental protection would fall into this category); the transmission of information (the telecommunication satellites); and space research. Telecommunication satellites are also used for the traditional services — the processes of communication by telephone, telex and the transmission of radio and television programmes. Modern telecommunication satellites are also used for high-speed data transmission.

Most communication satellites are placed in geostationary orbit. The geostationary orbit is located 35,780 kilometres (22,240 miles) above the earth's equator which is equivalent to the circumference of the Earth. A satellite in geostationary orbit circles the earth at the same speed that the earth revolves and thus remains fixed above the same spot relative to the earth below. Up to one-third of the earth's surface can be covered by a satellite in this orbit. Thus, three satellites in this orbit can provide global telecommunication services.

Telecommunication satellites can provide different types of services. There is the point-to-point satellite which involves a transmitting gateway earth station which receives relevant information by conventional means, i.e. by wire, cable or radio, and then transmits the information to the satellite. The satellite then relays the information to other gateway earth stations which transmit the information by terrestrial means to the individual destinations. Distribution satellites enable several earth stations in a specified area to receive signals. Distribution satellites are used for navigational telecommunication. Direct broadcast satellites are powerful geostationary satellites whose signals can be received by domestic television sets either via an individual dish aerial or via communal aerials and cable. Until 1988 television broadcasts were largely confined to certain areas. This was so because, as already described, cable or microwave relays were necessary to transmit television signals beyond a given point.

The first European television distribution satellite channel started in 1982. In September 1993, there were about 20 satellites above Europe broadcasting regular television programmes and newsfeeds. These satellites provided approximately 215 channels with 49 in the English language. To listen and watch, one would need a number of fixed dishes, a multi-feed antenna, or a motorised multi-satellite system. The channels vary from those financed by advertising to "pay TV" service to "compilations" from existing terrestrial channels.

The launch of the experimental Orbital Test Satellite (OTS) by the European Space Agency in May 1978 enabled the Department of Posts and Telegraphs to participate in experiments using an Orbital Test Satellite earth station in Dublin. The earth station was provided jointly by the Department and the National Board for Science and Technology. The acquisition in 1981 of a 3-metre antenna earth station enabled the Department and the National Board of Science and Technology to perform a series of tests via the satellite with an earth station located at the University of Graz in Austria for high-speed data transfer via satellite as part of the STELLA project.[2]

Ireland joined the International Telecommunications Satellite Organisation INTELSAT in 1964.[3] INTELSAT, an intergovernmental body based in Washington DC, is responsible for the provision and operation of the space segment of the world's commercial satellite telecommunication systems consisting of satellites and related facilities. Ireland's use of the satellite system began in 1965 when two satellite circuits from Ireland to the United States were brought into service via the Early Bird satellite. These circuits were routed via an earth station in Goonhilly, Cornwall in England in which the Department of Posts and Telegraphs had made a financial investment. Since 1965 the number of satellite services used by Ireland had increased, thus justifying Ireland having an earth station of its own to cater for satellite telecommunication facilities on the North Atlantic route. The earth station (INTELSAT Standard A) which gives access to an INTELSAT Atlantic Ocean satellite is situated in Elfordstown, Midleton, County Cork, and was supplied by NEC Japan under a contract awarded in late 1982. The installation was completed in December 1983 and the station was opened for service in 1984.[4] The Elfordstown earth station provided Ireland with its first major international telecommunication link independent of the United Kingdom.[5] Apart from providing telephone circuits, the Elfordstown earth station is capable of providing a television channel and an associated sound channel and was equipped in 1984 to communicate with earth stations in Saudi Arabia and South Africa. For technical reasons, access to the Indian Ocean Region satellite of the INSTELSAT system which serves Australia, New Zealand and Japan cannot be effected from the Irish earth station. Telecommunication traffic on this route had been transmitted through United Kingdom earth stations until 1983 when Ireland joined with telecommunication administrations of the Netherlands, Belgium and the Nordic countries in co-ownership of an earth station in Burum in the Netherlands. This arrangement gave Ireland independent access to INTELSAT's Indian Ocean Region satellite.

In 1981 Ireland joined EUTELSAT, the European Telecommunications Satellite Organisation created in 1977 with headquarters in Paris, which has responsibility for the provision and operation of the space segment of the European satellite telecommunication system.

EUTELSAT currently operates eight satellites in orbit (four

EUTELSAT one and four EUTELSAT II) providing a variety of services including telephony, radio and television distribution, EBU services, satellite investigations, business services and mobile services.

By 1992, there were fifteen INTELSAT satellites (twelve INTELSAT V and three INTELSAT VI) in geostationary orbit providing telecommunication services to more than 330 earth station antennae in over 133 countries. The INTELSAT satellites serve the Atlantic, Indian and Pacific Ocean regions to provide global coverage.[6] Telecom Éireann's Standard A antenna in Elfordstown, County Cork, points to one INTELSAT V — Flight 15 Satellite in the Atlantic Ocean Region positioned 35,780 Km (22,240 miles) above a point on the Equator at 18 degrees west longitude.

Telecom Éireann's international telecommunication service became more versatile with the opening by the Taoiseach in June 1987 of the Galway Earth Station (INTELSAT Standard E-2) which was designed exclusively for satellite business communication. Since 1987 further earth stations have been constructed at Limerick (Castletroy) and Elfordstown. In 1989 an INTELSAT Standard F-3 earth station was commissioned at Castletroy to provide additional capacity for business services. A second and third earth station were opened at Elfordstown in 1991. The second earth station (INTELSAT Standard B) is to provide restoration of traffic normally carried on the PTAT submarine optical fibre cable between Ireland and the USA in the event of a fault on the cable. The third Elfordstown earth station is a EUTELSAT Standard T-2. It accesses the Eutelsat I — Flight 5 satellite located at 21.5 degrees east longitude. This earth station is to carry over 400 telephony circuits to some 20 different countries.

The national microwave digital network and the satellite earth stations in Galway, Limerick and Elfordstown facilitate the transmission of high-speed data, digitised voice, facsimile and high-resolution video signals on digital transmission paths. Satellite links are made through INTELSAT and EUTELSAT, the international communications satellite organisation.

By 1987, the space segment in Europe was provided by three satellite systems, EUTELSAT, INTELSAT and TELECOM 1.[7] In addition, INMARSAT (the international maritime satellite organisation) provides mobile satellite service to ships at sea, with the eventual possibility of extension to aircraft and land-based vehicles.

Under the Final Acts of the World Administrative Radio Conference for the planning of broadcast satellite stations in Geneva in 1977, Ireland was allocated the geostationary satellite orbital position of 31 degrees west longitude with five DBS channels (a position shared with the UK, Spain, Portugal and Iceland). The Satellite Communications Committee, established by the Minister for Posts and Telegraphs, reported in 1983 and concluded that a case existed for an Irish satellite network which would combine a direct broadcasting satellite service with provision for general telecommunication services. Following consideration of the Committee's report, the Government sought proposals for provision of a satellite system and establishment from it of an Irish Direct Broadcasting Satellite Service. National and international groups were invited to submit their proposals for the new television service. The Minister for Communications announced on December 10, 1986 that the Government had decided to enter into a formal commitment with Atlantic Satellites Ltd, an Irish company with 80 per cent of its shareholding owned by Hughes Communications Inc., one of the world's largest satellite manufacturers.[8] No satellite has been launched to date for this service at 31 degrees west longitude.

7

Current Developments in Telecommunication

More technical changes have taken place in the development of telecommunication in the last fifteen years than in the preceding decades. States involved in the regulation of the telecommunication business have, in recent years, been profoundly affected by a concourse of technological, economic and political influences. The emergence of the microchip and the convergence of computing and communications are changing the ways people communicate. Digital signals are replacing the analogue signals of the telephone with the encoded language of the computer. This facilitates the introduction of new computerised telecommunication services and will effectively blur the distinction between voice, image and data communications, all of which can now travel down a telephone line. Digital communication systems also facilitate the easy processing, transmission and storage of information.

New developments like microwave radio, cellular mobile telephony, optical fibres and electronic data transmission are improving the ability of persons to communicate. The convergence of the communications technologies has brought us teletext, which is a combination of television and print and facilitates the remote printing of texts; videotex, which is the combination of television and the telephone and facilitates the interrogation of data-bases operated by a variety of information providers; and informatics, which is the technology born from the marriage of telecommunication and computers. RTE began permanent transmission of its teletext service, Aertel, in June 1987. The convergence of the communications technologies also make possible the exchange of files between computers, electronic payments, teleshopping, remote surveillance of buildings, teleconferencing, access to emergency services for the isolated and digital television (high definition in the interactive mode).

CARRIER-SERVICE DEVELOPMENTS

Integrated Services Digital Network (ISDN)

New telecommunication systems are being implemented in Ireland. The Integrated Services Digital Network (ISDN) is one such system and is essentially an end-to-end switched digital service. The ISDN process was initially concerned with the digitisation of the switching centres and the long-distance links between these centres. With appropriate investment in equipment at both ends of the subscriber line, the local link from the switching centre to the subscriber can also be digitised. This additional investment is seen as an opportunity "to upgrade Europe's existing capital stock in telecommunications into a high-quality network infrastructure for multiple use for both voice and data".[1]

Two ISDN exchanges were installed in 1989 to facilitate the evaluation of tests.[2] It is expected that commercial ISDN will be offered to certain Telecom Éireann customers from December 1993.

ISDN, together with optical fibre, offer cheap high-speed transmission (almost a million times faster than over copper wires), and will provide the basis for Integrated Broadband Communications (IBC). "Integrated" means not only integrated services at the user and network levels, but also refers to the integrity of the whole network and to the proper working of all its essential con- stituents including existing and emerging services, like telephony, packet-switched data, satellite and mobile facilities. In relation to IBC, work under EC RACE projects on Aynchronous Transfer Mode (ATM) to provide flexible implementation of broadband communications (including multi-media applications) is contributing to agreement on a common European strategy and to emerging international standards.

Digital Cellular Mobile Telephony

Telecom Éireann joined other European network operators in research and development in relation to the pan-European digital cellular mobile telephone system GSM (originally Groupe Spécial Mobile and now designated Global Systems for Mobile Communications). The first GSM commercial facilities became available in Ireland in 1993. GSM began as a European standard for a single digital mobile telephone system designed to replace more than ten analogue systems which were in use, and in most cases incompatible with each other. GSM offers greatly improved speech clarity and roaming facilities — no perceptible breaks at the hand-over from cell to cell, or from an operator in one country to an operator in a neighbouring country. The GSM system allows for smaller, lighter handsets, and uses spectrum capacity more efficiently. Telephone calls made abroad will be charged at the prevailing rate in the country where they were made plus a per-centage administrative surcharge.

Cordless Telephones

Cellular telephones are intended for what is described as "off-site" use in cars or other forms of transport. Cordless telephones are designed for users whose movements are confined within a well-defined area. The cordless telephone user makes calls from a port-able handset linked by radio signals to a fixed base station. The base station is connected either directly or indirectly to the public net-work. The DECT (Digital Cordless Telecommunications) standard was developed by the European Telecommunications Standards Institute (ETSI) around 1992.

Cordless telephones within a defined area allow the user to make and receive calls in exactly the same way as any other telephone connected to the public network. Many sophisticated facilities are at present available on cordless telephones.

Value-Added Services

The convergence of data processing and telecommunication pro-cesses has facilitated greatly the handling of information. The service diversification made possible by the convergence of telecommuni-cation and data processing is termed value-added service — adding value to suit users' needs. Value-added services facilitate the delivery of information to the subscriber in an intelligent manner. Value-added services include message storing and forwarding, mailbox systems and message handling, telebanking, authorisation of payments (smart cards), trade electronic data interchange, tele-working, security and control. The French Minitel system, which is a videotex-based value-added service, illustrates the potential of value-added services for the general user. By 1988 three million Minitel videotex terminals with access to thousands of services had been installed by France Telecom in French homes. A Minitel terminal is a simple specialised terminal equipped with screen and keyboard. The range of services available by Minitel includes information-based services like electronic telephone directory databases; personal information like details of a bank account; transaction services like home shopping and home banking; communication services like electronic mail for private communications and computing and processing data in remote databases.

An Irish Minitel service was established in 1991. Minitel Communications Ltd is a joint venture between Allied Irish Bank Group, Credit Lyonnais, France Telecom, and Telecom Éireann. Minitel Communications Ltd markets and promotes third-party videotex services under a national umbrella, supplying residential users, and recruits and pays revenues to those supplying services to the system. Initial services include banking, teleshopping, tourist information, agricultural advisory service and travel timetables.

Electronic Data Interchange

By September 1989 several Irish companies were participating in pilot schemes involving electronic data interchange (EDI), a variant of electronic mail which handles the documentation associated with the sale and supply of goods and services. EDI has been defined as

> the replacement of the paper documents relative to an administrative, commercial, transport or other business transaction by an electronic message structured to an agreed standard and passed from one computer to another without manual intervention.[3]

It has been estimated that in international trade, the costs related to paperwork lie between 4 and 15 per cent of the value of the merchandise; EDI is one solution to the problem of the paper mountain.[4] EDI can be effected from computer to computer through the exchange of magnetic media (tapes, diskettes) or via switched telephone networks or leased lines. Uniform treatment is essential and the Commission of the European Communities has drawn up a Community action programme — the TEDIS programme — to promote the electronic transfer of trade data.[5] The main EDI service providers in Ireland in 1993 were Eirtrade Ltd, a subsidiary of Telecom Éireann; PostGEM Ltd, a subsidiary of An Post; and a joint venture between Telecom Éireann and An Post, Irish National Electronic Trading Agency Ltd (INET). (There are others — only the State entities are listed here.)

EIRPAC

In Ireland, services such as data transfer, electronic mail, information
retrieval, and videotex access have been available since Telecom
Éireann's Public Packet Switched Data Network Service (EIRPAC)
began operation in December 1984.[6] EIRPAC, the public data
network, breaks data from different sources into small packets and
then interlaces them so that several connections are made simultaneously through the same telecommunication lines. The EIRPAC
service replaced the two experimental networks, EURONET and
IPSS (International Packet Switched Service), which gave data users
access to databases in Europe and North America respectively.
EURONET, which became operational in 1979, was the telecommunication network developed on behalf of the European Communities by a consortium of telecommunication administrations.

Data and Special Services Network

DASSNET (Data and Special Services Network) is Telecom Éireann's
managed digital private circuit network. DASSNET, which came
into service in 1990, supports M.1020, M.1040 and 64 kbit/s leased
lines, and has nodes linked by optical fibre and microwave
technology. DASSNET is designed to provide fast and reliable access
to digital private circuits for industrial and commercial use through
a centrally-managed network. DASSNET is linked by optical fibre
cable to the United Kingdom and the US (via the PTAT-1 cable which
lands at Courtmacsherry Bay, Co. Cork), by an Intelsat satellite to
the US and by a Eutelsat satellite to mainland Europe.

Electronic Mail

A computer-messaging service — electronic mail — known as Eirmail was formally established by Telecom Éireann in September
1985.[7] Eirmail is accessible through EIRPAC, the public packet
switched network, either directly or via the public switched telephone network (PSTN) as well as through the telex network. The
international standards which enable electronic mail users to communicate with each other are CCITT X400 and CCITT X420, promoted by the International Telegraph and Telephone Consultative
Committee responsible for developing standards for international
telecommunication.

ELECTRONIC FUNDS TRANSFER

Electronic Funds Transfer at Point-of-Sale (EFTPOS) involves Electronic Funds Transfer (EFT), a method of transferring funds from one computer (e.g. at your bank), to another (e.g. at a retailer's bank) using telecommunication facilities. Access to the system is achieved using a card. There is a point-of-sale terminal (POS) that allows a record of a transaction (or sale) to be stored in its memory for possible later transmission to a central computer. EFTPOS therefore involves both the recording of the transaction as well as the payment. Four types of electronic funds transfer are in common use. There are transfers between computers at different banks, transfers between banks and other organisations, public access to terminals providing banking services and use of cards for making direct debit payment for goods and services over a telecommunication link. Cards, sometimes called smart cards, are used in the above services. A smart card is similar to a credit card and contains a microprocessor, memory and program and has many different applications.

VIDEO TELEPHONY

Video telephony involves the transmission and display of moving images via telecommunication links. Video telephony is also referred to as videophony. Although Bell Laboratories in the United States first demonstrated a visual telephone in 1950, the fruit of 40 years work, small visual telephones are only now becoming available on a test basis.

EXPERT SYSTEMS

The development of the computer based "expert systems" foreshadows further innovations in the field of telecommunication. "Expert Systems" may be defined as complex computer systems which emulate human expertise by making deductions from given information using the rules of logical inference.[8]

BROADCASTING

In the field of broadcasting, national and international telecommunication bodies are being affected by technical developments in several areas: satellites, optical fibre cables, domestic television receivers and video-recorders. The technologies of telecommunication, data processing and entertainment are converging rapidly. The new technologies will permit greater capacity, quality, reliability and the integration of all telecommunication services.

It was estimated by the UK Peacock Committee[9] in 1986 that if every development which could lawfully occur within the next 10 years did so, the following television "broadcast" channels would be available to the consumer: four terrestrial channels — BBC1, BBC2, ITV and Channel 4 which are received in Ireland (in addition, Ireland has RTE1 and RTE's Network 2); five channels each from the UK, Ireland, France, Belgium, Holland and Germany via DBS (direct satellite broadcasts) received on a 90 cm dish (although good reception of some of these services might require a larger dish in some areas); 12 channels could be available with the reception of TV transmissions from low-power satellites in the bands primarily intended for fixed point-to-point telecommunication; the number of channels via cable was stated to be "technically almost unlimited," depending on the method of distribution used, though 30 or 60 channel capacity systems were likely, some being used for sound broadcasting or data.

ELECTRONIC PUBLISHING

Proponents of electronic publishing argue that by the end of the century it would be possible using fibre-optic technology to create a grid connecting every household in the country, whereby the nation's television viewers could simultaneously watch as many different programmes as the nation's readers could simultaneously read different books, magazines and newspapers.[10] Each television set could be equipped with a television dial on which the code number of the desired programme or connection would be dialled. It is argued that the equivalent of a telephone meter would monitor receptions on each set linked to the code number of the item received. A central "black box" would be maintained by the network controllers into which programmes could be fed (either by lodging tapes or by direct feed for live transmission).[11] The proponents of this system of electronic publishing argue that "publishers" could produce programmes which they would have a right to have fed into the national network provided the programmes did not break the law of libel, good taste, decency and other regulatory controls. These publishers would then draw their programmes to the attention of the public. The consumer, by dialling a number, could obtain the programme he or she wished to see. In this context, the issue arises whether Telecom Éireann or any other provider of a telecommunication service would be allowed to operate as a "common carrier", obliged to sell its transmission service to any "publisher" willing to pay the going price. This issue would be a matter for the regulatory authorities in Ireland and within the European Communities. Essentially, the proponents of this system argue that this form of electronic publishing would be analogous to print publishing.

FURTHER DEVELOPMENTS

There will be further developments in telecommunication; those with an indomitable determination will, like Bell, Edison and Marconi, build on the labours of their predecessors and discover new applications that will extend man's contact with man and with the universe around him. In this context, it is fitting to note the words of Justice Felix Frankfurter of the United States Supreme Court in a patent case involving the Marconi Wireless Telegraph Company of America (1943):

> Seldom indeed has a great discoverer or inventor wandered lonely as a cloud. Great inventions have always been part of an evolution, the culmination of a particular moment of an antecedent process. So true is this that the history of thought records striking coincidental discoveries — showing that the new insight first declared to the world by a particular individual was "in the air" and ripe for discovery and disclosure. The real question is how significant a jump is the new disclosure from the old knowledge. Reconstruction by hindsight, making obvious something that was not at all obvious to superior minds, until someone pointed it out — this is too often a tempting exercise for astute minds.[12]

PART III

The Regulation of Telecommunication in Ireland: Development and Overview

The existing matter will be injurious to us so long as we ignorantly submit to it; but beneficial if we oppose to it a vivid creative energy — obtain the mastery over it by a thorough grounding in history and thus appropriate to ourselves the whole intellectual wealth of preceding generations.

von Savigny (1779-1861) in Introduction to
The System of Modern Roman Law

8

The Regulation of Telecommunication to 1922

DEFINITION OF "TELECOMMUNICATION" AND OTHER TERMS

The term "telecommunication" is not defined in Irish legislation. The term, however, is employed in the *Irish Telecommunications Investments Limited Acts 1981* and *1983*,[1] the *Telecommunications Capital Act, 1981*[2] and the *Postal and Telecommunications Services Act, 1983*. The term is defined in the constitution of the International Telecommunication Union as any transmission, emission or reception of signs, signals, writing, images and sounds or intelligence of any nature by wire, "radio, optical or other electromagnetic systems".[3] The term "telecommunication" is in fact the modern equivalent of the term "telegraphy". The term "telegraphy" — coined by combining the Greek words *tele* (far) and *graphein* (to write) is of venerable vintage and has been used in legislation since the last century to cover all aspects of telecommunication.

The Telegraph Act, 1863 defined "telegraph" as "a wire or wires used for the purpose of telegraphic communication, with any casing, coating, tube, or pipe, enclosing the same, and any apparatus connected therewith for the purpose of telegraphic communication".[4] *The Telegraph Act, 1869*[5] extended the definition of "telegraph" to include any apparatus for transmitting messages or other communications by means of electric signals. The 1869 Act also defined "telegram" as "any message or other communication transmitted or intended for transmission by a telegraph".[6] These definitions of "telegraph" and "telegram" are still in force today. Legislation[7] governing telecommunication in Ireland still refers to such terms. Although modern forms of telecommunication have been invented since these definitions were enacted, modern telecommunication services are still partly regulated by the *Telegraph Acts 1863 to 1916* provided such services fall within the general scope of the above definitions.[8] The term "telegraph" includes telephones,[9] apparatus for wireless telegraphy,[10] and broadcasting apparatus.[11] Thus, the term "telecommunication", simply defined, means communication transmitted over distances by electronic processes such as the telephone (and other related forms of communication), radio broadcasting and cable systems.

Although the *Telegraph Acts 1863 to 1916* regulate telegraphy, wireless telegraphy (radio) and broadcasting, separate legislation has been enacted to regulate wireless telegraphy and broadcasting. The *Wireless Telegraphy Acts 1926 to 1988*, with regulations made thereunder, govern wireless telegraphy (radio-communication);[12] the *Broadcasting Authority Acts 1960 to 1993*, the *Broadcasting (Offences) Acts 1968 and 1988*, the *Radio and Television Act, 1988* and the *Broadcasting Act, 1990*, together with regulations made thereunder, govern broadcasting.

The expression "telecommunication carrier service", used in this book to cover services like the telephone and related services, must be distinguished from the expression "common carrier". A common carrier has special common law obligations to his customers but, in view of distinctions that can be made between the transmission of intelligence and the transportation of goods (including the element of the bailment of the goods to be conveyed), a telecommunication carrier is not a common carrier in the strict sense in which that term is applied to carriers of goods.[13] The clearest statement to this effect in a common law context is the 1893 decision of the United States Supreme Court in *Primrose v Western Union* where the Court ruled that the telegraph company was not a common carrier:

> Telegraph companies resemble railroad companies and other common carriers, in that they are instruments of commerce; and in that they exercise a public employment, and are therefore bound to serve all customers alike, without discrimination. They have, doubtless, a duty to the public, to receive, to the extent of their capacity, all messages clearly and intelligibly written, and to transmit them upon reasonable terms. But they are not common carriers: their duties are different, and are performed in different ways; and they are not subject to the same liabilities.[14]

PHASES IN THE REGULATION OF
TELECOMMUNICATION LAW

The first phase in the development of telecommunication law in the United Kingdom of Great Britain and Ireland could be characterised as a period of little regulation by the State. The second phase commenced with the passing of the *Telegraph Act, 1863*[15] whereby the Government strove to regulate and facilitate the telecommunication business being operated by the private companies by virtue of special Acts of Parliament or charters. These private companies, however, still retained a considerable measure of freedom. The third phase commenced in 1868 when the *Telegraph Act, 1868*[16] empowered a department of State — the Post Office — to acquire, work and maintain telecommunication systems. The *Telegraph Act, 1869*[17] heralded another phase which was to last until the passing of the *Postal and Telecommunications Services Act, 1983*. The 1869 Act vested the telecommunication monopoly in the State.[18] The private companies operating the telecommunication business (telegraph companies) were then bought out gradually. However, it was not until January 1, 1912 that the Postmaster-General assumed control of the National Telephone Company, the last remaining private telecommunication company then operating in Ireland.[19] When broadcasting became regulated in Ireland by the *Wireless Telegraphy Act, 1926*, the existing legislative mould of a State telecommunication monopoly was continued. The broadcasting service became a branch of the Civil Service under the Minister for Posts and Telegraphs and remained so until the passing of the *Broadcasting Authority Act, 1960*.

The *Postal and Telecommunications Services Act, 1983*, authorised the establishment of two companies, An Post and Telecom Éireann, (to be formed pursuant to the *Companies Acts 1963 to 1983*), to run the postal and telecommunication carrier services respectively. This Act heralded a new phase that could be described loosely as the commencement of the liberalisation or deregulation phase. The *Broadcasting and Wireless Telegraphy Act, 1988* and the *Radio and Television Act, 1988*, which provided for independent radio and television services, may be regarded as further examples of liberalisation or deregulation policies. The institutions of the European Communities have, in recent times, acted as significant forces in ensuring that telecommunication carrier-related services (in particular) are further liberalised.[20]

THE DEVELOPMENT OF TELECOMMUNICATION LAW
TO 1863

The first statutory reference to telecommunication (telegraphy as it then was) was in the *Admiralty (Signals Stations) Act, 1815*.[21] This Act authorised the compulsory acquisition of lands for signal and telegraph stations. The terms "signal" and "telegraph stations" were not defined in the 1815 Act, but the mode of transmitting intelligence was then limited to visual telegraphy. The first telecommunication system which was used on certain railway lines in Britain in the late 1830s comprised an electric alarm and telegraph system which was used in exchanging messages along certain railway lines to improve the signalling, safety and timekeeping of trains. The potentiality of the telegraph was realised at an early stage by Parliament. In 1840, the Select Committee on Railway Communication noted:

> Circumstances may arise in which it may be very inconvenient to leave in the hands of a private company or an individual the exclusive means of intelligence which the telegraph affords, it cannot fail to be of paramount importance that the Government should be furnished with similar means of procuring and transmitting intelligence.[22]

These sentiments were to be echoed often by Governments in their justification for ensuring State control of telecommunication including broadcasting.

The *Railway Regulation Act, 1844*[23] provided for the establishment of "electric telegraphs for Her Majesty's Service" on railway land subject to "such reasonable remuneration" as might be agreed. Provision was also made for the railway companies to use such telegraphs for their own purposes, subject to the priority of the Government.[24] Electric telegraphs on railway lines (other than exclusive lines for Government services) were, subject to the priority of the Government, opened to the public.[25] The Electric Telegraph Company, a private company incorporated in 1846, soon developed effective control of the telegraph business in the United Kingdom without receiving any financial assistance from the State. The *Electric Telegraph Company Act, 1846* reserved to the Home Secretary the right to take possession of the company's telegraphs for one week in case of internal disturbances.[26] A statutory provision enabling the State to take control of the telecommunication network in certain circumstances became a permanent feature of telecommunication law and is reflected in current legislation.[27] While the telecommunication business in Britain and Ireland was in the hands of private companies, the telecommunication business in mainland Europe was run, almost from the beginning, as a state monopoly.

Rival companies to the Electric Telegraph Company soon came into existence: the British Electric Telegraph Company was promoted in 1849 and received its special Act in July 1850;[28] in 1851 the English and Irish Magnetic Company was incorporated to provide telegraph lines between England and Ireland.[29] In the late 1840s considerable legislation of a regulatory nature was passed governing public utilities.[30] For example, gasworks, waterworks and railway companies could not pay out dividends in excess of 10 per cent. Little was done at this stage to regulate the telegraph companies. However, in 1855, the *Electric Telegraph Consolidation Act* prohibited the distribution in any one year of a dividend above 10 per cent.[31] The United Kingdom Electric Telegraph Company was prohibited in 1862 from selling or transferring any portion of its undertaking without the direct authority of Parliament.[32] It was also prohibited from leasing any of its wires to another company without the consent of the Board of Trade.[33] Disquiet was expressed about the powers of the telegraph companies which had been sanctioned by private bill committees; there were allegations that the companies were interfering with private and public rights by the manner in which wires and posts were laid.[34] The Postmaster-General, Lord Stanley, admitted in the House of Lords that the powers given to the electric telegraph companies under private Bills had been most extensive and in some cases very eccentric and had been often used in an injurious manner.[35]

STATE INTERVENTION 1863 TO 1868

Telegraph Act, 1863

The *Telegraph Act, 1863*[36] was the first general Act to regulate the telecommunication business. This Act, as amended, together with subsequent *Telegraph Acts*,[37] still regulates certain telecommunication services in Ireland. The 1863 Act consolidated into one Act the powers under special Acts for the construction and maintenance of telegraphs. The 1863 Act permitted telegraph companies already authorised by special Acts of Parliament, or to be authorised by such special Acts, to execute necessary telecommunication[38] works

subject to restrictions.[39] These powers were later to be exercised by
the Postmaster-General and subsequently by the Minister for Posts
and Telegraphs[40] and Telecom Éireann (under the *Postal and Telecommunications Services Act, 1983*). Provision was also made in the
1863 Act for the Government to have control over the "transmission
of messages" in an emergency.[41] Similar provisions were later made
in relation to wireless telegraphy[42] and broadcasting.[43]

In the 1860s numerous arguments were advanced for State control
of the telegraphs. Many newspapers depended on the telegraph
companies for receipt of news. Indeed, some newspapers were
forced to accept what the telegraph companies were willing to
supply to them. This was resented by the larger newspapers and
proved to be a factor which influenced the nationalisation of the then
telecommunication business. It was argued that the conveyance of
news could not be left safely and conveniently in the hands of even
one telegraph company without strict Government supervision.[44]
Others argued that the telegraph companies should be taken over
directly by the Government and administered by the Postmaster-
General.[45] The Postmaster-General had considered that the conveyance of messages by the electric telegraph might have been
incorporated advantageously into the postal system but he had not
been prepared to take the matter further at that time.[46]

The Post Office had expanded rapidly in the period 1840-1860. The
penny post had been introduced in the 1840s. Rowland Hill had
introduced internal reform and a new system of Post Office Savings
Banks had been introduced in 1861. Many admired the efficiency of
the Post Office. By 1866 Gladstone could state: "I am far from
thinking very highly of our rank of administrators, but if we could
be judged by the Post Office alone, we might claim the very first place
in this respect."[47] The future problems of deficits, employee unrest
and allegations of poor service had not yet surfaced to spoil the
efficient image of the Post Office. Arguments for a measure of State
control of the telegraph service were put forward on the basis of the
high charges of the telegraph companies, the "vexatious delays" in
the delivery of messages and the fact that many areas were without
a service. The press was also dissatisfied with the charges of the
telegraph companies.[48] In September 1865, the Postmaster-General,
Lord Stanley, directed Frank Ives Scudamore, then an Assistant
Secretary of the Post Office, "to enquire, and report, whether in his
opinion, the electric telegraph service might be beneficially worked
by the Post Office, and whether it would then possess any advantage
over a system worked by the private companies, and whether it

would entail a very large expenditure beyond the purchase of existing rights".[49] Scudamore presented his report to the Postmaster-General in July 1866 and recommended the purchase of the telegraph business by the Post Office.[50] Scudamore was of the view that little improvement could be expected from the companies, structured as they were, in his view, to earning dividends and engaged in wasteful competition.

Telegraph Act, 1868

The preamble to the *Telegraph Act, 1868*[51] recited the fact that there were insufficient means of communication by electric telegraph within the United Kingdom of Great Britain and Ireland and that important districts were without any such means of communication. Further, the preamble recited that it would be advantageous to the State, as well as to merchants and traders, and to the public generally, if a more expeditious system of telegraphy were established. The preamble recited that the Postmaster-General was accordingly empowered "to work telegraphs in connection with the administration of the Post Office". The Act was permissive only and placed the Postmaster-General in the same position as a newly formed telegraph company.

Introducing the 1868 Bill in the House of Commons,[52] the Chancellor of the Exchequer stated that, in general, with the exception of postal communications, the administration of the internal affairs of the State had been left to private enterprise. He believed that it had been with the entire assent and approbation of the community that postal communication had been a monopoly in the hands of the Government; telegraphic and postal communication might be considered as coming within the same category; it was only in the mode of conveying the communication that there was any difference. The Chancellor referred to the "backwardness" of the Union in relation to telegraphic communication, the complaints of high rates, the vexatious delays, the inaccurate rendering of messages and the absence of telegraphic communications in whole districts.[53] The Government, for the first time in modern history, was entering into a field of endeavour which had hitherto been the preserve of private enterprise. The 1868 Act did not confer on the Postmaster-General any rights which the telegraph companies themselves did not possess, or give the Postmaster-General any greater powers over private property. Specifically, the 1868 Act authorised the Postmaster-General to acquire the whole or part of the business of any telegraph company for an agreed sum.[54] Failing agreement between the parties, compensation was to be agreed by arbitration.[55]

THE BEGINNINGS OF STATE MONOPOLY

Following the enactment of the *Telegraph Act, 1868*[56] the Post Office immediately set about the purchase of available telegraph undertakings. Many interests were, however, bitterly opposed to any State plans to nationalise the telecommunication business. Commentators attempted to prognosticate on the consequences of nationalisation. Nationalisation, according to one commentator, would, in effect, result in the

> . . . abandonment of further telegraph enterprise; in the stagnation and dreary routine inseparable from official regulations; in the interference by the Government with commercial business. . . . [A reduction in tariffs] would be paid for by the rejection of all improvements . . . by the absence of all desire or inducement to improve; and . . . by the dependence of the press on the whim or favour, or perhaps prejudice, of a Government official.[57]

A Select Committee of Parliament in 1869 was of the view that it was not desirable that the transmission of messages for the public should become a legal monopoly of the Post Office. The Select Committee considered that such a monopoly would stifle the stimulus which would otherwise prompt the Post Office to salutary action.[58] [One hundred and ten years later in 1979 many of the foregoing sentiments were expressed in the *Report of the Posts and Telegraphs Review Group*[59] which argued that the telecommunication carrier business be taken out of the Civil Service and entrusted to a statutory company run on commercial lines.][60] The telegraph companies argued that the Post Office already had more duties than it could properly perform and that the Government had shown no special aptitude for telegraphic work.[61]

Several factors influenced the Government to vest the telecommunication monopoly in the Postmaster-General. The realisation that private companies could undercut the Post Office on remunerative routes, thus causing a financial loss to the Post Office, was one consideration. It was also perceived at the time that the Post Office had not abused the postal monopoly, considered to be similar in principle to the telegraph business. The pro-monopoly lobby had also argued that profits from remunerative telegraph routes were necessary to finance the unremunerative routes in remote areas. The Chancellor of the Exchequer argued that unless the Post Office had a monopoly, the purchase of the telegraphs pursuant to the 1868 Act "was a waste of money at the immense price that the Government was called upon to pay".[62] The sum of £6.73m had been paid by the Postmaster-General in the purchase of the interests and property of the various telegraph companies and in entering into appropriate arrangements with the railway companies. The purchase price of the telegraph companies was based on 20 years of the net profits up to June 30, 1868.[63] The Marquess of Lansdowne, speaking for the Government in the House of Lords on the nationalisation issue, pleaded that it was only fair that the Government should be protected against being exposed to ruinous loss and that the Government would be ready at all times "to adopt manifest improvements, and give the utmost accommodation to the public".[64] Others, however, argued wistfully that "the principle of non-monopoly . . . was one of the utmost consequence to the well-being of the community".[65]

STATE MONOPOLISATION 1869 TO 1922

Telegraph Act, 1869

The principle that the monopoly in telegraphic communication was somewhat akin to the postal monopoly found favour with the Government and was recited in the preamble to the *Telegraph Act, 1869*. The preamble recited, *inter alia*:

> [I]n order to protect the public revenue . . . similar powers to those conferred upon the Postmaster-General with respect to the exclusive privilege of conveying letters should be enacted with reference to the transmission of public telegraphic messages within the United Kingdom of Great Britain and Ireland. . . .[66]

Section 4 of the 1869 Act provided that the Postmaster-General was to have the exclusive privilege of transmitting "telegrams[67] within the United Kingdom of Great Britain and Ireland" and also to have "the exclusive privilege of performing all the incidental services of receiving, collecting or delivering telegrams," subject to certain exceptions.[68] By virtue of section 4 of the 1869 Act and subsequent judicial decisions, the Postmaster-General and his successor, the Minister for Posts and Telegraphs,[69] were vested with an exclusive privilege in relation to the transmission of telecommunication. Section 4 of the *Telegraph Act, 1869*[70] is still the legal basis for the present telecommunication monopoly of the Minister for Communications. The Act of 1869 also extended the Postmaster-General's power to purchase the undertaking of a telegraph company.[71] To further facilitate the acquisition by the Postmaster-General of the telegraph companies, the *Lands Clauses Consolidation Act, 1845* (a measure which deals specifically with compulsory purchase) was incorporated with the Act of 1869.[72]

Telegraph Act, 1878

The *Telegraph Act, 1878*[73] consolidated many of the protective clauses which had been authorised by special Acts of Parliament in relation to the telegraph companies in a general measure in favour of the Postmaster-General. The 1878 Act also provided for arbitration in case of "differences" between the Postmaster-General and persons whose consent was needed for the placing of telecommunication apparatus and plant.[74] Penalties were also stipulated where damage was caused to the telecommunication equipment of the Postmaster-General.[75]

The *Edison* Case

Following the patenting in 1876 of the telephone by Alexander Graham Bell, the Post Office in London was approached by Bell offering to exhibit the telephone to the Department in the hope that the Post Office would adopt the telephone and construct a network of telephone exchanges. The Post Office considered that the first practical telephones were not efficient instruments and that it did not appear that these telephones were likely to be very useful.[76] Subsequently in 1878 a company called the Telephone Company was registered in the United Kingdom to acquire and work Bell's patent. A rival company, the Edison Telephone Company, was formed in August 1879 to acquire and work the patents of Thomas Alva Edison. The Post Office then became concerned that the development of the telephone would affect the capital invested in the telegraph. Subsequently, the Postmaster-General, with the consent of the Treasury, informed the companies that their operations were in breach of the Postmaster-General's monopoly under section 4 of the *Telegraph Act, 1869* as they were operating without a licence.[77] The companies did not apply for a licence and legal proceedings were instituted by the Attorney General in November 1879 against the Edison Telephone Company and the Telephone Company. In June 1880 the two companies amalgamated under the title of the United Telephone Company Ltd.

The *Edison*[78] case came for hearing on November 29, 1880 and lasted five days before the Exchequer Division of the High Court consisting of Baron Pollock and Stephen J. The Attorney General appeared in person for the Postmaster-General. In court, each side lined up the most eminent scientists of the day. A telephone line was established between the Court and the United Telephone Company's Exchange at Palace Chambers, Westminster, and a telephone message was transmitted to the judges in court from the exchange in Palace Chambers. Delivering its judgment on December 20, 1880 the Court held that Edison's telephone was a "telegraph" within the meaning of the *Telegraph Acts 1863* and *1869*, although the telephone had not been invented in 1869. The Court also held that a conversation through the telephone was a "communication transmitted by a telegraph" and therefore a "telegram".[79] Edison's telephones were also held to infringe the exclusive privilege of the Postmaster-General granted by section 4 of the *Telegraph Act, 1869* and the exceptions set out in section 5 of the 1869 Act were held not to apply to Edison's telephones.

Anticipating the successful outcome of the *Edison* decision, the Postmaster-General submitted a memorandum to the Treasury outlining the necessity for allowing certain private companies to operate under licence and permitting at the same time the establishment of Post Office exchanges throughout the country "in a wide and comprehensive manner".[80] Adopting a restrictive view, the Treasury considered that the Post Office should not be authorised to establish a universal system of exchanges. The Treasury favoured the establishment of Post Office exchanges only to such a limited extent as would facilitate the Department to adopt an effective bargaining position with the companies over the issue of licences.[81]

After the *Edison* case the Government decided to license the companies which had been granted the telephone patents.[82] Licences were granted to such companies to "transmit telephonic communication" within certain specified districts.[83] There were no restrictions on the charges payable to the licensed companies. The Treasury also reluctantly agreed to permit the Post Office to establish a telephone-exchange network which would compete with the private companies.[84]

The telegraph system operated by the Post Office on a monopoly basis had become unprofitable by the 1880s and the Treasury doubted the capacity of the Post Office to compete effectively with private enterprise. Senior civil servants in the Treasury considered it somewhat unseemly for the Post Office to engage in tough competition with the remaining private telegraph companies. However, the Postmaster-General, Henry Fawcett, a firm believer in competition and free trade,[85] considered canvassing and advertising essential to establish a strong Post Office system. Notwithstanding the Postmaster-General's views, Treasury officials implied twice in 1882 that canvassing was beneath the dignity of a civil servant and refused to allocate the necessary funds.[86] The Treasury was so determined to limit the expansion of the Post Office telephone system that it even suggested raising the fees to discourage applications for service.[87] However, the Post Office and the Treasury agreed that competition between the telephone companies should be encouraged. The Postmaster-General, Henry Fawcett, stated in the House of Commons in July 1882 that it was "not in the interest of the public to create a monopoly in relation to the supply of telephonic communication".[88] The Treasury, aware of the unprofitable manner in which the telegraphs were being worked by the Post Office stated in June 1883 that it considered that it was a sound principle that the State

> as regards all functions which are not by their nature exclusively its own, should at most be ready to supplement, not endeavour to supersede, private enterprise and that a rough but not inaccurate test is not to act in anticipation of possible demand.[89]

The Treasury also opined wistfully:

> It is perhaps to be regretted that the Department [Post Office] ever travelled into functions outside its [postal] monopoly . . . the numbers in the Post Office are already those of a large army.[90]

Liberalisation of Licences

During the 1880s the press and members of Parliament strongly urged the Post Office to liberalise the terms of the basic licence issued to the telephone companies.[91] On June 13, 1884, *The Times* in a leading article commented that Parliament must liberate the telephone "from the bands of red tape in which it is being strangled and allow its future to be shaped by the operation of the ordinary law of political economy". Subsequently on August 7, 1884, the Postmaster-General announced in the House of Commons that licences were to be issued to telephone companies to transmit "telephone communications" anywhere within the United Kingdom.[92] The Government, however, was to receive 10 per cent of the gross receipts.[93] Despite rising public discontent with the telephone system the Government was still reluctant to proceed to buy out the telephone companies. The philosophy of fiscal rectitude propounded by the Treasury held sway: "My Lords are not prepared to embark upon another enterprise gigantic in itself, while the developments it might lead to are beyond their powers of prediction."[94] An official in the Secretary's Office of the Post Office pencilled the following words in the margin of this memorandum: "My Lords' powers of prediction are very limited. They cannot see beyond their noses at the present."[95]

Direct Government Intervention in Telephone Business

Public discontent with the existing telephone system run by the private telephone companies eventually forced the Government in the early 1890s to change its policies on the regulation of the telephone service. In consultation with the two then existing telephone companies, the National Company and the New Telephone Company, the Government proposed to take control of all the "trunk wire communications of the country" but leave the telephonic exchange business within defined areas in the hands of the private telephone companies.[96] That policy was carried into effect by the *Telegraph Act, 1892*:[97] section 1 of the 1892 Act referred to the Postmaster-General's intention to purchase and provide "the main lines of telephonic communications". This policy was reflected in an agreement in 1896 between the Postmaster-General and the National Telephone Company Limited[98] which had by 1896 absorbed the New Company. This agreement between the Postmaster-General and the National Telephone Company generally confined the right of the National Telephone Company to transacting "telephonic business" within "exchange areas". The company ceded rights in relation to telephonic communication which would have run to December 31, 1911.[99] The telephone system was to be open to the public as well as the subscribers of the company; the company's exchanges were to be connected with the Post Office and mutual accommodation was to be afforded for the transmission of messages by telephonic and postal means.[100] The licences of other companies were surrendered to the Postmaster-General in 1896.[101]

In 1898 a House of Commons Select Committee was appointed to inquire and report whether "the telephone service is, or is calculated to become, of such general benefit as to justify its being undertaken by municipal and other local authorities".[102] Other related matters were also to be examined by the Select Committee. The Committee considered that the telephone service

> already so essential to commercial men, and so well calculated under other conditions to benefit directly or indirectly all classes of the community ought no longer to be treated as the practical monopoly of a private company.[103]

The Committee was strongly of the opinion that effective competition with the National Telephone Company by either the Post Office or local authorities was necessary. The Committee also considered that a "really efficient Post Office service" afforded the best means "for securing such competition".[104] The Select Committee concluded that such competition should be carried on "by a distinct and separate branch of the Department, and in future be conducted under strictly business-like conditions, and by a staff specially qualified for such duty".[105]

In an effort to improve the facilities for telephonic communication, the Government passed the *Telegraph Act, 1899*,[106] part of which is still in force today. The Government was unhappy about the virtual monopoly enjoyed by the National Telephone Company and considered that more active competition in the provision of telephone service was essential for improvement. The Government policy, articulated by the Postmaster-General, the Duke of Norfolk, in the House of Lords in August 1899, was that there should be more active competition on the part of the Post Office and that the municipalities, should they desire to do so, should have facilities for providing a system of public telephonic communication.[107] Section 1 of the 1899 Act, repealed in 1983,[108] provided for a grant of two million pounds to the Postmaster-General for the purpose of the *Telegraph Acts 1863 to 1897*. In the House of Lords, the Postmaster-General stated that the two million pounds would allow the Post Office, "as quickly as possible, to enter into active competition" with the National Telephone Company in places where the Post Office had no telephone exchanges. Section 2 of the Act of 1899, the operative part of which is still in force, enabled local corporations and urban authorities to use their rates for providing a system for public telephonic communication. In Ireland, under section 2(3) of the 1899 Act, any expenses incurred by local corporations or urban authorities in the provision of a public telephone service were to be defrayed as expenses incurred in the execution of the *Public Health (Ireland) Acts, 1878 to 1896* for sanitary purposes, and money could be borrowed accordingly. This provision is still in force but such a local body requires a licence from the Minister for Communications by virtue of section 111(2) of the *Postal and Telecommunications Services Act, 1983*.

The Postmaster-General, the Duke of Norfork, was optimistic that this new measure would assist in remedying the defects in the telephone service. Speaking in the House of Lords when moving that the 1899 Bill be read a second time he stated:

> We trust that this Bill will tend in the direction of bringing the boon of telephonic communication to certain wide classes of the community who hitherto have been unable to enjoy it; that it has been framed as far as possible to give great benefits to the community without infringing unduly the rights of the [National Telephone Company] who have laboured for many years to promote telephonic communication, and that it will encourage municipalities to come forward and create the competition which we think is so desirable.[109]

Subsequently, certain municipalities were granted licences to operate telephone systems. However, by 1905, the municipal subscribers constituted only five per cent of the total number of subscribers.[110] Hull is the only municipality in the United Kingdom and Ireland to survive to the present time with its own telecommunication system.

Government Purchase of Assets of National Telephone Company

For some time, the expansionist wing of the Post Office had favoured the purchase of the assets of the National Telephone Company by the State. The Post Office Solicitor, Sir Robert Hunter, argued strongly in favour of the outright purchase. He denounced the Treasury trait of constantly referring back to the telegraph purchase. The assets of the private telegraph companies had been purchased by the Post Office at an inflated price and had been the subject of public and Treasury censure.[111] Sir Robert argued that the Treasury policy in relation to the telephone was "traditionalist" and out-moded and stated that while the earlier telegraph companies has been in a strong position to "extort" a high price from the Post Office because of their strong independent legal position which conferred upon them important wayleave powers, the National Telephone Company with its licence from the Post Office and the stipulation that the Post Office had the right to purchase the assets of the Company at certain specified dates was not in a similar position.[112]

By 1899, public dissatisfaction with the telephone system was again being expressed. One member of the House of Commons, Griffith-Boscawen, was typical of many both in and outside Parliament in his scathing attack on the poor state of the telephone service:

> Are we prepared to acquiesce in a state of affairs in which we lag so far behind the rest of the world? Are we willing for our trade to be handicapped by the fact that our telephone system is run not for the benefit of the public, but for the benefit of the shareholders of the National Telephone Company? What is the prime cause which makes us lag so far behind other countries? What precisely is it that places us under this disadvantage? It is the excessive cost of the telephone in this country.[113]

The speaker accused the private telephone company of failing to provide service to country districts because the company could not see any immediate prospect of a large return on such an invest-ment.[114]

The *Telegraph (Construction) Act, 1908*, which is still substantially in force, was introduced by the Postmaster-General, Sydney Buxton, to bestow on the Post Office "greater powers of obtaining wayleaves against unreasonable individuals".[115] Section 5 of the 1908 Act, which authorises the Postmaster-General (now Telecom Éireann by virtue of the *Postal and Telecommunications Services Act, 1983*, s. 8) to lop trees that obstruct a telegraphic line on a street or road, caused some opposition in both the House of Commons and the House of Lords. Mr. Goulding, MP, fearing that the beauty of the country could be depreciated, was of the opinion that the "Postmaster-General's servants were in no sense of the word woodmen".[116] Other sections of the 1908 Act facilitated the Postmaster-General in relation to the construction and maintenance of telegraph lines for telephonic and other telegraphic purposes. The *Telegraph (Construction) Act, 1911*[117] dealt with relations between the Post Office and the railway and canal companies and related in particular to telegraph and telephone lines which cross a railway or canal.

Public dissatisfaction with the telephone service forced the Postmaster-General to the conclusion that a single State-owned telephone system throughout the realm would ultimately remedy the defects in the service. After prolonged negotiations between the Postmaster-General and the National Telephone Company, an agreement was signed in 1905 fixing conditions whereby the State would take over the National Telephone Company's system when its licence expired in 1911. The *Telephone Transfer Act, 1911,*[118] repealed *in toto* by section 7 of the *Postal and Telecommunications Services Act, 1983*, made provisions for the transfer to the Postmaster-General of the plant, property assets and staff of the National Telephone Company and provided for further improvement of telephonic communication. The Postmaster-General, Herbert Samuel, in the House of Commons, stated that his Department was taking over 18,000 persons from the National Telephone Company with 2,000 persons of the 18,000 figure being pensionable with the company. After the transfer, 12,000 of the 18,000 received pension rights from the Post Office.[119] By 1908 in Ireland, the National Telephone Company owned 85 telephone exchanges while 33 exchanges were owned by the Postmaster-General.[120] With the exception of Hull, a single telephone system throughout the United Kingdom of Great Britain and Ireland owned by the State became a reality on December 31, 1911.

The *Telegraph (Construction) Act, 1916*[121] was introduced in the middle of the Great War to deal with "a few isolated cases" of what the Postmaster-General, Joseph Pearse, called "unpatriotic landowners who [were] . . . trying to bleed the Exchequer and extort money out of the Post Office in connection with wayleaves".[122] However, the Postmaster-General acknowledged that the Post Office had no experience of such unpatriotic landowners living in Ireland.[123] The 1916 Act attempted to simplify the procedure in relation to the resolution of disputes over wayleave rights by referring the dispute to the County, now the Circuit, Court.[124]

9

The Regulation of Telecommunication Carrier Services 1922-1993

THE REGULATION OF TELECOMMUNICATION CARRIER SERVICES IN SAORSTÁT ÉIREANN

When Saorstát Éireann (the Irish Free State) came into existence in 1922, the existing corpus of telecommunication law, as in other areas, was carried across the constitutional watershed and was to have full force and effect by virtue of Article 73 of the 1922 Constitution — subject to any inconsistencies between the earlier law and the Constitution of 1922 and until repealed or amended by an enactment of the Oireachtas. Two weeks after the 1922 Constitution came into force, the *Adaptation of Enactments Act, 1922* provided generally for the interpretation and adaptation of Acts of the Parliament of the United Kingdom.

The question of abolishing the Postmaster-General's Department in Ireland as a separate ministry and placing it under the control of the Minister for Finance was raised in January 1923 by the Executive Council.[1] It was argued that as the Post Office dealt largely with matters affecting the revenue of the State, and in fact acted as agent for the Finance Department in many matters, the Post Office should come under the control of the Finance Department. The Postmaster-General, James J Walsh, reacted swiftly and, within days of the Executive Council's first consideration of the issue, personally forwarded a memorandum to the Executive Council suggesting that some of the business performed by other Departments — like the business of tobacconists' and small traders' licences dealt with by the Department of Finance, the business of collecting rates and the distribution of outdoor relief managed by the Department of Local Government and the management of unemployment benefit which came under the aegis of the Department of Industry and Commerce

— might, to the greater advantage of the finances of the State, "be more economically fitted into Post Office machinery which [was] already available and which could take on such new businesses with but little extra cost".[2] The issue was settled in the Postmaster-General's favour by the *Ministers and Secretaries Act, 1924* which established the Department of Posts and Telegraphs and the powers, duties and functions of the Department were assigned to, and to be administered by, the Minister for Posts and Telegraphs.[3] The 1924 Act specified that the Department of Posts and Telegraphs would comprise the administration and business generally of services in connection, inter alia, with the telegraph and telephone together with the business, powers, duties and functions of the Postmaster-General.[4]

Government of Ireland Act, 1920

The early fluidity of certain constitutional structural arrangements of Saorstát Éireann raised issues relating to postal and telecommunication services concerning the whole island of Ireland. Up to 1925, responsibility for functions relating to postal and telecommunication services for the area described as the "Six Counties" was exercised directly from London. The UK *Government of Ireland Act, 1920*[5] purported to establish two parliaments, one for Northern Ireland and one for Southern Ireland. Section 3 of the 1920 Act provided that these Parliaments might, by identical Acts, establish a Parliament for the whole of Ireland, to be known as the Parliament of Ireland. The date at which the Parliament of Ireland was to be established was referred to in the 1920 Act as the date of Irish union.

Section 9(2) of the 1920 Act provided that certain matters including functions relating to the Post Office (which included telecommunication functions although not specifically referred to in the 1920 Act) were to be reserved matters until the date of Irish union and were then, unless Acts establishing the Parliament of Ireland otherwise provided, to be transferred from the Government of the United Kingdom to the Government of Ireland and were thereupon to cease to be reserved services. Section 9 (2) of the 1920 Act also provided, *inter alia*, that if before the date of Irish union, the Parliaments of Southern Ireland and Northern Ireland were by identical Acts to make provision for the transfer of reserved services to a Council of Ireland, such services were to be transferred in accordance with those Acts and would thereupon cease to be reserved services. The Attorney-General of Saorstát Éireann, John

O'Byrne, in a memorandum to the President of the Executive Council on April 28, 1925, considered that the suggested transfer of the postal and related services to the Government of Northern Ireland "would tend to defeat a possible transfer [of such services] to the Council of Ireland and to that extent [would detract] from the powers and jurisdiction of that body".[6] The Minister for Posts and Telegraphs, James J. Walsh, had more trenchant views on the subject. He considered that these services could be used, amongst other matters, "as a lever to get Irish unity"; the reserved services could be used in the nature of an inducement, but if these services were transferred to the Government of Northern Ireland without unity, the Minister considered that the Northern Government would become "a co-equal state with the same powers as we have" and there would be no inducement for them to unite with the Southern Government.[7] He concluded: "The more restricted their legislative and administrative powers remain, the better our chances of getting them in."[8] However, responsibility for the postal and telecommunication services were transferred subsequently from London to the Government of Northern Ireland and the separate administrations responsible for the two telecommunication services of the whole island of Ireland soon developed business-like relationships.

Telephone Capital Acts

The first telecommunication legislation of Saorstát Éireann was the *Telephone Capital Act, 1924* which received the King's assent on July 28, 1924.[9] The 1924 Act was the first of a series of Telephone Capital Acts later to be called *Telecommunications Capital Acts*[10] which authorised the Minister for Finance to issue out of the central funds such sums not to exceed a stipulated amount, as may be required for the development of the telephone service (as distinct from its operation and maintenance) in accordance with estimates of the Department of Posts and Telegraphs. The funds so provided were to be repaid by means of terminable annuities over a period generally not exceeding 25 years.[11] Leaving aside inflationary factors, the capital sum authorised by the *Telephone Capital Acts* grew in the latter half of this century. The *Telephone Capital Acts* also made provision for the preparation and audit of accounts and for a statement of the accounts to be laid before the Oireachtas.[12] In 1981 the fourteenth Capital Act, which authorised the remuneration of projects for the telecommunication service, departed from the nomenclature of similar previous Acts — the *Telephone Capital Acts*

— to become the *Telecommunications Capital Act, 1981*. The scope of the *Telecommunications Capital Act, 1981* was extended to make available capital monies up to a limit of IR£350m for the development of telex, data and telegram services in addition to the telephone service. The imminent formation of Telecom Éireann together with an expected financing of the telephone service of IR£100m "from private sources"[13] — references to monies expected from Irish Telecommunications Investments Limited, considered to be a vehicle for private financing — explains why the figure of IR£350m was the same amount as had been sanctioned under the *Telephone Capital Act, 1977*. Current expenditure for the day-to-day operation of the telecommunication service operated by the Department of Posts and Telegraphs was met out of monies voted by the Dáil annually.

Telecommunication Regulations

Regulation of the telecommunication services operated by the Minister for Posts and Telegraphs was primarily effected by the making of regulations. The *Telegraph Act, 1885*[14] empowered the Postmaster-General, and later the Minister for Posts and Telegraphs,[15] with the consent of the Commissioners of Her Majesty's Treasury, later the Minister for Finance,[16] to make regulations for the general conduct of the telecommunications business.[17]

The *Telegraph Act, 1885* was repealed in toto by the *Postal and Telecommunications Services Act, 1983*.[18] Section 90 of the 1983 Act now empowers Telecom Éireann, the telecommunication company established by the Minister for Posts and Telegraphs under the 1983 Act, to make schemes providing for the charges, terms and conditions in respect of any of the telecommunication services provided by the company. Existing regulations in force immediately before vesting day, January 1, 1984, were to have effect as if they were provisions of schemes made by the company.[19] The telecommunication services provided by Telecom Éireann are chiefly regulated by the *Telecommunications Scheme, 1992*.[20] Each subscriber to a telecommunication service signs an agreement for provision of service subject to any telecommunication scheme in force. The 1992 Scheme specifies the charges applicable for the service,[21] states that the subscriber is responsible for the safety of the telecommunication apparatus,[22] and provides for the termination of the agreement[23] or suspension[24] of telecommunication services in certain circumstances.

POST OFFICE (AMENDMENT) ACT, 1951 AND
TELEGRAPH ACT, 1953

Apart from the *Telecommunications Capital Acts*, the only primary
legislation of significance which impinged on the regulation of
telecommunication carrier service between the foundation of the
State and the enactment of the *Irish Telecommunications Investments
Limited Act, 1981* was the *Post Office (Amendment) Act, 1951* and the
Telegraph Act, 1953. The power to fix fees for telephone calls was,
prior to the *Postal and Telecommunications Services Act, 1983*, derived
from section 2 of the *Telegraph Act, 1885* which required that the fees
were to be fixed by regulation; the fees for telephone calls to places
outside the State, other than Great Britain and Northern Ireland, had
not been so determined and the Department of Posts and Telegraphs
did not want to have to make regulations each time the rates for such
calls were altered, undoubtedly due to the fact that the rates were
subject to frequent alterations and additions. Section 11 of the 1951
Act provided that foreign telephone rates were to be such as may be
determined by the Minister for Posts and Telegraphs with the consent of the Minister for Finance, and that notice of the rates were to
be published in *Iris Oifigiúil* at least 14 days before they came into
operation.

Indicative of the growing popularity of the telephone and its
attendant uses and abuses, the Minister for Posts and Telegraphs
found it necessary to be empowered by section 13 of the *Post Office
(Amendment) Act, 1951* to prosecute any person who sent by telephone any message of a grossly offensive, obscene or menacing
character, or messages which such person knew to be false.[25] Up to
then, the Minister was only empowered under the *Telephone Regulations, 1942*[26] to disconnect an offending subscriber's telephone
service.

The *Telegraph Act, 1953*[27] was enacted to remove certain statutory
limits[28] that prescribed the rates of charge for certain types of
telegram. The new rates of charge for telegrams were brought into
operation by statutory regulations to be made under section 2 of the
Telegraph Act, 1885. The 1953 Act was repealed in its entirety by the
Postal and Telecommunications Services Act, 1983.[29]

PRIVATE SECTOR FUNDING

Speculation as to possible "privatisation" of the State telecommunication carrier service achieved a certain currency in 1981. In essence, privatisation involves the transfer into private ownership of that which was previously owned by the State.[30] The Government's *Investment Plan 1981*,[31] subsequently outlined in more detail in the *Public Capital Programme 1981*, stated that the Government envisaged an extension to the existing partnership between private enterprise and the State.[32] The Government in its White Paper envisaged that private enterprise could provide capital assets for leasing by the State and "build projects by private capital and financed by tolls or charges".[33] The Government set a target of IR£200m for such suitable projects in 1981, mostly in relation to telecommunication development.[34] In February 1981, the Minister for Posts and Telegraphs, Albert Reynolds, proposed the formation of an investment company to raise IR£100m from private sector interests.[35] Subsequently, in April 1981, Irish Telecommunications Investments Limited (ITI Ltd) was incorporated under the *Companies Acts 1963 to 1977* but without reference to any other specific enabling legislation.

The primary function of the investment company was, in the Minister's words, "to obtain from the private sector, either by borrowing or leasing, up to IR£100m of the IR£221.8m required for the telecommunications development programme in 1981 and such other sums as might be required in subsequent years to finance telecommunications development".[36]

One object of ITI Limited as stated in its memorandum of association was "to give an opportunity to the private sector to invest in the development of the telecommunications service".[37] Another object was

> to sell or otherwise dispose of the property, assets and under-taking of the company or any part thereof, for such con-sideration as the company may think fit, and in particular for shares, stock, debentures or other securities of any other company whether or not having objects altogether or in part similar to those of the company subject in the case of [tele-communications buildings, plant and equipment] to the con-sent of the Minister for Posts and Telegraphs.[38]

As ITI Ltd was initially a private limited company, the articles of association provided that any invitation to the public to subscribe for any shares or debentures of the company was prohibited.[39] However, if references by Government Ministers to the term "privatisation"[40] were to be acted upon, it would have been relatively easy to change the status of ITI Ltd from a private limited company to a public limited company. [In July 1987 ITI Ltd became a public limited company to enable the company to issue securities to the public. Despite the status of the company, the public has not been invited to subscribe for any shares; the company has, however, issued securities in the form of bonds.]

Genuine privatisation, in this instance the transfer of the ownership of the telecommunication carrier service from the public sector to the private sector, was not carried into effect. The Minister for Posts and Telegraphs who was responsible for the formation of ITI Ltd referred in the Dáil in 1981 to "conflicting legal advice" in relation to the status of the company.[41] Subsequently, it was deemed necessary to introduce the *Irish Telecommunications Investments Limited Bill* in 1981. The primary purpose of the Bill was to provide for guarantees by the Minister for Finance of approved borrowings and leasing by ITI Ltd. Dr. Whitaker in the Seanad on the Second Stage of the Bill questioned the wisdom of the proposed legislation. He felt bound to ask

> whether there [was] any particular advantage in providing by this special legislation for a means by which the private sector can subscribe to State-guaranteed loans? They can do it without any legislation. They can do it anonymously. What is the advantage of doing it in this form? In what way does it bring anything into the Exchequer that could not be got in another way? I have to ask that because if the ideal of privatisation is to have real success, there must be access for the private investor to something more than he can get anonymously by subscribing to a national loan or taking up Government paper.[42]

The Bill was enacted on November 11, 1981. Section 2 of the *Irish Telecommunications Investments Limited Act, 1981* empowered the Minister for Finance to take up shares in the company up to the limit of the authorised share capital, i.e., IR£100; section 3 of the 1981 Act empowered the Minister for Finance to hold shares in the company for as long as he saw fit and to sell such shares after consultation with the Minister for Posts and Telegraphs.

Subsequently, in March 1983, the *Irish Telecommunications Investments Ltd (Amendment) Act, 1983* was passed which increased from IR£350m to IR£600m the limit on the company's approved borrowings which may be guaranteed by the Minister for Finance.

Section 7 of the Postal and *Telecommunications Services Act, 1983* provided for the repeal of the *Irish Telecommunications Investments Ltd Act, 1981* and the *Irish Telecommunications Investments Ltd (Amendment) Act, 1983* with effect from January 1, 1984 — the date of the vesting of Telecom Éireann. Section 97 of the Postal and Telecommunications Services Act, 1983 provided that the shares held on December 31, 1983 by nominees of the Minister for Posts and Telegraphs and the Minister for Finance were to be transferred to persons nominated by Telecom Éireann with the concurrence of these Ministers. Section 97(2) of the 1983 Act provided for amendment of the memorandum and articles of association of ITI Ltd to take account of the changes of ownership. Accordingly, ITI Ltd became a wholly owned subsidiary of Telecom Éireann. As stated above, in July 1987 the company was re-registered as a public limited company (plc).

Despite certain conjecture in that period in relation to privatisation, no concrete steps were taken towards the attainment of such an objective. Perhaps from a political viewpoint in relation to telecommunication, both the Fianna Fáil and Fine Gael/Labour Coalition Governments considered it prudent not to travel down the road of privatisation prior to the formation of the new semi-State companies, An Post and Telecom Éireann, which were intended to reduce the Civil Service by half. Although the formation of ITI Ltd and the enactment of the *Irish Telecommunications Investments Limited Act, 1981* were referred to as steps in privatisation, this was undoubtedly not so in a legal sense. In essence, what was involved was that private banks put up money for development of the telecommunication carrier infrastructure for a guaranteed return from the Government. This was public-sector borrowing by another name. One commentator neatly summed up the issues in relation to the formation of ITI Ltd and to references to so-called "privatisation" associated with that initiative:

> But this could never be seen as genuine "privatisation" by anyone. A semi-State investment company is to borrow the funds from the private sector and will own the assets which this money has been used to purchase. The end result is that both the assets and the liabilities i.e. the borrowings will not show up on the Government balance sheet. As far as the institutions providing the money are concerned, however, it is still another loan to the Government. . . . Merely tinkering with the nation's balance sheet achieves nothing, and we should learn one lesson

from the ill-fated "privatisation" exercise — politicians should decide on social issues making fully clear to the people of Ireland what is entailed politically before making half-baked pronouncements.[43]

ITI plc is now the treasury management subsidiary of Telecom Éireann and has been successful in raising finance in both the domestic and foreign markets for capital investment. ITI plc also provides training management and consultancy services to overseas clients.

REORGANISATION OF STATE TELECOMMUNICATION CARRIER SERVICES

In former times, knowledge and control of communication could be equated with a central power or government. With new technology, vast amounts of information became accessible to non-government agencies and private individuals. Inevitably, in this context, central government loses some of its status and power. It has been aptly stated that in recent times the "State is less governable, but not only at a technical or bureaucratic level".[44] Many argue that over the past two decades in particular the traditional instruments of government, particularly the Civil Service, have become less efficient. The telecommunication carrier services (the non-broadcasting service, i.e. telephone, telex and other related forms of telecommunication) undertaken as a branch of the Civil Service had deteriorated rapidly in Ireland in the late 1960s and 1970s.

The Postmaster-General and the Minister for Posts and Telegraphs acted not only as regulators but were themselves subject to severe regulation. As a department of State, as a potential income generator, often starved of capital, the Department of Posts and Telegraphs pursued policies under the direction of Government which often did not produce economical and efficient telecommunication services. Many considered that a Government department was an inappropriate agency to manage a business undertaking.[45] Others have, in the past, been more forthright about government management of the telecommunication service. In 1911, A.N. Holcombe in his doctoral thesis for Harvard University, *Public Ownership of Telephones on the Continent of Europe*, considered that public management of business undertakings was, at best, characterised by "hopeless mediocrity".[46] Holcombe quoted the views of Herbert Spencer: "Why should we hope so much from a state agency in new fields when in the old fields it has bungled so miserably?"[47] In an atmosphere of deteriorating service with a management directly under the control of a Government department, the spirit of deregulation inevitably gained momentum.

No serious attempt was made to reorganise the telecommunication carrier business until 1969. In that year the Public Service Organisation Review Group recommended a radical structural reorganisation of the Civil Service based on the concept of separate structures for policy formulation and execution of policy. The Group recommended that a Post and Telecommunications Office responsible for the day-to-day management of the postal and telecommunications services should be established as an executive unit of a new Department of Transport and Communications.[48] This recommendation was never implemented. Dr. Conor Cruise O'Brien as Minister for Posts and Telegraphs did moot in 1973 the establishment of a State-sponsored corporation on the lines of Córas Iompair Éireann or the Electricity Supply Board.[49] No firm proposals emerged from such consideration of the Minister.

By 1978 the telecommunication carrier service run as a branch of the Civil Service had become increasingly inefficient and undependable. In 1978, the Minister for Posts and Telegraphs set up the Posts and Telegraph Review Group. The terms of reference in relation to the telecommunication business were:

> To examine and report on the feasibility of giving to the telecommunications service such form of autonomous organisation as is likely to be most effective in meeting current public demand and providing for future development and expansion; and to make specific proposals regarding the nature, powers, and functions of the organisation recommended.[50]

The Group, in its report, stated that an efficient telecommunication service was essential for "the social and business purposes of the community".[51] It considered that the "restrictions, practices and precedents" within which the Civil Service functioned made the Civil Service an "unsuitable structure for management of a business such as telecommunications".[52] The Group recommended that the telecommunication service be taken out of the Civil Service and entrusted to a separate State-sponsored body in the form of a statutory company to be run on commercial lines. The Group also recommended that the monopoly vested in the Minister for Posts and Telegraphs be conferred on the new company, but modified to the extent that competition should be permitted for the supply of telecommunication equipment inside the subscriber's premises.[53]

The Government accepted in principle the basic recommendations of the Posts and Telegraphs Review Group. A Green Paper was issued in May 1980 containing proposals in general terms regarding the duties, powers and responsibilities of the proposed body to deal with telecommunication services.[54] A White Paper was subsequently issued containing the decisions of the Government on the re-organisation of the telecommunication services.[55]

POSTAL AND TELECOMMUNICATIONS SERVICES ACTS, 1983 AND 1984

The *Postal and Telecommunications Services Act, 1983* implemented the decisions set out in the White Paper and provided for the transfer of control and management of the postal and certain telecommunication services from the Minister for Posts and Telegraphs to two separate State-owned companies, An Post and Telecom Éireann. The 1983 Act did not (in general) consolidate or update the law in relation to the telecommunication carrier service. Having provided the appropriate mechanism for the establishment of a new State company, Telecom Éireann, the 1983 Act, *inter alia*, made consequential amendments in earlier legislation substituting Telecom Éireann, as appropriate, for the Minister for Posts and Telegraphs.

The 1983 Act which, inter alia, facilitated the process of liberalising the provision of telecommunication carrier-related services is considered in chapter 14, "Telecommunication Privileges, Powers and Duties" and in chapter 17, "Privileges, Powers and Duties of Telecom Éireann".

The *Postal and Telecommunications Services (Amendment) Act, 1984* was enacted to remedy the defective drafting of sections 56 and 57 of the 1983 Act. It had been the intention of the draftsman to transfer all potential liabilities by way of claims and court proceedings, extant on January 1, 1984, that had arisen in relation to the telecommunication carrier services to Telecom Éireann. The 1983 Act, however, only effected the transfer in relation to proceedings and claims brought by and against the Minister for Posts and Telegraphs and did not transfer liability, or the benefit of a cause of action, in which either the State or the Minister for Finance was a party. Section 2 of the 1984 Act remedied that defect.

It is appropriate to conclude this chapter with a brief reference to regulatory aspects associated with the management of Telecom Éireann since its incorporation on December 15, 1983. The first chairman of Telecom Éireann was Dr. Michael Smurfit who served 12 years between his chairmanship of the Interim Telecommunications Board and that of Telecom Éireann. This period could be characterised as one of stability and growth leading to the declaration of IR£94 million profits in 1992 albeit subject to a debt of IR£1 billion, much of which was inherited from the State on the vesting of the Company on January 1, 1984. Dr. Smurfit resigned in September 1991 at the time of the Department of Communications Telecom Inquiry[56] into the controversial purchase by Telecom Éireann of property in Ballsbridge for its proposed corporate headquarters. The Departmental Inquiry was followed by an Interim Report (July 1992) and Final Report (July 1993) to the Minister for Industry and Commerce by John A. Glackin, solicitor, pursuant to section 14(1) of the *Companies Act, 1990* into the ownership of certain companies involved in the sale of the Ballsbridge property to Telecom Éireann.[57] Mr. Glackin was satisfied that none of the Telecom Éireann executives or directors had been involved in any wrongdoing in relation to the purchse of the Ballsbridge property. Dr. Smurfit was replaced by Brendan Hynes who was removed from office in July 1992, pursuant to section 16(2)(b) of the *Postal and Telecommunications Act, 1993*, by the Minister for Communications, Máire Geoghegan-Quinn, as a result of difficulties within the board of directors. The third chairman, Ron Bolger, took up his appointment in December 1992. The first chief executive of Telecom Éireann was Tom Byrnes who resigned in 1985 and was replaced by Fergus McGovern.

The Departmental and Glackin Inquiries[58] were a powerful reminder of the regulatory role which could be played by Government outside the existing legal framework of telecommunication legislation.

10

Wireless Telegraphy

WIRELESS TELEGRAPHY ACT, 1904, THE TREATY OF 1921 AND THE WIRELESS TELEGRAPHY (RADIO) STATIONS

The ability to communicate by wireless telegraphy had been discovered by late 1894.[1] This discovery involved communication from a distance using electricity and without the aid of wires. The Wireless Telegraph and Signal Company (UK) was formed in 1897 and purchased certain telegraph patent rights. The Post Office argued at the time that the establishment of wireless telegraph stations would be in contravention of the Postmaster-General's telegraph monopoly.

Wireless telegraphy is a species of telegraphy.[2] Although the provisions of the *Telegraph Acts* apply to wireless telegraphy, separate legislation was enacted to regulate and control wireless telegraphy and broadcasting.[3] The *Wireless Telegraphy Act*, 1904[4] contained several features which were to become a permanent feature of wireless telegraphy law. Provision was made in the 1904 Act for licences to be issued for wireless telegraphy apparatus.[5] Penalties were prescribed for the establishment of a "wireless telegraph station" without a licence and for installing or working any apparatus for wireless telegraphy without a licence.[6] Provision was made for granting of search warrants and seizing of apparatus which appeared to be used or intended to be used for wireless telegraphy[7] in contravention of the Act. The 1904 Act was, however, a temporary measure and had to be renewed from year to year.[8] The Government was reluctant to settle important issues of policy which were raised by the introduction of wireless telegraphy, questions which affected defence, trade, internal communications and "the progress of invention".[9]

Meanwhile, new developments were fast taking place in wireless telegraphy; broadcasting services soon became a reality.[10] The British Broadcasting Corporation was granted a Royal Charter in

1922 and was also given the sole right of operating radio stations in the United Kingdom.

At the establishment of Saorstát Éireann in 1922, wireless telegraphy in the State was governed by Article 7 and Clause 2 of the Annex to the Treaty between Britain and Ireland signed on December 6, 1921 and by the *Wireless Telegraphy Acts, 1904 and 1906*.[11] After the transfer of the Post Office from the British Government in April 1922, permits were issued by the Postmaster-General of Saorstát Éireann for the installation and working of wireless receiving apparatus subject to certain conditions and the payment of a fee.[12] These permits were withdrawn on the outbreak of disturbances in July 1922 at the request of the military authorities and the sale, importation, and manufacture of wireless apparatus was also prohibited.[13] Military regulations prohibiting the holding by civilians of wireless or broadcasting apparatus were repealed in 1923.

The Wireless Telegraphy Act, 1904[14] regulated transmission as distinct from reception. The issue arose in the early days of Saorstát Éireann whether a user of a receiving apparatus only was obliged to take out a licence under the Act of 1904. This issue caused some administrative difficulties for the regulatory authorities of the new State. The Secretary of the Post Office informed the Executive Council in 1923 that about 35 ships whose port of registry was in Saorstát Éireann carried and used apparatus for wireless telegraphy.[15] The Secretary enclosed a copy of the British licence which the Department proposed to adopt; the Government was asked whether it had any objection to the licence. The Executive Council sought the advice of the Attorney General, John O'Byrne, who informed the Executive Council that under Article 11 of the 1922 Constitution, all the natural resources of the Saorstát including the air and all forms of potential energy were vested in the State and were to be controlled and administered by the Oireachtas in accordance with such regulations and provisions as might, from time to time, be approved by legislation in accordance with Article 11.[16] The Attorney General considered that wireless telegraphy would reasonably be held to come within the provisions of Article 11 and, accordingly, he could not advise the Minister for Posts and Telegraphs to issue any such licence without the authority of the Oireachtas. Further, the Attorney General drew attention to Article 7 of the Treaty and to the provisions in clause 2 of the Annex thereto.[17]

Article 7 of the Treaty provided that the Government of Saorstát

Éireann was to afford His Majesty's Imperial Forces in time of peace
such harbour and other facilities as were indicated in the Annex to
the Treaty or such other facilities as might from time to time be
agreed. Clause 2(a) of the Annex to the Treaty provided that wireless
stations for communication with places outside Ireland were not to
be established except with the agreement of the British Government;
submarine cables were not to be landed in Saorstát Éireann except
by similar agreement; the existing cable landing rights and wireless
concessions were not to be withdrawn save with the like consent; the
British Government were to be entitled to land additional submarine
cables or establish additional wireless stations for communication
with places outside Ireland; and that a Convention was to give effect
to these matters. Both Governments differed on the interpretation of
these provisions. The issue that provoked the disagreement was the
control of the coastal wireless radio stations which communicated
with ships at sea. The coastal stations at Valentia and Malin Head
remained under the control of the British authorities for some years
after 1922. The Department of Posts and Telegraphs operated them
for the British authorities and provided the staff, but the British
Government bore the cost of the staff and maintenance of the stations
and received appropriate revenue.[18]

The Attorney General of the Irish Provisional Government, Hugh
Kennedy (later to become Chief Justice), advised on March 13, 1922
that the issue of the wireless stations was "of the greatest
importance". The Attorney General was conscious of the fact that
during the recent World War messages were "jammed" from
particular message-sending stations. He did not know what was in
the minds of the signatories to the Treaty or what aspects of the
question were discussed; he would have to take the Treaty and
construe it as it stood. The Attorney General advised that the sole
object of the relevant provisions of the Treaty was to provide for
Imperial Defence, that any attempt to read commercial or non-
military control into those provisions was against the letter and spirit
of Article 7 of the Treaty, and that the suggestion that the British Post
Office had retained control of the wireless stations was not correct.[19]
He advised that any convention between the Governments must
limit itself to dealing with the provision of facilities for Imperial
Defence only and that the radio communication systems in Ireland
were to be "in all other respects used and developed under the
control of the Irish Government".[20]

On April 1, 1922 the *Provisional Government (Transfer of Functions)
Order, 1922*[21] provided for the transfer to the appropriate named

Ministers of the Irish Government of the functions in Ireland hitherto discharged by British Departments, including the functions of the Postmaster-General. But paragraph 11 of the Order stipulated that nothing in the Order should affect services in connection with wireless stations for communication with places outside Ireland or in connection with submarine cables to places outside the British Islands.

The issue of the wireless stations dragged on. John O'Byrne, Hugh Kennedy's successor as Attorney General, advised the Department of External Affairs in 1924 that the Convention mentioned in the Annex to the Articles of Agreement of the Treaty was not necessary to secure the handing over of the wireless stations; the Annex was merely intended to limit the establishment in the future of wireless stations for communication outside Ireland without the consent of the British Government. The Annex did not affect the handing over of the stations and the Attorney General could not understand why the stations had not been handed over already. The Attorney General advised that the Minister for Posts and Telegraphs should take steps to take over both stations from the British.[22] In correspondence between the Dublin and London Post Offices, Dublin asked for the handing over of the stations and London replied that in the opinion of its Government's Law Officers the Irish Government was not entitled to require the transfer.[23]

Attorney General John A. Costello in a memorandum to the President of the Executive Council in 1928 agreed with the opinion of his predecessors and advised that except in so far as the powers of the Oireachtas were limited or prescribed by the Treaty or by Article 11 of the new Constitution, the Oireachtas could deal in any way it liked with wireless telegraphy and wireless stations in the Saorstát.[24] He also advised that the provisions of the Treaty could have no bearing on wireless stations in existence at the date of the Treaty but only referred to wireless stations to be established after the Treaty.

No convention was ever entered into between the parties, but the Irish Government observed the spirit and letter of the Treaty by seeking appropriate consents of the British authorities. In July 1929, the Department of Post and Telegraphs sought the consent of the British authorities to grant landing facilities to the American Telephone and Telegraph Company for a new submarine cable from Cape Breton in Nova Scotia landing at points in Newfoundland, Mayo, Donegal and Scotland. The Dominions Office in London, in a courteous memorandum to the Minister for External Affairs on

July 12, 1929, stated that His Majesty's Government had no objection to the landing of the cable in the Irish Free State.[25]

By 1930, Attorney General Costello was becoming most impatient with the various Government departments involved with the wireless stations. In a memorandum to the Department of External Affairs in December 1930, the Attorney General stated that he could not understand why in a matter involving a question of the Treaty that there should be a lack of co-ordinated policy and action.[26] Referring to his own previous opinions and to the opinions of his predecessors on the issue, the Attorney General was "at a loss to understand why in the face of all these opinions effective steps [had] not been taken to take over the stations at Valentia and Malin Head as well as the disused stations".[27] Subsequently, the Solicitor to the Department of Posts and Telegraphs, Liam Lysaght, commenting on the Attorney General's memorandum noted that the Attorney General made "no allusion to the unproductive steps already taken [to solve the issue], some under [the Attorney General's] guidance".[28]

The Anglo-Irish Agreement of April 25, 1938 provided in Article 1 that the provisions of Articles 6 and 7 of the 1921 Treaty and of the Annex thereto were to cease to have effect. However, by 1947 the position still was that the Department of Posts and Telegraphs was being recouped by the British Post Office for any outgoings it discharged in relation to the disused wireless stations. In relation to the Malin and Valentia stations, the British Post Office still collected the revenue and reimbursed the Irish Department of Posts and Telegraphs for the salaries of staff and other outgoings discharged by it.

The Attorney General, Cearbhall Ó Dálaigh, in 1947 advised that the stations had not been given to the British Government by the Treaty of 1921 and, if they had been so given, all British rights to them terminated under the Anglo-Irish Agreement of April 23, 1938. He continued:

> If at present the stations are being operated by the [Irish] Post Office as "agents" for the British Government it seems to me that this arrangement is without warranty or authority in our law and it should cease forthwith. No further accounts should be furnished or monies paid over. The stations should be dealt with simply for what they are, that is to say, as Government property; and any notification to the British Government otherwise to the effect that these stations are Irish Government property and are being dealt with as such is liable to be

> misconstrued as a derogation from our rights. . . . Our position
> is clear; we are in possession as full owners and we intend to
> exercise our rights as such.[29]

This saga demonstrates the vital importance which Governments
attach to external modes of communication. Advances in the
technology of telecommunication solved the problem of the British
Government: Valentia and Malin Head wireless stations had become
of little strategic importance to the British Government in the context
of external telecommunication facilities.

WIRELESS TELEGRAPHY ACTS 1926 TO 1988

The Irish authorities benefited from regular contact with the
Postmaster-General's Department in London concerning developments in wireless telegraphy and broadcasting. For example, in May
1925 the Secretary of the General Post Office in London in a
confidential letter to his counterpart in Dublin gave advance details
of the UK Government's legislative proposals in relation to certain
amendments to the UK *Wireless Telegraphy and Signalling Bill, 1925*.
The Secretary in London added:

> It is essential that the information therein given shall not
> become public property. . . . So far as we have made suggestions
> for alterations . . . they are merely provisional and have not yet
> been submitted to the Parliamentary Draftsman for con-
> sideration. Any leakage of information would therefore be
> extremely inconvenient — to say the least of it.
> . . . [I]t is no trouble to give you any information we can for
> confidential use and I hope you will not hesitate to ask me
> whenever I can properly be of assistance.[30]

The fruits of these communications influenced the drafting of Irish
legislation.

A Wireless Telegraphy Bill was introduced and passed in the Dáil
in 1926. The *Wireless Telegraphy Act, 1926* consisted of two parts. Part
1 made provision for the regulation and control of wireless
telegraphy; Part 11 related to broadcasting. Part 1 was modelled on
the provisions of the *Wireless Telegraphy Act, 1904* and the withdrawn
UK *Wireless Telegraphy and Signalling Bill, 1925*, modified to meet the
conditions of Saorstát Éireann. There had been considerable

criticism of the 1925 Bill in the United Kingdom: members of Parliament moved a motion requesting the House to decline a Second Reading of the Bill "which [gave] immense power to a Government Department, would inflict excessive risks for infringement of regulations made under such powers, and created new rights of search which unduly infringe the liberties of the subject whilst at the same time discouraging scientific research and experiments in the new industry". The UK Government withdrew the Bill deciding to appoint a Committee to inquire into the future of broadcasting.[31]

Although the Irish Act of 1926 received the Royal Assent on December 24, 1926, the Admiralty, War Office and Air Ministry in London expressed concern with certain aspects of the legislation. While the British authorities were consulted when the legislation was in Bill form, the Dominions Office in London did not raise matters of concern until April 14, 1927.[32] The Dominions Office was concerned principally with the interpretation of "ships of war" which were exempted from the licensing requirements under section 3(6) of the 1926 Act and argued for a general licensing exemption for military aircraft, whether belonging to the Royal Air Force or the Fleet Air Arm. The "special position of the Royal Navy in relation to the Irish Free State" was recited by the Dominions Office as a justification for the exemption. Section 3(6) of the 1926 Act provided that licensing requirements were not to apply to apparatus for wireless telegraphy kept by or in possession of the Minister for Defence for the purpose of the Defence Forces, or to any ship of war belonging to the Government of Saorstát Éireann or any other country or state.[33] The Irish Government in its reply[34] assured the Dominions Office that fleet auxiliaries including oil and provision ships would, in practice, be regarded as being ships of war and hence exempted from the licensing requirements of the 1926 Act. Straining the plain meaning of section 3(6) of the 1926 Act,[35] the Irish Government also confirmed that military aircraft whether belonging to the Royal Air Force or Fleet Air Arm would, in practice, be exempted from the licensing requirements. The Irish Government confirmed that "a Bill to amend the *Wireless Telegraphy Act, 1926* would be desirable" and that the matters referred to by the Dominions Office would be borne in mind when the draft of the amending Bill was being prepared.[36]

No substantive amendments were, in fact, made to the 1926 Act until the enactment of the *Wireless Telegraphy Act, 1972*. An assurance was also given to the Dominions Office that "the British forces at

Berehaven, Cobh and Lough Swilly and all premises occupied by them" would be regarded as exempt, so far as service wireless telegraphy installations were concerned, from the provisions of sections 7 (obligation to furnish certain information by way of declaration) and section 8 (issue of search warrants) of the 1926 Act.[37] It was not until 1990 that the Minister for Communications was empowered to recognise (for the first time) wireless telegraphy licences granted in other countries as being valid in Ireland.[38]

The 1926 Act, as amended,[39] is still the principal Act regulating wireless telegraphy today. The expression "wireless telegraphy" is defined in the 1926 Act as meaning

> the emitting and receiving or emitting only or receiving only, over paths which are not provided by any material substance constructed or arranged for that purpose, of electric, magnetic or electro-magnetic energy of a frequency not exceeding 3 million megahertz, whether or not such energy serves the conveying (whether they are actually received or not) of communications, sounds, signs, visual images or signals, or the actuation or control of machinery or apparatus.[40]

The expression "apparatus for wireless telegraphy" is defined as meaning

> apparatus capable of emitting and receiving, or emitting only or receiving only, over paths which are not provided by any material substance constructed or arranged for that purpose, electric, magnetic or electro-magnetic energy, of a frequency not exceeding 3 million megahertz, whether or not such energy serves the conveying (whether they are actually received or not) of communications, sounds, signs, visual images or signals or the actuation or control of machinery or apparatus, and includes any part of such apparatus, and also includes any other apparatus which is associated with, or electrically coupled to, apparatus capable of so emitting such energy.[41]

The *Wireless Telegraphy Acts* and the regulations made thereunder at present regulate all communications made by wireless telegraphy.[42] In particular, regulations have been made governing broadcasting receiving apparatus (television licences);[43] radio experimenters' licences;[44] business radio and radio links;[45] wired broadcast relay licences (cable television);[46] personal radio licences (citizens' band radio);[47] television programme retransmission service;[48] control of radio interference from various apparatus and equipment;[49] and the mobile radio community repeater service.[50] The *Wireless Telegraphy Act, 1926*[51] provides for the granting of licences,[52] creates offences[53] and provides for Government control of wireless telegraphy in emergencies.[54]

The *Wireless Telegraphy Act*, 1956 amended the 1926 Act to provide that a vehicle "shall itself be deemed to be a place separate and distinct from the premises" in which the vehicle is ordinarily kept.[55] The 1956 Act was enacted swiftly following a decision of the High Court. That court, sitting as a Divisional Court, held in *Mullen v Minister for Posts and Telegraphs*[56] that a District Justice was wrong in law in dismissing a summons for possession of a radio receiving set in a car without a licence contrary to the provisions of the *Wireless Telegraphy Act 1926*. Haugh J in his judgment stated that the prohibition on possession of wireless receiving apparatus anywhere within the State contained in section 3(1) of *Wireless Telegraphy Act, 1926* was "in its clearest terms, absolute".[57] Haugh and Murnaghan JJ also held that section 5 of the *Wireless Telegraphy Act, 1926* which authorised the Minister for Posts and Telegraphs to grant a licence for apparatus for wireless telegraphy "in any specified place" could not be interpreted as meaning, inter alia, a vehicle. The same judges were also of the opinion that the *Wireless Telegraphy (Receiving Licence) Regulations 1937*[58] were outside the powers conferred by the 1926 Act insofar as they purported to extend the meaning of the word "place" in the Act. Although the Solicitor to the Department of Posts and Telegraphs, Frank Connolly, and the Attorney General, Patrick J. McGilligan, queried whether the decision of the Divisional Court represented the correct view of the law, they advised amending legislation with retrospective effect to remove the doubts raised.[59] The judgments of the Divisional Court were delivered on January 19, 1956; the *Wireless Telegraphy Act, 1956* was enacted into law on February 21, 1956, with the amending section deemed to have come into operation immediately after the commencement of the 1926 Act.

The *Wireless Telegraphy Act, 1972* substantially amended the 1926 Act and now enables the Minister for Communications to obtain information concerning the sale and letting of television sets. The objective of the Act, as stated by the Minister to the Dáil, was to reduce to a minimum the "evasion of payment of licence fees on television sets".[60] The Opposition spokesperson in the Dáil noted that the proposed Act was another intrusion "into persons' private affairs".[61] Television dealers were required to register with the

Minister,[62] maintain records of transactions and supply the Minister with relevant particulars.[63] The Minister was also empowered to restrict the manufacture or importation of certain apparatus for wireless telegraphy.[64] The foregoing provisions were based on the UK *Wireless Telegraphy Act, 1967*. Amendments were also made to the *Wireless Telegraphy Act, 1926*; presumptions were created relating to possession of apparatus for wireless telegraphy;[65] criminal offences were created and existing penalties were increased.[66]

The obligation on television dealers to register with, and supply information to, the Department of Posts and Telegraphs was first mooted in 1925. The Minister for Finance, ever anxious to increase the revenue of the State, requested the Parliamentary Draftsman to include a section in the *Wireless Telegraphy Bill, 1925* giving power to the Minister for Posts and Telegraphs to make regulations requiring all dealers in wireless telegraphy apparatus in the Saorstát to keep a record of the names and addresses of persons to whom wireless sets and wireless parts were sold as well as the type of sets involved.[67] It was also proposed that dealers would have to furnish the Department with appropriate details within a certain period. The Minister for Finance considered that the information thus obtained would greatly facilitate the Department of Posts and Telegraphs in checking evasion of the licence fee and in restricting the necessity of domiciliary visits. The Solicitor to the Department of Posts and Telegraphs, George R. Reid, while fully sympathising with the intentions of the Department of Finance, considered that the proposed regulations would be "both unworkable and of little use".[68] He wrote of the great trouble that would be caused to traders, the clerical labour involved and the ease with which persons could give false names. The Minister for Posts and Telegraphs concurred with the views of the Solicitor and stated that the Department should oppose the proposal.[69] In deference to the representations of the Department of Posts and Telegraphs, the Minister for Finance agreed not to proceed with his proposals.[70] The enactment of the provisions in question into legislative form in the United Kingdom by virtue of the UK *Wireless Telegraphy Act, 1967* renewed Irish interest in this area.

The *Broadcasting and Wireless Telegraphy Act, 1988*, was introduced primarily to prohibit broadcasting in the State save under and in accordance with a licence issued by the Minister for Communications. The 1988 Act also amended and extended the Wireless Telegraphy Acts 1926 to 1972. The range and level of penalties pertaining to wireless telegraphy were also updated.[71]

11

State Broadcasting: Regulation by the Government and Ministers for Posts and Telegraphs, 1926-1953

DEVELOPMENT OF BROADCASTING LAW IN SAORSTÁT ÉIREANN

The establishment of an Irish broadcasting service was, understandably, not a matter of priority for the new Irish State. However, the reception in Ireland of broadcasting signals from the United Kingdom prompted the Irish Government into action. The press media were critical of the early inertia of the new Irish Government in this area. *The Irish Times* in January 1924 opined:

> [T]he situation [in relation to broadcasting] is at once ridiculous and irritating. The wonderful development of "broadcasting" has turned the whole of Western Europe into a vast auditorium. Every owner of a comparatively cheap apparatus can "listen" in to the music of the most famous singers and orchestras and the words of great statesmen and preachers. Only the citizens of the Saorstát, like Moore's Peri — "at the gate of Eden stand disconsolate". Their Government, through its Postmaster-General, has refused on the one hand to allow them to tap the sweet voices of the outer world, and on the other, to provide them with any home-made pleasures of the same kind. The absurdity and stupidity of this situation are aggravated by the fact that some — perhaps many — people in the Free State own receiving sets and are defying Mr. Walsh's [the Postmaster-General] threats of pains and penalties.[1]

The development of Government policy including the various tensions over the early form of regulation of the Irish broadcasting service will be reviewed here.

The Postmaster-General of Saorstát Éireann, James J. Walsh, published a statement in the national press in April 1923 to the effect that he hoped "to be in a position to grant licences for the establishment of wireless broadcasting stations in the Free State".[2] Persons and firms interested in the manufacture and supply of broadcasting apparatus were invited to apply to the Secretary of the General Post Office so that necessary arrangements could be made.

In November 1923, a White Paper was issued by the Post Office.[3] The first question posed in the White Paper was whether broadcasting should be "worked as a Post Office monopoly". The first Postmaster-General of the Irish State concluded that the broadcasting service should not be run by his Department. He was firmly of the opinion that the "business of arranging concerts and general entertainment was not one which a State Department ought to undertake".[4] [Thirty seven years later when introducing the *Broadcasting Authority Bill, 1959* establishing a statutory authority to control and operate the Irish broadcasting service, the Minister for Posts and Telegraphs, Michael Hilliard, submitted that this statement of principle by the first Postmaster-General of the State was well founded.][5] The 1923 White Paper concluded that an Irish Broadcasting Company should be established; the capital for the company would be provided by industrial firms and the smaller manufacturers and traders would be permitted to have shares in the company.[6] This arrangement was identical to that then in operation in Britain.[7]

Postmaster-General Walsh, and the Secretary of the Department, P.S. O'Hegarty, were influenced in their formulation of policy by the Sykes Committee Report (1923) in the United Kingdom.[8] The following sentiments expressed by the Sykes Committee were often reiterated by Ireland's first Postmaster-General and the Secretary of his Department. Emphasising the disadvantages of direct Government operation of the broadcasting service, the Sykes Committee stated:

A Minister might well shrink from the prospect of having to defend in Parliament the various items in Government concerts. If a Government Department had to select the news, speeches, lectures, etc, to be broadcast, it would be constantly open to suspicion that it was using its unique opportunities to advance the interests of the political party in power; and in the endeavour to avoid anything in the slightest degree controversial, it would probably succeed in making the service intolerably dull.[9]

These specific charges were often laid against the controllers of the Irish broadcasting service — the Minister for Posts and Telegraphs and ultimately the Government of the day.

Arrangements were made to implement the proposals in the 1923 White Paper: the White Paper stated that "constituent firms have agreed to join in the broadcasting scheme under licence from the Post Office". The broadcasting company was to erect and operate a broadcasting station in Dublin; a licence was to be issued to the company for five years and be "renewable thereafter at the pleasure of the Postmaster-General". The Postmaster-General was to issue licences for wireless receiving sets and the new broadcasting company would receive a share of the fee charged for licences. An assurance was given in the White Paper that "no monopoly [would] be created as all manufacturers [would] be at liberty to share in the operations of the proposed company".

The Dáil subsequently established a committee in 1923 to examine the White Paper. The committee was requested to consider in particular the proposal "by which it [was] intended that the State should pass over the right to license and tax incoming wireless apparatus to a clearing house under the control of a private company".[10] Three interim reports were issued.[11] In the final report, the Committee stated that "broadcasting should be a State service purely — the installation and the working of it to be solely in the hands of the Postal Ministry".[12] The Committee came to this view because it regarded broadcasting to be of "incalculable value" as an instrument of "popular education"; the use of broadcasting for entertainment was considered to be "of vastly less importance than its use as ministering alike to commercial and cultural progress".[13] The Dáil Committee rejected the objection of the Postmaster-General to the running of a broadcasting station as a State department. The Committee considered that the operation of a broadcasting station by the State would not involve a new principle; it argued that the State for some time had combined "subsidised national culture with entertainment" and instanced the National Library, National Museum and the National Gallery. The Dáil Committee considered that should its recommendations that the broadcasting service be run by the Department of Posts and Telegraphs not be acceptable to the Dáil, then the Committee would recommend that broadcasting be developed "by means of a company, in which the State would have, directly or indirectly, a controlling interest".

The Secretary of the Postmaster-General's Department, P.S. O'Hegarty, in his evidence to the Special Committee on Wireless Broadcasting demonstrated that he shared the same ideological philosophy as his Minister: the Secretary stated that broadcasting was not an undertaking which a Government department "could do well or ought to undertake".[14] He considered private enterprise would operate the broadcasting service more economically and efficiently than a Government department.[15]

Other senior public servants expressed similar views. In 1924, the Secretary to the Executive Council, D. O'Hegarty, foresaw public criticism which would be directed against the Government if the State undertook the broadcasting service itself.[16] He argued that the Government should secure itself against criticism by placing between itself and the public a board which would be "sufficiently competent to act as a buffer" and that it would be much safer if a company could be secured which would contract to supply programmes up to a required standard. Whether these proposals were acceptable or not, the Secretary to the Executive Council argued that care would have to be taken that the operations of all the broadcasting stations and all receiving stations were susceptible to being closed down or controlled by the Government in time of war or emergency.[17]

In the subsequent Dáil Debate on the Final Report, Ernest Blythe, Minister for Finance, expressed his anxiety that the State would not be committed to providing a new service and thus incurring additional expenditure.[18] Postmaster-General Walsh vigorously rejected the Committee's view that amusement was only a subsidiary element in the function of broadcasting:

> It is said by the Committee that one of its main reasons for State control is that amusement is only subsidiary. Well my information from people who have had experience in other countries is entirely contrary to that. I am assured that the ordinary user of receiving sets feels that anything else but music jars on his nerves. . . . [T]he people want amusement through broadcasting; they want nothing else, and they will have nothing else. If you make amusement subsidiary then you will have no broadcasting. . . .[19]

The Postmaster-General argued trenchantly against State control:

> Every country in the world decided against State control, and
> not one but this young State, which is struggling to get on its
> legs, has been made the stalking horse for what I consider to be
> a foolish and ill-advised experiment. There is one country an
> exception to those which I mentioned in the production of
> concerts and public amusement, and that is Russia. In Russia,
> the State had quite a lot of enthusiasm for this particular line at
> one time, but information of late indicates that there it is found
> it can be better conducted by private enterprise. Therefore, we
> stand alone to the world.[20]

The views of the Postmaster-General were not accepted by the
elected representatives; the Final Report with its recommendations
that the broadcasting service should be run as a State service by the
Postmaster-General's Department was adopted by the Dáil on May
7, 1924.[21]

Part II of the *Wireless Telegraphy Act, 1926* empowered the Minister
for Posts and Telegraphs to establish, maintain and operate broadcasting stations. The word "broadcast" was defined in the 1926 Act
as meaning "the transmitting, relaying or distributing of *broadcast
matter*"[22] (emphasis added). That definition of "broadcast" was
amended in 1988 to mean

> the transmission, relaying or distribution by wireless tele-
> graphy of communications, sounds, signs, visual images or
> signals, intended for direct reception by the general public
> whether such communications, sounds, signs, visual images or
> signals are actually received or not.[23]

The expression "broadcast matter" retained a relevance until the
coming into force of the *Radio and Television Act, 1988* and was
defined in the 1926 Act to mean and include

> any lectures, speeches, news, reports, advertisements, reci-
> tations, dramatic entertainments, and other spoken words and
> any music (whether vocal or instrumental) and other sounds
> approved by the Minister as suitable for being broadcasted
> from a broadcasting station maintained under [the Wireless
> Telegraphy Act, 1926] [or the Broadcasting Authority Act, 1960
> and also includes images].[24]

The words within the square brackets were added by section 34(c) of the *Broadcasting Authority Act, 1960*.

Section 17(2) of the 1926 Act authorised the Minister for Posts and Telegraphs to receive, transmit, relay or distribute for broadcasting stations such broadcast matter as he should "think proper". The Minister for Finance, Ernest Blythe, in his consideration of the draft Bill informed the Executive Council that he considered that "the absolute control over the matter to be broadcasted given to the Minister for Posts and Telegraphs" was "an excessive privilege".[25] In the context of the 1922 and 1937 Constitutions, this power was indeed "an excessive privilege" and it is surprising that the definition of broadcast matter was never adverted to in the context of the constitutional and other challenges to the broadcasting monopoly in the 1980s.[26] However, for the record, the Minister for Finance had not objected to the "excessive privilege" of the Minister for Posts and Telegraphs on the grounds of freedom of expression but because the Minister for Posts and Telegraphs was an extern Minister, i.e. was not a member of the Executive Council. The Minister for Finance also considered that the Minister for Posts and Telegraphs should only control broadcasting in conjunction with the statutory advisory committee which was to be established under the 1926 legislation.[27] The Executive Council did not agree with the Minister for Finance and the Minister for Posts and Telegraph's untrammelled powers in relation to the control of broadcasting matter continued until modified with the passing of the *Broadcasting Authority Act, 1960* and the establishment of Radio Éireann in 1960.[28]

The broadcasting service on its establishment became a branch of the Department of Posts and Telegraphs under the control of the Minister for Posts and Telegraphs. Part II of the *Wireless Telegraphy Act, 1926* regulated broadcasting until the enactment of the *Broadcasting Authority Act, 1960*. The Minister for Posts and Telegraphs was himself subject to regulation by the Minister for Finance in relation, inter alia, to the finances of the broadcasting service. Both Ministers were subject to direction by the Government.

Much was expected of the national broadcasting station. Being a branch of the Civil Service and therefore under direct ministerial control, aspects of Government policy were expected to be fostered and developed. Maurice Gorham, the Director of Broadcasting from 1953 to 1960, wrote of this period:

[Radio Éireann] was expected to revive the speaking of Irish; to foster a taste for classical music; to revive Irish traditional music; to keep people on the farms; to sell goods and services of all kinds, from sausages to sweep tickets; to provide a living and a career for writers and musicians; to reunite the Irish people at home with those overseas; to end partition. All this in addition to the broadcaster's normal duty to inform, educate and entertain and in a programme time amounting (if advertising time was excluded) to some 5.5 hours a day.[29]

RELATIONSHIP BETWEEN THE TWO BROADCASTING SERVICES IN THE ISLAND OF IRELAND DURING THE SECOND WORLD WAR

The importance of broadcasting as a propaganda tool for Governments is illustrated by the relationship between the two broadcasting services in this island during the Second World War. The Dominions Office in London in 1940 endeavoured to seek ways of improving relations between the United Kingdom and Ireland. The Dominions Office considered whether items of special Irish or Catholic interest might be stressed in BBC programmes in Northern Ireland in order to win a greater audience in what may be described as the southern part of the island of Ireland.[30] The hope was that the Dublin Government could be persuaded to join in the war effort on behalf of the Allies. In pursuit of the UK Government's Irish objectives, the UK Ministry of Information issued the following directive to the BBC in May 1940:

> It is generally inadvisable to engage in controversy or propaganda about the partition of Ireland. If, however, there is important Irish news which makes it inevitable that the question will be raised, the point to be consistently made is that Partition is a problem for the Irish themselves to solve: the British Government would be ready to accept any agreement reached by the different sections of the Irish people. In other words, the agitation against the British Government and people on this point is made at the wrong address.[31]

The Northern Ireland authorities were most unhappy with this and other related developments. When the Northern Ireland Prime Minister, J.M. Andrews, learned about the format for a regular Irish broadcast programme he wrote immediately to the Director General of the BBC:

I understand . . . that the object of the broadcasts will be to interest "Ireland" both North and South, and Irishmen everywhere, in the war effort, by telling them and the world how Irishmen are helping in the present struggle.

This, in my view, would be an insidious from of propaganda which would entirely misrepresent the position of Northern Ireland in the United Kingdom and would slur over the neutral and most unhelpful attitude which Éire has taken up during the war.

I feel sure that, if I am correctly informed of the position, you would not approve of any such proposal, and I feel strongly that steps should be taken to put a stop to propaganda of this character in whatever quarter it may originate.[32]

The Prime Minister added in his own handwriting, "Why not leave Éire 'to plough her lonely furrow'?"[33] The Director General of the BBC, F.W. Ogilvie, a former Vice-Chancellor of Queen's University Belfast, wrote to the Prime Minister about the BBC's concern with the "tens of thousands of men and women" who have left Éire and "joined His Majesty's forces" and had "thrown their lot — plough-teams, lives and all — with our common cause".[34] The Northern Ireland Prime Minister retorted:

My opinion, for what it is worth, continues to be that, as Éire stands out of the War and refuses even to lend the ports, she should be left alone. I am speaking of the Empire's interest, for I am firmly of the opinion that a policy of appeasement which has never succeeded with Éire never will succeed and that it is only through strength that she will be got to change her ways.[35]

Programmes were broadcast on BBC radio in Northern Ireland with a Southern Irish flavour despite the protestation of many Northern Unionists. The policy of the UK Government on the issue at that time was unambiguous. The Director General of the UK Ministry of Information wrote in March 1942 to George Marshall, the Northern Ireland Regional Director of the BBC, that the UK Government was in favour of "cultivating the goodwill of Éire listeners by indirect means such as Irish Half Hour and other programmes. . . ."[36]

Tension between the Northern Ireland authorities and the Government in London were heightened over a programme broadcast on Radio Éireann in August 1942 from St. Mary's Hall,

Belfast. Although Radio Éireann's outside broadcasting equipment had been used, certain facilities (including the use of certain telecommunication lines) had been leased from the Post Office in Northern Ireland. The programme was *Question Time* with the popular Joe Linnane acting as compère. Joe Linnane asked a competitor on the programme to name the great compilers of fairy stories. The competitor answered, "Winston Churchill", and the audience broke out into loud cheers and laughter. Whenever this particular competitor came to the microphone he was enthusiastically applauded. Professor Rex Cathcart in his history of the BBC in Northern Ireland, *The Most Contrary Region*, noted that Unionist listeners were outraged, "the more so as Radio Éireann officials seemed to have connived at his answer and not to have gonged it as wrong or inappropriate".[37] Questions were asked in Westminster. At a meeting in the Postmaster-General's Department in London to discuss the issue it was agreed that it be put to the Dublin Government that the BBC in Northern Ireland would not make any requests for broadcasts from "each other's territories" for the duration of the war. However, at the request of the Minister for Posts and Telegraphs in Dublin this was limited to a period of six months.[38]

A shift in the UK Government's attitude to the Dublin Government came in 1943, when the war effort was going better for Britain. A general election was called by the Dublin Government and the BBC proposed a fairly full coverage of the election. Brendan Bracken, Tipperary-born Minister of Information in London, turned down the proposal "in the most emphatic terms": "The public would be horrified if they heard anything from the BBC about de Valera and those lousy neutrals: people of Irish stock overseas are heartily ashamed of Éire's attitude. . . ."[39]

Professor Cathcart sums up the end of this saga, the change of heart of the Government and the Ministry of Information in London towards Ireland: "Courting Éire was no longer necessary."[40]

ADVERTISING AND THE QUEST OF COMMERCIAL INTERESTS FOR PARTICIPATION IN BROADCASTING

Apart from the views of the first Postmaster-General of Saorstát Éireann and the Secretary of his Department who supported the principle that private enterprise would operate the broadcasting service more economically and efficiently than a Government Department,[41] Governments and senior civil servants subsequently demonstrated a marked antipathy to the active participation of commercial interests in broadcasting.

In April 1933, the Minister for Posts and Telegraphs, with a view to raising additional revenue for the broadcasting service, entered into an advertising contract with the Athlone Radio Publicity Company. The contract provided for the supply of sponsored programmes on Radio Éireann for six hours per week. The Athlone Radio Publicity Company defaulted in July 1933 and the contract passed under the terms of a guarantee bond to the New Ireland Assurance Company which arranged for the performance of the contract by the International Broadcasting Company (Ireland), described in a memorandum from the Department of Posts and Telegraphs to the Executive Council in April 1934 as "a nominally Saorstát company but whose interests were almost exclusively British".[42]

The question of the renewal of the contract with the International Broadcasting Company (Ireland) for a service of advertising (sponsored) broadcast programmes prompted the Department of Posts and Telegraphs and the Government in 1934 to review policy in relation to advertising and the participation of commercial interests in broadcasting. The Department of Posts and Telegraphs argued that the continuance of advertising programmes must be considered from other points of view besides revenue. The Department considered that with the exception of the Irish Hospitals' Trust programmes, the advertisements which were being broadcast on Radio Éireann were largely of a kind which was "undesirable for broadcasting from State stations, in as much as they relate[d] to patent medicines, cosmetics, and other articles in respect of which the appeal of the advertisement [was] to the credulity or vanity of listeners".[43] Further, the advertisements related almost exclusively to foreign products and although the policy of the Department was to accept such advertisements only when the articles advertised could not compete effectively with any similar articles produced within the State, the Department considered that the fact that advertisements related to articles of foreign origin created the impression in the public mind that the State broadcasting stations were being exploited in the interests of foreign trade.

Many of the advertisements broadcast by Radio Éireann were designed to attract listeners in Great Britain. The Department considered that in order not to embarrass unduly the programme contractors in carrying out their contractual obligations, the Department reluctantly tolerated these advertisements and sponsored programmes which were designed to attract listeners in Great Britain. Nevertheless, the Department considered that such programmes designed for listeners outside the State "[were] incompatible with the Government's policy of economic and cultural development and [were] generally derogatory to the national tone of the broadcasting programmes".[44] The Department of Finance, ever ready to ensure that a source of finance was not lost to the State, objected to the abandonment of revenue from advertising programmes and requested the Department of Posts and Telegraphs to make arrangements to ensure a continuance of such revenue "by an un-interrupted maintenance of the unobjectionable part of the sponsored programmes on the most favourable financial basis that [could] be made with the contractors".[45] The Cabinet in 1934 agreed with the views of the Department of Posts and Telegraphs that the contract held by the International Broadcasting Company (Ireland) for a service of advertising (sponsored) broadcast programmes should not be renewed but decided that the Minister for Posts and Telegraphs would make arrangements for advertising in broad-casting programmes subject to the conditions that only Saorstát products and enterprises should be advertised.[46] This decision was, on the instructions of the Minister for Posts and Telegraphs, inter-preted as meaning that sponsored programmes as part of broad-casting policy should be discontinued except in special cases such as the Irish Hospitals' Trust programmes.[47]

A proposal that the Cork Broadcasting station should be leased to a private company for the purpose of commercial broadcasting was considered by the Cabinet in September 1934. Dr. John Charles McQuaid, then President of Blackrock College, Dublin, later to become Archbishop of Dublin, wrote to the President of the Executive Council, Eamon de Valera, in February 1934 enclosing a memorandum from George Shanks of the Industrial Broadcasting Corporation of Ireland Limited (which had changed its name from the International Broadcasting Company). Dr. McQuaid stated that George Shanks was "very shrewd and very honourable: a good Catholic with singularly right views on our nation".[48] Dr. McQuaid was of the opinion that the scheme proposed by the Industrial Broadcasting Corporation of Ireland was very interesting in view of the broadcast once made by Eamon de Valera in the context of "our cultural vocation" and because the proposed scheme seemed a means of realising de Valera's ideal.[49] The essence of the memor-andum of George Shanks[50] which Dr. McQuaid sent to Eamon de Valera was that the tastes and opinions of the Irish people were not sufficiently catered for by one broadcasting station. Two broadcasting stations were essential: one broadcasting station should revive and foster "the ancient Irish culture and be of an educational nature, the second station should broadcast programmes of more ordinary type as well as help the building up of the State by means of its intercourse with neighbouring nations and commercial propaganda". The proposal was that the Cork broadcasting station which then relayed Athlone programmes should be separated from Radio Éireann, given to a private company as a commercial enterprise and put under the auspices of the Minister for Industry and Commerce. The commercial station was to establish "a definite link" with a leading national newspaper "in order to circularise the world with true facts about Ireland and increase its circulation in the Free State". The memorandum argued that the imprisonment of the wireless was contrary to its natural state and referred to the regulation of broadcasting in the United States where private commercial broadcasting services were successful.

No reference was made in the 1934 memorandum to the Roman Catholic Church involvement. However, a letter from F. O'Reilly, K.C.S.G., Executive Secretary of the Catholic Truth Society, to Most Rev. J.M. Harty, Archbishop of Cashel, on August 18, 1934 elaborates on the religious dimension to the application for private broadcast facilities.[51] In the letter, George Shanks of the Industrial Broadcasting Corporation of Ireland was quoted to the effect that so far as he could ascertain, the Minister for Posts and Telegraphs, Gerry Boland, was still opposed to a station for commercial broadcasting but that it was considered that there was a possibility of obtaining a concession for a broadcasting station "if it were put under a definitely Catholic flag". However, the writer of the letter informed the Archbishop that he felt certain that the President of the Executive Council, Eamon de Valera, would not listen to any proposals about Catholic broadcasts unless he was satisfied that these proposals had the full sanction of the bishops. The scheme for the proposed broadcasting station should show the amount of capital that would be required, and the manner in which the capital would be raised, the system of ensuring that the directorate would always remain Catholic and the system of providing control by the bishops of Catholic broadcasts and censorship of all other broadcast matter to ensure that nothing was released that was likely to give offence to any section of the community. The writer argued that the bishops would want a veto on the transfer of shares with voting rights and that five to fifteen hours per week would be devoted to Catholic broadcasts. The writer also referred to a conversation with Cardinal McRory when the Cardinal expressed the view that a commercial company would be a better proposition than a Catholic hour over the "Government station" as "it would ensure that there would be no Protestant broadcasts".[52] Reference was made to the greatest contribution that Ireland could make to a world culture which was to spread the Catholic faith and that the Committee of the Bishops should have power "to forbid broadcasting of any item, commercial or otherwise, not in consonance with Catholic culture".[53]

The Bishops did not enter into a public debate on the issue. In this context, John Horgan has noted that the Government's hostility to the idea of broadcasting operated by private enterprise interests could not, it appears, "be breached even by so imposing a Trojan horse".[54] The Department of Posts and Telegraphs was emphatically opposed to leasing the existing Cork broadcasting station to a private company for commercial broadcasting. In his memorandum for members of the Government in September 1934,[55] the Minister for Posts and Telegraphs referred to a fundamental misconception on the part of the promoters and the Department of Industry and Commerce on the issue of the promoters proceeding to negotiate with the international regulatory agency, Union Internationale de Radiodiffusion, for another wavelength or an increase in power. The Department of Posts and Telegraphs emphasised that all questions of wavelength and powers of wireless stations including broad-casting stations were the "jealously guarded prerogatives of Govern-ments" and that any negotiations for a change in wavelengths or power of broadcasting stations situated within Saorstát Éireann must be conducted by the Government with the other interested Governments.

The 1934 commercial broadcasting saga gave the opportunity to the Department of Posts and Telegraphs to outline its broadcasting policy to the Government:[56] the aim of the Department was to furnish to all the inhabitants of Saorstát Éireann a national broad-casting service to which the inhabitants could tune in easily and receive "in a really satisfactory manner". The Department admitted that such an ideal had not been achieved but was being pursued assiduously. The Department stated that there was no possibility whatever of obtaining two exclusive wavelengths from the inter-national regulatory agency. The considered view of the Department was that the project for a commercial broadcasting station must constitute "a further serious obstacle in the path of providing the whole of Ireland (including Northern Ireland) with an Irish programme easily receivable at all times of the year". If the Department's aim of providing a satisfactory service were achieved, "no listener would be able to offer as an excuse for listening to outside programmes (that may and undoubtedly do often contain subtle propaganda) the fact that he could not tune easily and satisfactorily to an Irish programme". The Department concluded by putting the issue in stark terms: which was to be regarded as being of paramount importance — its efforts towards perfecting reception of a national broadcasting service all over Ireland, and as wide an area as possible of Great Britain and the rest of Europe; or the exploitations of a commercial service, the benefit of which would be mainly to English advertisers. The memorandum finally concluded: "The two schemes seem to be mutually destructive." The Cabinet, at its meeting on October 10, 1934, agreed with the Department of Posts and Telegraphs and refused to approve the commercial broadcasting project.[57]

The issue of "commercial broadcasting" was again considered by the Cabinet in November 1938. The Minister for Posts and Telegraphs in a memorandum to the Government stated that his Department had been "continuously pressed by various groups of people, financiers and speculators mainly, requesting that they be allowed to undertake a service of international advertising from Éire radio stations".[58] The Minister for Posts and Telegraphs, Oscar Traynor, in 1938 agreed with his predecessor as to the undesirability of sponsored programmes associated with advertisements of foreign goods intended for listeners outside the country. The Minister stated that the quality of the sponsored programmes of the Irish Hospitals' Trust had, in fact, tended to stiffen the opposition to any extension of such broadcasting. The Minister considered that the Hospitals' Trust, with an Irish directorate and, he presumed, mainly under Irish management, might reasonably be expected to possess some "normal national outlook in the framing of the programmes to accompany their sweepstakes announcements". However, he stated that the Director of Broadcasting had considerable and continuous trouble with the Hospitals' Trust in his efforts to raise their programmes "to a proper standard". The Minister was of the opinion that the publicity section of the Trust seemed "to have no conception of radio entertainment of a higher order than jazz, crooning, songs reflective of, or associated with, London night life. . . ."[59] The Cabinet in 1938 adopted the views of the Minister for Posts and Telegraphs: international radio advertising from the stations within the State was undesirable both on national and departmental grounds and was not to be permitted; the restriction already imposed confining radio advertising to advertisements of products and enterprises of the State was sound in principle and was to be maintained; and the erection and operation of a commercial station by a private company should not be allowed even if it were practicable to acquire a separate wavelength for a such a purpose.[60]

Subsequently, the Minister for Posts and Telegraphs, Oscar Traynor, in a memorandum to the Taoiseach in August 1939 referred again to applications received by his Department in relation to international commercial broadcasting which were almost wholly concerned with the broadcasting from this State of advertisements of British products intended, not for listeners in the State, but for those in Great Britain. The Minister was of the opinion that such broadcasting could not reasonably be allowed in the face of strong opposition which was certain to come from the British Government. The Minister stated that the British Government was completely opposed to international broadcasting which, in Europe, was indulged in by only two countries, France and Luxembourg. Luxembourg was only able to broadcast internationally because France acquiesced and France, apparently, was subjected at every International Radio Conference to strong pressure from Britain to stop the broadcasting from Luxembourg.[61]

In 1944 the Cabinet again considered the issue of commercial broadcasting. On this occasion the proposal came from Ferndale Pictures Ltd, London, advertising agents who had received the sole concession for radio productions on behalf of the Radio Guild. The Radio Guild was an organisation of representatives of business which included the radio industry and advertising agencies in Great Britain. Ferndale Pictures Ltd proposed to lease 24 hours weekly from Radio Éireann for sponsored programmes. The Minister for Posts and Telegraphs noted in his memorandum for the Government that the proposal was hardly one in which a Government decision was necessary.[62] Nevertheless, the Minister considered that the Government should be aware of such a proposal. The memorandum for the Government circulated by the Minister for Posts and Telegraphs provides an overview of the regulatory stance adopted by the Department in relation to commercial broadcasting, advertising and issues relating to presentation of standards in the fostering of Irish culture.

Initially, Ferndale Pictures Ltd was reluctant to agree to the conditions imposed by Radio Éireann in connection with sponsored programmes arguing that it was thinking primarily of 47 million

British listeners and that the company would find it impossible to make the programmes acceptable to (a) the British sponsor, (b) the British public, (c) the Director of Broadcasting and (d) the Irish public. Later the proposers agreed to accept all the usual conditions imposed by Radio Éireann including the exclusion of such items as cosmetics and alcohol, and the ban on jazz. The Department submitted that regardless of any promises made by Ferndale Pictures Ltd, the proposers would constantly endeavour to broadcast programmes with a popular appeal in England "which would be entirely unsuitable for the Irish public". Reference was made to the endless trouble which was experienced in getting the Irish Hospitals' Trust Ltd to produce a higher standard of programme than "jazz, crooning and the like" and that a greater respect for national culture could not be expected from a British combine. The best the Department could hope for was that their programmes would be "neutral" — not offensive to Irish taste but not stressing Irish culture. It was claimed by the Department that the international prestige of Radio Éireann would be considerably lowered and that the station could come to be regarded as another "Luxembourg". The consistent refusal of the Department to permit the use of Radio Éireann for international commercial programmes was also cited together with the fact that the British Administration might object. This latter objection was argued on the basis that, if the proposers were successful, the BBC would inevitably be forced to permit advertising from their own stations and this would affect the Department adversely. It was argued that the British interests involved in this proposal might also like to obtain commercial broadcasting facilities in order to break the BBC monopoly in England and develop commercial broadcasting from British stations after the war. It was anticipated that there would be considerable opposition from the newspapers which would make capital "of the giving of a virtual monopoly to an English firm". The argument in favour of the proposal was the revenue it would yield, estimated at IR£54,000, but it was stressed by the Department that the financial perspective had never been regarded as an overriding consideration in deciding whether to permit advertising programmes. The memorandum concluded forcefully:

> [T]he national broadcasting station has a most important cultural and educational function in the national life and any proposal, however profitable financially, the adoption of which would tend to hamper or prejudice the most effective

performance of this function or to injure the prestige of the station, should not be entertained.[63]

The Cabinet agreed with the Department that the proposal of Ferndale Pictures Ltd in relation to leasing 24 hours weekly from Radio Éireann for sponsored programmes should not be entertained.[64] This decision may be contrasted with the inauguration in September 1989 of Atlantic 252 (Radio Tara), a joint venture between RTE and the Luxembourg broadcasting company on long-wave and aimed mainly at UK audiences.

The issue of relaxing certain restrictions on advertising programmes came before the Cabinet again in May 1949. For decades, advertisements of cosmetics and patent medicines had not been permitted on Irish radio. Irish advertising agents argued in 1949 that the policy stance adopted by the Department of Posts and Telegraphs in relation to cosmetics was out of date as cosmetics were "used by women as widely and normally as soap and other preparations". The Department had maintained that advertisements relating to cosmetics and patent medicine were regarded as appealing to the vanity or credulity of listeners and associated musical programmes were generally considered unsuitable for broadcasting from the national station. The Department agreed that there might be something in the contention of the advertising agents that the Department was out of date in relation to the advertising of cosmetics. However, in relation to patent medicines, the Department considered that it could not set itself up as a judge of the merits of individual patent medicines and the only safe course was to exclude them altogether from radio advertising. The Cabinet in May 1949 agreed with the proposal of the Minister for Posts and Telegraphs in relation to sponsored programmes broadcast by Radio Éireann: participation in such programmes was to be confined to companies and organisations registered in Ireland, including the Six Counties; only articles manufactured or produced in, or services given in Ireland were to be advertised; no products or services were to be specifically excluded from broadcast advertisements but the Minister for Posts and Telegraphs was to exercise discretion in this regard.[65]

In 1950, the Industrial Corporation of Ireland Limited applied for facilities for the establishment of a commercial radio station at Cork and Blackstone Advertising Company Ltd applied for facilities to broadcast advertisements for United States' firms from the Athlone radio station. Again, the Minister for Posts and Telegraphs reiterated the Department's long-held policy that the use of broadcasting for commercial purposes was "derogatory to national dignity" and only tolerable for purely internal advertising because of the revenue it brought in.[66] Technical arguments relating to the unavailability of wavelengths and shortage of studio accommodation were also raised. The Cabinet agreed with the recommendation of the Minister for Posts and Telegraphs and refused both applications.[67]

The quest by the commercial lobby for participation in radio and television broadcasting during the period 1950 to 1988 will be considered in the next chapter.

IRISH CULTURE AND THE IRISH LANGUAGE

The fostering of Irish culture and the Irish language and the official innate distaste for certain prevailing "foreign-based" cultures prompted the Department of Posts and Telegraphs and its Minister to initiate reviews of policy in these areas. These reviews were initiated because of the Department's association with broadcasting. In 1945, the Minister for Posts and Telegraphs, Patrick J. Little, proposed a Council of Culture in which the radio broadcasting service would play an effective role. The Minister in a submission to the Taoiseach, Eamon de Valera, put the issue in these terms:

> [A]s the stress of the national struggle grows less acute and the public mind less concerned with national defence, it becomes highly desirable to pay attention to the problems of Irish culture whose importance is not by any manner or means yet properly appreciated. The talents of our people and what remains of our folk culture need to be exploited to the full, if we are to avoid absorbing more than is good for us of foreign ideas and ways of life. There is a danger that with the defence situation no longer intense, politics will run to seed and that even the language movement will suffer unless a widespread cultural renaissance is achieved, something that will stimulate and fill the people's minds with interest in the treasures and possibilities of their own land. Such a revival might easily prove to be one of our best safeguards in time of national emergency, a way to future national unity and a very desirable and valuable invisible export. Incidentally, it would improve substantially the quality of our broadcasting programmes which naturally reflect the cultural standards of the people.[68]

The task of the Council of Culture was to be the same task as Thomas Davis envisaged: the combining of the best of the nation's traditions with the best of modern development.[69] Propaganda was to be placed at the head of the list of suggested activities of the Council.[70] Specifically, the terms of reference of the proposed Council envisaged by the Minister for Posts and Telegraphs were stated as follows:

> To plan and supervise the task of increasing popular interest and participation in all forms of cultural activity; of supplying people with wider opportunities of hearing and seeing the best works of art through whatsoever media; of providing people when organised into cultural groups (eg. music groups, dramatic societies, etc) with expert direction and training; of encouraging the creative efforts of Irish artists; and of stimulating local action designed to improve the appearance and amenities of the countryside.[71]

The Council was to be called An Comhairle le Saíocht Naisiúnta or Comhairle an Dáibhísigh. The Minister for Posts and Telegraphs took the issue so seriously that he wrote an impassioned letter in his own hand to the Taoiseach, Eamon de Valera, on January 16, 1946.[72] Addressing the Taoiseach as "My dear Chief", the Minister stated that he was so anxious to make a success of the proposed Council of Culture that he asked the Taoiseach "as a special favour" to give it his "personal interest"; the Minister considered that the proposed initiative was "extremely important if Ireland [was] to survive culturally". But the Minister had "grave misgivings that [the scheme would] receive rough handling and niggardly treatment from Finance — and so the scheme [would] only limp and maybe fail".[73] Little effective action was taken by the Government on this issue.

Radio was seen as an effective potential medium in assisting in the development of the Irish language and culture. The Taoiseach, Eamon de Valera, raised these issues directly with the Minister for Posts and Telegraphs in 1945 and suggested that a radio station should be dedicated to broadcasting solely in Irish.[74] The issues were considered by a committee within the Department of Posts and Telegraphs — all of the members of the committee being Irish language enthusiasts. Apart from concluding that an all-Irish broadcasting station would not be likely to increase appreciably the listening public for Irish programmes and that in fact increased facilities for the reception of radio broadcasting would be likely to have an injurious effect on the position of the Irish language in the Gaeltacht, the departmental committee reported that serious engineering and wavelength difficulties existed in relation to an all-Irish broadcasting station which appeared to be insoluble. Group listening of programmes in Irish from Radio Éireann was suggested and one of the immediate aims of the Minister in 1945 was to educate persons in the Gaeltacht to use the radio sets intelligently. The Minister opined: "I would hate to see the sets used, as gramophones were used formerly in the Gaeltacht, for purveying musical trash."[75]

An all-Irish radio station, Raidio na Gaeltachta, was inaugurated on April 2, 1972. Subsequently, in 1993, a commitment was given in the Programme for Partnership Government (Fianna Fáil and Labour) (1993) that Teilifís na Gaeilge would be established. The new headquarters for the service was to be based in the Connemara Gaeltacht; the new television service would provide between two and three hours per day in Irish for children and adults at times best suited to the viewer. The Foundation Committee was chaired by Professor Gearóid Ó Tuathaigh, Vice-President of University College, Galway.

OFFICIAL PROPAGANDA: THE FAILURE OF THE SHORTWAVE RADIO STATION

The importance of broadcasting for official propaganda purposes and as a perceived process of public communication with Irishmen and women around the world is illustrated in the various policy developments relating to the ill-fated shortwave broadcasting project. In this context, propaganda related to matters concerning Irish affairs as distinct from any official view on foreign issues. The Department of Posts and Telegraphs was anxious at all times to observe the spirit and the letter of the *International Convention Concerning the Use of Broadcasting in the Cause of Peace* (1936).[76] A clear example of such policy was stated on behalf of the Taoiseach, Eamon de Valera, in 1952. Whilst confirming that the Irish people "naturally sympathise[d] with all peoples rightly struggling to be free", the Taoiseach's office stated in a communication which was circulated to the Department of Foreign Affairs and the Director of Broadcasting (Radio Éireann) that

it has always been a rigid rule of the Irish broadcasting authorities not to permit the Irish stations to be used for the

dissemination of views which [were] either directly or indirectly of a political propagandist nature in regard to foreign
countries.[77]

Long-distance broadcasting, for example, inter-continental, is
effected on high-power shortwave transmissions. A shortwave
broadcasting service was mooted by the Department of Posts and
Telegraphs in 1936, but the President of the Executive Council
decided that further consideration of the matter should be
deferred.[78] It was not possible during the war years to obtain any of
the complex radio components necessary for a high-powered
shortwave station, but in 1946 the Government was determined to
establish a high-power shortwave station. In the Dáil on April 30,
1946 while introducing his broadcasting estimate, the Minister for
Posts and Telegraphs, Patrick J. Little, stated that expenditure for the
year would exceed revenue by IR£119,000 which was accounted for
by expenditure for the shortwave radio which the Department
hoped to open by the end of April 1947. A 100-kw Marconi transmitter was installed in a new building beside the medium-wave
transmitter at Athlone; aerials were stretched over 40 acres so that
directional broadcasts could be carried to the United States. In
February 1948 the Government changed; the new Minister for
Finance, Patrick McGilligan, announced in his budget speech that
for economic reasons the Government had decided not to proceed
with the shortwave project together with the proposed transatlantic
air service.

Many expressed disappointment at the abandonment of the
shortwave project. The Irish National Association of Australasia in
a letter to the Taoiseach in November 1948 expressed an intensity
and a yearning "for the establishment of a medium" which would
convey information regarding "the culture of the Homeland". The
writer warned that Ireland's spiritual empire would soon become "a
tawdry figment of the rhetorician".[79] The Taoiseach in his reply to
the Irish National Association of Australasia in January 1949 stated
that the Government decision not to proceed for the time being with
the shortwave radio did not imply total abandonment of the project
and that the matter would receive further consideration in the light
of prevailing circumstances.[80]

The Department of External Affairs in a memorandum for the
Government in May 1949 argued that the provision of facilities for
direct communication with countries overseas was most important
from the external affairs viewpoint.[81] The Department considered

that without such communication facilities, political action abroad was liable to be brought to a standstill particularly at moments of crisis. The memorandum referred to the Government's inability to rely on the established press agencies to get its point of view across abroad; official releases had been suppressed and sometimes only such material was carried that suited the British and American interests who owned these agencies. The memorandum also stated that the commercial cable companies could not be relied upon in all circumstances. The Department of External Affairs stated in its memorandum that it no longer entrusted messages to the Western Union cable company because, on one occasion, it held up an important official statement from the Department to its legation for as long as five days. In the context of broadcasting, the Department argued that it could only reach overseas countries through the medium of British short-wave transmitters and referred to a recent occasion when the BBC reserved a right of censorship over material sent out in that way.[82] This instance of censorship is not elaborated upon in the memorandum, but the *Irish Press* on May 19, 1949 in a report on the shortwave radio proposals referred to two occasions in which the BBC when relaying addresses of John A. Costello deleted portions of Mr. Costello's speeches relating to the partition of the country. The Department of External Affairs concluded that the only satisfactory remedy for this state of affairs was a shortwave transmitter; long distance wireless facilities were essential if the State was to be sure of propagating its viewpoint "quickly, widely and fully abroad".[83] The Cabinet, meeting on May 17, 1949, decided that the necessary steps should be taken to begin "shortwave broadcast transmissions to the United States of America of an emergency half-hour programme daily, as soon as it [was] practicable to do so".[84] The expenditure involved was to be met either by economies by the Minister for Posts and Telegraphs or by an increase in the receipts in connection with the broadcasting service.

The Minister for Posts and Telegraphs, James Everett, in a subsequent memorandum to the Government on October 18, 1949 stated that the cost of the shortwave project could not be met by savings on the Post Office or broadcasting votes as these had been "rigidly pruned" prior to Government approval.[85] The Minister considered it wrong in principle that the radio licence fees should be raised to meet the expenses connected with overseas programmes which the listeners paying the fees could not hear. The Minister argued that as the Department of External Affairs initiated the short-wave radio project as a matter of international policy, the expenditure should be borne ultimately by the Exchequer and recorded as a "service rendered to the Department of External Affairs".[86]

The Minister for Finance, Patrick McGilligan, in a memorandum of October 18, 1949 considered that the "somewhat detached attitude of the Department of Posts and Telegraphs" was not entirely justified arguing that it was the Department of Posts and Telegraphs which had proposed the retention of the shortwave broadcasting station. The Minister for Finance noted that there was an estimated deficit of IR£33,000 on the broadcasting service for 1949 and argued that the Department of Posts and Telegraphs must put the broadcasting service on at least a self-supporting basis either by economies or by increases in the amount of the licence fee.[87] In a further memorandum to the Government on April 24, 1950, the Minister for Posts and Telegraphs, James Everett, disclosed that enquiries made in the United States had revealed that there was practically no demand for shortwave radio sets for domestic listening; stressed once again the primary responsibility of the Department of External Affairs; and recommended that if the shortwave broadcasting service were to be opened, a Department of External Affairs section should be established within the broadcasting service with responsibility for the supply of speech material, for the conduct of shortwave programmes and that all material not of a propagandist character should rest with the Director of Broadcasting.[88]

In 1956 the Government abandoned the shortwave project at a cost in excess of IR£142,000. Broadcasting transmissions to North America had in fact commenced in 1947 but were never received there with clarity. Broadcasts by countries on nearby wavelengths caused serious interference. A Government statement in May 1956 stated that since 1947 the prospects for shortwave broadcasting had progressively deteriorated.[89] World Broadcasting Frequency Conferences between 1947 and 1950 failed to obtain agreement on radio frequencies due to the prevailing international tension. The Government considered in 1956 that it would be unjustifiable to embark on expenditure with a prospect of negligible results.[90] In Gorham's words the aerials and other apparatus became "little more than scrap".[91] However, the project led to a doubling up of Radio Éireann's resources: a new service, a symphony orchestra, a light orchestra together with staff script-writers, outside broadcast units and a professional repertory company remained as a permanent legacy from the days of the failed short-wave radio project.

BROADCASTING: THE QUEST FOR INDEPENDENCE
FROM GOVERNMENT 1947-1953

By the 1950s, Ireland was one of the few democratic countries in the world where broadcasting was operated as part of the Civil Service. Deeply conscious of this fact, the Department of Posts and Telegraphs favoured, from time to time, the assignment of the broadcasting function to an independent board. A Posts and Telegraphs Departmental Committee reported unanimously to the Minister for Posts and Telegraphs in 1947 in favour of the estab- lishment of a broadcasting public utility board which would operate under licence from the Minister for Posts and Telegraphs.[92] The Minister, Patrick J. Little, aware that opposition would come from certain members of the Government to any proposal to establish an independent board to run the broadcasting service, withheld a pro- posal to the Government in relation to the establishment of such a board.

Little's successor as Minister for Posts and Telegraphs in the Coalition Government, James Everett, raised the issue in his first Dáil Estimates Debate on wireless broadcasting in 1948 and posed the question whether the system of control and operation of the broadcasting service was the best one.[93] Stating that his short time in the Department had not given him the opportunity of coming to a definite conclusion, the Minister nevertheless was unhappy with the concept of the national broadcasting service being operated as part of the civil service:

> A civil servant, by tradition and training, feels the need to anticipate difficulties to save the Department possible em- barrassments. In fact, safety must be his keynote. This emphasis on safety imposes a rigidity in the material broadcast which is fatal in such a service.[94]

In 1948, Everett as Minister for Posts and Telegraphs decided that apart from laying down policy in general terms for the staff of Radio Éireann, he proposed to give the broadcasting service "the widest measure of freedom possible to do their job".[95]

Four years later in 1952, after a change in Government, the Minister for Posts and Telegraphs, Erskine Childers, proposed to the Government that the operation of broadcasting should be controlled by an independent board instead of being part of the machinery of Government.[96] The Minister justified such a proposal to secure a more flexible broadcasting organisation, greater freedom of expression and a reasonable expansion of the broadcasting service. On the issue of flexibility, the Minister decried the rigidity of the control mechanism in relation to the Department's broadcasting functions. On the issue of freedom of expression, the Minister argued that it was difficult to honour or to appear to honour "the constitutional liberty of the radio as an instrument of public opinion (under Article 40.6.1.i of the Constitution) so long as broadcasting remained a Government concern".[97] The Minister continued:

> The direct link with the State inevitably entails some restriction on speech matter, to the detriment of programme interest and freedom of view, varying from Minister to Minister and from Government to Government. Suspicion persists among whatever party happens to constitute the Opposition that the radio is or will, on critical occasions, be used for the advantage of the Government of the day, no matter what measures are taken to demonstrate the contrary.[98]

The Minister for Finance, Seán MacEntee, opposed the proposals of the Minister for Posts and Telegraphs and considered that the reference of the Minister for Posts and Telegraphs to Article 40.6.1.i of the Constitution was "inappropriate". The Minister for Finance was of the view that so long as there was only one broadcasting organisation in the country, or until everyone was free to establish a broadcasting organisation of his own, there would inevitably be "some restrictions on speech matter" over the radio.[99] Where there was a restriction on speech, there would be suspicion of bias. Both Ministers referred to the BBC and their references were coloured by the nature of their arguments. In the context of the freedom-of-expression argument, the Minister for Finance, referring to the fact that the BBC was frequently accused of bias in the presentation of home and foreign news stated that the BBC was "widely believed to have been actuated in its policy during the recent war and for some years afterwards by a desire to propagate Communism in Europe and extreme 'leftish' principles at home".[100] Accordingly, the Minister argued that if these criticisms were well founded, "the model independent broadcasting organisation has put a very one-sided interpretation on the right of free expression".[101]

The compelling justification for the proposals presented by Childers as Minister for Posts and Telegraphs was starkly simple: the Minister could not defend the existing broadcasting service in

Ireland. He argued that while the officials of the broadcasting service
were, in general, "energetic and competent", they could not
surmount "basic deficiencies"; Radio Éireann had the shortest
broadcasting day in Europe and had only a single programme to
cater for all levels of taste in entertainment and education and the
broadcasting service was housed in "makeshift accommodation".[102]
The Minister concluded his appeal to the Government by referring
to broadcasting as "one of the most potent media for fostering
distinctive national characteristics" and by stating his conviction that

> broadcasting can be such an influence for good and [have] such
> a powerful effect on modern life that no Government can afford
> to lose the opportunity of keeping it technically and artistically
> at as high a point of efficiency as possible.[103]

The central objection of the Minister for Finance, Seán MacEntee,
to the establishment of an independent board to run the
broadcasting service did not relate to financial issues but to the issue
of control; the broadcasting monopoly "with its wide intellectual
appeal, must be under immediate public control":[104]

> Certain groups in the country are endeavouring to exercise an
> influence on broadcasting policy quite disproportionate to their
> members or to the value of any ideas they are capable of
> contributing to it. The mere faddists and pseudo-intellectuals
> in these groups can be regarded with a certain degree of
> indifference; but there are others who are not above the
> suspicion of desiring to use the radio, as they use other media,
> for subversive purposes of one kind or another. Such people
> are more likely through their tireless and many-sided propa-
> ganda to attain their ends if the service is withdrawn from the
> supervision of a Minister answerable to Dáil Éireann than they
> are while the present system is maintained.[105]

The arguments of Childers did not prevail at that time and the
Cabinet decided in July 1952 on a compromise by authorising the
Minister for Posts and Telegraphs to establish a Council or
Committee "to advise or assist the Minister for Posts and Telegraphs
in the conduct of the broadcasting service and to be responsible,
under the Minister for the general control and supervision of the
service".[106] Comhairle Radio Éireann, a non-statutory body of five
persons, was accordingly established in 1953 and, subject to the

control of the Minister for Posts and Telegraphs, ran the broadcasting service up to the establishment of Radio Éireann in 1960. In
the absence of appropriate legislation, the five members of the
Comhairle were appointed as temporary civil servants.[107]

The print media expressed disappointment with the Government
decision that an autonomous body was not to be established for the
service: "No amount of window dressing can disguise the fact that
without legislation the Minister for Posts and Telegraphs remains
directly responsible for broadcasting."[108] The dilemma facing the
civil-servant broadcasters was stated aptly by *The Leader* (1952):

> Civil servants responsible to Parliament through their Minister
> for their official words or actions are naturally guided by
> extreme caution. The good civil servant avoids as far as possible
> creating a problem that may have unpleasant political con-
> sequences for his Minister. In this respect a broadcasting service
> has an amplitude of pit-falls, and the more carefully the traps
> are avoided the more arid and colourless the programmes are
> likely to be.[109]

However, the efforts of Childers in reforming the broadcasting
service were praised in the printed media.[110]

PROHIBITION ON BROADCASTING OF DISCUSSIONS ON POLITICAL ISSUES

In the context of the right to express freely convictions and opinions
and the specific reference to radio in the framework of rightful liberty
of expression in Article 40.6.1.i of the Constitution, it is noteworthy
that up to the mid-1950s political parties in the State effectively
prevented political discussion on the radio. This reluctance did not
extend to monologues from Ministers of the Government. In this
context, the caustic comments of the radio correspondent of *The Irish
Times* in 1945 in a review of Irish broadcasting are apposite:

> When a crisis develops in our foreign relations, national
> defence, transport system or food and fuel supplies, the
> Government remembers that it has a broadcasting station, and
> the Taoiseach or one of his Ministers goes down to the studio
> and delivers a message to the people. When his address has
> been given, the speaker leaves in a flurry of attention from
> excited officials. . . .[111]

Yet certain civil servants in the Department of Posts and Telegraphs and various Ministers for Posts and Telegraphs were anxious from time to time to extend the frontiers of expression. As early as 1926, the Minister for Posts and Telegraphs, James J. Walsh, favoured the broadcasting of the Budget Debate and made a submission to the Ceann Comhairle of the Dáil advocating that the broadcasting of "an interesting debate like that of the budget . . . would greatly stimulate interest in the proceedings of the Oireachtas".[112] In March 1926 the Cabinet decided that speeches in the Dáil should not be broadcast.[113]

A proposal initiated by the Broadcasting Advisory Committee to allow a statement from each of the principal political parties to be broadcast prior to the 1932 General Election was rejected by the Minister for Finance. In 1937, the Minister for Posts and Telegraphs, Oscar Traynor, sought the views of the Executive Council on the relaxation of the prohibition on party-political broadcasts in the then forthcoming election. The Director of Broadcasting favoured such a relaxation; the Secretary of the Department, however, recommended that "in view of the obvious dangers in an inflammatory atmosphere such as ours, the prohibition on political broadcasts should be continued. . . ."[114] The Cabinet at its meeting on June 1, 1937 decided that the prohibition on political broadcasts should not be relaxed.[115] This fear of unbridled expression coupled with a reference to an inflammatory atmosphere articulated by the Secretary of the Department of Posts and Telegraphs was to surface frequently and is one of the justifications for section 31 of the *Broadcasting Authority Act, 1960*.[116]

In 1948 the Minister for Posts and Telegraphs, James Everett, again proposed that a limited number of party-political broadcasts would be allocated each year to the various parties in accordance with their representation in the Dáil and that special party-political broadcasts would be allocated at times of General Elections.[117] The Minister suggested that the matter be considered by the Dáil Committee on Procedure and Privileges. Certain members of the Dáil Committee, however, considered it generally undesirable to have "uncensored statements" broadcast on "political matters".[118] Deputy Gerry Boland stated that the Fianna Fáil party was entirely opposed to political broadcasting; the Parliamentary Secretary to the Taoiseach, Liam Cosgrave, stated that the Fine Gael party was indifferent to the proposal; Deputy Michael Keyes stated that the Labour Party did not favour the proposal; Deputy James Pattison on behalf of the National Labour party stated that no decision had been taken by that party on the issue; Deputy Patrick Halliden stated that the Clann na Talmhan party did not favour the proposal while the Independent members of the Dáil, by a majority, were in favour of political broadcasts.[119] The Committee on Procedure and Privileges recommended by a majority that it was "opposed in principle to the proposed initiation of political broadcasts".[120] Everett regretted the all-party decision against "loosening up the rigid limitations on the use of the radio".[121]

Apart from purely political broadcasts, the Minister, James Everett, considered that there was room for considerable relaxation of the attitude maintained towards discussions and debates before the microphone "of matters in which there [was] some element of controversy". The Minister was conscious of the value of public expression of conflicting views:

> Listeners have a keen appreciation of these live topics and, provided the decencies are observed, I do not think a discussion of them on the radio does any harm. On the contrary, it may do positive good in educating public opinion or in providing an additional vent for the expression of conflicting views.[122]

The Minister for Posts and Telegraphs in 1951 again sought to widen the scope of the broadcasting of political matter that had been confined to important addresses from Ministers on special occasions in announcing policy or making national appeals and very brief news reports of Dáil proceedings. In a memorandum for the Government in July 1951 the Minister, Erskine Childers, stated that he considered that Radio Éireann "should broadcast interesting political matter in the same manner as the newspapers, with the proviso that balance between the political groups be maintained as far as possible".[123] In fact, this was an overstatement because in the body of his submission the Minister proposed that the Director of Broadcasting would "take pains" to ensure that political broadcasts would not be used "for the purpose of reflecting on the private character of individuals".[124] This and other restraints on freedom of expression proposed by the Minister emphasised, in fact, the differing treatment of the broadcast medium from that of the printed word. In an effort to persuade his Cabinet colleagues, the Minister for Posts and Telegraphs stressed that "political broadcasting" was permitted subject only to provisos relating to the security of the State and fair allocation of time in Australia, New Zealand, Belgium, Holland, Great Britain, Norway, Finland and other countries.[125]

The Cabinet on August 8, 1951 in a wide-ranging consideration of the issue agreed to extend the broadcasting of political matter by permitting special weekly reports of proceedings in Dáil Éireann and Seanad Éireann on the basis that over a period of two weeks, the Government and the Opposition should receive approximately one-half of the total time but with speeches by the Taoiseach and other members of the Government and leaders of the Opposition parties receiving more attention than speeches by other members of either House of the Oireachtas.[126] For the first time, the Cabinet agreed that discussion groups "should be allowed to debate freely questions in which political viewpoints [were] involved".[127] The adjective "freely" in the decision as recorded in the Cabinet minutes of August 8, 1951 was quite inappropriate in the light of the restrictions which the Cabinet placed on the broadcasting of such discussions. Firstly, where scripts of such discussions were not furnished to the Director of Broadcasting in advance, the discussions were to be recorded in advance to permit editing and "to ensure a reasonable balance in the expression of views".[128] Further restrictions were placed by the Cabinet on discussion of political issues. The Cabinet stipulated that it was understood that

(i) in addition to discharging his obligations in regard to public order, morality and the maintenance of the authority of the State, the Director of Broadcasting would take pains to ensure that broadcasts of political matter would not be used for the purpose of reflecting on the private character of individuals,
(ii) when the Director was in doubt as to the wisdom of any statement touching on the relations between Ireland and other States, he would seek the advice of the Department of External affairs,
(iii) comment on religious organisations would be excluded.[129]

In a further effort to regulate the broadcasting of political issues the Cabinet directed that a record was to be kept of the time allocated in the news bulletins to the various political interests.[130] However, the specific recommendation of the Minister for Posts and Telegraphs that reports of political speeches made elsewhere than in the Dáil and Seanad should be broadcast in the news bulletins was rejected by the Cabinet.[131] Maurice Gorham, the Director of Broadcasting, defended the prohibition by Radio Éireann on the reporting of speeches made at political meetings (with the exception of extracts from those made at the annual conventions of the principal political parties).[132] He stated that "political speeches" at such meetings were liable from time to time to contain "political attacks" which it would be better to exclude from the national broadcasting service. However, speeches at political meetings relating to a matter of wide national interest could be reported at the discretion of the Director of Broadcasting.[133]

In a strange development, the Cabinet on November 5, 1951 decided that persons who were members of Dáil Éireann or of Seanad Éireann should not be included in any broadcast discussion groups.[134] *The Irish Times* on December 4, 1953 noted that this ban on broadcasting by politicians had been "so rigorous that a Dáil deputy could not broadcast on Hamiltonian equations, or town-planning under the T'ang dynasty even if he was an acknowledged master on these themes." The public justification for the ban as expressed by the Minister for Posts and Telegraphs, Erkine Childers, in the Dáil in 1953 was that the State "should have a little experience in greater freedom of discussion before [the Government] added the additional normal facility available in every western democracy of including Deputies and Senators in discussions".[135] The ban was lifted in December 1953 with the Minister announcing that "Radio Éireann would be free to invite Deputies and Senators to take part in broadcasts for which they are specially qualified".[136] The Minister admitted that "this new freedom will rid our broadcasting system of an undesirable limitation and enable it to deal more adequately with contemporary affairs".[137]

The issue of party-political broadcasts by leaders of political parties was directed by the Cabinet in 1951 to be referred to the Dáil Committee on Procedure and Privileges.[138] Minister Childers in his draft submission to the Ceann Comhairle as chairman of the Committee on Procedure and Privileges which was submitted for Cabinet approval in 1952 stated, with some degree of under-statement, that "in accepting the principle of broadcasts by political parties, [the Committee on Procedure and Privileges] will not be introducing an innovation among the nations".[139] Lest the Govern-ment was in any doubt where he stood on the issue Childers under-lined the following passage in his submission: "I am very strongly of the opinion that the time is long past when we should continue to restrict the use of the broadcasting service in a manner which clearly distinguishes our attitudes towards freedom of discussion from that of other countries."[140] The issue was withdrawn from the Cabinet in April 1952 "until further notice".[141]

The chairman of the newly appointed Comhairle Radio Éireann,

C.J. Brennan, took up the issue in 1953 and Comhairle Radio Éireann, the five-member body, considered that a direct approach to the political parties would be more appropriate than consideration by the Committee on Procedure and Privileges.[142] Little progress was achieved until the General Election of 1954. Gorham has written that Radio Éireann was determined in 1954 to run a series of party-political election broadcasts. Fifteen talks by nominees of the political parties were subsequently broadcast between April 26 and May 14, 1954. Noting that Radio Éireann was not obliged to transmit party political broadcasts, Gorham stated that these broadcasts caused more trouble than many series with much greater programme value. He concluded: "But it is only by tackling this sort of enterprise that a national broadcasting service can feel that it is really doing its job."[143] Further party-political broadcasts followed in the General Election of 1957 and subsequent General Elections; the frontiers of expression had been enlarged. Sound broadcasting of the Dáil commenced in March 1987. The Dáil approved the televising of its proceedings on March 30, 1990; the live coverage commenced with the 1991 budget.[144]

12

Broadcasting Regulation
1953-1993

THE SEARCH FOR A REGULATORY FORMULA

During the period 1950 to 1960, one person played a most significant role in the regulation of broadcasting: León Ó Broin, Secretary of the Department of Posts and Telegraphs. He was a theoretician as well as a maker of public policy. He never relented in the task of framing an effective regulatory strategy — one of the most difficult of governmental arts. Ó Broin's steadfast views were to shape broadcasting legislation until the enactment of the *Radio and Television Act, 1988* which provided for commercial broadcasting.

Public interest in television in Ireland was heightened by the opening in December 1949 of the BBC transmitter at Sutton Coldfield. This transmitter enabled television programmes to be received at places along the East coast of Ireland. Up to 1955 television reception in Ireland from the United Kingdom was intermittent and unsatisfactory; the early owners of television sets in Ireland were classified by the Department of Posts and Telegraphs as "mainly radio enthusiasts and people with sufficient money to indulge a craving for novelty".[1] Dáil questions on the subject in the early 1950s were answered to the effect that the Department of Posts and Telegraphs was keeping in touch with developments abroad but that it was not possible to give any estimate as to when an Irish television service could be established.

The advent of television posed many problems of a regulatory nature for the Irish Government; looming over all other issues was the question of finance; how could the State cope with such an expensive service? The regulatory issue of public versus private operation of an Irish television service was intimately bound up with the financial problem. The regulatory issues facing the State in the decade between 1950 and 1960 were reminiscent of similar problems facing the first Government of the State over the establishment of an

Irish radio broadcasting service in the period 1922 to 1926.[2]

The first issue of a regulatory nature was to secure international agreement for the allocation of any necessary wavelengths. In 1952, at the Stockholm International Radio Conference, Ireland was allocated television and VHF (sound) frequencies for stations in or near the following places: Dublin, Cork, Galway, Kilkenny and Ballyshannon. Under the Plan agreed at the conference, Ireland provisionally selected the 405-line standard of definition (as used by Britain), mainly because of the likelihood of there being considerable interchange of programmes between Ireland and Britain. [The 525-line standard was used in the US and the 625-line standard was used in mainland Europe generally except France.]

A Departmental Television Committee established by the Minister for Posts and Telegraphs, chaired by the Secretary of the Department, León Ó Broin, and also composed of Maurice Gorham and T.J. Monaghan, reported to the Minister in September 1953.[3] In its report, marked "secret", the Committee concluded that while it was probably true that television was not essential to national life, it was nevertheless an invention of enormous potentiality for good as well as evil and would be a desirable asset if it could be afforded. The Committee concluded that an Irish television service was impracticable at that time on strictly financial grounds. However, the Committee articulated a fundamental principle which the Department of Posts and Telegraphs firmly held for many years in discussions on the future regulatory regime for any Irish television service: television was too important a medium to be entrusted to commercial interests which could not be expected to make it "an instrument for promoting Irish culture and national consciousness but would seek to attract large audiences by importing standardised mass entertainment from abroad".[4]

The 1953 Television Committee considered the issue of a television service being provided by means of a permanent link with the BBC *via* its station at Belfast. While technically feasible, the Committee considered that such a permanent link would almost certainly prove to be a considerable and constant source of embarrassment:

> Plays and music-hall shows, as well as newsreels displaying royalty or royal occasions, would provide endless headaches for an Irish television organisation that no precautions or prior arrangements could avoid.[5]

In 1955 the Minister for Posts and Telegraphs, Michael Keyes, formally proposed to the Government the establishment of a statutory public-service organisation to provide broadcasting services. He declared that a broadcasting service organised legally on a rigid Civil Service pattern, with ultimate Government responsibility for every word broadcast, could not and did not function satisfactorily: "It lacked life at every point; its inevitable neutrality in the treatment of issues of importance made it dull in the extreme."[6]

Although the Minister considered that some of the "taboos" which were stifling the broadcasting service had been lessened in recent years, particularly with the establishment of the non-statutory Comhairle Radio Éireann, he considered that the status of members of the Comhairle as temporary civil servants was an inappropriate status for the governing body of broadcasting. The Minister feared that future Ministers for Posts and Telegraphs might not be so ready to relinquish their power to intervene in broadcasting details, and that Radio Éireann could be "thrust into the arena of party politics".[7] The Minister submitted that in the context of the trusteeship of broadcasting for the national interest, there was a good argument in favour of appointments to the statutory broadcasting board being made by the President "on the nomination of a body set up on the lines of the Council of State".[8] Alternatively, the Minister considered that the good sense of successive Governments may be relied upon to make a satisfactory choice of persons. The Cabinet agreed in principle in October 1955 to establish a broadcasting service as a statutory public service organisation.[9] However, wrangling between the Departments of Posts and Telegraphs and Finance over the financing of such a body ensured the shelving of the issue.

Several factors forced Keyes as Minister for Posts and Telegraphs in the Coalition Government of Fine Gael and Labour in 1956 to reconsider formally the regulatory position concerning an Irish television station. A permanent BBC television station had been established at Divis near Belfast in July 1955 which enabled BBC television programmes to be received over a considerable part of what may be termed Southern Ireland. In September 1955 the first British commercial television station was opened in London under the Independent Television Authority (ITA). The Pye Organisation (which included some 56 companies operating mostly in the United Kingdom) submitted a scheme to the Minister for Posts and Telegraphs for establishing a commercial television station to be operated by an associate company of Pye (Ireland) Ltd to serve the city of Dublin and a radius of about 20 miles.

The original Departmental Television Committee, joined by S.Ó Droma, prepared a supplementary report but did not make any recommendation for or against the establishment of an Irish television service.[10] The Committee considered that the question whether the costs involved were too great was one which must in the final analysis be decided by the Government on grounds of public policy and in the light of the overall financial position of the State. The Committee reiterated its opposition to an Irish television service being entrusted to commercial interests. The Committee emphasised that the programmes being received in Ireland from exclusively British sources were frequently objectionable "on national and moral grounds ... [and] were entirely British in outlook and uncensored".[11] The Committee, in its report which was circulated to members of the Government in June 1956, contained selected extracts from an address by His Holiness, Pope Pius XII, to delegates of the European Broadcasting Union in October 1955.[12] The sentiments expressed by the Pope were later to be echoed by subsequent Taoisigh and Ministers for Posts and Telegraphs. Pope Pius XII had stated:

> The good and bad which can come from television broadcasts is both incalculable and unforeseeable. Consequently, you must do your utmost to prevent it from spreading evil and error, making of it an instrument of information, of formation, of transformation. ... You must try to overcome difficulties of an economic or juridical nature which would prevent the extension of such a beneficial medium. Study carefully the administrative, legal and technical means of ensuring its spreading but above all give attention to the moral and the true good of man and of the family.[13]

Minister Keyes in his submission to the Government circulating the Television Committee's report, stated that in the prevailing conditions of 1956 he did not propose that any expenditure be incurred on the establishment of an Irish television station. The Minister agreed with the Departmental Television Committee that the commercial applications should be rejected and that an announcement should be made that when conditions permitted a television service to be established in the State, such a service would be based on public ownership and management. However, the Minister for Finance, Gerard Sweetman, saw no prospect of it being possible for the Exchequer "in the foreseeable future to undertake the expense of setting up and maintaining a State television service".[14] The Minister for Finance was strongly of the opinion that the Government should not be asked to commit itself "in even the vaguest way to the proposition that any television service established here would be based on public ownership and management".[15] The Cabinet rejected the views of the Minister for Finance and agreed with the Minister for Posts and Telegraphs that any television service in Ireland should be based on public ownership and management. However, the Cabinet decided that the establishment of a publicly-owned television service would involve expenditure which was beyond the resources available to the State, regard being had to other commitments and that a television service would furthermore be "undesirable on the ground that it would encourage imports of luxury goods to the detriment of the national economy".[16]

Policy in relation to television and sound broadcasting was reconsidered following the change of Government in March 1957. Two private groups, the Michelson Group and the McLendon Investment Corporation, had offered to provide and operate television services without cost to the State on condition that they first obtain the concession to conduct international commercial broadcasting from Ireland.[17] The new Minister for Posts and Telegraphs, Neil Blaney, asked the Departmental Television Committee to examine the issue with a view to suggesting to the Government "a specification" which might be given to all parties interested setting out the conditions under which the Government was prepared to have television and international commercial broadcasting established.[18] The Minister's direction appeared to signify a definite shift in Government policy: several members of the new Cabinet appeared willing to consider the involvement of private enterprise in the establishment of any national television service and any international radio broadcasting service.

The Departmental Television Committee chaired by León Ó Broin made it clear in June 1957 that it was not recommending the establishment of a television service in Ireland at that time. The Committee did so on the grounds that even with the involvement of private interests in commercial television, the State would be involved in considerable cost for the provision of the public-interest part of the service and in greater cost if for any reasons the commercial interests did not find it possible to continue. In relation to international commercial broadcasting, the Committee recommended its rejection insofar as international commercial radio broadcasting involved the establishment of special commercial stations with special wavelengths to be controlled and operated by private interests. The Committee did so as such commercial radio broadcasting would involve a flouting of Ireland's international obligations by using a wavelength not allocated to Ireland.[19]

The Department of Posts and Telegraphs prepared its first major policy document for the new Fianna Fáil Government in June 1957. A draft was first circulated to the Departments of Finance, Industry and Commerce and External Affairs for their concurrence in its terms.[20] The draft repeated much of what the Departmental Television Committee had recommended. The Department recommended the rejection of international radio broadcasting but stated that the Minister proposed to increase the power of the Athlone radio transmitter beyond 150 kw on an experimental basis to reach the Irish in Britain. The Department admitted that such an increase in broadcasting power would involve a breach of the internationally agreed Copenhagen Convention on broadcasting,[21] but confessed that such a breach was not as serious as taking over a new wavelength. In relation to television, the Department side-stepped the crucial issue of public versus private operation of any new television service by merely asking the Government for direction as to whether any steps should be taken to prepare for a television service.[22]

The Department of Industry and Commerce in a confidential memorandum formally replied to the Secretary of the Department of Posts and Telegraphs that "the Minister" had no observations to offer in relation to the draft memorandum.[23] However, the previous day, July 25, 1957, the new Tánaiste and Minister for Industry and Commerce, Seán Lemass, wrote an official letter to the Minister for Posts and Telegraphs, Neil Blaney, which was scornful of the Posts and Telegraphs draft memorandum for the Government. Lemass stated it was just the type of memorandum, as a member of the Government, he hated to get "because it [did] not convey a clear picture and [appeared] to be, in some respects, self-contradictory".[24] The memorandum dealing with commercial radio broadcasting was, he said, "somewhat less than frank". The reference to increasing the power of the Athlone radio transmitter thus "serving Irish people in Britain" rang "a trifle phoney". Lemass drew attention to the self-contradictions in the Posts and Telegraphs memorandum. The Posts and Telegraphs memorandum advised that it could not recommend to the Government to break the Copenhagen Convention in relation to international radio broadcasting, yet pointed out that it would be a breach of the Convention to increase the power of the Athlone transmitter so that Radio Éireann could be received in Britain.

In relation to television broadcasting, Lemass wrote that the memorandum for Government of the Department of Posts and Telegraphs was "even more confused".[25] The memorandum had stated that practically every other European country had a television service but stated that there was no urgency about providing a service in Ireland. Posts and Telegraphs had also stated that British television programmes were being received increasingly in the State, but argued that because an Irish service would have to use British programmes it would be undesirable. Lemass suggested that the television issue be put to the Government in the following "clear form": "(1) A State TV service [to be] ruled out on grounds of cost. (2) A TV service must, therefore, be based on commercial advertising, and be provided by private enterprise."

Finally, the Tánaiste and Minister for Industry and Commerce suggested to the Minister for Posts and Telegraphs that he should seek authority from the Government to make a public announcement that proposals for a commercial television service be provided and operated by private enterprise would be considered subject to the following conditions:

(1) No cost to the Government;
(2) Suitable machinery for the supervision and control of programmes;
(3) Free time for public services;
(4) Nation-wide coverage;
(5) Encouragement of Irish language.

Lemass argued that Government authority should also be sought so that proposals for a television service deemed most satisfactory under the foregoing headings would be approved.[26]

Ó Broin personally drafted the reply of the Minister for Posts and Telegraphs.[27] He conceded that the draft memorandum for Government was the result of several attempts to reconcile or set out conflicting views on a rather difficult subject and agreed that the draft needed further recasting. Thanking Lemass for his views on television which would be "valuable in our further consideration of the matter", Ó Broin (through his Minister) stood firm on the major issues. The letter to Lemass stated that it would be an over-simplification of the TV problem to put it to the Government as a Hobson's choice between a State TV service that we cannot afford and a commercial service provided and operated by private enterprise. There is no problem in getting the latter kind of service quickly — but we believe it would mean that the 26 Counties would, in effect, become an extra-territorial British ITA region with the programme contractor much more strongly entrenched than in any British region since he would own the television stations.[28]

The issue of the future of broadcasting was discussed between the Secretaries of the Departments of Finance, Posts and Telegraphs and Industry and Commerce in July 1957.[29] Dr. Whitaker, Secretary of the Department of Finance, stated that his Department had no objection to the proposal to increase the power of the Athlone transmitter but queried whether additional expenditure on sound broadcasting would result in a worthwhile increase in listening to Irish programmes, particularly in view of the advent of television. The querying of the necessity for additional finance infuriated Ó Broin. The Secretary of the Department of Posts and Telegraphs stated that he was "tired of answering this sort of questioning of broadcasting needs by the Department of Finance". Ó Broin stated that he had expected a more sympathetic approach. He stated that the broad facts were that broadcasting had been starved of funds, that it had started operation in a Post Office building and was still operating with great difficulty from another Post Office building in Henry Street, Dublin, and that it was only since the amount of money provided for programmes had been increased in recent years that it had been possible to have the programmes taken seriously and to secure a larger listening audience.[30] However, Ó Broin secured some measure of agreement from Dr. Whitaker who stated that his Department recognised that television would have to come sooner or later and that he personally could not imagine a television service in Ireland without a good deal of public control.[31]

The issue of television was again taken up by Ó Broin in a memorandum to his Minister in September 1957.[32] In this memorandum, Ó Broin expounds his own regulatory philosophy and presents, in a persuasive style of writing, his apologia for his vision of the future of television broadcasting in Ireland. First, he queries whether Ireland must have television at all. He states that the reason is not that all or most Western European countries have television and that Ireland should not be out of step with them. Unless television were intrinsically good, Ireland should be prepared to stand out of the line. Was television intrinsically good? Yes, answered Ó Broin. Television had become "the means by which the family takes enjoyment together"; the State should welcome television.

However, Ó Broin opined that there were two important factors which modified the conclusion about the State welcoming television. The two issues were related to each other; the first was the use to be made of television, the second was the financial factor. Ó Broin stated that even before any Papal pronouncements,[33] "we were aware that this new medium would have to be used with the greatest circumspection". He continued:

> [Television] can be an instrument of evil as well as of good. Its power to influence people is so enormous that the Government that permits TV to operate within its territory assumes a responsibility for ensuring that it operates at best to uplift the public, and when it can't do that, to leave them no worse than they were. In no circumstances can the Government allow it to debase the public. What we in Ireland have hitherto successfully done in the realm of sound, we must repeat in the realm of vision.[34]

Ó Broin acknowledged that, for financial reasons, a substantial amount of commercial programming would have to be permitted on any Irish television service. However, stating that "we are unashamedly a Christian people", he expected, as a result of the Pope's pronouncement,[35] a committee to be appointed by the Hierarchy "to watch developments" in Ireland, which "may make it unavoidable that we go on our way and avoid entanglement with groups that are primarily in the game for the money they can made out of it". In conclusion, Ó Broin stated that he believed that the Government would not be acting unwisely if it took a decision in principle in favour of having a publicly-controlled television service as the memorandum for Government recommended.

The Cabinet decision on broadcasting in 1957 reflected, in part, Ó Broin's concern about public control. The Government decided that it was desirable that an Irish television service should be established as early as practicable, that any such service should be under public control and that, so far as possible, the service should be provided without cost to the Exchequer in respect of either capital or operating expenses.[36] The Government also decided that a Cabinet Committee comprising the Tánaiste and the Ministers for Finance, External Affairs and Posts and Telegraphs should examine the matter further and report to the Government.

The Cabinet Committee on Television recommended in January 1958 that a concession for a television service be granted exclusively to one privately-owned interest, that a suitable authority be established to act for the Government in the control of television after the contract to provide the service had been awarded, that this authority should also control Radio Éireann, and that consideration be given to granting an international commercial sound broadcasting licence concession.[37]

The Tánaiste and Minister for Industry and Commerce, Seán Lemass, played a leading role in the Cabinet Committee. Lemass clearly envisaged a significant role for private enterprise in both the radio and television services in Ireland. Ó Broin wrote to his new Minister, Seán Ormonde, on seeing a draft of the Cabinet Committee's recommendations. Ó Broin stated "how profoundly unhappy" he felt about the decisions of the Cabinet Committee:

> I fear that [the decisions of the Cabinet Committee] will, in effect, involve abandonment of every feature that we have considered essential or valuable for Irish television and may be a source of constant trouble to every Minister for Posts and Telegraphs responsible to the Dáil for the service.[38]

Ó Broin expressed alarm to his Minister about the possible award of the international commercial radio concession as this would involve a breach of the Copenhagen Convention. The Copenhagen Convention governed the use of wavelengths in the long and medium bands and had been signed in 1948 by 25 European states including Ireland. Ó Broin continued:

> [T]he fundamental objection to these applicants is that they are asking us to do something we cannot legally do. That should end the matter. We cannot consistently preach the rule of law in international affairs at the United Nations and in Áras an Uachtaráin and then break the international radio conventions we have solemnly signed.[39]

The new Minister for Post and Telegraphs, Seán Ormonde, forwarded a copy of Ó Broin's memorandum to the Tánaiste, Seán Lemass. In an official letter to the Minister for Posts and Telegraphs, the Tánaiste retorted that a public service television provider was "out of the question for financial reasons".[40] He continued: "The Government have decided to proceed on the basis of a commercial service and this question must now be regarded as settled." On the issue of the question of any breach of the Copenhagen Convention, Lemass put it that the Cabinet Committee "clearly understood that the acceptance of a proposition which included commercial sound broadcasting involved withdrawal from the Copenhagen Convention".[41]

The Department of Posts and Telegraphs in its formal memorandum for Government reacted strongly against the implementation of the Cabinet Committee's proposals.[42] The Department considered that the recommendations, if approved, would result in the deliberate creation of a private monopoly in television. Such a monopoly was undesirable because television was "more powerful in its impact on the public than the press, the cinema or the radio".[43] The Department also argued that any television authority (as envisaged by the Cabinet Committee) would only exercise negative external supervision and could have no effective control of programme operation. In relation to the Cabinet Committee's proposal to grant an international commercial sound broadcasting licence, the Department considered that the establishment of an Irish international commercial broadcasting service would involve a flagrant breach of the Copenhagen Convention:

> This course would involve abandonment of the international rule of law designed to secure the orderly utilisation of radio frequencies and thereby to prevent chaos in the broadcasting spectrum. All the European signatory States to the Convention, including those of the Eastern bloc have, in their own and in the general European interest, recognised the importance of maintaining adherence to the Convention and Ireland would be the first of the twenty five signatories to denounce it.[44]

THE TELEVISION COMMISSION

The Minister for Health, Seán MacEntee, in an effort to reach a satisfactory compromise in relation to the conflicting views of members of the Cabinet, recommended the establishment of a commission to consider and report on the establishment of any television service in Ireland.[45] The Government agreed and appointed in March 1958 a commission under the chairmanship of Mr. Justice George D. Murnaghan.

The Television Commission was requested to make recommendations on the issue of establishing a television service "on the basis that no charge shall fall on the Exchequer, either on capital or on current account, and the effective control of televised programmes must be exercisable by an Irish public authority to be established as a television authority".[46]

Many persons and organisations submitted written and oral evidence to the Commission. One submission that was never published or even referred to in the Commission Report was a handwritten memorandum by Ó Broin. In his confidential submission to the Television Commission, he argued strongly that the Irish television and sound broadcasting service should be controlled and operated directly by a Television Authority as a semi-State body detached from the Civil Service and the Post Office.[47] He stated that he would personally view with dismay the handing over of a monopoly to private commercial interests of a powerful medium which has such an impact in the formation of public opinion "and in the raising of cultural and educational standards which could cause such immense damage if not operated in the public interest".[48] Ó Broin argued that the whole tendency of commercial broadcasting would be to make money by holding large audiences with "standardised entertainment of a certain elemental character and in disregard of cultural and minority interests".[49] The Departmental Secretary informed the Commission on discussions he had had with the BBC: the BBC was prepared to place at the disposal of an Irish public service television authority, at little or no charge, a large selection of documentaries, discussions, educational, scientific, agricultural, childrens, sports and other programmes in which relay fees for artistes were not involved. The Secretary firmly stated that the BBC programmes would be made available to an Irish television service only if it were controlled and operated as a public-service organisation. He warned that BBC programmes "could not, of course, be got by Irish television if it were operated by a commercial organisation".[50] The Secretary argued that although there should be the maximum separation from day-to-day State supervision both for the television and sound broadcasting service, overriding responsibility for certain legally prescribed matters of broad policy and technical conditions would be retained by the Minister for Posts and Telegraphs and the Government. He envisaged the relationship between the Minister for Posts and Telegraphs and any new authority as being similar to the relationship between the British Postmaster-General and the BBC.

Archives[51] released in 1990 from the Department of the Taoiseach provide an insight into how the Vatican endeavoured in a secret manner to influence the development and regulation of broadcasting in Ireland in the period prior to the publication of the *Report of the Television Commission*.[52] In July 1958, Monsignor Georges Roche, Prelate of the Papal Household and Superior General of Opus Cenaculi, together with Monsignor Andrea Deskur, Assistant Secretary of the Vatican Commission on Cinema, Radio and Television, called on Seán MacEntee, Minister for Health, in Dublin with a letter of introduction from Fr. Michael Browne, the Master General of the Order of Preachers in Rome and brother-in-law of Seán MacEntee.[53] The prelate had submitted a confidential and comprehensive memorandum to the Television Commission and had been charged to express informally the Pope's great personal interest in the fact that the Irish Government proposed to establish a television service because of the great service which His Holiness believed broadcasting under the auspices of an Irish Government could render in combating irreligion and materialism.[54] The prelates stated that His Holiness considered that by reason of its geographical situation Irish television could be of great service to the Christian religion provided that a transmitter be installed which would be sufficiently powerful to transmit its programmes to trans-oceanic territories. The prelates hoped that when the type, power and site of broadcasting transmitters were being determined this consideration would be given great weight. The prelates stated that it would be greatly appreciated if an opportunity were given to the Pontifical Commission on Radio and Television to study the report of the Television Commission before the Government made a decision in regard to it. The Taoiseach, Eamon de Valera, agreed that a copy of the report of the Television Commission should be sent to either of the prelates through Ireland's Ambassador at the Vatican and, if possible, in advance of the final signatures of the members of the Commission.[55] Monsignor Deskur and Monsignor Roche gave oral evidence before the Commission in July 1958. Their evidence, *inter alia*, suggested that an independent international broadcasting system would help Ireland's prestige in the cultural field.[56]

In September 1958 Monsignor Roche, in an atmosphere of secrecy, handed the Irish Ambassador to the Holy See proposals for a full television service and a sound broadcasting service based in Ireland for transmision abroad.[57] The proposals were in the names of five non-Irish laymen. Monsignor Roche informed the Irish Ambassador that if the broadcasting scheme which had been submitted were to be adopted, Ireland would become a centre from which would radiate programmes conforming to the ideals of Christendom and western civilisation which would compete with Communist propaganda.[58] The prelates assured the Ambassador that no doubt existed as to the availability of the necessary funds or the technical experience. The Television Commission made no public reference to the Vatican intervention or the written submissions which appeared to have the approval of the Vatican. However, the Minority Report (part of which was never published) disagreed with the omission from the Majority Report of any serious consideration of international commercial sound broadcasting as a potential revenue-raiser for the effective financing of an Irish commercial television service.[59]

The narrow terms of reference of the Commission — the stricture that the establishment of a television service was to be on the basis that no charge was to fall on the Exchequer — created certain divisions among the members of the Commission. In an *Interim Report* in December 1958, the Commission (by a majority) considering, *inter alia,* that it would be unfortunate if a growing number of viewers "had formed the habit of viewing not only the BBC programme, but also an alternative programme emanating from outside the Republic" before a television service was established in Ireland, recommended that the Government should immediately take steps to facilitate the speedy acquisition of sites for transmitting stations to give national coverage for the television organisation which was to be decided upon at a later stage.[60] The *Interim Minority Report of the Commission* disagreed with the majority on this issue: the minority argued that the recommendation of the Majority Report would involve expenditure for the acquisition of sites for transmitters necessarily falling on the Government.[61] The Department of Posts and Telegraphs favoured the acquisition of sites; the Department of Finance objected principally on the grounds of cost. The Minister for Finance stated that he was not impressed by the argument advanced in favour of urgent action, i.e., that the viewing habits of the Irish public were likely to be determined on a long-term basis by exposure to non-Irish programmes.[62] The Government decided in March 1959 that a site at Kippure, County Wicklow, should be acquired for a television transmitter to service the Dublin area.[63]

The Report of the *Coimisiún um Athbheochan na Gaeilge* on

Television was published in March 1959 — a matter of weeks before the publication of the Television Commission Report.[64] The Taoiseach, Eamon de Valera, requested the Minister for Posts and Telegraphs to examine the report and to submit a memorandum to the Government containing comments with such recommendations as the Minister desired. The Taoiseach's request gave the Department of Posts and Telegraphs, and the Secretary of the Department in particular, a further opportunity to present arguments in favour of the public-service concept of television broadcasting. Although there is no documentary evidence to prove where the Taoiseach's sympathy lay, de Valera gave the Department of Posts and Telegraphs every opportunity to present its case in Cabinet. The Department of Posts and Telegraphs in its memorandum for Government endorsed many of the realistic recommendations of the Irish Commission's report.[65] The Minister agreed with the Commission that television had great potentialities for the revival of the Irish language. The Minister noted that "no country except Monaco and Luxembourg" had given the television concession to "a foreign concern". Reference was made to the fact that commercial interests were not "in television to help Irish or Irish culture but to increase their profits". The Radio Éireann experience of sponsors "in providing only the lowest common denominator in foreign entertainment" was also recited. The Department disagreed, however, with the Commission's proposal that "Irish should be the language of administration for the service generally", noting that this was unrealistic. The Minister concluded forcefully by advocating for a television authority which would itself operate the programmes, sell advertising time and which would not be dominated by "the commercial element".[66]

Eamon de Valera was inaugurated as President of Ireland on June 25, 1959. His successor as Taoiseach was Seán Lemass, the former Tánaiste and Minister for Industry and Commerce. The Television Commission had finalised its work on May 8, but it was not until July that the Department of Posts and Telegraphs presented the Government with the Minister's view on the report.[67]

The Television Commission considered that if there had to be an Irish television service within the terms of reference it must (for some time) be provided by private enterprise. The Minister favoured the reservation to the report signed by six members (out of nineteen) that the transmitting system should be owned by the proposed Authority. The Minister agreed with the views expressed by the six members that the Authority would have little difficulty, if permitted to do so, in raising the necessary capital within the State.[68]

The Commission stressed the urgency of starting an Irish television service and recommended that the Government should immediately have the necessary negotiations undertaken and a contract signed in order that the necessary installations be put in hand by the private contractor in advance of the enactment of legislation.[69] The Minister for Posts and Telegraphs agreed on the question of urgency but saw difficulty in entering into any commitment with a private group that would enable them to proceed with the establishment of television installations before the Oireachtas had an opportunity of discussing the matter. The Minister stated that apart from other considerations, broadcasting was by law a State monopoly (and there was no provision, it was claimed, for broadcasting from a private broadcasting station) and it appeared to him that it would be improper to assume or anticipate the approval of the Oireachtas for such an important charge.[70] The argument that it would be improper for a Minister of the Government to assume or anticipate the approval of the Oireachtas on a matter relating to broadcasting policy was a new weapon in the Department's regulatory approach.

The Commission recommended separate bodies initially to control radio and television.[71] The Minister argued that the two services of radio and television should be complementary rather than competitive and that this could best be secured from the outset by one body. The Minister argued that interests of a national and cultural kind would be safeguarded, to some extent, by unified control and operation of both broadcasting services.

The Minister emphasised that the Commission's report was made on the basis of the terms of reference which were interpreted as precluding consideration or recommendation of any arrangement involving a charge on the Exchequer, even by way of loan. The Minister quoted from the Majority Report (and emphasised the following quotation by underlining it) that "if the necessary capital monies were available there [was] little or no doubt that television should, if possible, be provided as a public service". The Minister also referred to the considerable misgivings expressed in the Report about the operation of a monopoly service by a private group.[72] The Commission's opinion that "viewed conservatively" a television service could be self-supporting within a few years, together with the misgivings of the Commission on the issue of a private mono-poly, made it "difficult" for the Minister to defend the establishment of a private monopoly in television on the plea that the State was unable to advance the capital involved then estimated at IR£1.5m over a few years.[73] The Minister stated that when the original policy of "no charge on the Exchequer" was formulated in 1957, capital had been scarce — but matters had improved and it was acknowledged that television could now pay its way. The Minister's principal anxiety (and the Minister assumed that this "would weigh heavily with the Government") was "to ensure that programmes catering for cultural and national interests would be a first consideration, instead of being the last, or of being ignored, or obstructed".

In the "national interest", the Minister requested the Government to direct that the policy of "no charge" on the Exchequer be modified to one of "no ultimate charge"; that both the control and operation of the television service be carried out by the proposed Authority itself; and that a single authority should control both sound broadcasting and television.

The Minister for External Affairs, Frank Aiken, and the Minister for Industry and Commerce, Jack Lynch, had no observations to offer on the Post Office memorandum. The Minister for Education, Patrick J. Hillery, supported the Minister for Posts and Telegraphs adding his "serious concern" on the question of opening Irish television "to the advertising of non-Irish goods" as he considered that such a step would "tend to have a demoralising influence on national morale".[74]

Dr. T.K. Whitaker, Secretary of the Department of Finance, articulated in June 1959 the view of the Department of Finance on the issue of the regulation of television.[75] First, he considered that the Department of Finance's attitude would be that television was not high in the list of priorities for urgent expenditure. Secondly, the Department of Finance would not regard the terms of reference laying down that there was to be no charge on the Exchequer as meaning that there should not be even an initial charge. The Department considered that the latter interpretation was too narrow and that no ultimate charge would be a reasonable interpretation.

The Minister for Finance in a subsequent formal memorandum for Government reiterated the points which Dr. Whitaker had already articulated.[76] It was claimed that it was reasonable to assume that the inauguration of an Irish television service would result in expenditure by private persons on television sets and accordingly private savings would be seriously affected to the detriment of capital availabilities generally. Further, the Minister argued that experience in other countries had indicated that the provision of television would result in a substantial fall in cinema attendance that would have "bad effects" both in terms of employment and in the loss of revenue from cinema entertainments tax — then over IR£1m per annum. The Minister argued that on economic grounds the provision of television in Ireland should be postponed until the Programme of Economic Expansion was well under way. However, on the structure of any organisation that would provide a television service, the Minister for Finance stated he "would not dissent" from the Posts and Telegraphs recommendation that a Television Authority should be a state-sponsored body which would provide and operate the national television service, to be financed by licence fees and advertising revenue.

The Department of Posts and Telegraphs was very pleased with the Finance memorandum. In a briefing note for the Minister for Posts and Telegraphs "to assist the Minister in the discussions at Government", the Department noted that the points raised by Finance were "fair and reasonable — in fact . . . remarkably reasonable coming from the Minister whose official attitude might be expected to be to get a television service at the lowest possible costs".[77]

The views of Ó Broin ultimately prevailed in Cabinet. The Government at its Cabinet meeting on July 31, 1959 decided that the policy of "no charge" on the Exchequer in connection with the establishment of a television service should be modified to one of "no ultimate charge", the control and operation of the television service was to be carried out by a Television Authority itself, and that both sound broadcasting and television should be controlled by a single authority.[78]

THE BROADCASTING AUTHORITY ACT, 1960

The *Broadcasting Authority Act, 1960* established a single statutory authority, Radio Éireann (later to become Radio Telefís Éireann (RTE)),[79] to control and operate the existing sound broadcasting service and the proposed television service. The Authority was to "establish and maintain a national television and sound broadcasting service" and was invested with "all such powers as [were] necessary for or incidental to that purpose".[80] The Irish television service was inaugurated on December 31, 1961. The powers and duties of RTE will be considered in chapter 19.

THE BROADCASTING (OFFENCES) ACT, 1968

The *Broadcasting (Offences) Act, 1968* was the next major legislation to regulate broadcasting after the *Broadcasting Authority Act, 1960*. The 1968 Act enabled Ireland to ratify the Council of Europe Agreement entitled "European Agreement for the Prevention of Broadcasts transmitted from Stations outside National Territories". This Agreement was signed on behalf of Ireland, subject to ratification, on March 9, 1965. Contracting parties were obliged to take appropriate measures to make punishable as offences in accordance with domestic law the establishment or operation of broadcasting stations on board ships, aircraft and marine structures outside national territories; the 1968 Act prohibited broadcasting from ships, aircraft or marine structures in sea waters adjacent to the State or in tidal waters in the State.[81] Broadcasting from Irish registered ships operating anywhere was made unlawful.[82] Certain acts facilitating broadcasting from ships, aircraft or marine structures were also prohibited.[83] [The provisions of the 1968 Act served as a model for many of the provisions of the *Broadcasting and Wireless Telegraphy Act, 1988* which provided for the prohibition of unlicensed broadcasting in the State.][84]

The Minister for Posts and Telegraphs, Erskine Childers, was determined that "any kind of pirate broadcasting station, irrespective of the kind of programme transmitted, [would] have to be suppressed".[85] There have been no prosecutions to date under this Act, but unlawful radio broadcasting from within the State was to become extensive in the late 1970s and 1980s.

BROADCASTING REVIEW COMMITTEE REPORT, 1974

In 1971 a Broadcasting Review Committee was appointed under the chairmanship of Mr. Justice George D. Murnaghan with the following terms of reference:

> To review the progress of the television and sound broadcasting services since the enactment of the *Broadcasting Authority Act 1960*, with particular reference to the objectives prescribed in that Act, and to make any recommendations considered appropriate in regard to the further development of the services.[86]

The Committee recommended in 1974 a new legislative declaration on the purpose of broadcasting in Ireland.[87] The Committee favoured, inter alia, the inclusion of the following concepts in such a legislative declaration:

> Broadcasting should be concerned with safeguarding, enriching and strengthening the cultural, social and economic fabric of the whole of Ireland.[88]

The Committee also considered that the broadcasting service should be essentially Irish in context and character and should also

> actively contribute to the flow and exchange of information, entertainment and culture within Ireland, and between Ireland and other countries, especially her partners in the European Economic Community; and provide for a continuing expression of Irish identity.[89]

The Committee recommended that broadcasting continue to be a public service[90] and that a Broadcasting Commission be established which would be responsible for the review of programme structures and performance, deal with complaints of partiality, licensing of broadcasting and cable operations.[91] The consolidation of existing broadcasting legislation was also recommended by the Committee.[92]

The Broadcasting Commission proposal was never implemented. It is argued later in this book that there is merit in the establishment of a single quasi-judicial body with wide ranging powers which would function as a regulatory authority for all telecommunication services.[93]

THE BROADCASTING AUTHORITY (AMENDMENT) ACT, 1976

The *Broadcasting Review Committee Report, 1974*[94] influenced the drafting of the *Broadcasting Authority (Amendment) Act, 1976*. The 1976 Act had two main purposes: firstly to expand the duties of the RTE Authority in the light of developments since the Authority had been established in 1960; secondly to provide "greater autonomy and freedom for the broadcasting service within clearly defined statutory restraints and obligations, while at the same time

improving public control in certain areas".[95] The power of the
Minister for Posts and Telegraphs to prohibit the broadcasting of any
class of matter was restricted by the 1976 Act.[96] A Broadcasting
Complaints Commission was established.[97] Provision was made
that a member of the RTE Authority could only be removed by the
Government for stated reasons and then only if resolutions asking
for his removal were passed by both Houses of the Oireachtas.[98]
Prior to the passing of the 1976 Act the Minister had an unrestricted
power to dismiss all or any members of the Authority.[99]

Much of the debate on the *Broadcasting Authority (Amendment) Bill,
1975* in the Seanad, where the Bill was first introduced, was taken
up with the issue of what is now described as trans-frontier
broadcasting. Then the issue was described as open broadcasting.
The Minister for Posts and Telegraphs, Dr. Cruise O'Brien, in his
speech on the Second Stage of the Bill stated that the Government
favoured the use of the second proposed network for transmitting
BBC 1 or Ulster Television, if negotiations with the British authorities
which had been going on for some time were successful.[100] Section
6 of the Bill was designed to empower the Minister for Posts and
Telegraphs to direct the RTE Authority to rebroadcast programmes
from any source other than the Authority, as specified by the
Minister. Under section 6(2) of the Bill, the Authority would have
been obliged to comply with the Minister's directions. When the Bill
was being debated in the Seanad, several Senators argued that
rebroadcasting a foreign channel in its entirety without any form of
control would be in breach of Article 40.6.1.i of the Constitution
which specified that the State shall ensure that organs of public
opinion "shall not be used to undermine public order or morality or
the authority of the State".[101] John Kelly, TD, then Parliamentary
Secretary to the Taoiseach, considered that the arguments against
re-broadcasting the BBC were "unreasonable and hypocritical".[102]
He argued that re-broadcasting BBC was

> so minimal, so tiny, so imperceptible compared with the sub-
> stantial cultural conquest which has been made that it is not
> worth arguing about and, above all, not worth arguing about
> in the very emotional terms we heard used. . . .[103]

The Minister for Posts and Telegraphs sought the guidance of the
public in a survey; a survey jointly sponsored by the Department of
Posts and Telegraphs and RTE in 1975 showed a clear preference for
a second RTE Channel (RTE 2) — "selected from BBC 1, BBC 2, the

15 ITV companies, other overseas sources, and additional home-produced material" over the rebroadcasting of BBC.[104] The Minister accepted the findings of the survey and agreed to delete section 6 of the Bill and other related provisions.[105] The second RTE channel was later inaugurated on November 2, 1978 and was designated "Network 2" by RTE in 1988.

ILLEGAL COMMERCIAL RADIO STATIONS AND THEIR EVENTUAL LEGALISATION

Illegal radio stations commenced operating on a commercial basis in Dublin in 1975 and soon flourished in major towns in Ireland. During 1976 and subsequently, "search and seize operations" under the *Wireless Telegraphy Acts, 1926 to 1972* were carried out by the Department of Posts and Telegraphs against many illegal radio stations. The maximum penalty for the possession of transmitting apparatus without a licence was IR£50 and elaborate precautions were often taken to thwart the efforts of the Department in enforcing the law.

The pettiness of the fines, the fact that the seized apparatus was rarely forfeited under the discretionary power vested in the District Court under section 3(3) of the *Wireless Telegraphy Act, 1926,* and the inaction of the Government in enacting appropriate legislation encouraged the "pirate broadcasters" to continue broadcasting despite successful prosecutions against them. All the foregoing factors undoubtedly encouraged the "pirate broadcasters" to post-pone a constitutional challenge to the broadcasting monopoly of the Minister for Posts and Telegraphs. Article 40.6.1.i of the Constitution certainly could have been invoked by those seeking to broadcast on the premise that the Constitution, albeit subject to appropriate restrictions, gave citizens the right to broadcast similar to their rights to publish the printed word.

A measure to suppress illegal broadcasting stations in the form of the *Broadcasting and Wireless Telegraphy Bill, 1979* was introduced in the Dáil in April 1979. The main purpose of the 1979 Bill was to prevent the making of broadcasts from anywhere within the State, unless in accordance with a licence issued by the Minister for Posts and Telegraphs. Offences were to be created prohibiting anyone providing accommodation, equipment or programme material for, to advertise by means of, or to take part in, such broadcasting. The Bill was broadly on the lines of the *Broadcasting (Offences) Act, 1968* which had been enacted to suppress broadcasting from ships, aircraft and marine structures. The 1979 Bill also provided for amendments and extensions to the *Wireless Telegraphy Acts, 1926 to 1972*. The Bill had not been debated when the Dáil was dissolved in May 1981, consequently lapsed, and was not re-introduced.

The continuing popularity of the "pirate" radio stations forced the Government to shift its policy from mere suppression of the un-lawful broadcasting stations towards a policy of making legislative provision for commercial local broadcasting (in addition to RTE) and, at the same time, suppressing the unlicensed stations. The first legislative attempt to break the *de facto* broadcasting monopoly of RTE and introduce local broadcasting was made in the *Independent Local Radio Bill, 1981*. The 1981 Bill proposed the establishment of an Independent Local Radio Authority which would operate broad-casting transmitters for local radio services under licence from the Minister for Posts and Telegraphs. The envisaged Radio Authority would enter into contracts with other interested parties for the provision of programmes to be broadcast on the authority's trans-mitters. This 1981 Bill was presented by the Minister for Posts and Telegraphs in May 1981, the same month as the Dáil was dissolved.

The *Independent Local Broadcasting Authority Bill, 1983* which was substantially based on the *Independent Local Radio Bill, 1981* but included provisions for the regulation of television services as well as radio, was introduced by Fianna Fáil in opposition on private members' business. The Coalition Government stated in the Dáil in June 1983 that it was the intention of the Government to proceed "at an early date with legislation for the orderly development of local community radio services".[106] This statement ensured the defeat of the Fianna Fáil measure. Ideological differences between the partners in the Coalition Government about the regulation of broadcasting delayed the publication of the Government's own legislative broadcasting proposals. However, in June 1985, the Coalition Government introduced in the Seanad its *Broadcasting and Wireless Telegraphy Bill, 1985* which was based primarily on the 1979 Bill and at the same time introduced in Dáil Éireann its *Local Radio Bill, 1985* which envisaged the provision of local sound broadcasting services with an emphasis on community and an RTE involvement. The Minister for Communications, Jim Mitchell, also announced the establishment of an interim Local Radio Commission (An Coimisiún um Radio Áitiúil) — a body which was incapable of effective action because of legislative inaction. The Labour Party strongly advocated involvement both by RTE and the broader community in any local radio broadcasting régime. Ideological differences among the Coalition partners in Government resulted in neither of the 1985 measures being enacted into legislation.

The subsequent Fianna Fáil Government became determined to achieve "a major and radical development of . . . broadcasting services" within the State[107] and accordingly introduced in November 1987 its *Sound Broadcasting Bill, 1987* and its *Broadcasting and Wireless Telegraphy Bill, 1987*. The Minister for Communications, Ray Burke, stated in the Dáil in December 1987 that up to 70 pirate radio stations had been operating in the country for the past ten years. Admitting that the authorities had tolerated "a situation of lawlessness in the airwaves for over 10 years", the Minister stated that this situation represented "an indictment of the legislative process that we have for so long failed to respond to a demand which we all know exists among the public for evolution in our radio services".[108]

The Government's approach to its proposed legislation was stated to be influenced by two major developments: firstly, the radio frequencies for broadcasting, particularly VHF (very high frequencies) were no longer as scarce as they had been; secondly, the existing regulatory framework was considered to be no longer relevant.[109] The *Sound Broadcasting Bill, 1987* which had envisaged a direct licensing arrangement between the Minister for Communications and sound broadcasters underwent a transformation at the end of the Committee Stage in the Dáil, became styled as the *Radio and Television Bill* and provided for the establishment of an Independent Radio and Television Commission which would regulate private radio and television services. The central objective of the transformed Bill was stated by the Minister for Communications, Ray Burke, "to create an environment and framework which would allow individuals and organisations the maximum opportunity to become involved in broadcasting and to meet and respond to public demand and requirements in the broadcasting sphere".[110] The Minister for Communications, articulating the policy of the Government, emphasised that it was not the function of the State to provide the new broadcasting services; the State sought merely to provide the framework and opportunity to allow the public to decide what they wanted to see and hear and to provide for the "emergence of diversity" in the broadcasting service.[111] The reason for the transformation between the *Sound Broadcasting Bill, 1987* as published and its subsequent enactment as the *Radio and Television Act, 1988* was the strong opposition against the proposed direct ministerial involvement in the granting of broadcasting licences. The opposition parties argued for an independent regulatory broadcasting authority and forced the minority Government to concede on this issue and provide for the establishment of an Independent Radio and Television Commission, which would have the function of entering into contracts for the provision of sound broadcasting services and a television programme service additional to the services provided by RTE.

The *Broadcasting and Wireless Telegraphy Bill, 1987* was based on the *Broadcasting and Wireless Telegraphy Bill, 1985* and was not debated at any length in the Dáil and Seanad because of its uncontroversial nature and the measure of agreement between all the parties on the need to restore a degree of regulation to the airwaves. The purpose of the *Broadcasting and Wireless Telegraphy Act, 1988* was to prohibit broadcasting in the State save under and in accordance with a licence issued by the Minister for Communications, to amend and extend the *Wireless Telegraphy Acts 1926 to 1972* and the *Broadcasting (Offences) Act, 1968* and to provide for other related matters. The Independent Radio and Television Commission was established on October 17, 1988[112] and is empowered by section 4 of the *Radio and Television Act, 1988* to select and regulate persons other than RTE in relation to the provision of certain broadcasting services. The powers and duties of the Independent Radio and Television Commission will be examined in chapter 21.

BROADCASTING ACT, 1990 AND THE BROADCASTING AUTHORITY (AMENDMENT) ACT, 1993

Century Radio was launched as a national private radio service on September 4, 1989 but ceased operating due to financial difficulties in 1991. Commentators have suggested that lack of advertising revenue lay at the heart of difficulties which Century Radio experienced in its first year of existence.[113] Century Radio promoters argued that the biggest single obstacle to the station's success had been "the distortion of the advertising marketplace" caused by the dual-funded system under which RTE operated whereby RTE received income from advertising revenue together with licence fees.[114]

RTE's dual-funding status led to what was termed an "uneven playing pitch" with the commercial broadcasting stations competing with RTE using their advertising revenue alone. The newspapers also complained about the "uneven playing pitch" in relation to advertising and lobbied the Minister for Communications about the unfairness of RTE's dual-funded status.

The Minister for Communications promised a remedy. *The Broadcasting Bill, 1990* provided that the Minister for Communications, with the approval of the Minister for Finance, was authorised to pay, in each financial year, out of monies provided by the Oireachtas up to 25 per cent of an amount equivalent to net television licence fee receipts to the Independent Radio and Television Commission, with the remainder being paid to RTE. The Independent Radio and Television Commission was to be required to disburse the amounts received solely for the purpose of supporting the establishment and operation of sound broadcasting services and the television programme service to be established under the *Radio and Television Act, 1988*. The Bill also provided that the daily times for broadcasting advertisements and the maximum period to be given to advertisements in any one hour was to be determined by the Minister for Communications. The Minister was also to be authorised to direct by order that total revenue to be derived by RTE from advertising, sponsorship and commercial promotion in its broadcasts was not to exceed an amount to be determined in such order.

The proposals caused a political furore. Newspapers reported that the Government Coalition of Fianna Fáil and the Progressive Democrats was "strained" by the rift over the *Broadcasting Bill*.[115] The Irish Congress of Trade Unions warned that some elements in the Bill were "totally unacceptable".[116] *The Irish Times* commented in its leading article that Government decisions in relation to the Bill represented "the most politically inept performance" by the Government since it was sworn into office.[117]

The Minister for Communications, Ray Burke, defended his proposals in the Dáil stating that the primary purpose of RTE's State subvention (in the form of licence fees) was to enable RTE to meet certain public-service obligations.[118] However, he argued that the effect of the State subvention went further. It allowed RTE to sell its advertising time at, in effect, "below cost" rates, thereby artificially dominating the market.[119] The Minister stated that the commercial broadcasting stations were obliged to perform certain public-service obligations — like, for example, devoting not less than 20 per cent of broadcasting time to news and current affairs programmes[120] but they did so without the benefit of any licence fee income. At the same time, the commercial broadcasting stations competed with the below-cost selling of advertising time by RTE. The Minister also argued that the print media was equally affected by RTE's dual-funding system.

The Opposition argued that the principle of alienating any percentage of the television licence fees on a permanent basis to sustain commercial radio stations was fundamentally flawed.[121] Such a proposal, if implemented, would subsidise and encourage inefficiency among the commercial broadcasting providers.

Dr. Garret FitzGerald argued that the concept of capping RTE's revenue in the manner contemplated in the Bill was designed "to intimidate the Broadcasting Authority" and was "undemocratic and undesirable".[122] Dr. FitzGerald hoped that the capping provision would be removed by a subsequent Government that would ensure that public broadcasting in Ireland was made "immune to the maximum extent possible to the kind of political pressures which always tend to be designed to limit their critical faculty".[123]

The Minister for Communications was forced to omit the provision in relation to the payment of licence-fee income to the commercial "independent" broadcasting services. Instead of giving the Minister flexibility in relation to determining the total daily time for advertising as envisaged in the Bill, section 3 of the Broadcasting Act, 1990 imposed a statutory limit on the amount of revenue which could be derived by RTE from advertising sponsorship and other forms of commercial promotion in broadcasting and limited the amount of time which could be devoted to broadcast advertising on RTE services to 7.5 per cent of total daily transmission time and to five minutes in any one hour.

The *Broadcasting Authority (Amendment) Act, 1993* introduced by the Coalition Goverment of Fianna Fáil and Labour, repealed the "cap" provision on RTE's revenue from advertising in the 1990 Act and restored the situation with regard to broadcast advertisements on RTE's services to that which had existed prior to the enactment of the 1990 Act, i.e. that the total daily times and the maximum time in any one hour for broadcast advertisements fixed by RTE was to be subject to the approval of the Minister for Arts and Culture.

Other provisions in the *Broadcasting Act, 1990* related to an extension of the remit of the Broadcasting Complaints Commission, the drawing up of codes of practice relating to advertising and other commercial promoters and the prohibition on interception of certain broadcasting transmission services. These issues will be dealt with in further detail in the next part of this book.

The *Broadcasting Authority (Amendment) Act, 1993* also provided that RTE must make specific amounts available for programmes commissioned from the independent television production sector in each financial year.[124] The amount to be set aside for this purpose is £5m in 1994, rising in stages to £10m in 1998 and 20 per cent of television expenditure in 1999 and thereafter or £12.5m, whichever is the greater. The amount of £12.5m will be adjusted annually in line with changes in the Consumer Price Index.[125]

Eilish Pearce in a perceptive article published when the Dáil was considering the *Broadcasting Bill, 1990* argued that Governments in Ireland viewed an independent broadcasting service as a rival in "consensus forming".[126] It is inevitable that there is tension between the Government of the day and any truly independent public broadcasting service. The earnest opposition to the proposals of the Minister for Communications particularly in proposing that licence fees be given to the private broadcasting sector, the Minister's subsequent withdrawal of some of his proposals and the dilution of others, demonstrate in part the public regard for RTE and the concept of an independent public service ethos in broadcasting.

13

Cable Television

Cable television systems are relay systems in which, at present, television and sound programmes are distributed over wired networks to individual service points located in houses, hotels and other such locations. The demand for cable television in Ireland has been linked with fortuitous "off air" availability of British broadcasting programmes in what was called the multi-channel area.[1] Cable systems will form an important role in telecommunication systems of the future and will be capable of carrying a wide range of entertainment and other services. New wideband cable systems can carry channels with two-way communication capability (interactive) that facilitate the flow of information in both directions.[2]

The term "telegraph" as defined in the *Telegraph Acts, 1863 and 1869*[3] includes cable used for communication purposes. Cable systems connected to apparatus for wireless telegraphy also come within the definition of "apparatus for wireless telegraphy".[4]

Television relay cable systems developed slowly in Ireland. In 1960, the Radio Éireann Authority was opposed to the Minister for Posts and Telegraphs licensing the relay of British programmes in Ireland until the Irish television station had become established.[5] It was considered that the unrestricted development of cable television to enable viewers to receive television programmes other than from the national television station would have an adverse effect on Radio Éireann advertising revenue. The Minister accepted this argument at that time. Private interests in 1961 sought permission from the Minister for Posts and Telegraphs to set up cable systems which would relay both programmes from the national station and British television stations. The Government decided in October 1961 that restricted use of the television relay systems should be permitted on conditions to be determined by the Minister for Posts and Telegraphs. The Minister decided that multi-channel cable television systems to serve up to ten homes in a single building, or block of flats, should be permitted. In the autumn of 1965 the Minister for Local Government, Neil Blaney, raised the question of providing multi-channel cable television for Ballymun housing estate, Dublin, where it was argued, a "special position" existed. In Ballymun, the housing scheme then consisted of 450 two-storey houses surrounded by 34 blocks of flats of from 4 to 15 storeys high. The Government decided that Radio Éireann should provide a multi-channel wired television system for Ballymun.[6] In March 1970, the Government announced that the maximum number of permitted outlets per system should be raised from ten to five hundred.

Subsequently it was decided that the Minister for Posts and Telegraphs would license certain cable television relay systems. Licences were to be issued only to RTE,[7] local authorities and those interested directly with housing schemes or local areas concerned. RTE was permitted to engage in the cable television relay business to compensate for loss of advertising revenue which would follow from an anticipated decline in the viewing of RTE's programmes. It was anticipated that the "foreign" channels would attract many viewers away from RTE. A division within RTE, called RTE Relays and later to be incorporated, was established to manage RTE's cable relay business.[8] The Government decided in October 1972 to permit private contractors to provide multi-channel communal aerial systems.

The Broadcasting Review Committee (1974) in its second *Interim Report*[9] made a number of recommendations concerning cable television. It was recommended that cable television be regulated by statute, so that, *inter alia*, (a) no one operator would have a monopoly, (b) RTE programmes would necessarily be carried, and (c) a contribution would be made to RTE's finances. Regulations were subsequently made by the Minister for Posts and Telegraphs in 1974.[10]

The Minister for Posts and Telegraphs, Dr. Conor Cruise O'Brien, in the Dáil in 1975 succinctly summed up the State's policy or lack of policy in relation to cable television:

> The whole history of cable television in this country has been a history of the abandonment of a series of more or less artificial lines of defence in which public policy and the institutional interest of RTE appeared intertwined and in continuous retreat.[11]

The regulation of local programme matter[12] for distribution on cable systems was provided for subsequently by the *Broadcasting Authority (Amendment) Act, 1976* which inserted an appropriate provision in the *Wireless Telegraphy Act, 1926*.[13]

The Cable Systems Committee which reported to the Minister for Communications in December 1984 recommended that cable systems should be regarded as an integral part of Ireland's communications infrastructure[14] and that communications, entertainment and interactive services should be provided by private enterprise.[15] However, the Committee considered that because of the strategic importance of the new interactive cable technology, some State encouragement and support would be required to enable such developments to occur.[16] The Committee recommended that the 15 per cent fee which cable licensees paid to the Minister for Communications and which was used as a contribution towards the finances of RTE to offset a reduction in RTE advertising potential as a consequence of the development of cable television, should not be extended to embrace charges for non-broadcast, interactive or other additional services.[17] The Committee recommended a new regulatory framework for cable communication services and considered that the licensing mechanism should be utilised to encourage the adoption of new technology in cable systems. In particular, the Committee recommended that all existing licences currently in force be revoked; new regulations should be made providing for a fixed term licence with more stringent technical conditions. The Committee considered that the term of the new licence should depend on whether the licensee undertook to provide two-way communication capability on cable.[18] The Committee's recommendations have not, in general, been implemented.

With the development of cable telecommunication systems, the advent of entertainment and interactive services, including the use of cable to receive satellite broadcasts, much of the existing basis for regulation of cable broadcasting may be challenged. The primary basis for regulation of broadcasting to date is that the broadcasting frequency is a limited resource. However, the Cable Systems Committee Report in 1984 noted that the limited resource argument did not apply to cable communication systems: "Cable systems make available a man-made frequency spectrum which when exploited will conserve the natural frequency spectrum, a limited resource, and will provide an orderly electronic highway to business and the home."[19] However, the Restrictive Practices Commission in 1986 concluded that cable television was, in general, a local national monopoly.[20] The Commission did not consider it practical or economically viable to have more than one television cable available to each household.[21] However, the Commission did note that if there were no existing licences and Dublin were being cabled for the first time then, ideally, there should be between two and five independent licence holders, each allocated a sensible geographical area.[22]

Professor Ithiel de Sola Pool has argued in the context of cable telecommunication services that spectrum shortage was no longer a technical problem but a man-made one.[23] However, what was lacking was a legal and economic structure to create incentives to use extant technologies in ways that would provide broadcasting in abundance. Assuming in the future that cable systems become carriers not only for entertainment but also for business, education and security purposes, the issue of the exercise of monopoly power could become increasingly relevant. This very issue worried the Restrictive Practices Commission and is reflected in their 1986 Report into cable television systems in the Greater Dublin area.[24] It had been submitted to the Commission that cable television and broadcasting were developing into two separate media. To allow one company to control both media was to over-concentrate power. The submission argued that society, to be free and democratic, needed a diversity of opinions. The argument was expressed that if control of cable communications systems were exercised by the national broadcasting service (RTE), then there would be a risk that, in the future, there might not be a full diversity of views available in society. The Commission noted that broadcasters in other countries were prohibited from being involved in a cable television company serving the same geographical area.[25] However, the Commission did conclude, subject to certain recommendations being accepted and positive future action,[26] that the objectives of the common good and the interests of the subscribers could be achieved with the then arrangement whereby RTE controlled Cablelink Ltd — the licence holder in 1986 for approximately 95 per cent of the cable systems in the Dublin area serving approximately 193,000 homes.[27] In the context of future interactive services being available via cable systems, the Commission favoured a situation where cable systems would be in direct competition with Telecom Éireann, the national telecommunication-message carrier.[28] In 1990, Eircable Limited, a subsidiary of Telecom Éireann, acquired 60 per cent of the issued share capital of Cablelink Limited. The remaining 40 per cent of the issued share capital is owned by RTE.

An answer to monopoly concerns would be to separate ultimately the cable carrier from the programmers, advertisers and others who wished to transmit via the cable service. In effect, a separation of powers could be brought about between the carrier of the cable system and those supplying the programmes; the cable carrier would thus become similar to a common carrier. In 1973 a US Cabinet Committee on Cable Communications reached this same conclusion. The Committee looked forward to a system in which

> cable would function much like the Postal Service — or more appropriately like the United Parcel Service or a trucking company that for a fee will take anyone's package — or, in the case of cable, anyone's television programming and distribute it to the people who wish to have it. The key point is that the distributors would not be in the business of providing the programming themselves, but would distribute everyone else's programs to viewers that wanted to see them.[29]

In fact, in 1986 the Irish Restrictive Practices Commission recommended that independent programme makers should have access to cable on a reasonable basis. The Commission argued that consideration should be given to the leasing of a channel to a suitable operator.[30] The *Competition Act, 1991* which prohibits anti-competitive agreements and practices and the abuse of a dominant position may also be releveant here.

The powers and duties of cable television carriers are considered in chapter 20.

PART IV

Telecommunication
Privileges, Powers and Duties

We have reached the stage when virtually anything we want to do in the field of communications is possible, the constraints are no longer technical, but economic, legal or political. Thus, if you want to transmit the ENCYCLOPEDIA BRITANNICA around the world in one second, you can do so. But it may be a lot cheaper if you're prepared to wait a whole minute — and you must check with the Britannica's lawyers first.

Arthur C. Clarke, "Beyond the Global Village",
Address on World Telecommunications Day,
United Nations, New York, May 17, 1983

Legislation is static; broadcasting fluid and volatile; broadcasters [are] always impatient of curbs and on occasions ingenious in evading them.

Dr. Conor Cruise O'Brien, *Second Stage of*
Broadcasting Authority (Amendment) Bill, 1975,
79 Seanad Debates, col. 795, March 12, 1975

14

Introduction

The regulation of telecommunication including broadcasting in Ireland highlights fundamental issues. One such issue is the form of statutory control that determines who may enter the tele-communication business or service. This form of control is classically exercised by the creation of a statutory monopoly or some form of privilege. Another issue is the degree of control exercised over those who have been granted such a monopoly or privilege.

By the reign of Elizabeth I, a monopoly essentially embraced the exclusive grant of patents and franchises by the Queen to her servants and courtiers.[1] Such exclusive grants resulted in the raising of prices of necessary commodities. The hardship caused by the high prices in victuals and implements of trade and commerce resulted in the celebrated *Case of Monopolies*[2] which prohibited and declared illegal exclusive grants or franchises. The monopolist not only caused a rise in prices but also restrained trade and manufacturing because of the exclusive nature of his grant. This element of exclusiveness by royal sanction which, in effect, precluded persons from pursuing a livelihood, gave birth to the common law principle that "*prima facie* trade must be free".[3] This concept is implicit in Lord Coke's definition of a monopoly:

> A monopoly is an institution or allowance by the King, by his grant, commission or otherwise, to any person or persons, bodies politic or corporate, of, or for the sole buying, selling, making or using anything; whereby any person or persons, body politic or corporate, are sought to be restrained of any freedom or liberty, they had before or hindered in their lawful trade.[4]

A distinction must be made between a monopoly in the public-utility field which has received legal sanction from the State in the interest of proper management of a scarce resource, or the avoidance of unnecessary duplication of investment and overexpansion with possible resultant injury to the public, and those monopolies created by individual or corporate efforts from "something which was before of common right".[5]

The economists Cournot (1838), Dupuit (1844) and Marshall (1927) suggested that there were some industries and services where a monopoly was likely to form as a matter of course or where competition would be destructive. Such industries or services could be identified by the presence of decreasing costs or increasing returns to scale. John Stuart Mill in 1848 was among the first economists of note to consider the concept of natural monopolies. Mill noted that a great economy of labour would be obtained if, for example, London were supplied by a single gas or water company instead of the then existing plurality.[6] At the turn of the last century, other noted economists developed theories on the concept of natural monopolies.[7] Today, in essential terms, a natural monopoly may be defined as an industry or service in which multi-firm production or provision of services is more costly than production or provision by a single entity.[8] Judge Richard Posner defined natural monopoly in this way: "If the entire demand within a relevant market can be satisfied at lowest cost by one firm rather than two or more, the market is a natural monopoly...."[9] The justification for any "natural monopoly" is that competition cannot effectively work in that sector and that only one provider of the service is appropriate.

It has long been assumed that the provision of basic tele-communication services is a "natural monopoly". In economic terms, in the context of telecommunication services, the explanation is that because economies of scale are so pervasive, one provider of a basic telecommunication service can run the service better than two: basic fixed costs are so high that duplicating services would be uneconomic. Electrical power, for example, can be distributed by means of a tree-like network, but in telephony, in general, an individual pair of wires must be provided and the network is "reconfigured" from call to call. The State telecommunication monopoly is also justified on the basis that the electro-magnetic spectrum, so essential for transmission of radio communications and the broadcasting service, is finite, owned by the State (pursuant to Article 10 of the Constitution) and the allocation of a scarce resource — the frequency spectrum — is best controlled by the State by the creation of a monopoly and associated privileges and regulated by a licensing system. This assumption as to scarce resources is now being challenged to a certain extent in relation to some tele-communication services including the cable television service.

It is also necessary in this context to distinguish between the telecommunication network and certain telecommunication services, for example, value-added or enhanced telecommunication services and customer telecommunication equipment. The latter may not come within the definition of a natural monopoly but may come within the definition of the legal telecommunication monopoly of the Minister for Communications.[10]

Irish law regulating the telecommunications carrier service has made a distinction in the *Postal and Telecommunication Services Act, 1983* between what may be described as certain basic telecommunication services and customer premises equipment. Section 87(1) of the 1983 Act[11] granted Telecom Éireann an exclusive privilege, subject to certain exceptions,[12] of transmitting telecommunication messages up to "a connection point, in the premises of a subscriber" for any telecommunication service. Telecommunication customer-premises equipment, insofar as it lies behind the "connection point", was thus determined to be outside Telecom Éireann's exclusive privilege.

It was not until 1992, prompted by liberalising measures from the European Communities,[13] that Irish law distinguished indirectly between what may be described as "basic" telecommunication services and value-added or enhanced telecommunication services.[14] *The European Communities (Telecommunications Services) Regulations, 1992*, which amended the *Postal and Telecommunications Services Act, 1983*,[15] restricted Telecom Éireann's exclusive privilege to offering, providing and maintaining the public telecommunication network and offering, providing and maintaining voice telephony services.[16] The subsequent licence of the Minister for Communications to persons to provide certain public telecommunication services in competition with Telecom Éireann does not refer to value-added or enhanced services by name, but defines the telecommunication services being liberalised (which are, in essence, value-added services) as public telecommunication services involving the transmitting, receiving, collecting or delivering of telecommunication messages (other than the exceptions to Telecom Éireann's privilege specified in section 87(3) of the *Postal and Telecommunications Services Act, 1983* and certain other exceptions)[17] which

> (a) include facilities which are integral to the [telecommunication] service provided but which are additional to anything necessary for the purpose of conveying a telecommunications message, and which facilities consist of message processing,

conversion, storage, re-direction, replication or other such message handling; and

(b) do not involve the commercial provision to the public of the direct transport and switching of speech in real time between network termination points, nor the conveying of messages by telex, mobile radio-telephony, paging or satellite services.[18]

Value-added telecommunication services include the basic telecommunication transmission facility and an additional service ("value-added"). Examples of value-added services include (a) database or computer bureau services including executive information systems, payroll services, human resource management and legal information services; (b) videotex services; (c) electronic mail — message/voice store and forward and message/voice store and retrieval services; (d) electronic data interchange services; (e) electronic bulletin board services; (f) electronic funds transfer/point-of-sale services; and (g) videoconference services. However, persons providing these value-added services must use the telecommunication links provided by Telecom Éireann within the State and the international links provided by Telecom Éireann or other network operators licensed by the Minister for Communications for any international conveying of telecommunication messages to or from the State.[19]

Certain forms of statutory regulation in relation to telecommunication are prescriptive in nature: statutory and other regulatory provisions specify what the regulated telecommuni- cation service can and must do, e.g., what services they must provide and what prices they may lawfully charge; in essence, their duties and powers are prescribed. The State is the main regulator: the State prescribes by statute and otherwise the criteria which regulate Telecom Éireann, RTE, the Independent Radio and Television Commission and other providers of telecommunication services.[20] Telecom Éireann itself further regulates telecommunication services for its customers; this regulation is achieved by means of delegated legislation in the form of schemes which are statutory instruments.[21] The Independent Radio and Television Commission also has regulatory functions in relation to the private (non-State owned) broadcasting services.[22]

The telecommunication monopoly of the Minister for Communications, together with his powers and duties, will be considered in the next chapter. This will be followed by an examination of the privilege, powers and duties of Telecom Éireann, other providers of telecommunication carrier-related services, RTE, the Independent Radio and Television Commission and other broadcasting service providers.

In the final part of this book, the law relating to the privileges, powers and duties of telecommunication service providers will be reviewed generally.

15

Privileges, Powers and Duties of the Government, the Minister for Communications and the Minister for Arts and Culture

BACKGROUND

The *Ministers and Secretaries Act, 1924*[1] provided that the Department of Posts and Telegraphs would comprise the administration and business generally of public services in connection with posts, telegraphs and telephones together with the powers, duties and functions in connection with these public services and, in particular, the business, powers, duties and functions of the Postmaster-General. The *Postal and Telecommunications Services Act, 1983* provided for the reorganisation of postal and telecommunication services and the constitution of two new companies, An Post and Telecom Éireann, for that purpose. The long title of the 1983 Act stated that the Act was to make provision for the assignment to the new companies of the functions heretofore exercised by the Minister for Posts and Telegraphs. Functions of the Minister for Posts and Telegraphs were assigned by substituting the postal company and the telecommunication company for the Minister for Posts and Telegraphs in earlier legislation which provided for the administration of the postal and telecommunication services.[2]

Vesting day for the two new companies was January 1, 1984.[3] Provision was made in the *Ministers and Secretaries (Amendment) Act, 1983* for the establishment on December 31, 1983 of a Department of Communications and for the transfer of functions of the Minister for

Posts and Telegraphs and of the Minister for Transport to the Minister for Communications: the office of the Minister for Posts and Telegraphs was thereby abolished.[4] In 1993, the functions of the Minister and the Department responsible for telecommunication, with the exception of certain functions relating to broadcasting, were transferred to the Minister for Transport, Energy and Communications and the Department of Transport, Energy and Communications respectively.[5] Certain functions relating to broadcasting were in 1993 assigned by the Government to the Minister for Arts, Culture and the Gaeltacht.[6] [However, as stated in chapter 1, for the purpose of convenience, the expressions "the Minister for Communications" and "the Minister for Arts and Culture" are used throughout this book in place of the current full titles of the relevant Ministers.]

DESCRIPTION OF THE STATE TELECOMMUNICATION MONOPOLY

The statutory basis for the State telecommunication monopoly or, as it is styled, exclusive privilege, is section 4 of the *Telegraph Act, 1869*.[7] That section, as amended,[8] provides as follows:

> The Minister for Communications by himself, or by his deputies, and his and their respective servants and agents, shall have the exclusive privilege of transmitting telegrams; and shall also have the exclusive privilege of performing all the incidental services of receiving, collecting or delivering telegrams, except as provided by section 87(1) of the *Postal and Telecommunications Services Act, 1983*.

The term "telegram" includes any message or other communication sent by a telecommunication system.[9] Communication by means of the telephone together with wireless telegraphy,[10] as well as broadcasting,[11] are included in the legal definition of the term "telegram". Thus, subject to the exception specified in section 4 of the 1869 Act which refers to the exclusive privilege granted to Telecom Éireann, the entire telecommunication monopoly is vested in the Minister for Communications. This includes, in the context of the telecommunication carrier service, all basic and value-added services and all associated telecommunication services like the provision of telecommunication equipment.[12] This exclusive privilege

in the context of broadcasting was exercised directly by the Minister
for Posts and Telegraphs until 1960 when the broadcasting authority
then known as Radio Éireann was established. The *Broadcasting
Authority Act, 1960*[13] specified that the Minister for Posts and
Telegraphs would no longer exercise any of the powers conferred
on him by Part II of the *Wireless Telegraphy Act, 1926*. Part II of the
1926 Act had authorised the Minister to acquire, establish, maintain
and work broadcasting stations. In effect, from 1960, the Minister
was not empowered to acquire, establish, work and maintain any
broadcasting station. However, arguably, the Minister could have
licensed others to broadcast.[14]

The Postmaster-General and his successor, the Minister for Posts
and Telegraphs, retained the full exclusive privilege in relation to
the telecommunication carrier services of telephone, telex and
associated services until 1983. In the *Postal and Telecommunications
Services Act, 1983*,[15] the Minister for Posts and Telegraphs divested
himself of certain carrier-related functions of an exclusive nature in
relation to telecommunication messages which, subject to certain
exceptions,[16] were assigned to Telecom Éireann. The term "telecommunications" is not defined in the 1983 Act, but the exclusive
privilege of which the Minister divested himself only relates to
"telecommunications messages" and then only up to a connection
point in the subscriber's premises. In essence, from 1984 onwards
the Minister was no longer empowered to operate the telecommunication carrier services — the telephone and associated services.
However, the Minister still retains licensing functions in relation to
these telecommunication services. In certain circumstances, the
Minister may grant a licence to a person to provide a telecommunication service which is within[17] or outside[18] the exclusive
privilege granted to Telecom Éireann and has already done so.[19] The
Minister for Communications thus has licensing responsibility for
basic and value-added telecommunication services including
telecommunication equipment in addition to wireless telegraphy
and broadcasting licensing responsibilities. It is understood that the
intention of the Government is that the licensing function of the
Minister will be assigned to an independent public regulatory body.

POWERS AND DUTIES OF MINISTER FOR COMMUNICATIONS IN RELATION TO TELECOM ÉIREANN AND OTHER PROVIDERS OF TELECOMMUNICATION SERVICES

The Minister for Communications has considerable duties and functions in relation to telecommunication services operated by Telecom Éireann. Part VII of the *Postal and Telecommunications Services Act, 1983* is headed "Functions of Minister for Posts and Telegraphs" — now by virtue of the *Ministers and Secretaries (Amendment) Act, 1983*, and the transfer of ministerial functions,[20] the Minister for Communications. Most of the Minister's functions in relation to the telecommunication services operated by Telecom Éireann are not specified in Part VII of the 1983 Act but are contained in the body of the Act and in the memorandum and articles of association of the company. The Minister has also certain functions and powers under the Wireless Telegraphy Acts in relation to wireless telegraphy and under the broadcasting legislation in relation to broadcasting.

Section 110 of the *Postal and Telecommunications Services Act, 1983* provides that the Minister may issue directions to Telecom Éireann to comply with policy decisions of a general kind made by the Government concerning the development of the telecommunication service.[21] The Minister may direct the company to do (or refrain from doing) anything which he may specify from time to time as necessary in the national interest or to enable the Government or State to become a member of an international organisation or a party to an international agreement.[22] The Minister may also direct Telecom Éireann to perform such work or provide or maintain such service for a State authority as may be specified in the direction; the company must comply with any such direction given to it. The Minister may also stipulate, in consultation with Telecom Éireann and with the consent of the Minister for Finance, financial targets to be achieved by Telecom Éireann including payment of dividends in respect of his shares in the company.[23]

The Minister retains licensing functions in relation to the telecommunication carrier services. He may, by order, with the consent of the Minister for Finance, provide for the grant of a licence to any person to provide a telecommunication service of a class or description relating to transmitting, receiving, collecting and delivering of telecommunication messages within the State up to and including a connection point in the premises of a subscriber for any such service.[24] Thus, the Minister is empowered to license a rival entity to Telecom Éireann which could, in law, provide a similar service to that of Telecom Éireann. However, certain conditions must be fulfilled before the Minister can grant such a licence; the Minister must consult with Telecom Éireann;[25] the grant of any such licence must be in the public interest[26] and must be consistent with the reasons specified in section 87(2) of the 1983 Act for the grant of the exclusive privilege to Telecom Éireann.[27] The Minister is also empowered, after consultation with Telecom Éireann, to grant licences to any person to provide international telecommunication services.[28] The Minister for Communications has in fact licensed[29] others to compete directly with Telecom Éireann, i.e., within the scope of Telecom Éireann's exclusive privilege. An Post, the national postal company, has been licensed to provide a public national and international telecommunication mail service.[30] This service essentially relates to the electronic transmission of messages (other than voice messages), e.g., messages in legible form. Providers of value-added telecommunication services have also been licensed to compete with Telecom Éireann.[31] Telecom Éireann itself has been licensed by the Minister to provide international telecommunication services.

The Minister has other functions under the *Postal and Telecommunications Services Act, 1983*. The memorandum and articles of association of Telecom Éireann cannot be altered without the prior approval of the Minister, given with the consent of the Minister for Finance and, where appropriate, the consent of the Minister responsible for the public service.[32] Telecom Éireann requires the consent of the Minister and the Minister for Finance before it divides the shares in its share capital into several classes or attaches thereto any preferential, deferred, qualified or special rights, privileges or conditions.[33] Shares in Telecom Éireann have been issued to the Minister in consideration of the transfer of assets. The 1983 Act provides that the Minister may exercise all the rights and powers of a holder of such shares.[34] The Minister may not transfer or alienate any of his shares in Telecom Éireann.[35] Except where money is borrowed from the Minister for Finance, borrowing by Telecom Éireann requires the consent of the Minister for Communications and the Minister for Finance.[36] The aggregate of temporary borrowing of Telecom Éireann shall not exceed such amount as has been approved by the Minister with the consent of the Minister for Finance.[37] The Minister for Finance, in consultation with the Minister, may guarantee certain borrowings of Telecom Éireann.[38] Accounts of all monies received or expended by Telecom Éireann, including a profit and loss account and a balance sheet, must be in such form as may be approved of by the Minister with the consent of the Minister for Finance.[39] Audited accounts are to be presented to the Minister who shall cause copies thereof to be laid before each House of the Oireachtas.[40]

Telecom Éireann must make an annual report to the Minister. Copies of the report are to be laid before each House of the Oireachtas.[41] The Minister, with the consent of the Minister for Finance, may direct that every annual report shall contain information regarding the cost-effectiveness of the operations of the company.[42] Pursuant to section 33(3) of the 1983 Act, the company must, if so required by the Minister for Communications, furnish information to the Minister on the policy and operations of the company — other than day-to-day operations. The Minister appoints employees to be directors of Telecom Éireann pursuant to section 15 of the *Worker Participation (State Enterprises) Act, 1977* as amended by section 19 of the *Worker Participation (State Enterprises) Act, 1988.*[43]

The Minister may on his own initiative, and must on the application of Telecom Éireann, issue a certificate in respect of specified land or property certifying, as he thinks proper, that the land or property vested in Telecom Éireann or did not so vest.[44] The certificate of the Minister is to be conclusive evidence of the facts certified.[45] The Minister may authorise Telecom Éireann to acquire compulsorily land, easements or other rights over land for the purpose of providing a site for, or approaches to, any building or structure intended to be used by the company.[46] The Minister also has certain functions in relation to the compulsory acquisition procedure, e.g., in the appointment of an arbitrator and publishing prescribed notices.[47]

Other miscellaneous powers of the Minister in relation to Telecom Éireann are specified throughout the *Postal and Telecommunications Services Act, 1983*. Telecom Éireann must submit to the Minister a scheme or schemes for the granting of pensions.[48] The Minister may direct Telecom Éireann to provide certain telecommunication services in the public interest.[49] The Minister may certify that Telecom Éireann took over rights and liabilities from the Minister for Posts and Telegraphs which arose by virtue of contracts or commitments.[50] Telecom Éireann requires the consent of the Minister to grant a licence to any person to provide a telecommunication service within the exclusive privilege granted to the company.[51] Where the company refuses to grant such a licence the applicant has a right of appeal to the Minister.[52] The company may not increase any charge under a scheme relating to its telecommunication services without the concurrence of the Minister.[53] The Minister has power to make regulations in relation to pre-cabling of housing and industrial estates for telecommunication services.[54] The 1983 Act also enables the Minister to make regulations prohibiting the provision or operation of overhearing facilities in relation to apparatus connected to the network of Telecom Éireann.[55]

Certain other functions of the Minister are specified in the memorandum and articles of association of Telecom Éireann. The chairman and other directors of Telecom Éireann are appointed and may be removed by the Minister with the consent of the Minister for Finance.[56] The Minister, with the consent of the Minister for Finance, may determine a greater number of directors than the twelve specified in the articles of association.[57] The chairman and other directors are paid such remuneration, allowances and expenses as the Minister may determine with the approval of the Minister responsible for the public service.[58] The directors must prepare and submit annually to the Minister five year rolling business plans for the company in a form agreed with the Minister with the consent of the Minister for Finance.[59] The Minister may direct the directors of the company to convene an extraordinary general meeting.[60]

The approval of the Minister, given with the consent of the Minister for Finance, is required before the company invests in any other undertaking.[61] The Minister, with the consent of the Minister responsible for the public service, must approve the terms, conditions and remuneration of the chief executive of the company.[62] The directors must have regard to Government policy concerning remuneration and conditions of employment of which the Minister may notify the company from time to time with the consent of the Minister responsible for the public service. The books of account of the company are to be open for inspection of the Minister for Communications or his duly appointed representative.[63] The Minister, with the consent of the Minister for Finance, must approve the appointment of auditors.[64]

WIRELESS TELEGRAPHY FUNCTIONS OF THE
MINISTER FOR COMMUNICATIONS AND THE
MINISTER FOR ARTS AND CULTURE

The expression "wireless telegraphy" covers communications sent by means of electric, magnetic or electro-magnetic energy and thus includes communications sent without the aid of wires, e.g., by radio.[65] In 1993 wireless telegraphy functions were divided between the Minister for Communications and the Minister for Arts and Culture.[66] The Minister for Communications is the principal regulatory authority for wireless telegraphy; the wireless telegraphy functions of the Minister for Arts and Culture relate principally to the management of television licence fee arrangements and related prosecution functions.[67]

The Minister for Communications is empowered to grant licences[68] and prosecute any person who keeps or possesses[69] apparatus for wireless telegraphy without a licence.[70] The Minister may prosecute persons who install, maintain, work or use apparatus otherwise than in accordance with a licence granted under the Act.[71] The 1926 Act also provides for the issue of search warrants relating to apparatus for wireless telegraphy.[72]

An Post, however, has been empowered (a) to issue on behalf of the Minister for Arts and Culture and, on payment of the appropriate fee, licences for television sets;[73] (b) to collect fees for, and sell, television licences and to identity persons in possession of unlicensed or incorrectly licensed sets;[74] and (c) to exercise certain powers under the *Wireless Telegraphy Act, 1972* in so far as the Act relates to the registration of television dealers and the supply of information by the dealers.[75] While so empowered, An Post has been authorised to prosecute persons for possession of television sets without a licence and television dealers who contravene the *Wireless Telegraphy Act, 1972* in relation, for example, to notifying the Minister for Arts and Culture in relation to details of sales and letting of television sets.[76]

The Minister for Arts and Culture may, by order, empower RTE to exercise functions in relation to the granting of licences in respect of wireless telegraphy apparatus for receiving only and in relation to the collection of fees and prosecution functions in relation to these matters.[77] No such order has been made to date.

The Minister for Communications is empowered by order under section 6 of the *Wireless Telegraphy Act, 1926* to make regulations in relation to all licences granted under the *Wireless Telegraphy Acts*. The

Minister for Arts and Culture is empowered to make regulations in relation to television sets.[78] Regulations have been made governing broadcasting receiving licences (television licences),[79] experimenter's licences,[80] business radio and radio link licences,[81] wired broadcast relay licences (cable television),[82] personal radio licences (citizens band radio),[83] and television programme re-transmission licences.[84] Regulations may not be made in relation to fees without the prior consent of the Minister for Finance.[85] The Minister for Communications, the Minister for Arts and Culture and An Post (in relation to television sets) may require any person to furnish information concerning wireless telegraphy apparatus.[86]

Regulations governing licences provide generally that whenever the Minister for Communications is satisfied that the holder of a licence has failed to observe any of the conditions imposed on the licensee, or has done anything in contravention of the wireless telegraphy code, the Minister may suspend or revoke the licence by notice in writing sent to the holder of the licence.[87] Regulations governing licences also provide that the Minister may, by notice published in *Iris Oifigiúil*, revoke in whole or in part all licences.[88]

The Minister may after consultation with the Minister for Enterprise and Employment make regulations in respect of wireless telegraphy on ships and aircraft.[89] No such regulations have been made to date.

The Minister for Communications may make regulations for the purpose of ensuring that the use of certain apparatus does not cause undue interference with wireless telegraphy.[90] The Minister must first publish a draft of any such regulations and have them placed for sale by the Stationery Office and invite representations suggesting variations of the draft regulations which may be made to the Minister.[91] The Minister is empowered to appoint an advisory committee to advise him in relation to the making of the regulations.[92] It is a criminal offence to work or use apparatus that does not comply with the requirements applicable to it under regulations.[93] Where the Minister is of the opinion that the relevant apparatus does not comply with the requirements applicable to it under the regulations, he may serve notice on any person who manufactured or imported the apparatus in the course of business prohibiting the person after the expiration of a stated period from selling the apparatus (otherwise than for export), or offering or advertising it for sale, or letting it on hire or advertising it for such hire.[94] The Minister may similarly prohibit the selling of apparatus for export to countries or territories specified in the relevant regulations or offering or advertising it for sale — where the Minister is of opinion that the apparatus does not comply with the requirements applicable to it under regulations.[95] There is authority to inspect and make tests on such apparatus.[96] The Minister may by order declare that RTE or any other body specified in the order shall have all the powers which the Minister may exercise in relation to the prohibition of persons from selling such apparatus.[97] There is provision for the issue of a search warrant to search for relevant apparatus and to examine and test all such apparatus found in the place named in the warrant.[98]

Regulations have been made under the *Wireless Telegraphy Act, 1926*[99] relating to interference with wireless telegraphy and the radiation of electro-magnetic energy.[100] [RTE has been invested with powers appropriate for the investigation and detection of interference with wireless telegraphy apparatus for receiving only.[101]] The Minister for Communications (and the Minister for Arts and Culture in relation to television sets only) may, by order, require persons who are in possession of any apparatus or equipment capable of radiating, in conditions specified in the order, radio frequency power equal to or greater than an amount specified in the order, to notify the relevant Minister of certain information including descriptive particulars of the apparatus or equipment and the address of the premises at which it has been or is to be installed.[102] The Minister for Communications, with the consent of the Minister for Enterprise and Employment, may, by order, for the purpose of preventing or reducing the risk of interference with wireless telegraphy or for such other purposes as the Minister may specify, prohibit the importation, sale, letting on hire, or manufacture, whether or not for sale of apparatus of a certain class or description.[103] Certain criminal offences have been created in relation to these provisions.[104] Persons may, in certain circumstances, be exempt from the above prohibition by licence.[105] An order was made in 1981 in relation to the control of the sale, letting on hire or manufacture, and importation of certain types of radio transceivers.[106]

The Minister for Communications (and the Minister for Arts and Culture in relation to television sets only) may impose special conditions on licensees under the *Wireless Telegraphy Act, 1926* for the purpose of conserving the radio frequency spectrum or avoiding undue interference with wireless telegraphy apparatus.[107] Failure to comply with such conditions is an offence.[108] The Minister for Arts and Culture has powers under the *Wireless Telegraphy Act, 1972* to obtain certain information as to the sale or hire of television receiving sets.[109] The Minister has, however, empowered An Post to exercise on his behalf the functions conferred on him by the *Wireless Telegraphy Act, 1972* in so far as the Act relates to the registration of television dealers and the supply of information to him by dealers.[110] A person shall not act as a television dealer unless, prior to his so acting, he has given to An Post a notice in the prescribed form containing certain information including specifying where records which he is required to keep under the Act are to be kept and made available for inspection.[111] Registered dealers must make a record of certain particulars relating to the sale and letting of a television set and must give to An Post a notice in a prescribed form containing certain information in relation to the transaction within a specified time.[112]

Challenges to the constitutionality of the *Wireless Telegraphy Acts, 1926 to 1988* are considered later in this chapter in the context of the powers and duties of the Government and Minister for Arts and Culutre relating to broadcasting other than RTE.[113] This is because the challenges to the Wireless Telegraphy Acts arose in the context of unlawful broadcasting.

POWERS AND DUTIES OF THE GOVERNMENT AND
MINISTER FOR ARTS AND CULTURE IN RELATION
TO BROADCASTING BY RTE

Certain functions under the *Broadcasting Authority Acts, 1960 to 1993* in relation to RTE are exercised by the Government. The members of the Authority are appointed by the Government and may be removed from office by the Government for stated reasons if resolutions are passed by both Houses of the Oireachtas calling for such removal.[114] The period of office of a member of the Authority shall be such period, not exceeding five years, as the Government may determine.[115] The Minister for Arts and Culture must lay the terms of appointment and remuneration of the members of the Authority before both Houses of the Oireachtas.[116] The Government appoints the Chairman.[117] The consent of the Minister is necessary before the Authority appoints or removes the Director-General or alters his remuneration or his terms and conditions of office.[118] Superannuation schemes of the Authority must be approved by the Minister with the concurrence of the Minister for Finance.[119] Disputes concerning entitlement to superannuation benefit must be submitted to the Minister who must refer the dispute to the Minister for Finance whose decision is final.[120]

RTE operates its broadcasting transmitters and other apparatus under licence from the Minister for Communications.[121] The licence must be laid before each House of the Oireachtas.[122] The Minister for Arts and Culture controls the total number of broadcasting hours on the television service and sound broadcasting service.[123] The total daily times for broadcasting advertisements, while fixed by the Authority, must have the consent of the Minister.[124]

The consent of the Minister for Arts and Culture is required before the RTE Authority can appoint advisory committees or advisers to the Authority in relation to the performance of its functions.[125] It was proposed in the Heads of the *Broadcasting Bill, 1959* that the Authority should be empowered to appoint advisory committees. Subsequently, the Government decided that the appointments should be made by the Minister. The Department of Posts and Telegraphs strongly urged that the responsibility for such appointments should be transferred back to the Authority.[126] The Department, ever anxious to protect its Minister, argued that if the Minister appointed the committees there would be opportunities for attacks on the Minister about television and broadcasting, arrangements for sports, religion and other such matters for which he would have no actual responsibility. The Department recalled its experiences with the Broadcasting Advisory Committee set up under the *Wireless Telegraphy Act, 1926*: the advice the committee often gave was ignored on the ground of undue expense or otherwise; most of the Committee members felt "they were just wasting their time and many showed this feeling by not attending the meetings".[127] The Department adverted to another danger which had to be considered. It would be "impossible to get a formal committee on such matters as religion or sport". The Department stated that the Catholic Church would not take part in a formal committee on religion and that the Gaelic Athletic Association would not take part in a committee on sport.[128] The 1960 Act empowered the Minister, after consultation with the Authority to appoint advisory committees or advisers.[129] The *Broadcasting Authority (Amendment) Act, 1976* changed that position by empowering the Authority with the consent of the Minister to appoint advisory committees or advisers.[130] The 1960 advice from the Department of Posts and Telegraphs ultimately prevailed.

The Minister for Finance, on the recommendation of the Minister, is empowered to make advances to the Authority for capital purposes.[131] The Minister with the approval of the Minister for Finance, pays to the Authority out of monies provided by the Oireachtas an amount in respect of each financial year equal to the total of the receipts in that year in respect of broadcasting licence fees less collection costs and other expenses.[132]

When the *Broadcasting Authority Bill, 1959* was being drafted, the Minister for Finance made it abundantly clear to his Government colleagues that he reserved the right to suggest at a future stage that a proportion of the licence fees should be retained to meet the general purposes of the Exchequer. The Minister for Finance was of the view that outlay on radio and television was "a form of sumptuary expenditure" which should be liable to be taxed to assist the ordinary revenue of the State as was the case with motoring. The Minister for Finance considered it essential that the State's right to impose such taxation should be asserted and that neither the public nor the members of the Broadcasting Authority should be left under the impression that the Authority would always be given the full licence fees to spend as it pleased.[133] The broadcasting licence fee has not been used to date as a form of general taxation to augment the ordinary revenue of the State. The issue of the distribution of the licence fee arose in the context of the *Broadcasting Act, 1990*, when the Minister for Communications proposed to allot a share of the licence fee to the independent broadcasting service providers. The vehemence of the opposition to this proposal forced the Minister to abandon his scheme.

The Minister for Arts and Culture is vested with considerable powers over what may be termed RTE management matters. For example, the Minister in consultation with the Minister for Finance must approve the form of accounts of the RTE Authority.[134] The Authority requires the consent of the Minister before it borrows money.[135] The Minister may from time to time seek information regarding the performance of the Authority's functions.[136]

The Minister's power to give directions[137] to RTE are considered in chapter 16 "Censorship of the Broadcasting Media in Ireland including Section 31 of the Broadcasting Authority Act, 1960" and in chapter 26, "Freedom of Expression". The Minister's functions in relation to the Broadcasting Complaints Commission are examined in chapter 22.

POWERS AND DUTIES OF THE GOVERNMENT, THE MINISTER FOR COMMUNICATIONS AND THE MINISTER FOR ARTS AND CULTURE RELATING TO PRIVATE (NON-STATE OWNED) BROADCASTING SERVICES

RTE and the private broadcasting services in Ireland are (in general) regulated by separate statutory codes. RTE is regulated pursuant to the *Broadcasting Authority Acts, 1960 to 1993* and the *Broadcasting Act, 1990*. The private non-State-owned broadcasting services are regulated pursuant to the *Radio and Television Act, 1988*. The powers of the Minister for Arts and Culture in relation to these private broadcasting services will be considered here. Unlicensed broadcasting which is governed by the *Broadcasting (Offences) Acts 1968 and 1988* and the *Wireless Telegraphy Acts, 1926 to 1988* will also be considered briefly.

The Government appoints the chairman[138] and members of the Independent Radio and Television Commission which regulates the private broadcasting services[139] and may remove from office a member of the Commission for stated reasons if resolutions are passed by both Houses of the Oireachtas calling for his removal.[140] The Minister for Arts and Culture exercises considerable powers of an administrative and management nature over the Commission[141] similar to those powers (specified in the foregoing section) over RTE.

The Minister for Arts and Culture exercises considerable powers over the actual core functions of the Independent Radio and Television Commission. However, under the *Radio and Television Act, 1988*, the frequency management function of issuing broadcasting licences remains with the Minister for Communications while the Commission actually selects and regulates persons to provide broadcasting services.

The régime of the Independent Radio and Television Commission may be considered briefly. The Commission on its own initiative invites "expressions of interest" in the sound broadcasting services.[142] In relation to the television programme service, it is the Minister for Arts and Culture who takes the initiative and directs the Commission to invite applications.[143] The Commission makes a report of its findings to the Minister for Communications who, in consultation with the Commission, specifies the geographical areas in relation to which applications for sound broadcasting contracts are to be invited and the Commission must comply with the Minister's direction.[144] In the context of the television programme service, the applications relate to a television distribution system which uses channel capacity on wired broadcast relay systems and television programme re-transmission systems (MMDS) licensed under section 6 of the *Wireless Telegraphy Act, 1926* supplemented by a conventional terrestrial UHF transmission.[145] Taking into consideration the Commission's report and the availability of radio frequencies for sound broadcasting, the Minister for Communications may limit the number of areas which he may specify in relation to which applications for sound broadcasting contracts are to be invited.[146] The Commission then proceeds to invite applications for the provision of a sound broadcasting service in each area specified by the Minister or in relation to the single television programme service and then enters into appropriate contracts.[147] The Minister for Communications then issues a licence to the Commission under section 4(3) of the 1988 Act in respect of the sound broadcasting transmitter to which the contract relates and appropriate apparatus of the television programme service contractor.

Pursuant to section 4(5) of the 1988 Act, the benefits of the licence of the Minister for Communications to the Commission are conveyed to the sound broadcasting contractor through his contract with the Commission. Any broadcasting transmitter which is established, maintained and operated in accordance with the Commission's contract will, pursuant to section 4(5) of the 1988 Act, be deemed to be licensed for the purposes of the *Wireless Telegraphy Acts, 1926 to 1988*. Any member of the public may, by virtue of section 4(6) of the 1988 Act, inspect every licence issued by the Minister to the Commission.

Under section 7 of the 1988 Act, the Minister for Communications is empowered to vary any term or condition of a licence in relation to a sound broadcasting transmitter. Pursuant to section 7(2) of the Act, the Minister may so act in the interests of good radio frequency management;[148] for the purpose of giving effect to an international telecommunication agreement to which the State is a party and which has been ratified by the State;[149] in the public interest;[150] for the safety or security of persons or property;[151] on a request from the Commission after consultation with any affected sound broadcasting contractor;[152] or on request from the Commission on behalf of a sound broadcasting contractor.[153] The natural justice requirements of the Constitution are reflected in the procedure which the Minister must adopt when proposing to vary any term or condition of a licence; these provisions are set out in section 7(3) of the 1988 Act and include notice in writing of the Minister's intention and the opportunity of the affected party to make representations. The requirements of due process specified above do not relate to a variation of a term or condition of a licence necessitated in the interests of safety or security of persons or property.[154]

Dr. Colum Kenny and others have argued that the Minister for Arts and Culture ought to have been obliged by statute to publish details of the applicants for licences. However, the Commission has held public hearings before awarding licences and this has facilitated public trust in the licensing process. Public access to the licensing records of the Minister for Communications pursuant to section 4(6) of the 1988 Act in relation to the broadcasting service is also an innovative feature in the telecommunication licensing regime.

Section 16 of the 1988 Act empowers the Minister for Arts and Culture, at the request of the Commission and after consultation with RTE, to require RTE to co-operate with sound broadcasting contractors and the television programme service contractor in the use of any mast, tower, site or other installation. This provision was justified on the basis that RTE owns sites, masts and other facilities which have been developed since the inception of broadcasting in the State in 1926 and that these facilities are used within the framework of international frequency agreements. It was argued that use of the allocated frequencies by the broadcasting contractors may necessitate the use of the physical facilities owned by RTE for transmission purposes.[155] There is provision in section 16(2) of the 1988 Act for payment by the broadcasting contractors to RTE as the Minister may direct. The Minister for Communications when introducing this measure considered that the role here of the relevant Minister would be that of an arbiter but he argued correctly that the Minister could appoint and take advice from a professional arbiter.[156]

Unlicensed Broadcasting

Unlicensed broadcasting in Ireland is governed by the *Broadcasting (Offences) Acts, 1968 to 1988* and provisions of the *Wireless Telegraphy Acts, 1926 to 1988*, and comes within the responsibilities of the Minister for Communications.

Essentially, the *Broadcasting (Offences) Act, 1968* prohibited the establishment or operation of broadcasting stations on board ships, aircraft and marine structures. The *Broadcasting and Wireless Telegraphy Act, 1988*[157] in conjunction with the *Wireless Telegraphy Acts 1926 to 1972*, inter alia, make unlawful the broadcasting from any premises or vehicle in the State unless made pursuant to and in accordance with a licence issued by the Minister for Communications.[158] The facilitating of unlawful broadcasting is also illegal.[159]

The constitutionality of the "search and seize" provisions of section 8 of the *Wireless Telegraphy Act, 1926* in relation to unlicensed wireless telegraphy apparatus was unsuccessfully challenged in *Walsh and Others trading as Cork Broadcasting Company v Ireland and Attorney General* (1978).[160] Hamilton J, in *Walsh*, in the era of the flourishing of unlicensed broadcasting stations (the pirate radio stations), dismissed an application for a mandatory injunction directing the Minister for Posts and Telegraphs to hand over broadcasting apparatus which had been seized pursuant to a search warrant under the *Wireless Telegraphy Act, 1926* pending a criminal prosecution. The plaintiffs in their plenary summons sought a declaration that those provisions of the *Wireless Telegraphy Act, 1926* that provide for the seizure of wireless telegraphy apparatus were unconstitutional. Refusing relief, Hamilton J stated that before establishing an unlicensed broadcasting service, the plaintiffs had done nothing to challenge the constitutionality of the 1926 Act. He considered that it was not a proper case to grant any relief at the interlocutory stage. The plaintiffs did not proceed with their case.[161]

The constitutionality of the *Wireless Telegraphy Act, 1926* was again unsuccessfully challenged in *Nova Media Services v Minister for Posts and Telegraphs* (1983)[162] and *Sunshine Radio Ltd v Ireland* (1983).[163] In *Nova*, officials of the Department of Posts and Telegraphs, pursuant to a warrant under section 8 of the 1926 Act, had searched the plaintiffs' premises and seized unlicensed apparatus for wireless telegraphy (broadcasting apparatus) found on the premises. The plaintiffs issued proceedings claiming the relevant provisions of the Act to be inconsistent with the Constitution and in violation of the EC Treaty. They then applied to the High Court for interlocutory relief restraining the defendants from interfering with their ability to broadcast and seeking the return of their equipment pending trial of the full action. The plaintiffs contended that: (i) the defendant Minister had abused his power under the Act to the extent of creating a broadcasting monopoly in favour of the State broadcasting station; (ii) the Act was in violation of Articles 38, (trial of offences) 40.6.1.i (freedom of expression) and 45 (directive principles of social policy) of the Constitution; and (iii) they would suffer irreparable loss to their business if the interlocutory relief they sought was refused.

Murphy J in the High Court refused the applications. He held that the evidence had not established that the Minister had abused his regulatory power under the Act. Further, the High Court held that although the plaintiffs' constitutional claims constituted a stateable case involving difficult questions of law calling for detailed consideration, the balance of convenience lay in favour of the defendants. Murphy J also held that while the defendants might not suffer financial loss if the plaintiffs were successful in their applications, it would only be in extraordinary cases that the courts would restrain a Minister from performing a duty laid on him by legislation passed for the common good. The implicit representations over a number of years that the plaintiffs' activities would be regularised did not amount to such an extraordinary case.[164]

Another challenge to the regulatory scheme governing unlicensed broadcasting came in the form of a challenge to section 7 of the *Broadcasting and Wireless Telegraphy Act, 1988*. Section 7 of the 1988 Act enables the Minister for Communications, if of opinion that an illegal broadcast is emanating from any premises or vehicle, to serve a notice on Telecom Éireann and the Electricity Supply Board requiring that neither entity shall, for the duration of such notice, offer to provide or maintain, to a connection point in the premises specified in the notice, telecommunication or electricity service, as the case might be. In *Cooke v Minister for Communications* (1989),[165] the Supreme Court affirmed the refusal of the High Court[166] to grant an interlocutory injunction restraining the compliance by the Electricity Supply Board and Telecom Éireann with notices issued by the Minister for Communications pursuant to section 7 of the Act. The applicant had challenged the compatibility of the said section 7 with the Constitution of Ireland and with the EEC Treaty. Although the Supreme Court refused to restrain (by injunction) at the interlocutory stage preventive measures authorised by the 1988 Act, the Court acknowledged that the matter raised a constitutional issue of great importance.

16

Censorship of the Broadcasting Media Including Section 31 of the Broadcasting Authority Act, 1960

INTRODUCTION

Before considering the existing law on censorship of the broadcasting media in Ireland,[1] it is appropriate to review previous forms of regulation governing censorship of the mass media in Ireland. Such a review will place the "section 31" form of censorship in context.

Censorship of expression has been an integral part of the regulation of the broadcasting service in Ireland since the inception of Radio Éireann in 1926. Censorship of expression on the broadcasting service was effected by the issuing of instructions by the Cabinet and the Minister for Posts and Telegraphs. There was no specific legislation governing censorship of expression on the broadcasting service until the enactment of section 31 of the *Broadcasting Authority Act, 1960*. Replying to a query from the Secretary of State for Dominion Affairs in London, the Governor General, T.M. Healy, stated in January 1927 that his Ministers desired him to state that they had forbidden the broadcasting in the Irish Free State "of any controversial matter particularly matters of a political or theological character".[2] The Governor General also stated that the Broadcasting Station Director had the responsibility of ensuring that no objectionable matter was allowed to be broadcast. All matter to be broadcast whether talks, lectures, songs or recitations had first to be submitted to and passed by the Station Director. No matter could be broadcast by any person that had not previously been approved. The Governor General concluded by stating that the arrangement had worked well in practice and that no difficulty had been experienced in regard "to the modification of matter considered to be controversial or undesirable".[3]

Censorship of expression on the broadcasting service up to the enactment of the *Broadcasting Authority Act, 1960* was not confined to State authorities. Dr. John Charles McQuaid, Archbishop of Dublin, wrote in his own hand a personal letter to the Minister for Posts and Telegraphs, Patrick Little, in November 1941 requesting the Minister's "kind cooperation in a system of censorship of religious addresses".[4] The Archbishop added that the existing scheme which provided for leave to broadcast "in relation to religious matter" had proved useful both to the Ministry and "to Archbishop's House". The Archbishop suggested that when leave had been obtained, the regulation would require that the manuscript be first submitted to the Vicar-General in charge of ecclesiastical censorship and only then accepted by the Ministry. The Archbishop concluded that such a procedure would ensure the prudent handling of all questions in addresses that purport "to give a Catholic viewpoint".[5] The Archbishop also requested that the regulation would apply to "all persons" if they purported to give the Catholic viewpoint in a broadcast, and that the Archbishop's authority must first be obtained by a charity before the then current "five-minute" appeal could be booked for broadcasting.[6] The Minister agreed.[7]

The ecclesiastical and civil systems of censorship of broadcast expression sometimes ran into difficulties. The Primate of All Ireland, Dr. D'Alton, refused to supply a script for his sermon on the occasion of the consecration of Cavan Cathedral in September 1947. The Minister for Posts and Telegraphs took the matter up directly with the Archbishop.[8] Dr. Patrick Lyons, Bishop of Kilmore, followed suit in relation to a proposed sermon at a Solemn High Mass to be broadcast from St. Patrick's, Dundalk on Sunday, September 28, 1947. Minister Little, writing to Dr. Lyons stated that there was a standing instruction that nothing was to be broadcast unless the text had been obtained beforehand:

> In view of the wide influence of broadcasting on the public mind and having regard to the grave responsibility of the authorities, both in the international as well as in the home sphere, for the proper use of the medium, Your Lordship will appreciate the necessity of applying the rule even to persons in high positions.[9]

The Minister concluded by stating that "we would not dare to interfere with any statement of a theological nature".[10]

Dr. Lyons persisted in his refusal to give the script of his sermon in advance. He stated that his objection was based on a principle derived from the highest of all sources, referring to St. Paul's words on bishops.[11] On the issue of censorship, the Bishop wrote:

> This is exactly where the shoe pinches. Bishops object to having their sermons censored, even in other countries where the Church is being persecuted. It ought not to be necessary in Catholic Éire.[12]

The Minister suggested an interview. Dr. Lyons travelled to the General Post Office, Dublin on September 24, 1947 four days before the proposed broadcast. The Minister read "the substance" of the Bishop's proposed sermon and regarded this on that occasion "as meeting requirements". The sermon was to last twenty-two minutes.[13]

Another form of censorship of the broadcasting service was documented by Maurice Gorham, Director of Broadcasting at Radio Éireann, in a memorandum to the Secretary of the Department of Posts and Telegraphs in January 1955.[14] The Minister for Finance, Gerard Sweetman, personally telephoned Radio Éireann to say that he was making an important speech, at short notice, on a bank dispute and that he would like his speech to be well reported on the 6.30 news programme that evening and that nothing else about the bank dispute was to be mentioned in that programme. Maurice Gorham rightly considered that it was most undesirable for a Minister to make a direct request for the exclusion of items from the news. Allegations in relation to this form of censorship were also made against Charles Haughey, as Minister for Agriculture, in 1966 (during a period of farmers' unrest). This led to the statement of the Taoiseach, Seán Lemass, in the Dáil about RTE being "an instrument of public policy".[15]

Censorship of expression in the Irish State in the interest of State security goes back to the foundation of the State when a military censorship of publications was operated for a period during the civil war of 1922-23.[16] Subsequently, the *Public Safety Act, 1927*, which was passed following the murder of the Minister for Justice, Kevin O'Higgins, gave the Minister for Justice extensive powers in relation to publications connected with illegal organisations. The 1927 Act was repealed at the end of 1928. The emergence of political violence in 1931 led to the enactment of the *Constitution (Amendment No. 17) Act, 1931* which made unlawful certain activities in relation to publications issued or published on behalf of an unlawful organisation.[17]

Following the declaration of the 1939 national emergency, the Government enacted the *Emergency Powers Act, 1939* which gave the Government extensive powers of censorship. As the national broadcasting service, Radio Éireann, was under the direct control of the Minister for Posts and Telegraphs, it was administratively possible to implement a rigorous form of censorship (at any time) without any special legislative measures.

Pursuant to the 1939 Act, the *Emergency Powers (No. 5) Order, 1939* empowered, *inter alia*, an authorised person to give directions to the proprietor of a newspaper "prohibiting such proprietor from publishing either permanently or during a specified period, in such newspaper or in any poster or placard in connection with such newspaper any specified matter or any particular class or classes of matter" — words which are somewhat similar to the words of section 31 of the *Broadcasting Authority Act, 1960*.

Prompted by the fact that statements by certain members of the Oireachtas had been censored and that action which had been taken against *The Irish Times* for ignoring the Press Censor's orders would lead to a Dáil Debate on censorship, the Minister for Co-ordination of Defensive Measures circulated in January 1940 a paper for the information of members of the Government entitled "Neutrality, Censorship and Democracy".[18] That paper represents an apologia for censorship, particularly in relation to public statements arguing against the State's neutrality, public statements supporting or attacking the belligerents in the war and statements which might cause offence to Governments of friendly states. However, it articulated issues which are relevant today to the legal and policy issues regulating censorship of the mass media including broadcasting. The paper considered the arguments that would be presented by certain members of the Dáil against censorship: Ireland is a democratic country; censorship is neither democratic nor necessary; according to international law people in a neutral state can think and say what they please about belligerents and "if democracy is to survive they must be allowed to do so"; and it is not only a gross violation of the personal rights guaranteed in Article 40 of the Constitution to prevent citizens and particularly representatives of the people and newspapers from expressing their opinions, but dangerous from the perspective that this power might

be used by the executive to suppress the organisation of public
opinion which articulates the safeguarding of vital interests of the
nation. Acknowledging that there would be some who would say
that individual citizens and public representatives should be
allowed the freedom to talk offensively about the belligerents and
advocate the declaration of war on one or other of them, the paper
firmly advocated that such persons should not be permitted to
articulate such views:

> Freedom of this kind might have had certain usefulness in other
> countries in olden times in providing an outlet for a certain type
> of people who like blowing off steam, but in our country and
> in our circumstances it would be positively dangerous. If we
> were a nation of Dillons, words would only lead to words. But
> we are not. And if a competition . . . were allowed to start
> between gentlemen who would confine themselves to words,
> they would very quickly get supporters who would wish to use
> stronger arguments, and it might very well be that we would
> have a civil war to decide the question as to which of the
> European belligerents we should declare war upon.[19]

Not all members of the Government were in favour of a repressive
régime of media censorship and the Minister for Industry and
Commerce, Seán MacEntee, in February 1940 circulated each
member of the Government with a memorandum which contained
a passage from a speech made in the House of Lords by the
Parliamentary Under-Secretary of State for the Colonies, the
Marquess of Dufferin and Ava, in opposition to a motion that
"careful censorship of news-film in wartime" was necessary.[20] In the
memorandum MacEntee did not emphatically state his own views
on the issue of censorship but lest any member of the Government
was in any doubt about where he stood on the issue, he underlined
in toto the following extract from the House of Lords speech:

> I do believe that if every time an abuse of freedom is committed,
> we allow that to be an opportunity for further Government
> control, further censorship, further denial of liberty, then I do
> believe that you are going to erode in a very few years perhaps
> the whole rock of personal liberty. . . . It is easy to take little
> examples, little slips, and say, "Therefore we will step in,
> therefore we will control." Once you start doing that, I firmly
> believe you are on a slippery slope indeed. I believe there is

nothing more worth fighting for, either in the field or in politics, than the personal liberty of the public, liberty of expression and freedom.[21]

By 1941 all press telegrams were censored and letters were subject to censorship but some journalists, particularly visiting American and English journalists, often escaped the censorship net by using the "unrestricted telephone" service between Ireland and Britain. The Controller of Censorship in a memorandum for the Government on January 25, 1941 drew the attention of the Government to "the most alarming and irresponsible stories" that had been sent across the Irish sea by telephone.[22] One of these alarming stories which had been "traced to its source" related to a visiting representative of the Associated Press who telephoned the London office of his paper from Dublin "to the effect that German planes ... were bombing the city at the time he was speaking and that the German Minister had been given his passport". The London office relayed the news to New York where it was broadcast on one of the American radio systems.[23] In those circumstances, the Controller of Censorship had little difficulty in persuading the Government to make it a criminal offence to send a press message out of the country without submitting it for censorship. However, the subsequent *Emergency Powers (No. 67) Order, 1941* in fact prohibited any person in the State from sending "by post, telegraph, telephone or any other means whatsoever" to any person outside the State, any communication relating, inter alia, to an event connected with the war or the supply of commodities in the State.[24]

This 1941 prohibition was repealed in 1942 and replaced by a more wide-ranging power which was, however, confined to journalists. Article 9(1) of the 1942 Order prohibited any journalist from sending, by any means whatsoever, to any newspaper or press agency outside the State any communication in relation to any matter, other than exempted communications which related exclusively to sporting and social events and matters declared by an order to be exempted matter, unless approved by an authorised person.[25] The Office of the Controller of Censorship considered that if any section of the press set out to make the existing processes of censorship impossible, resort would have to be made to prohibit altogether, or for a definitive period, the publication of any specified newspaper which published matter in contravention of censorship regulations and to direct the seizure of printing and other related machines of such a newspaper.[26] Fortunately, with the end of the war, that form of rigorous public censorship of the mass media was brought to an end with effect from May 11, 1945.[27]

The *Offences Against the State Act, 1939* could be used as a form of regulation in relation to processes of telecommunication. Section 10(1) of the 1939 Act provides that it shall not be lawful, inter alia, to publish or distribute any document[28] which is or contains or includes an incriminating document,[29] or a treasonable document[30] or a seditious document.[31] The word "document" is very widely defined in the 1939 Act to include the usual textual attributes as well as devices for recording sound and visual images associated with the processes of broadcasting. A "seditious document", for example, under the *Offences Against the State Act, 1939* includes a document containing matter calculated to undermine the public order or the authority of the State.

The *Official Secrets Act, 1963* is also a potent regulatory instrument which could be used as a form of censorship. The 1963 Act inhibits freedom of expression in broadcasting and in the printed media although one must state that prosecutions under the Act are very rare indeed. Section 4 of the 1963 Act prohibits the communication of official information without authority. Section 9(1) of the 1963 Act prohibits any person, in any manner prejudicial to the safety or preservation of the State to obtain, record, communicate to any other person or publish, or have in his possession or control, any document or other record with information relating, inter alia, to security matters and any other matter whatsoever, information as to which would or might be prejudicial to the safety or preservation of the State.

Accordingly, there is in force legislation which, inter alia, prohibits the broadcasting of matter calculated to undermine the public order or the authority of the State. In fact, in addition to the provisions of the *Offences Against the State Act, 1939*, there is a specific statutory prohibition on the RTE Authority from including in its broadcasts anything which "may reasonably be regarded as being likely to promote, or incite to, crime or as tending to undermine the authority of the State".[32] A similar duty is imposed on the private commercial broadcasting services pursuant to section 9(1)(d) of the *Radio and Television Act, 1988*. The *Wireless Telegraphy Act, 1926* prohibits the sending by wireless telegraphy (which includes the process of broadcasting) any message or communication subversive of public order.[33] The issue therefore arises whether the specific prohibitions on freedom of speech contained in section 31 of the *Broadcasting Authority Act, 1960* were necessary.

SECTION 31 OF THE BROADCASTING AUTHORITY ACT, 1960

The Minister for Arts and Culture is empowered by statute to direct the RTE Authority and all other broadcasting services to refrain from broadcasting certain matter: section 31(1) of the *Broadcasting Authority Act, 1960*, as amended by section 16 of the *Broadcasting Authority (Amendment) Act, 1976*, provides the Minister with this enabling power. Section 31(1) of the 1960 Act, as amended, provides as follows:

> (1) Where the Minister [for Arts and Culture] is of the opinion that the broadcasting of a particular matter or any matter of a particular class would be likely to promote, or incite to, crime or would tend to undermine the authority of the State, he may by order direct the Authority to refrain from broadcasting the matter or any matter of the particular class, and the Authority shall comply with the order.

An order made by the Minister remains in force for a period not exceeding twelve months; this period may be extended for a period not exceeding twelve months by an order made by the Minister or by a resolution passed by both Houses of the Oireachtas.[34] Every order must be laid before each House of the Oireachtas and may be annulled by resolution of either House.[35]

The original section 31(1) of the *Broadcasting Authority Act, 1960* provided that the Minister "may direct the Authority in writing from broadcasting any particular matter or matter of any particular class". The Government's approach to the issue was articulated in the debate in the Dáil by the Minister for Posts and Telegraphs, Michael Hilliard:

> [T]he main intent is to give me and the Government an over-riding authority to veto programmes in certain circumstances in the public interest. The Government have an ultimate responsibility in this regard for a national broadcasting service and I think that the Government cannot get away from that responsibility.[36]

The Minister for Posts and Telegraphs argued at the second stage of the Bill in the Dáil that section 31(1) was not intended to provide the Minister with a general power of censorship.[37] The Minister argued that as the broadcasting service would be a national one, "there must be reserved to the Government some means of ultimate control over broadcasts which might be inimical to the national interest".[38] The Minister justified the power to issue a directive by stating that a situation could arise whereby the Authority may not be in a position to possess information that would be at the disposal of the Government in relation to the implications that a broadcast may have in respect of the State's relationship with other countries or in relation to a crisis within the State.[39]

The philosophy of the Department of Posts and Telegraphs on the power of veto expressed in section 31(1) of the 1960 Act may be gleaned from briefing notes prepared for the Minister at appropriate stages of the Bill.[40] The Department correctly noted that there was likely to be criticism of the section in general and in detail. The Department argued that the principle of a Government veto was accepted in legislation or regulations governing other broadcasting organisations which were generally recognised as providing models of independence as regards programming. In this regard, reference was made to the BBC. The briefing notes added that the Department could have attempted to do as many other countries had tried to do "and filled a few extra sections with clauses to the effect that the Authority may not broadcast what is indecent, obscene, subversive of public order or likely to injure our relations with other countries and so on".[41] The Department considered that no purpose would be served in solemnly admonishing a responsible public authority in such a manner. A more substantive reason was also specified by the Department. Such provisions could not be exhaustive in the sense of covering every kind of "delicate situation" likely to arise in which the broadcasting of a certain programme or programmes would be "embarrassing to the Government and damaging to the national interest".[42] In the Seanad, Senator Dr. Sheehy Skeffington argued that section 31(1) was "unnecessary and potentially dangerous" as it gave the Minister a complete veto over every item and every class of item and gave the Minister the power to exercise that veto completely and without reference to the Authority.[43] Senator Patrick Donegan argued that the Minister was vesting himself with a dictatorial power, not only by his ability to issue a directive but by the mere fact that he had the power to issue a directive.[44] Senator Donegan did argue, however, that some Ministerial power was necessary lest for example, "we might have Sinn Féin trouble," but argued that the power expressed in section 31(1) was excessive.[45]

Section 31(2) of the *Broadcasting Authority Act, 1960* provides that the Minister for Communications may direct the Authority in writing to allocate broadcasting time for any announcement by or on behalf of any Minister of the Government in connection with the functions of that Minister of the Government, and the Authority shall comply with the direction. This issue is also considered in chapter 26 "Freedom of Expression". In the original Bill, as published, there was an additional subsection, section 31(3) which provided that the Authority may, subject to the consent of the Minister, announce that a direction had been granted under this section. In effect this would have permitted the Minister to operate a form of censorship in a secret manner. In fact, the Government requested the Minister for Posts and Telegraphs to consider an amendment to the then proposed subsection 31(3) to the effect that the Authority could not, without the consent of the Minister, announce that a direction had been given under that section.[46] The Minister for Posts and Telegraphs, Michael Hilliard, in a letter to the Taoiseach, Seán Lemass, correctly stated that the proposed amendment would put the provision in a harsher form without changing its meaning or effect.[47] Lemass replied firmly to the Minister on the day he received the Minister's letter:

> It is not the intention to allow the Broadcasting Authority to be independent of the Government in respect of official announcements. In this matter the legislation must provide without ambiguity that the Authority must do what the Government tells it to do.[48]

Subsequently, influenced by the fact that the then BBC Charter gave full discretion to the BBC in the context of making such announcements in relation to any direction from the Postmaster-General, section 31(3) of the Bill was deleted.

The original section 31 of the 1960 Act, in effect, gave the Minister a general power of censorship which was not confined to matters relating to incitement of crime or the undermining of the authority of the State. In a speech delivered in 1961, the Minister for Posts and Telegraphs stated that no Irish broadcasting service could be regarded as acceptable which did not maintain proper moral standards.[49] He stated that the Government and the Oireachtas took the view that no Irish public body would countenance the presentation of morally objectionable material and for that reason no provision for censorship was written into the *Broadcasting Authority Act, 1960*. Given the power of the Minister for Posts and

Telegraphs under the original section 31(1) of the 1960 Act, it is difficult to understand the Minister's justification for stating that no provision for censorship was written into the 1960 Act.

In oral argument in the High Court in *State (Lynch) v Cooney*,[50] where, *inter alia*, the constitutionality of the amended section 31 was successful in the High Court, but not on appeal to the Supreme Court, O'Hanlon J enquired from counsel for the Minister and the Attorney General whether section 31 in its original form would have been unconstitutional. Niall McCarthy, S.C. (as he then was), replied for the respondents that the original section had contained a very wide power indeed and he would not have felt comfortable in defending it in relation to Article 40.6.1.i of the Constitution.[51] O'Hanlon J took this issue up in his judgment:

> Initially s. 31 of the Act of 1960 gave to the Minister in absolute terms an overriding power to direct the Authority to exclude from being broadcast such matters as the Minister thought fit. At first sight that absolute power seems to be out of harmony with the constitutional guarantees of freedom of expression and with the very limited qualifications to which the exercise of this right may be subjected; perhaps it was a realisation of this difficulty of reconciliation which inspired the enactment of the amending provisions of 1976.[52]

THE EARLY WRITTEN DIRECTIVES TO RTE

Early in 1960, the Taoiseach, Seán Lemass, considered that policy directives of "a very general character" should be given to the new Broadcasting Authority. The directives

> would convey the views of the Government on how particular problems likely to arise should be dealt with, and would imply that the persistent ignoring of these views would probably involve corrective action by the Government.[53]

The Taoiseach personally listed the subjects which the policy directives should include:

> 1. The "image" of Ireland and of the Irish to be presented, including the avoidance of stage-Irishisms, playboyisms, etc. The "image" should be of a vigorous progressive nation, seeking efficiency.

2. The handling of social problems, either general or local. The desirable course would be to encourage objective presentation of facts and constructive comment. The "God-help-us" approach should be ruled out.
3. The presentation of features and comments on events abroad involving criticism of the policies of other Governments. The attitude to events in Iron-Curtain countries would require particular definition.
4. The coverage of events in Northern Ireland, with particular reference to criticism of the Northern Ireland administration, and the encouragement of anti-Partition sentiment.
5. The presentation of plays and features which emphasise sex.
6. The policy to be followed in covering sporting events, and the prominence to be given to national games.
7. The utilisation of the service for religious instruction, and the facilities to be given to non-Catholic Churches.
8. The utilisation of the service for instruction in scientific subjects, and the subjects which are suitable for such instruction.[54]

The Secretary of the Government, M. Ó Muimhneacháin, "respectfully" submitted to the Taoiseach that the "*need*" for any "general policy directives" was open to question (emphasis in original). The Secretary referred to appropriate sections of the legislation including the general duty of the Authority in respect of the national aims of restoring the Irish language and of preserving and developing the national culture[55] and in particular section 31 which empowered the Minister for Posts and Telegraphs to issue directions to the Authority.[56] However, the Secretary reassured the Taoiseach that apart from the statutory provisions he had quoted, the Government would have the last word on policy at all times, since the members of the Authority would be appointed by the Government;[57] the Government was empowered to remove at any time a member from office[58] and would have the function of appointing the chairman.[59] The Secretary to the Government, with acute perception, also doubted the advisability of the Taoiseach giving such directives and emphasised the word "advisability" by underlining it. The Secretary argued that the giving of such directives could be represented both at home and abroad as an illiberal action calculated to hamper unduly the freedom of the Broadcasting Authority and reflecting an attitude of distrust on the part of the Government towards a body which was appointed by it.

With an eye on the Constitution, the Secretary in the language of polite but vigorous disagreement stated that it might even be suggested that the giving of such directives would be out of harmony with the spirit of Article 40.6.1.i of the Constitution, which (subject to general safeguards) guarantees liberty of expression for organs of public opinion including the radio.

Lemass replied to the Secretary of the Government on the following day, April 5, 1960. The Taoiseach stated that he considered it only fair and proper that the Director and members of the Broadcasting Authority should be informed of the Government's views as to how "certain difficult aspects of national policy" should be treated, particularly as it was certain that persistent departure from them would force the Government to take action, either on its own initiative or under pressure from public opinion. The Taoiseach continued: "On these matters it is not enough to have the last word, if we do not have the first also. . . ."[60]

However, the Taoiseach relented and decided that many of the matters referred by him above could well be incorporated in an address by the Minister for Posts and Telegraphs to the members of the Authority at their first meeting, although he considered that it might be necessary to supplement the Minister's remarks privately in a couple of matters in relation particularly to partition and religion.[61]

The Taoiseach took a personal interest in the drafting of the Minister's address and many of the Taoiseach's own words and phrases were incorporated in the final draft of the address.[62] The address can be considered to be in the nature of a direction to the Authority as to how the Government perceived the role of the new broadcasting service. In a sense, the address can be considered from a legal perspective as an endeavour or exercise at prior restraint of the Broadcasting Authority by the Government. First, the address emphasised the power of television as a medium thus reinforcing the view that because of its pervasiveness television must be regulated:

> There can be no doubt that [television] is today one of the most effective media for influencing, for good or evil, the minds and hearts of men, women and children. To an extent which may, from some points of view, be alarming it helps to determine the standards of judgment which will be applied to moral, political, social and economic questions. Those, in every country, who are charged with the task of providing and administering

broadcasting, including television services, may well feel therefore that the responsibility which rests on them is one of fundamental importance and that their power to advance and improve every sector of national life is correspondingly great.

The address then moved to the Irish context and the Government's expectations of the Authority. The Minister referred to the sovereign right of the Irish nation, affirmed in the very first article of the Constitution, "to develop its life, political, economic and cultural, in accordance with its own genius and traditions".[63] Broadcasting was stated to be a most important instrument in the promotion of such development and "Irish broadcasting must play its part in the development of . . . national life".[64] Accordingly, the address noted that the people of Ireland no less than the Oireachtas would confidently expect that the programmes broadcast by Radio Éireann in their general content and in the manner of their presentation would "be in harmony with the highest traditions and ideals of the Irish people".[65]

After referring to the general statutory duties of the Authority, including a reference to the restoration of the Irish language, the Minister then dealt with the issue of morality — the censorship of that which is morally objectionable. He stated that no Irish broadcasting service could be regarded as acceptable which did not maintain worthy standards from the moral point of view. The Minister referred to the express guarantees in the Constitution to protect the family and to guard with special care the institution of marriage. Features which "would tend towards the debasement of moral standards or towards the exaltation of violence or cruelty" were to be excluded from programmes.[66] The Minister stated that the Government had no doubt about the exclusion of these facets from the Irish broadcasting service. Hence "no provision for censorship was included in the Broadcasting Authority Act [1960]".[67] However, the Authority was to maintain "a proper liaison with regard to filmed material with the national film censor".[68]

On the issue of censorship of television films, the Government decided in January 1960 that consideration was to be given to the question of providing statutory provision in the *Broadcasting Authority Act, 1960* for liaison with the official Censor of Films.[69] The Ministers for Posts and Telegraphs and Justice considered the issue and agreed that statutory provision for liaison between the Authority and the official Censor of Films need not be made. The Minister for Posts and Telegraphs was "satisfied" that the Authority

would be "very glad" to avail of the help and advice of the official
Film Censor and that the Authority would establish the necessary
liaison without being placed under a statutory duty to do so.[70]

On the issue of foreign policy, the Minister in his address to the
first meeting of the Broadcasting Authority warned the Authority
about the danger of Ireland being seen to speak with "two voices".
Ireland was firmly committed to the ideal of peace and friendly
co-operation. When Ireland's voice was raised in the councils of the
nations, it re-affirmed Ireland's adherence "to the principle of
peaceful settlement of disputes and acceptance in international
affairs of the rule of law".[71] The Minister continued:

> You will, I feel sure, appreciate that, in its position in respect of
> international affairs, Ireland should not appear to speak with
> two voices and that the national broadcasting service will be
> expected to be in harmony with the accepted national policy.
> That policy should, particularly, be borne in mind where any
> matter arises that involves the question of critical comment on
> the policies of other Governments.[72]

The issue of the exercise of the powers authorised by section 31 of
the 1960 Act arose in relation to a proposed visit of RTE cameramen
and reporters to Vietnam in 1967. Having consulted with the
Minister for Posts and Telegraphs, Erskine Childers, the Taoiseach,
Jack Lynch, spoke to the Chairman of the RTE Authority and
informed him that "in the opinion of the Government, the best
interests of the nation would not be served by sending a news team
to Vietnam" and that such a visit "would be an embarrassment to
the Government in relation to its foreign policy". The proposed visit
was abandoned by RTE. The Taoiseach made it clear in the Dáil that
had the proposed visit to Vietnam not been abandoned by RTE, then
it would have been a matter for consideration whether the terms of
section 31 of the 1960 Act should be invoked.[73]

The issue whether Sinn Féin was to be permitted access to the
national broadcasting service arose shortly after the establishment
of the Broadcasting Authority, then styled Radio Éireann. Sinn Féin
sought an allocation of time for party political broadcasts on television in September 1961, on the calling of the General Election. The
new Broadcasting Authority immediately wrote to the Taoiseach,
Seán Lemass, in relation to the constitutional position concerning the
possible assignment of broadcasting time to Sinn Féin.[74]

The Attorney General, Andreas O'Keeffe, advised that he doubted if it could be shown positively that Sinn Féin was itself "unconstitutional", although he was of the opinion that in practice "that close identification of its leading personnel with the IRA leads naturally to the inference that its aims are the same as those of the IRA" which was "an unconstitutional army".[75] The Attorney General suggested that the Director General of the Broadcasting Authority could state that it would be contrary to the spirit of the Constitution to allot time to an organisation which aims at the alteration of the Constitution by a means outside the Constitution itself. However, the Attorney General noted that as none of the elected Sinn Féin deputies had taken their seats in the Dáil, the allocation of broadcasting time would not be warranted. The matter was resolved at official level by the decision of the Party Whips that party-political broadcasts should be confined to political parties actually represented in the Dáil.

The Taoiseach took the issue further in his letter to the Director General of the Broadcasting Authority.[76] The Taoiseach stated that he would regard it as undesirable that the Authority should at any time entertain a request for broadcasting facilities for Sinn Féin or any similar organisation without a written assurance, which the Authority should be free to publish, that the organisation so applying recognises and accepts the authority of the Oireachtas under which the Authority functions and does not seek to alter the Constitution of Ireland otherwise than in accordance with the terms of the Constitution.[77] Radio Éireann accordingly refused broadcasting time to Sinn Féin during the election campaign. In a letter to Sinn Féin, the Authority regretted that it could not entertain Sinn Féin's request as the elected representatives of Sinn Féin did not take their seats in the 16th Dáil and the Authority had no evidence that Sinn Féin recognised and accepted the authority of the Oireachtas under which Radio Éireann itself functions.[78]

SINN FÉIN, THE NORTHERN IRELAND PROBLEM AND SECTION 31 DIRECTIVES

The conflict in Northern Ireland and its impact on what may be described as the southern part of Ireland caused many difficulties for those regulating broadcasting in Ireland. The dilemma and sense of grave frustration of the regulators can be illustrated by reference to correspondence between the Minister for Justice, Desmond O'Malley, and the Minister for Posts and Telegraphs, Gerard Collins,

in July 1970.[79] The Minister for Justice commenced the correspondence by stating that he was writing to protest "very strongly
against the irresponsible behaviour of RTE in glamorising persons
who [were] well known to have engaged in subversive or criminal
activities". The Minister for Justice made reference to certain individuals who had appeared on television and who were openly
identified as members of the IRA. The Minister continued:

> When is this going to stop? Is the RTE Authority going to sit
> back and allow the television and radio stations to be used by
> this minority to brainwash the public? If the answer to that is
> "yes" then I am faced with the unfortunate necessity to raise the
> question of enforcement of the law. If they will not maintain
> some reasonable effort at fair play they must at least observe
> the law of the land and, if nothing else can be done, I propose
> to raise immediately the question of prosecuting them the next
> time that they publish seditious matter.[80]

O'Malley concluded by stating that he would be glad to know
"whether anything [was] going to be done. . . ."[81]

In his reply, the Minister for Posts and Telegraphs stated that he
was in general agreement with much of what the Minister for Justice
had said.[82] In relation to the IRA, the Minister for Posts and
Telegraphs felt bound to point out that in the past year or two the
newspapers appeared to have been tacitly released from the
obligation not to refer to the IRA by name and that there had been
innumerable instances of the newspapers giving generous and
favourable publicity to the IRA. The Minister referred to an extensive
report in *The Irish Times* of July 7, 1970 ("far longer and more
comprehensive than RTE would have given") of a statement by the
"Army Council of the IRA" Dublin with a photograph of the Chief
of Staff of the IRA speaking at a press conference. The Minister stated
that any foreigner reading that article would assume that the IRA
"was a legitimate recognised army in the State" and that many of his
fellow citizens must be feeling that "it has Government blessing as
well as toleration".[83] The Minister continued:

> I don't know what the Department of Justice has done about all
> these matters, but until the situation which has been allowed to
> develop is changed, RTE cannot reasonably be forbidden to
> publish news items about the IRA which the newspapers —
> their competitors — freely publish. These matters are news and

it would be absurd of RTE to draw a veil over them while the newspapers flaunt them.

So what RTE will be required to do — and I am sure the Authority will be very willing to do it — is to report facts on the subject, in a "played-down" way and to avoid as far as possible making the illegal organisations sound attractive or appealing to the impressionable.

When the Department of Justice decides to enforce the law in regard to the IRA and its satellites, I shall be happy to deal further with the problem as far as RTE is concerned.[84]

Several features of this correspondence are noteworthy. There is no reference by either Minister to the Minister for Posts and Telegraph's specific power enshrined in section 31 of the *Broadcasting Authority Act, 1960* to direct the RTE Authority to "refrain from broadcasting any particular matter or matter of any particular class".[85] Secondly, the broadcasting service was directly equated to that of the printed media by the Minister for Posts and Telegraphs. However, in this context it should be noted that the Minister for Posts and Telegraphs was, in effect, defending himself. Above all else, the correspondence demonstrates a sense of frustration at a growing problem — IRA militancy and the reporting of IRA activities in the media.

The first *public* directive was issued by the Minister for Posts and Telegraphs to the RTE Authority on October 1, 1971. The Minister, Gerard Collins, directed the Authority to refrain from broadcasting

any matter of the following class, i.e., any matter that could be calculated to promote the aims or activities of any organisation which engages in, promotes, encourages or advocates the attaining of any particular objective by violent means.

The catalyst for the Minister's action was the interviewing on September 28, 1971 "of members of an illegal organisation" on a television programme "7 Days" which the Minister and the Government considered "to be prejudicial to the public interest".[86] The wording of the directive was, however, exceedingly vague. Dr. Conor Cruise O'Brien, a future Minister for Posts and Telegraphs, then an opposition deputy, staunchly criticised the directive. Radio and television, he argued, had become "less free in relation to the State" because of the application of this directive.[87] He also argued that it was "undesirable that there should be special rules for RTE and that the consequences of certain instruments of the law should be applied only to RTE".[88] Deputy Cruise O'Brien subsequently adopted a different attitude when he became a Minister of the Government.

In 1972 the Minister for Posts and Telegraphs and the Government became increasingly concerned with what they regarded as undue publicity on radio and television for members of subversive organisations. The Minister articulated these views in the Dáil on June 8, 1972 in a reply to a parliamentary question by Deputy L'Estrange in relation to a news programme on May 22, 1972 when a prominent member of the republican movement was given "equal time" to comment on a speech of the Taoiseach, Jack Lynch.[89] The Minister admitted that while the direction under section 31 of the *Broadcasting Authority Act, 1960* may not have been breached it seemed that an undue amount of time had been given by RTE on radio and television to members of subversive organisations, people who had no mandate from the electorate and represented nobody but themselves. They had been allowed to express their viewpoints and philosophies which were clearly unacceptable to the vast majority of the Irish people. The Minister stated that he was reluctant to intervene in programming matters but the Authority had its duties under the Act and he had his duties and responsibilities in the last resort in relation to the performance by the Authority of its statutory functions.[90]

In the light of the foregoing, it is surprising that no one raised the issue of prosecuting RTE under the *Offences Against the State Act, 1939,* legislation which, *inter alia,* prohibits the publication of certain material issued by or emanating from an unlawful organisation.[91] Any such prosecution would, however, raise the most serious issues relating to freedom of expression and Article 40.6.1.i of the Constitution.

Dr. Garret FitzGerald, TD (then in opposition), chided the Minister for Posts and Telegraphs and the Government on their concept of the national interest in the context of the directive under section 31 of the 1960 Act:

> [Y]ou could not allow a Government of one party in Parliament to have the undisputed power to determine that something should not be broadcast in the national interest. There is some-thing inherently unbalanced about the idea of a Government deciding what is in the national interest. The Government can decide what is in the Government's interest. They can have a

view of what is in the national interest. You cannot legally
define the national interest as what a Government want. To do
so would be to destroy democracy completely.[92]

Dr. FitzGerald argued that both he and the Fine Gael party
considered that the power to issue a directive should be constrained
by the necessity to have the directive countersigned by the leader of
one of the opposition parties.[93]

The alleged failure of the RTE Authority to observe the terms of
the 1971 directive led to its dismissal.[94] In November 1972, the British
Prime Minister visited Northern Ireland and issued a policy
statement on the future developments of the region. RTE sent Kevin
O'Kelly, a journalist, to interview the IRA Chief of Staff in relation
to policy enunciated by the British Prime Minister. Subsequently on
Sunday, November 19, 1972 a summary of the IRA Chief of Staff's
comments and points of view were broadcast in a current affairs
programme. The Gardaí subsequently arrested the IRA Chief of Staff
and searched the house of the journalist. The journalist was later
convicted for contempt of court when he refused to identify the
speaker on the tape recording and was sentenced to three months
imprisonment, later reduced on appeal to a fine.[95]

The Minister for Posts and Telegraphs, Gerard Collins, then wrote
to the Chairman of the RTE Authority, Donall Ó Móráin, requesting
him to summon a meeting of the Authority as a matter of immediate
urgency for the purpose of enabling the Authority to consider the
action it proposed to take in connection with the matter.[96] The
Authority met and at the end of a ten-hour discussion informed the
Minister that it had done everything possible to lay down guidelines
in accordance with the directive of October 1, 1971 despite the
ambiguities in that directive. The Authority stated that it was
satisfied that the RTE staff had shown a remarkable sense of duty
and a genuine commitment to reporting impartially and accurately.
The Authority did concede, however, that the interview with the IRA
Chief of Staff, demonstrated a lapse in editorial judgment in the
context of the 1971 directive. Subsequently, the Minister appeared
on television and announced the dismissal of the Authority pursuant
to section 6 of the *Broadcasting Authority Act, 1960*. Explaining the
stance adopted by the Government, the Minister for Posts and
Telegraphs in the Dáil considered that the response of the Authority
to his request as to what action the Authority proposed to take in
relation to the broadcast was

a long winded and waffling reply which admitted that the
programme should not have been broadcast in the form in
which it was broadcast but offered no apology, no expression
of regret, no indication that the Authority as such accepted
responsibility and no adequate assurance that this sort of thing
would not be allowed to happen again.[97]

The Minister stated that members of the Authority "had proved
themselves clearly to be unfit to hold office" and that what was at
stake was "a matter of vital national interest affecting the lives and
deaths of citizens of Ireland".[98] The Taoiseach, Jack Lynch, described
the dismissal as an exercise in democracy and as an act which was
taken because the Government saw the need for protecting the
community.

Professor T.W. Moody, a member of the dismissed Authority and
an eminent historian, argued the Authority's case in a letter to *The
Irish Times* on November 27, 1972. Professor Moody dealt succinctly
with the competing interests involved in relation to the regulation
of the content of what is broadcast. He stated that it was inevitable
in a democratic society that conflicts of judgment should arise
between Government and any broadcasting body invested by
Parliament with large disciplinary powers and a monopoly of
broadcasting. Conflicts between the Government and the Authority
had arisen in public and in private before October 1971. Sometimes,
the Authority gave way; more often it held its ground. But inherent
difficulties were aggravated when the Minister invoked for the first
time section 31 of the *Broadcasting Act, 1960* in October 1971.
Professor Moody stated that there was no inclination on the part of
the Authority to flout the Government or to question its right to be
concerned about the broadcasting service. The Authority's collision
with the Government was due to contradictions between the
Government's views and the Authority's efforts to fulfil its
obligations under the Broadcasting Act in the field of news and
current affairs programmes. Professor Moody argued that the
Authority endeavoured to give due weight to two competing claims;
on the one hand the freedom of public expression and debate; on the
other the protection of society and the State against subversion.
Professor Moody acknowledged that the Government's decision
may have been democratic but he doubted whether the democratic
process has been strengthened by its outcome:

A democratic society needs to face disagreeable truths and the best service the communications media can render at a time of grave crisis may well be to help it to do so. The danger is that the directive, as interpreted by its authors, may render this impossible in Ireland.

The second public directive was made on October 18, 1976 by Dr. Conor Cruise O'Brien, then Minister for Posts and Telegraphs, who directed the RTE Authority to refrain from broadcasting

> matter of the following class; i.e. interviews or reports of interviews with spokesmen for;
> (a) The Irish Republican Army (Provisional or Official),
> (b) Organisations classified as unlawful in Northern Ireland,
> (c) Provisional Sinn Féin.

The 1976 Directive was not in the form of a statutory instrument and did not purport to repeal the earlier directive of October 1, 1971. Both orders remained in force until the enactment of the *Broadcasting Authority (Amendment) Act, 1976*. The Minister for Posts and Telegraphs considered that the unrestricted power to prohibit the broadcasting of any class of matter which the Minister enjoyed under the original section 31 of the 1960 Act had proved to be "too formidable" to be "entrusted to any Minister in relation to so sensitive a matter as broadcasting".[99] The Minister sought to limit that power by prohibiting the broadcasting of matter which fell into certain defined categories. The Minister accepted the recommendation of the Broadcasting Review Committee, chaired by Mr. Justice George D. Murnaghan, that there should be statutory provisions for Government directives in relation to the "control" of broadcasting.[100] The Review Committee argued, and the Minister agreed, that any use of such directives should be "public, clear and specific and should be subject to subsequent parliamentary confirmation and review".[101]

The Minister for Posts and Telegraphs, when introducing the amendment to the original section 31 in 1975, justified this form of State censorship on several grounds. He argued that broadcasting frequencies were scarce and thus had to be controlled by the State on behalf of the community.[102] The principal justification was that the State had a duty to see that broadcasting was not used to endanger the security of the State or lives of the citizens.[103] Dr. Conor Cruise O'Brien in 1979 elaborated his views on the role of the Minister responsible for broadcasting in the context of violence in

Northern Ireland and the consequent coverage of this phenomenon
on radio and television. The passage is lengthy, but worthy of
inclusion as it is a considered view of a respected statesman:

> Not long after I became Minister, the Irish national television
> service broadcast a programme about violence in Northern
> Ireland. The only violence shown or alluded to in any way, in
> the course of that programme, was violence by British soldiers.
> No IRA men, as far as the programme was concerned, had ever
> contributed to the programme's subject matter: "Violence in
> Northern Ireland."
>
> I viewed that programme in the presence of the then chairman
> of the authority and the then director-general. At the end of it,
> I enquired whether the IRA had been in actual physical
> occupation of the station when the programme was made and
> when it was broadcast. It transpired that this was not the case.
> But the IRA propagandists had contrived . . . to penetrate the
> station and attain a spiritual occupation sufficient to secure the
> making and transmission of such a programme.
>
> In these conditions, I retained the power to issue directives. I
> not merely retained it, but used it. I directed the Authority to
> refrain from broadcasting interviews with spokesmen for the
> IRA (both wings) and for Provisional Sinn Féin. I took the view
> that, since all such spokesmen were there to serve the purposes
> of an illegal private army, broadcasts by them constituted
> incitement of violent crime, and thus infringed broadcasting
> law. I could have left that decision to the Authority itself. In the
> circumstances I have described, I thought it safer to act
> myself.[104]

One distinguished academic lawyer who justified the section 31
power was the late Professor John Kelly. Writing in 1978 he argued
that section 31 was "a minimum power which no Irish government
could have refrained from invoking over recent years". Professor
Kelly, while admitting the force of some of the contrary arguments,
continued:

> We must maintain a minimum consensus about murder and a
> few other things, and allow nothing to weaken that consensus,
> or dilute people's natural abhorrence of cruelty by presenting
> its perpetrators as excusable. I think the values of public
> enlightenment must take second place to this.[105]

Section 31 of the 1960 Act was considered by the 1980 Joint Oireachtas Committee on RTE.[106] Wesley Boyd, the Director of News in RTE, in response to a question from the Committee as to how RTE coped with the broadcasting prohibition stated in evidence that he did not consider that any journalist or broadcaster would attempt to defend section 31. Journalists and broadcasters did not like section 31 but as it was the law of the land it must be observed. He argued that section 31 inhibited coverage of some events, particularly events in the North of Ireland. However, section 31 did not inhibit journalists and broadcasters to the extent that people were being denied knowledge of what is happening in the North of Ireland because RTE still carried statements from legal and illegal organisations; RTE referred to their activities; RTE published their claims or denials of responsibility for certain events. Boyd argued that section 31 was not a complete inhibition but he considered it prevented the presentation of a complete and balanced picture of what was happening. He concluded that most responsible journalists considered that it would be of benefit to the public if searching interviews could be held with certain people who were active "in certain activities North and South of the Border".[107]

The 1981 Oireachtas Committee noted that no complaint had been received from any Minister or Government Department or anybody else alleging that there had been a breach of the Ministerial directive on the part of the Authority.[108] The Committee itself, without any elaboration or reference to any programme, stated it was of the opinion that the section had not been fully observed by RTE in early May 1981.[109] While the Committee noted the journalists' views on the problems caused by section 31, it concluded that the section was "a necessary contribution to public order at this troubled time in our history".[110] The Committee also believed that the spirit as well as the letter of the section should be observed by RTE at all times.

Orders under section 31 of the 1960 Act, as amended, have remained continuously in force from 1971 up to the date of writing. The present order[111] prohibits RTE and the "independent" private broadcasting services[112] from broadcasting any matter which is

> (1) an interview, or report of an interview, with a spokesman or with spokesmen for any one or more of the following organisations, namely,

>> (a) the organisation styling itself the Irish Republican Army (also the I.R.A. and Óglaigh na hÉireann),

(b) the organisation styling itself Sinn Féin,

(c) the organisation styling itself Republican Sinn Féin,

(d) the organisation styling itself the Ulster Defence Association,

(e) the organisation styling itself the Irish National Liberation Army (also the INLA),

(f) the organisation styling itself the Irish Peoples Liberalisation Organisation (also the IPLO),

(g) any organisation which in Northern Ireland is a proscribed organisation for the purposes of section 28 of the Act of the British Parliament entitled the *Northern Ireland (Emergency Provisions) Act, 1991*,

(2) a broadcast, whether purporting to be a political party broadcast or not, made by, or on behalf of, or advocating, offering or inviting support for, the organisation styling itself Sinn Féin or the organisation styling itself Republican Sinn Féin,

(3) a broadcast by any person or persons representing, or purporting to represent, the organisation styling itself Republican Sinn Féin.

The organisations proscribed within the meaning of section 21 of the *Northern Ireland (Emergency Provisions) Act, 1978* are the Irish Republican Army (Provisional and Official), Cumann na mBan, Fianna na hÉireann, Saor Éire, Ulster Volunteer Force, Ulster Freedom Fighters, Red Hand Commandoes and the Irish National Liberation Army.

RTE, in its interpretation[113] of the section 31 order, states that the broadcasting of matter consisting of factual reportage relating to organisations described in the order is not prohibited. Further, statements from these organisations, or from a spokesman or spokesmen for them, on significant developments, including the acceptance or denial of responsibility or denial of responsibility for violence or other unlawful activity may be reported. Directions to RTE staff also provide that appropriate use of mute film or stills to illustrate such reportage is permitted at the discretion of the Director of News, but sound recording or sound-on-film of a spokesman or spokesmen for any one or more of such organisations, or interviews or reports of interviews with such persons, is not permitted. In the context of the section 31 prohibition, the RTE "guidelines" do not refer to the provision in the *Offences Against the State Act, 1939* which, inter alia, makes it an offence to publish or distribute a document (which includes a sound track or film)[114] issued by or emanating from an unlawful organisation or appearing to be so issued or appearing to aid or abet any such organisation or calculated to promote its formation.[115] Amended guidelines were issued by RTE following the *O'Toole* case.[116] The guidelines, issued in September 1993, allowed journalists and presenters to interview members of Sinn Féin, or Republican Sinn Féin, but only generally after referral to a Divisional Executive who may consult with the Director General. The amended guidelines provide that the lawfulness of a contribution from a Sinn Féin member depends on his or her status, the capacity in which he or she is speaking and the content of what is said or expected to be said.

LEGAL CHALLENGES TO SECTION 31

The constitutionality of section 31 of the 1960 Act and of a 1982 Order was challenged in the *State (Lynch) v Cooney* (1982).[117] Much of the legal argument and the judgment of the High and Supreme Courts in this case dealt with the administrative-law issue of the reviewability of the Minister's opinion that the broadcasting of a particular matter of a particular class would be likely to promote, or incite to, crime or would tend to undermine the authority of the State. The issue of freedom of expression received little attention. However, O'Hanlon J having considered that the Minister's opinion was not reviewable concluded that section 31(1) of the *Broadcasting Authority Act, 1960* was unconstitutional because it contained in-sufficient safeguards for the rights of freedom for the expression of convictions and opinions guaranteed by Article 40.6.1.i of the Constitution — particularly in the context of the protection of freedom of the press, the radio and television from the control of the Executive.[118]

The Supreme Court, discharging the declaration of invalidity of O'Hanlon J, stated that Article 40.6.1.i of the Constitution placed on the State the obligation to ensure that organs of public opinion including the press, radio and television were not to be used to undermine public order or public morality or the security of the State. O'Higgins CJ, delivering the judgment of the Court, continued:

> Therefore, it is clearly the duty of the State to intervene to prevent broadcasts on radio and television which are aimed at such a result or which in any way would be likely to have the effect of promoting or inciting to crime or endangering the

authority of the State. These, however, are objective deter-
minations and obviously the fundamental rights of citizens to
express freely their convictions and opinions cannot be curtailed or prevented on any irrational or capricious grounds.[119]

The quotation above is virtually a paraphrase of the second paragraph of Article 40.6.1.i. of the Constitution. The Constitution thus
sanctions prior restraints of expression which may "undermine"
public order, morality or the authority of the State. Prior restraint of
expression has aroused the ire of writers and legal scholars over the
centuries. Yet the courts in *Lynch* could easily have found that the
proposed election address did not come within those prohibited
categories of undermining public order or the authority of the State.
In this context, Sinn Féin (the political party to which Mr. Lynch
belonged) had agreed to submit the script to RTE of the relevant
party political broadcasts in advance of any broadcast for vetting by
RTE.[120]

The legal challenge to the section 31 orders was taken a stage
further in the case of *Purcell v Ireland* (1991).[121] Ms. Betty Purcell and
sixteen other journalists and producers of radio and television
programmes complained to the European Commission of Human
Rights that, inter alia, the then current section 31 order,[122] as applied
to them, constituted an unjustifiable interference with their freedom
of expression and was a serious infringement of their right in a
democratic society to receive and impart information to the public,
and of their right to receive information without unnecessary
interference by a public authority. The journalists invoked Article 10
of the European Convention on Human Rights which provides:

> (1) Everyone has the right to freedom of expression. This right
> shall include freedom to hold opinions and to receive and
> impart information and ideas without interference by public
> authority and regardless of frontiers. This Article shall not
> prevent States from requiring the licensing of broadcasting,
> television or cinema enterprises.

The European Commission of Human Rights concluded that the
order constituted an interference with the exercise of the applicants'
right under Article 10, para 1, of the Convention to receive and
impart information and ideas. The question then arose as to whether
this interference was justified, as the Irish Government had
maintained, by any of the restrictions which may be imposed on the
exercise of the freedom of expression in accordance with Article 10,

paragraph 2 of the Convention. To be justified under this provision, the condition or restriction must be "prescribed by law". Based on the case law of the European Court of Human Rights,[123] the Commission concluded that the restrictions were "prescribed by law" within the meaning of Article 10, para 2, of the Convention.

The issue then arose whether the impugned restrictions had a legitimate purpose under Article 10, paragraph 2, and were "necessary in a democratic society" for achieving that purpose.[124] In this context, the Commission in its decision quoted the words of Henchy J in *State (Lynch) v Cooney*[125] that Sinn Féin, although a registered political party, was "an integral dependent part of the apparatus of the Provisional IRA, an illegal terrorist organisation which, by both its avowed aims and its record of criminal violence, is shown to be committed to, amongst other things, the dismantling by violent and unlawful means of the organs of State established by the Constitution". The Commission noted that the impugned order did not prohibit the reporting of the activities of any of the listed organisations; it only banned live interviews with their spokesmen. The Commission concluded in this context that the impugned restrictions on the applicants' freedom to receive and impart information had a legitimate aim under Article 10, paragraph 2, of the Convention.

On the issue whether the impugned restrictions "were necessary in a democratic society", the Commission, noting the margin of appreciation of contracting States, considered that its sole task was to examine whether the reasons underlying the section 31 order were relevant and sufficient under Article 10, paragraph 2,[126] i.e. whether the Minister had convincing reasons for assuming the existence of a pressing social need for imposing the impugned restrictions on the applicants.

The Commission emphasised, as the Court had done on several occasions,[127] that freedom of expression constituted one of the essential foundations in a democratic society. But the Commission also emphasised that the exercise of that freedom carried with it duties and responsibilities (Article 10, para 2, of the Convention) and that the defeat of terrorism was a public interest of the first importance in a democratic society. The Commission, influenced by the power and domination of the broadcast media, concluded that given the scope of the restrictions imposed on the applicants and the overriding interests that they were designed to protect, they could reasonably be considered "necessary in a democratic society" within the meaning of Article 10, para 2, of the Convention. Accordingly, the Commission reasoned that the complaints made by the individual applicants were manifestly unfounded and must be rejected in accordance with Article 27, para 2, of the Convention. The writer considers this issue later[128] in the general context of a consideration on restrictions on freedom of expression.

In the context of broadcasting censorship, the inevitable tension which exists between the regulator and the regulated can be illustrated by the *Jenny McGeever* case. Jenny McGeever, a journalist with RTE, allowed Martin McGuinness of Sinn Féin to be heard on the "Morning Ireland" radio programme on March 16, 1988. The journalist was suspended from duty and an internal enquiry was ordered following a formal complaint from the Government.[129] It was reported that the Cabinet discussed the issue on the day of its occurrence and the Minister for Communications later demanded a full explanation of the incident from RTE and was said to be "angry" over the matter.[130] Commenting on the case, *The Irish Times* leader writer noted that the episode showed, once again, the "unreal and ultimately the truth-destroying nature of the section 31 management".[131] The censorship provision was described as "a blunt instrument, wholly incapable of being adapted to the multiplicity of complex situations in which broadcast journalists find themselves".[132]

For many years, RTE adopted a rigorous and conservative interpretation of the section 31 order. The *Marcus Free* case (1987), a decision of the Broadcasting Complaints Commission, illustrates that conservative approach.[133] Marcus Free's complaint related to a person who telephoned the RTE "Live Line" radio programme in October 1987 which dealt with a book on wild flora. The caller sought to ask a question on mushrooms but stated that he was a member of Sinn Féin. The call was terminated. Marcus Free complained that the caller did not come within the terms of the section 31 order because he was neither a spokesman for Sinn Féin nor did he represent or purport to represent Sinn Féin (as prohibited by the section 31 order) but was simply a radio listener with an interest in mushrooms who happened to be a member of Sinn Féin.[134] Accordingly, he considered that RTE had breached its statutory duty of fairness[135] and had, in effect, misinterpreted the section 31 order. RTE denied breach of any statutory duty or any misinterpretation of the section 31 order. The Commission (chaired by Ercus Stewart, SC) agreed with RTE and dismissed the complaint.

The judgments of O'Hanlon J (High Court) and the Supreme Court in *O'Toole v RTE* (1993)[136] ameliorated, to a certain extent, the conservative interpretation by RTE of the section 31 order.[137] In effect, RTE had interpreted the order as banning members of Sinn Féin per se from the airwaves as distinct from spokesmen and persons representing or purporting to represent Sinn Féin. In fairness to RTE, the distinction is not necessarily as clear cut as it might appear. In *O'Toole*, RTE refused to broadcast interviews with the plaintiff in his capacity as the chairman of a strike committee at a bakery in Dublin in 1990 on the grounds that he was a member of Sinn Féin. O'Hanlon J held that the section 31 order did not prohibit the broadcast of any material emanating from or spoken by a person solely on the grounds that he was a member of the Sinn Féin party. O'Hanlon J reasoned that if a Ministerial order had been made prohibiting all access to the airwaves at all times by a person who was a member of Sinn Féin, the validity of such an order would have to be considered and would in the judge's opinion be open to considerable doubt as a valid exercise of the powers conferred on the Minister under section 31 of the Broadcasting Act, 1960 as amended.[138] The judge also invoked the statutory obligations to observe rules of fairness and impartiality in broadcasting news and in its treatment of current affairs[139] by stating that this obligation was infringed by RTE when it refused on arbitrary grounds to allow the views of workers involved in a major industrial dispute, which was arousing widespread public attention, to be put forward on their behalf by the plaintiff — the person they had appointed their spokesman.

The Supreme Court unanimously upheld the decision of the High Court. Finlay CJ in his judgment said that the submission on behalf of Mr. O'Toole that the ban constituted an addition or amendment of the terms of the order, rather than a method of implementing it, was valid and correct. O'Flaherty J in his judgment considered that someone speaking on an innocuous subject on the airwaves, even though he is a member of an organisation including in its objectives a desire to undermine public order or the authority of the State, was neither outside the constitutional guarantee of freedom of expression nor within the Ministerial order. The liberal sentiments expressed by O'Flaherty J may pave the way for a greater appreciation of freedom of expression in Ireland.[140]

RTE's conservative approach to the "section 31" issue is further illustrated by the case of *Brandon Books Publishers Ltd v RTE* (1993).[141] RTE had refused to accept a radio advertisement for a book of short stories (not overtly of a propagandist nature) by the Sinn Féin President, Gerry Adams, on the basis that it was in breach of the relevant section 31 order.[142] Carney J, in a conservative judgment, reasoned that although since the case of *O'Toole*,[143] an ordinary member of Sinn Féin might broadcast on a range of topics, nevertheless that so far as Mr. Adams was concerned his public persona was such that he could not be divorced in the public mind from advancing the cause of Sinn Féin. Carney J argued that greater expertise in relation to the making of the judgment on these matters must lie with the national broadcasting authority rather than the courts, and it must be asked whether the exercise of such a judgment by the Broadcasting Authority was reviewable by the courts. To a certain extent, the core issue was side-stepped.

In the hearing of the *Brandon Books* case, an RTE executive was reported[144] as giving evidence to the effect that if the advertisement for Mr. Adams's book had been carried by RTE, it could have the effect of popularising Sinn Féin and undermining the authority of the State as the man could not be separated from his position as president of his party. [In this context, one must not forget that Sinn Féin is a legitimate political party in Ireland.]

A similar case was taken by Brandon Books Ltd against the Independent Radio and Television Commission (IRTC) which had informed the independent radio stations that to broadcast an advertisement for a collection of short stories by Gerry Adams would contravene the section 31 order.[145]

A comparative reference may be made to the United Kingdom's equivalent of the section 31 order. In the 1980s the UK Government became increasingly concerned about exposure of Sinn Féin spokesmen on the broadcasting services. The Prime Minister, Margaret Thatcher, expressed the view at a press conference on July 16, 1985, that the terrorists should not be given the "oxygen of publicity". On July 29, 1985, the Home Secretary, Leon Brittan, wrote to the chairman of the BBC seeking to suppress a programme in which Martin McGuinness, a Sinn Féin spokesman, and Gregory Campbell, a unionist, were interviewed as examples of how on both sides of their conflict there were people who were prepared to support violence. The Home Secretary released his letter to the press before it had been received by the chairman of the BBC. The BBC Board of Governors cancelled the programme although it was shown one month later with 30 seconds altered.[146]

The murder of eight soldiers near Omagh in Northern Ireland when a bomb destroyed their bus in August 1988 prompted the UK Government into further action. On October 19, 1988 the Home Secretary, pursuant to section 29(3) of the UK *Broadcasting Act, 1981* and clause 13(4) of the Charter, Licence and Agreement made between the Home Secretary and the BBC on April 2, 1981 issued certain notices to the BBC and the IBA. Section 29(3) of the 1981 Act provided that the Secretary of State might, at any time, in writing, require the Authority to refrain from broadcasting any matter or classes of matter as specified in the notice. The 1981 Royal Charter to the BBC contained a similar provision. The notice directed the BBC and the IBA to refrain from broadcasting

> any matter which consists of or includes any words spoken, whether in the course of an interview or a discussion or otherwise, by a person who appears or is heard on the programme . . . where (a) the person speaking the words represents or purports to represent [one of the specified organisations] or (b) the words support or solicit or invite support for such an organisation. . . .

Words spoken in the course of proceedings in Parliament, or by or in support of a candidate at a parliamentary, European parliamentary or local election pending that election, were not covered by the notice. No such exemption applies in Ireland (excluding Northern Ireland). The specified organisations included five Republican paramilitary groups and three illegal Loyalist paramilitary groups, Sinn Féin, Republican Sinn Féin and the Ulster Defence Association.

The Home Secretary in a statement made on October 19, 1988 in both Houses of Parliament stated, inter alia, that the restrictions followed "very closely the lines of similar provisions which have been operating in the Republic of Ireland for some years".[147] Four factors influenced the Secretary of State in issuing the directive.[148] Firstly, offence had been caused by the appearance of apologists for terrorism, particularly after a terrorist outrage. Secondly, such appearances had afforded terrorists undeserved publicity which was contrary to the public interest. Thirdly, it was claimed that the appearances had tended to increase the standing of terrorist organisations and to create a false impression that support for terrorism was itself a legitimate political opinion. Fourthly, it was claimed that broadcast statements were intended to have, and did in some cases have, the effect of intimidating some of those at whom they were directed. The Home Office in a letter dated October 24, 1988[149] further defined and explained the notices by stating that the correct interpretation was that the notices applied only to direct statements and not to reported speech and that the person caught by the notices was the one whose words were reported and not the reporter or presenter who reported them. The Home Office confirmed that the notices permitted the showing of a film or still picture of the initiator speaking the words together with a voice-over account of them, whether in paraphrase or verbatim.[150] Genuine works of fiction were not to be covered by the restrictions.[151] The Home Office confirmed that a member of a prohibited organisation could not be held to represent that organisation in all his daily activities. Whether at any particular time such a person was representing the organisation concerned would depend upon the nature of the words spoken and the particular context. Accordingly, the Home Office stated that where such a person was speaking in a personal capacity or purely in his capacity as a member of an organisation which did not fall under the notices, (for example, an elected Council), it followed that the prohibition on broadcasting would not apply.[152]

Thus, in the United Kingdom the directives do not restrict the reporting of statements made by those who are the subject of the directive. What is prohibited is the direct appearance on radio and television of those members of the relevant organisations while actually making their statements — what has been described as "actuality reporting". This contrasts with the Irish prohibition where, inter alia, interviews or reports of interviews with a spokesman for the relevant organisation are prohibited. The UK prohibition can be described as limited and modest in comparison to the Irish prohibition.

In *Brind v Secretary of State* (1990),[153] the plaintiff journalist applied for judicial review of the Home Secretary's decision to issue the directives on the grounds that the directives were ultra vires section 29(3) of the UK *Broadcasting Act, 1981* and clause 13(4) of the BBC licence and agreement made between the BBC and the Secretary of State. It was also claimed that the Home Secretary had acted in breach of the right to freedom of expression recognised in Article 10 of the Convention for the Protection of Human Rights and Fundamental Freedoms and had acted without necessity, disproportionately and perversely. Furthermore, it was claimed that the directives were in conflict with the duty to preserve impartiality imposed on the IBA under s. 4(1)(f) of the 1981 Act and on the BBC under its licence.

A Divisional Court refused the application. The Court of Appeal dismissed the plaintiff's appeal. The House of Lords, affirming the decision of the Court of Appeal held, *inter alia*, that the judicial rule of construction that subsequent domestic legislation was to be read to conform with the provisions of the European Convention on Human Rights, (provided it was reasonably capable of bearing such a meaning) did not extend to the interpretation of secondary legislation. Applying the conventional principles of judicial review, the House of Lords held that the Home Secretary's "media ban" was a valid exercise of his "discretionary authority".[154]

The orders of the Irish and British Governments in relation to the broadcasting services constitute a curtailment of freedom of expression. A review of such curtailments of expression and certain conclusions are considered in chapter 26.

To conclude this chapter describing censorship of the broadcast media, we will consider the Minister for Communications' ultimate power of censorship — the assumption by the Minister of direct control over every mode of telecommunication including broadcasting. Section 10(1) of the *Wireless Telegraphy Act, 1926* provides that if at any time the Government is of the opinion that a national emergency has arisen of such a character that it is expedient in the public interest that the Government should have full control over the sending and receiving of messages, signals and other communications by means of wireless telegraphy and of signalling stations capable of being used for communicating with ships at sea, the Government may, if they so think fit, publish in *Iris Oifigiúil* a notice declaring that such emergency has arisen. Section 10(2) of the 1926 Act empowers the Minister for Communications to make regulations governing the matter.

The Minister for Communications has power in an emergency declared under section 10 of the *Wireless Telegraphy Act, 1926* to suspend a licence of RTE and operate any service being provided by the Authority under the suspended licence.[155] The Minister has similar powers in relation to the private commercial broadcasting services but in addition he may require such broadcasting services to be operated "as he directs".[156] In relation to the telecommunication carrier service, where an emergency has arisen in which it is considered expedient "for the public service" that the Government should have control over "the transmission of messages", possession may be taken by the State of any telecommunication company or part of it, on behalf of the Government.[157]

17

Privilege, Powers and Duties of Telecom Éireann

DESCRIPTION OF PRIVILEGE

Confusion arises from time to time over the precise legal title of the national telecommunication carrier service. The correct title is necessary in legal agreements and in court proceedings. The certificate of incorporation describes the private limited company as Bord Telecom Éireann or, in the English language, the Irish Telecommunication Board. Telecom Eireann (without an accent on the "E" of Eireann) and Telecom Ireland are registered business names only. Telecom Éireann is used throughout this book as an abbreviation of Bord Telecom Éireann.

Certain aspects of what is termed "the exclusive privilege"[1] of Telecom Éireann in relation to telecommunication services have been considered in chapter 14. The privilege (subject to exceptions) is confined to transmitting, receiving, collecting and delivering telecommunication messages within the State up to and including a connection point in the premises of a subscriber for such a service.[2]

Telecom Éireann's privilege was restricted in 1992 (pursuant to liberalising measures from the European Communities)[3] to offering, providing and maintaining the public telecommunication network and to offering, providing and maintaining voice telephony services.[4] This restriction, effected by the *European Communities (Telecommunications Services) Regulations, 1992*[5] (which implemented those liberalising measures) was not, however, to be construed as affecting the offer, provision or maintenance by Telecom Éireann within the State of telex services, mobile radio telephony services, paging services and satellite services which were within the exclusive privilege of Telecom Éireann by virtue of section 87 of the *Postal and Telecommunications Services Act, 1983*.

The words "transmitting, receiving, collecting and delivering" have their origin in the monopoly-creating section of the *Telegraph*

Act, 1869[6] which is the statutory basis for the Minister's overall privileges in relation to telecommunication. The words defining the privilege of Telecom Éireann are more appropriate to the age when "telegrams" were physically received, collected and delivered than to modern-day conditions. Certain services have been excepted from Telecom Éireann's privilege. Section 87(3) of the *Postal and Telecommunications Services Act, 1983* sets out these exceptions:

(a) services provided and maintained by a person solely for his own domestic use,

(b) services provided and maintained by a business for use between employees for the purposes of the business and not rendering a service to any other person,

(c) services provided and maintained by a person by means of apparatus situated wholly in a single set of premises occupied by him,

(d) the operation of a broadcasting station under licence granted by the Minister [for Communications],

(e) radio communications systems provided under licences granted under the *Wireless Telegraphy Acts, 1926 to 1972*,

(f) cable television systems licensed under the Wireless *Telegraphy Acts, 1926 to 1972*,

(g) services provided in accordance with the terms and conditions of a licence granted by [Telecom Éireann] under section 89 or by the Minister [for Communications] under section 111.

These exceptions are similar to the original services which were excluded from the Postmaster-General's exclusive privilege by virtue of section 5 of the *Telegraph Act, 1869*.

The Oireachtas, mindful perhaps of the potential constitutional vulnerability of monopolies, set out in the 1983 Act the justification for granting an exclusive privilege to Telecom Éireann.[7] That exclusive privilege was granted because of Telecom Éireann's primary purpose of providing a national telecommunication service, its general duty to ensure that charges for services are kept at the minimum rates consistent with meeting approved financial targets having regard to the area and population of the State and the state of development of telecommunication technology and because a viable national telecommunication system involved subsidisation of some loss-making services by profit-making services.[8]

The privilege of Telecom Éireann is considerably qualified by the exceptions specified above, and by the licensing powers of the Minister for Communications. The 1983 Act enables the Minister to license persons to provide telecommunication services which may be within the exclusive privilege of Telecom Éireann or outside it.[9] Section 89 of the 1983 Act provides that Telecom Éireann may, with the consent of the Minister, grant on the application of any person, a licence to such person, to provide a telecommunication service within the exclusive privilege granted to Telecom Éireann. This power has not been exercised since the enactment of relevant EC directives.[10]

Under section 111 of the 1983 Act, the Minister for Communications may, by order, with the consent of the Minister for Finance, provide for the grant of a licence to any person to provide a telecommunication service of a kind within the exclusive privilege granted to Telecom Éireann. The Minister may also grant licences to any person to provide a telecommunication service of a kind not within the exclusive privilege granted to Telecom Éireann.[11]

As discussed earlier, the Minister for Communications has made an order which has enabled a licence to be issued to provide telecommunication services within the so-called exclusive privilege of Telecom Éireann.[12] Up to 1992, many licences had also been granted by the Minister to persons, including Telecom Éireann, to provide limited telecommunication services, for example, supplying telecommunication terminal equipment.[13] In October 1992, the Department of Communications announced that consequent on the implementation of *Directive 88/301/EEC*,[14] the requirement for a licence under section 111(2) of the *Postal and Telecommunications Services Act, 1983* in relation to telecommunication terminal equipment intended for connection to the public telecommunication carrier network had been abolished.[15] The Minister for Communications also stated that he had decided to discontinue the requirement for a licence to install and maintain such equipment.[16]

POWERS OF TELECOM ÉIREANN

It is appropriate here to refer to Telecom Éireann's powers in relation to the construction and maintenance of telecommunication plant and systems. Telecom Éireann is empowered, subject to certain conditions,[17] (1) to place and maintain any telecommunication apparatus under, over, along or across, or any post in or upon, any street or public road and when placed, to alter or remove the same;[18]

(2) to alter the position in any street or public road of any pipe (not being a main) for the supply of water or gas;[19] (3) for any of the purposes mentioned above, to open or break up any street or public road and (4) to place and maintain telecommunication apparatus under, in, above, along or across any land or building, or any railway or canal, or any estuary, or branch of the sea, or the shore or bed of any tidal water, and may alter or remove the same.[20] Related powers and the conditions under which these powers must be exercised are set out in the *Telegraph Acts 1863 to 1916*, the *Postal and Telecommunications Services Act, 1983* and the *Telecommunications Scheme, 1992*.[21]

DUTIES OF TELECOM ÉIREANN

The principal statutory objects of Telecom Éireann are prescribed by section 14 of the *Postal and Telecommunications Services Act, 1983*. Those objects are

(a) to provide a national telecommunications service within the State and between the State and places outside the State,
(b) to meet the industrial, commercial, social and household needs of the State for comprehensive and efficient telecommunications services and, so far as the company considers reasonably practicable, to satisfy all reasonable demands for such services throughout the State, and
(c) to provide such consultancy, advisory, training and contract services inside and outside the State as the company thinks fit.

The statutory objectives of the company were based on the 1981 White Paper, *Reorganisation of Postal and Telecommunications Services*.[22] A general duty is also imposed on Telecom Éireann by section 15(1) of the 1983 Act: the company is charged with conducting its affairs to ensure that

(a) charges for services are kept at the minimum rates consistent with meeting approved financial targets, and
(b) revenues of the company are not less than sufficient to

(i) meet all charges properly chargeable to revenue accounts (including depreciation of assets and proper allocation to general reserve) taking one year with another,
(ii) generate a reasonable proportion of capital needs, and
(iii) remunerate capital and repay borrowings.

These duties in relation to financial matters were also based on the 1981 White Paper.[23] Section 15(2) of the 1983 Act specifies, however, that nothing in section 14 of the Act, which outlines the principal objects of the telecommunication company, or in section 15, in relation to the general duty of the company, shall be construed as imposing on the company, either directly or indirectly, "any form of duty or liability enforceable by proceedings before any court to which it would not otherwise be subject". The (UK) *Telecommunications Act, 1981* made similar provision in relation to the public corporation known as British Telecommunications.[24]

Prior to the passing of the 1983 Act, the extent of the Minister's duty to provide a telecommunication carrier service was not clear. The question of whether there was a duty on the Minister for Posts and Telegraphs to provide a postal and telephone service was raised in the *State (Post Office Officials Association) v The Minister for Posts and Telegraphs*.[25] Industrial action had been taken by the Post Office Workers' Union with effect from midnight on February 18, 1979. This action involved the withdrawal by the Union's members of their services at post offices and telephone exchanges throughout the State. The Post Office Officials' Association, which represented a small minority of employees in post offices and telephone exchanges, sought an order of *mandamus* in the High Court against the Minister compelling him, *inter alia*, to provide a postal and telephone service, and to direct the opening of the doors of post offices and telephone exchanges. McMahon J refused the application. He stated that the application had not disclosed what duty, if any, rested on the Minister in relation to providing a postal or telephone service. He stated that it might be that the legislature had not imposed any duty. McMahon J stated that in the absence of any authority that the Minister was under an absolute duty to provide a service in all circumstances, it seemed he could not make the order of *mandamus* sought. However, Telecom Éireann is under a contractual duty with each of its customers to provide a telecommunication service, subject to certain conditions and limitations.[26]

The essence of the principal statutory objects of Telecom Éireann is to provide what may be described as a universal telecommunication service. Such a service consists of the provision and exploitation of a nation-wide telecommunication carrier network service having a general geographical coverage, and being available to any user upon request within a reasonable period of time at reasonable prices. In the context of the telephone service, the concept of a universal telecommunication service was advocated in the

United States by American Telephone and Telegraph's (AT&T) Theodore Vail as early as 1907.[27] The goal of providing a universal telecommunication carrier service throughout the United States was embraced by Congress in the US *Communications Act, 1934.*[28]

Ireland's nearest neighbour, the United Kingdom, in its *Telecommunications Act, 1984* was unambiguous about the social aspect of British Telecom's objectives. The social objectives are

> to secure . . . throughout the United Kingdom . . . such telecommunication services as satisfy all reasonable demands for them including, in particular, emergency services, maritime services and services in rural areas;[29]
>
> to promote the interests of consumers, purchasers and other users in the United Kingdom (including, in particular, those who are disabled or of pensionable age) in respect of the prices charged for, and the quality and variety of, telecommunication services provided and telecommunication apparatus supplied.[30]

This particular definition of universal service and its associated social-service dimension came too late to influence the drafting of Ireland's *Postal and Telecommunications Services Act, 1983.*

One of the tasks facing the regulators of telecommunication in Ireland and the European Communities is to address the often irreconcilable conflict between the twin policy goals of competition and universal service. Particularly in the context of the national telecommunication carrier network (as distinct from competition in value-added services and customer- premises (terminal) equipment etc), it would be imprudent to forsake the traditional goal of universal service. If that goal were to be abandoned, there would be a distinct probability that a considerable segment of the people of Ireland would be excluded from the benefits of the Information Age, thereby creating, in effect, an information elite. The absence of any efficient national telecommunication carrier service whose principal task is to provide a universal service could infringe a person's constitutional right to communicate.[31]

The European Communities (Telecommunications Services) Regulations, 1992,[32] which provided for the liberalising of aspects of telecommunication carrier services — in essence valued-added or enhanced telecommunication services[33] — imposed specific duties on Telecom Éireann in relation to providers of telecommunication services in the context of access to the public telecommunication network. Telecom Éireann must ensure in relation to telecommunication service providers (including Telecom Éireann itself when providing a telecommunication service[34] which is not within its exclusive privilege)[35] that, *inter alia*, conditions (including charges payable) governing access to the public telecommunication network are objective, non-discriminatory and are published.[36]

In relation to the provision of leased lines, the 1992 Regulations stipulate that Telecom Éireann must meet requests for leased lines within a reasonable period of time; there are to be no restrictions on their use other than those relating to (a) provision of voice telephony services, (b) the security of network operations, (c) the maintenance of network integrity, and (d) in justified cases, the interoperability of services and data protection.[37]

It is noteworthy that there are no significant qualifications on the additional duties, identified in the foregoing paragraph, which were imposed on Telecom Éireann by the 1992 Regulations.[38] The concept specified in the 1983 Act[39] that duties and objects specified in that legislation in relation to the provision of telecommunication services were not to be construed as imposing on Telecom Éireann, either directly or indirectly, any form of duty or liability enforceable by proceedings before any court (to which it would not otherwise be subject), held little sway in the 1992 era of consumer sovereignty.

In 1992, the European Commission in its review of the telecommunication services sector advocated its support for full liberalisation of the intra-Community public telephony services with points of presence (interconnection points) for service providers on the territory of Member States.[40] The Commission argued that the conditions under which new entrants would compete would be fixed by national regulatory bodies which would also be empowered, in particular, to set appropriate access charges. The charges could include a contribution to the costs of maintaining universal service.[41] In June 1993, the European Council of Telecommunication Ministers supported the Commission's intention to liberalise all public voice telephony services on January 1, 1998, but Luxembourg and Belgium could apply for extensions to the year 2000, and Ireland, Greece, Portugal and Spain were given until 2003 to comply.[42]

In an effort to ensure greater competition in the markets for telecommunication network infrastructure (switching and transmission equipment) and pursuant to *EC Council Directive 90/531/ EEC*,[43] implementing regulations[44] have extended to the telecommunication carrier sector the rules already in force for public procurement in other sectors. The Directive applies to utilities (including telecommunication) works contracts the estimated value of which is not less than 5,000,000 ECU (approximately IR£3,845,460) — the same threshold as that for the existing "works" directive for public authorities. In the case of supplies contracts, however, the threshold for the "Utilities" is 400,000 ECU (approximately IR£307,637) — except in the case of the telecommunications sector for which the figure is 600,000 ECU (approximately IR£461,455). In June 1993 the Council of the European Communities adopted *Directive 93/38/EEC* coordinating the procurement procedures of entities operating in the water, energy, transport and telecommunication sectors.[45]

The regulation of Telecom Éireann, particularly in the context of the European Communities, is considered further in chapter 25, "The Jurisprudence of the Courts and International Influences".

18

Privileges and Duties of Other Providers of Telecommunication Carrier-Related Services

LIBERALISATION IN IRELAND

Subject to certain exceptions, the Postmaster-General and the Minister for Posts and Telegraphs enjoyed their *de jure* monopoly[1] under section 4 of the *Telegraph Act, 1869* over all aspects of the telecommunication carrier service until technology and international deregulation policies, particularly those emanating from the European Communities,[2] forced a change in that regime. The first telecommunication carrier-related activity to be liberalised was the provision, installation and maintenance of private automatic branch exchanges (PABXs) for connection to the general public network. This form of liberalisation had been authorised for many years by the Minister for Posts and Telegraphs prior to the establishment of Telecom Éireann in January 1984. This form of liberalisation was followed by the licensing of modems on privately-leased telecommunication lines — provided the equipment was type-approved.

The danger of "cream-skimming", and the conservation of the unity and integrity of the network resulted in the Government in 1983 granting Telecom Éireann a privilege to provide telecommunication services up to a connection point in the premises of a customer.[3] Any telecommunication service inside the connection point of the subscriber was thus outside Telecom Éireann's privilege. Although there was a specific licensing mechanism whereby persons could be licensed to provide telecommunication services *within* Telecom Éireann's so-called exclusive privilege, the Minister for Communications, John Wilson, stressed categorically in 1982 in the

Dáil that "there [was] no intention at present of issuing such a licence".[4] John Wilson's successor, Jim Mitchell, stated in the Dáil in 1983 that the issue of such licences was "not contemplated".[5] Technology and the liberalising forces of the European Communities persuaded the Government to license competitors to Telecom Éireann, i.e., to grant licences to others to provide telecommunication services within the exclusive privilege of Telecom Éireann.[6]

On its vesting in 1984, Telecom Éireann was granted an exclusive licence in relation to the provision of the first domestic telephone set. However, from 1984 onwards, pressure from suppliers of telecommunication equipment — together with the liberalising policies of the European Communities[7] — forced the Minister for Communications to further liberalise this segment of the provision of telecommunication services. Prohibitions on the supply of telecommunication terminal equipment were eased by the Minister for Communications on July 1, 1990 when the markets in telephone sets and payphones were liberalised. In consequence, from July 1 1990, telephones and payphones (in addition to all other terminal equipment) could, subject to conditions, be supplied to the market by suppliers licensed by the Minister for Communications.[8] In 1992, licensing requirements in relation to the supply, installation and maintenance of terminal equipment was stated to have been "abolished". Telecommunication terminal equipment intended for connection to the public network, however, had to be approved by the Minister for Communications for the purpose of ensuring the safety of users, network personnel and the networks.[9]

The *European Communities (Telecommunications Services) Regulations, 1992,*[10] made pursuant to liberalising measures of the European Communities,[11] specifically stipulated that telecommunication terminal equipment was not to be connected to or used in conjunction with the public telecommunication network of Telecom Éireann unless such equipment was of a type that had been approved by the Minister for Communications.[12] A person who places on the market, or connects to or uses in conjunction with the public telecommunication network, or who causes or permits to be so connected or used, telecommunication terminal equipment which has not been approved by the Minister for Communications shall be guilty of an offence and shall be liable on summary conviction to a fine not exceeding IR£800 or to imprisonment for a term not exceeding 12 months or to both.[13] The District Court is empowered to grant search and seizure warrants where, *inter alia,* equipment is being used in contravention of the 1992 Regulations.[14]

COMPARISON WITH THE UNITED STATES

Ireland's efforts at liberalisation of telecommunication terminal equipment may be compared with those of the United States. Up to 1947, virtually all US telephone companies required both business and residential subscribers to make use of chiefly carrier-provided, installed and maintained telephone equipment. They did so by imposing restrictions on the sale of "foreign attachments", i.e., attachments "foreign" to those of the telephone carrier. The restrictions on customer equipment choice were rationalised as necessary to safeguard the technical integrity of the public-switched network but were widely regarded as efforts to ensure "captive markets" for the carrier-service providers.

The first major break in this policy took place in 1947 when the US Federal Communications Commission (FCC) sanctioned the direct connection of telephone recording and answering devices to the public-switched network.[15] In 1948, the Hush-a-Phone Corporation filed a complaint with the FCC challenging the lawfulness of American Telephone and Telegraph (AT&T) tariff prohibitions on the use of a plastic, sound-muffling device that could be clipped on to a telephone mouthpiece in order to facilitate communications in noisy work environments. [AT&T was then the biggest corporation in the world.] The FCC agreed with AT&T that permitting the use of this device could give rise to such alleged harms as a "blasting effect" or the instrument handset being "not well-seated on the ear". However, the Court of Appeal for the District of Columbia Circuit in 1956 overturned the FCC's decision and directed the removal of the relevant tariff restrictions on the basis that they constituted an "unwarranted interference with the telephone subscriber's right to use reasonably his telephone in ways which are privately beneficial without being publicly detrimental".[16]

A decade later, the FCC in its *Carterfone* ruling ordered broad changes in AT&T's "foreign attachments" regulations. In 1960, the Carter Electronics Corporation attempted to market a cradle that would connect an ordinary telephone to a mobile radio transmitter. When AT&T threatened to suspend telephone service to customers using the "carterfone," Carter initiated a regulatory proceeding that lasted eight years before the FCC concluded that Bell's regulation had been unreasonable and discriminatory since its inception.[17] The Carterfone decision did not initially apply to embedded plant; it gave subscribers the right to use additional terminals of their own choosing, but not necessarily to replace existing equipment.[18]

Subsequently, in 1975, the FCC unequivocally applied *Carterfone* to embedded plant.[19] In 1976-77, the FCC adopted its "registration program", which authorised the interconnection of terminal equipment meeting relatively minimal standards sufficient to safeguard the network from technical harms.[20]

In 1980, the FCC adopted new rules governing carrier provision of terminal equipment as part of its *Second Computer Inquiry*.[21] The decision in that proceeding deregulated the business of retailing, installing and maintaining terminal equipment. The *Second Computer Inquiry* also required the Bell System companies to establish separate subsidiaries to handle regulated and unregulated operations, ostensibly to minimise the potential for anti-competitive cross-subsidisation. Contemporaneously, AT&T and its local telephone operating companies established a network of retail telephone equipment outlets, "phone centres", and AT&T's manufacturing arm, Western Electric, began marketing its terminal equipment through a diversity of retail outlets.

In the celebrated antitrust suit against AT&T which culminated in the Modified Final Judgment,[22] it was claimed, *inter alia*, that AT&T had foreclosed the equipment market through a bias towards its subsidiary Western Electric. It was alleged that the bias allowed AT&T to overcharge for Western Electric's equipment and earn excess profits at the expense of the ratepayer. Ultimately, however, Judge Greene acknowledged that the US Government's case on procurement bias against AT&T was not extremely strong.[23]

Throughout the world (including Ireland), the operators of the telephone carrier service monopolised the terminal equipment market ostensibly on the grounds of preserving the integrity of the network. Outside influences forced the providers of the telephone carrier services to open up the supply, installation and maintenance of terminal equipment to "outsiders". The courts in the United States, and the directives of the European Communities in the Irish context, were the agents of change.

VALUE-ADDED TELECOMMUNICATION SERVICES

The *European Communities (Telecommunications Services) Regulations, 1992*[24] limited the scope of Telecom Éireann's exclusive privilege and curtailed the discretion of the Minister for Communications in licensing value-added telecommunication services. The expression "value-added" or "enhanced" telecommunication services is not defined in the 1992 Regulations. However, the licence for such services refers to the provision of public telecommunication services by licensees which include facilities that are *additional* to anything necessary for the purpose of conveying a telecommunication message, and which facilitate processing, conversion, storage, redirection, replication or other such message handling.[25] Certain conditions are stipulated in the licence including the prohibition on the commercial provision to the public of the direct transport and switching of speech in real time between network termination points and the obligations on licensees to utilise the telecommunication links provided by Telecom Éireann or other network operators licensed by the Minister for Communications for any international conveying of telecommunication messages to or from the State.[26]

19

Privilege, Powers and Duties of Radio Telefís Éireann (RTE)

PRIVILEGE OF RTE

The *Wireless Telegraphy Act, 1926* authorised the Minister for Posts and Telegraphs, with the sanction of the Minister for Finance, to "acquire or establish such or so many broadcasting stations in such places in Saorstát Éireann" as the Minister from time to time considered proper.[1] The Minister was also empowered, with the sanction of the Minister for Finance, to "maintain and work all broadcasting stations" acquired or established by him and to receive, transmit, relay, or distribute "such broadcast matter" as he thought proper.[2]

The *Broadcasting Authority Act, 1960*, which established a broadcasting authority, later to be designated as Radio Telefís Éireann (RTE),[3] also provided that the Minister for Posts and Telegraphs was not empowered to exercise any of the powers previously mentioned in relation to broadcasting stations after the establishment day of the new authority.[4] Section 16 of the 1960 Act, as amended, provided that the Authority "shall establish and maintain a national television and sound broadcasting service and may establish and maintain local broadcasting services...." The 1960 Act also specifically empowered the Authority to establish, maintain and operate broadcasting stations and to "acquire, install and operate apparatus for wireless telegraphy".[5] These powers were specifically to be exercised by the Authority under licence from the Minister.[6]

O'Hanlon J in his judgment in the High Court in *State (Lynch) v Cooney*[7] (1982) noted that as no other lawful television or sound broadcasting service had been established since the passing of the *Broadcasting Authority Act, 1960*, it was correct to state that the RTE Authority at that time enjoyed a monopoly in broadcasting. Since

1988, RTE, pursuant to a licence from the Minister for Communications,[8] enjoys a privilege which is no longer of an exclusive nature of providing national radio and television services. From 1988, the "privilege" of providing broadcasting services has been shared between RTE and private enterprise.

POWERS AND DUTIES OF RTE

The main functions of the RTE Authority are set out in the *Broadcasting Authority Act, 1960* as amended.[9] The Authority is charged with establishing and maintaining a national television and sound broadcasting service and is also empowered to establish and maintain local broadcasting services. The Authority has all such powers as are necessary for or incidental to those purposes; incidental powers specified in the 1960 Act, as amended, included the authorisation to provide for the distribution by cable of programmes broadcast by the Authority and such other programmes as the Authority might decide.[10]

Under the 1960 Act, the Authority was obliged in performing its functions to bear constantly in mind certain "national aims" which were defined as the restoration of the Irish language and the preservation and development of the national culture.[11] The Minister for Posts and Telegraphs, Dr. Conor Cruise O'Brien, in the Seanad on the Second Stage of the *Broadcasting Authority (Amendment) Bill, 1975* considered that these two concepts were ambiguous in that they assumed "as obvious and acceptable to all the people certain concepts which are not in fact clear and which, if understood in a narrow sense, are not acceptable to many people in Ireland".[12] The Minister accepted many of the 1974 Broadcasting Review Committee recommendations on widening the scope of the duty of the Authority.[13] The *Broadcasting Authority (Amendment) Act, 1976* subsequently provided that in performing its functions, the Authority must in its programming

> (a) be responsive to the interests and concerns of the whole community, be mindful of the need for understanding and peace within the whole island of Ireland, ensure that the programmes reflect the varied elements which make up the culture of the people of the whole island of Ireland, and have special regard for the elements which distinguish that culture and in particular for the Irish language,

(b) uphold the democratic values enshrined in the Constitution, especially those relating to rightful liberty of expression, and
(c) have regard to the need for the formation of public awareness and understanding of the values and traditions of countries other than the State, including in particular those of such countries which are members of the European Economic Community.[14]

The Minister for Posts and Telegraphs intended that the duty expressed above would reflect a wider consensus based on "the growing recognition of the diverse interests and concerns of the people of Ireland".[15] A similar duty was imposed in 1988 on the proposed private television service but not on the private commercial radio services.[16] In many ways, these statutory duties imposed on the RTE Authority and on the private television service in Ireland appear to be aimed at developing the complete citizen. The complete Irish citizen should be responsive to the interests and concerns of the whole community, should be mindful of the need for understanding and peace within the whole island of Ireland, should be a person who appreciates the culture of the people of the whole island of Ireland, should uphold the democratic values enshrined in the Constitution, and should be aware of the need for the formation of public awareness and understanding of the values and traditions of countries other than Ireland.

The Irish Language

When the broadcasting legislation was being drafted in 1959, the Minister for Education, Patrick J. Hillery, suggested that the legislation should provide that all programmes be compatible with an Irish outlook and tradition.[17] Conscious of the fact that the new Authority would have to rely on imported films and tape-recordings, the Minister for Posts and Telegraphs, Michael Hilliard, considered that it would be impracticable for the Authority to comply with such a legal requirement.

The Television Commission (1959) had recommended that broadcasting programmes should bring the Irish language in gradually and be presented to the people in an attractive and efficient way and that eventually all staff dealing with the production and transmission of programmes should be bilingual.[18] The Interim Report of Coimisiún Um Athbheochan na Gaeilge on the use of Irish in the proposed television service recommended, *inter alia*, a stipulation that a satisfactory percentage of programmes should be in Irish, that the percentage should be gradually increased and that Irish should be the language of administration generally; persons without a competent knowledge of Irish were to be employed temporarily only. The Minister for Posts and Telegraphs made it clear that he did not propose to impose a specific statutory obligation of that kind on the Authority. He considered that implementation of the national policy in this regard could best be secured by the appointment of suitable persons to the Authority in due course.[19]

The general statutory duty imposed on the RTE Authority and in particular the duty on the Authority to have, inter alia, special regard for the Irish language was considered in the case of *An t-Aire Poist agus Telegrafa v Cáit Bean Uí Chadhain*.[20] This involved a case stated by Judge Gleeson of the Circuit Court to the Supreme Court pursuant to section 16 of the *Courts of Justice Act, 1947*. The defendant had been convicted in the District Court for possession of a television set without a licence. On appeal, the Circuit Court judge accepted that the defendant did possess a television set without a licence, but also accepted that the defendant was a native Irish speaker, that Irish was used by her and her nine children as the language of the home, that only five per cent of programmes shown on RTE in the preceding year were in Irish and that because of the lack of programmes in Irish the defendant had refused to obtain a television licence. Judge Gleeson accepted her submission that RTE had not fulfilled its statutory duty to have special regard for the Irish language when performing its functions in relation to programming. He was satisfied that the defendant was accordingly not guilty of the offence of possession of a television set without a licence.

Judge Gleeson stated that he would thus allow the appeal unless the Minister sought a case stated to the Supreme Court, in effect, forcing the Minister to request a case stated to the Supreme Court. Judge Gleeson posed the question for the Supreme Court whether the defendant was correct in defending herself on the grounds that the RTE Authority did not fulfil its statutory duty. The Circuit Judge then postulated that if the answer to that question were in the affirmative, whether the RTE Authority had a statutory duty to have some of its programmes in Irish and, further, whether such a duty would be fulfilled with approximately 5 per cent of RTE's programmes in Irish.

In the majority judgment, Henchy J of the Supreme Court considered that only one question need be answered — could the defendant when charged with the offence of possession of a television set without a licence use the defence that RTE had not fulfilled its duties as set out in section 17 of the *Broadcasting Authority Act, 1960*. Henchy J, with whom Griffin J agreed, had no difficulty whatsoever in stating that the defendant could not use such a defence: "Is furast an cheist sin a fhreagairt: ní cead di sin a dhéanamh." ["It is easy to answer that question: she is not allowed to do that."][21] The Circuit Judge's view that he had jurisdiction to take RTE's statutory duty into account in the case before him was swiftly disposed of by Henchy J: "Bhí dul amú air sa tuairim sin." ["He was mistaken in that opinion."] Walsh J dissented as he considered that no questions of law were involved. Henchy J did state that if the defendant wished to raise the question of a statutory duty, she could do so in the High Court, but before she did so, she should remember the wide discretion that section 17 gave the Authority. In so stating Henchy J drew particular attention to the expressions "within the whole island of Ireland" and "the people of the whole island of Ireland" in section 17 of the 1960 Act. Whilst he did not wish to prejudge the matter, Henchy J considered that it would be difficult to state that the duties of the Authority were not being fulfilled merely because a certain percentage of the programmes were not in Irish. Henchy J, with whom Griffin J agreed, held that the other questions raised by the Circuit Judge were extraneous to the issues affecting the defendant's case. [It is of interest to note that the entire case from the District to the Supreme Court was conducted in Irish. Equally all the judgments were in Irish. Unfortunately, the judgments have not been reported.]

Objectivity and Impartiality

News and the treatment of current affairs broadcast by RTE must be reported and presented in an objective and impartial manner and without any expression of the Authority's own views.[22] When the original section of the 1960 Act was being amended by the 1976 Act, objections were raised to the inclusion in the legislation of references to impartiality and objectivity. The Minister for Posts and Telegraphs, Dr. Conor Cruise O'Brien, appreciated that objectivity and impartiality were "probably philosophically unattainable by human beings".[23] Nevertheless he considered it desirable, on balance, that a public corporation should have the obligation enjoined on them "to move in that direction". The Minister considered that the obligation on the Authority to be objective and impartial was a means of "subjecting the Authority to a continuous reference to the

Broadcasting Complaints Commission".[24] This is undoubtedly correct.

The broadcast treatment of current affairs must be fair to all concerned but in this context, two or more related broadcasts may be considered as a whole provided that the broadcasts are transmitted within a reasonable time.[25]

The duty of objectivity is interpreted by RTE as the "setting forth of an actual external situation uncoloured by the feelings or subjective views of the broadcaster".[26] Impartiality is interpreted "as being fair and just in reporting and presenting the facts without favouring any particular interest or interests involved".[27] The requirement to be "fair to all interests" is seen by RTE as "requiring the programme-makers to present, in an equitable manner, views of persons or interests involved in a significant way in a particular issue".[28]

The statutory duties of objectivity and impartiality are considered further in chapter 30.

Crime, the Authority of the State, Pornography and Violence

There is a statutory prohibition on the RTE Authority from including in any of its broadcasts anything which "may reasonably be regarded as being likely to promote, or incite to, crime or as tending to undermine the authority of the State".[29] These words were based on the final sentence of Article 40.6.1.i. of the Constitution. Dr. Cruise O'Brien, as Minister for Posts and Telegraphs, gave an interesting insight into his meaning of the expression "tending to undermine the authority of the State".[30] The Minister considered whether the word "security" should be used instead of "authority". However, he chose "authority" because it had a broader meaning. The Minister stated that anything which undermined the security of the State also undermined its authority. But he stated that you could have certain programmes which would cast doubt on the legitimacy or effectiveness of the democratic State which would not be construed as a direct threat to the security of the State, but which would nevertheless undermine its authority. The Minister instanced examples of programmes reflecting not on individuals in Parliament, nor on the Government of the day, as such, but on Parliament as a whole, on the judiciary, on the army, on the Garda. The Minister stated that all these programmes would not necessarily threaten security but they would undermine the authority of the State.[31]

Pursuant to an EC Council Directive of 1989,[32] regulations made by the Minister for Communications in 1991 prohibit RTE, (and any other entity in Ireland providing a licensed television programme service) from broadcasting television programmes that may seriously impair the physical, mental or moral development of minors, in particular those that involve pornographic or gratuitous violence.[33] However, the regulations stipulate that other programmes which might impair the physical, mental or moral development of minors may only be shown where the broadcaster ensures, by selecting the time of the broadcast, or by any technical means, that minors would not normally be expected to hear or see such broadcasts.[34]

The 1991 Regulations also stipulate that a broadcast shall not contain any incitement to hatred on the grounds of race, sex, religion or nationality.[35]

Privacy

The RTE Authority is specifically obliged not to "unreasonably encroach on the privacy of an individual" in its programmes and in the means employed to make such programmes.[36] This specific statutory duty was imposed on the Authority by the 1976 Act. Although the legislation did not expressly provide that a person could sue the Authority in damages for breach of its statutory duty where a person's privacy was encroached upon in a radio or television programme of the Authority, it is submitted that such a person could do so under the general law.[37] A complaint could also be made to the Broadcasting Complaints Commission.[38] Senator John Horgan considered that this statutory obligation on RTE was unfair because RTE was "lumbered with a statutory restriction which did not apply to other agencies".[39] Subsequent to the enactment of the 1976 Act, RTE itself in a direction to staff banned the "use of surreptitious recording and filming" devices except in the most exceptional cases[40] and the Director-General was to authorise such exceptions. To constitute an exception, the activity under investigation must be gravely anti-social; the broadcasting of matter relating to the activity must be recognised as serving an important public purpose which could not be achieved by other means; the use of the devices in question must be indispensable and must not contravene the law.[41] Use of certain radio devices without a licence is prohibited by the *Wireless Telegraphy Acts*.[42]

Transmission of European Works

Pursuant to a 1989 EC Directive,[43] regulations made by the Minister for Communications in 1991 direct that RTE (and any other television programme service provider in Ireland) shall, where practicable and by appropriate means, reserve for European works "a majority proportion of its transmission time, excluding the time appointed to news, sporting events, games, advertising and teletext services".[44] This obligation is qualified by the provision that regard should be had to RTE's (and any other television programme service provider) informational, educational, cultural and entertainment responsibilities to its viewing public;[45] the obligation was to be achieved progressively.[46] The regulations provide that when the above obligation cannot be attained, the relevant proportion of transmission time for European works is not to be lower than the average proportion of transmission time devoted to European works, if any, in 1988.[47] "European works" are defined in the EC Council Directive (but not in the 1991 Regulations) as meaning works originating from Member States of the Community, European Third countries party to the European Convention on Transfrontier Television of the Council of Europe and works originating from other European Third countries.[48]

Subject to qualifications similar to those expressed above in relation to "European works" in general, RTE (and any other television programme service provider) must, where practicable and by appropriate means, reserve at least 10 per cent of television transmisssion time for European works created by producers who are independent of broadcasters, or reserve 10 per cent of its programming budget for European works which are created by producers who are independent of broadcasters.[49]

Other Powers and Duties

The RTE Authority is obliged to conduct its affairs so as to secure that its revenues meet both current expenditures and make "suitable provisions" for capital requirements.[50] The duties of the Authority in respect of accounts and audits,[51] annual reports,[52] borrowing powers[53] and advertising[54] have already been considered under the heading of the powers of the Minister for Communications.[55] The Authority is authorised to acquire land by agreement and compulsorily, if necessary, and dispose of land.[56] Every broadcast made by the Authority must be recorded in sound form and retained by the Authority for at least 180 days or for such other period as shall be agreed between the Authority and the Broadcasting Complaints Commission.[57]

RTE (and any other television programme service provider) are prohibited from broadcasting a film, unless otherwise agreed between its rights holders and RTE (or such other television programme service provider) until two years have elapsed since the film was first shown in cinemas in one of the Member States of the European Community or one year where the film was co-produced by RTE (or any other television service provider).[58]

The general competition law of the EEC has affected RTE in relation to its listings of television programmes.[59] In effect, RTE is being forced to share its listings information with others.

INDEPENDENCE OF RTE

From a legal viewpoint, subject to the constraints already discussed, the RTE Authority is independent of Government. The Government, from time to time, has had other views. The restrictive view of RTE's functions, expressed in the Dáil in 1966 by the Taoiseach, Seán Lemass, achieved considered notoriety:

> Radio Telefís Éireann was set up by legislation as an instrument of public policy and as such is responsible to the Government. ... [T]he Government reject the view that Radio Telefís Éireann should be, either generally or in regard to its current affairs and news programmes, completely independent of Government supervision. [I]t has the duty, while maintaining impartiality between political parties ... to sustain public respect for the institutions of government and, where appropriate, to assist public understanding of the policies enshrined in legislation enacted by the Oireachtas. The Government will take such action ... as may be necessary to ensure that Radio Telefís Éireann does not deviate from the due performance of this duty.[60]

This often-quoted dictum has had a considerable influence on the psyche of the Irish broadcaster. Peter Feeney, a producer in RTE, stated that Lemass's statement was "burnt into the consciousness of every serious broadcaster".[61] The Lemass view of RTE was firmly rejected in the Dáil by a subsequent Taoiseach, Dr. Garret FitzGerald,

almost 20 years later. Controversy over the appointment of a
director-general to RTE prompted the Taoiseach to deny categorically that the Government had "any intention of, or would tolerate
a politicisation of RTE".[62] He continued:

> On this subject I have a very strong view which I have held since
> the establishment of RTE as our national broadcasting service.
> I believe that it is of vital importance that RTE be free from
> political control, influence or bias — that it be as independent
> as we can make it. It is not, and should never be, an arm of
> Government policy. On this point I find myself, and remain, in
> disagreement with the statement by the former Taoiseach, Mr.
> Seán Lemass, that RTE should be an "instrument of public
> policy".
> No Government of which I am leader will take any step that
> will weaken the independence of RTE.[63]

An inevitable tension exists between Government and broadcasters. From time to time in Ireland as in other democracies this
tension becomes public.[64] An example of such tension was the
political storm which followed the questioning of Seamus Brennan,
then Minister for Transport and Tourism on September 22, 1989 in
the context of a discussion on the decision to take operating rights
from Aer Lingus and give them to Ryanair. The Minister was asked
whether Tony Ryan of Ryanair was a contributor to Fianna Fail party
funds. The Government immediately sought an apology from RTE.
The Director-General of RTE apologised by letter and a subsequent
apology was broadcast on radio. The Director-General stated that
the implication "was that you, as Minister, could be influenced in
any decision by anything other than the relevant issues. . . . an
implication for which no evidence was provided". Dr. Cruise
O'Brien wrote that the Director-General's apology to the Minister for
Transport and Tourism

> constitute[d] a denial of freedom to question, and consequently
> an abdication of the most important function of broadcasting
> in relation to the political health of our democracy. That
> apology weakens to a significant degree the defences of the
> people against possible abuses of power.[65]

Dr. Ronan Fanning has argued that the relationship between
journalists and politicians must always be potentially adversarial.[66]

In a sense, the RTE Authority is a mediator between the professional broadcasters and the Government: the RTE Authority is ultimately accountable to the Government in the sense that a member of the Authority can be removed from office by the Government (subject to resolutions being passed by both Houses of the Oireachtas)[67] and the Government and Dáil are accountable to the public. However, the RTE Authority is independent of Government, although the Authority is, in a limited sense, also acting in a manner akin to a trustee in the public interest.

20

Cable Television and Multi-Point Distribution Systems Providers

PRIVILEGES, POWERS AND DUTIES OF CABLE TELEVISION PROVIDERS

The history of cable television in Ireland and the various reports and inquiries[1] relating to cable services have been considered in chapter 13. The privileges, powers and duties of cable operators will be considered here. Cable television systems come within the definition of apparatus for wireless telegraphy.[2] Hence, the *Wireless Telegraphy Acts, 1926* to 1988 regulate cable television. The term "telegraph" as defined in the *Telegraphs Acts 1863 and 1869*[3] includes cable used for communication purposes. Hence the Telegraph Acts 1863 to 1916 still partly regulate cable services. However, the *Wireless Telegraphy (Wired Broadcast Relay Licence) Regulations, 1974 to 1988*[4] (the governing regulations) specifically regulate cable. Only cable systems with more than 100 service points must be licensed under the *Wireless Telegraphy Acts.*[5]

A cable television operator receives a licence from the Minister for Communications for a defined area.[6] The licence authorises the licensee to install, maintain, work and use appropriate (wireless telegraphy) apparatus[7] at the places specified in the licence and to connect the apparatus with service points in the area (described in the licence) to the intent that the relevant programmes may be received by wire at service points in the area. Although the licence does not purport to be exclusive for a particular area, in effect, only one licence is granted for a defined area; hence the cable licensee enjoys an exclusive licence, i.e. has a monopoly within a defined area. In several cases, cable licensees have succeeded in obtaining orders in the High Court directing the Minister for Posts and Telegraphs and his successor, the Minister for Communications, to prosecute unlicensed operators within a "licensed" area.[8] In *Connaught (Multi-Channel TV) Limited*,[9] the Minister for Communications undertook in the High Court to take all feasible steps necessary to enforce the *Wireless Telegraphy Acts 1926 to 1972* against unlicensed persons who kept and used wireless telegraphy apparatus to rebroadcast television signals and who interfered with the signal reception or relayed services of Connaught (Multi-Channel) TV or provided an "illegal service" to an area or areas covered by a cable television licence of Connaught (Multi-Channel) TV. In effect, the cable licensees were enforcing their exclusive privileges. The issue of the constitutionality of a local monopoly for cable television operators in the context of the constitutional guarantee of freedom of expression in Article 40.6.1.i of the Constitution will be considered in chapter 26 "Freedom of Expression".

A distinction is made in the governing regulations between two cable services. Firstly, there is the "basic service" which is defined as meaning television programmes and sound programmes relayed by the licensee which a person is obliged to pay for in order to become a subscriber to a relay service.[10] The basic service includes the national television and sound programmes of RTE and approved local programmes as may be required by the Minister to be relayed.[11] The discretionary service is defined as meaning television programmes or sound programmes relayed by the licensee which a subscriber may accept or refuse, at his discretion, without affecting the relay of basic services to that subscriber.[12]

Cable television operators must pay to the Minister for Communications a fee of five per cent gross revenue less installation charges and value added tax[13] paid to the cable television operator in respect of basic service only. In this context, the Minister for Communications may require a certificate from an auditor.[14] The approval of the Minister for Communications is required for any proposed charge and any variation of the charge for the basic service.[15] Although it is not expressly provided for or authorised in the governing regulations, the Minister for Posts and Telegraphs (and his successors) have issued proceedings against cable television operators for recovery of licence fees on the basis that such fees were owed as a contractual debt.

The Minister for Communications determines, to a certain extent, what programmes the cable operator may transmit. Firstly, the television cable operator must relay "live" the national television and national sound programmes of RTE, and any "local programmes" as may be required by the Minister. These may be termed the "must-carry" provisions. Secondly, the cable operator has a discretion to transmit other programmes as may be specified by the Minister for Communications.[16] However regulations made in 1991 provide that subject to certain conditions, nothing in earlier regulations shall be construed as restricting retransmission in Ireland of any television broadcasts from Member States of the European Communities or from States (being non-Member States of the European Communities) who are parties to the *European Convention on Transfrontier Television.*[17]

The cable television operator must maintain a record of the names and addresses of possessors of television sets connected to the cable service and the record must include particulars of the dates on which the programmes were first transmitted to such connection points and the dates on which such transmission ceased.[18] Such information and any information in relation to the cable service must be furnished to the Minister upon request.[19]

The cable television operator, inter alia, (a) must not place any restrictions on the make or type of apparatus which may be used to receive the relayed programmes, (b) must not use or allow to be used the cable wires for any purpose other than the relay of the authorised programmes, (c) shall not originate or receive any programme, message, or item for transmission except the authorised programmes, (d) shall not refuse to connect a person to the cable service unless the Minister for Communications agrees and (e) shall not use any frequency channels other than approved frequency channels.[20]

If and when required by the Minister for Communications, the cable television operator must delete any advertising matter from a programme received by him or insert advertising or other matter in a programme or programmes relayed to subscribers.[21]

MULTI-POINT MICROWAVE DISTRIBUTION SYSTEMS PROVIDERS

Ireland was the first European country to embark on multi-point microwave distribution systems (MMDS) for the retransmission of television and radio signals. MMDS, which is also known in the television industry as "wireless cable", is a local telecommunication delivery system capable of distributing video, voice and data signals by radio from a central transmitter to individual locations. To receive MMDS signals, a subscriber requires an MMDS receiver antenna, a downconverter and generally a decoder.

The *Wireless Telegraphy Acts 1926 to 1988* and the *Wireless Telegraphy (Television Programme Retransmission) Regulations, 1989,*[22] in particular, regulate MMDS in a manner similar to cable television. A licence from the Minister for Communications authorises licensees to install, maintain, work and use appropriate apparatus for the retransmission of television programme services and for such other purposes as are specified in the licence. However, an MMDS licensee may not install or agree to the installation of an MMDS service in any area in which a cable television service licence has been issued, except with the prior approval of the Minister for Communications and the cable television licensee.[23] Like cable television, a licence does not purport to be exclusive for a particular area. However, in practice, only one licence is granted for a defined area. This is because of physical restraints on available frequencies. Hence the MMDS licensee enjoys an exclusive licence, i.e. has a monopoly within a defined area.

The fee paid by an MMDS licensee on the grant of a licence is £20,000.[24] In addition, the amount of the renewal fee is five per cent of the annual gross revenue, excluding installation charges and value-added tax arising from the provision of television programme services.[25] There is an automatic renewal procedure for a total period of ten years.[26]

As in relation to cable television services, the regulations provide a "must carry" obligation: the Minister for Communications determines to some extent what programmes the MMDS licensee may transmit.[27] The licensee must furnish appropriate information to the Minister[28] and, on request, permit an authorised officer to inspect any record kept by the licensee in connection with the subject matter of his licence. The licensee must maintain a record of the names and addresses of each possessor of a television set at each subscriber reception area, and such record must include the date service was first provided and the date (if any) when the re-transmission to such subscriber ceased.[29] Within six months of commencing retransmission, the licensee must transmit to the Minister for Communications names and addresses of each subscriber in possession of a television set and the total number of subscribers.

INTERCEPTION OF CABLE AND MMDS SERVICES

The *Broadcasting Act, 1990* (sections 9 to 15) prohibits unauthorised connections to the cable television network and to the MMDS distribution system. In effect, the unlawful interception of cable television and MMDS signals has been made a specific criminal offence. The word "interception" is defined essentially as taking cable television or MMDS signals without the agreement of the licensed operator of the service.[30]

Section 9(1) and 9(3) make it a criminal offence to: (a) intercept a cable or MMDS television service; (b) suffer or permit or do any other thing that enables the interception of the cable or MMDS service by any person; (c) possess, manufacture, assemble, import, supply or offer to supply equipment which is designed or adapted for the purpose of enabling interception; and (d) publish information with the intention of enabling any person to intercept the service.[31]

21

The Powers and Duties of the Independent Radio and Television Commission and Private Broadcasting Service Providers

THE INDEPENDENT RADIO AND TELEVISION COMMISSION

The *Radio and Television Act, 1988*, originally presented by Fianna Fáil Minister for Communications, Ray Burke, as the *Sound Broadcasting Bill, 1987*, envisaged a *direct* licensing arrangement between the Minister for Communications and sound broadcasters. This did not find favour with the opposition parties and, subsequently, the 1987 Bill was transformed at the Committee Stage in the Dáil,[1] became the *Radio and Television Bill* and provided for the establishment of the Independent Radio and Television Commission. Accordingly, the Independent Radio and Television Commission owes its existence partly to the fact that the Government of the day was in a minority position in voting terms in the Dáil and that some form of independent broadcasting commission was demanded by the opposition parties.

The constitution of the Commission is similar to that proposed for the Local Radio Commission in the *Local Radio Bill, 1985* by the Coalition Government of Fine Gael and Labour parties. The conventional and routine legislative statutory provisions regulating the Commission are set out in the schedule to the *Radio and Television Act, 1988*. Many of these provisions have been considered earlier in the context of the powers and duties of the Minister for Communications in relation to the Commission. Of note is the statutory duty on

a member of the Commission who has any interest in any company
or concern with which the Commission proposes to make any
contract, or any interest in any contract which the Commission
proposes to make, to disclose to the Commission the fact and nature
of the interest and not to take part in any deliberation or decision of
the Commission relating to the contract.[2] Such disclosure must be
recorded in the minutes of the Commission.[3] There is also a statutory
duty on the Commission to make an annual report of its proceedings
to the Minister for Arts and Culture during the preceding year and
to submit such information regarding the performance of its
functions as the Minister may from time to time require.[4]

The functions of the Commission are set out in section 4 of the
Radio and Television Act, 1988. The Commission is empowered to
select persons (excluding RTE) who wish to provide broadcasting
services and to regulate the broadcasting services to be provided by
such persons.[5] Some of the functions of the Commission have been
considered earlier in the discussion on the powers and duties of the
Minister for Communications in relation to broadcasting services
other than RTE.[6] Some further functions and powers of the
Commission may be considered here.

The Commission must ensure that every sound broadcasting
contractor and the television programme service contractor comply
with the provisions of the *Radio and Television Act, 1988.*[7]

Section 4(8) of the 1988 Act provides that the Commission is to
have all such powers as are necessary for or incidental to the
performance of its functions under the 1988 Act. Some of these
powers are specified: the power to require sound broadcasting and
the television programme service contractors to enter into financial
bonds with the Commission; the power to direct a contractor to
record any or all of the programmes broadcast by him in the case of
a sound broadcasting contract, or provided by him in the case of a
television programme service contract, and to retain such recordings
for a period of 90 days after the recording is made and to submit the
recordings to the Commission should the Commission so request.
The Commission is also specifically empowered under section 4(10)
of the Act of 1988

> (a) to make such contracts, agreements and arrangements and
> do all such other things as are incidental or conducive to the
> objects of the Commission;
> (b) to acquire and make use of copyrights, patents, licences,
> privileges and concessions;

(c) to compile, prepare, publish and distribute with or without charge, such magazines, books and other printed material and such aural and visual material as may seem to the Commission to be incidental or conducive to its objectives;

(d) subject to the consent of the Minister [for Arts and Culture], to arrange for the provision of services with or without charge for and on behalf of any Minister of the Government by a sound broadcasting contractor or the television programme service contractor;

(e) to require sound broadcasting contractors and the television programme service contractor to co-operate with the Garda Síochána, local authorities and health boards in the dissemination of relevant information to the public in the event of major emergencies.

Section 4(10)(d) of the 1988 Act, which authorises the Commission, subject to the consent of the Minister for Arts and Culture, to require contractors to provide services for and on behalf of any Minister of the Government, would facilitate broadcasting by members of the Government and is similar to the obligation imposed on the RTE Authority pursuant to section 31(2) of the *Broadcasting Authority Act, 1960*.

PRIVILEGES, POWERS AND DUTIES OF PRIVATE BROADCASTING SERVICE PROVIDERS

The legislation regulating broadcasting services, other than those services provided by the semi-state authority RTE, was deferred for many years because of legislative inaction and ideological differences over the form of regulation among the partners in the Coalition Government of the early 1980s.[8] The regulation of what may be loosely described as private broadcasting service providers is governed by the *Radio and Television Act, 1988*, the broadcasting contract between the Independent Radio and Television Commission and the private broadcasting service providers, and the licence issued by the Minister for Communications to the Independent Radio and Television Commission in relation to each broadcasting service.

The *modus operandi* whereby contracts are awarded for sound broadcasting services and for the single television programme service has already been considered.[9] In the case of the sound broadcasting contractor, the Independent Radio and Television Commission receives a licence from the Minister for Communications pursuant to section 4(3) of the 1988 Act in respect of the sound broadcasting transmitter. The position is similar in respect of the single private television programme service contractor. However, any television programme service is to be distributed using channel capacity on wired broadcast relay and television programme re-transmission systems.[10] There are thus several regulatory regimes applicable to the independent broadcasting services: first, the *Radio and Television Act, 1988*; second, the contractual formalities; and thirdly, the licensing process.

The principal statutory duties of the private providers of broadcasting services (which include any non-profit community-based radio services) relate to the content of their programmes. Every sound broadcasting contractor and the single television programme contractor has a statutory duty under section 9(1) of the *Radio and Television Act, 1988* to ensure that

> (a) all news broadcast by him is reported and presented in an objective and impartial manner and without any expression of his own views;
> (b) the broadcast treatment of current affairs, including matters which are either of public controversy or the subject of current public debate, is fair to all interests concerned and that the broadcast matter is presented in an objective and impartial manner and without any expression of his own views.

However, there is a proviso in section 9(1)(b) to the effect that should it prove impracticable in relation to a single broadcast to apply these standards of objectivity and impartiality, then two or more related broadcasts may be considered as a whole if the broadcasts are transmitted within a reasonable period of each other. [The issue of the constitutionality of these standards is considered in chapter 30.] The requirements of objectivity and impartiality do not prevent a sound broadcasting contractor from transmitting political party broadcasts — provided that in the allocation of time for such broadcasts, the broadcasting contractor does not give an unfair preference to any political party.[11]

A further duty imposed on sound broadcasting contractors, subject to certain exceptions, is that not less than 20 per cent of broadcasting time and, if the sound broadcasting service is provided for more than 12 hours in any one day, two hours of broadcasting time between 07.00 hours and 19.00 hours is dedicated to the broadcasting of news and current affairs programmes. This proviso does not apply to any television programme service contractor.[12] Section 15 of the *Radio and Television Act, 1988* authorises the Commission to grant a derogation in whole or in part from this obligation on the private sound broadcasting service (relating to news and current affairs programming) where it is satisfied that there is a reasonable plurality of sources of news and current affairs programming available to the public in question from other sound broadcasting services. The rationale behind the derogation principle is that the specified quota of broadcasting time that must be devoted to the broadcasting of news and current affairs imposed on sound broadcasting contractors by section 9(1) of the 1988 Act could impede the development of specialised radio services.

This obligation to devote not less than 20 per cent of broadcasting time to news and current affairs is unduly onerous. Its constitutionality is queried later in chapter 26 in the context of an examination of the constitutional guarantee of freedom of expression. Such an obligation would be justifiable if it were imposed on RTE services only which are maintained partly by public funds. In the United Kingdom there is no requirement that all services licensed by the Independent Television Commission or the Radio Authority (which does not include the BBC) provide news. In the United Kingdom the necessity for every cable programme service, satellite channel or local radio service to devote time to news was considered to run counter to the government's policy to foster expansion and diversity in those areas.[13]

Every broadcasting contractor must comply with the requirement specified in section 9(1)(d) of the 1988 Act that nothing is broadcast by him which may reasonably be regarded as offending against good taste or decency. Surprisingly, this requirement has never been imposed by statute on the RTE Authority. Section 9(1)(d) of the 1988 Act also imposes on every sound broadcasting contractor the duty of ensuring that nothing is broadcast which may reasonably be regarded as being likely to promote or incite crime or as tending to undermine the authority of the State. There is a similar prohibition imposed on the RTE Authority under section 18(1A) of the *Broadcasting Authority Act, 1960* as amended by substitution by section 3 of the *Broadcasting Authority (Amendment) Act, 1976*. A dual enjoiner similar to that imposed in section 9(1)(d) of the 1988 Act in relation, *inter alia*, to good taste and promoting or inciting crime was contained in section 4(1)(a) of the UK *Broadcasting Act, 1981* and has been re-enacted in section 6 of the UK *Broadcasting Act, 1990*. This enjoiner was considered in *Attorney General ex rel McWhirter v Independent Broadcasting Authority*[14] where it was stated that the courts will not interfere with a decision of the Authority to transmit a programme which is alleged to contravene this requirement unless it is shown that the Authority had misdirected itself in law or reached a conclusion that it could not reasonably reach.[15]

A further duty imposed on every independent broadcasting contractor by virtue of section 9(1)(e) of the 1988 Act is to ensure that in programmes broadcast by him and in the means employed to make such programmes, the privacy of the individual is not unreasonably encroached upon. A similar duty is imposed on the RTE Authority under section 18(1) of the *Broadcasting Authority Act, 1960* as amended by substitution by section 3 of the *Broadcasting Authority (Amendment) Act, 1976*. There is no authoritative definition of privacy in Irish law but in *Kennedy and Arnold v Ireland* (1987),[16] where in the context of rights guaranteed by the Constitution, it was held that telephone tapping by the State of the plaintiffs' telephones infringed their right of privacy, Hamilton P adopted for the purposes of that case what he described as the definition of Brandeis J — "the right to be let alone".[17]

Every broadcasting contractor must comply with any code governing standards and practice in relation to the duties considered above which the Independent Radio and Television Commission may prepare.[18]

Certain statutory duties in relation to programming are imposed on the private television programme service contractor which do not apply to the private sound broadcasting service contractors. Section 18(3) of the *Radio and Television Act, 1988* provides that the Independent Radio and Television Commission must ensure that the television programme service provided under the 1988 Act shall in its programming

> (a) be responsive to the interests and concerns of the whole community, be mindful of the need for understanding and peace within the whole island of Ireland, ensure that the programmes reflect the varied elements which make up the culture of the people of the whole island of Ireland, and have special regard for the elements which distinguish that culture and in particular for the Irish language;
> (b) uphold the democratic values enshrined in the Constitution especially those relating to rightful liberty of expression;

(c) have regard to the need for the formation of public awareness and understanding of the values and traditions of countries other than the State, including in particular those of such countries which are members of the European Community; and

(d) includes a reasonable proportion of news and current affairs programmes.

The obligations imposed by virtue of section 18(3)(a),(b) and (c) above are identical to the obligations imposed on the RTE Authority by section 17(a),(b), and (c) of the *Broadcasting Authority Act, 1960* as amended by substitution by section 13 of the *Broadcasting Authority (Amendment) Act, 1976*. The 20 per cent quota requirement in relation to news and current affairs has not been extended to the television service, primarily according to the Minister for Communications (when introducing the legislation) because television, particularly in the news area, involves a much higher order of costs than radio. Accordingly, it was considered that a more flexible approach should be adopted which is now specified in section 18(3)(d) of the 1988 Act which requires the television programme service contractor to provide only "a reasonable proportion of news and current affairs programmes".

Section 18(4)(a) provides that the Independent Radio and Television Commission must ensure that the private television service will have a reasonable proportion of its programmes produced in the State or in another Member State or the European Communities. In the Seanad, when introducing the provision, the Minister for Communications, Ray Burke, admitted a preference for programmes of Irish origin but realised that European Communities' obligations precluded "a purely national discrimination".[19] Further, section 18(4) provides that the Commission must ensure that a reasonable proportion of the television programme service is devoted to original programme material produced in a Member State of the European Communities, by persons other than the contractor, his subsidiary, his parent or existing broadcasting organisations.

The sound broadcasting contractors are authorised specifically to include advertising in their programmes but must comply with any appropriate code governing standards and practices in advertising.[20] Advertising in this context is to be construed as including reference to advertising matter contained in sponsored programmes.[21] However, certain categories of advertisements are prohibited by the 1988 Act: no advertisement may be broadcast which is directed towards any religious or political end or which has any relation to an industrial dispute.[22] A similar prohibition is imposed on the RTE Authority by section 20(4) of the *Broadcasting Authority Act, 1960.* The total daily times for broadcasting advertisements in a sound broadcasting service is regulated by the 1988 Act: the time allotted for broadcasting advertisements is not to exceed a maximum of 15 per cent of the total daily broadcasting time and the maximum time to be given to advertisements in any hour is not to exceed a maximum of ten minutes.[23]

Every sound broadcasting contractor and the television programme service contractor is obliged by section 11(1) of the *Radio and Television Act, 1988* to give due and adequate consideration to any complaint which is not of a frivolous or vexatious nature, made by a member of the public in respect of the broadcasting service provided by the contractor. Every broadcasting contractor must keep due and proper records of all such complaints and of every reply made or of any action taken in relation to the complaint.[24] Every broadcasting contractor must, if requested by the Independent Radio and Television Commission, make available for inspection by the Commission all records kept by him in relation to complaints.[25] In 1992, the Minister for Communications, pursuant to section 11 (3) of the 1988 Act directed that complaints made by members of the public in relation to any sound broadcasting service and any television programme service contractor may be investigated by the Broadcasting Complaints Commission.[26] The Broadcasting Complaints Commission is considered in the next chapter.

Each broadcasting contractor must comply with any order made under section 31(1) of the *Broadcasting Authority Act, 1960* as amended by substitution by section 16 of the *Broadcasting Authority (Amendment) Act, 1976.*[27] Section 31(1) of the 1960 Act, as amended, provides that where the Minister for Arts and Culture is of the opinion that the broadcasting of a particular matter or matter of a particular class would be likely to promote or incite to crime or would tend to undermine the authority of the State, he may by order direct the RTE Authority from broadcasting the matter or any matter of the particular class and the Authority must comply with the order of the Minister. This issue is considered in some detail in chapter 16.

The Broadcasting Contract

The second layer of regulation of the private broadcasting services is effected by the Independent Radio and Television Commission *via* the broadcasting contract between the Commission and the broadcasting contractor.[28] No television programme service contract has been issued to date by the Commission; accordingly, this section is devoted to a consideration of the sound broadcasting contract. However, the same principles would probably apply to a television programme contractor.

The sound broadcasting contractor is authorised by the contract to have the right and duty to establish, maintain and operate sound broadcasting transmitters subject to the terms and conditions of the *Radio and Television Act, 1988*, the contract with the Commission, and the licence issued by the Minister for Communications to the Commission. Sound broadcasting contracts were specified to be for a period of seven years with the right to renew the contract for a further period of seven years on terms similar to those specified in the contract between the parties with such variations (if any) as the Commission considers reasonably proper. Neither the contract nor any right or interest may be assigned by the contractor without the prior consent in writing of the Commission.

Detailed rules are prescribed by the Commission in relation to what may be described as "cross ownership". The aggregate interests of all "restricted investors" must not, without the prior written consent of the Commission, exceed 25 per cent of the voting rights in the contractor, excluding any such "restricted investor" that owns or controls less than 1 per cent of any such rights. The term "restricted investor" is defined, *inter alia*, as another sound broadcasting contractor, a person who beneficially owns or controls not less than 5 per cent of the voting rights in another sound broadcasting contractor, the proprietor of any newspaper, whether international, foreign, national or local, a television programme service contractor, a national or international broadcasting agency or communications company, a political party or an elected representative of any such political party, a religious denomination or a recognised representative of any such religious denomination, or a person not normally resident in a Member State of the European Communities.

The justification for these restrictions must be the hope that a flourishing marketplace of ideas will emerge from a diversity of many voices. The Commission was acting to ensure that there would be genuine multiplicity and diversity. Restrictions on newspapers, other broadcasting contractors, religious denominations and political parties may be justified, as such multiple ownership might lead to a monopoly in a particular area both in economic and informational senses. However, such entities should not be prohibited, *per se*, from ownership of radio stations.

In the context of programming, the broadcasting contractor must provide to the satisfaction of the Commission the quality, range and type of programme required by the 1988 Act as proposed by the contractor in his application for the award of the contract. The Commission may, by notice, require the contractor to submit written proposals of any schedule of programmes proposed to be broadcast by the contractor. In such a circumstance, the contractor is not to publish or cause to be published any portion of its proposed programme schedule in advance of Commission approval. Pursuant to such notice, the Commission may give reasonable directions to the contractor in relation to the content of its existing programme schedule and the contractor shall amend its programmes accordingly. The contractor is authorised by the Commission (in the contract) to include in the broadcast programmes party political broadcasts, but the party political broadcasts shall be at the time or times and according to a method of allocation approved by the Commission by prior notice in writing to the broadcasting contractor. Persons nominated for election to the European Parliament, Houses of the Oireachtas, Údarás na Gaeltachta or local authorities are prohibited from presenting programmes until such time as the election has been completed.

The broadcasting contract stipulates that the programmes broadcast by the contractor shall, at all times, be such as in the opinion of the Commission are of a high general standard in all respects and in particular in respect of their content and quality and contain proper proportions of material of Irish origin and of Irish performance.

The contractor is specifically enjoined not to include in any programme broadcast by him in any manner whatsoever whether by way of sound, words or music, any defamatory, seditious, blasphemous or obscene matter or any matter which constitutes an injurious falsehood or slander of title, or any tort or an infringement of any copyright or a contravention of the provisions of the *Official Secrets Act, 1963* or a criminal offence or contempt of court or breach of parliamentary privilege. The contractor must indemnify the Commission by appropriate insurance in respect of claims incurred by the Commission up to a certain limit.

Recordings must be made of all programmes broadcast by the contractor and retained for at least 90 days. Sponsored programmes must be limited to such percentage of total broadcasting time as the Commission determines from time to time. The contractor must co-operate with the Garda Síochána, local authorities, health boards and other State and semi-state agencies in the dissemination of relevant information to the public in the event of major emergencies. The contractor undertakes that it will not, in its programmes and in the means employed to make such programmes, unreasonably encroach on the privacy of an individual.

Any person nominated by the Minister for Communications, the Commission, or where relevant Telecom Éireann, is to be permitted to enter at all reasonable times on any premises owned or occupied by the broadcasting contractor for the purpose of inspecting and testing any transmitter or apparatus for wireless telegraphy, provided reasonable advance notice of access is given.

In the context of commercial matters, the accounts of the broadcasting contractor for such period and as to business formats are to be as the Commission shall reasonably approve. Information in relation to the financial position, operations, income and expenditure of the contractor are to be furnished to the Commission for the purposes of the discharge of the Commission's functions under the 1988 Act. Facilities for the examination of the contractor's books, accounts and records are also to be afforded to the Commission for the purposes of the discharge of the Commission's functions under the 1988 Act.

Breach of the broadcasting contract may give rise to termination or suspension of the contract by the Independent Radio and Television Commission.

Licence of Minister for Communications

The provisions in the licence issued by the Minister for Communications to the Independent Radio and Television Commission in respect of the radio frequency to be used by the contractor constitute a third layer of regulation[29] of the private broadcasting service providers. The benefit of the Minister's licence to the Commission is conveyed by section 4(5) of the *Radio and Television Act, 1988* to the sound broadcasting contractor through the contract with the Commission. Further, by virtue of the Commission's contract with the contractor, the right of the contractor to broadcast is specifically subject to the terms and conditions of the Minister's licence.

The licence of the Minister for Communications prescribes, inter alia, technical details in respect of the broadcasting service. Some general regulatory provisions are also stipulated. The sound broadcasting transmitters must at all reasonable times be subject to inspection and tests by officers of the Minister. All relevant records are to be available for inspection. Transmitters must be installed and used to ensure that no avoidable interference with any State or other authorised apparatus for wireless telegraphy and no avoidable injurious affection to any telecommunication apparatus or service of Telecom Éireann (wherever placed and by whomsoever used) is caused by the use of any transmitter or an associated apparatus. Messages, other than broadcast matter, must not be transmitted from broadcasting transmitters. All reasonable steps must be taken to ensure that access to the sound broadcasting transmitters cannot be obtained by unauthorised persons at any time. The provisions of the International Telecommunication Convention[30] and of any international convention or international agreement to which the State may be or become a party during the continuance of the licence must be complied with.

The regulatory provisions stipulated in the contract between the Commission and the providers of the private commercial broadcasting services together with the regulatory provisions of the licence issued by the Minister to the Commission which binds both the Commission and, by virtue of the Commission's contract, the broadcasting service provider, are in the nature of secondary legislation and must be construed as such, particularly, for example, in the context of their constitutionality.[31]

22

Powers and Functions of the Broadcasting Complaints Commission

INTRODUCTION

In the United Kingdom, the BBC established a Programme Complaints Commission in 1971. Subsequently, in February 1974, the Minister for Posts and Telegraphs, established an Irish Broadcasting Complaints Committee on a non-statutory basis. The Irish Broadcasting Complaints Committee had a wide brief. It was entrusted with the function of deciding whether a programme against which a complaint had been made offended against any of the provisions set out in an RTE *Code of Policy on Current Affairs and Public Service Broadcasting*. The Code included (*inter alia*) an obligation on RTE "generally to reflect the mores and respect the values of the society in which it operates" and to "respect the standards of taste, decency and justice".[1]

In March 1977, pursuant to section 4 of the *Broadcasting Authority (Amendment) Act 1976*, a Broadcasting Complaints Commission was established. The Commission consists of a Chairman and not less than two other members who are appointed by the Government.[2] Any member may be removed from office by the Government for stated reasons, if, and only if, resolutions are passed by each House of the Oireachtas calling for his or her removal.[3] This security of tenure was specifically enacted to "demonstrate the independence of the Commission".[4] Some Dáil Deputies considered this rather pretentious as it tended to put the Commission on the same footing as the judiciary. Dr. Conor Cruise O'Brien, as Minister for Posts and Telegraphs, assured the Dáil that because of the Commission's function in relation to impartiality of broadcasting, the Commission needed "an equivalent protection". However, it was not intended to indicate some judgment as regards status or as conveying some attempt at glorification of the Commission. The protection was purely "functional".[5]

FUNCTIONS OF THE BROADCASTING COMPLAINTS COMMISSION

The Broadcasting Complaints Commission has jurisdiction to deal with complaints relating to all radio and television services in Ireland.[6] However, its jurisdiction is more limited than that of the former Broadcasting Complaints Committee. The Commission may investigate and decide on limited categories of complaints. A complaint may be made to the Commission that in broadcasting news specified in the complaint a broadcasting service did not comply with the statutory requirement that news is to be reported and presented in an objective and impartial manner and without any expression of the RTE Authority's own views, or, in the case of the private broadcasting services, the broadcasting contractor's own views, whether via radio or television,[7] and without reference to anything which may reasonably be regarded as "being likely to promote, or incite to, crime or as tending to undermine the authority of the State".[8]

The Commission has jurisdiction to consider a complaint relating to the broadcasting of a programme that did not comply with the statutory requirement that the broadcast treatment of current affairs, including matters which are either of public controversy or the subject of current public debate, was fair to all interests concerned, was presented in an objective and impartial manner and without any expression of the Authority's own views.[9] In relation to any programme, a complainant may allege infringement of the statutory prohibition on the broadcasting of a programme which was likely to promote or incite to crime or tended to undermine the authority of the State.[10]

A further category of complaint which the Commission may consider relates to a breach of a Ministerial order under section 31(1) of the *Broadcasting Authority Act, 1960* where the Minister for Arts and Culture has directed the broadcasting services to refrain from broadcasting certain matter or certain matter of a particular class.[11] The statutory duty of the broadcasting services that in their programmes and in the means employed to make such programmes they must not "unreasonably encroach on the privacy of an individual" may also be the subject of a complaint to the Commission.[12]

Advertisements may also be the subject of a complaint to the Commission where any advertisement contravenes the codes drawn up by the RTE Authority or the Independent Radio and Television Commission governing standards and practices in broadcast advertising.[13] The Commission may investigate a complaint alleging that any matter, whether written, aural or visual, concerned with news or current affairs which was published, distributed or sold by the RTE Authority, was not presented in an objective and impartial manner.[14]

The *Broadcasting Act, 1990* granted jurisdiction to the Commission to investigate and decide on a complaint by a person that an assertion was made in a broadcast of inaccurate facts or information which constituted an attack on that person's honour or reputation.[15] This extension of the jurisdiction of the Commission was necessitated by an EC Directive on Broadcasting Activities[16] and the Council of Europe Convention on Transfrontier Television.[17]

A complaint must be made to the Broadcasting Complaints Commission in writing.[18] However, in general, the complaint must first be made to the relevant broadcasting service not more than 30 days after the date of the offending broadcast.[19] When the Commission proposes to investigate a complaint, the Commission must afford the broadcasting service an opportunity to comment on the complaint.[20] The consideration by the Commission of a complaint made to it is to be carried out by the Commission in private.[21] The Commission has no power to award costs or expenses to any party.[22]

The Minister for Posts and Telegraphs, Dr. Conor Cruise O'Brien, justified the establishment of the Broadcasting Complaints Commission by expressing concern about the risk of erosion of RTE's freedom under the then existing system where the Minister was the recipient of complaints concerning alleged breaches of the RTE's responsibilities and when the Minister had "unlimited power" to judge and act on such complaints.[23] As the Minister was a political figure, Dr. Cruise O'Brien considered that it was clearly undesirable that a Minister should be the sole judge of impartiality in cases that may involve comment on party politics and politicians. The Minister argued that the Authority could not be left as the sole judge whether or not they were discharging their responsibilities. The Minister stated that the Oireachtas would be the ultimate judge of the Authority's conduct. (Pursuant to section 2 of the *Broadcasting Authority (Amendment) Act, 1976*, a member of the Authority can be removed for stated reasons, only if resolutions are passed by both

Houses of the Oireachtas calling for his removal.) The Minister concluded that it would be impracticable and undesirable to bring every instance of alleged failure in this area before the Oireachtas.[24]

The Minister for Posts and Telegraphs envisaged the Commission as a quasi-judicial body.[25] However, he emphasised that the complaints procedure would be "very informal" and he hoped, consistently inexpensive.[26] He stated that the Commission was not intended as a substitute for recourse to the courts. Should any matter be broadcast which was damaging to an individual or group of persons, "the injured should have the ordinary recourse in law".[27] Indeed the Minister confirmed that if a person considered his or her private or personal interests to be damaged seriously, the Commission procedure would not be his form of recourse because it was not intended as any substitute for ordinary legal recourse.[28] Action in the courts is not precluded by any complaint to the Commission.

The Commission has several powers to provide relief to successful complainants. Unless the Commission considers it inappropriate, it must publish particulars of its decision in such manner as it considers suitable.[29] Where the Commission considers that the publication should be by the relevant broadcasting service, the particulars must be published by the broadcasting service in such manner as shall be agreed between the Commission and the relevant service.[30] The decisions of the Commission are published in the RTE Guide and sometimes in the national media. This is a limited remedy in the sense that a principle of proportionality should demand that where the Commission decides that a breach of statutory duty has occurred on the part of the broadcasting service, such decisions should be published at the start or end of an appropriate broadcasting programme. However, pursuant to European influences,[31] section 8 of *Broadcasting Act, 1990* has given the Commission jurisdiction to award a powerful remedy to a limited category of complainant. In addition to publication of a decision in the printed media, where the Commission finds in favour, in whole or in part, of a complainant in relation to a broadcast of inaccurate facts or information in relation to a person which constituted an attack on that person's honour or reputation, the relevant broadcasting service must (unless the Commission considers it inappropriate) broadcast the Commission decision at a time and in a manner corresponding to that in which the offending broadcast took place.[32]

The Commission must submit a report to the Minister for Communications of its activities during the year under review.[33] The

Report must contain such statements as the Commission thinks fit giving particulars of decisions made by it.[34] Copies of the Report must be laid before both Houses of the Oireachtas.[35] If the Authority informs the Commission that it does not accept a decision of the Commission, the Commission's report for the year shall contain a statement giving particulars of the decision.[36]

In its early years of operation, the Commission received very few complaints. This prompted the Commission to raise the question of whether it was sufficiently known to the public. The Commission considered, however, that it could fulfil its role even if it did not receive any complaints because its very existence may have helped prevent any legitimate cause for complaint.[37] However, by 1986, the Commission considered that the public was sufficiently aware of its existence.[38]

DECISIONS OF THE BROADCASTING COMPLAINTS COMMISSION

A reference to some of the significant decisions of the Commission illustrates the strictures under which broadcasters operate in Ireland. Robert Herbst complained in 1982 about a "Today Tonight" television programme on El Salvador.[39] The Commission considered that the RTE reporter concerned had been consistently critical of the El Salvador and the US Governments' involvement, with little or no suggestion (apart from an interview with Mr. W. Clarke of the US Government) that there was any argument at all to be advanced on the other side. The Commission (chaired by Vincent Landy, SC,) decided that the complete failure of the programme to disclose not merely what the case for the El Salvador and US Governments was but that there were many people who (rightly or wrongly) supported their case amounted in the opinion of the Commission to a failure to observe the standards of objectivity and impartiality required by section 8(1)(b) of the *Broadcasting Authority Act, 1960* as amended by section 3 of the *Broadcasting Authority (Amendment) Act, 1976*.

Most of the complaints made to the Commission to date have not been upheld. Those complaints which have been upheld have been accepted by the RTE Authority with a notable exception. The RTE Authority refused to accept a decision of the Commission in relation to a complaint made by Bruce Arnold concerning a segment of the "Late Late Show" transmitted by RTE 1 on January 28, 1984.[40] The segment of the programme complained of concerned that part in which Seán Doherty, TD, appeared and made a number of points connected with telephone tapping which had been made public by the Coalition Government in 1983. Mr. Arnold complained of the treatment given to this subject on the "Late Late Show" on the basis that it constituted a form of trial by television from which critical witnesses were excluded and also that Seán Doherty was given *carte blanche* to clear himself at Mr. Arnold's expense. Mr. Arnold complained that RTE had failed to comply with its statutory duties specified in section 18(1)(a) and (b) of the *Broadcasting Authority Act, 1960* as amended by section 3 of the *Broadcasting Authority (Amendment) Act, 1976* (objectivity, impartiality and fairness to all interests concerned) which related to the broadcasting of news and current affairs.

RTE submitted that the programme could not amount to the broadcasting of "news", that the interview with Mr. Doherty was in a "chat-show" format and was not a "current affairs" programme. The Commission rejected RTE's contention that the interview on the "Late Late Show" was not within the remit of the Commission. The Commission decided that the screening of any particular item in the context of an entertainment programme or chat show did not place a subject like Mr. Doherty's interview or its contents outside the competence of the Commission. The Commission upheld RTE's contention that the programme did not come within the definition of "news" (section 18(1)(a) of the 1960 Act), but decided that the screening in question did constitute a current affairs broadcast. The Commission (chaired by Ercus Stewart, SC), noted the air of incredulity in the questioning of Mr. Doherty by the presenter and that this was communicated to the audience and the viewers. The Commission held that despite this the programme displayed a distinct lack of balance in that several serious allegations by Mr. Doherty went unchallenged and that this was evident in particular in that part of the discussion which related to the tapping of telephones. The Commission, upholding the complaint, held unanimously that the programme was not fair to all interests concerned as required by statute[41] and in particular to those persons accused by Mr. Doherty of propagating falsehoods.[42] The RTE Authority refused to accept the Commission's decision on the basis that the programme complained of did not in the view of the RTE Authority constitute a current affairs broadcast. The Commission rejected RTE's contention and still maintained that the segment of the programme at issue did constitute "current affairs".[43]

The segment of the "Late Late Show", the subject of Mr. Arnold's complaint, did constitute a current affairs broadcast. The *Broadcasting Authority Act, 1960* imposes, *inter alia,* a duty on RTE that its "broadcast treatment of current affairs, including matters which are either of public controversy or the subject of current public debate" is fair to all interests concerned and is presented in an objective and impartial manner.[44] A current affairs broadcast does not depend on any particular label given to a programme. The *dicta* of the German Constitutional Court in the *First Television Case* (1961) are instructive here. The Court noted that the influence of broadcasting in forming public opinion was by no means limited "to news programmes, political commentary, or series about past, present or future political problems; it also occurs in radio plays, musical presentations, the transmission of cabaret shows, and even in the ways scenes are presented within a programme".[45]

Reference may be made to another decision of the Commission which considered the statutory duty imposed on RTE that the RTE Authority shall not, in its programmes, and the means employed to make such programmes, unreasonably encroach on the privacy of the individual.[46] Dr. J. Gerard Byrne, a consultant child psychiatrist, complained that, during a "Today Tonight" (current affairs television) programme broadcast on November 7, 1985 on child sexual abuse, young children were clearly identifiable as having been victims of sexual abuse. The Christian names of the children and the family name were given. As a child psychiatrist Dr. Byrne was concerned at this invasion of their privacy, even if their parents had consented.[47] The Commission (chaired by Ercus Stewart, SC) was unanimous that this programme was a gross violation of the children's right to privacy. The normal cautious way of protecting the anonymity of persons was not even followed; the very young children were readily identifiable. The Commission upholding the complaint held unanimously that a delicate subject had been handled in a very indelicate and insensitive manner, that the programme was not fair to all interests concerned and constituted an invasion of privacy.[48]

Another decision of the Commission considered the statutory prohibition on the RTE Authority from including in any of its broadcasts anything which may reasonably be regarded as being likely to promote or incite to crime.[49] Mr. J.A. Barnwell complained in 1987[50] of an "Evening Extra" programme which was broadcast after a High Court ruling relating to the "Well Woman Centre" and "Open Line Counselling" clinics in Dublin.[51] Mr. Barnwell alleged that the programme featured a one-sided interview conducted in a non-adversarial way with two interviewees, both of whom spoke strongly in favour of supporting and supplying information to Irish women seeking abortion facilities in the United Kingdom. The complainant submitted that no spokesperson or representative was invited to put the other side of the case, i.e. the pro-life or anti-abortionist cause, and that a number of remarks broadcast during the interview advocated a deliberate defiance and flouting of the law as enunciated and enshrined in various legally binding constitutional and statutory provisions. The Commission (chaired by Ercus Stewart, SC) decided that the programme sought to elicit the reaction of the clinics to the judgment of the High Court and, to that extent, the requirement of balance was not applicable. However, the Commission upheld the complaint (in part) by considering that certain parts of the programme could be construed as constituting a breach of section 18(1A) of the *Broadcasting Authority Act, 1960*[52] as being likely to promote, or incite to, crime.[53]

Public figures who considered that they have been unfairly treated have also complained to the Commission. Professor Martin O'Donoghue, a former Minister of the Government, complained about an interview with Dr. Patrick Lynch, a former professor of economics at University College Dublin, which was broadcast in a programme called "Hanley's People" on January 30, 1989.[54] In the course of the programme, the presenter, David Hanley, attributed a quote to the Minister for Finance, Albert Reynolds, TD, that "[w]hat happened in 1977 in the election [was] criminally irresponsible". The presenter added: "[T]hat was done with the connivance of an economist now teaching in Trinity." Professor O'Donoghue contended that the programme was unfair and was not impartial or objective for several reasons. He maintained he was clearly identifiable as "the economist now teaching in Trinity". Professor O'Donoghue claimed that the comments lacked objectivity and impartiality and that they purported to attribute or were understood to attribute responsibility for all aspects of the 1977 General Election to him. He considered that the words "criminally irresponsible" suggested that he was irresponsible to the point of criminal recklessness, and that the words indicated that he was guilty of bad faith and incompetence as well as condoning wrongdoing or misbehaviour. Professor O'Donoghue considered that the manner of the questioning did not allow Dr. Lynch to give an adequate response and that the comments were an expression of the Authority's own views.[55]

RTE denied that the programme lacked objectivity and impartiality and stated that the programme did not express the Authority's own views. RTE also considered that the professor's role in Government, as an elected representative, was fairly open to public comment. RTE stated that the remark about the 1977 General Election was a paraphrase of a quotation from an interview with Albert Reynolds, TD, which had appeared in a Sunday newspaper.

The Commission (chaired by Ercus Stewart, SC) decided that Professor O'Donoghue was clearly identifiable as the person referred to as having "connived" with criminally irresponsible action. There was no reason why the words as quoted in the *Sunday Tribune* could not have been quoted accurately. The words "criminally irresponsible" in the opinion of the Commission were not a paraphrase and carried a different and more prejudicial meaning than those admitted of by the words used by Mr. Reynolds. To that extent, the Commission considered that the presentation was unfair and therefore upheld the complaint.[56]

A complaint to the Commission by Marcus Free relating to the banning of Sinn Féin from RTE is considered in chapter 16.

GENERAL OBSERVATIONS

Colin Munro, writing in 1983 about the early work of the UK Broadcasting Complaints Commission, pondered whether "the mountains [had] been in labour to bring forth a mouse".[57] He submitted that the UK Commission in 1983 was an inappropriate object for the extravagant hopes and fears expressed concerning it.[58] These views could be applied to the early years of the Irish Broadcasting Complaints Commission. Certainly, the Commission's powers were limited; hence some may have doubted its value as a statutory regulatory agency. If the Commission had the power to insist that the appropriate broadcasting service publish a short synopsis of its decision at the start or end of a particular programme when it holds in favour of a complaint, a very powerful form of relief would be available. There is a provision in the *Broadcasting Act, 1990* that the RTE Authority must (unless the Commission considers it inappropriate) broadcast the decision of the Commission at a time and in a manner corresponding to that in which the offending broadcast took place where the Commission finds in favour of a complainant, in whole or in part, in relation to a broadcast of in- accurate facts or information in relation to a person which con- stituted an attack on that person's honour or reputation.[59] If this provision is interpreted liberally by the Commission, a significant remedy may be available.

The 1981 Joint Oireachtas Committee on RTE recommended that legislation be introduced to alter the functions of the Broadcasting Complaints Commission so that it may

(a) be responsible for the conduct of scientific investigations of the social consequences of broadcasting;
(b) give guidance to Government and RTE on the impact of various types of programmes;
(c) be consulted in the preparation of broadcasting guidelines;
(d) deal with individual complaints of breaches of guidelines;
(e) give a response within 14 days to significant public charges of breach of guidelines; and
(f) be funded directly from the Exchequer.[60]

These additional functions are somewhat similar to the role of the (UK) Broadcasting Standards Council which, *inter alia*, in 1990 examined the portrayal of violence on television, and in 1991 in its *Annual Survey* looked at aspects of taste and decency, under which the use of "bad" language falls.[61] There is merit in the 1981 proposals.

PART V

The Regulation of Telecommunication: General Analysis and Conclusions

Certainly ... we may question whether television will ever bring us the multitude of voices that would enhance our political and cultural life. Newton Minow's prophesied wasteland appears to become more arid year by year as television becomes even more homogenised, and the few oases dry up, one after another. I join those who lament television's apparent inability to promote creativity and variety. But I fear direct government intrusion into program content even more.

US Judge David L. Bazelon, "The First Amendment and the New Media — New Directions in Regulating Telecommunications," 31 *Fed Comm LJ* 201, 209

Since the printing of the Guttenberg Bible, political elites have feared each new information system. For ages, books were kept out of the hands of peasants lest they get revolutionary ideas. When they were permitted to read, their texts were carefully censored. Mass printing has never produced a revolution, nor did it create Nazism, Fascism or Communism. Guns and political cruelty produced all three, aided afterward by propaganda channels of totalitarians. It is far more likely that the explosive diversity of the new communication technologies will prepare the way for democratic governance.

Leonard R. Sussman, *Power, The Press and the Technology of Freedom: The Coming Age of ISDN*, Freedom House, USA, 1989

23

General Analysis of Development of Telecommunication Law in Ireland

INTRODUCTION

Telecommunication law in Ireland reflects the spirit of the people who enacted it and the spirit of the times in which the enactments were made. There is merit in Pound's analysis of the legal process as a form of "social engineering". Law is an instrument whereby a society may shape and control the behaviour of members of that society with the object of achieving the goals set out by that society. Dr. Johnson in his letter to Boswell summed up admirably the social influence on the development of law: "Laws are formed by the manners and exigencies of particular times. . . ."[1] A study of the regulation of telecommunication by the State illustrates that prevailing views as to how society was to be shaped or controlled often had a considerable influence on the mould of telecommunication legislation. These social influences were particularly evident when the telecommunication monopoly was first vested in the State in 1869.[2] Social influences were again relevant when the issue of who was to run the fledgling radio service at the foundation of the State was being considered.[3]

In general, telecommunication statute law, particularly the *Telegraph Acts 1863 to 1916*, evolved in a haphazard manner as statutory responses to immediate specific needs. Each statute amended a previous statute; no attempt was ever made to consolidate telecommunication legislation into a single statutory code. The reorganisation of the telecommunication carrier services in 1983 presented the Oireachtas with an opportunity to consolidate the entire telecommunication statutory code in so far as it related to the telecommunication carrier system. However, the existing enactments were largely amended or adapted and the opportunity to consolidate was lost. The haphazard manner in which the telecommunication statutory code evolved from 1863 to the present time may partly explain why the draftsmanship of the *Telegraph Acts 1863 to 1916* is uniformly poor. Lord Loreburn, the Lord Chancellor, in the House of Lords in 1909 in a case concerning the interpretation of the *Telegraph Act, 1869*[4] relating to the telecommunication monopoly of the State, was moved to declare that the language of the statutory provisions in the 1869 Act relating to the monopoly was "clumsy".[5] He went further and stated that the case

> afford[ed] an admirable illustration of the dangers to which great interests in [the] country [were] exposed by the slovenly manner in which even public Acts of Parliament are expressed.[6]

The present formulation of the telecommunication privileges for the carrier service in the *Postal and Telecommunications Services Act, 1983* is largely based on those provisions criticised by the House of Lords.[7]

The statute law relating to telecommunication should be up-dated and consolidated. The period between the establishment of the Posts and Telegraphs Review Group in 1978 and the *Postal and Telecommunications Services Act, 1983* was an appropriate period in which consolidation could have been undertaken. One is tempted to speculate that the reason why such consolidation was not carried into effect was the fact that no similar consolidation had been attempted in the United Kingdom up to the introduction of Ireland's *Postal and Telecommunications Services Bill, 1982*. Several opportunities had presented themselves to the United Kingdom Parliament for such consolidation. For example, an opportunity for consolidation arose in 1969 when the British Post Office with responsibilities for both postal and telecommunication services became a nationalised corporation, having been a Department of State under the Postmaster-General up to 1969. A further opportunity presented itself in 1981 when the UK *Telecommunications Act, 1981* provided for the establishment of a separate state-owned corporation called British Telecom. It was not until the UK *Telecommunications Act, 1984* which provided for the privatisation of British Telecom that the *Telegraph Acts 1863 to 1916* were repealed in general in the United Kingdom and replaced by a single statutory code entitled the

Telecommunications Code. By then, Ireland's re-organisation of the telecommunication carrier service had been effected by the *Postal and Telecommunications Services Act,1983.*

Ireland has been, and in many senses still is, linked to the United Kingdom by historical, legislative and cultural ties. Telecommunication law in Ireland reflects these ties: the influence of English law on Ireland's present telecommunication law is still pervasive. The State's reliance on legislative precedents of the United Kingdom has irked Irish jurists and parliamentarians alike. In the Dáil on the Second Stage of the *Postal and Telecommunications Services Bill, 1982* Professor John Kelly, TD, articulated this sense of frustration:

> When did we invent something here, let alone a major structural administrative reform in which the English had not preceded us? Let the Minister name one. It is shaming and I should expect the Minister to be foremost in being ashamed about it. We were long enough learning about other countries. We hardly know where they are. . . .[8]

It was noted earlier that the initial proposals for broadcasting in 1923 were largely based on arrangements in existence in the United Kingdom;[9] the *Wireless Telegraphy Act, 1926* was largely modelled on the provisions of the *Wireless Telegraphy Act, 1904* and the withdrawn UK *Wireless and Signalling Bill, 1925;*[10] the *Wireless Telegraphy Act, 1972* was substantially based on the UK *Wireless Telegraphy Act, 1967;*[11] the salient provisions of the *Broadcasting Authority Act, 1960* were based, *inter alia*, on the Royal Charter of the British Broadcasting Corporation and the UK *Television Act, 1954.*[12] The obvious fondness of Ireland's civil servants for studying relevant UK legislation and making proposals to Ministers on the basis of British legislation is perhaps understandable given our common language, our shared common law system, our small population and shortage of administrators and parliamentary draftsmen.

In the United Kingdom, in recent years there has been a definite shift in legislative policy in relation to the regulation of modes of telecommunication. Although the UK *Telecommunications Act, 1981* (which established British Telecom) transferred to British Telecom an exclusive privilege in relation to telecommunication systems, the 1981 Act provided that the exclusive privilege was not to be infringed by anything done under licence granted by the Secretary of State.[13] (Section 87 of Ireland's *Postal and Telecommunication Services Act, 1983* is phrased in similar terms.) The UK *Telecom-*

munication Act, 1984 provided for the privatisation of British Telecom
(by the sale of over 50 per cent of its equity), the abolition of British
Telecom's exclusive privilege and its replacement by a public telecommunication operator's licence. Mercury Communications
Limited was licensed to provide a public telecommunication service
in competition with British Telecom. A new regulatory body, the
Office of Telecommunications (OFTEL), was established by the 1984
Act to regulate and promote fair and effective competition and to
benefit consumers.

The UK Government in its White Paper, *Competition and Choice:
Telecommunications Policy for the 1990s* (1991),[14] provided for a further
radical overhaul of the telecommunication carrier service in the
United Kingdom. The Government decided to end the duopoly
policy of licensing only two providers of telecommunication carrier
services — British Telecom (BT plc) and Mercury Communications
Ltd. Any application for a licence to offer telecommunication
services over fixed links within the United Kingdom was to be
considered on its merits.[15] The Secretary of State for Trade and
Industry noted that the general presumption would be that such
licences should be granted unless there were specific reasons to the
contrary.[16] The provision of satellite services *via* telecommunications
systems not connected to the public switched network at either end
was to be authorised by means of a class licence.[17] The cable
television companies were to be allowed to provide voice telephony
services in their own right rather than as agents of British Telecom
or Mercury. The Government considered the cable television
companies as a valuable source of competition with the main service
providers of telecommunication carrier services.[18] Fearing that cable
operators would be unlikely in practice to make greater use of the
main public telecommunication operators' network if, for example,
British Telecom or Mercury were to be allowed to obtain a national
franchise to provide entertainment services, the UK Government
stated that it did not intend to remove the existing restrictions on
British Telecom and other public telecommunication operators from
conveying entertainment services in their own right until after
2001.[19] However, national public telecommunication operators like
British Telecom would be able to continue to apply through associate
companies for franchises to provide entertainment services in local
areas.[20] The Director General of OFTEL announced in the White
Paper that he had decided to proceed with the early introduction of
equal access by which customers could exercise a choice as to the
trunk operator that carries their call. He expected this process to be

introduced within two years from 1991 and to be available to a majority of telephone users within about five years.[21] It was not necessary for the UK Government to amend the UK *Telecommunications Act, 1984* to implement the foregoing changes in policy. Many of the foregoing changes could be effected in Ireland by means of licensing powers of the Minister for Communications pursuant to existing legislation.[22]

Reference may also be made to the current regulation of broadcasting in the United Kingdom. The UK *Broadcasting Act, 1990* established the Independent Television Commission (ITC), a new Radio Authority and provided for the reform of the legal framework for independent television, cable and radio broadcasting. New regulatory concepts were introduced in the 1990 Act. Part IV of the 1990 Act provided for the privatisation of the Independent Broadcasting Authority's transmission system. The function of collecting television licence fees was transferred to the BBC.[23] The principle that the Independent Television Commission must award the licence to the applicant who had submitted the highest bid (subject to certain qualifications) was another novel element in the jurisprudence related to broadcasting in the islands of Ireland and Great Britain.[24]

It remains to be observed whether the current legislative policies of the United Kingdom will influence the development of telecommunication legislation in Ireland. Relying on the experiences of the past, it is likely that, in time, provided the UK policies prove to be successful, such policies will continue to influence the development of telecommunication law in Ireland.

ANALYSIS OF FACTORS INFLUENCING DEVELOPMENT OF LAWS REGULATING TELECOMMUNICATION CARRIER SYSTEMS

Ideology[25] played little part in the early development of telecommunication law. Factors which influenced and prompted state regulation and subsequently state monopolisation of the telecommunication carrier business were essentially pragmatic. It was earnestly hoped that the Postmaster-General and his Department would operate the telecommunication carrier system more efficiently than the existing private companies — thus benefiting the community. Professor C.R. Perry in *The Victorian Post Office* (1992) stated correctly that the activities of the Post Office were understood usually as a means to shore up weaknesses in the existing economic structure rather than as frontal attacks on the entire edifice. Professor Perry concludes that in general the Post Office did not challenge the conventional wisdom that private enterprise was to be preferred to state management.[26]

The "efficiency" argument once put forward as a raison d'être for state control and regulation was in 1979[27] put forward as a raison d'être for a fundamental shift in legislative policy: the spirit of deregulation and privatisation was abroad. The reason for the shift in legislative policy was that by 1979 the telecommunication carrier service was authoritatively stated to be in "a crisis".[28] Although much good work had been done since the foundation of the State, the telecommunication carrier service had been starved of capital and could not satisfy the demands made upon it.

Conscious of the fact that privatisation of the telecommunication carrier service would engender a debate "which would run deeply at public, political and trade union levels", entail a "slower legislative process" and "heavy delay before any action could be taken", the Posts and Telegraphs Review Group in 1979 recommended that the telecommunication carrier service be taken out of the control of the Civil Service and entrusted to a state-owned statutory company run on commercial lines.[29]

Deregulation may be described as the demise of "command and control" regulatory provisions by which a superintending body requires or proscribes specific conduct by regulated entities. The deregulation and liberalisation of telecommunication processes in the United States and United Kingdom together with the concept of privatisation (a political concept from Britain which in general involves the transfer of ownership of goods and services from the public service to the private sector)[30] are influencing legislative policy in Ireland; the *Radio and Television Act, 1988* is one example of an aspect of the deregulation philosophy. It is noteworthy that in the United States the judicial arm of government played a significant role in the restructuring of the United States telecommunication carrier services. The Modified Final Judgment of 1982 ended more than 30 years of continuous antitrust litigation between the Government and the American Telephone and Telegraph Company (AT&T).[31] Similar restructuring could be effected in Ireland by a successful challenge to the various telecommunication oligopolies and privileges. Many would consider the judiciary to be an inappropriate major decision maker in relation to the regulation of telecommunication. The economic, technological and analytical resources available to the courts are limited.

Ideological factors did come to the fore in the Dáil in the debates on the *Postal and Telecommunications Services Bill, 1982.* In 1982 the Labour Party, then in opposition, at first opposed the Bill. In essence the Labour Party argued for continued State control of the postal and telecommunication carrier services. The Labour Party, in particular, was opposed to any form of privatisation.[32] Subsequently, after a change in Government, the Fine Gael Minister for Posts and Tele-graphs, under some pressure from his Labour Cabinet colleagues, gave assurances on the sensitive issue of privatisation: "It should be stressed that the postal and telecommunications services will firmly remain within the public sector and there is no possibility of privatisation of the company without further legislation."[33]

However, the *Postal and Telecommunications Services Act, 1983,* as passed by Dáil Éireann did allow indirectly for privatisation. Section 21 of the Bill, as passed by the Dáil, provided: "No issue of share capital shall be made [except as set out in the Act] unless the Minister [for Communications] with the consent of the Minister for Finance, has authorised such issue." The Minister [for Communications], could thus have authorised the issue of share capital in An Post and Telecom Éireann to the public. On the Committee Stage of the Bill in the Seanad, the Minister, under pressure from the Labour Party and Senator Mary Robinson in particular, introduced a Government amendment which deleted the words "unless the Minister with the consent of the Minister for Finance has authorised such issue".[34] Thus, privatisation could only be achieved by further legislation. However, deregulation — in this instance, allowing others to compete with the state-owned telecommunication carrier company, Telecom Éireann — can be achieved easily by the Minister for Communications by means of his licensing powers. Licences can and have been granted by the Minister to allow others enter into direct competition with Telecom Éireann.[35]

ANALYSIS OF FACTORS INFLUENCING THE DEVELOPMENT OF LAW REGULATING BROADCASTING

The paramount factor which influenced the early development of broadcasting legislation in Ireland was the principle that the broadcasting service must be subject to direction by the State. Reference was made earlier to the 1923-1924 Dáil Committee on

Broadcasting which recommended that the new broadcasting service should be operated only as a State service under the supervision of the Department of Posts and Telegraphs or, alternatively, should that recommendation not have been acceptable to the Dáil, it was proposed that a company in which the State would have a controlling interest would operate the broadcasting service.[36] Both the Postmaster-General and senior civil servants objected strongly to these proposals. In memorable speeches to the Dáil on the debates on the Reports of the Special Committee on Broadcasting[37] the Postmaster-General, James J. Walsh, objected to direct State control of the proposed broadcasting service. He objected to the Department of Posts and Telegraphs having to do "the showman [differentiating] between rival organ-grinders, rival tenors and people of that kind, and even rival politicians who want to get control and preferential treatment".[38]

The fledgling State's first Postmaster-General opined that if the Dáil so determined that the Department of Posts and Telegraphs would operate the broadcasting service, then it would be done but it would be "at a price" and it would be "a very dear price".[39] Senior civil servants had also argued against direct State control. The Department of Finance argued that a State-controlled company would operate at a loss; the State could not operate as economically as a private firm and the proposals would increase considerably the number of civil servants.[40]

Despite all the objections, the Dáil was not prepared to allow the broadcasting service pass into the hands of private enterprise. The Dáil adopted the Report of the Special Committee on Broadcasting and subsequently the *Wireless Telegraphy Act, 1926* was passed which set up a broadcasting service under the direct control of the Minister for Posts and Telegraphs. Dr. Ronan Fanning in his book The Irish Department of Finance has argued that the enactment of the *Wireless Telegraphy Act, 1926* illustrated the powerlessness of the Department of Finance to resist successfully "new expenditure when political considerations affecting national prestige were adjudged paramount".[41]

In chapters 11 and 12 we have seen how the ideological issue of public versus private enterprise operating broadcasting services surfaced regularly since the inception of broadcasting. When the establishment of the national television service was being considered in the late 1950s, the Television Commission, based on its terms of reference, recommended that a television service be established for Ireland by "private enterprise, financed mainly by revenue from advertisements".[42] The Government was, however, reluctant to allow control of the broadcasting service to pass to private interests. The Government justified its rejection of the Commission's recommendations on several grounds. Firstly, the monopoly of such an "important medium of communication" should not be handed over to private interests. Secondly, the "capital position" of the State had improved since the terms of reference of the Commission had been set, and the Government considered that the broadcasting service would "soon pay its own way". Above all else there was the Government's fear that "effective public control" of the broadcasting service would be lost if the national television service were operated by private interests.[43]

Ideological factors came to the fore again on the publication of the Government's *Local Radio Bill, 1985*.[44] The 1985 Bill was designed to provide a statutory basis for independent local radio services and envisaged the establishment of a two-tier structure. One tier would comprise a local professionally-run radio service "operating on a sound commercial basis and serving relatively large catchment areas such as a major city, a county or groupings of counties".[45] Broadcasting contractors were to establish, maintain and operate broadcasting transmitters.[46] The Minister justified this policy decision on economic grounds.[47] The Labour Party vigorously opposed the Bill on ideological grounds; it was argued that the Bill involved denationalisation or privatisation of broadcasting which "since its inception had been in the public domain".[48] The 1985 measure was not enacted into legislation owing primarily to the ideological difference between the partners in Government.

Ideological differences came to the fore again in the debates on the *Sound Broadcasting Bill, 1987* which was later to become the *Radio and Television Act, 1988* which established the Radio and Television Commission. Opposing the Government measure, the Labour Party spokesman in the Dáil argued that the concept of broadcasting as a public service should be maintained.[49] The Labour party argued strongly against releasing broadcasting "into the marketplace" from an ethos of public service accountability.[50] The *Radio and Television Act, 1988* did represent a shift in legislative policy from the absoluteness of the public trusteeship model of broadcasting to that motivated (at least to a certain extent) by the marketplace.

Ireland's geographical proximity to the United Kingdom together with the fortuitous overspill of British radio and television signals influenced the development of broadcasting law in Ireland. These factors forced the Government into legislative action. This was evident when radio broadcasting was introduced in Britain in the 1920s and subsequently when television broadcasting was introduced. In 1959 when legislative provision was being made for RTE, the Minister for Posts and Telegraphs frankly admitted that the "whole issue could perhaps have been shelved for a few years if the matter lay entirely in our hands". However, he continued:

> [B]roadcasting has little respect for frontiers, natural or artificial and shortly after the . . . Government took office in 1957 the rapid development of British television coupled with increasing purchases of television sets here to receive British programmes made the establishment of an Irish service a matter of urgency.[51]

Many civil servants and perhaps some of their political masters respected established British systems. For example, in the 1950s the threat to the BBC's monopolistic position from commercial interests in Britain was viewed with some alarm by senior civil servants at the Department of Posts and Telegraphs. Dr. León Ó Broin, Secretary of the Department, writing in 1953 at a time when broadcasting in Ireland was controlled directly by the Department of Posts and Telegraphs stated that he was "incensed that any body of opinion can be found to defend the commercial television idea in opposition to the really excellent job being done by the BBC". He stated that the commercial lobby would be resisted in Ireland:

> It will be very much more difficult with Britain gone commercial. Our new Radio Council,[52] like most cultured people, has taken a dim view of the quality of the limited number of sponsored programmes that we put out on the sound broadcasting side and has been pressing for their removal, although it involves abandoning much needed revenue.[53]

The marked antithesis to the commercial broadcasting lobby of civil servants regulating broadcasting may also be gleaned from correspondence between Maurice Gorham, the Director of Broadcasting, León Ó Broin and Maurice Moynihan, Secretary to the Government. Writing in February 1958 to Ó Broin, the Director of Broadcasting deplored the Ministerial sympathy with the idea of commercial television (free of cost to the Exchequer) and commercial broadcasting from Ireland to other countries coupled with continued strict Government control of the finances and Government control of the broadcasting content of Radio Éireann.[54] Hoping that this scenario would not come to pass, Gorham added: "This may merely be a nightmare." On receipt of this letter, Ó Broin took the issue so seriously that he immediately wrote to the Secretary to the Government, enclosing a copy of Gorham's letter. Ó Broin added:

> [T]he function of broadcasting has never been understood in this country with the result that the service has been starved and its possibilities as a builder of national morale and as a promoter of culture in the best sense of the word have been left unexploited.[55]

Ó Broin's detestation of the idea of commercial broadcasting was not disguised. He wrote that if the trend which Gorham feared continued, Radio Éireann would "remain the shabbiest of Cinderellas while our new ugly sisters [the commercial broadcasting service] (and how ugly they may be) show off their finery".[56]

Ó Broin suggested to the Secretary to the Government that the correspondence should be shown to the Taoiseach, Eamon de Valera. The correspondence was read aloud to the Taoiseach on receipt of Ó Broin's letter.[57] The "nightmare" scenario did not, however, materialise and the semi-State authority then known as Radio Éireann was established in 1960 pursuant to *Broadcasting Authority Act, 1960*.

It was not until 1988 that the commercial lobby succeeded in its quest for participation in broadcasting with the enactment of the *Radio and Television Act, 1988* which provided for the establishment of commercial radio and television.

The development of broadcasting law in Ireland has been influenced by a strong desire to protect Ireland's culture from the bombardment of cultural influences from Ireland's nearest neighbour — the United Kingdom. Ireland's problem is mirrored in Canada in its desire to protect Canadian culture from influences of the United States. A Royal Commission on Broadcasting in Canada in 1957 stressed that the regulation of broadcasting in Canada was necessary if "we want to have radio and television contribute to a Canadian consciousness and sense of identity, if . . . we seek to avoid engulfment by American cultural forces. . . ."[58] The (Canadian) *Broadcasting Act, 1958*, enacted as a result of the Royal Commission Report, made the Board of Broadcast Governors responsible, *inter alia*, for "the provision of a varied and comprehensive broadcasting service of a high standard that is basically Canadian in content and character".[59] In this context, it is noteworthy that subsequent legislation in Canada enacted that the broadcasters' mandate was "to safeguard, enrich and strengthen the cultural, political, social and economic fabric" of Canada.[60]

Many rightly value cultural diversity. Yet despite being members of the European Communities, there is merit in legislation seeking to reinforce an individual nation's social and cultural values. There is considerable merit in the statement of the RTE Authority's mandate expressed in 1976 and influenced undoubtedly by Dr. Conor Cruise O'Brien, then Minister for Posts and Telegraphs.[61] The analysis of Peter W. Johansen in 1973 in the analogous context of a threat to the Canadian nation's existence coming from a deluge of mass media from foreign powers has relevance to the Ireland of today:

> Political theorists tell us that the cohesiveness of a nation is directly related to the ratio of internal to external communication within the system. The integration of a nation's people is dependent in part upon a shared experience and knowledge of each other. It is apparent "that unless people are aware of each other and know a good deal about one another, they are not likely to enter into social or political partnership."[62] This knowledge of each other is not to be had from foreign media. There must be a truly national system of communi- cation. Native communication is needed to articulate and reinforce social values that arise out of the population itself. External messages will acculturate a population to external values — not necessarily inferior or wrong values, but not *their* values.[63]

In general, since the inception of broadcasting, Irish Governments appeared to be committed to the concept of retaining, at least in part, some system of public-service broadcasting. The concept of public-service broadcasting is difficult to define but certain core principles associated with the concept may be considered here. Firstly, broadcasting is regarded as a national asset which should be used, to some extent, for the national good rather than for the exclusive benefit of narrow interest groups. Secondly, there is the notion of a broadcasting authority which is appointed as a trustee in the national interest and, thirdly, that the broadcasting authorities should be free of Government intervention in their operational affairs and in the content of their programmes. The UK Broadcasting Research Unit has embodied eight principles in the concept of public-service broadcasting.[64] These are:

(i) geographic universality;

(ii) catering for all interests and tastes;

(iii) catering for minorities;

(iv) concern for national identity and community;

(v) detachment from vested interests and government;

(vi) one broadcasting system to be directly funded by the corpus of users;

(vii) competition in good programming rather than for numbers; and

(viii) guidelines to liberate programme makers and not to restrict them.[65]

It would be unreasonable to insist that all broadcasting stations in Ireland observe such duties. However, there is merit in at least one national broadcasting service being obliged to fulfil a public-service broadcasting function. RTE in Ireland effectively provides such a public broadcasting service. Such a role should continue to be carried out by RTE.

SINGLE REGULATORY BODY WITH RESPONSIBILITY FOR TELECOMMUNICATION

There is merit in the establishment of a single regulatory board or commission with responsibility for the regulation of all aspects of telecommunication in Ireland. Telecommunication regulatory functions (including, where applicable, those of a licensing nature) are exercised by the Minister for Communications, the Minister for Arts and Culture, the Independent Radio and Television Commission, Telecom Éireann, RTE, the Broadcasting Complaints Commission and the Ombudsman. Potential conflicts of interest may arise: the Minister for Communications is one of the principal regulators of telecommunication services, yet is also one of the major shareholders in Telecom Éireann, a company that is competing in certain telecommunication services with private telecommunication companies.[66]

The Restrictive Practices Commission in 1986 noted that the Minister for Communications had "many widespread and potentially conflicting interests" as the licensor and Minister responsible for the broadcasting services, as licensor of cable system operations and satellite services, and as licensor and with Ministerial responsibility for Telecom Éireann.[67] Directive 88/301/EEC of 16

May 1988 on competition in the markets in telecommunication terminal equipment provided that Member States must ensure from July 1, 1989 that responsibility for drawing up technical specifications for terminal equipment, monitoring their application and granting type-approval was entrusted to a body independent of public or private telecommunication undertakings offering goods or services in the telecommunication sector.[68] The Minister for Communications is effectively responsible for this aspect of regulation.

A single regulatory entity could be comprised of a board or a commission appointed by the Government. The mandate of such a body could be specified in terms of regulating telecommunication in Ireland, so as to make available, so far as possible, to all the people of Ireland efficient nation-wide telecommunication services. The agency would monitor violations of any of the duties imposed on the providers of telecommunication services. The board would be authorised to exercise price control functions in the interests of the consumer. Within the limits of international law, the board would assign bands of frequencies to the providers of telecommunication services. For the proper conduct of its business, the board could hold public enquiries, grant hearings on matters within the scope of its jurisdiction, and have power to require the attendance and testimony of witnesses and the production of records. In September 1993, the Minister for Communications, Brian Cowen, proposed the establishment of an independent Irish telecommunications regulatory authority with its own powers of enforcement. He stated that the Governmnet would develop an appropriate regulatory framework which would encourage competition, choice and efficiency but which would also take account of public-service requirements and social needs. Appropriate legislation would be prepared.[69]

In the context of a single regulatory agency, one is fortified by the arguments of Commissioner Nicholas Johnston of the US Federal Communications Commission who argued that it was a necessity (not merely an intellectual luxury) that any issue of communications policy be considered in its broadest inter-disciplinary context with the full sense of its interrelationships and impact on all other communications policy issues.[70] In particular, he argued that mass communications issues should not be carved out and treated separately from the problems of private communications systems.[71]

24

The Case For and Against Regulation

THE CASE AGAINST STATE REGULATION

Before considering further the regulation of telecommunication (including broadcasting) in Ireland, the case against State regulation will first be considered briefly. In simple terms, there is the argument that the economic theory of marketplace performance should dictate that the State plays no part in the business of regulation.

In the context of broadcasting, Mark Fowler, chairman of the Federal Communications Commission (FCC) (1981-1987) has been one of the most influential exponents of the case against any form of regulation.[1] He urged the FCC to move away from the trusteeship doctrine in the regulation of broadcasting. The trusteeship doctrine has been a central theme in the regulation of broadcasting in the United States since the inception of broadcasting; the broadcaster is a trustee for the people. The same doctrine permeates the Irish system of broadcast regulation. Under the trusteeship doctrine, the legislature and the Minister for Communications determine the rules which decide how the broadcaster is to serve the community. Indeed, there is merit in the argument that both the prime vehicles of telecommunication expression, the national telecommunication carrier service, Telecom Éireann, and the national public-service broadcasting service, RTE, are held to a certain extent in trust for the State. Chairman Fowler advocated a marketplace approach and the abandonment of the trusteeship doctrine.[2]

Under the marketplace philosophy, the Government would defer to a broadcaster's judgment about how best to compete for viewers and listeners, and how best to attract and sustain the public's interest. Under the marketplace rationale, the public's interest defines the public interest in broadcasting. The public interest should be measured by the success and failure of stations in the marketplace, their programmes and their schedules, one against the other, as well as against competing technologies. Many argue that the reasons articulated to justify the different treatment of broadcasting from the press are not sufficient to sustain the trusteeship obligations. Those who argue against the trusteeship doctrine submit that the arguments offered to sustain the doctrine — the scarcity of outlets as well as the impact of broadcasting (the pervasiveness rationale) — do not justify a system where the government endeavour to tell broadcasters what the people want or what the people should want. In short, broadcasters should have the same editorial freedom as that enjoyed by other media: "the freedom to achieve or fail, the freedom to upset or amuse, the freedom to tantalise or bore, the freedom to dismay or inspire."[3]

In the context of broadcasting, it could also be argued that those who do not use the airwaves efficiently (including those who incur excessive operating costs) could, in a free market, be bought out by more efficient entities. Further, an auction of the radio spectrum would enable the State to obtain further value for its use. It could be argued that there should be no necessity for broadcasters to seek a renewal of their authority to broadcast. There should be no content regulation and no ownership restrictions on broadcasters, apart from those applying to the media generally.

The case against State regulation often revolves around a perceived superiority of market forces over administrative decision-making. In relation to the allocation of the radio spectrum, it has been argued that administrative decisions in the form of licensing are arbitrary and are often mistaken in determining what is the best interests of users.[4] Auctions of the radio spectrum have been put forward as the most sensitive market option for distributing the radio spectrum. Following an auction, the successful bidder would obtain a right to the radio spectrum for a defined period of time; property rights could be established and be capable of transfer.

Further, it could be argued that the business of providing telecommunication carrier-related services should not be carried out directly or indirectly by the State: telecommunication carrier-related functions should be provided directly by the marketplace.

JUSTIFICATIONS FOR THE REGULATION OF
TELECOMMUNICATION BY THE STATE

A compelling argument can be made, however, to those who argue against any form of regulation by the State. The trusteeship model on which much of the regulation of broadcasting in Ireland is based ought not to be replaced by market forces only. An open-marketplace approach might simply involve a shift from trustees who are controlled in the public interest to private monopolistic or oligopolistic interests. Such a shift may have serious implications for the expression of a diversity of viewpoints.

The auctioning of the radio spectrum would not be practical in a small country like Ireland. A free market could create substantial costs to users; a free market would still require active regulation, for example, to monitor interference.

However, that is not to say that all is well with the existing regime of regulation. Suggestions for reform will be considered in subsequent chapters.

A classic form of regulation is the determination by the State (or other public authority) of who may enter a particular business or service and, secondly, the imposition of restrictions for whatever reason on the providers of such a business or service.

The State's primary telecommunication monopoly is expressed in statutory form in section 4 of the *Telegraph Act, 1869*.[5] There is, however, a strong justification for arguing that Article 10 of the Constitution of Ireland (1937) (which replaced Article 11 of the 1922 Constitution) provides a constitutional foundation for the thesis that the State owns certain of the basic resources which the tele-communication services utilise to effect communication at a distance. Article 10.1 of the Constitution reads:

> All natural resources,[6] including the air and all forms of potential energy, within the jurisdiction of the Parliament and Government established by this Constitution, and all royalties and franchises within that jurisdiction belong to the State subject to all estates and interests therein for the time being lawfully vested in any person or body.

Article 10.3 stipulates:

> Provision may be made by law for the management of the property which belongs to the State by virtue of this Article and

for the control of the alienation, whether temporary or permanent, of that property.

Telecommunication services depend on electro-magnetic energy for the transmission of messages by wire (including cable), by optical-fibre, and through the air — the frequency spectrum. Electro-magnetic energy is a form of energy and is a natural resource. The frequency spectrum is equally regarded as a natural resource.

This book describes the provisions made by law for the management of the natural resources associated with the processes of telecommunication. Control of the alienation of the natural resources (permitted by Article 10) has been effected to date in the various legislative codes dealing with telecommunication.[7]

In the United States, the Supreme Court has recognised that the electro-magnetic spectrum is a natural resource within the public domain, the ownership of which is vested in the people of the United States.[8] Congress has stated that the purpose of broadcasting regulatory legislation was "to maintain control of the United States over all [broadcasting] channels . . . and to provide for the use of the channels but not for the ownership thereof".[9] In any consideration of the constitutionality of certain public-interest restrictions in broadcasting, it must not be overlooked that, as outlined in the foregoing paragraphs, the broadcasting channels are owned by the State; newspaper facilities are owned by private publishers.

A distinction must be made between the use of electro-magnetic energy — which the Electricity Supply Board (ESB) makes available for all to use — and the frequency spectrum which is more exclusive and which is essential for the broadcasting service. The generation of electro-magnetic energy in the form of electricity is already regulated.[10] A virtual monopoly in relation to its generation has been given to the ESB.[11] Assuming that the basic "raw material" involved in the telecommunication process is vested in the State by virtue of Article 10 of the Constitution, Article 10 cannot stand alone and must be interpreted in the light of other provisions of the Constitution.[12] Thus, the State is obliged under Article 10.3 to manage the frequency spectrum for the common good. This may well entail the licensing of others in such a manner as befits the common good.

The telecommunication privileges conferred by statute restrict entry into the market for those willing to provide telecommunication services. Further, the providers of telecommunication services are subject to statutory restrictions in the manner in which they provide the appropriate telecommunication service. Several reasons have been advanced over many years for such form of regulation. Firstly, there is the consideration of continuing the advantages of a natural monopoly and of providing a universal telecommunication service; secondly, there is the allocation of inherently scarce resources; thirdly, there is the issue of providing for the protection of consumers from those who may provide sub-standard services, the security of telecommunication networks, promoting network interoperability and ensuring the privacy of citizens; fourthly, there is the question of maintenance of a system of keeping tariffs for telecommunication services down to a regulated minimum; fifthly, there is the protection of national sovereignty and security. Many of these reasons could be stated to be comprehended (in whole or in part) within the concept of the "common good".

The concept of "natural monopoly" in telecommunication has already been referred to earlier.[13] In essence, a "natural monopoly" comes into existence when high fixed costs yield economies of scale to such an extent that relevant telecommunication services can best be provided at lowest cost by a single entity. It is argued that two or more entities attempting to compete in this market would produce undesirable economic results. In any consideration of the concept of "natural monopolies" in telecommunication services, a distinction must be made between the telecommunication carrier service, which depends largely on a single network and broadcasting and cable services where existing facilities can be shared by several service providers. The European Commission as early as 1973 in its observations under Article 20 of the EEC Treaty in the *Sacchi* case[14] noted the fact that different competition criteria could distinguish the traditional broadcasting services (radio and television) from the emerging cable services because the technical reasons which justify a monopoly for radio transmission — the limited number of available frequencies and the obstacles to the transmissions of televised programmes beyond frontiers — were practically eliminated by the technology of cable television.[15]

As stated earlier, a further distinction should be made in the context of any consideration of a justification for telecommunication privileges between basic and value-added telecommunication services and between basic telecommunication carrier equipment and terminal equipment in the premises of a customer.[16] The "natural monopoly" argument in relation to the public telecommunication carrier service is that as a result of "economies of scale" and "economies of scope" a single monopoly supplier is more efficient than if the market were to be served by several suppliers.

This justification for some privileges of an exclusive nature can be understood readily in relation to the basic public telecommunication carrier network but recent technological advances in micro-electronics, satellites and specialised networks are challenging the notion of an absolute unified basic network. The justification for a single monopoly supplier of telecommunication services loses its force when applied to customer premises equipment and certain value-added telecommunications services — both of which lie within the exclusive privilege of the Minister for Communications. In fact, since July 1, 1990 the market for telephones and payphones has been liberalised in Ireland.[17] The supply of other telecommunication terminal equipment had been gradually liberalised before that date. Value-added services were liberalised formally in 1992.[18]

A complete liberalisation of the telecommunication carrier network service (as distinct from regulated competition) could diminish the concept of "universal service" which is enshrined as one of the principal objects of Telecom Éireann — the national telecommunication carrier service — by virtue of section 14(1)(b) of the *Postal and Telecommunications Services Act, 1983*.[19] Aspects of this issue are considered in the next chapter under the heading of "The European Communities".

25

The Jurisprudence of the Courts and International Influences

Irish law in relation to telecommunication has been and will continue to be affected by many influences. Conscious of the role of telecommunication in facilitating the completion of the internal market, the institutions of the European Communities have evolved many pro-competition policies which are having and will continue to have a profound effect on the future development of Irish telecommunication processes. New technologies will force constant re-examination of the definition or re-definition of the public-service character of certain telecommunication and the distinction between the basic telecommunication network service and other value-added services which may be appropriate for private sector investment. The extent to which any public-service entity is performing its role and whether its performance could be improved by subjecting that public entity to greater competition will constitute another influence. Ideological arguments in relation to any deregulation policies to be implemented by Government will also play an increasing role in determining the future of telecommunication processes.

THE EARLY YEARS

The pace of technological change together with the haphazard manner in which legislation concerning telecommunication evolved presented interesting opportunities for judicial interpretations. For example, the question arose in 1880 in *Attorney General v The Edison Telephone Company*[1] whether communications by telephone came within the exclusive privilege (monopoly) of the Postmaster-General under section 4 of the *Telegraph Act, 1869*. The telephone had not been invented in 1869 and for the Attorney General and Postmaster-

General to succeed it was necessary to prove that the telephone was "a telegraph" within the meaning of the *Telegraph Acts 1863 and 1869* and that a telephone conversation was a "message or a communication by a telegraph" and therefore a "telegram" within the meaning of the Acts of 1863 and 1869.[2] In the *Edison Telephone Company* case it was held that the telephone was a "telegraph" and a telephone conversation was "a telegram" within the definitions of the Acts of 1863 and 1869 and accordingly, in the circumstances of the case, the telephone business being operated by the Edison Telephone Company of London infringed the Postmaster-General's exclusive privilege.

Professor Atiyah has argued[3] that the decision in the *Edison Telephone Company case,* and the Privy Council ruling in 1932 in *Re Regulation and Control of Radio Communication in Canada*[4] which held, *inter alia,* that broadcasting fell within the meaning of the word "telegraphs" in the context of the relevant legislative framework, were courageous decisions which were difficult to reconcile with the traditional canons of interpretation. Professor Atiyah contended that these decisions could be justified if the courts had power to extend statutes by analogy. At face value these decisions seem extraordinary and appear to merit the epithet "courageous" by Professor Atiyah. However, upon closer examination, while the courts appear to have been influenced by several factors, the ratio decidendi in both cases can be fully justified on traditional criteria. The term "telegraph" is defined in the *Telegraph Acts* as including any apparatus for transmitting messages and other communications by means of electric signals.[5] Electric signals are used for the transmission of telephone messages; accordingly, it was not difficult to conclude that a telephone was a telegraph within the meaning of the *Telegraph Acts.* Further, as the term "telegram" is defined to mean any message or other communication transmitted or intended for transmission by a telegraph,[6] it followed that a telephone message was a "telegram" within the legislative framework of the *Telegraph Acts.* In the *Edison Telephone Company* case, the Exchequer Division consisting of Pollock B and Stephen J appear to have been influenced by the fact that the legislature in 1869 used language which in their view embraced future discoveries "as to the use of electricity for the purpose of conveying intelligence".[7] In fact, in the parliamentary debates on the *Telegraph Bill, 1869* some members of Parliament were critical of the potential scope of the Postmaster-General's monopoly. Mr. Walter, MP, complained that the Bill would confer on the Government "the exclusive right of conveying messages of an incorporeal character not only by wires, but by any other means which the ingenuity of mankind might hereafter devise".[8]

The Court in *Edison* appears to have been influenced also partly by the doctrine of "consequentialism", i.e., the social and legal consequences that would flow from its decision if the State's monopoly were to be defeated.[9] Stephen J, for the Court, could be stated to have articulated that premise thus:

> It is difficult to suppose that the legislature intended to grant a monopoly so liable to be defeated or that its language was meant to be so construed as to be limited to the then state of, perhaps, the most progressive of all sciences.

The House of Lords in 1909 in *Postmaster-General v National Telephone Company*,[10] a case which also involved a challenge to the Postmaster-General's monopoly, was influenced partly by the consequences that could flow from its decision. It had been argued by the National Telephone Company that private telephone lines connecting two or more separate and independent persons or businesses were not within the exclusive privilege of the Postmaster-General. The House of Lords held that such communications were within the exclusive privilege of the Postmaster-General. Lord Loreburn LC, with whom the other Law Lords[11] agreed, put the issue this way:

> In the present case the Government bought the telegraphs and acquired a monopoly of telegraphic communication which includes telephonic communication about forty years ago for a great sum of money; and today your Lordships have to consider how far that monopoly extends not in regard to trivial or frivolous invasions but in regard to claims so far reaching that, if admitted, they go a considerable way towards destroying the value of the monopoly itself. . . .[12]

Irish judges likewise had considerable difficulty in interpreting the words "telegram"[13] and "telegraph". In *Postmaster-General v Great Southern and Western Railway Co*[14] (1909-1910), the Postmaster-General successfully contended that the words "telegraph materials" used in certain deeds entered into between the defendants and the plaintiff included telephone materials. As Gibson J (in the Divisional Court) put it, the Postmaster-General claimed "in the absence of a controlling context, all the references in

the deeds to telegraphs embrace telephony".[15] Dodd J noted at first
instance in the (Irish) King's Bench Division that the "controversy"
had become "acute" because in 1911 the Post Office was to take over
all the telephones.[16] Dodd J added:

> The Post Office [intended] to carry on the [telecommunication]
> business with public offices for the reception of customers, and
> all the appliances which such a system demands. The [Great
> Southern and Western Railway Co] say "non in haec foedera
> venimus" ["we do not enter these treaties"].

Although Dodd J (at first instance)[17] dismissed the action of the
Postmaster-General, his observations on the meaning of the words
"telegram" and "telegraph" are of interest — particularly as these
words still have particular significance in the statutory code
regulating telecommunication in Ireland. Since the *Great Southern
and Western Railway Co* case is an important but unreported
judgment, more extensive quotation than normal is justified. Dodd
J said:

> The curious thing is that there was no ordinary meaning of the
> word [telegram], apart from its use in electrical science. The
> vocabulary of electrical science had to be made. The word
> "telegram" does not appear in Webster's Dictionary of 1849.
> The words to describe the various units of electricity had to be
> invented, and the international courtesy in naming ohms, and
> volts, and ampères and farads, and such like is a matter of
> history. The word "telegram" when introduced was challenged
> by purists as being wrong in composition. It does not appear in
> the Telegraph Act of 1863, nor in the Telegraph Act of 1868. A
> periphrasis is adopted, "a message sent along or across the
> wires". But one single word was needed to describe the thing,
> and so it came, as the phrase is, to stay.
>   Writers and draughtsmen avoided it for a time, but it was too
> convenient to be set aside. It had come to be applied either to
> the message itself or to the paper sent out to the addressee
> enclosed in the official envelope labelled telegram. . . .
>   It did not include the telephone at first, for telephones were
> not in existence, and it could not well include what did not exist,
> but it was capable of carrying the meaning if the context
> demanded it. . . .
>   The word "telegram" does not lend itself readily to

abbreviation and there are not wanting indications that it will disappear from use.

A "wire" has come in commercial language largely to supersede telegrams. Shall I send you a wire? No; 'phone me, I am on the 'phone — seems likely to be the language of the future.

American writers, I notice, use the inverted comma before 'phone to indicate it is a contraction. But this will disappear. Macaulay, with tears in his pen, besought his sister not to adopt the corruption, "cab", but to cling to the more polite "cabriolet"; but the plastic force of a people's habits was powerful to establish the shortened word.

There is one slight matter on this etymological subject that is of some moment. When telephones came into use it was easy to refer to that method of transmission by telegraph as telephonic — but no word was either invented or adopted to describe the use of telegraphic wires other than a telephonic use, so the generic word "telegraph" has come to be applied to that portion of the service leaving the word "telephonic" to the other. Telegraphic gets, therefore, now, in ordinary language, a meaning that contrasts it with "telephonic" but that is due to the meagreness of language. . . .[18]

Gibson J in the Divisional Court in the same case stated that the problem was "not easy of solution".[19] He too analysed the words "telegraph" and "telegram":

The verb "telegraph" has always had a wide signification; it covers all kinds of distance signals—semaphores, flags etc. The noun "telegram" suggested in 1852 in America, and in 1858 in England, as a legitimate coinage has, as far as I know, never in popular use been applied to purely oral messages. What we have here to consider is the meaning of "telegraph" and "telegraphic" in connection with electric telegraphy. In ordinary speech I have no doubt that "telegraph" and "telegram" would, as between members of the public, denote ordinary telegraphy and not telephony. If any one said he sent a telegram to a friend, no one would suppose an oral telephone message was meant. A contract by a merchant with Lloyds to insure against mistakes in business telegrams — a possible risk — would hardly be construed as extending to mistakes in oral business intercourse by telephone. The convenience of everyday life has appropriated a specific meaning to "telegraph" and "telegram"; and this is exemplified in the [*Telegraph Act, 1892*]. . . .

But though the popular and natural meaning of "telegraph" and "telegram" does not in common parlance cover telephone, it by no means follows that these expressions are to be similarly restricted in a contract between the Postmaster-General and a Railway Company with regard to wayleaves and the exercise of the powers and rights of the former which, if necessary, could be enforced against the Company by means of compulsory acquisition.[20]

Gibson J was of the opinion that in the relevant clauses of the wayleave grant between the parties, the reference to "telegraph materials" did include telephone materials. [In fact Dodd J so held at first instance.] Madden J delivered a concurring judgment and Kenny J agreed with his brother judges that the judgment of Dodd J should be reversed on other grounds.

The meaning of the word "telegram" arose in oral argument in *Nova Media Services Ltd v Minister for Posts and Telegraphs* (1983)[21] because the Minister's telecommunication privilege is specified in section 4 of the *Telegraph Act, 1869*[22] as "transmitting telegrams", but the case did not turn on that issue and there is no reference to the matter in the judgment of Murphy J.

In *Re Regulation and Control of Radio Communication in Canada (1932)*[23] the issue arose whether the Parliament of Canada had exclusive legislative power to regulate and control broadcasting in Canada. The essence of the matter was whether broadcasting (radio communication) came within the following provisions: ". . . telegraphs, and other works and undertakings connecting the Province with any other of the Provinces, or extending beyond the limits of the Province".[24] The Privy Council had no difficulty in ruling that the undertaking of broadcasting was an undertaking "connecting the Province with other Provinces and extending beyond the limits of the Province". Almost as a secondary ground for so holding, the Privy Council considered that broadcasting fell within the description of "telegraphs". The Privy Council stated[25] that the word "telegraph" in everyday speech is accepted as an "electrical instrument which by means of a wire connecting that instrument with another instrument makes it possible to communicate signals or words of any kind". Viscount Dunedin delivering the judgment of the Privy Council took refuge, however, in the original meaning of the word "telegraph" as given in the Oxford Dictionary which corresponded with the statutory definition in the *Telegraph Acts 1863* and *1869* as "an apparatus for transmitting messages to a distance, usually by signs of some kind".[26] The Privy Council too was concerned with the consequential aspects of deciding the case the other way. This would have led to "confusion and in-efficiency".[27] Their Lordships were pleased to note that in fact "it [was] a matter of congratulation that the result arrived at [seemed] consonant with common sense".[28]

FOUR CONSTITUTIONAL PROVISIONS

Four provisions of the Constitution of Ireland are particularly relevant to the law relating to telecommunication. Article 10 of the Constitution, considered in the previous chapter, provides that all natural resources including all forms of potential energy belong to the State and that provision may be made by law for the management and control of the alienation, whether temporary or permanent, of that property. In the previous chapter it was argued that electro-magnetic engergy, which is the essence of telecommunication, is a natural resource within the terms of Article 10.

Article 40.6.1.i of the Constitution provides that the State guarantees liberty for the exercise, subject to public order and morality, of the right of the citizens to express freely their convictions and opinions. The second paragraph of Article 40.6.1.i qualifies further the free expression rights. The education of public opinion is stated to be a matter of such grave import to the common good that the State must endeavour to ensure that the organs of public opinion including the radio, the press and the cinema, while preserving their rightful liberty of expression including criticism of Government policy, shall not be used to undermine public order or morality or the authority of the State. This guarantee is considered in chapter 26.

The third constitutional provision is Article 40.3.1 which provides that the State guarantees in its laws to respect and, as far as practicable, by its laws to defend and vindicate the personal rights of the citizen. This latter provision may be described as the judicial law-making clause of the Constitution. This view is based on Kenny J's dictum in *Ryan v Attorney General* (1965)[29] that the personal rights which may be invoked to invalidate legislation are not confined to those specified in Article 40 but include those rights which result from the Christian and democratic nature of the State. The right to communicate, considered in chapter 27, and the right to privacy in telephone conversations,[30] considered in chapter 28, stem from Article 40.3.1.

Article 40.3.2 of the Constitution may also play a role in the regulation of telecommunication. This Article provides, *inter alia*, that the State shall, in particular, by its laws protect as best it can from unjust attack, and in the case of injustice done, vindicate the person and good name of every citizen. These provisions are explored in subsequent chapters.

CHALLENGES TO THE STATE'S TELECOMMUNICATION PRIVILEGES: JURISPRUDENCE OF THE IRISH COURTS

The State's telecommunication privileges — in essence the telecommunication monopoly powers of the State — have been challenged unsuccessfully in several cases in the form of constitutional attacks on the regulatory legislation governing telecommunication.

In *Walsh v Ireland* (1978),[31] considered in chapter 15, the attack on the constitutionality of the provisions of the *Wireless Telegraphy Act, 1926* which provided for the seizure of wireless telegraphy apparatus (broadcasting equipment in this case) was easily disposed of by Hamilton J who considered that *Walsh* was not a proper case to grant any relief at the interlocutory hearing. The plaintiffs never pursued their case.

The *Nova* and *Sunshine Radio* cases (1983),[32] considered in chapter 15, represented a more serious challenge to the regulation by the Minister for Posts and Telegraphs of telecommunication (radio broadcasting in these cases). The plaintiffs, inter alia, contended that the Minister for Posts and Telegraphs had abused his powers under the *Wireless Telegraphy Act, 1926* to the extent that no statutory regime of regulation had come into existence in relation to radio broadcasting and, in effect, an unauthorised monopoly had been created in favour of RTE, the national broadcasting service. In addition to claiming that the relevant provisions of the *Wireless Telegraphy Act, 1926* were inconsistent with the Irish Constitution, the plaintiffs claimed that the relevant provisions violated the EEC Treaty and the European Convention for the Protection of Human Rights and Fundamental Freedoms. These were serious issues and although Murphy J, in dismissing the interlocutory application on the balance of convenience argument, considered that the plaintiffs had made out a stateable case, the plaintiffs never pursued their case. The paltry nature of the fines for illegal broadcasting[33] and the relatively permissive attitude of the authorities in the years prior to the enactment of the *Broadcasting and Wireless Telegraphy Act, 1988,* provided little incentive to the unlawful radio stations to launch a major constitutional attack on the Minister's monopoly powers.

The monopoly powers of the Minister for Posts and Telegraphs were also challenged unsuccessfully in *Attorney General v Paperlink Ltd* (1983).[34] In *Paperlink* the challenge related to the postal monopoly powers of the Minister. The right to communicate which was determined in *Paperlink* is explored later in chapter 27. Apart from the right to communicate, Costello J in *Paperlink* adopted a conservative approach to the issue of the constitutionality of granting of privileges of a monopoly nature by the Oireachtas in the commercial sphere. Essentially, the view adopted by Costello J was that these issues were matters for the legislature. Accordingly, Costello J dismissed the arguments of the postal courier company in relation to the unconstitutionality of the monopoly of the Minister for Posts and Telegraphs.

The ultimate fear of undue concentration is that economic power will be controlled by the few. Telecom Éireann was originally granted its privilege of an exclusive nature specifically because of its primary purpose of providing a national telecommunication service.[35] Justification for the granting of such a privilege (and in the case of Telecom Éireann it is a limited privilege which is in certain respects shared by others) could be based on the public order standard of Article 40.6.1 and the "common good" standard of Article 43. Walsh J, in his extra-judicial writing, has given an interesting insight into the meaning of the phrase "common good". In his Foreword to *Cases and Materials on The Irish Constitution* he argues:

> . . . the common good must be understood principally as the satisfaction of the greatest proportion of interests of all the persons in so far as this is possible with the least sacrifice, the least friction, and the least waste. In other words, the common good includes the general conditions of personal and family security, peace, economic prosperity and public service, which can best satisfy everybody's interests.[36]

In the United States, despite an abiding and widespread fear of the evils that flow from monopoly,[37] exclusive privileges of public entities granted by the legislature in the public interest, subject to appropriate regulation for the general welfare, have been justified under the US Constitution on the grounds of public interest, convenience and necessity.[38]

THE EUROPEAN COMMUNITIES

The primary international influence on the regulation of telecommunication in Ireland is the law which emanates from the
institutions of the European Communities. For many years, it was
considered that Article 90(2) of the EEC Treaty somehow immunised
the State telecommunication administrations from the effects of EC
law. Article 90 of the EEC Treaty appeared to sanction, to a certain
extent, undertakings to which the State has granted special or
exclusive rights. Article 90 may be quoted in full:

> 1. In the case of public undertakings to which Member States
> grant special or exclusive rights, Member States shall neither
> enact nor maintain in force any measure contrary to the rules
> contained in this Treaty, in particular to those rules provided
> for in Article 7 and Articles 85 to 94.
> 2. Undertakings entrusted with the operation of services of
> general economic interest or having the character of a revenue-
> producing monopoly shall be subject to the rules contained in
> this Treaty, in particular to the rules on competition, in so far
> as the application of such rules does not obstruct the per-
> formance, in law or in fact, of the particular tasks assigned to
> them. The development of trade must not be affected to such
> an extent as would be contrary to the interests of the Com-
> munity.
> 3. The Commission shall ensure the application of the pro-
> visions of this Article and shall, where necessary, address
> appropriate directives or decisions to Member States.

The status of State telecommunication monopolies was considered by the Court of Justice in Case 155/73 *Sacchi* (1974).[39] In
Sacchi, the Court of Justice held that Article 90(1) of the Treaty
permitted Member States to grant television organisations the
exclusive right to broadcast television transmissions including cable
transmission. The Court held that the fact that an undertaking to
which a Member State grants exclusive rights within the meaning of
Article 90 has a monopoly is not, as such, incompatible with Article
86 of the Treaty (prohibition on abuse of a dominant position). The
Court also held that the grant of an exclusive right to transmit
television signals does not as such constitute a breach of Article 7 of
the Treaty which prohibits any discrimination on grounds of
nationality. However, discrimination by undertakings enjoying

such exclusive rights against nationals of Member States by virtue of their nationality would be incompatible with Article 7 of the Treaty. In *Sacchi* the Court concluded that the provision of a television signal must, by reason of its nature, be regarded as provision of a service. The Court held that the transmission of television signals including those in the nature of advertisements came, as such, within the rules of the Treaty relating to services. The Court also held that trade in material, sound recordings, films and other apparatus used in the dissemination of television signals was subject to the rules of the Treaty relating to freedom of movement for goods.

Subsequently, the Court of Justice concluded in *Case 52/79 Debauve* that the transmission of television signals by cable came likewise within the rules of the Treaty relating to services.[40]

The Court of Justice in *ERT, Case 260/89* (1991),[41] a case involving ERT, a Greek radio and television undertaking to which the Greek State had granted exclusive rights, confirmed the *Sacchi* judgment that Community law does not prevent the granting of a television monopoly in the public interest and on the basis of non-economic considerations. However, the Court held that the arrangments for organising and operating such a monopoly must not infringe the provisions of the Treaty on the free movement of goods and services or the competition rules.

In *ERT*, the Court also considered that the limitations imposed on the power of Member States to apply the provisions referred to in Articles 56 and 66 (right of establishment and freedom to provide services) of the EEC Treaty for reasons of public policy, public safety and public health, must be assessed in the light of the general principle of freedom of expression entrenched in Article 10 of the European Convention on Human Rights.

Any derogation claimed under Article 90(2) would, in the pro-competition climate of present times, be subject to the strictest scrutiny, and would only apply in the most exceptional circumstances. The Court of Justice has confirmed in *Italy v EC Commission* (the British Telecom case)(1985)[42] the Commission's view that telecommunication administrations were undertakings within the meaning of Article 86. The Court considered that the measures at issue (a regulation promulgated by British Telecom which prohibited private message-forwarding agencies in the United Kingdom from relaying telex messages received from or intended for other countries) were not covered by Article 90(2) of the Treaty and that the applicant had failed to demonstrate that the

Commission's censure of the offending schemes of British Telecom
had put the performance of the particular tasks entrusted to British
Telecom in jeopardy from the economic point of view. In Case
C/18/88, RTT (Belgium) (1991) a case involving the Belgium telecommunication carrier service which held a monopoly for
establishing and running the public telecommunication network
and a company which sold terminal equipment, the EC Court stated
that the exclusion or restriction of competition in the telephone
equipment market by Belgian law could not be regarded as justified
by the task of providing a public service of general economic
interest.[43]

The EC Court of Justice favours a narrow interpretation of existing
monopoly rights and disfavours the extension of a service monopoly
as new telecommunication technologies are developed. In the *International Air Couriers* case (1985),[44] which related to value-added
services in the postal field and issues under Articles 90 and 86 of the
EEC Treaty, the Commission stated that it regarded Member States'
postal and telecommunications authorities as commercial undertakings since they supplied goods and services for payment and that
"any extension" by one or more of these undertakings of their
dominant position might constitute an abuse under Article 86 of the
EC Treaty.

An important case in the evolution of EC telecommunication case
law is *France v Commission*.[45] The Court of Justice upheld the validity
of most of the telecommunication terminal equipment directive[46]
which provided in general for the withdrawal of the special
privileges that telecommunication carrier operators enjoyed in
Member States in relation to the supply and maintenance of telecommunication terminal equipment. The Court confirmed the
power of the Commission to legislate under paragraph 3 of Article
90 without having to persuade the Council of Ministers to adopt its
proposal.

The services directive for telecommunication,[47] adopted before
the judgment was given in *France v Commission*, was also substantially upheld by the Court of Justice in *Spain, Belgium and Italy v
Commission*[48] in a similar manner to *France v Commission*, but relying
on Article 86 (abuse of dominant position).

The *Corbeau* case (1993),[49] (relating to the extent of the postal
monopoly in Belgium), which considered Articles 86 and 90 of the
EC Treaty, is relevant to the status in law of telecommunication
privileges. Mr. Corbeau had been prosecuted for carrying on the
business of collecting mail from clients in Liege and delivering the

mail not later than mid-day the following day. The Court of Justice recognised that the post office did come within Article 90(1); that it was dominant by virtue of its exclusive rights; but that this did not in itself infringe Article 86 (abuse of dominant position). However, taking Article 90(1) and 90(2) into consideration, the Court stated that the competition rules applied in so far as they did not interfere with the accomplishment of the Post Office's task. There was an obligation on the Post Office to provide a universal service which would require cross-subsidisation. Obviously, this justified some limitation on competition. But the Court considered that this did not authorise a prohibition on the services which were better than those of the post office in certain circumstances. The Court of Justice remitted the case back to the national court for an examination whether the relevant specific services were dissociable from a service operated in the public interest and which would not jeopardise the economic stability of the post office.

Telecommunication in Ireland is being regulated increasingly by EC law. The EC Commission Green Papers on telecommunications services (1987) and satellites (1990),[50] together with the tele-communication policies adopted by the Council of Ministers in its Resolution of June 1993[51] will determine much of Ireland's legis-lative programmes in relation to telecommunication carrier-related activities. The June 1993 Resolution supported the Commission's intention to prepare before January 1, 1996 the necessary amendments to the Community regulatory framework in order to achieve liberalisation of all public voice telephone services by January 1, 1998. Ireland together with Spain, Greece and Portugal, were granted an additional transition period up to 2003 to achieve the necessary structural adjustments in particular, in relation to tariffs. It may be stated, in general that certain *de jure* public network privileges of an exclusive nature of the national telecommunication carrier administrations are, at present, permissible under EC law.[52] The basic network aspect of Telecom Éireann's privilege is in accord-ance with present EC policy. As stated, the present *de jure* service privileges of the national telecommunication carriers are being restricted. Only the switched voice-telephony service (and certain other limited telecommunication services) may be provided at present on the basis of exclusive rights; all other telecommunication carrier-related services, including, in particular, value-added services within and between Community States, must be provided on a competitive basis. In this context, a major liberalisation measure was implemented in Ireland in 1992.[53] In order to ensure open non-discriminatory access for service providers, and users of tele-communication carrier-related services, certain interconnect and access obligations were imposed on national telecommunication administrations. This concept is known as Open Network Provision and its first phase has already been implemented in Ireland.[54] The terminal equipment exclusive privilege of national telecom-munication administrations has been abolished. This has already been effected in Ireland.[55] Finally, European standardisation procedures are to be streamlined.

In relation to satellite communications, the European Commission in its Green Paper (1990)[56] has proposed four major changes: (a) full liberalisation of the earth segment including both receive-only and transmit/receive terminals, subject to appropriate type approval and licensing procedures where justified to implement necessary regulatory safeguards; (b) free (unrestricted) access to space segment capacity, subject to licensing procedures in order to safeguard those exclusive or special rights and regulatory provisions set up by Member States in conformity with Community law and based on the consensus achieved in Community telecommunication policy; (c) access should be on an equitable, non-discriminatory and cost-oriented basis; (d) full commercial freedom for space segment providers, including direct marketing of satellite capacity to service providers and users, subject to compliance with the licensing pro-cedures mentioned above and in conformity with Community law, in particular competition rules; and (e) harmonisation measures as far as required to facilitate the provision of Europe-wide services. [This latter provision concerns in particular the mutual recognition of licensing and type-approval procedures and frequency coordination].[57]

The European Commission has set out guidelines on the application of EC competition rules which aim at clarifying the application of Community competition rules to the market participants in the telecommunication sector.[58] The Commission adopted its first formal decision, according with the guidelines in a joint venture involving Telecom Éireann and Motorola Ireland Ltd, a subsidiary of the US Motorola Group, which had jointly set up a company, Eirpage Limited, to provide a nationwide wide-area radio-paging service interconnected to Telecom Éireann's fixed tele-communication network.[59] Following the principles set out in the guidelines, this cooperation between two potential competitors was found to fall under Article 85(1) (prohibition on prevention, restriction or distortion of competition within the common market).

The Commission considered, however, that it also made possible the rapid introduction of a new paging service previously unavailable to consumers and businesses in Ireland. The Commission also considered that the market for the sale of paging receiving equipment might also be expected to benefit as subscribers to the Eirpage service were free to use any brand of compatible receiving units on the system, which had been so constructed as to allow the broadest possible range of compatibility. Under those circumstances, the Commission concluded that the joint venture could be exempted under Article 85(3) of the EEC Treaty.[60]

The Treaty on European Union (Maastricht, 1992), *inter alia*, outlines broad principles on further developments.[61] With a view to enabling citizens of any European Union, economic operators and regional and local communities to derive the full benefit from the establishment of a Europe without internal frontiers, the Treaty provides that the Community is to contribute to the establishment and development of trans-European networks in telecommunications. Within the framework of a system of open and competitive markets, action by the Community is to be directed at promoting the inter-connection and inter-operability of national networks as well as access to such networks.[62] This stance on trans-European networks with an emphasis on interconnection and inter-operability is justified given that the EC was characterised in 1992 in relation to the telecommunication carrier service as having "twelve technically diverging national networks".[63]

In broadcasting, developments in cable television networks and satellite-based broadcasting are converging with the mainstream technological development of the telecommunication carrier network infrastructure. Conscious of this fact, the EC is developing its audio-visual policy. EC broadcasting policy is developing along three main lines. Firstly, efforts are being made to harmonise technical standards and technological developments. Secondly, there is the drive to create a common market for broadcasting especially by satellite and cable.[64] Thirdly, the EC seeks to promote a European audio-visual industry.

The EC is interested principally in laying down rules guaranteeing freedom of transmission in broadcasting. In *Council Directive 89/552/EEC* of 3 October 1989 on the pursuit of television broadcasting activities, the Council of the European Communities acknowledged that its Directive does not affect the responsibility of Member States with regard to the organisation (including the systems of licensing and taxation), financing and the contents of television programmes. The Council specifically acknowledged that cultural development in the Member States and the preservation of cultural diversity remained unaffected.[65]

COUNCIL OF EUROPE AND THE EUROPEAN CONVENTION ON HUMAN RIGHTS

The Council of Europe, established pursuant to the Statute of the Council of Europe (1949), exerts a significant influence on the regulation of telecommunication in Ireland. The primary influence of the Council of Europe is via the European Convention on Human Rights signed by Ireland in 1950 and ratified in 1953.[66]

In the context of telecommunication, the substantive rights and freedoms granted by the European Convention on Human Rights together with its protocols (First and Fourth Protocols) are mainly the rights to respect for private and family life, home and correspondence (Article 8), the freedom of thought, conscience and religion (Article 9) and of expression (Article 10). Article 8 of the Convention is considered in chapter 28 on interception of telecommunication.

Article 10 of the Convention has the potential for playing a pivotal role in the regulation of telecommunication and provides as follows:

> (1) Everyone has the right to freedom of expression. This right shall include freedom to hold opinions and to receive and impart information and ideas without interference by public authority and regardless of frontiers. This Article shall not prevent States from requiring the licensing of broadcasting, television or cinema enterprises.
> (2) The exercise of these freedoms since it carries with it duties and responsibilities, may be subject to such formalities, conditions, restrictions or penalties as are prescribed by law and are necessary in a democratic society, in the interests of national security, territorial integrity or public safety, for the prevention of disorder or crime, for the protection of health or morals, for the protection of the reputation or rights of others, for preventing the disclosure of information received in confidence or for maintaining the authority and impartiality of the judiciary.

Article 10 of the Convention guarantees a fundamental right —

the right to freedom of expression. This right includes the freedom to hold opinions, the freedom to receive information and ideas, the freedom to impart information and ideas (the right to communicate) without interference by public authority and regardless of frontiers. Any interference by public authority with this right, e.g., by a law, would result in a violation of Article 10 unless such interference fell within one of the exceptions specified in Article 10(2) of the Convention.

It is submitted that Article 10(1) of the Convention covers all types of expression which imparts or conveys opinions, ideas or information. This obviously includes expression via any telecommunication medium, the telephone, telex and associated means of communication and broadcasting. In *Groppera Radio AG*, (1990) (a case involving a ban on the retransmission by cable in Switzerland of programmes broadcast from Italy) the European Court of Human Rights held that broadcasting over the air and cable retransmission were included in the right enshrined in the first two sentences of Article 10(1).[67]

In the context of the compatibility of broadcasting monopolies and the Article 10 rights, the European Commission of Human Rights in *Sacchi v Italy*[68] considered that it no longer was disposed to sustaining "purely and simply" its former statement that Article 10 authorises a public broadcasting monopoly. In *Groppera Radio AG* (1990) the Court of Human Rights held that the licensing clause in Article 10(1) of the Convention was of limited scope. Its purpose was to make it clear that States are permitted to control by a licensing system the way in which broadcasting is organised in their territories, particularly in its technical aspects.[69] It is unlikely, however, because of the fear of creating private broadcasting oligopolies, that the Court would hold that notwithstanding the freedom of expression enshrined in Article 10(1), individual freedom of expression implies the right without authorisation to disseminate broadcasting programmes. The Commission and the Court may be more inclined to reinterpret the licensing clause as authorising an appropriate legal framework of regulation rather than as authorising and legitimising a public monopoly.

In *Autronic AG v Switzerland* (1990) the Court of Human Rights held that Article 10 concerned not only the content of information but also the means of transmission or reception, since any restriction imposed on the means of transmission or reception interfered with the right to receive and impart information.[70] The reception of television programmes by means of a dish or other aerial was considered by the Court to come within the right laid down in the first two sentences of Article 10(1). The Court held that the Swiss administrative and judicial decisions that prevented Autronic AG, the Swiss company specialising in home electronics, from receiving by means of a private dish aerial uncoded television programmes intended for the general public from a Soviet telecommunication satellite amounted to "interference by public authority" with the exercise of freedom of expression. The interference did not fulfil the conditions set out in 10(2) of the Convention.[71]

Article 10 of the Convention and the jurisprudence of the European Court of Human Rights will play a significant role in the future regulation of telecommunication. Although the Convention itself is not a code of legal principles which are, *per se*, enforceable in the domestic courts,[72] this does not prevent the jurisprudence of the European Court from having a persuasive effect as O'Hanlon J illustrated in relation to freedom of expression in *Desmond v Glackin*.[73]

THE INTERNATIONAL TELECOMMUNICATION UNION

The impelling forces of self-preservation and commerce spurred states to effect cross-border telecommunication. The first treaty of note related to the early days of the telegraph — the first effective mode of telecommunication. In May 1865, after two and a half months of arduous negotiations, the first international telegraph convention was signed by the 20 participating states and countries; and the International Telegraph Union had been established. This marked the birth of what was later to be styled as the International Telecommunication Union (ITU). The ITU is a worldwide organisation within which governments and the private communication sector co-ordinate the establishment and operation of telecommunication networks and services; it is responsible for the regulation, standardisation, co-ordination and development of international telecommunication as well as the harmonisation of national policies.

The International Telecommunication Constitution (Geneva, 1992) sets out the purposes of the ITU. The latest constitution and convention enter into force on July 1, 1994. However, the provisions relating to the new structure and working methods have been applicable from March 1, 1993 given the importance of maintaining the pre-eminence of the ITU and the development of world telecommunication and of ensuring that the work of the ITU continues to be relevant to the needs of the telecommunication community. Unlike other treaties, the convention of the ITU has been re-negotiated *de novo* at regular intervals. The ITU's legal status is based on two types of text having treaty status and therefore binding on all ITU members. They consist of the Constitution and Convention of the ITU signed on December 22, 1992 (Geneva) and the Administrative Regulations (Radio Regulations and Inter- national Telecommunications Regulations) annexed to the Convention. The Radio Regulations were signed in 1979 (Geneva) and have been partially revised since then by World Administrative Radio Conferences.

The International Telecommunications Regulations were signed on December 9, 1988 (Melbourne) and entered into force on July 1, 1990. Ireland has played a significant role in the activities of the ITU and the ITU has adapted itself to a significant degree to meet modern conditions and respond to the needs of its members.

GERMAN AND ITALIAN JURISPRUDENCE

Irish and British courts have exerted little influence on the development of telecommunication law. This contrasts with, for example, the courts in the United States and the constitutional courts of Germany and Italy which have exerted a profound influence on the development of telecommunication law.[74] The German Con-stitutional Court (Bundesverfassungsgericht), which sits at Karlsruhe, and the Italian Constitutional Court (Corte Con-stituzionale) in Rome, have ruled on the issue of public versus private ownership of broadcasting systems and other related issues. The US Supreme Court has also dealt with the role of the broadcaster in the overall context of the First Amendment to the US Constitution (freedom of speech and of the press).

The post-war constitutions of both Germany and Italy and their determination to avoid the repression of earlier totalitarian regimes may explain the role of their judiciary in the regulation of broad-casting. Article 5 of the German Basic Law of 1949 (Grundgesetz) provides:

> Everyone shall have the right freely to express and disseminate his opinion by speech, writing and pictures and freely to inform himself from generally accessible sources. Freedom of the press and freedom of broadcasting by means of broadcasts and films are guaranteed. There shall be no censorship.

Article 5(2) provides that the foregoing rights are limited by general laws together with laws for the protection of youth and reputation. In the *Third Television* case (1981),[75] the Bundesverfassungsgericht rejected the complete deregulation of broadcasting and its absolute comparison with the position of the press. Yet the court accepted that private broadcasting had a distinctive role. The court's decision paved the way for the private television legislation in Germany of the 1980s.

In the *Fourth Television* case (1986), the Bundesverfassungsgericht in a significant contribution to the development of German broadcasting law emphasised the important role of the media in providing information for citizens and so contributing to the working of democracy.[76] In the context of the relationship between public and private broadcasters the *Fourth Television* decision envisaged the relationship between public and private broadcasters as having complementary rather than competitive roles. Public broadcasters had a central responsibility to inform and educate, and to provide a comprehensive service. Such high standards were not expected of private broadcasters but private broadcasters enjoyed their complementary role because of the role of public broadcasting authorities in discharging certain fundamental responsibilities in a modern democracy. It has been argued that the *Fourth Television* ruling may be regarded as constituting a constitutional guarantee for the continued existence of public broadcasting.[77] The German Constitutional Court insisted that public broadcasting should enjoy adequate financing to enable it to discharge its responsibilities. However, in its sixth broadcasting judgment (1991),[78] the German Constitutional Court reasoned that Land (State) legislatures were free to choose any broadcasting system, public, private or a dual broadcasting system of public and private services, as long as the chosen system guarantees the free formation of opinions and programme output was representative of social forces and their views.

The Italian Constitutional Court (Corte Constituzionale) has been anxious to prevent the development of private broadcasting oligopolies, which would allow media owners to exercise an undue influence on public opinion. As expected in modern democracies, there are similarities between the constitutions of Ireland and Italy, in relation, *inter alia*, to freedom of expression. Article 21 of the 1947 Italian Constitution provides that "[e]veryone has the right to express himself freely verbally, in writing and by other means". Article 41 of the Italian Constitution, which has similarities to Article 45.3.1 and 2 of the Irish Constitution (directive principles of social policy in relation to private enterprise), postulates a freedom of private economic enterprise to be conducted in conformity with social utility and in such a way as not to damage security, liberty and human dignity.

In its 1988 judgment in relation to broadcasting,[79] the Italian Constitutional Court considered that the role of public broadcasting was to permit a wide variety of opinions and perspectives for the benefit of all citizens; parliament had a responsibility to ensure that the public broadcasting services had sufficient funds to enable them to carry out their role. In relation to private broadcasting which was constitutionally permissible, the balance between various competing constitutional interests could be satisfied by ensuring that the private channels were not all owned by one group.

Both the German and Italian Constitutional Courts in the *Fourth Television* case[80] and in the 1988 judgment[81] respectively stressed implicitly the importance in the context of their respective constitutions of the continued existence of public broadcasting institutions. It is also of note that neither court considered the broadcast media in the same context as the printed press. Further, neither court was prepared to leave all to the marketplace. Irish courts would probably adopt a similar stance.

The reference to "the education of public opinion" being a matter of "such grave import to the common good" in Article 40.6.1.i of the Constitution of Ireland (although not framed as a constitutional right), and the obligation on the State (by its laws) to protect as best it may from unjust attack and in the case of injustice done to vindicate the good name of the citizen (Article 40.3.2), for example, may well offer the courts the opportunity to protect the continued existence of the institution of public broadcasting in Ireland. A form of public-service broadcasting should exist side-by-side with private broadcasting services.

UNITED STATES' COURTS AND THE TELECOMMUNICATION CARRIER SERVICE

In the United States, the judicial arm of government has played a significant role in the restructuring of the telecommunication carrier service in the form of American Telephone and Telegraph Company (AT&T or Bell System) — the world's largest privately-held corporation.[82] For three quarters of a century the United States Government confronted AT&T in legal challenges over AT&T's

alleged monopolistic power and predatory behaviour. The AT&T monopoly derived originally from patents for telephone inventions. When these patents ran out, AT&T's *de facto* monopoly was extended by classic industrial tactics that prompted application of the US antitrust laws. These tactics included the use of improvement patents, the acquisition of competing enterprises and the abuse of franchises in relation to telephone exchange operations.[83]

The US Department of Justice filed its most celebrated antitrust action against AT&T in 1974 pursuant to the Sherman Act.[84] That case was resolved by a settlement (a negotiated consent decree, referred to as the Modified Final Judgment or MFJ) between the Department of Justice and AT&T.[85] Judge Harold H. Greene, District Court Judge for the District of Columbia, was the trial judge. The consent decree entered into in 1982 effected the largest divestiture in the legal history of the United States; AT&T was split into eight separate corporate entities. In return, AT&T retained Western Electric and was allowed to engage in unregulated commerce, a diversification which had been prohibited by an earlier consent decree. The 1982 consent decree attempted to isolate the regulated monopoly components of the AT&T system from components of that system which should have been competitive. The approach was that AT&T, shorn of its control of local monopoly telephone service, would compete effectively with other suppliers of long-distance telecommunication service to the (divested) seven regional Bell Operating Companies (RBOCs) which held local monopolies.

The decree contained a provision which permitted any of the parties to return to the court at any time to request it to construe, modify or enforce the decree.[86] Another provision gave the court the authority to grant waivers from the restrictions which prohibited the regional companies from engaging in any activity other than the local telephone business.[87]

Several major criticisms[88] have been made justifiably in relation to the 1982 decree of Judge Harold H. Greene. Of particular concern to Ireland is the criticism that the Modified Final Judgment imposed too much regulatory responsibility on the court — in effect on a single judge. Professor Louis Schwartz put the issue in this way:

> Vindicating justice is a different and perhaps higher function than managing vast enterprises. Boredom and mortality set a temporal limit on a single judge's administrative policy; that of his successor will almost be accidentally determined by political influences on appointment and assignment.[89]

A "restructuring" could (in effect) be carried out in Ireland by the High Court (and Supreme Court) by means of a successful challenge to the various telecommunication oligopolies and privileges.[90] However, many would rightly consider the judiciary to be an inappropriate major decision-maker in relation to the regulation of telecommunication. The economic and technological resources available to the courts are limited.

26

Freedom of Expression

INTRODUCTION

The right to communicate, considered in the next chapter, and freedom of expression, are linked. Much of what is written in this chapter on freedom of expression relates also to the right to communicate.

Article 40.6.1.i. of the Constitution provides that the State guarantees liberty for the rights of the citizens to express freely their convictions and opinions, subject to public order and morality. The meaning of "convictions" and "opinions" has given rise to some academic debate.[1] It has been argued, for example, that expression and communication of facts are excluded from the guarantee in Article 40.6.1.i by virtue of the use in that subsection of the words "convictions and opinions".[2] It is perhaps somewhat artificial to separate conviction and opinion totally from the realm of fact.

In Article 40.6.1.i of the Constitution, the organs of public opinion, such as radio and television,[3] are referred to in terms of "preserving their rightful liberty of expression including criticism of government policy". The electronic media thus receive implicit constitutional protection.

One function of the electronic media (as part of the wider media) which may be inferred from Article 40.6.1.i is to provide the public with an uninterrupted flow of information about politics and society which may sometimes act as a "check" on government. The word "criticism" connotes implicitly a "checking" process. The dissemination of articulate and balanced reports on matters of public concern must ensure that the government in all its branches (executive, legislative and judicial) remains accountable to the people. Any legislative or other measure that hampers the media in its "rightful liberty of expression" must be constitutionally suspect. Justice White's dictum in the US case of *Red Lion* (1969) that "it is the right of the viewers and listeners, not the right of the broadcasters, which is paramount"[4] should apply in Ireland.

In any consideration of freedom of expression, we must distinguish between the primary telecommunication carrier service operated by Telecom Éireann whereby, subject to limited restrictions, the citizen can communicate freely and express his convictions and opinions, and the broadcasting services which are subject to more severe restrictions.

In relation to the telecommunication carrier service, Telecom Éireann is authorised to prohibit the transmission of objectionable messages.[5] In addition, the *Post Office (Amendment) Act, 1951* specifically makes it an offence for any person to send, by means of the telecommunication system operated by Telecom Éireann, any message or other matter which is grossly offensive or of an indecent, obscene or menacing character, whether addressed to an operator or any other person.[6] The issue of indecency is considered in the next chapter. It is also an offence for any person to send a telecommunication message which such person knows to be false or to make persistent use of Telecom Éireann's telecommunication system for the purpose of causing annoyance, inconvenience or needless anxiety to another.[7] Penalties for these offences range up to IR£50,000 on indictment, or five years imprisonment, or to both the fine and imprisonment.[8] Similar prohibitions apply to messages sent by wireless telegraphy (which includes broadcasting) with an additional prohibition on messages or communications subversive of public order.[9] In chapter 28 it is argued that interception of telecommunication by the Minister for Justice is a legitimate restraint on freedom of expression, provided that appropriate safeguards are maintained.

A central feature in the regulation of broadcasting in this State has been the restriction, based on one premise or another, on freedom of expression. In chapter 16, censorship of the broadcasting media in Ireland was considered. There is also the licensing regime which delimits the modes of telecommunication which are available. The State may also control absolutely all the modes of telecommunication in a national emergency.[10] Then there is also direct programme-content regulation by the State and the Independent Radio and Television Commission. Programme-content regulation includes section 31 of the *Broadcasting Authority Act, 1960*, already considered,[11] the duties of fairness and impartiality[12] and the prohibition on editorialising.[13]

FREEDOM OF EXPRESSION: THE WIDER CONTEXT

The antithesis to the State's content regulation of telecommunication including broadcasting is that the State should not attempt in any circumstance to regulate verbal utterances. This concept is best expressed by those who believe in what Voltaire is supposed to have said, that although they may not agree with what is being said they must "defend to the death" the right to say it.

The concept that freedom of expression enhances the social good by promoting the discovery of truth was espoused by John Milton in *Areopagitica* in 1644. Arguing against the licensing of printing he wrote:

> And though all the winds of doctrine were let loose to play upon the earth, so Truth be in the field, we do injuriously by licensing and prohibiting to misdoubt her strength. Let her and Falsehood grapple; who ever knew Truth put to the worse, in a free and open encounter?[14]

Milton's contribution to the "jurisprudence" of freedom of expression was his statement that unrestricted debate would lead to the discovery of truth. The notion that truth would always prevail in any encounter with falsehood is, however, simplistic. John Stuart Mill, philosopher and economist, writing 200 years after Milton, correctly stated in *On Liberty* that

> the dictum that truth always triumphs over persecution is one of those pleasant falsehoods which men repeat after one another till they pass into common-place, but which all experience refutes. . . . It is a piece of idle sentimentality that truth has any inherent power denied to error of prevailing against the dungeon and the stake.

Mill contended, however, that government could not "prescribe opinions" or "determine what doctrines or what arguments people should hear". He argued that not even if the government and the populace were at one on an issue should coercion regarding freedom of expression be allowed:

> [T]he peculiar evil in silencing the expression of an opinion is that it is robbing the human race; posterity as well as the existing generation; those who dissent from the opinion, still more those

who hold it. If the opinion is right, they are deprived of the opportunity of exchanging error for truth, if wrong, they lose what is almost as great a benefit, the clearer perception and livelier impression of truth, produced by its collision with error.[15]

A criticism of Mill's thesis is that he overvalued intellectual discussion and the necessity for persons to be able to debate public affairs energetically.

The most powerful judicial expression of the argument that free speech promotes the discovery of truth was the dissent of Justice Oliver Wendell Holmes in *Abrams v United States* (1919):

> But when men have realised that time has upset many fighting faiths, they may come to believe even more than they believe the very foundations of their own conduct that the ultimate good desired is better reached by free trade in ideas — that the best test of truth is the power of the thought to get itself accepted in the competition of the market, and that truth is the only ground upon which their wishes safely can be carried out. That at any rate is the theory of our Constitution.[16]

The First Amendment of the United States Constitution provides that Congress "shall make no law . . . abridging the freedom of speech, or of the press". The *Abrams* dissent of Justice Holmes stands as the foundation of one of the cardinal tenets of contemporary jurisprudence in relation to freedom of expression as articulated by the United States Supreme Court. There is validity in Justice Holmes's marketplace analogy that restrictions on the supply of ideas inhibit the discovery of truth and may damage democracy itself.

The truth-discovery rationale of freedom of expression as enunciated by Holmes has been subject to criticism. Dean Lee Bollinger of the University of Michigan Law School in his perceptive analysis of US First Amendment jurisprudence, *The Tolerant Society*, noted that Holmes's faith in the outcome of the market was perhaps "a secular analogue to the comforting illusion of prior centuries that the King spoke with divine authority".[17] John Wigmore, a law professor and dean at Northwestern University Law School, may be taken as typical of scholars who criticise the truth-discovery rationale. Writing shortly after the *Abrams* (1919) decision, Wigmore argued that the value of free speech was overemphasised by many:

the rationale enunciated by Holmes was without proper proportion.[18] Wigmore argued that oversensitivity to the dangers of free
speech meant that the right was "being invoked more and more in
misuse", for and on behalf of "impatient and fanatical minorities —
fanatically committed to some revolutionary belief, and impatient of
the usual process of rationally converting the majority".[19] Other
legal scholars have argued that objective "truth" does not exist[20] and
that the way "free" discussion operates in practice contravenes the
open market of ideas which the truth-discovery rationale assumes.[21]

Undoubtedly as a philosophical concept, Justice Holmes's
doctrine contained certain weaknesses. In essence, Holmes was
emphasising the theory that the idea which ultimately survives in
the struggle of ideas represents the truth. How long would
"ultimately" take? In Nazi Germany, many ideas ultimately
prevailed for a period but could hardly be stated to represent
objective truth. Further, Justice Holmes's theory implicitly accepts
not that what survives is the truth, but that what is true will survive.

Holmes's analogy with the economic concept of the marketplace
is attractive but has its limitations. Is there such a phenomenon as
perfect competition in any sphere of activity? There is inequality
among the communicators in the marketplace of ideas. Such
inequality could result in the ideas of the rich, the powerful and the
articulate becoming paramount thus distorting the ability of "truth"
to prevail in the marketplace. The truth-discovery rationale of
freedom of expression is not absolute. Justice Holmes argued that
the actual scope of the guarantee afforded by the US First
Amendment depended on the precise context in which the speech
occurred. In words now immortalised, Justice Holmes himself
delineated boundaries on the guarantee of free speech:

> [T]he most stringent protection of free speech would not protect
> a man falsely shouting fire in a theatre and causing a panic. It
> does not even protect any man from an injunction against
> uttering words that have all the effect of force.[22]

The analogy of the fire in the theatre may be inapt as it constitutes
a statement of a falsehood, but Justice Holmes's thesis was that there
must be some limits to free speech. The governing principle for
Justice Holmes was

> whether the words used are used in such circumstances and are
> of such a nature as to create a clear and present danger that they

will bring about the substantive evils that Congress has a right to prevent.[23]

For Holmes, it was "a question of proximity and degree".[24] The great champion of free speech, John Stuart Mill, also conceded in *On Liberty* (1859) that his theory would permit punishing the statement that corn dealers are starvers of the poor "when delivered orally to an excited mob assembled before the house of a corn dealer". Inflammatory speech may cause a government to consider that public order considerations outweigh concerns for the intellectual development of man.

A further function of freedom of expression is based on citizen participation in a democracy; persons cannot intelligently make independent judgments in a self-governing society unless they are permitted to hear all possible views in relation to the issue in question.[25] It may be argued that if a society has chosen to be self-governing, then the government cannot label certain information or expression of opinion within that self-governing community as too dangerous or wrong for that society to hear. Such a form of censorship makes a mockery of the notion of self-government.[26] US Justice Brandeis in *Whitney v California* (1927) expressed what may be described as a representative judicial view of this free-speech theory:

> Those who won our independence believed that the final end of the State was to make men free to develop their faculties; and that in its government the deliberative forces should prevail over the arbitrary. . . . They believed that freedom to think as you will and to speak as you think are means indispensable to the discovery and spread of political truth; . . . that the greatest menace to freedom is an inert people; that public discussion is a political duty; and that this should be a fundamental principle of American government.[27]

Public discussion is a vital element in a democracy.

In the context of broadcast discussion of public issues, the United States Supreme Court reiterated in 1984 in *Federal Communications Commission v League of Women Voters*[28] (a case that dealt with issues of permissible broadcast regulation) that freedom of "expression on public issues 'has always rested on the highest rung of the hierarchy of First Amendment values (the constitutional guarantee of freedom of speech and of the press)'".[29] In the context of the Irish

Government's prior restraint as expressed in section 31 of the *Broadcasting Authority Act, 1960*,[30] the following passage from the opinion of the US Supreme Court in *League of Women Voters* is noteworthy:

> The freedom of speech and of the press guaranteed by the Constitution embraces at least the liberty to discuss publicly and truthfully all matters of public concern without previous restraint or fear of subsequent punishment. . . . Freedom of discussion, if it would fulfil its historical function in this nation, must embrace all issues about which information is needed or appropriate to enable members of society to cope with the exigencies of their period.[31]

There is merit in the argument that political speech or at least discussion on public issues should receive some sort of preferred status in the constitutional protection of freedom of expression. The rationale of Justice Brennan for the United States Supreme Court in *New York Times v Sullivan* (1964)[32] (although that case related to a civil libel action brought by a public official) could be applied to the regulation of broadcast and printed expression in Ireland:

> [W]e consider this case against the background of a profound national commitment to the principle that debate on public issues should be uninhibited, robust and wide open, and that it may well include vehement, caustic and sometimes unpleasantly sharp attacks on government and public officials. . . .[33]

A further function of free expression may be stated as the enhancement of the development of personality and self-respect, thus enabling a person to relate effectively to others. Steven Shriffrin has correctly stated that "the private daily communications of millions of individuals profoundly affect public opinion".[34] Freedom of expression also provides a vital outlet for emotion which can act as a safety valve. Those who articulate this view in the context of the justification for freedom of expression believe that peaceful persuasion and change may be achieved and pent-up violence avoided. Dr. Conor Cruise O'Brien, as Minister for Posts and Telegraphs, on the second stage of the *Broadcasting Authority (Amendment) Bill, 1975* postulated that thesis in the following way *before* arguing for a limitation on free expression in broadcasting:

> [The] State should . . . leave purely verbal utterances strictly alone. Language, it is urged, can be a safety valve for feelings which might otherwise find more dangerous expression; debate, using even the most heated forms of argument, has a cleansing power; even the most detestable ideas — the advocacy of genocide for example — should be allowed the widest possible public expression, and then be met by reasoned argument.[35]

LIMITATION ON FREE EXPRESSION: THE IRISH POSITION

Dr. Conor Cruise O'Brien, as Minister for Posts and Telegraphs, argued for a limitation on free expression in the context of broadcasting in 1975 when he considered that the weakness of the doctrine that freedom of expression "is an absolute whose untrammelled exercise will necessarily be beneficial to society and that the State has no right to interfere with it" was that it assumed that discourse consisted of rational argument alone.[36] Conscious of the fact that "language can be used to inflict pain and arouse cruelty, to instil fear into one group and arouse hatred in another", the Minister argued that restrictions must be applied to freedom of expression. The Minister justified greater State regulation over broadcasting than over the press because

> the electro-magnetic spectrum, unlike newsprint and ink, is public property and cannot readily be bought and sold in separate consignments and that therefore broadcasting has to be controlled in some degree at least by the State on behalf of the community, basically through an inherent monopoly in the allocation of frequencies, combined with responsibility to the people in the matter of how these frequencies were used.[37]

Dr. Cruise O'Brien argued that as the State was allocating the use of a public asset, the Government had a responsibility to ensure that broadcasting was not used to endanger either the security of the State which licensed broadcasting or the lives of the citizens who pay the licence fees. Dr. Cruise O'Brien was also influenced by the fact that broadcasting had, of all the media, by far the greatest capacity to generate emotion.[38] This is an example of the pervasiveness rationale which will be considered in chapter 29.

In Ireland, the constitutional basis for any regulation of freedom of expression and free speech pursuant to Article 40.6.1.i of the Constitution must be, in the words of O'Higgins CJ in *State (Lynch) v Cooney*, "the overriding considerations of public order and public morality".[39] The specific words of the second paragraph of Article 40.6.1.i of the Constitution, which provide that the education of public opinion being a matter of such grave import to the common good, the State must endeavour to ensure that the organs of public opinion, such as the radio, the press, the cinema, while preserving their rightful liberty of expression, including criticism of Government policy, are not to be used to undermine public order or morality or the authority of the State, sanction a form of prior restraint.

The principal architect of the 1937 Constitution, Eamon de Valera, considered that a form of prior restraint in the context of public order, morality or the authority of the State was necessary for the common good. The perceived necessity for a form of prior restraint may be gleaned from the following exchange during the Dáil debate on the draft Constitution in 1937:

> *Mr. de Valera*: I say that the right of citizens to express freely their convictions and opinions cannot, in fact, be permitted in any State. . . . If we believe in order, are we going to permit the free expression of such opinion as that it is inconsistent with man's nature that he should be governed at all? Are we going to have anarchical principles, for example, generally propagated here? I say no.
> *Dr. Rowlette*: (Deputy for Dublin University) Why not?
> *Mr. de Valera*: I say no.
> *Dr. Rowlette*: Because you disagree with them?
> *Mr. de Valera*: It is clearly a matter of the whole question of government and order.
> *Dr. Rowlette*: Not at all.
> *Mr. de Valera*: I say it is. I say you should not give to the propagation of what is wrong and unnatural the same liberty as would be accorded to the propagation of what is right.[40]

De Valera's thesis on prior restraint can be rebutted. John Stuart Mill in *On Liberty* (1859) wrote (with some overstatement) that "all silencing of discussion [was] an assumption of infallibility". Walter Bagehot put the issue in similar terms. He argued that persons with strong opinions can hardly understand why they cannot make use of the State to crush the errors they hate and replace them with the tenets they approve.[41] There is merit in the Irish test enunciated in *Attorney General v X* that the harm involved must be "real and substantial".[42] There is also merit in the "clear and present danger" test adopted by Justice Holmes;[43] accordingly, in deciding whether or not to exercise prior restraint, it must be considered whether, in the particular circumstances, the expression in question is likely to be of such a nature so as to create a clear and present danger of offending against public order or public morality. One could argue that the case of *State (Lynch) v Cooney*[44] afforded the Supreme Court an opportunity of adopting the above tests that would have been more fitting perhaps than the approach adopted by the Court.

In relation to the sensitive issue of freedom of expression (Article 40.6.1.i of the Constitution), *State (Lynch) v Cooney*[45] demonstrated that judges are reluctant to disturb the existing restrictions on broadcast media: the balance of convenience rests with maintaining the status quo. In appropriate cases, judges have a natural tendency to defer to the views of the legislature and the executive. Further, Irish judges appear to have no special interest in enlarging the existing modes of telecommunication based on the guarantee of freedom of expression. An *ad hoc* balancing approach is used in the interpretation of Article 40.6.1.i of the Constitution (freedom of expression). Perhaps the balancing-of-interests approach is the least dogmatic and the approach most likely to be adopted by a collegiate court which consists of persons of diverse backgrounds and interests. However, the *ad hoc* balancing approach has the effect in practice of only making small adjustments to the existing corpus of law.

The Supreme Court in *State (Lynch) v Cooney*[46] avoided any philosophical debate on an approach to the issue of freedom of expression. The Court avoided any serious debate on prior restraint of expression. Prior restraint of expression has been condemned in general because it is broader in its effect and more easily and effectively enforced than subsequent punishment. Everything that is publicly uttered or published is open to scrutiny. Banned expression is never allowed to come alive and be tested against other opinions.

The Irish Government is practising a form of selective exposure to "Sinn Féin" speech. *An Phoblacht/Republican News*, the newspaper of Sinn Féin, is permitted but "Sinn Féin" speech on radio and television is not permitted. *An Phoblacht/Republican News* regularly carries interviews and information about legal and illegal activities. The question may be asked why is the Government practising a form of selective censorship? There is a sense of frustration in Government and among the general public about the inability to rid the country of persons of violence. It is submitted that the Government want to be seen to be doing something on the issue and the section 31 form of regulation allows the Government to push an awkward issue from the radio and television media.

In the context of any concern over Sinn Féin speech and other speech prohibited by the section 31 order,[47] it must not be forgotten that there is already a heavy duty imposed on broadcasters to ensure that no matter may be broadcast which may reasonably be regarded as "likely to promote, or incite to crime, or as tending to undermine the authority of the State".[48] There is also the specific prohibition in the *Wireless Telegraphy Act, 1926* (which, inter alia, applies to broadcasting communication) on sending any message or communication subversive of public order.[49] The penalties range up to IR£20,000 and include imprisonment.[50] The section 31 orders — the blanket prohibition on, for example, Sinn Féin speech — far exceeds any prohibition to the effect that nothing is to be broadcast which is likely to promote or incite to crime or as tending to undermine the authority of the State. There is merit in establishing a new specific criminal offence (in addition to the common law) prohibiting any person from expressing in any broadcasting medium anything which may be likely to promote or incite to crime, or to undermine the authority of the State.

The decision of the European Commission of Human Rights in *Purcell v Ireland* (1991)[51] was considered in chapter 16. In the context of freedom of expression and the rights enshrined in Article 10 of the European Convention on Human Rights and the case law of the European Court of Human Rights, it is difficult to justify the decision of the Commission in *Purcell*. Shortly after the *Purcell* decision, the European Court of Human Rights delivered its judgment in the cases of *The Observer and The Guardian v United Kingdom* and *The Sunday Times v United Kingdom (No 2)* (1992).[52] The Court reiterated certain major principles on the restrictions that may be applied to freedom of expression in the context of what is necessary in a democratic society.

Firstly, the Court noted that freedom of expression constituted one of the essential foundations of a democratic society and was as applicable to ideas which offended, shocked or disturbed as to those which were inoffensive. The exceptions to the freedom had to be narrowly interpreted and the necessity for any restrictions had to be established convincingly.

Secondly, those principles that governed freedom of expression were of particular importance as far as the press was concerned. While the press must not overstep the bounds set, inter alia, in the interests of national security or for maintaining the authority of the judiciary, it was nevertheless incumbent on the press to impart information and ideas on matters of public interest. Not only did the press have the task of imparting such information and ideas; the public also had a right to receive them. Were it otherwise the press would be unable to play its vital role of public watchdog.

Thirdly, the adjective "necessary" in paragraph 2 of Article 10 implied the existence of a "pressing social need". The contracting states had a certain margin of appreciation in assessing whether such a need existed but the Court was empowered to give the final ruling on whether a restriction was reconcilable with freedom of expression as protected by Article 10.

Fourthly, the Court's task was to look at the interference complained of in the light of the case as a whole and determine whether it was "proportionate to the legitimate aim pursued" and whether the reasons adduced by the national authorities to justify it were "relevant and sufficient". Article 10 did not in terms prohibit the imposition of prior restraints on publication as such. However, the dangers inherent in prior restraints were such that they called for the most careful scrutiny on the part of the Court. This was especially so as far as the press was concerned for news was a perishable commodity and to delay its publication even for a short period might well deprive it of all its value and interest.

Substitute the word "media" for "press" in the above analysis and it is submitted that the section 31 order (as currently phrased)[53] would offend against those criteria and should be held to be in contravention of the Convention.

Public order is a paramount value in society. This is recognised specifically by the constitutional obligation on the State, pursuant to Article 40.6.1.i of the Constitution, to ensure that the organs of public opinion must not be used to undermine public order or morality or the authority of the State. Once public order has been breached, chain reactions may follow. The Supreme Court in *State (Lynch) v Cooney*[54] was confronted with the difficult issue of policy — when may speakers be silenced who are associated with an organisation that supports violence as a means of achieving political action?

The ultimate evil that is sought to be prohibited in the banning of certain broadcast speech in the section 31 order is, in effect, subversive advocacy. This issue has troubled Irish authorities since the foundation of the State; Irish authorities have consistently adopted a conservative and cautious approach to this issue. This issue has already been considered in chapter 16. However, it is appropriate in this context to refer again to the jurisprudence in the United States with their written constitutional guarantees of free expression — albeit without the qualifications that limit the free expression guarantees in Article 40.6.1.i of the Constitution of Ireland. In *Brandenburg v Ohio* (1969),[55] the US Supreme Court revisited the issue of subversive advocacy. In *Brandenburg*, a Ku Klux Klan leader had been convicted for violating the Ohio *Criminal Syndicalism Statute of 1919*. This law prohibited "advocating . . . the duty, necessity or propriety of crime, sabotage, violence or unlawful methods of terrorism as a means of accomplishing industrial or political reform". The US Supreme Court reasoned that the Court's own jurisprudence[56] had fashioned the principle that the constitutional guarantee of free speech and free press did not permit a State to forbid or proscribe advocacy of the use of force or of law violation except where such advocacy was directed to inciting or producing imminent lawless action and was likely to incite or produce such action. This test bears a strong similarity to the "clear and present danger" test as a pre-condition for censorship laid down by a unanimous US Supreme Court in *Schenck* (1919).[57] Quoting from *Noto v United States* (1961), the US Supreme Court noted that "the mere abstract teaching . . . of the moral propriety or even moral necessity for a resort to force and violence, [was] not the same as preparing a group for violent action and steeling it to such action".[58] The Court reasoned that a statute that failed to draw the above distinction intruded impermissibly upon the freedoms guaranteed by the First and Fourteenth Amendments. The constitutional defect was that such a statute swept within its condemnation speech which the US Constitution had immunised from government control.[59] Finding the Ohio statute unconstitutional and within the condemnation of the First and Fourteenth Amendments, the Court concluded that it was confronted with a statute which, by its own words and as applied, purported to punish mere advocacy. Mere advocacy has been banned in the section 31 order.

Though most abhor any form of violence, it can be argued that the current section 31 order[60] is in excess of what is required by the public-order requirements in Article 40.6.1.i of the Constitution of Ireland. Interviews or reports of interviews with spokesmen of named organisations including Sinn Féin are banned simpliciter. The banning of interviews or reports of interviews with spokesmen inciting to crime is justified. One recalls the passion of Justice Holmes, then seventy-nine years of age, who as a justice of the US Supreme Court, in *Abrams* (1919)[61] reasoned that we should be eternally vigilant against attempts to check "the expression of opinions that we loathe and believe to be fraught with death, unless they so imminently threaten immediate interference with the lawful and pressing purposes of the law that an immediate check is required to save the country".[62]

The current section 31 order[63] is overly broad. The order prohibits, for example, the broadcasting speech of a Sinn Féin spokesman on the merits of prayer as a basis for spiritual renewal. The order prohibits all the broadcasting speech of spokesmen of named organisations. There is thus a considerable waste of communication and expression freedoms. In the United States, the practical effect of the overbreadth doctrine in constitutional law is that it enables the Court to invalidate a law on its face and to do so in the earliest possible case — without waiting for an unconditional application. For example, in *Gooding v Wilson* (1972)[64] the US Supreme Court, in a five to two decision, invalidated a Georgia statute on its face on the basis that it was capable of being applied to protected as well as unprotected speech.

The State should point with exactness to the speech that violates the law. Judge Learned Hand of the US District Court in one of the early free-speech cases in the American tradition, *Masses Publishing Co v Patten* (1917),[65] described succinctly the philosophy of exactitude:

> The tradition of English-speaking freedom has depended in no small part upon the merely procedural requirement that the State point with exactness to just that conduct which violates the law. It is difficult and almost impossible to meet the charge that one's general ethos is treasonable.[66]

The *dicta* of Judge Hand leads to the next issue, the focus on the character of speakers under the section 31 order. Is it sufficient to justify the prohibition of broadcasting speech on the basis that the ethos of some members of the banned group may possibly be treasonable? If the law allowed the character of speakers to be taken into consideration, then the section 31 order could be justified on some basis of association. The Constitution does not permit the State to ban speech merely on the basis of the character of the speaker. What is prohibited under the section 31 order is the act of communication rather than the content of the communication. Concern ought to shift from the character of the speaker to the content of his or her speech. This is important particularly where the view would prevail that the speaker belongs to a legitimate political party, for example, Sinn Féin.

The section 31 order could be amended to accommodate the concerns expressed in this chapter. The speaker could be prohibited from expressing explicit words promoting or inciting to crime or undermining the authority of the State.[67] The prohibition would relate to action words which urged direct concrete action. The statutory power to issue the section 31 order should remain.[68]

The Irish Times argued in a leader column commenting on the decision of the High Court in *O'Toole v RTE* (1992) that access to the airwaves should be allowed "for all but the overt supporters of violence" and that provision should be made "for exemplary sanctions against those who would use [the airwaves] to seek support for it or for their sponsors".[69]

The time has come to test the maturity of Irish broadcasters by not renewing the section 31 order for a trial period of years. In the alternative, the section 31 order should be amended prohibiting speakers from expressing explicit action words, promoting or inciting certain crime.

FREEDOM OF EXPRESSION AND THE SCARCITY
RATIONALE

A primary justification for State control in Ireland over freedom of expression in the context of broadcasting is that the frequency spectrum is a finite natural resource which is State-owned and must be regulated for the common good. This scarcity rationale in relation to broadcasting has not been tested in the Irish Courts but has been upheld consistently by the United States Supreme Court albeit with less vigour with the passage of time. In *National Broadcasting Co v United States* (1943) the Supreme Court in a majority opinion adopted the scarcity rationale as a justification for regulation: "Unlike other modes of expression, radio inherently is not available to all. That is its unique characteristic and that is why, unlike other modes of expression, it is subject to governmental regulation."[70] The dissenting opinion concurred with the majority on this issue. In *Red Lion Broadcasting Co v FCC* (1969)[71] where, *inter alia*, the plaintiffs had argued that technological advances had produced a far more efficient and productive utilisation of the radio spectrum than had been possible when the US *Communications Act, 1934* was passed,[72] a unanimous Supreme Court defended the scarcity rationale and stated that demand for the radio spectrum had grown to the point where not all demand would be satisfied if the radio spectrum were free. Yet again in 1984 in *FCC v League of Women Voters of California*[73] the US Supreme Court upheld the scarcity rationale but with less conviction than it had done so in the past:

> The prevailing rationale for broadcast regulation based on spectrum scarcity has come under increasing criticism in recent years. Critics including the incumbent Chairman of the Federal Communications Commission charge that with the advent of cable and satellite television technology, communities now have access to such a wide variety of stations that the scarcity doctrine is obsolete. (See, eg. Fowler and Brennan, "A Marketplace Approach to Broadcast Regulation", 60 Tex L Rev 207, 221-226, (1982)). We are not prepared however, to reconsider our long-standing approach without some signal from Congress or the Federal Communications Commission that technological developments have advanced so far that some revision of the system of broadcast regulation may be required.[74]

The absoluteness of the scarcity justification is being eroded with the passage of time: advances in technology can enable higher frequencies to be exploited and can also enable more intensive use to be made of a given band of frequencies. The Minister for Communications stated in the course of the Dáil Debates on the *Radio and Television Act, 1988* that radio frequency planning carried out by his Department, particularly in VHF, had ensured that frequencies for broadcasting were no longer as scarce as they had been.[75]

In the context of scarcity, a distinction must be made here between over-the-air broadcasting and cable telecommunication services. Cable television involves signals being sent along "wide-band" cables directly to individual receivers and permits the simultaneous transmission of a large number of television programmes. Fewer scarce resources are utilised in this process because the radio waves are transmitted by cable instead of through the air.

In relation to the issue of scarcity, the question of the con-stitutionality of a local cable television monopoly in the context of the First Amendment of the US Constitution (freedom of speech and the press) has been considered in the United States. In *City of Los Angeles v Preferred Communications Inc* (1986),[76] a cable company alleged that the city of Los Angeles violated its First Amendment and other rights in refusing to grant it a cable franchise to serve a part of the city. Preferred Communications Inc had sought to bypass the city's franchising regulations by asking relevant utility companies to provide space on their poles for the purpose of establishing a cable system. The utility companies refused because Preferred had not been awarded a cable franchise by the city of Los Angeles. The city justified its refusal on the grounds that the cable company had not participated in the cable franchise auction held to award the franchise. The cable company based its complaint on the allegation that since sufficient excess physical capacity and economic demand existed in the franchise area, the city's auction system discriminated unconstitutionally against First Amendment speakers. The Supreme Court acknowledged that cable television "plainly implicate[d] First Amendment interests" which would ordinarily require a balancing of those interests against "competing societal interests". However, the Supreme Court declined to engage "in the balancing process" without a further development of the disputed issues in the case. The court called for a greater inquiry into the factual basis of the city's policy, including an investigation of such indicia as traffic congestion, disruption and aesthetic blight caused by a second cable operator and economic demand for competing cable systems.[77]

One US Federal Court of Appeals in 1982 in *Omega Satellite Products v City of Indianapolis* (1982)[78] had denied a claim based on First Amendment and Sherman Act (Antitrust) grounds to invalidate a city's grant of an exclusive cable franchise. Judge Richard Posner in his opinion wrote of the possibility of a competitive "free-for-all", wasteful duplication of facilities, higher prices and higher costs.[79] In his *Economic Analysis of Law*,[80] Judge Posner considered extra-judically a city acting as agent for its residents, soliciting bids for cable services, setting as the city's goal the best possible contract for its subscribers, and granting an exclusive franchise to the entity that had submitted the best proposal. The result would be a monopoly-provided service but one which would eliminate wasteful duplication and higher costs.[81]

Accordingly, at the time of writing, there is a mixed pattern of jurisprudence in the United States on whether the US First Amendment (freedom of speech and of the press) requires a city to grant more than one cable franchise — assuming adequate space on telephone poles and ducts. In Ireland, it is submitted that the courts in general would initially favour the views of Judge Richard Posner and accept a monopoly-provided cable service in a local area thus (probably) eliminating wasteful duplication and higher costs.

The last seminal work of Ithiel de Sola Pool was aptly titled *Technologies of Freedom*.[82] Professor Pool examined the new modes of communications and concluded they would not necessarily centralise control of the providers of information. On the contrary, Professor Pool argued that the new technologies would be engines of freedom. He urged that the new technologies be regarded as "the press", and not common carriers subject to regulatory action by the government. Dr. Pool argued:

> Networked computers will be the printing presses of the twenty-first century. If they are not free of public control, the continued application of constitutional immunities to [the] non-electronic [press] . . . may become no more than a quaint archaism, a sort of Hyde Park Corner where a few eccentrics can gather while the major policy debates take place elsewhere.[83]

Arthur C. Clarke, an acknowledged telecommunication sage, made the optimistic point in 1983[84] that he saw journalists and transmitters becoming totally independent of national communications carrier systems in ten years. "The implications of this are profound," said Clarke,

> and not only to media news gatherers who will no longer be at the mercy of censors or inefficient (sometimes non-existent) postal and telegraph services. It means the end of closed societies and ultimately . . . the unification of the world.

Clarke said the old debate about free flow of information "will soon be settled — by engineers, not politicians".

Coase noted in 1959 that the scarcity rationale was not convincing on economic grounds.[85] Virtually all resources are limited and scarce; the price mechanism, in effect, determines in general who uses scarce resources. Coase argued that the problem was that "no property rights were created in these scarce frequencies".

The advent of cable, satellite and other technologies has ensured that broadcasting is no longer as "scarce" a resource as it had been. However, regulators must make a choice between two or more potential broadcasters who wish to use the same broadcast frequency. Two or more newspapers can physically operate in the same area at the same time; market forces will determine their survival. But two broadcasters cannot operate on the same frequency at the same time. If they did so, neither would be heard. Thus, there is what may be described as an allocational scarcity. For as long as there are more persons seeking to broadcast than there are frequencies available, there will be a need for regulation of some description.

THE PROHIBITION ON EDITORIALISING IN BROADCASTING

All the broadcasting media in Ireland are prohibited from editorialising; neither the RTE Authority nor the private broad-casting contractors may express their own views in relation to the news broadcast by them, or in relation to the broadcast treatment of current affairs including matters that are either of public controversy or the subject of current public debate.[86]

In the context of the guarantee of freedom of expression enshrined in Article 40.6.1.i of the Constitution, it is appropriate to consider how the issue of broadcast editorialising was dealt with in the United States in the context of the United States Constitution's prohibition on Congress enacting legislation abridging the freedom of speech, or of the press.[87] In the United States, the principle of editorialising was carried over from the print media into the new broadcasting medium by the first radio licensees. In 1940, however, the Federal Communications Commission (FCC) in its *Mayflower* decision[88] prohibited the practice of broadcast editorialising stating that partisan communication was contrary to the public interest:

> A truly free radio cannot be used to advocate the causes of the licensee. . . . It cannot be devoted to the support of principles he happens to regard most favourably. In brief, the broadcaster cannot be an advocate.[89]

The constitutionality of this provision was not challenged but the FCC in effect reversed this decision in 1949. By then the nation had returned to relative stability after World War II and commercial television was becoming available. In an opinion dealing with broadcast editorialising and fairness in the presentation of controversial issues of public importance, the FCC found that "overt editorialising within reasonable limits and subject to the general requirements of fairness . . . [was] not contrary to the public interest".[90] The FCC decided that its objective of achieving fairness in the discussion of controversial issues would not be defeated by permitting commercial broadcast licensees to editorialise.[91]

The FCC, however, directed that editorials had to be "fair" and the programming in general had to be "balanced". The US *Public Broadcasting Act of 1967* which amended the US *Communications Act of 1934*, however, provided that "no non-commercial educational broadcasting station may engage in editorialising or may support or oppose any candidate for political office".[92] Some Congressmen (perhaps like some Dáil Deputies and Senators) were unwilling to trust a potentially critical medium: "There are some of us who have very strong feelings because we have been editorialised against."[93] The prohibition on editorialising by non-commercial educational broadcasting licensees was held in 1984 to violate the First Amendment.[94] Justice Brennan, delivering the opinion of the US Supreme Court, stated that were a similar ban on editorialising applied to newspapers and magazines the Court would not hesitate to strike it down as violative of the First Amendment. The Court, however, agreed with the Government that because broadcast regulation involved "unique considerations", the same approach that had been applied to other media had not been followed in cases relating to the regulation of broadcasting. This was so principally because of the fact that broadcasting frequencies were a scarce resource. However, the Court considered that broadcasters "are entitled under the First Amendment to exercise 'the widest journalistic freedom consistent with their public [duties]'".[95] Justice Brennan argued that the editorial had traditionally played an historic function by informing and arousing the public and by criticising and cajoling those who hold government office in order to help launch new solutions to the problems of the time. Justice Brennan continued:

> Preserving the free expression of editorial opinion, therefore, is part and parcel of "our profound national commitment . . . that debate on public issues should be uninhibited, robust and wide-open".[96]

The majority opinion, as articulated by Justice Brennan, emphasised that the disposition of that case rested upon a narrow proposition. The Court stressed that it had not held that Congress or the Federal Communications Commission were without the power to regulate the content, timing, or character of speech by non-commercial broadcasting stations. The Court emphasised that it only held that the specific interests sought to be advanced by the ban on editorialising were either not sufficiently substantial or were not served in a sufficiently limited manner to justify the substantial abridgement of important journalistic freedoms which the First Amendment jealously protected. Justice Rehnquist dissenting, with whom the Chief Justice and Justice White joined, argued that it was plainly rational for Congress to have determined that taxpayer monies should not be used to subsidise management's views or to pay for management's exercise of partisan politics. Further, he argued that Congress's prohibition was strictly neutral.

The issue of the prohibition on editorialising in the context of Article 40.6.1.i. of the Constitution (freedom of expression) came to the fore on the introduction of legislation providing for private commercial broadcasting services. When the *Sound Broadcasting Bill, 1987* was published, there was no prohibition on the expression of the sound broadcasting contractors' own views in relation to the reporting of news or in relation to the broadcast treatment of current affairs. The opposition parties strongly advocated that such a statutory duty should be imposed on the independent broadcasting companies. The views of the Minister for Communications were unequivocal: "On the question of the editorial view, it is not my intention, and it never was my intention, that the station would have the right to an editorial view."[97] The Minister explained that the editorial prohibition did not appear in the original Bill because of advice he had received from the Attorney General's Office that such a provision would be contrary to the freedom of expression provisions in Article 40.6.1.i of the Constitution. The legal advice contained the analogy that a prohibition on the expression of the broadcasting contractors' own views would be tantamount to preventing newspapers from carrying editorials.[98] However, the Minister shared the views of the Opposition on the matter and consulted further with the Attorney General's Office. The advice tendered to the Minister at that stage was that there was a risk that the provision would be declared unconstitutional but that such "a risk [was] very small indeed".[99] Accordingly, the Minister pursuant to section 9(1) of the *Radio and Television Act, 1988* prohibited each sound broadcasting contractor and, by virtue of section 18 of the 1988 Act, any television programme service contractor, from presenting their own views in relation to the news broadcast by them and in their treatment of current affairs including matters of public controversy and the subject of current debate.

The 1988 Irish legislation on broadcast editorialising in relation to the private commercial broadcasting services is more restrictive than the 1960 legislation governing RTE. The prohibition on the RTE Authority from expressing its own views in relation to current affairs does not apply to any broadcast in so far as the broadcast relates to any proposals concerning policy relating to broadcasting which is controversial in a public sense or the subject of current debate and which is being considered by the Government or the Minister for Communications.[100] No similar exemption applies to the broadcasting services licensed under the *Radio and Television Act, 1988*.

The absolute ban on editorialising on the private local broadcasting stations in Ireland[101] in relation to news and current affairs (including matters which are either of public controversy or the subject of current public debate) constitutes an unjustifiable prior restraint on expression and violates Article 40.6.1.i. of the Constitution (freedom of expression).[102] Similar arguments could be applied to the national taxpayer-funded broadcasting service, RTE, but (adopting the view of US Justice Rehnquist, now US Chief Justice)[103] it can be argued that it is quite proper for the Oireachtas to determine that taxpayer monies should not be used to subsidise management's views. Assuming that all broadcasters in Ireland would continue to be obliged to operate within the confines of the fairness and impartiality obligations (or some modification thereof), allowing the private local broadcasters to editorialise (albeit subject to some form of regulation) would only increase the diversity of expression in broadcasting which should be in the public interest and would be in keeping with those who believe in the paramountcy of the guarantees enshrined in Article 40.6.1.i of the Constitution on freedom of expression.

Rules on editorialising could, in general, provide that no undue prominence is given to the views of the persons providing the broadcasting service, could prohibit, for example, the expression of views of persons providing the services in relation to matters pertaining to industrial disputes, any improper exploitation of any susceptibilities of viewers and listeners and any abusive treatment of the religious views and beliefs of others.[104]

In the context of the sensitive issue of political editorialising by a broadcasting station, reference may be made to the sensible rules adopted by the FCC.[105] These rules provide that where a broadcast licensee in an editorial either endorses or opposes a legally qualified candidate, the licensee must transmit to the other candidates, within 24 hours, notification of the date and time of the editorial, a script or a tape and an offer of a reasonable opportunity for the candidate, or a spokesman to respond. Assuming that the fairness and impartiality criteria were to continue to apply in Ireland, the esssence of the FCC's rules ought to apply to broadcasters engaged in political editorialising.

RIGHT OF REPLY

In the context of the constitutional protection of freedom of expression (Article 40.6.1.i), the constitutional obligation on the State in its laws to protect as best it may from unjust attack and, in the case of injustice done, to vindicate the good name of the citizen (Article 40.3.2) and the statutory duties of fairness, objectivity and impartiality enshrined in broadcasting legislation,[106] should the ordinary citizen have a right of reply in the broadcasting media? The United States Supreme Court in *Miami Herald Co v Tornillo*[107] unanimously held that a right-of-reply law, requiring editors to print a reply by a political candidate who had been subjected to adverse comment in their paper, did violate the First Amendment (freedom of speech and the press): there had been an impermissible interference with the freedom of the press by the right-of-reply law. The compulsion-to-print-reply requirement might have led to the omission of other material which the editors wished to publish in the particular edition of the paper and might in the future have encouraged them to omit controversial matter.

A right of reply has, to a limited extent, become a feature of Irish broadcasting law pursuant to EC Council Directive 89/552/EEC in relation to television broadcasting activities.[108] Article 23 thereof provides that any legal person, regardless of nationality, whose legitimate interests, in particular reputation and good name, have been damaged by an assertion of incorrect facts in a television programme, must have a right of reply or an equivalent remedy. Provision must also be made whereby disputes as to the exercise of the right of reply or the equivalent remedies can be subject to judicial review.[109] Pursuant to section 8 of the *Broadcasting Act, 1990*, where the Broadcasting Complaints Commission finds in favour in whole or in part of a complainant in relation to the broadcasting of in-accurate facts or information in relation to a person which constituted an attack on that person's honour or reputation, the RTE

Authority must, unless the Commission considered it inappropriate, broadcast the Commission decision at a time and in a manner corresponding to that in which the offending broadcast took place.

O'Hanlon J stated in *O'Toole v RTE* (1992)[110] that no member of the public has an automatic right to be heard on radio or television and a general power has to be left in the hands of the Broadcasting Authority (subject to statutory constraints such as the obligations of fairness and impartiality)[111] to regulate programmes and determine their content. He also stated that those responsible for the day-to-day running of the broadcasting services must be allowed scope to carry out their functions in a professional manner and to the best of their ability.

The limited right-of-reply enshrined in section 8 of the *Broadcasting Act, 1990* should constitutue a sufficient safeguard to meet any constitutional requirements.

FREEDOM OF EXPRESSION AND THE BROADCASTING LEVIES

We have seen earlier[112] that a fee of IR£20,000 is payable to the Minister for Communications on the granting of a multi-point microwave distribution system (MMDS) licence,[113] a fee of 5 per cent of gross revenue (excluding installation charges and VAT) is payable as a renewal fee to MMDS licensees,[114] and a fee equivalent to 5 per cent of gross revenue (excluding installation charges and value added tax) must be paid by a cable television licensee.[115] The issue arises whether and in what circumstances such a fee could be open to a constitutional challenge on the basis of an unjustifiable levy on the constitutional guarantee of freedom of expression enshrined in Article 40.6.1.i of the Constitution.

The levies, to the extent to which they are unrelated to cable and MMDS purposes, may be vulnerable to constitutional challenge. In *Minneapolis Star and Tribune Co v Minnesota Commissioner of Revenue* (US) (1983)[116] the issue arose whether a state tax on ink and newsprint constituted a tax on First Amendment speakers (freedom of speech and of the press). The newpaper claimed the tax violated the freedom of the press and equal-protection guarantees of the First and Fourteenth Amendments of the US Constitution. The US Supreme Court held that a special tax on a First Amendment speaker will be found unconstitutional unless it is deemed necessary to achieve an overriding governmental interest of compelling importance. The raising of general revenue is not sufficient justification for such a special tax.

In *City of Los Angeles v Preferred Communications* (1986) the US Supreme Court stated that cable television "implicate[d] First Amendment interests".[117] The Supreme Court noted that through original programming or by exercising editorial discretion over what stations or programmes to include in its repertoire, cable television partakes of some of the aspects of speech and the communication of ideas as do the traditional enterprises of newspaper and book publishers, public speakers and pamphleteers.[118] The same could be stated of MMDS providers. Though cable and MMDS fees payable to the Minister for Communications are not invalid per se, the proper use of the licence fee would be to defray regulatory costs and for some telecommunication-related function. But if the fees are used for general revenue purposes, they may be open to constitutional challenge as an infringement of Article 40.6.1.i of the Constitution.

FREEDOM OF EXPRESSION AND THE MUST-CARRY OBLIGATIONS

We have seen in the earlier consideration of cable television and multi-point microwave distribution systems (MMDS) services[119] that "must-carry" provisions are an integral element in the regulation of cable and MMDS service.[120] The Minister for Communications designates certain television programme services that must be retransmitted. The issue arises whether these "must-carry" provisions are in accordance with the constitutional rights of both broadcasters and citizens and, in particular, whether these provisions offend against the constitutional guarantee of freedom of expression enshrined in Article 40.6.1.i of the Constitution.

The "must-carry" rules in the United States where cable television services were obliged to carry local television services (in addition to any other programming), have raised issues of constitutional importance in the context of the First Amendment. In *Quincy Cable TV Inc v FCC* (1985)[121] the Court of Appeals (District of Columbia Circuit) declared that the must-carry rules, as written, were unconstitutional under the First Amendment. The "must-carry" rules were held to have abridged cable operators' constitutional rights to "speak" and also to have conferred an unconstitutionally overbroad right of preferential carriage to every one of more than

1,200 local broadcasters, regardless of whether the survival of each station was essential to the statutory scheme of local broadcasting.[122]

The court in *Quincy* in its search for a regulatory formula in relation to cable rejected any application of the scarcity rationale noting that cable does not use the airwaves to deliver its programmes to its subscribers. The *Quincy* Court also rejected an economic scarcity argument based on the concept that cable was a natural monopoly. The court was sceptical of cable's status as a natural monopoly, suggesting that the pattern of one cable system to a specified area was primarily a result of municipal franchising policies. The court noted that economic scarcity had been rejected as a ground for infringing First Amendment rights in *Miami Herald Publishing Co v Tornillo* (1974).[123]

The court in *Quincy* referred to the so-called *O'Brien* test[124] which relates to an exacting level of scrutiny. The *O'Brien* test has a relevance to the saving clause in Article 40.6.1.i of the Irish Constitution (the proviso relating to "public order or morality or the authority of the State".) In the context of regulations governing constitutional rights, *O'Brien* established the following test:

> [A] government regulation is sufficiently justified if it is within the constitutional power of the government; if it furthers an important or substantial government interest; if the government interest is unrelated to the suppression of free expression; and if the incidental restriction on alleged First Amendment freedoms is no greater than is essential to the furtherance of that interest.[125]

The *Quincy* court considerd that the "must-carry" rules failed even a relaxed *O'Brien* test. The court held that the FCC had failed to prove that the "must-carry" rules served an important government interest. The FCC had asserted that the interest served by the rules was preserving free locally-oriented television, but this had not been proved to the court's satisfaction. Finally, the Court indicated that it had "not found it necessary to decide whether any version of the rules would contravene the First Amendment" leaving the door open for the FCC to draft new rules. The FCC declined to appeal the *Quincy* decision.[126]

It is permissible (and appropriate) in constitutional terms that the Minister for Communications should be empowered to determine that a designated number of broadcast channels be carried on cable and MMDS services. The Minister thus facilitates the achievement of a greater diversity of viewpoints. Cable and MMDS services have certain local monopoly characteristics. It would be inappropriate and outside the constitutional framework that the private power of a cable or MMDS operator should control exclusively the bulk of channels of electronic communications in a particular area. However, if the Minister for Communications endeavoured to determine everything that cable and MMDS viewers see and hear, this would be constitutionally overbroad and would, arguably, infringe Article 40.6.1.i of the Constitution.

FREEDOM OF EXPRESSION AND NEWS OBLIGATIONS

The statutory duty on private (non-RTE) sound broadcasters to provide a 20 per cent quota of news and current affairs programming is an onerous obligation.[127] However, it is noted that the Independent Radio and Television Commission may authorise a derogation from this requirement provided it is satisfied that there is a reasonable plurality of sources of news and current affairs programmes available to the public in question from other sound broadcasting services.[128] The Minister for Communications, Ray Burke, justified the news and current affairs obligation by stating that one of the important reasons for establishing additional broadcast services was to encourage "great plurality in sources of news, information and matters of current debate" which were "very desirable in a democracy".[129] This restriction is not in keeping with the avowed intentions of the Minister for Communications of adopting a "minimalist approach" to the private broadcasting services and of allowing persons "the freedom to be involved themselves and decide for themselves what they want to listen to".[130] Local radio stations in particular should not be obliged to mirror the public-service obligations of *national* radio or television. Listeners should determine the issue — not the legislature. It is always open to listeners to complain to the Independent Radio and Television Commission about a radio station's performance; any such complaints could influence the issue of a renewal of a licence.

It is difficult to justify the 20 per cent news and current affairs quota obligation on the local commercial broadcasting stations in the context of the State's guarantee for the right of citizens to express freely their convictions and opinions pursuant to Article 40.6.1.i of the Constitution. It is noteworthy that the US Federal Communications Commission, even in its pre-deregulatory period, never required that a station broadcast a specific minimum percentage of news or current affairs programmes.

FREEDOM OF EXPRESSION AND GOVERNMENT SPEECH

Section 31(2) of the *Broadcasting Authority Act, 1960* provides that the Minister for Communications may direct the RTE Authority in writing to allocate broadcasting time for any announcements by or on behalf of any Minister of the Government in connection with the functions of that Minister of the Government, and the Authority shall comply with that direction.

The Government's decision to invoke section 31(2) of the 1960 Act in June 1992 to enable the Taoiseach to make an RTE broadcast urging a "yes" vote on the Maastricht referendum was challenged unsuccessfully in *McCann v An Taoiseach* (1992).[131] The *McCann* case and the case of *McKenna v An Taoiseach* (1992)[132] which sought unsuccessfully an injunction, *inter alia*, restraining the Government from advocating an affirmative vote in the Maastricht Treaty referendum without setting out impartially the arguments of both sides, raised the issue of the role of government speech. Dr. Gerard Quinn, in a perceptive article on this general issue,[133] has argued that a healthy concern for the integrity of the marketplace of ideas and information and the proper role of "government speech" is long overdue. He argues that if any ethic ought to dominate this area it should be that all are equal and ought therefore to have an equal chance of presenting their case to the public. He concludes by stating that only when the marketplace has been purged of undue corporate influence and over-zealous "government speech" can a free market exist allowing the people to decide.

Should the Government use section 31(2) of the *Broadcasting Authority Act, 1960* to advocate a certain course in a referendum of the people without furnishing a right of reply to others on the same medium, then the issue would arise as to whether such use was in accordance with Article 40.6.1.i of the Constitution (freedom of expression).

27

The Right to Communicate

THE RIGHT TO COMMUNICATE UNDER IRISH LAW

In *Paperlink* (1984)[1] "the very general and basic human right to communicate" was considered to be one of the personal unspecified rights of the citizen protected by Article 40.3.1 of the Constitution. The right to communicate was also recognised in *Kearney v Minister for Justice* (1987) where Costello J examined the right in the context of interception of written communications to a convicted prisoner.[2] In *Attorney General for England and Wales v Brandon Book Publishers Ltd* (1987),[3] which concerned an application to restrain publication of a book by a former member of the British Secret Service, Carroll J said, *inter alia*, that what was at stake was "the very important constitutional right to publish *now* and not in a year or more when the case has worked its way through the courts" (emphasis in original).[4] Professor William Binchy and Raymond Byrne have noted that Carroll J in her judgment used the words "expression", "publish", and "communicate" to express the type of liberty protected by the Constitution.[5] No distinction was made between these terms. This contrasts with Costello J's approach in *Paperlink*[6] where he distinguished between Article 40.6.1.i. (the right to express freely convictions and opinions) and the right to communicate under Article 40.3.1. The right to communicate, according to Costello J, may involve the communication of information and not merely the expression of convictions and opinions.[7]

The right to communicate has not been defined in a legal context; arguably, it should never be defined in any absolute sense. Costello J in *Paperlink* noted that the right to communicate can take many forms.[8] There is substance in the argument advanced by Le Duc that "the right to communicate is not a single unified doctrine; rather it is a descriptive term for a number of individual and specific communication rights".[9] Nevertheless, the scope of any such right must be examined: Costello J's analysis in *Paperlink*[10] that a right to communicate must inhere in the citizen by virtue of his human personality illustrates the human and social dimensions of the right to communicate.[11] This foundation of the right to communicate has received widespread acceptance in fora that are discussing this emerging right. A formulation of the right to communicate by a working group of UNESCO experts has expressed the right in the following terms:

> Everyone has a right to communicate. Communication is a fundamental social process which enables individuals and communities to exchange information and opinions. It is a basic human need and the foundation of all social organisation. The right to communicate belongs to individuals and the communities which they compose.[12]

The right to communicate implies access, participation and the concept of two-way communication, but does not exclude a one-way process of communication. The parameters of the fledgling right to communicate were examined by Jean D'Arcy in 1977 and summed up in the following words:

> The right to hear and be heard, to inform and to be informed, together may be regarded as the essential components of a "right to communicate". . . . The realisation of a "right to communicate" is a desirable object for a democratic society so that each individual may know he is entitled to be informed and to be heard, regardless of where he may live or work in his own country.[13]

Others too have framed the constituents of a right to communicate with a different emphasis: Henry Hindley has listed "the right to speak, the right to be heard, the right to a reply, the right to make a reply and the right to listen" as the essential components of a "right to communicate".[14] The "right not to communicate" or "a right not to be informed" is an additional perspective for inclusion in a right to communicate. There is also the right to receive communications including information.[15] In fact, the right to receive communications and information makes the right to communicate meaningful. Justice Brennan of the US Supreme Court put the issue succinctly: "It would be a barren marketplace of ideas that had only sellers and no buyers."[16] In fact, the *Magill* series of cases[17] (in relation to listings of television programmes available to viewers in Ireland, and the effect of general competition law of the EC upon RTE) can be considered from the perspective of communications companies being forced to share information with others.

The concept of access and participation — the two-way interactive process — was emphasised in the Final Report of the *International Commission on the Study of Communication Problems* (the MacBride Commission) (1980). The concept was expressed in the following words:

> Communication, nowadays, is a matter of human rights. But it is increasingly interpreted as the right to communicate, going beyond the right to receive communication or to be given information. Communication is thus seen as a two-way process, in which the partners — individual and collective — carry on a democratic and balanced dialogue. The idea of dialogue, in contrast to monologue, is at the heart of much contemporary thinking, which is leading towards a process of developing a new area of social rights.
>
> The right to communicate is an extension of the continuing advance towards liberty and democracy. In every age, man has fought to be free from dominating powers — political, economic, social, religious — that tried to curtail communication. Only through fervent, unflagging efforts did peoples achieve freedom of speech, of the press, of information. Today, the struggle still goes on for extending human rights in order to make the world of communications more democratic than it is today. But the present stage of the struggle introduces new aspects of the basic concept of freedom. The demands for a two-way flow, for free exchange, for access and participation, make a qualitatively new addition to the freedom successively attained in the past.[18]

The right to communicate is specifically recognised in Article 10 of the European Convention on Human Rights. This issue has been considered in chapter 25 under the heading of "The Council of Europe and the European Convention on Human Rights". There is also Article 19 of the Universal Declaration of Human Rights, as qualified by Articles 19, 20 and 29, of the International Covenant on Civil and Political Rights.

The most comprehensive statement of the right to communicate which draws all the above strands together in one encapsulation is the Bratislava Declaration (1993) produced by a forum of non-governmental organisations (NGO) on human rights at the World

Conference on Human Rights (WCHR), (Vienna, June 1993).[19] That declaration considered that the declaration on the right to development, approved by the General Assembly of the United Nations in 1986, established that participation, including the free access to the process of communication, was the basis of the full enjoyment of all human rights. The Bratislava Declaration also observed that private corporations and governments everywhere could dominate world information flows and exert a homogenising influence over ideas and culture. The drafters[20] of the declaration were convinced that individuals and groups must have adequate resources for satisfying the human need to communicate in the practice of democracy; that those who wish to use channels and technologies of communication and information (including access to the frequency spectrum) should have fair and equitable access to them without discrimination; and that the most diverse segments of the population should have media channels sufficient to allow them to take part in public affairs. The declaration sought the affirmation and strengthening of the right to communicate in international legal instruments considering the right to communicate "as an inalienable right of individuals and peoples and as a fundamental instrument in the democratisation of society". The declaration recited the belief that the right to communicate goes beyond freedom of opinion, expression and the press and comprises, but is not limited to

> the right of individuals and groups to inform and to be informed, including the general right of access to government information and information held by and about public authorities; the right to speak and to be heard; the right to a reply and to make a reply; the right to see and to be seen; the right to assemble and to participate in public communication; the right of free access to any and all receivers of the communication process; the right to language; the right to knowledge; as well as the right to privacy, also to be selective and to be silent.

The declaration also recited its belief that the right to communicate includes also

> fair and equitable access to media distribution channels and to adequate resources for the satisfaction of the human need to communicate in the practice of democracy and in the exercise of any other human right and fundamental freedom.

In time the components of the above right to communicate will most likely be recognised by Irish law. A right to communicate is, as stated at the start of the chapter, a right recognised as a constitutional right in Ireland — but it has yet to be developed; a cohesive jurisprudence has yet to emerge. Should the Oireachtas fail to develop and safeguard the right to communicate, the High Court and the Supreme Court, under their "law-making" powers implicit in Article 40.3.1 of the Constitution (unenumerated rights),[21] will (in time) develop this right to its proper potential.

There is a heavy onus on the State to guarantee the exercise of the citizen's right to communicate; in essence, the State "guarantees in its laws to respect, and as far as practicable by its laws to defend and vindicate" the citizen's right to communicate under Article 40.3.1 of the Constitution.

Should the regulators of telecommunication services restrict a person's right to communicate, i.e. place restrictions which could not be justified on public-good criteria, (as considered in the next section of this chapter) then these restrictions would be open to legal challenge.

The right to communicate under Article 40.3.1. of the Constitution may yet be regarded as the apex and amalgam of other recognised freedoms and rights and may be regarded as wider in scope than Article 40.6.1.i whereby the State guarantees, subject to public order and morality, the right of the citizens to express freely their convictions and opinions.

CONSTRAINTS ON THE RIGHT TO COMMUNICATE

The freedom to exercise the right to communicate is not, of course, absolute, and may be subject to legitimate constraints.[22] The legal constraints on the right to communicate may be classified as coming within the public order, public morality and the authority of the State criteria that qualify the guarantee of freedom of expression in Article 40.6.1.i of the Constitution. Several of these constraints are considered in the last chapter, chapter 26, "Freedom of Expression" and in subsequent chapters, e.g., chapter 30, "The Statutory Duties of Objectivity and Impartiality in Broadcasting Services". Another constraint is the licensing regime in wireless telegraphy which is considered in chapter 15. These constraints qualify the right to communicate and the constitutional guarantee of freedom of expression.

There are also other competing constitutional rights. For example, the right to communicate may be diminished legitimately where the "speaker" intrudes in an intolerable manner upon any person's right to privacy. The US Supreme Court put the issue succinctly in *Rowan v Post Office Department* (1970) in the context of offensive mailings: "[T]he right of every person 'to be let alone' must be placed in the scales with the right of others to communicate. . . . A mailer's right to communicate must stop at the mailbox of an unreceptive addressee."[23]

Indecency and Obscenity

A significant constraint that qualifies both the right to communicate and the constitutional guarantee of freedom of expression relates to the area of indecency and obscenity.

The "public morality" qualification on free speech,[24] the constitutional obligation on the State to endeavour to ensure, inter alia, that the media must not be used to undermine public morality,[25] and the stipulation in Article 40.6.1.i of the Constitution that the publication or utterance of, inter alia, indecent matter is an offence, limit both the right to communicate and freedom of expression in relation to any facility for telecommunication.

No specific prohibition in relation to indecency or obscenity has been imposed on RTE because it was considered at its establishment that no purpose would be served in admonishing solemnly a responsible public authority in such a manner.[26] The authorities were not taking the constitutional prohibition on the utterance of indecent matter into account, but may have had in mind the prohibition on the sending by wireless telegraphy[27] of any message or communication of an indecent, obscene or offensive character[28] which would apply to radio and television in so far as the indecent or obscene matter constituted a message or communication. On conviction on indictment for sending such a message or communication, a person is liable to a fine of IR£20,000, or a term of imprisonment for 12 months, or both a fine and imprisonment.[29] However, the private broadcasting services in Ireland are specifically obliged to ensure, *inter alia*, that anything that might reasonably be regarded as offending against good taste or decency is not broadcast.[30]

In relation to the national telecommunication carrier service, Telecom Éireann is authorised by statute to prohibit the transmission of objectionable messages.[31] It is an offence to send, by means of the telecommunication systems operated by Telecom Éireann, any message or other matter which is grossly offensive or of an indecent, obscene or menacing character, whether addressed to an operator or any other person.[32] In such circumstances, Telecom Éireann is also authorised to suspend telecommunication services or refuse to provide such service to a subscriber.[33]

The expression "grossly offensive" in the formula used in Irish postal regulations prohibiting the posting of postal packets with words, marks or designs "of an indecent, obscene or grossly offensive character"[34] was considered in the Supreme Court in *Dillon* (1981).[35] Henchy J, delivering the principal judgment, applied the maxim *noscitur a sociis* (a word or expression is known from its companions), and considered that the expression "grossly offensive character" meant being obnoxious or abhorrent in a way that brought it close to the realm of indecency or obscenity.

Pollock CB stated in *R v Webb* (1848) that the word "indecently" had no definite legal meaning. He remembered that in the older Courts of Justice the judge retired to a corner for a necessary purpose, even in the presence of ladies, and concluded that that perhaps would in 1848 be considered "indecent".[36] In *R v Stanley* (1965)[37] the Court of Criminal Appeal (England and Wales) held that the words "indecent or obscene"[38] conveyed one idea, *viz.* that of offending against the recognised standards of propriety, "indecent" being at the lower end of the scale and "obscene" at the upper end of the scale.[39]

In Ireland, as stated above, Article 40.6.1.i of the Constitution declares specifically that the publication or utterance of, *inter alia*, indecent matter is an offence which shall be punishable in accordance with law. Although statute law does not replicate exactly the words specified in Article 40.6.1.i, a person could be charged with such an offence contrary to the Constitution. Accordingly, a person in Ireland has a right not to hear indecent speech on any facility for telecommunication.

The dictionary definition of "indecent" is very broad and includes such descriptions as unbecoming, in extremely bad taste, unseemly, offending against propriety or delicacy, immodest, suggesting or tending to obscenity.[40] "Obscene" is defined in the *Shorter Oxford English Dictionary* as offensive to modesty or decency, expressing or suggesting lewd thoughts, offensive to the senses or mind, disgusting and filthy.[41] The term "indecent" is broader than the term "obscene" and gives a prosecuting authority a greater latitude than would be the case if the constitutional prohibition related only to obscene matter. An indecent matter may not be obscene, but an obscene matter would also be indecent.

This consideration of indecent matter is particularly relevant in relation to certain modern commercial telephone services and computer bulletin boards. (A computer bulletin board is a system through which computer readable information is sent or retrieved by users through a telephone line). The restrictive position under Irish constitutional law can be contrasted with the liberal attitude adopted by the US Supreme Court. In *Sable Communications v FCC* (1989)[42] the US Supreme Court upheld a law[43] as constitutional insofar as it banned "obscene" commercial telephone messages, but declared that the part of the law that banned "indecent" commercial telephone messages was unconstitutionally broad. In effect, companies like Sable Communications were permitted to provide paying customers with sexually-oriented "indecent" messages — provided that those messages were not obscene — the criteria for obscenity being legally more difficult to reach than indecency. The US Supreme Court noted in *Sable* that the telephone medium required the listener to take affirmative steps to receive the indecent communication. In broadcasting, the indecent communication can intrude on the privacy of the home without prior knowledge. In *Sable*, the Court reiterated the dictum of *Butler*[44] that the "government may not reduce the adult population . . . to . . . only what is fit for children". The court was also influenced by the FCC rules involving the use of credit cards to obtain services, the use of special access codes and the scrambling of indecent messages as an acceptable means of restricting access of children to indecent messages while allowing proper access to adults:

> Because the statute's denial of adult access to telephone messages which are indecent but not obscene far exceeds that which is necessary to limit the access of minors to such messages, we hold that the ban does not survive constitutional scrutiny.[45]

There have been many successful criminal prosecutions in Ireland of persons who have sent messages over the telephone which were considered grossly offensive or of an indecent or obscene character.[46] However, all of these criminal prosecutions were based on the evidence of complainants who were recipients of such uninvited speech and who had requested that relevant telephone calls be intercepted and monitored by Telecom Éireann pursuant to section 98(2) of the *Postal and Telecommunications Services Act, 1983*.

28

Interception of Telecommunication

INTRODUCTION

The preamble to the English Ordinance of 1657 establishing a General Post Office noted that a General Post Office was

> the best means to discover and prevent many dangerous and wicked designs which have been and are being daily contrived against the peace and welfare of the Commonwealth. . . .

Government today still relies on the Post Office and its sister institution, the national telephone company, Telecom Éireann, to acquire intelligence about crime and matters pertaining to the security of the State.

The interception of telecommunication will be examined here under two headings: firstly, the interception of telecommunication messages by the Minister for Justice and, secondly, the interception of telecommunication by other parties. The expression "interception" in general relates to the obtaining of information about the contents of a communication sent by means of a telecommunication system without the consent of the parties involved. However, the term "intercept" is defined by statute in a narrow sense,[1] and this definition will be considered later in this chapter when discussing the statutory law on interception of telecommunication. The related process known as "metering", which involves the use of a device which registers the numbers dialled on a particular tele- communication instrument — generally a telephone — together with the time and duration of calls, but which does not record details of the contents of any telecommunication as such, will also be examined.

PARLIAMENTARY CONSIDERATION OF INTERCEPTION OF TELECOMMUNICATION BY THE MINISTER FOR JUSTICE

The Dáil was informed in 1972 that warrants for the interception of telephone calls had been issued by every Minister for Justice since the foundation of the State — with the knowledge and approval of every Government.[2] In fact, the purpose of what became the *Interception of Postal Packets and Telecommunications Messages (Regulation) Act, 1993* ("the *Interception Act, 1993*") was "to place on a statutory basis the conditions under which the *existing power* (emphasis added) of the Minister for Justice to issue warrants authorising the interception of . . . telecommunications messages [was] to be exercised. . . ."[3]

One of the earliest references in the Dáil to interception of telecommunication by the State was in 1927 when Professor Magennis, TD, raised "the spectre" that his telephone calls were being intercepted.[4] The Minister for Posts and Telegraphs, J.J. Walsh, stated that he had often concluded that his predecessors "in the British days" were engaged in the interception of telephone messages.[5] The Minister assured the Deputy that no such practice existed in the Department of Posts and Telegraphs. The Minister had given a general and definite instruction that no tapping whatever of any communication passing through the Post Office whether in the form of telegrams, letters or telephone calls should occur.[6]

Another early reference in the Dáil to interception of communications by the State was in 1928 when Seán Lemass, then in Opposition, in a parliamentary question, asked the Minister for Posts and Telegraphs on behalf of Deputy De Valera, whether it was the practice of the Post Office to supply the Minister with copies of telegrams received or sent by political opponents.[7] The Parliamentary Secretary to the Minister for Posts and Telegraphs replied that it was not "the practice and has not been the practice at any time, for officers of the Post Office Department to divulge the information contained in telegrams or letters passing through the Post Office".[8]

In 1949 in reply to a parliamentary question the Parliamentary Secretary to the Minister for Posts and Telegraphs confirmed that officials of the Post Office listened into and recorded private telephone conversations.[9] He stated that this was done in "very exceptional cases and where the public interest" required it. He stated that it was only done in obedience to a warrant issued by the Minister for Justice.

The so-called Dáil criteria for interception of postal communications, telegrams and telephone messages came into existence in 1957.[10] The Minister for Justice, Oscar Traynor, stated that interceptions were made on "the authority of the Minister for Justice in exercise of a long standing power", the existence of which was "explicitly recognised in section 56 of the *Post Office Act, 1908*".[11] The Minister stated that each warrant was issued on the personal authority of the Minister for Justice which was given "only where the warrant [was] required for security purposes or for the prevention or detection of serious crimes, information as to which could be got in no other way".[12]

The Taoiseach, Jack Lynch, during the period of the "Arms Crisis" in 1970 on a motion in the Dáil for the nomination of members of the Government delineated further criteria which governed the issue of warrants by the Minister for Justice.[13] He stated that the warrant under the *Post Office Act, 1908* may be issued "only where required for security purposes or for the prevention or detection of serious crime information as to which could be got in no other way". The Taoiseach stated that the interception procedure was circumscribed by other conditions. The request for the warrant must come from the Commissioner of the Garda Síochána, or the Deputy Commissioner. The officials of the Department of Justice must advise that they are satisfied that the information concerned could be obtained in no other way.[14]

EARLY JUSTIFICATION OF AUTHORITY OF MINISTER FOR JUSTICE

Prior to the enactment of the *Interception Act, 1993* the legal authority for the power of the Minister for Justice to intercept telecommunication messages was variously described in the Dáil as "a long standing power",[15] "a general residual common law power",[16] and "a statutory power".[17] The statutory power was stated in the Dáil[18] by the Minister for Justice, Charles Haughey, in 1964 to be section 56 of the *Post Office Act, 1908*.[19] Section 56 of the *Post Office Act, 1908*, repealed in 1983,[20] prohibited the opening of postal packets including telegrams,[21] but also provided that the prohibition was not to extend to the opening, detaining or delaying of a postal packet (including a telegram) "in obedience to an express warrant in writing under the hand" of the Minister for Justice.[22] Section 56 could not be construed as a power enabling the Minister for Justice to intercept telecommunication messages.

Section 98 of the *Postal and Telecommunications Services Act, 1983* prohibited the interception of telecommunication messages. But the prohibition on interception[23] of telecommunication messages in the 1983 Act did not apply to a person acting in pursuance of a direction issued by the Minister for Communications under section 110 of the 1983 Act.[24] Section 110 of the 1983 Act allows the Minister for Communications to direct Telecom Éireann to "do (or refrain from doing) anything which he may specify from time to time as necessary in the national interest".

Section 110(1)(c) of the 1983 Act enables the Minister for Communications to require Telecom Éireann to "perform such work or provide or maintain such services for a State authority as may be specified in the direction". These provisions are wide enough for the Minister for Communications to direct Telecom Éireann to intercept telecommunication messages. Telecom Éireann is obliged to comply with every direction given to it by the Minister under section 110 of the 1983 Act. The Minister for Justice, Padraig Flynn, informed the Seanad in 1992 that interceptions were carried out by appropriate officials in Telecom Éireann on foot of a direction under section 110 of the *Postal and Telecommunications Services Act, 1983* in conjunction with a warrant issued by the Minister for Justice.[25] However, section 110 of the 1983 Act could not be described as a statutory authority which empowers the Minister for Communications or the Minister for Justice to intercept telecommunication messages.

Prior to the *Interception Act, 1993* there was statutory authority for the interception of telecommunication in relation to foreign telegrams under the *Official Secrets Act, 1963*.[26] Other general authority was exceedingly vague. The power to intercept could not be described in modern Ireland as in the nature of a prerogative or common law power.[27] As a general statement of law, it may be stated that public officials may perform lawfully only such things for which express authority may be found in some statutory or common law rule.[28] The Minister for Justice had not been so authorised to intercept communications. The fact that the Minister for Justice had intercepted communications for a very long period did not make the activity lawful.[29] Interception activities performed by the State do not become lawful merely because they can be demonstrated in some way to have been in the interest of the State.[30]

EUROPEAN CONVENTION ON HUMAN RIGHTS

The jurisprudence of the European Court of Human Rights exerted a major influence on the drafting of the Irish *Interception Act, 1993.* Prior to the enactment of the 1993 Act, the administrative practices in relation to interception of communications by the State in Ireland were almost certainly in breach of Article 8 of the *European Convention on Human Rights* which provides as follows:

1. Everyone has the right to respect for his private and family life, his home and his correspondence.

2. There shall be no interference by a public authority with the exercise of this right except such as is in accordance with the law and is necessary in a democratic society in the interests of national security, public safety or the economic well-being of the country, for the prevention of disorder or crime, for the protection of health or morals, or for the protection of the rights and freedoms of others.

In several cases[31] the European Court of Human Rights considered that telephone conversations were covered by the concepts of "private life" and "correspondence" referred to in paragraph 1 of Article 8 of the European Convention.

The *Malone* case (1984)[32] was of considerable significance to Ireland because administrative practices and the statutory law in the United Kingdom outlined in *Malone* (which impinged on the question of interception of telecommunication) were almost identical at the relevant time with such practices and statutory law in Ireland. The European Court of Human Rights (which included Mr. Justice B. Walsh in its composition) held unanimously that there had been a breach of Article 8 by the United Kingdom in relation to the interception of telephone communications of the applicant.[33]

The principal issue in *Malone* was whether the interferences were justified under the terms of paragraph 2 of Article 8, i.e. whether they were in accordance with the law and "necessary in a democratic society" for one of the purposes enumerated in that paragraph. The European Court of Human Rights held that it could not state with any reasonable certainty what elements of the power in England and Wales to intercept communications were incorporated in legal rules and what elements remained within the discretion of the executive. The Court reasoned in *Malone* that the minimum degree of legal protection to which citizens were entitled under the rule of law in a democratic society was thus lacking.

The case of *Malone* may be contrasted with that of *Ludi v Switzerland* (1992).[34] In *Ludi*, an investigating Swiss judge, acting on information from the German police that Mr. Ludi was planning to buy drugs in Switzerland, opened a preliminary enquiry and ordered his telephone communications to be intercepted. Mr. Ludi was subsequently convicted. The European Court of Human Rights had no doubt that the telephone interception had been an interference with Mr. Ludi's private life and correspondence. However, the Court found that interference had been in accordance with the law (Article 171(b) and 171(c) of the Berne Code of Criminal Procedure) and necessary in a democratic society for the prevention of crime.[35]

INTERCEPTION OF POSTAL PACKETS AND TELECOMMUNICATIONS MESSAGES (REGULATION) ACT, 1993

In *Kennedy v Ireland* (1987),[36] the telephone tapping case involving two journalists, Hamilton P held that the right to privacy, although not specifically guaranteed by the Constitution of Ireland, was one of the personal rights of the citizen which flowed from the Christian and democratic nature of the State. Further, the President of the High Court held that the constitutional right to privacy included the right to hold private telephone conversations without deliberate, conscious and unjustified intrusion by servants of the State. The right to privacy was held, however, not to be an unqualified right but was subject to the requirements of public order, public morality and the common good.[37] Accordingly, interception of telecommunication messages by the Minister for Justice, (pursuant to the *Interception Act, 1993*) in the interests of public order and the exigencies of the common good, (subject to the comments about initiating the interception process before a judge) appears to be in accord with constitutional criteria.

The purpose of the *Interception Act, 1993* was to place on a statutory basis the conditions under which the Minister for Justice issued warrants authorising the interception of postal packets and telecommunication messages and to regulate the procedure for the issue of authorisations. Under the Act, the only purposes for which interceptions may be authorised are those of criminal investigation or in the interests of the security of the State.[38]

There is a specific definition of "interception" in the *Interception*

Act, 1993, in relation to telecommunication messages as follows:

> an act —
> (i) that consists of the listening or attempted listening to, or the recording or attempted recording, by any means, in the course of its transmission, of a telecommunications message, other than such listening or recording, or such an attempt, where either the person on whose behalf the message is transmitted or the person intended to receive the message has consented to the listening or recording, and
> (ii) that, if done otherwise than in pursuance of a direction under section 110 of the [*Postal and Telecommunications Services Act, 1983*], constitutes an offence under section 98 of that Act.[39]

If the listening or recording of the telecommunication message is with the consent of either the sender or receiver of the message, then this does not constitute "interception" within the meaning of the *Interception Act, 1993*. Secondly, there is a link in the definition to a direction given under section 110 of the *Postal and Telecommunications Services Act, 1983*, (the mechanism whereby the Minister for Communications directs Telecom Éireann to carry out the interception process on behalf of the Minister for Justice). Thirdly, there is a link to section 98 of the 1983 Act. In effect, this latter provision ties down the interception to telecommunication messages being transmitted by Telecom Éireann — because section 98 (the prohibition on general interception) only applies to messages transmitted by Telecom Éireann. This latter requirement represents a flaw in the interception legislation as telecommunication messages such as communications via business radio and private telecommunication systems transmitted by parties other than Telecom Éireann may be outside the scope of the prohibition and the process of interception by the Minister for Justice.

The *Interception Act, 1993* sets out in detail the procedure in relation to applications for, and the issue of, warrants authorising interceptions. The Act introduces two principles for controlling the exercise of the power of the Minister for Justice in respect of interceptions. First, the principle of entrusting supervisory control over the interception of telecommunication by the State to a judge, which commended itself to the European Court of Human Rights in *Klass*,[40] is enshrined in the 1993 Act.[41] Second, the principle of the necessity for protection in domestic law against arbitrary interference by public authorities with the rights safeguarded by paragraph 1 of Article 8 of the Convention on Human Rights which the European Court of Human Rights emphasised in *Malone*[42] is given effect to in the 1993 legislation by the establishment of a Complaints Referee to whom complaints that a person's communications have been intercepted improperly may be made.[43] The Irish legislation is similar in many respects to the UK *Interception of Communications Act, 1985* which itself was introduced primarily to conform to the jurisprudence of the European Court of Human Rights in the light, particularly, of *Malone*.

Although there is to be judicial control over the interception process, that process itself is not initiated before a judge in the same manner as a person would apply for a warrant to search premises. The question arises whether Ministerial control over the interception process is in accordance with the Constitution of Ireland. There is also the issue whether provision should have been made for admissibility of evidence obtained in the interception process.

In the United States, the Fourth Amendment to the US Constitution (the prohibition against unreasonable searches and seizures), governs not only the seizure of tangible things but extends to the interception of telephone messages. The Fourth Amendment protects people, and not simply places, against unreasonable searches and seizures.[44] Article 40.5 of the Constitution of Ireland (prohibition on forcible entry) differs in several respects from the US Fourth Amendment. Article 40.5 reads: "The dwelling of every citizen is inviolable and shall not be forcibly entered save in accordance with law." The phrase "save in accordance with law" must mean authorised by process of law, i.e., by the Constitution, statute or the common law.

The Minister for Justice is empowered specifically by section 2(1) of the *Interception Act, 1993* to intercept telecommunication. It may be argued, however, that the issuing of a warrant by the Minister for Justice to intercept telecommunication has certain attributes that are normally associated with the process of administration of justice.[45] The question whether the exercise of this power by the Minister for Justice is an unconstitutional exercise of a power which is more appropriate to the judicial arm of government is a matter which may be raised in an appropriate case. Two factors should be borne in mind. It is in large measure the duty of the State to gather evidence for criminal prosecutions. It is the duty of the courts to consider the evidence presented by the State and ultimately to determine the guilt or innocence of persons charged with such offences. Arguably, the Minister for Justice's powers should be examined in the light of the function of the executive arm of government to gather evidence for criminal prosecutions.

On the other hand, there is the extra-judicial view of Walsh J, based on Article 40.5 of the Constitution of Ireland (inviolability of the dwelling), that interception of telecommunication messages without a judicial authorisation is unconstitutional.[46] It would have been more appropriate had provision been made in the legislation to the effect that the judicial arm of government would authorise interception of telecommunication rather than be involved in a merely supervisory capacity after the event. This would have ensured that the interception process was in accord with the practical and, perhaps in the context of the exercise of judicial power, the constitutional demand that a neutral and detached authority be interposed between the law enforcement officers and the citizens. It would also have tended to give greater assurance to the public that the decisions were fair. These considerations influenced the development of the statutory law on interception of communications in the United States.[47]

INTERCEPTION OF TELECOMMUNICATION MESSAGES BY PERSONS OTHER THAN THE STATE

Interception of telecommunication messages by parties other than the State (subject to certain exceptions) contravenes section 98 of the *Postal and Telecommunications Services Act, 1983*, as amended by section 13 of the *Interception Act, 1993*. The provisions of section 98 of the *Postal and Telecommunications Services Act, 1983* when read in conjunction with the 1993 Act enhance, to a limited extent, the protection of privacy in Ireland by enacting a general prohibition on interception of telecommunication messages while they are in the course of transmission by the national network carrier, Telecom Éireann. Section 98(1) of the *Postal and Telecommunications Services Act, 1983* provides as follows:

A person who—
(a) intercepts or attempts to intercept, or
(b) authorises, suffers or permits another person to intercept, or
(c) does anything that will enable him or another person to intercept telecommunications messages being transmitted by [Telecom Éireann] or who discloses the existence, substance or purport of any such message which has been intercepted or

uses any information obtained from any such message shall be guilty of an offence.

The penalty on conviction on indictment is up to IR£50,000 or imprisonment for a term not exceeding five years or to both the fine and imprisonment.[48] By 1993, the definition of "interception" in the 1983 Act was considered too restrictive; the consent of both the person transmitting the message and the person intended to receive that message was required before the listening or recording ceased to be unlawful. Under, the *Interception Act, 1993*, the consent to the listening or recording of either the person transmitting the message or the person intended to receive the message will suffice to take the listening or recording out of the interception prohibition. Thus, as amended, the definition of "intercept" in the 1983 Act reads as follows:

> listen to, or record by any means, in the course of its transmission [by Telecom Éireann], a telecommunications message but does not include such listening or recording where either the person on whose behalf the message is transmitted or the person intended to receive the message has consented to the listening or recording.[49]

The statutory prohibition on interception of telecommunication messages does not apply to certain persons carrying out certain specified duties.[50] The prohibition does not apply to any person acting pursuant to an investigation by a member of the Garda Síochána, where there is a complaint relating to a suspected offence under section 13 of the *Post Office (Amendment) Act, 1951*.[51] This provision refers to telecommunication messages of an obscene, menacing or similar character. The statutory prohibition on interception does not extend to any person acting "in the course of and to the extent required by his operating duties or duties for or in connection with the installation or maintenance of a line, apparatus or equipment for the transmission of telecommunications messages by [Telecom Éireann]".[52] The statutory prohibition on interception does not apply to a person acting in pursuance of a direction issued by the Minister for Communications under section 110 of the *Postal and Telecommunications Services Act, 1983*[53] or under other lawful authority.[54]

Section 98 of the 1983 Act appears to have been modelled on section 86 of the *Australian Telecommunications Act, 1975*. However, interception in the 1975 Australian Act refers to "information passing over a telecommunications system" whereas the 1983 Act refers to "telecommunications messages". Difficulties may arise on the interpretation of the word "message" in the 1983 Act.

As discussed earlier, the principal deficiency concerning the prohibition on interception of telecommunication is that the prohibition only applies to telecommunication messages transmitted by Telecom Éireann. Other jurisdictions provided for prohibition on interception of private communications systems. The Canadian Criminal Code made it unlawful for anyone to intercept wilfully a private communication by means of an electro-magnetic, acoustic, mechanical or other device.[55]

Use of any form of radio equipment to intercept communications would infringe the *Wireless Telegraphy Acts*[56] and regulations. It is an offence under the *Wireless Telegraphy Acts*[57] for any person to keep, possess, work or use any apparatus for wireless telegraphy without a licence. It is also an offence for a person to work or use apparatus for wireless telegraphy otherwise than in accordance with the terms and conditions of the licence.[58] The expression "wireless telegraphy" is defined to include all forms of radio communication.[59] The improper disclosure of the purport of any message, communication or signal sent by wireless telegraphy is an offence.[60] There is also a specific provision in licences granted under the Wireless Telegraphy Acts that the holder of a licence shall not divulge communications received by means of licensed apparatus.[61]

The interception of cable and MMDS services is considered in chapter 20.

THE PROCESS OF "METERING"

The process known as "metering" involves the use of a printer meter, pen register or similar device which records the electronic impulses which are made when an incoming or outgoing telephone call is dialled. These devices activate a computer printout which records the time, date and number dialled. The printer tape does not show whether any actual conversation took place over the telephone. These devices are used for operational reasons. These records could, however, prove an invaluable aid to law enforcement personnel.

The process known as "metering" is outside the scope of the prohibition on interception of telecommunication messages and outside the remit of the Minister for Justice's power to intercept telecommunication messages.[62] The definition of "interception" in section 98 of the 1983 Act relates only to listening to or recording a telecommunication message. However, section 98(2A) of the *Postal and Telecommunications Services Act, 1983* (inserted by the *Interception Act, 1993*), prohibits specifically a person employed by Telecom Éireann from disclosing any information concerning the use made of telecommunication services provided for any other person (including, for example, the "fruits" of any metering process) unless the disclosure is made

(a) at the request or with the consent of that other person,
(b) for the prevention or detection of crime or for the purpose of any criminal proceedings,
(c) in the interests of the security of the State,
(d) in pursuance of an order of a court,
(e) for the purpose of civil proceedings in any court, or
(f) to another person to whom he is required, in the course of his duty as such employee, to make such disclosure.

A person is liable on indictment for breach of section 98 (2A) of the 1983 Act to a fine not exceeding IR£50,000 or imprisonment to a term not exceeding five years, or to both fine and imprisonment.[63]

Section 98(2A) of the 1983 Act does not specifically authorise employees of Telecom Éireann to release the "fruits" of any metering process to law enforcement personnel. The section merely provides, inter alia, that such disclosure in the circumstances described shall not be a criminal offence. This provision is based on a similar provision in the UK *Interception of Communications Act, 1985*,[64] which in turn was based on a provision in the UK *Data Protection Act, 1984* which provides for disclosure of information made for the prevention or detection of crime, for the purpose of criminal proceedings, in the interests of national security or on the order of a court.

In the interests of Telecom Éireann employees who provide the metering information to law enforcement personnel, and in the interests of the general public so that they may be assured that "the system cannot be abused," the Minister of State at the Department of Justice, William O'Dea, introduced an amendment to the 1993 legislation at the Report Stage[65] providing that a request by a member of the Garda Síochána or an officer of the Defence Forces to a person employed in Telecom Éireann to make disclosure of metering information must be in writing and be signed by a member of the Garda Síochána not below the rank of chief superintendent or an officer of the Permanent Defence Forces who holds an army rank not below that of colonel.[66]

The question arises whether the metering process — the use of a telephone-tracing device — without the consent of relevant parties for any purpose other than operational reasons or in pursuance of an order of a court infringes any constitutional right of the citizen. In particular, does the use of a telephone-tracing device infringe Article 40.5 — inviolability of the dwelling — where a telephone is located in the dwelling? Based on *Kennedy v Ireland*,[67] the citizen arguably has a right of privacy against arbitrary government (and perhaps other) intrusions in relation to a person's telephone calls. Does such a right extend to information relating to telephone calls?

Courts in the United States have been divided to some extent on the question whether telephone-tracing devices are regulated by the Fourth Amendment of the US Constitution — the prohibition on unreasonable searches and seizures. A similar provision exists in the constitutions of individual US states. The US Supreme Court held in *Smith v Maryland* (1979)[68] that the utilisation of an electronic "pen register" (a device that identifies telephone numbers called, together with relevant date and time) did not constitute a search or necessitate a warrant under the US Constitution; there was no "expectation of privacy". In *Smith*, the telephone company used a "pen register" at the request of the police to record the numbers dialled from the house of a man suspected of placing threatening calls to a robbery victim. Two tests featured in *Smith*. The first test related to whether the individual had shown that he sought to preserve something private; the second test was whether the individual's subjective expectation of privacy was one that society was prepared to recognise as reasonable. In relation to the first test, the Court found that the caller could not have entertained an actual expectation of privacy in the numbers he dialled. The Court doubted that persons in general entertained any actual expectation of privacy in the numbers they dialled. Such persons should realise that the telephone company has facilities for making permanent records of the numbers which persons dial.

In relation to the second test, the *Smith* court reasoned that if any such expectation of privacy existed, it was not one that society would recognise as reasonable; the telephone user must assume the risk that the telephone company might reveal relevant information to the police.

The reasoning of the Supreme Court in *Smith* is not convincing, unlike the reasoning of the Colorado Supreme Court which reached a different conclusion in *People v Sporleder* (1983)[69] in holding that warrantless use of a pen register violated the state constitution. [The State Constitution contained provisions similar to the US Constitution]. The State court held that the telephone subscriber had a legitimate expectation of privacy in the numbers dialled; thus, a pen register constituted an illegal search and seizure in the absence of a search warrant, exigent circumstances or consent. The court considered that the telephone was "a necessary component of modern life" and that disclosing to a telephone company the numbers dialled did not alter the caller's expectation that those numbers would be used only for internal telephone company business purposes. The individual had the right to expect that the information would otherwise remain private.

It would have been preferable (as a minimum requirement) if the legislature in Ireland had provided specifically that, for the purposes of criminal investigation and in the interests of the security of the State, the Minister for Justice was authorised to issue a warrant (subject to safeguards as in the *Interception Act, 1993*) authorising the national telephone company to hand over details of telephone calls (the fruits of any metering process) to appropriate law enforcement personnel. This would have afforded a greater degree of protection to the citizen's right of privacy in his or her telephone conversations.

29

The Pervasiveness Rationale in Broadcasting

PERVASIVENESS RATIONALE IN IRELAND

In addition to the argument over the finite nature of the frequency spectrum, State regulation of expression in the context of broadcasting has also been justified on the basis of the pervasiveness of broadcasting—described here as the pervasiveness rationale. The broadcast medium that gains access to the living room is such a powerful medium that its content must be regulated in the public interest. The pervasiveness rationale has been propounded by governments as a justification for controlling modes of tele-communication since practical systems of telecommunication became possible. A Bill regulating communications proposed under the regime of Louis-Philippe (1830-1848) illustrates an early adoption of the pervasiveness justification:

> Governments have always kept to themselves the exclusive use of things which, if fallen into bad hands, could threaten public and private safety: poisons, explosives are given out only under State authority and certainly the telegraph in bad hands, could become a most dangerous weapon. Just imagine what could have happened if the passing success of the Lyons silk workers' insurrection had been known in all corners of the nation at once.[1]

In effect, the pervasiveness rationale as a justification for regulation represents the application of old beliefs to the new media. Edmund Burke saw in the press "the grand instrument of the subversion of order, morals, religion and human society itself".[2] Sir James Macintosh commented in 1803 on the role of the press in the great change that had taken place in the discussion of public affairs: "The multiplication of newspapers has produced a gradual revolution in our government by increasing the number of those who exercise some sort of judgment on public affairs."[3] Brougham's analysis in 1831 of the press in the pre-reform era could, perhaps, be applied to the broadcasting media of today: "[The press] alone rivalled the House of Commons in that it was the only organ of public opinion capable of dictating to the Government, since nothing else could speak the sense of the people."[4] Broadcasters are often perceived as mediators between parliament and people, the rulers and the ruled. This is so because of the pervasiveness and influence of the broadcasting medium.

An early illustration of the perceived power of the broadcasting medium to arouse passions was the censoring in March 1927 of the message of the President of the Executive Council to the International Broadcasting Corporation which operated radio station WGL. The President of the Executive Council, William T. Cosgrave, had been invited to send a message to be broadcast by the United States International Broadcasting Corporation, but the members of the corporation's board of directors decided on reading the text that it must be censored or not broadcast at all.[5] Eamon De Valera had already broadcast on the same radio station in the same month. *The New York Herald Tribune* in its edition of March 18, 1927 printed the censored passage highlighting, in retrospect, the differing treatment of the printed word over the broadcast word. The censored paragraph, which incidentally referred to the interruption of communications during the years 1922-1923, read as follows:

> Mr. De Valera's insane campaign of destruction in 1922-23 by which he endeavoured to wreck the Treaty between Ireland and Great Britain cost the State no less than 75 million dollars in Army expenditure and 28 million dollars in compensation for direct destruction of life and property of which 23 million dollars have already been paid. For nearly two years the normal life of the country was practically at a standstill while Mr. De Valera's dupes in the name of freedom strained every nerve to deprive their country of life and liberty. Their honesty of purpose may be judged from the fact that banks were a special object of their attack and that from these they robbed hundreds of thousands of dollars. Rails were torn up, roads broken and bridges destroyed, telephone and telegraph wires cut and stolen and communication by every means repeatedly interrupted; the total cost to the State in direct expenditure taking no account of consequential losses to farmers and business men being over 103 million dollars.

The early influence of the pervasiveness rationale on the Government may be gleaned from a statement made by the Minister for Posts and Telegraphs to the Seanad on the Second Stage of the *Broadcasting Authority Bill, 1959*:

> Broadcasting is the most powerful and pervasive medium of communication yet devised. It is unsurpassed in speed, range and economy either for disseminating information, news and ideas or for bringing music, plays, variety and discussion to a widely scattered audience.[6]

The same sentiment was expressed trenchantly by President de Valera at the opening of the new broadcasting service, Telefís Éireann, on December 31, 1961:

> I must admit that sometimes when I think of television and radio and their immense power, I feel somewhat afraid. Like atomic energy, it can be used for incalculable good but it can also do irreparable harm. Never before was there in the hands of men an instrument so powerful to influence the thoughts and actions of the multitude.[7]

The average amount of television viewing time in Ireland in 1992 was 3.23 hours per day for persons aged 4 years and upwards. For those aged 15 years and upwards, the average daily viewing time in 1992 was 3.33 hours.[8] However, in 1987-1988 the average American home watched television for an average of 6 hours 59 minutes each day.[9] The 1981 Joint Oireachtas Committee on RTE,[10] chaired by Senator Eoin Ryan, SC, with Senator Patrick Cooney as Vice-Chairman (both lawyers), noted that whatever the reality was about television viewing, it was evident that television was "an all-pervasive force" that occupied a large portion of our leisure time.[11] The Oireachtas Committee also stated that the role of RTE as the national public service station was of particular significance and that for everybody RTE was in some way identified with "the orthodox, not to say official, mainstream of thinking in the country".[12] Accordingly, RTE's ability to influence thinking "through a variety of ways, overt and hidden, [was] immense".[13] In the context of a consideration of the pervasive influence of television, the Committee was convinced that there was an excessive level of violence in RTE transmissions and that no programme with any significant element of violence should be screened before 10.00 p.m.

The Committee stated that it was gratified with RTE's assurance that the amount of material with violent scenes was being phased down.[14] The Committee hoped that this process would be continued and accelerated.[15]

Dr. Conor Cruise O'Brien, as Minister for Posts and Telegraphs, justified the greater extension of control by the State over broadcasting than over the printed media by reference partly to the pervasiveness rationale:

> [B]roadcasting of all the media, both through sounds and images, has by far the most immediate impact on people and situations, has by far the greatest capacity to generate emotion, and its capacities in these regards have aroused and held the fascinated attention of people interested in promoting and justifying violence and strongly desirous of access to broadcasting for precisely these ends.[16]

The pervasiveness rationale, in essence, is the fundamental justification for the ministerial power enshrined in section 31 of the *Broadcasting Authority Act, 1960*.[17] The prohibition against undermining public order, public morality or the authority of the State applies to all communications media including the printed word and is enshrined in Article 40.6.1.i and under general law; yet no order similar to the section 31 order is in force to regulate the content of the printed word.

In *Purcell v Ireland* (1991),[18] the European Commission of Human Rights was influenced by the power and domination of the broadcast media in its decision that the complaints made by the Irish journalists and producers in relation to the section 31 order were unfounded:

> In contemporary society radio and television are media of considerable power and influence. Their impact is more immediate than that of the print media, and the possibilities of the broadcaster to correct, qualify, interpret or comment, on any statement made on radio or television are limited in comparison with those available to journalists in the press. Live statements could also involve a special risk of coded messages being conveyed, a risk which even conscientious journalists cannot control within the exercise of their professional judgment.[19]

The Minister for Communications on the Second Stage of the *Radio and Television Bill, 1988* reiterated the traditional arguments in relation to the differing treatment between broadcasting and the printed media in terms of the pervasiveness of the broadcasting media. Referring to the elements of broadcasting's potential, he instanced the fact that "[broadcasting] would allow for greater and easier access than the printed word" and referred to "the relative immediacy and one-way nature of its communication". The Minister continued:

> The recognition of these elements left a clear awareness that broadcasting could be a major force for good or bad in society — or at least that it would be a very influential medium. In these circumstances it was almost inevitable that Governments would seek to retain some control over how it developed.[20]

The "pervasiveness" of broadcasting remains a primary justification of the executive branch of government for much of the regulation of the content of what is broadcast in Ireland.

THE PERVASIVENESS RATIONALE IN THE UNITED STATES

The pervasiveness rationale has played a part in the United States as a justification for the regulation of the content of broadcasting. The argument has been made successfully that recipients of broadcast speech constitute members of a captive audience on the basis that such speech is "in the air" and thus unavoidable. US Judge Bazelon, a noted authority on telecommunication law, commented on this issue in 1969 in a case concerning whether cigarette commercials were sufficiently controversial to require broadcasters to provide reply time pursuant to the (US) Fairness Doctrine:

> Written messages are not communicated unless they are read, and reading requires an affirmative act. Broadcast messages in contrast are "in the air." In the age of omnipresent radio, there scarcely breathes a citizen who does not know some part of a leading cigarette jingle by heart. Similarly an ordinary habitual television watcher can *avoid* these commercials only by frequently leaving the room, changing the channel, or doing some other such affirmative act. It is difficult to calculate the subliminal impact of this pervasive propaganda, which may be

heard even if not listened to, but it may reasonably be thought greater than the impact of the written word.[21]

The notion of the pervasiveness of the broadcast medium and the need to protect the captive audience was developed by Chief Justice Burger in *Columbia Broadcasting System Inc v Democratic National Committee* (1973):

> In a very real sense listeners and viewers constitute a "captive audience" . . . The "captive" nature of the broadcast audience was recognised as early as 1924 when Commerce Secretary Hoover remarked . . . that the "radio listener does not have the same option that the reader of publications has — to ignore advertising in which he is not interested — and he may resent its invasion of his set."[22]

However, this concept of a "captive audience" has its limitations. A distinction must be made between, for example, radio on a bus, where one truly cannot avoid the broadcast message except by plugging one's ears or by avoiding public transport, and broadcasting received in the home, where the viewer or listener can avoid an offensive programme or advertisement by changing the channel or turning the radio or television off. Also, account must be taken of the affirmative act of initially inviting the broadcast medium into the home.

The pervasiveness rationale been used by the United States Supreme Court to justify content regulation of the broadcast media. In *FCC v Pacifica Foundation* (1978),[23] a New York radio station, affiliated with the Pacifica network, had broadcast George Carlin's "Filthy Word" monologue concerning his thoughts on words "you couldn't say on the public . . . airwaves". The Federal Communications Commission ruled that Pacifica could be penalised for broadcasting the monologue and, on appeal, the Supreme Court held in a five-to-four decision that it was constitutional to punish a radio station for broadcasting the "indecent" words, although a printed version of the monologue could not be challenged on constitutional grounds. The majority opinion explained the different treatment between the printed and broadcast media:

> The reasons for these distinctions are complex, but two have relevance to the present case. First, the broadcast media have established a uniquely pervasive presence in the lives of all

Americans. Patently offensive indecent material presented over the airwaves confronts the citizen, not only in public, but also in the privacy of the home, where the individual's right to be left alone plainly outweighs the First Amendment rights of an intruder.[24]

The majority in *Pacifica* considered that because the broadcast audience was constantly tuning in and out, prior warnings could not completely protect the listener or viewer from unexpected programme content. The Court argued that to say that one may avoid further offence "by turning off the radio when he hears indecent language is like saying that the remedy for an assault is to run away after the first blow".[25] In his dissent, Justice Brennan argued that the Court's opinion misconceived the privacy interest of one who voluntarily brings radio communication into his home, and that it ignored the constitutional rights of those who wish to transmit and those who wish to receive broadcasts that some may find offensive.[26]

Although the pervasiveness rationale above was linked to the right of privacy, the US Supreme Court considered other aspects of the pervasiveness rationale when it considered the effect of broadcasting on children:

> [B]roadcasting is uniquely accessible to children, even those too young to read. Although Cohen's written message ["Fuck the Draft"] might have been incomprehensible to a first grader, Pacifica's broadcast could have enlarged a child's vocabulary in an instant. Other forms of offensive expression may be withheld from the young without restricting the expression at its source. Bookstores and motion picture theatres, for example, may be prohibited from making indecent material available to children. We held in *Ginsberg v New York* 390 US 629, that the Government's interest in the "well-being of its youth" and in supporting "parents' claim to authority in their own household" justified the regulation of otherwise protected expression. *Id.*, at 639 and 640. . . . The ease with which children may obtain access to broadcast material, coupled with the concerns recognised in *Ginsberg*, amply justify special treatment of indecent broadcasting.[27]

There is some objective support for the proposition that television exerts a greater influence on behaviour than the printed word. A 1982 report issued by the US National Institute of Mental Health concluded that there is little doubt that exposure to television violence results in attitudes that foster aggressive behaviour and increased aggressive behaviour itself in both children and adolescents.[28] Although there are some critics who disagree,[29] most of the research concludes that constant exposure to violence on television increases the degree to which children will engage in aggressive behaviour.[30] A 1986 study found a significant relationship between exposure to violence on television at the age of eight and the seriousness of criminal acts performed by the same individuals at age 30.[31] It can, therefore, be argued that television has a greater pervasive influence than the printed word and therefore at least in relation to minors should be subject to more stringent regulation.

In the context of the broadcast medium's power to arouse, the pervasiveness rationale, and constitutional implications for the regulation of broadcasting, reference may be made to *Zamora v Columbia Broadcasting System* (1979).[32] In *Zamora* a 15-year-old boy and his parents sued three television networks alleging that negligent programming had resulted in the boy becoming involuntarily addicted to and "completely subliminally intoxicated" by viewing television violence. The teenage plaintiff had been convicted of murdering his 83-year-old neighbour. He and his parents alleged he "developed a psychopathic personality" and had become "desensitised to violent behaviour" as a result of the network's failure "to use ordinary care" to prevent the teenager from "being 'impermissibly stimulated, incited and instigated' to duplicate the atrocities he viewed on television".[33]

The court in *Zamora* rejected the contention that the networks had a duty to avoid making "violent" shows and that such programming could constitute negligence.[34] The court held that imposing a duty on the defendants would violate public policy. The court recognised that allowing such a claim would create potentially crushing and unpredictable liability which would "give birth to a legal morass through which broadcasting would have difficulty finding its way".[35] The court focused on rights under the First Amendment of the US Constitution (freedom of speech and the press) and noted that the right of the public to view programming "should not be inhibited by those members of the public who are particularly sensitive or insensitive".[36]

Courts should be slow in imposing liability, for example, in negligence on the broadcasting media for speech or acts emanating from such media which allegedly result in damage to a viewer.

CONCLUSION

The pervasiveness rationale may well justify the regulation of the content of broadcasting in limited circumstances, particularly in relation to minors. However, it is difficult in law to justify the entire regulation of broadcasting on the pervasiveness rationale alone. Although the rationale for regulating broadcasting based on the scarcity of frequencies may not be as valid today as in former times and the pervasiveness rationale (as a basis for regulating broadcasting) may not have a strong constitutional justification, broadcasting should still be subject to regulation by the State.

An unregulated "free for all" in broadcasting would not be satisfactory. There is no guarantee that, without a system of regulation, private broadcasting would enable a significant number of social groups and ideological movements to express their opinions. Citizens could have difficulty in exercising any right to be informed, and to hear the expression of different considerations and opinions if the broadcasting media were to be dominated solely either by the State or market forces.

Broadcasting is a "culture-creator" in our society. To have the broadcasting services owned by the few or as subsidiaries of other's financial interests could skew the way in which cultural information and indeed information of any kind is collected and distributed.[37] The US Supreme Court in *Metro Broadcasting Inc v FCC* (1990), which upheld measures to increase the number of minority owners of broadcast stations, has recognised the importance of "multiculturalism" and the need to take active steps to nurture diversity in broadcasting.[38] In the context of the importance of diversity in broadcasting and the need for some form of regulation, the writer adopts the words of Professor Patricia Williams:

> We think freedom of expression as something creative, innovative, each word lives a birth of something new and different. But it is also the power to manipulate one's resources to sanction what is not pleasing. The property of the communications industry is all about the production of ideas, images and cultural representations, but it also selectively silences even as it creates. Like all artistic expression, it is a crafting process of production and negation, in the same way that a painting may involve choices to include yellow and blue while leaving out red and green.[39]

The regulation of broadcasting in Ireland may be founded, inter alia, on Article 40.6.1.i of the Constitution (freedom of expression). Regulation is necessary to achieve a plurality of voices. In relation to the argument that the broadcasting media is being more strictly and more unjustifiably regulated than the print media, and therefore being discriminatory, the different forms of regulation may be justified on the basis that the historical treatment of the press has resulted in a certain balance that is basically sufficient to guarantee the circulation of a diversity of considerations and opinions;[40] the same cannot be said of broadcasting at this stage in its development in Ireland. Hence, subject to constant review, the State should provide a regulatory scheme in relation to broadcasting that would contibute to the formation of public opinion while simultaneously reflecting its diversity and allowing the public a significant choice. Taking the issue a stage further, based on Article 40.6.1.i of the Constitution, the "grave import" of "[t]he education of public opinion" for "the common good," there is a constitutional warrant for the continued existence in Ireland of at least one public-service radio and television service.

30

The Statutory Duties of Objectivity and Impartiality in Broadcasting Services

DEVELOPMENT OF CONCEPTS OF OBJECTIVITY AND IMPARTIALITY

The statutory imposition of the duties of objectivity and impartiality was first expressed in these islands in section 3 of the UK *Television Act, 1954* which established the Independent Television Authority.[1] Therefore, it was not surprising that there was also general acceptance in the parliamentary debates on the *Broadcasting Authority Bill, 1959* of the necessity for imposing a statutory duty of objectivity and impartiality on the new Irish broadcasting authority. Section 18(1) of the *Broadcasting Authority Act, 1960* obliged the RTE Authority "to secure" that when it broadcast any information, news or feature which related to matters of public controversy or was the subject of current public debate, the information, news or feature was presented objectively and impartially and without any expression of the Authority's own views.[2]

The judicial inquiry in relation to a programme on illegal money lending which was broadcast on television on November 11, 1969[3] considered the issue of the standard of journalistic care in broadcasting; the standard of care impinges on the operation of the objectivity and impartiality obligations. The Judicial Tribunal (composed of Mr. Justice Seán Butler, Mr. Justice Denis Pringle and District Justice Cathal Ó Floinn),[4] sat for 49 days at the Four Courts, Dublin, and heard evidence from 141 witnesses including eight witnesses who were allowed to give evidence *in camera*. The Tribunal found that many of the facts presented on "7 Days", the news and current affairs programme which was under scrutiny, were not authentic, that the purported estimation of 500 unlicensed moneylenders stated in the programme was wildly inaccurate and that other matters stated in the programme did not amount to a fair representation of the facts. The Tribunal set out the following principles on the standard of journalistic care in the presentation of facts:

(1) A journalist must make every effort to ensure that the facts he presents are true and accurate.
(2) To do this he should try to check the facts at every possible stage.
(3) Where it is not possible to check the facts, he should evaluate critically the source from which they come.
(4) While he may accept statements from obviously reliable and trustworthy sources, he should be doubtful about information of a factual nature which he cannot check coming from a source which is not shown by experience or otherwise to be reliable and accurate.
(5) The evaluation of such a source involves checking into the background of the informant, his means of knowledge and his reputation for veracity.
(6) Where an editor, or other journalist responsible for the presentation of fact, relies on the investigation and judgment of a subordinate or researcher, he must be satisfied as to the experience of that person and his suitability for the task.[5]

The Tribunal considered that the "7 Days" team had failed to apply these principles. Some 14 years later, the *Broadcasting Review Committee, 1974* (chaired by Mr. Justice George D. Murnaghan) endorsed the above statement of principle relevant to the standard of journalistic care in the presentation of facts in the context of broadcasting.[6] Peter Feeney has argued that the "7 Days" tribunal symbolically "came to be regarded as the re-establishment of control of broadcasting by politicians".[7] The judicial inquiry with its full panoply of the law may not have been warranted; a lesser form of inquiry should have sufficed. The judicial inquiry was an effective reminder to the broadcasters of the Government's own power: a precedent of admonition had been generated.

There is a constant tension between Government and broadcasters in relation to the duties of objectivity and impartiality. For example, the Minister for Justice, Desmond O'Malley, in 1970 wrote to the Minister for Posts and Telegraphs, Gerard Collins, stating that the "left-wing bias" in RTE was so notorious that he would not take up the Minister's time by illustrating its many manifestations. The Minister for Justice stated that it was clear

> that an altogether disproportionate number of RTE staff at key points were biased to varying degrees to the left and when subjects of current interest come up, they not only put their own slant on them but [were] in a position to pick most of the guests from amongst people of like manner.[8]

The Minister for Justice concluded by stating that he would be glad to know whether anything was going to be done about the matter. Replying, the Minister for Posts and Telegraphs agreed in general with much of what the Minister for Justice had stated and gave an assurance that in so far as his powers enabled him to do so, he would see to it that "a proper balance [was] maintained in programme presentation".[9] However, the Minister for Posts and Telegraphs stated that so far as left-wing bias in RTE was concerned, it was necessary to move with "some care".[10] The Minister for Posts and Telegraphs was in no doubt that the left-wing and "even some pretty extreme elements of it [had] a good footing in RTE" but that it would be very easy in attempting to deal with that situation "to do a lot more harm than good".[11] The Minister stated that it was perfectly natural that an exciting service like RTE would attract very many young people to its staff and without considering the possibility of deliberate infiltration "by hard line communists," the probability was that a great number of these young people would be of left-wing sympathies. The Minister stated that there could be no question of eliminating these influences in RTE but that what could and would be done was to ensure to the utmost extent possible that they would not be able by their influence to bring about the presentation of programmes biased in favour of their views. The Minister continued by stating that breaches of the statutory requirement of objectivity and impartiality would occur from time to time but he intended to leave the RTE Authority in no doubt of "the absolute need to enforce the rule as fully and efficiently as [was] possible". The Minister concluded by emphasising that if "prejudiced and unbalanced presentation" did occur, he would certainly take it up with the Authority "very firmly".[12]

The *Broadcasting Review Committee Report* in 1974 in its chapter entitled "News and Current Affairs" which considered, *inter alia*, the issues of objectivity and impartiality, referred to the nature of television, which can provide an increased sense of the actuality of events and which can enhance "the risks of exaggeration and distortion".[13] The 1974 Committee stated that it could not regard RTE's treatment of Northern Ireland's affairs throughout the period since 1968 as having conformed to an adequate standard of objectivity and impartiality.[14] The Committee emphasised that one of the most important duties of the RTE Authority was to ensure impartiality and to guard against imbalance or overemphasis in the sphere of news and current affairs, and in the exercise of this duty a programme series was to be evaluated over a period of time.[15]

The *Broadcasting Authority (Amendment) Act, 1976* expanded the provision in the 1960 Act in relation to objectivity and impartiality. The 1976 Act imposed on the RTE Authority the duty of ensuring that all news broadcast by it was reported and presented in an objective and impartial manner and without any expression of the Authority's own views, that the broadcast treatment of current affairs, including matters which are either of public controversy or the subject of current public debate, was fair to all interests concerned and that the broadcast matter was presented in an objective and impartial manner and without an expression of the Authority's own views.[16] Further, the same broadcasting standards in relation to objectivity and impartiality were extended to any written, aural or visual material which related to news or current affairs including matters which were either of public controversy or the subject of current public debate which the Authority may publish or distribute.[17] The then current practice within RTE whereby the impartiality requirement was considered to be fulfilled if all significant views were aired in two or more related programmes, if these programmes were broadcast over a reasonable period, received statutory backing.[18] Similar statutory duties were subsequently imposed on private commercial radio services pursuant to the *Radio and Television Act, 1988.*[19]

O'Hanlon J delivered the first judicial analysis of the fairness and impartiality obligations[20] in *O'Toole v RTE* (1992),[21] a case where RTE (in the context of the section 31 orders banning spokesmen of, inter alia, Sinn Féin from the airwaves)[22] had refused to broadcast interviews with the chairman of a strike committee in Dublin on the grounds that he was a member of Sinn Féin. O'Hanlon J reasoned that the statutory obligation to present news and discussions of current affairs in a fair and impartial manner would, in his opinion, be breached if RTE acting on its own authority decided that it would not allow expressions of the views of any individuals based on the race, colour or creed of such person or persons. He would place in the same category a prohibition directed against membership of any organisation, such as Sinn Féin which was not a proscribed organisation. O'Hanlon J argued that while access to broadcasting time had to be regarded generally as a privilege and not as a right, he considered a decision by the RTE Authority to single out a particular person or group and impose a blanket prohibition against his, her or their views on any topic whatever, expressed in their personal capacity, would be difficult in law to justify. This was so having regard to the constitutional guarantees of freedom of expression contained in Article 40.6.1.i of the Constitution and the dominant position of RTE in radio and television.[23] In fact, the Supreme Court, on appeal, noted that the ban constituted an addition or amendment to the terms of the order rather than a method of implementing it.[24]

The statutory duty of objectivity and impartiality should ensure that there is at least a two-way dialogue, that more than one viewpoint in relation to matters, either of public controversy or the subject of current public debate, are available to the public audience. In a political sense, this duty mirrors a form of parliamentary democracy and of parliamentary debate.

Some doubt the capacity of the mass media to be objective and impartial. Majid Tehranian has argued that mediated communication is manufactured communication: mediated realities are reconstructed realities.[25] Tehranian submitted that professional neutrality in the mass media was a myth which has served as an ideology of self-justification for media institutions, professionals and their sponsors:

> [The myth of professional neutrality in the mass media] has mystified the fact that media institutions are no exception to any other institution in society; they serve the interests of those who control them. As A.J. Liebling aptly put it, "The freedom of the press belongs to those who have one!"[26]

A human being with his or her chequered emotions and multi-faceted personality will always find it difficult to achieve objectivity and impartiality. It is all the more difficult if an employer of media presenters has a fixed ideology. The concept of "fairness" and "impartiality" are subjective and difficult to enforce. But such concepts can be enforced on a-case-by-case basis. This has been the essence of the common law for centuries. The concept of fairness is not more difficult to apply as a guide to man's behaviour than the test for negligence, the public interest standard and the concept of the reasonable man.

The duty of the RTE Authority and of the private commercial broadcasting services in relation to impartiality[27] is qualified by reference to the statutory prohibition on the broadcasting bodies from including in any of their broadcasts or published material anything which may reasonably be regarded as being likely to promote, or incite to, crime or as tending to undermine the authority of the State.[28] Further, both the RTE Authority and any private commercial television service, but not surprisingly the private radio broadcasting services, are enjoined, inter alia, to uphold the democratic values enshrined in the Constitution.[29] Accordingly, taking the foregoing enjoiners into consideration, both RTE and any private commercial television service in Ireland could not in their broadcasts be neutral in any contest between democracy and dictatorship.

The impartiality obligation imposed on RTE[30] was considered by the Joint Committee on State-Sponsored Bodies in 1981.[31] The Committee, in its report, quoted extensively from the RTE staff guidelines on impartiality.[32] In any consideration of the fairness and impartiality obligations it is useful to note the guidelines of the national public broadcasting service:

> Broadcasting must generally reflect the mores and respect the values of the society in which it operates, acknowledging its standards of taste, decency and justice. It cannot, therefore, be just a channel for any and all opinions, nor can it be neutral in its basic philosophy and attitudes. It must, however, be impartial. It must seek to widen and deepen the knowledge of the audience in programming which includes such critical examination of public issues as is considered necessary to fulfil the needs of impartial objective enquiry.

The foregoing guidelines noted by the 1981 Committee were still current in 1993.[33] The 1981 Committee concluded that in controversial matters it was essential that "mainstream opinions get adequate representation on programmes" and that as a general rule *"pro* and *con* standpoints" should be presented in the same programme.[34]

The 1981 Committee received a number of complaints alleging breaches by RTE of its statutory duty to be objective and impartial

and to be fair to the interests of all concerned.[35] It is noteworthy that
the complaints received by the Committee related to the treatment
of sexual morality and religion.[36]

In the context of the disturbances in Northern Ireland, the 1981
Committee did disagree with the use of the word "killed" by RTE
newsreaders and journalists; the Committee considered that the
word "murdered" would more accurately describe what had taken
place.[37] Wesley Boyd, as Director of News, stated in evidence that
the word "killed" was regarded as a more neutral and acceptable
word in certain circumstances where it may not be clear that the
killing in question was murder.[38] Mr. Boyd stated that there was no
rigid rule on the issue and that quite often the matter was left to the
journalist covering the story to decide which word to use.[39]

The issue of the use of appropriate words used by RTE to describe
the actions of the IRA in Northern Ireland and elsewhere which
result in injury and death led to a renewed debate in the national
media in April 1993.[40] Dr. Conor Cruise O'Brien stated that the nub
of the matter was the avoidance of the word "terrorist" in relation to
people who planned and perpetrated the Warrington Bombings
(1993) where two boys died. RTE was reported to have stated: "We
have generally avoided using the word 'terrorist' because it goes
against the historical tradition in this country".[41] One agrees with
Dr. Conor Cruise O'Brien: we must call murder "murder" and use
the word "terrorist" to describe the IRA when appropriate.

The statutory obligations of objectivity and impartiality will
always be controversial.[42] The tongues of broadcasters are undoubtedly bridled by these statutory restrictions; the tongues of
broadcasters may also be bridled at the thought of any past or
possible future painful public encounters with regulatory
authorities in the form of inquiries or decisions of the Broadcasting
Complaints Commission.

In the context of the fairness and impartiality obligations in Irish
broadcasting law, reference may be made to the statutory provisions
in relation to party political broadcasts. Section 18(2) of the
Broadcasting Authority Act, 1960 provides that nothing in the section
which deals with the impartiality obligation shall prevent the RTE
Authority from transmitting political party broadcasts. The *Radio
and Television Act, 1988* contains a similar provision but with the
proviso that broadcasting contractors shall not, in the allocation of
time for such broadcasts, give an unfair preference to any political
party.[43] The wording of the statutory provisions in Ireland which
refers to "party political broadcasts" has avoided many of the

problems which have arisen in other jurisdictions in relation to broadcast time for candidates seeking office. Section 315 of the US *Federal Communications Act, 1934*[44] provided that if any licensee permitted any person who was a legally qualified candidate for any office to use a broadcasting station, he must afford equal opportunities to all other such candidates for that office in the use of such broadcasting stations. In 1959 the Federal Communications Commission in its *Lar Daly* decision,[45] affirmed by the Court of Appeals for the Seventh Circuit, held that a candidate's appearance on a regularly scheduled newscast was a "use" within the meaning of the 1934 Act and his opponents had a right to demand equal time at the same cost. The effect of that decision was to require three broadcasters to divide a total of 17 minutes and 44 seconds broadcast time among other candidates because Mayor Richard Daley had been shown performing various functions including accepting the Party nomination and greeting Venezuela's President at the local airport. Congress acted swiftly to amend the existing law and provided, *inter alia*, that an appearance of a legally qualified candidate on a bona fide broadcast was not to be deemed "use" of a broadcasting station within the appropriate regulatory framework.[46] In fact, the effect of that legislative provision operates in Ireland because although there is no similar statutory wording, the fairness and impartiality provisions in Irish law would apply to any broadcast exposure given to legally qualified candidates for public office.

In relation to a remedy by an aggrieved person who claims a breach of duty by a broadcasting service of its statutory duty to be objective and impartial, the Broadcasting Complaints Commission may investigate and decide on such a complaint.[47] Apart from finding in favour of a complainant, in so far as the complaint relates to a broadcast of inaccurate facts or information in relation to the complainant which constituted an attack on that persons's honour or reputation, then (unless the Commission otherwise directs) the Commission decision (including any correction of inaccurate facts or information) is to be broadcast at a time and in a manner corresponding to that in which the offending broadcast took place.[48]

Other remedies may be considered. The issue arises whether an aggrieved person could sue for damages for breach of statutory duty. In the context of the duties of objectivity and impartiality, there have been no reported cases in Ireland on that issue. The Attorney General could act (as guardian of the public interest) in so far as any breach of duty complained of affected the public in general.[49] However, in

Wilson v Independent Broadcasting Authority,[50] the Scottish Outer
House (Lord Ross) granted an interim interdict to three individuals
preventing the broadcast of relevant programmes stating that
section 2(2)(b) of the *Independent Broadcasting Authority Act, 1973*[51]
placed on the Independent Broadcasting Authority (IBA) a duty to
ensure that programmes broadcast by it maintained a proper balance
and that in the circumstances the IBA was prima facie in breach of
that statutory duty.

There have been several cases in Ireland where unsuccessful
attempts have been made to prevent RTE from broadcasting certain
information including parts of programmes.[52] In *O'Toole v RTE*[53]
(considered earlier in this chapter and in chapter 26), the statutory
duties of fairness and impartiality were relevant factors in O'Hanlon
J's decision in holding that it was unlawful for RTE to ban a member
of Sinn Féin from the airwaves in certain circumstances. Assuming
that in the relevant circumstances the absence of objectivity and
impartiality had affected particular persons (as distinct from the
public at large), an action would lie against the broadcasting services
in Ireland for damages for breach of statutory duty. A complainant
could also call in aid Article 40.3.2 of the Constitution (the obligation
on the State, inter alia, in its laws to vindicate the good name of every
citizen) and McCarthy J's dicta in *[X] v RTE*[54] that the constitutional
guarantee of the good name of every citizen might be vindicated in
damages. However, it would be difficult for a person to restrain
publication of a broadcast in advance in the light of the constitutional
guarantee of freedom of expression in Article 40.6.1.i.[55]

THE FAIRNESS DOCTRINE IN UNITED STATES

The Irish statutory obligations of objectivity and impartiality (the
Irish Fairness Doctrine) may be contrasted with the so-called
Fairness Doctrine in the United States. The US Doctrine was
determined by the Federal Communications Commission.[56] The
Fairness Doctrine required broadcast licensees to devote a
reasonable percentage of time to the coverage of public issues and
to cover those issues in a fair manner. In essence, the US Fairness
Doctrine required the presentation of contrasting points of view on
public issues. US Chief Justice Burger summarised the doctrine for
the US Supreme Court in *Columbia Broadcasting System Inc v
Democratic National Committee* (1973)[57] when he stated that the
Fairness Doctrine was

formulated under the Commission's power to issue regulations consistent with the public interest, the [Fairness] Doctrine imposes two affirmative responsibilities on the broadcasters: coverage of issues of public importance must be adequate and must fairly reflect differing viewpoints.[58]

In August 1987, the FCC abolished the Fairness Doctrine. The FCC concluded that the Fairness Doctrine contravened the First Amendment of the US Constitution (freedom of speech and press) and thereby disserved "the public interest".[59] The FCC based its conclusion on the following grounds:[60] (a) the Fairness Doctrine chills speech; (b) the Fairness Doctrine is not narrowly tailored to achieve a substantial governmental interest; (c) the changes in the electronic marketplace provide a basis for Supreme Court reconsideration of the diminished protection provided to the electronic media;[61] and (d) because the roles of print and electronic media are identical, the same First Amendment principles should be applied to each.[62]

Pursuant to a petition for review, the District of Columbia Circuit Court of Appeals held that the FCC's decision was neither arbitrary, capricious nor an abuse of discretion.[63] Denying the petition for review, the Court did not consider in any detail the fundamental issue of whether the Fairness Doctrine violated the First Amendment. The Court avoided the constitutional issue and did not preclude Congress from restoring the doctrine.

THE CONSTITUTIONALITY OF THE IRISH FAIRNESS DOCTRINE

Many of the arguments of the US Federal Communications Commission (considered above) could be applied in Ireland in the context of the constitutionality of the Irish objectivity and impartiality statutory obligations (the Irish Fairness Doctrine). In particular, it could be argued that the Irish provisions chill the right of citizens to express freely their convictions and opinions. Secondly, it could be argued (to a limited extent) that as the roles in society of the print and electronic media are comparable, the electronic media should not be subject to more stringent content regulation than the printed word.

In the context of the constitutionality of the Irish Fairness Doctrine, it is appropriate to call in aid the views of distinguished US judges whose views have been crystallised in the "seething cauldron" of the instant case. Judge Tamm in *National Broadcasting Co* (1974) argued, that properly understood, the US fairness doctrine was a balancing influence between the public's right of access to the broadcast media and the right of broadcast licensees to transmit their own message.[64] US Chief Justice Burger in *CBS v Democratic National Committee* (1973) dealt with the balancing concept. The Chief Justice submitted that the role of the Government as an "over-seer" and ultimate arbiter and guardian of the public interest and the role of the broadcaster as a journalistic "free-agent" called for a delicate balancing of competing interests.[65]

In an objective and absolute sense and examined strictly against the unequivocal wording of Article 40.6.1.i. of the Constitution of Ireland which provides that the State guarantees liberty, subject to public order and morality, of the right of citizens to express freely their convictions and opinions, it is difficult (at first) to justify the constitutionality of the fairness, objectivity and impartiality statutory provisions particularly when the printed media are not subject to such restrictions. However, the writer argues that such provisions are constitutional.

In an effort to seek arguments to sustain the view as to the constitutionality of the fairness, objectivity and impartiality provisions (subject to the comments below on their amendment), some comfort may be taken from Article 40.3.2 of the Constitution which provides, inter alia, that the State shall, in particular, by its laws protect as best it may from unjust attack and, in the case of injustice done, vindicate the person and good name of the citizen. But leaving aside the issue of one's good name, what is the justification in constitutional terms in insisting that in the broadcasting media, views on issues relating to current affairs must always be impartial? The public order and public morality qualifications in Article 40.6.1.i. are limited in scope: the adjective "public" is a significant qualification on "order"; public order refers to the maintenance and observance of law or constitutional authority. Undoubtedly some views in relation to matters of public controversy may raise public-order concerns. But, many issues in relation to matters of public controversy have nothing to do with public order. However, Article 40.6.1.i. refers to the education of public opinion being a matter of such grave import to "the common good". It could be argued that the fairness and impartiality obligations represent a delicate compromise between the freedom of expression rights of the broadcasters and the right of the public to be informed. Further, the acknowledgment of the people of Ireland in the preamble to the Constitution when enacting the Constitution to endeavour

> to promote the common good, with due observance of Prudence, Justice and Charity, so that the dignity and freedom of the individual may be assured, true social order attained, the unity of [the] country restored and concord established with other nations

would justify the implicit acceptance that all the constitutional guarantees must be examined in the light of the common good. Walsh J, writing extra-judicially, considered that the common good could have priority over the individual interest.[66] He noted that the common good includes the common conditions of personal and family security, peace, economic prosperity and public service which can best satisfy everybody's interests. In general, and subject to the views expressed below on their amendment, the statutory obligations of fairness, objectivity and impartiality come within the common-good standard and accordingly are constitutional.

Another argument in favour of the constitutionality of the fairness, objectivity and impartiality obligations and against an absolute interpretation of Article 40.6.1.i. is what may be described as the balancing-of-constitutional-rights approach. The approach of US Justice Frankfurter in his dissent in *Bridges*[67] is relevant to the interpretation of Article 40.6.1.i. Sowing the seed to another general approach to First Amendment cases (freedom of speech and of the press), Justice Frankfurter argued that other interests protected by the US Constitution were also at stake and that he would not give any special deference to the interests protected by the First Amendment:

> Free speech is not so absolute or irrational a conception as to imply paralysis of the means for effective protection of all the freedoms secured by the Bill of Rights. . . . In the cases before us, the claims on behalf of freedom of speech and of the press encounter claims on behalf of liberties no less precious.[68]

There is a compelling sense of logic in the approach of the United States Supreme Court in *Red Lion* (1969)[69] to the then so-called US Fairness Doctrine. The Court was concerned that without a Fairness Doctrine, broadcasters could exercise "unlimited private censorship" and have unfettered power to make time available only to the highest bidders, to communicate only their own views on public issues, people and candidates, and to permit on the air only those with whom they agreed.... Freedom of the press from governmental interference under the First Amendment [freedom of speech] does not sanction repression of that freedom by private interests.[70]

Although, at the time of writing, the US Fairness Doctrine has not been resurrected, the articulation by the Federal Communications Commission in 1949 on the significance of the Fairness Doctrine in the broadcasting of controversial issues of public importance is instructive:

The public has a paramount right in a free society to be informed and to have presented to it for acceptance or rejection the different attitudes and viewpoints concerning vital and often controversial interests which are held by the various groups which make up the community. It is the right of the public to be informed, rather than any right on the part of the Government, any broadcast licensee or any individual member of the public to broadcast his own particular views on any matter, which should be the foundation of the system of broadcasting.[71]

A multiplicity of voices should ensure the presentation of contrasting views, thus ensuring fairness and impartiality, leaving it up to the listener and viewer to make up his or her own mind. Judge Learned Hand (1943) observed that

right conclusions are more likely to be gathered out of a multitude of tongues, than through any kind of authoritarian selection. To many this is, and always will be, folly; but we have staked upon it our all.[72]

The same judge also wrote in 1952: "[W]e must not yield a foot upon demanding a fair field and an honest race to all ideas."[73] To achieve "a free trade in ideas",[74] there must be a market to which a person with ideas can have access. The US Supreme Court has stated that the purpose of freedom of speech and the press is to assure "the widest possible dissemination of information from diverse and antagonistic sources".[75]

In a medium which is not open to all, the obligation of fairness and impartiality should not give way to a form of private censorship. The system of checks and balances that once was confined to regulating governmental power should, in this context, include the broadcasting media. In this context, there is merit in the analysis of Jerome Barron: large private media interests act as private censors; wealth buys media access and communication power, and the marketplace of ideas may be overwhelmed by the wealthy. In that situation, the right of freedom of expression of most citizens is a right to listen and watch and the free and open debate necessary in a democracy goes unfulfilled.[76] Without the obligations of fairness and impartiality, the issues and points of view broadcast may represent the private interest of the broadcasters rather than the public interest. There is great merit in the dictum that "it is the right of the viewers and listeners, not the right of the broadcasters, which is paramount".[77]

The obligation to report news and matters of public controversy in an objective and impartial manner accords with accepted reputable journalistic practices and should not chill the speech of a broadcaster who acts in the public interest. The duty of being fair to all the interests concerned does ensure that alternative views are aired which does, in effect, create a diversity of viewpoints and maintain a check on monied interests obtaining access to unchallenged viewpoints. Thus, taking the common good into account, the restraints imposed by the fairness, objectivity and impartiality clauses of Irish broadcasting legislation, subject to the comments below on their amendment, do not infringe Article 40.6.1.i of the Constitution.

SUGGESTED STATUTORY AMENDMENTS

The concepts of fairness, objectivity and impartiality lie at the heart of public-service broadcasting. However, these obligations[78] as laid down at present are unduly onerous. There is merit in a qualification. Broadcasters should not be expected to be impartial between, for example, justice and injustice, tolerance and intolerance. Objectivity and impartiality should not require absolute neutrality on every issue or a detachment from fundamental democratic principles. In this context, the words of the preamble to the Constitution whereby the people of Ireland seek "to promote the common good, with due observance of Prudence, Justice and Charity, so that the dignity and freedom of the individual may be assured, [and] true social order attained" are worthy of consideration.

The unduly onerous nature of obligations could be overcome by the use of the adjective "due" which would qualify the concepts of fairness, objectivity and impartiality.[79] The word "due" is used here in the sense of proper or requisite. The concepts of fairness, objectivity and impartiality still stand, but the qualification of "due" would enable broadcasters to bear in mind, for example, the words of the preamble to the Constitution quoted above.

There may be circumstances where the obligations of objectivity and impartiality may not be necessary. If, for example, a licence for a local radio station (as distinct from a national radio service) were to be awarded to persons with the specific object of spreading the Christian gospel, the statutory obligations of fairness, objectivity, impartiality and the prohibition on editorialising[80] would cause legal difficulties for such a licensee. The prohibition on editorialising could, for example, prevent a local church that owned a radio station from broadcasting its own religious services. The legislature in the United Kingdom, after much deliberation,[81] overcame this difficulty by providing that due responsibility is to be exercised with respect to the content of religious programmes, and that in particular any such programmes do not involve any improper exploitation of any susceptibilities of viewers or listeners, or any abusive treatment of the religious views and beliefs of those belonging to a particular religion or religious denomination.[82]

31

Prohibition on Advertising in the Broadcast Media

Both RTE and the private broadcasting services are prohibited, *inter alia*, from broadcasting any advertisement which is directed towards any religious or political end or which has any relation to an industrial dispute.[1] This chapter will deal principally with these restrictions which do not apply to the printed media. There is also a considerable body of legislation that restricts, controls or otherwise affects advertising in Ireland. For example, the *Venereal Diseases Act, 1917*[2] makes it an offence to advertise in any way any preparation or substance of any kind as a medicine for the prevention, care or relief of venereal disease. However, these restrictions apply to all communications media and so are not peculiar to broadcasting. RTE and the Independent Radio and Television Commission set out these general restrictions in their respective comprehensive codes dealing with advertising in broadcasting services.[3]

The Government in 1960 rejected the recommendation of the Television Commission (1959) that there should be no additional restriction on advertising on television compared to advertising generally in any other medium in Ireland.[4] When establishing the Radio Éireann Authority pursuant to the *Broadcasting Authority Act, 1960*, the Minister for Posts and Telegraphs argued that the national broadcasting service should not be drawn into industrial or labour disputes.[5] The essence of the issue was expressed by the Minister for Posts and Telegraphs when he stated that if advertisements directed towards religious ends were permitted, the Authority would have to accept advertisements from any religious group including advertisements which the majority of viewers might consider "very objectionable and offensive".[6] The justification for the prohibition on advertisements directed towards political ends was based on the principle that the national broadcasting service should not be used in any way to further the interests of one party as against another.[7] The Minister accepted that many would argue that political parties should be free to advertise on television but he argued that there were "poor parties" that were entitled to representation in Ireland which would not be in a position to pay for an advertisement on television.[8] The Minister and his Department may have been influenced by the fact that the UK *Television Act, 1954*, which provided for the UK Independent Television Authority, specifically prohibited the broadcasting of advertisements that were directed towards any religious or political end or which had any relation to any industrial dispute.[9]

In the context of broadcast advertising, the 1974 *Broadcasting Review Committee Report* considered that because of its access to a mass audience, television was "a powerful advertising medium".[10] However, the 1974 Committee considered that advertising occupied too great a place in RTE's revenue and programming. The Committee was of the view that in a broadcasting service that relies on advertising for as large a proportion of its revenue as did RTE, programme planning and content were inevitably affected and the goals of range and balance become more difficult to attain.[11] However, with the exception of a reference to alcoholic drink, advertising aimed at young people and RTE's code of standards for advertisements, the 1974 Report did not make any specific recommendations in relation to the regulation of the content of broadcast advertising. The Committee considered the arguments for and against advertising on television. One argument against advertising was that a commercially influenced service was, in its own way, the counterpart of ideologically controlled services in the sense that it tended to reduce the ability of people to influence their society's development on truly democratic lines.[12] *The Annan Report* (UK 1977) summarised effectively the position of those who argue against advertising on broadcasting. Advertising was described as "an undesirable type of propaganda which cons the public, creates anti-social wants, promotes materialism, feeds off fears of sickness and off social envy, degrades the use of the English language and presents a stiflingly banal view of life".[13]

The principal argument in favour of advertising was stated in the Irish *Broadcasting Review Committee Report* (1974) as the imparting of information to the public as to the various choices available in goods and services as well as on such matters as road safety and health.[14] The Committee concluded that advertising on television should be restricted in regard to the times at which it is inserted in the programme schedule, and that the overall time devoted to it should be reduced.[15]

The issue of restrictions on broadcast advertisements arose again in the context of the private broadcasting services authorised pursuant to the *Radio and Television Act, 1988*. Official thinking on the issue had not changed in the intervening period between the *Broadcasting Authority Act, 1960* and the enactment of the 1988 legislation. The Minister for Communications argued that it would be inappropriate "to reduce spiritual values to pure commercial terms" and argued that in the context of the numerous religious sects in existence it would be in the public interest to prevent them exploiting the new broadcast media to propagate their messages.[16] Two years later the UK *Broadcasting Act, 1990* removed the ban on religious advertising which had been a feature of UK broadcasting legislation since the advent of commercial broadcasting. However, religious programmes, which include advertisements, must not involve any improper exploitation of the audience or of any abusive treatment of the religious views of others.[17] In relation to appeals for donations, the UK Independent Television Commission is obliged to draw up a code giving guidance (inter alia) on the rules to be observed.[18] In the context of political advertising, the Minister for Communications argued in 1988 that it would not be in the public interest or in the interests of democracy that "political ends should be sold across the broadcast media". The Minister argued that broadcast advertising in relation to industrial disputes would not generally be conducive to the fostering of good industrial relations or to the resolution of industrial disputes particularly where there might be "a wide disparity between the resources available to either side in any such dispute".[19]

The restrictions on the content of advertisements described above exceed the requirements laid down in the EC Council Directive on broadcasting.[20] Article 12 of the Directive which Member States were obliged to bring into force, as appropriate, not later than October 3, 1991 provides that television advertising shall not

(a) prejudice respect for human dignity;
(b) include any discrimination on grounds of race, sex or nationality;
(c) be offensive to religious or political beliefs;
(d) encourage behaviour prejudicial to the protection of the environment.

Article 13 of the Directive prohibits broadcast advertising for cigarettes and other tobacco products. The broadcast advertising for alcoholic beverages is regulated in Article 15. Certain rules relating to the protection of children and young persons are specified in Articles 16 and 22. Most of these prohibitions are contained in existing Irish legislation and codes of standards of RTE and the Independent Radio and Broadcasting Commission.[21]

In the context of freedom of expression and Article 40.6.1.i of the Constitution, commercial speech and advertising do deserve a measure of protection under the Constitution. It may be helpful here to adopt a definition of commercial speech as expression (spoken, written, printed, broadcast or otherwise) which "does no more than propose a commercial transaction"[22] or which "relate[s] solely to the economic interests of the speaker and its audience".[23] Commercial speech should not necessarily receive the same protection as ordinary speech, such as speech related to the exposition of thought and action. Accordingly, commercial speech may be regulated to a greater degree than ordinary speech;[24] false and misleading advertising, for example, should not receive constitutional protection.

Commercial speech and advertising are not synonymous. All advertising does not necessarily constitute commercial speech and perhaps vice versa. An advertisement could express social grievances and appeal for funds but would not constitute commercial speech and should receive greater protection in the context of Article 40.6.1.i than pure commercial speech.

The absolute restrictions on broadcast advertising in relation to any religious or political end in particular are difficult to justify in the context of Article 40.6.1.i of the Constitution. In view of the sensitivity of industrial disputes, of how easily words can inflame the participants, the prohibition on broadcast advertising in relation to an industrial dispute may be justified on the grounds of the common good.

In relation to the prohibition on religious advertising,[25] it is difficult, in constitutional terms, to justify how a novel containing sensational passages on sex and violence may be advertised in the broadcast media but not a children's book of bible stories. Broadcast advertising for religious lectures or exhibitions of Christian resources are also covered by the prohibition. The *News of the World* may be advertised but not *The Church Times*. It is possible to regulate religious advertisments by prohibiting any improper exploitation of the susceptibilities of viewers or listeners and any abusive treatment of the religious beliefs of others.[26] Equally, (subject to appropriate safeguards), it is difficult, in constitutional terms, to justify the absolute prohibition on advertisements directed towards a political end.[27]

The absolute prohibition on advertising in relation to any religious or political end violates Article 40.6.1.i of the Constitution.

32

Whither Now?

We have the entered the era of cyberspace. "Cyberspace" is a term (coined by novelist William Gibson in *Neuromancer*) which is used to describe the place without physical walls or indeed physical dimensions where telephone conversations occur, where electronic signals are routed, stored, and transferred both in real-time and delayed.

Increasingly, electronic impulses (the essence of telecommunication) are determining many facets of our lives. The fact that these impulses can be manipulated, modified and erased (often in cyberspace) is anathema to a legal system that is wedded to tangible things, and that relies on documentary evidence. We have separate legal "pigeonholes" for many aspects of telecommunication law — the carrier-related services, broadcasting and wireless telegraphy (radio). Yet signals, electronic impulses, in short, telecommunication, in a digital environment will not differentiate between wire, video and data. The electronic networks that operate today contain component parts of publishing, broadcasting and carrier-service telephony — but no one model applies. This hybrid demands new thinking. Ultimately, this may demand that a single unified statutory code should regulate all forms of telecommunication.

The architecture of the Constitution may need to be strengthened in an age reconstituted by the microchip. Professor Eli Noam in the first Ithiel de Sola Pool Memorial Lecture, (1990)[1] noted that computer networks and network associations acquire quasi-governmental powers as they necessarily take on such tasks as mediating their members' conflicting interests, creating their own rules of admission, access and expulsion, even establishing their own de facto taxing mechanisms. Professor Noam concluded that "networks become political realities".[2] Individual rights in such circumstances may need to be defended in the name of the Constitution.

Certain technologies may soon become indispensable to man. It may be that minimal access to basic telecommunication facilities may become as significant a constitutional right as the right to vote, access to the courts, or to primary education. Indispensability of telecommunication facilities (including broadcasting) should not, however, provide the Government with the right to impose unnecessary forms of regulation including, in particular, unnecessary forms of content regulation.

In the context of content regulation, however, some restrictions on the freedom of expression of broadcasters like, for example, the statutory obligations imposed on all the broadcasting services in Ireland of fairness, objectivity and impartiality[3] reflect a public-service commitment that is part of the constitutional dimension of being, in the words of Article 40.6.1.i of the Constitution, for the "common good" and are in accordance with the Constitution.

Other statutory restrictions such as the absolute prohibition on editorialising, the 20 per cent news and current affairs programming quota in the private radio broadcasting services, the absoluteness of the must-carry obligations on cable television and multi-point microwave distribution services[4] and the absolute prohibition on broadcast advertising in relation to any religious or political end infringe Article 40.6.1.i of the Constitution.[5]

Judges are sometimes inclined to the view that the use of modern technology involves the assumption of risk and somehow impairs the effect of a constitutional guarantee. Hamilton P held in *Kennedy v Ireland*,[6] the telephone tapping case, that the constitutional right to privacy included the right to hold private telephone conversations without deliberate, conscious and unjustified intrusion by the State. However, Hamilton P also reasoned that an "individual must accept the risk of interference with his communications". The assumption-of-risks argument in relation to the modern telecommunication technologies should not entail the watering down of any constitutional rights. There is merit in (US) Justice Harlan's *dictum*:

> Since it is the task of the law to form and project, as well as mirror and reflect, we should not . . . merely recite . . . risks without examining the *desirability* of saddling them upon society.[7]

Constitutional guarantees should not be shackled on mere technological grounds. A classic example of the shackles of technology restraining a constitutional guarantee is the case of *Olmstead v United States* (1928)[8] where the US Supreme Court held that telephone tapping involved no "search" or "seizure" within the meaning of the US Constitution's Fourth Amendment's prohibition on "unreasonable searches and seizure". The majority of the US Supreme Court argued that the Fourth Amendment "itself shows that the search is to be of material things — the person, his papers or his effects" and reasoned that "there was no searching" when a telephone in a suspect's house was tapped because the Constitution's language "cannot be extended and expanded to include telephone wires reaching to the whole world from the defendant's house or office". The Court reasoned that the intervening wires were not "part of his house or office any more than are the highways along which they are stretched".[9] *Olmstead* was overruled in 1967 in *Katz* when the US Supreme Court held that the Fourth Amendment applied to telephone tapping and electronic eavesdropping on the basis that the Fourth Amendment "protects people not places".[10] The US courts now accept that in the context of the First Amendment (freedom of speech), as well as the Fourth Amendment's purposes of protecting privacy, any invasion of a person's confidential telephone communications was a "search" with or without physical trespass.

   In the light of the comments on cyberspace and the difficulties (real and perceived) that modern processes of telecommunication pose for constitutional rights and guarantees, it is fitting to conclude this chapter and this book with a call for a constitutional amendment in Ireland.[11] A suggested constitutional amendment which could be inserted as a preface to the section entitled "Fundamental Rights" reads as follows:

   The rights, whether specified or unspecified, protected by this Constitution shall be construed as fully applicable without regard to the method or medium in relation to, or through which, communications, by whatever technological means, are originated, conveyed, stored or controlled.

Notes on Chapters

PART I: INTRODUCTION

1: *The Electronic Age*

1. *R & D in Advanced Communications Technologies for Europe (RACE)*, Communication from the Commission to the European Parliament and Council of Ministers, COM(93) 118, Brussels, 1993 pp. 1 and 2.
2. See *Tourism, Transport and Communications (Alteration of Name of Department and Title of Minister) Order, 1993* (S.I. No. 17 of 1993).
3. See *Broadcasting (Transfer of Departmental Administration and Ministerial Functions) Order 1993* (S.I. No. 13 of 1993) and *Gaeltacht, (Alteration of Name of Department and Title of Minister) Order 1993* (S.I. No. 22 of 1993).
4. *Many Voices, One World*, London, Kogan Page Ltd, UNESCO, 1988 preface, pp. xvii and xviii.
5. *Ibid.*
6. S. Handel, *The Electronic Revolution*, Middlesex, England, Pelican, 1967.
7. *Understanding Media*, Sphere Books Edition, London, 1968, p. 79.
8. Joint Committee on State-Sponsored Bodies, 18th Report, Radio Telefís Éireann, Dublin, Stationery Office, 1981, (Prl. 9945).
9. *Ibid.*, para 123.
10. *Ibid.*, para 124.
11. D.F. Wildman, in R. Abelman & S.M. Hoover (eds.), *Religious Television: Controversies and Conclusions*, Norword, NJ., Ablex, 1990, p. 275.
12. See First Supplementary Report of the Television Committee, 1956 in File S.14996A, *Television General*, National Archives, Dublin.
13. *Ibid.*
14. *Irish Television Drama*, RTE, 1987.
15. Wesley Burrowes, *The Riordans*, Dublin, 1977, p. 18.
16. Brother Vivian Cassells, *Irish Independent*, February 23, 1978.
17. *The Irish Times*, February 25, 1978.
18. Michael D. Higgins, "The Tyranny of Images", *The Crane Bag*, vol. 8, No. 2 1984, pp. 133 and 141.
19. *The Irish Times*, February 14, 1966.
20. *Evening Press*, February 16, 1966.

21. *Ibid.*
22. Maurice Earls, "The Late Late Show, Controversy and Context", in M. McLoone and J. McMahon, *Television and Irish Society*, Dublin, RTE/IF, 1984, p. 113.
23. See, for example, J. Bryant, (ed.), *Television and the American Family*, East Sussex and Hillsdale (US), Lawrence Erlbaum, 1990, and the authorities cited therein. See also M. Medved, *Hollywood v America*, New York and London, Harper Collins 1993.
24. See *The Times*, March 18, 1993.
25. *Broadcasting Guidelines for RTE Personnel*, RTE, 1989.
26. Anthony Comstock, *Traps for the Young*, New York, 1883.
27. Howard Rosenberg, "Nervous in the Naked City", *Media Studies Journal*, The Freedom Forum Media Studies Center, Columbia University, New York, Winter, 1992, p. 10.
28. See generally, Alexei Izyumov, "Raskolnikov's Regret: Covering Crime in Russia", *Media Studies Journal*, The Freedom Forum Media Studies Center, Columbia University, New York, Winter 1992, 183-194.
29. *Ibid.*
30. J. Bryant (ed.), *Television and the American Family, op. cit.*
31. Robert Abelman, "From The Huxtables to The Humbards: The Portrayal of Family on Religious Television", in J. Bryant (ed.), *Television and the American Family, op. cit.*, p. 166.
32. See Report of the President's Commission on Market Mechanisms, (The Brady Commission) (Washington DC: US Government Printing Office, January 8, 1988); *Fortune*, February 1988 p. 18; "Calculating Computers Role", *Washington Post*, November 29, 1987, pp. H1, H4-H5.
33. XXVII *Punch*, 1854, p. 143 quoted in Lord Asa Briggs, "The Pleasure Telephone", in Ithiel de Sola Pool, (ed.), *The Social Impact of the Telephone*, Cambridge, Mass, MIT Press, 1977, p. 50.
34. *Ibid.*
35. Mary Kelly, *Twenty Years of Current Affairs on RTE*, in M. McLoone and J. McMahon, (eds.), *Television and Irish Society*, RTE/IFI, 1984, p. 95.
36. Bernard Lynch, *A Priest on Trial*, London, Bloomsbury, 1993.
37. T.S. Eliot, "Burnt Norton", in *Four Quartets* (1935).
38. See chapter 7.
39. Telecomputer is the expression used by G. Gilder in *Life After Television*, New York, London, Norton & Co. 1992.
40. A. Toffler, *The Third Wave*, Pan Books, 1980.
41. T.S. Eliot, *The Rock*.
42. *Scientific American*, September 1991, p. 38.
43. George Orwell, *Nineteen Eighty-four*, London, Martin Secker & Warburg, 1949.
44. William Gibson, *Neuromancer*, Grafton Paperbacks, London, 1986.

45. *Scientific American*, September 1991, p. 112.
46. See generally, B. Clough and P. Mungo, *Approach Zero: Data Crime and the Computer Underworld*, London and Boston, Faber and Faber, 1992.
47. George Gilder, *Life After Television*, New York and London, W. Norton, 1992, p. 45.

PART II: THE DEVELOPMENT OF TELECOMMUNICATION IN IRELAND

2: *The Early Development of Telecommunication: The Telegraph*

1.   See generally the list of sources including the bibliography at the end.
2.   Referred to by William Tegg in *Posts and Telegraphs Past and Present*, London, William Tegg & Co., 1878, p. 144.
3.   Lettre sur un nouveau telegraphe, (An VI).
4.   Robert Britt Horwitz, *The Irony of Regulatory Reform*, Oxford University Press, 1989, p.91.
5.   *Voice Across the Sea*, William Luscombe Publisher Ltd, 1974, p. 22.
6.   The legal regulation of the telegraph companies is considered in chapter 8.
7.   14 & 15 Vict. c.118.
8.   See J.W. O'Neill, "Telecommunications in Ireland during the First Half of the Twentieth Century", The Institute of Electrical Engineers, Irish Branch, paper read in Trinity College, Dublin on February 15, 1951, p.4.
9.   *Voice Across the Sea*, William Luscombe Publisher Ltd, London, 1974, p. 35.
10. Henry Field, *History of the Atlantic Telegraph*, New York, 1865.
11. *Voice Across the Sea, op. cit.*, p. 63.
12. *Ibid.*, p. 62-63.
13. *Report of the Joint Committee appointed by the Lords of the Committee of Privy Council for Trade and the Atlantic Telegraph Company to inquire into the Construction of Submarine Telegraph Cables: together with the Minutes of Evidence and Appendix*, 1861, HMSO.
14. See D. de Cogan, (University of East Anglia), "From Technical Wonder to Profitable Investment: the Economics of North Atlantic Telegraphy", paper presented to the American Historical Association, Fall Meeting, Oct. 1986, not published.
15. Station diary at Heart's Content, Newfoundland (now in Provincial Archives of Newfoundland & Laborador); service letter, R. Collett to J. Dean, October 22, 1866.
16. See paper by D. de Cogan, (University of East Anglia), "Cable landings in and around Newfoundland", not published.
17. See D. de Cogan, "James Graves and the Valentia Telegraph Station", *Electronics and Power*, July 1984, and J. Graves, *36 years in the Telegraph*

Service, not published; the original manuscript is in the possession of the Graves family.

18.   Quoted by D. de Cogan in "James Graves and the Valentia Telegraph Station", *ibid.*

19.   "Ocean Telegraphy", *The Telegraphist*, December 1885, pp. 1, 2.

20.   D. de Cogan, "From Technical Wonder to Profitable Investment: the Economics of 19th Century North Atlantic Telegraphy", *loc. cit.*

21.   D. de Cogan, (University of East Anglia) "The Early History of British Empire Communications", not published.

22.   D. de Cogan, (University of East Anglia) paper entitled "An introduction to the technology of the Valentia Cable Station", 1986, not published.

23.   Chapter 8.

24.   (31 & 32 Vict. c. 110).

25.   See report by Frank Scudamore, *Re-organisation of the Telegraph System of the United Kingdom* (Cmnd. 304), HMSO, 1870.

26.   S. 4 of the Telegraph Act, 1869 (32 & 33 Vict. c. 73), still extant but amended by s. 8 of the *PTS Act, 1983.*

27.   *Scudamore, op. cit.,* p. 26.

28.   *Ibid.,* p. 32.

29.   *Ibid.,* p. 57.

30.   *Ibid.,* p. 86.

31.   *Ibid.,* p. 88.

32.   *Ibid.,* p. 89.

33.   *Special Report from the Select Committee on the Electric Telegraph Bill, 1868*, Parliamentary Papers, 1867-1868 Vol 11, col. 1864.

34.   See J. Kieve, *The Electric Telegraph: A Social and Economic History*, David and Charles, 1973, p. 178.

35.   See H.G. Swift, *A History of Postal Agitation*, 1929, p. 128.

36.   *Fortnightly Review*, December 1875, 833.

37.   See *Telegraph (Foreign Written Telegram) Regulations 1980 and 1981.*

3: *The Telephone and Radio Communication*

1.   Post Office records, *Telephone Companies Departmental Policy and History of Relations 1878-90*, E. 13267/1889, London.

2.   *Attorney General v Edison Telephone Company of London* (1880) 6 QBD 244.

3.   See J.W. O'Neill, "Telecommunications in Ireland during the final half of the 20th Century", I.E.E Branch paper, 1951 and A.J. Litton, "The Growth and Development of the Irish Telephone System", *Journal of the Statistical and Social Inquiry Society of Ireland*, 1961-62, p. 81.

4.   See *Litton, op. cit.,* p. 81.

5.   E. Davies, *Telecommunications, A Technology for Change*, HMSO, London, 1983, p. 16.

6.   Katherine M. Schmitt, "I'm your old Hello Girl", *Saturday Evening Post*, July 12, 1930, p.3.
7.   *Voice Across the Sea*, William Luscombe Publisher Ltd, London, 1974, p. 126.
8.   *Hansards Parliamentary Debates*, Fourth Series, v. 31, March 1, 1895, cols. 219-220.
9.   *The Times*, January 14, 1902, p. 7.
10.   *Historical Summaries of Post Office Services to 30 September 1906*, London, n.d., p. 53.
11.   *Ibid.*, p. 54.
12.   Post Office Records, London, C.7, Hicks Beach to A. Chamberlain, June 11, 1901.
13.   See *Litton, op. cit.*, p. 83.
14.   Modern Library Edition (1933).
15.   "The First and Only Century of Telephone Literature" in Pool (ed.), *The Social Impact of the Telephone*, M.I.T. Press, 1977, p. 213.
16.   Editorial, *The Irish Times*, December 10, 1908.
17.   The economic and political reasons are discussed in chapter 8.
18.   Paid pursuant to the *Telephone Transfer Act, 1911* (1 & 2 Geo 5 ch. 26), repealed by s. 7 of the *PTS Act, 1983*.
19.   See *Litton, op. cit.*, p. 85.
20.   File S.1342, "Military Action Against Irregulars, Postal and Telegraphic Communications", National Archives, Dublin.
21.   File S.6921, "Telephone Capital Bill, 1927", National Archives, Dublin.
22.   D. de Cogan, "The Commercial Cable Co. and their Waterville Station", *IEE History of Technology Weekend*, Trinity College, Dublin, July 1987, referring to Conor O'Brien, *From Three Yachts*; William Phillips, *Revolution in Ireland*, Longman, 1923; Robert Brennan, *Allegiance*, Browne & Nolan, 1950, p. 352.
23.   D. de Cogan, *op. cit.* in paper entitled "An introduction to the technology of the Valentia Cable Station" (1986).
24.   File S. 6921, *loc. cit.*
25.   León Ó Broin in *Just like Yesterday, An Autobiography*, Gill and Macmillan, (n.d.) p. 59.
26.   7 *Dáil Debates*, col. 2982, June 20, 1924.
27.   *Ibid.*
28.   *Ibid.*, col. 2983.
29.   File S.1908 entitled "Post Office Services, Transfer to Provisional Government 1922", National Archives, Dublin.
30.   See *loc. cit.*, n. 26.
31.   *Ibid.*, col. 2984.
32.   *Ibid.*, col. 2983.
33.   7 *Dáil Debates*, cols. 2979-2981, statement of Minister for Finance (Ernest Blythe) at Second Stage of *Telephone Capital Bill, 1924*.
34.   See report of interview of Irish Postmaster-General, James J. Walsh, with the British Postmaster-General held in London on February 8,

1922 in File S. 1908 "Post Office Services, Transfer to Provisional Government, 1922", National Archives, Dublin.

35. Speech of the President of the Executive Council in File S.1966 "General Post Office, Re-building 1929", National Archives, Dublin.

36. *Ibid.*

37. See *Litton, op. cit.*, p. 82.

38. J.W. O'Neill, "Telecommunication in Ireland during the first half of the twentieth century", *The Institution of Electrical Engineers*, Irish Branch, paper delivered at Trinity College, Dublin on February 15, 1951.

39. Message in tribute to Marconi read at the dinner of the Institute of Electrical Engineers, January 13, 1902, commemorating the first transatlantic wireless signal — recounted in O.E. Dunlap Jr, *Communications in Space*, Harper & Row, New York, 1962, p. 13.

40. J.W. O'Neill, *op. cit.*

41. See M. Gorham, *Forty Years of Irish Broadcasting*, The Talbot Press Ltd, 1967.

42. 7 *Dáil Debates*, col. 2984, June 20, 1924 (Second Stage of *Telephone Capital Bill, 1924*).

43. See "A simple guide to the electromagnetic spectrum and broadcasting" Appendix F in *Report of the Committee on Financing the BBC*, London, HMSO, Cmmd. 9824, 1986, pp. 168-176.

44. This technique is referred to as "radiodetermination" which is defined in the ITU Radio Regulations (1982) Article 1, para 10, as "determination of position, velocity and/or other characteristics of an object, or the obtaining of information relating to these parameters, by means of the propagation properties of radio waves".

45. See C.A. Codding and A.M. Rutkowski, *The International Telecommunication Union in a Changing World*, Artech House Inc., Washington DC, 1982, ch. 12, "Frequency Management".

46. See generally, Eugene Foster, *Understanding Broadcasting*, Addison-Wesley, Reading, Mass., 1982.

4: Telecommunication Carrier Services 1930-1993

1. 38 *Dáil Debates*, col. 127, April 22, 1931.

2. *Ibid.*, cols. 149-150.

3. *Ibid.*

4. Extract from Cabinet Minutes and associated papers in File S. 3157, National Archives, Dublin.

5. *Ibid.*, memorandum dated July 4, 1940 submitted by the Minister for Posts and Telegraphs to the Cabinet.

6. Memorandum entitled "Submarine Cables with Landing Places in An Saorstát" presented by the Department of Industry and Commerce and associated with Cabinet Minutes and other papers in File S. 3157, National Archives, Dublin.

7.   See File entitled "Communications — External and Internal; Emergency measures in the event of invasion or internal attack", File S. 11992 in National Archives, Dublin (Memorandum from the Department of the Taoiseach, dated December 16, 1941).

8.   See memorandum of the Departments of Defence and Post and Telegraphs dated February 8, 1941 entitled "Emergency Organisation" in File S.11992, National Archives, Dublin.

9.   Memorandum dated June 15, 1939 "Staffing of Censorship to be established in time of war" in File S.11306, "Censorship in Time of War — Organisation 1939, Establishment, Staff, etc," National Archives, Dublin.

10. Memorandum dated August 1939 "Postal and Telegraph Censorship" in File S.11306, *ibid*.

11. Memorandum dated January 25, 1941 in File S. 11586A, "Censorship of publications (including newspapers and periodicals)", National Archives, Dublin.

12. *Ibid*.

13. Article 2(1), (S.I. No. 20 of 1940).

14. *Emergency Powers (No. 359) Order, 1945*.

15. *Litton, op. cit.* pp. 86-87.

16. Memorandum from the Department of the Taoiseach dated December 16, 1941 in File No. S.11992, "Communications — External and Internal, Emergency Measures in the event of invasion and internal attack", National Archives, Dublin.

17. *Ibid*.

18. *Ibid*.

19. See León Ó Broin, Just like yesterday, An Autobiography (former Secretary to Department of Posts and Telegraphs) Gill and Macmillan, 1986.

20. *Ibid.*, p. 190.

21. *Ibid.*, p. 139.

22. Extract from minutes dated January 7, 1943 in File S.13086A "Telephone Developments Post-War Plans," Cabinet papers, National Archives, Dublin.

23. File S. 13086A, supra.

24. *Ibid*.

25. *Ibid*.

26. *Ibid*. See incidentally *Fitzsimons v Telecom Éireann* [1991] IR 536 where the plaintiff's husband was killed when he came into contact with loose telephone wires dangling from a pole.

27. Memorandum of Department of Posts and Telegraphs, dated November 16, 1944 in File S. 13086A, *ibid*.

28. File S. 13086B, "Telephone Developments, Post-War Plans", Cabinet Papers, National Archives, Dublin.

29. File S. 13086B, *ibid*.

30. Memorandum dated October 21, 1946 in File S. 13086B, *ibid*.

31. Memorandum dated October 18, 1946 in File S. 13086B, *ibid*.
32. *Ibid*.
33. Cabinet Minutes dated October 22, 1946 in File S. 13086B, *ibid*.
34. 103 *Dáil Debates*, cols. 200 *et seq*. October 23, 1946.
35. *Litton, op. cit*., p. 87.
36. 103 *Dáil Debates*, cols. 201-202, Minister for Posts and Telegraphs on the Second Stage of the *Telephone Capital Bill, 1946*, October 23, 1946.
37. 103 *Dáil Debates*, col. 369, November 6, 1946.
38. *J.W. O'Neill, op. cit*.
39. Memorandum dated February 23, 1951 in File S. 13086C "Telephone Developments, Post-War Plans", National Archives, Dublin.
40. Statement of Minister for Posts and Telegraphs on Second Stage of *Telephone Capital Bill, 1951*, 126 *Dáil Debates*, cols. 1014 and 1017.
41. *Ibid*., col. 940.
42. The Chancellor of the Exchequer, Michael Hicks Beach, noted in 1901 that "telephone communication was not desired by the rural mind". Post Office Records, London, C. 7, Hicks Beach to A. Chamberlain, June 11, 1901.
43. See n. 39 supra.
44. See *Litton, op. cit*., p. 88.
45. See *Litton, op. cit*., p. 90.
46. See *Litton, op. cit*., p. 91.
47. Report and Accounts for year ended April 2, 1987, Bord Telecom Éireann, p. 21.
48. 7 *Dáil Debates*, col. 2984, June 20, 1924.
49. See *Litton, op. cit*., p.89.
50. 206 *Dáil Debates*, col. 659, December 5, 1963, Minister for Posts and Telegraphs on Second Stage of the *Telephone Capital Bill, 1963*.
51. 269 *Dáil Debates*, col. 874, December 4, 1973, Minister for Posts and Telegraphs, Dr. Cruise O'Brien, on Second Stage of *Telephone Capital Bill, 1973*.
52. *Report of Posts and Telegraphs Review Group 1978-79*, Stationery Office, Dublin (Prl. 7883) para 4.5.
53. *Ibid*.
54. *Ibid*.
55. 159 *Dáil Debates*, col. 22, July 3, 1956, Mr. Keyes at the Second Stage of the *Telephone Capital Bill, 1956*.
56. *Just Like Yesterday, An Autobiography*, Gill and Macmillan, 1968, p. 163.
57. *Ibid*., p. 162.
58. *Ibid*., p. 163.
59. *Ibid*., p. 164.
60. *Ibid*.
61. *Ibid*.
62. 269 *Dáil Debates*, col. 869, December 4, 1973, on Second Stage of *Telephone Capital Bill, 1973*.
63. *Ibid*., col. 870.

64. *Ibid.*, cols. 870-871.
65. A. Mullen, "Digitalisation of the Telecommunications Network" in *Engineering in Telecom Éireann*, Bord Telecom Éireann, 1984, p. 1.
66. *Report of Post and Telegraphs Review Group 1978-1979*, presented to the Minister for Posts and Telegraphs, May 1979, Stationery Office, Dublin (Prl. 7883) p.1.
67. *Ibid.*
68. See *Mullen, op. cit.*
69. See *Mullen, op. cit.*
70. W. Fay, "The Irish Telex Network — An Overview" in *Technical Journal*, Bord Telecom Éireann, 1986, p. 11.
71. *Ibid.*
72. *Ibid.*, p.12.
73. *Telecommunications in Europe*, The European Perspectives Series, Commission of the European Communities, Brussels, 1988, p. 40. See also T.G. Drumm, "Switching Systems in the Irish Telephone Network" in *Engineering in Telecom Éireann*, Bord Telecom Éireann, 1984, pp. xiv, xv.
74. J.M. Dwyer, "The Provision of the Irish Digital Radio Link Network" in *Technical Journal*, Bord Telecom Éireann, Spring, 1986, p. 7.
75. *Ibid.*, p. 10.
76. T. Callendar, "New Telecommunications Services" in *Engineering in Telecom Éireann*, Bord Telecom Éireann, 1984 p. xvii.
77. B.T. Corkery, "The Eircell System" in *Technical Journal*, Spring 1987, Bord Telecom Éireann, p. 69.
78. See J.M. Dwyer, "The Provision of the National Digital Transmission Network" in *Engineering in Telecom Éireann*, Bord Telecom Éireann, 1984, p. xxxvi.
79. G. Devitt, "Optical Fibre Systems in Ireland" in *Technical Journal*, Spring 1987, Bord Telecom Éireann, p. 30.
80. *Ibid.*, p. 5.
81. T. Doyle and J. Styles, "The Portmarnock-Holyhead Optical Fibre Submarine Cable System" in *Technical Journal*, Spring 1987, Bord Telecom Éireann, pp. 3, 12.
82. See A.P.G. Ó Broin, "Videoconferencing Service Development", in *Technical Journal*, Spring 1987, Bord Telecom Éireann, p. 22.
83. See T. Doyle and J. Styles, "The PTAT-1 Transatlantic Submarine Cable". *Technical Journal*, Winter 1989/1990, Bord Telecom Éireann, p. 4.

5: Radio and Broadcasting

1. See R. Cathcart, *The Most Contrary Region: The BBC in Northern Ireland 1924-1984*, Belfast, The Blackstaff Press, 1984.
2. *Evening Telegraph*, Dublin, September 16, 1924.
3. See M. Gorham, *Forty Years of Irish Broadcasting*, Dublin, The Talbot Press Limited, 1967.

4.   *Ibid.*, pp. 23-24.
5.   *Ibid.*
6.   Both the Minister and the Secretary of the Department, P.S. O'Hegarty, were from Cork.
7.   38 *Dáil Debates*, col. 249, April 23, 1931.
8.   See File S.5111/11, "President's Speech at Opening of Athlone Broadcasting Station", February 6, 1933, National Archives, Dublin.
9.   *Ibid.*
10. *Ibid.*
11. M. Gorham, *Forty Years of Irish Broadcasting*, Dublin, The Talbot Press, 1967, p. 132.
12. File S.11992 entitled "Communications - External and Internal, Emergency Measures in the event of invasion or internal attack", National Archives, Dublin.
13. *Ibid.*
14. *Ibid.*
15. *Ibid.*
16. *Ibid.*
17. *Ibid.*
18. *From Semaphore to Satellite*, ITU, Geneva, 1965, p. 193.
19. See memorandum for the Government entitled "Television" dated March 15, 1951 in File S. 14996A, National Archives, Dublin.
20. Communication dated April 20, 1951 in File S. 14996A, *loc. cit.*
21. *Ibid.*
22. *The Irish Times*, January 1, 1962, p. 3. The full text of the President's speech is reproduced in Appendix 1 of M. McLoone and J. McMahon (eds.), *Television and Irish Society*, Dublin, RTE-IFI, 1984.
23. A.P.G. Ó Broin, "Cable Television Networks at Limerick and Shannon" in *Technical Journal*, Spring 1987, Dublin, Bord Telecom Éireann, p. 36.
24. See *O'Keeffe v An Bord Pleanála*, [1992] ILRM 237.
25. C. Corbett, "History of the [Aviation Communications] Service 1936-1986" in S. O'hAllmhurain and Aviation and Marine Radio Officers Association, (eds.), *Aviation Communications Service 1936-1986*, 1986.
26. *Ibid.*, p. 8.
27. *Ibid.*, p. 30.
28. *Ibid.*, p. 34.
29. Statistics from the Department of Transport, Energy and Communications, Shanwick Radio, Co. Clare.

6: *Telecommunication via Satellite*

1. *From Semaphore to Satellite*, ITU Geneva, 1965 p. 291.
2. J.M. Dwyer, "The Role of Satellite Communications in the Development of the Irish Telecommunications Network 1984/1986", Dublin, Department of Posts and Telegraphs, 1983.
3. For a brief outline of the development in Ireland of telecommunication satellite services, see J.M. Dwyer, "Communications via Satellite" in *Engineering in Telecom Éireann*, Dublin, Bord Telecom Éireann, 1984.
4. J.M. Dwyer, "Communications Via Satellite" *ibid.*, p. xxxvii.
5. L.M. Garvey, "The Elfordstown Earth Station" in *Technical Journal* Spring 1987, Dublin, Bord Telecom Éireann. In the annual *INTELSAT Earth Station Performance Report* (1985) Elfordstown was ranked as No. 1 among the 301 earth stations covered by the Report. The No. 1 ranking was the result of a 100 per cent record of availability and continuity of service during 1985.
6. *Garvey, loc. cit.*, p. 70.
7. *Green Paper on the Development of the Common Market for Telecommunications Services and Equipment*, Brussels, Commission of European Communities, COM (87) 290 final p. 39.
8. See Statement on behalf of the Department of Communications dated December 10, 1986, issued by the Government Information Services.

7: *Current Developments in Telecommunication*

1. Herbert Ungerer, *Telecommunications in Europe*, European Perspective Series, Commission of the European Communities, Brussels, 1988 p. 49.
2. See J. Ryan, "Field Trial with Integrated Service Digital Network (ISDN) in Telecom Éireann", in *Technical Journal*, Winter 1989/1990, Dublin, Telecom Éireann, p. 64.
3. *Simplification of International Trade Procedures Board* (SITPRO): document (88) 06.
4. *Ungerer, op. cit.* p. 58.
5. Council Decision of October 5, 1987 introducing a communications network, Community programme on trade electronics data interchange system (TEDIS), 87/449/EEC, OJ.L. 285, 8.10.1987.
6. This service is regulated by the *Telecommunications Scheme, 1992* (S.I. No. 19 of 1992).
7. *Ibid.*
8. See T. Johnston, "Expert Systems and Public Policy," in *Inter Media*, Journal of the International Institute of Communications, July-September 1984, vol. 12, p. 43.
9. *Report of the Committee on Financing the BBC*, London, 1986, HMSO, Cmnd. 9824, p. 174.

10.   See consideration of the submission of Peter Jay and others in the
       Report of the Committee on Financing the BBC, loc. cit. pp. 112-115.
11.   *Report of the Committee on Financing the BBC,* loc. cit p. 113.
12.   *Marconi Wireless Telegraph Company of America v United States,* 320 US
       809 (1943).

PART III: THE REGULATION OF
TELECOMMUNICATION IN IRELAND: DEVELOPMENT
AND OVERVIEW

8: *Development and Regulation of Telecommunication up to 1922*

1.   Repealed by s. 7 of the *PTS Act, 1983.*
2.   The *Telephone Capital Acts 1924 to 1977* and the *Telecommunication
      Capital Act, 1981* are cited together as the *Telecommunications Capital
      Acts 1924 to 1981.* See section 4(2) of the 1981 Act. The term
      "telecommunications" in this legislation appears to relate only to the
      telephone, telex and related means of telecommunication. However,
      this is not so stated in the legislation.
3.   Annex 1 of the *Constitution of the International Telecommunication Union,*
      Nice, 1989, published by the General Secretariat of the ITU, Geneva,
      1989. A similar definition is contained in the Canadian Federal
      Interpretation Act R.S.C. 1970, c.1-23, s.8. Aspects of the term "tele-
      communication" are defined in *Council Directive of 28 June 1990 (Tele-
      communication Services) 90/387 EEC,* Article 2.
4.   26 and 27 Vict. c.112, s.3.
5.   32 and 33 Vict. c.73, s.3.
6.   *Ibid.,* s. 3.
7.   *Telegraph Acts 1863 to 1916;* this collective citation is referred to in s.
      2(2) of the *PTS Act, 1983.*
8.   *AG v Edison Telephone Company of London* (1880) 6 QBD 244.
9.   *AG v Edison Telephone Co. of London* (1880) 6 QBD 244 where it was held
      that a telephone is a "telegraph" within the meaning of the *Telegraph
      Acts of 1863 and 1869.* See also the judgments of the Divisional Court,
      King's Bench Division, Gibson, Madden and Kenny JJ in *Postmaster
      General v Great Southern & Western Railway Co.,* unreported, January
      31, 1910. This case is considered in chapter 25.
10.   See *Edison,* supra, at p. 249 where the Court considered that "any
      apparatus for transmitting messages by electric signals is a telegraph,
      whether a wire is used or not". See also the definition of "wireless
      telegraphy" in s.2 of the *Wireless Telegraphy Act, 1926,* as amended by
      s. 2(1)(b) of the *Broadcasting and Wireless Telegraphy Act, 1988* and see
      Re Regulation and Control of Radio Communication in Canada [1932] AC
      300, 316 (PC).

11. See *Re Regulation and Control of Radio Communication in Canada* [1932] AC 300 (PC) at pp. 315, 316. Professor P.S. Atiyah in his Chorley Lecture 1984 entitled "Common Law and Statute Law" (1985) 48 *MLR* 1, 19 describes the *Edison Telephone Co* case and the Privy Council ruling in *Re Regulation and Control of Radio Communication in Canada* as courageous decisions, being examples of dramatic statutory construction which are difficult to reconcile with the traditional canons of interpretation. He argues that they could easily be justified "if the Court had the power to extend statutes by analogy". This issue is discussed further in chapter 25.

12. See chapter 10.

13. See *Dickson v Reuters Telegrams Co* (1877) 3 CPD 1, 7 (CA), where Bramwell LJ expressed the view that telegraph companies were not common carriers. In *MacAndrew v Electric Telegraph Co* (1855) 17 CB 3 it was assumed, but not decided, that telegraph companies might be called carriers or bailees of the telegrams.

14. 154 US 1, 14 (1893).

15. 31 & 32 Vict. c.110 still in force, as amended by ss. 7 & 8 of the *PTS Act, 1983*.

16. 31 & 32 Vict. c.110, s. 4.

17. 32 & 33 Vict. c.73.

18. S. 4 as amended by the *PTS Act, 1983*, s.8.

19. See A.J. Litton, "The Growth and Development of the Irish Telephone System" in *Journal of the Statistical and Social Inquiry Society of Ireland 1961-1962*, pp.79 to 115.

20. See, for example, *Commission Directive of 16 May 1988 on competition in the markets for telecommunications terminal equipment*, OJEC, No.L, 131/73, 27.5.88; *Council Directive of 28 June 1990 on the establishment of the internal market for telecommunications services through the implementation of open network provision* (90/387/EEC) OJEC, No. L. 192/1, 24.7.90, and *Commission Directive of 28 June 1990 on competition in the markets for telecommunication services* (90/388/EEC) OJEC, No. L. 192/10 (24.7.90).

21. 55 Geo. 3 c. 128.

22. *Report from the Select Committee on Railway Communication*, July 1840, S.C.R. 1840, p.8.

23. 7 & 8 Vict. c.85, ss. 13 and 14.

24. S. 13, *ibid*.

25. S. 14, *ibid*.

26. 9 Vict c. xliv. In April 1848 these powers were exercised to obstruct the chartist lines of communication.

27. See notes 41, 42, 43 *infra*.

28. 13 & 14 Vict. c 186, Private Act.

29. 14 & 15 Vict. c. 118 Private Act. By 1850 in Ireland there were 500 miles of railway but no telegraph. See J. Kieve, *The Electric Telegraph — A Social and Economic History*, Newton Abbot, David & Charles, 1973.

The British Electric Telegraph Company and the English and Irish Magnetic Telegraph Company amalgamated in 1857 to form the British and Irish Magnetic Telegraph Company, generally called "the Magnetic". This was a limited liability company under the *Joint Stock Act, 1856.*

30. See, for example the *Railways Clauses Consolidation Act, 1845* (8 & 9 Vict. c. 20), *Gasworks Clauses Act, 1847* (8 & 9 Vict. c. 15), and the *Waterworks Clauses Act, 1847,* (10 & 11 Vict. c. 17).
31. 18 & 19 Vict. c.cxxiii, s. 10.
32. *Electric Telegraph Act, 1862* (25 & 26 Vict).
33. CXXXI, s. 74.
34. See, for example, 166 *Hansard,* col. 2090, May 23, 1862, when Lord Redesdale presented petitions complaining of the powers of the electric telegraph companies.
35. *Ibid.,* cols. 2091-2092.
36. 26 & 27 Vict. c.122.
37. *Telegraph Acts 1863 to 1916.*
38. 26 & 27 Vict. c.122, s. 6.
39. *Ibid.,* ss. 8-25.
40. *Telegraph Act, 1868,* (31 & 32 Vict. c.110) s.2; *Telegraph Act, 1892* (55 & 56 Vict. c.59) s.5; *Ministers and Secretaries Act 1924,* s.1 (ix).
41. S. 52 as amended by s.8 of the *PTS Act, 1983.*
42. *Wireless Telegraphy Act, 1926,* s. 10.
43. *Broadcasting Authority Act, 1960,* s. 16(3)(b) and s. 4(11) of the *Radio and Television Act, 1988.*
44. *Quarterly Review* (1854), vol. 95 pp.149-151.
45. John Lewis Ricardo, MP for Stoke, one-time Chairman of the Metropolitan Railway and a director of the London and Westminster Bank submitted a memorandum to the Chancellor of the Exchequer entitled "In Support of the Expediency of the telegraphic communications being in the hands of H.M. Government and administered by the Post Office"; *British Parliamentary Papers* 1867-8, vol. 41,48.
46. Lord Stanley of Alderley, Postmaster-General, 152 *Hansard,* Third Series, March 4, 1859, Lords, cols. 1262-1263.
47. J. Morley, *The Life of William Ewart Gladstone,* vol. 2, London, 1903, p. 182.
48. See *British Parliamentary Papers,* 1867 vol. 41, 51 *et seq.*
49. *British Parliamentary Papers,* 1867 vol. 41, p.3 *et seq.*
50. *Ibid.*
51. 31 & 32 Vict. c.110. The preamble to an Act of Parliament is often enlightening. Termes de la Ley has stated that the preamble to a statute "is a key to open the minds of the makers of the Act, and the mischiefs which they intend to remedy by the same". See *Sussex Peerage Case,* 11 Cl & F 143; *per* Lord Blackburn; *Westham v Iles,* 8 App. Cas. 388.
52. 191 *Hansard,* cols. 678-682, April 1, 1868.

53. *Ibid.*
54. S. 4 of *Telegraph Act, 1868* (31 & 32 Vict. c. 110), repealed by s. 7 of the *PTS Act, 1983.*
55. S. 8 of 1868 Act, repealed by the *Statute Law Revision (No. 2) Act, 1893* (56 Vict. c. 14).
56. 31 & 32 Vict. c. 110.
57. *Railway Times*, Third Series, April 18, 1868, pp. 428-9.
58. 192 *Hansard*, col. 1978, June 23, 1868; 193 *Hansard* Third Series cols. 1563-1564, July 21, 1868.
59. *Report of Posts and Telegraphs Review Group, 1978-1979*, Dublin Stationery Office (Prl.7883).
60. *Ibid.*
61. Pamphlet entitled *Government and Telegraphs — Statement of the case of the Electric and International Telegraph Company against the Government Bill for Acquiring Telegraphs*, May, 1868.
62. 198 *Hansard*, Third Series, col. 767, July 26, 1869.
63. 198 *Hansard*, cols. 1135-1136, August 3, 1869.
64. *Ibid.*, cols. 1136-1137.
65. *Investors Guardian*, July 10, 1865.
66. 32 & 33 Vict. c.73. The preamble was repealed by the *Statute Law Revision (No. 2) Act, 1893*, (56 & 57 Vict. c.14).
67. The expression "telegram" is defined in s. 3 of the *Telegraph Act, 1869* (32 & 33 Vict. c.73) as meaning any message or other communication transmitted or intended for transmission by a telegraph. The term "telegraph" is defined in section 3 of the *Telegraph Act, 1863* (26 & 27 Vict. c.112) as amended by s.3 of the *Telegraph Act, 1869* (32 & 33 Vict. c. 73) as including "any apparatus for transmission of messages or other communications by means of electric signals". A conversation through the telephone is a "message" or at all events "a communication transmitted by a telegraph" and therefore a "telegram". See *AG v Edison Telephone Co* (1880) 6 QBD. 244. Electro-magnetic energy is the basis for transmission of all forms of telecommunication.
68. Exceptions were set out in s. 6 of the *Telegraph Act, 1869* (32 & 33 Vict. c. 73).
69. *Ministers and Secretaries Act, 1924* and Eighth Part of Schedule to the Act.
70. As amended by s. 8 of the *PTS Act, 1983.*
71. S. 7 of Act, repealed by s. 7 of the *PTS Act, 1983.*
72. S. 10 of 1869 Act repealed by s. 7 of the *PTS Act, 1983.*
73. 41 & 42 Vict. c. 76.
74. Ss. 3 and 4 of *Telegraph Act, 1878* (41 & 42 Vict. c. 76) as amended by s. 8 of the *PTS Act, 1983.*
75. S. 8 of the 1878 Act as amended by s. 8 of the *PTS Act, 1983.*
76. Evidence of Sir John Cameron Lamb, Assistant Secretary of the Post Office in *Report from the Select Committee on the Telephone Service*, HMSO, July 1895, p.1.

77. *Ibid.*, p.21, licences were provided for in s. 5 of the *Telegraph Act, 1869* (32 & 33 Vict. c.73) now repealed by s. 7 of the *PTS Act, 1983*.
78. *AG v Edison Telephone Company of London* (1880) 6 QBD 244.
79. *Edison* case, *ibid.*, p. 258.
80. Memorandum dated March 6, 1880 contained in Enclosure LIV, Telephone Policy, Bundle R, (1880-91) *Telephone Policy Box* C.22, Post Office Central Archives, Post Office, London.
81. See *ibid.*, Treasury letter, 21421, December 16, 1880.
82. Evidence of Sir Robert Hunter, Solicitor to the Post Office, Minutes of Evidence, *Report from Select Committee on Telephones*, HMSO, 1898, p.2.
83. *Ibid.*, col. 40 p.4.
84. Post Office Records, London, Post 30/542, E 13267/1889, Treasury to Post Office, December 16, 1880.
85. See Henry Fawcett, "Modern Socialism" in *Essays and Lectures*, London, 1872.
86. Post Office Records, London, Post 30/603, E4522/1892, Treasury to Postmaster-General, July 24, 1882.
87. Post Office Records, London Post 30/542, E 13267/1884, Treasury to Post Office, November 11, 1882.
88. 272 *Hansard*, Third Series, July 17, 1882.
89. Post Office Records, London, Post 30/603, E 4522/1892, Treasury to Postmaster-General, June 25, 1883.
90. *Ibid.*
91. Evidence of Sir Robert Hunter, Solicitor to the Post Office; *Report from Select Committee on Telephones*, HMSO, 1898.
92. *Ibid.*, p. 3.
93. *Ibid.*
94. Post Office Records, London, Bundle R. File 70, Treasury to Post Office, June 27, 1890.
95. *Ibid.*
96. Evidence of Sir Robert Hunter, Solicitor to the Post Office; *Report from the Select Committee on Telephones*, HMSO, 1898, col. 49, p. 4.
97. 55 & 56 Vict c. 59.
98. The agreement was dated March 25, 1896 and is set out in E.G.M. Carmichael, *The Law relating to The Telegraph, The Telephone and Submarine Cable*, London, Knight & Co, 1904, Appendix A.
99. Under the licence granted by the Postmaster-General to the company in 1884.
100. Agreement between Postmaster-General and National Telephone Company Ltd dated March 25, 1896, *loc. cit.*
101. Evidence of Sir Robert Hunter, *loc. cit.* col. 51.
102. *Report from the Select Committee on Telephones*, HMSO, 1898, p.ii.
103. *Ibid.*, p. vii.
104. *Ibid.*, p.xiii.
105. *Ibid.*
106. 62 & 63 Vict. c. 38.

107. 75 *Hansard* (Lords) col. 1244, August 3, 1899.
108. S. 7 of *PTS Act, 1983*.
109. 75 *Hansard* (Lords) col. 1245, August 3, 1899.
110. *Kieve, op. cit.*, p.213.
111. See H. Parris, *Constitutional Bureaucracy*, Allen and Unwin, London, 1969, pp. 103-4.
112. See memorandum entitled "As to the Proposed Position with the National Telephone Company", Telephone Policy Bundle "N", *Telephone Policy Box C. 23*, Post Office Central Archives, London.
113. 73 *Hansard* (Commons), col. 129, June 20, 1899.
114. *Ibid.*
115. 189 *Hansard* (Commons), col. 1816, June 2, 1908.
116. *Ibid.*, col. 1815.
117. 1 & 2 Geo. 5 c. 39.
118. 1 & 2 Geo 5 c. 26.
119. 28 *Hansard* (Commons) col. 1512, August 11, 1911.
120. See A.J. Litton "The Growth and Development of the Irish Telephone System" in *Journal of the Statistical and Social Inquiry Society of Ireland*, 1961-62.
121. 6 & 7 Geo 5 c. 40.
122. 85 *Hansard* (Commons), col. 264, August 1, 1916.
123. *Ibid.*, col. 272.
124. S. 22(4)(a) and Schedule 5 of *Courts (Supplemental Provisions) Act, 1961*.

9: *The Regulation of Telecommunication Carrier Services 1922-1993*

1. See File S. 1933, "Posts and Telegraphs, Proposed Termination of Ministry, 1922", National Archives, Dublin.
2. *Ibid.*, memorandum dated January 8, 1923.
3. S. 1(ix) and Eighth Part of the schedule.
4. *Ibid.*
5. 10 & 11 Geo V. c. 67.
6. Memorandum dated April 28, 1926 to President of Executive Council in File S.4174, "P.O. Proposed Transfer of P.O. Services in Six Counties to Belfast Government", National Archives, Dublin.
7. *Ibid.*, memorandum dated December 24, 1924.
8. *Ibid.*
9. The last telecommunication legislation to receive the King's Assent was the *Telephone Capital Act, 1936*. The 1936 Act was also the first Act passed by the Dáil alone consequent on the abolition of the Seanad. The *Telephone Capital Act, 1938* was also the first telecommunication legislation to be signed by the President of Ireland.
10. The collective citation of *Telecommunications Capital Acts 1924 to 1981* was authorised by s. 4(2) of the *Telecommunications Capital Act, 1981*. Prior to the 1981 Act, the designation *Telephone Capital Acts* had been used.

11. See, for example, s. 2 of the *Telephone Capital Act, 1951* (No. 19 of 1951).
12. Ss. 3 and 4 of the Telephone Capital Act, 1924. Provisions similar to ss. 3 and 4 of the *Telephone Capital Act, 1927* as amended by s. 3(2) of the *Telephone Capital Act, 1963* were incorporated in each *Telephone Capital Act*, since 1927 including the *Telecommunications Capital Act, 1981*.
13. 328 *Dáil Debates*, col. 3058, May 14, 1981, Minister of State at the Department of Posts and Telegraphs on Second Stage of the *Telecommunications Capital Bill, 1981*.
14. 48 & 49 Vict. c. 58 s. 2.
15. S. 1(ix) and Eighth Part of Schedule of *Ministers and Secretaries Act, 1924*.
16. *Ibid.*, s. 1(ii) and First Part of Schedule.
17. S. 2 of the 1885 Act used the expression "telegram" and "telegraph" and see definitions of "telegram" and "telegraph" *supra*. The term "telegram" includes any communication sent by any form of electronic telecommunication technology.
18. S. 7 of the 1983 Act which provided that the repeal was to have effect from vesting day, January 1, 1984.
19. S. 92 of 1983 Act.
20. S.I. No. 19 of 1992 and amendments thereto.
21. See schedules to the *Telecommunications Scheme, 1992* (S.I. No. 19 of 1992) as amended by the *Telecommunications (Amendment) (No.4) Scheme, 1993* (S.I. No. 249 of 1993).
22. See Article 37 *ibid*.
23. Article 16 *ibid*.
24. Article 15 *ibid*.
25. S. 13 of the 1951 Act was amended and penalties were increased by ss. 4 and 8 of the *PTS Act, 1983*.
26. S.R.O. No. 62 of 1942.
27. See background details in File S. 14946 A2, D/T, "Post Rates General, Telegraph Bill, 1953", National Archives, Dublin.
28. See. S. 1 of *Telegraph Act, 1928*; s. 16 of the *Telegraph Act, 1868* as amended by the *Post Office and Telegraph Act, 1915*.
29. S. 7 of the *PTS Act, 1983*.
30. One muses whether the Government was influenced by the philosophy enunciated by Adam Smith in *The Wealth of Nations*, Book V, Chapter II Part 1:
    > In every great monarchy of Europe the sale of the crown lands would produce a very large sum of money, which if applied to the payment of the public debts, would deliver from mortgage a much greater revenue than any which those lands would have ever afforded to the crown.... When the crown land had become private property, they would in the course of a few years, become well improved and well cultivated."
31. *Investment Plan 1981* laid by the Government before each House of the

Oireachtas, January 1981, Dublin, Stationery Office, (Prl 9471).

32. *Ibid.*, para 2.67.
33. *Ibid.*
34. *Ibid.*, para 2.68.
35. 326 *Dáil Debates*, col. 1056, February 4, 1981, speech of Minister for Posts and Telegraphs, Albert Reynolds, on Budget Debate.
36. 96 *Seanad Debates*, col. 434, Second Stage of *Irish Telecommunications Investments Bill, 1981*, October 29, 1981, Patrick Cooney, the Minister for Posts and Telegraphs.
37. Clause 2(vi) of Memorandum of Association of Irish Telecommunications Investments Ltd.
38. Clause 2(xii) *ibid.*
39. *Companies Act, 1963*, s. 33.
40. Minister for Posts and Telegraphs, 96 *Seanad Debates*, col. 434 (1981) on Second Stage of *Irish Telecommunications Investments Limited Bill, 1981*.
41. 330 *Dáil Debates*, col. 1352, November 5, 1981, Albert Reynolds, then in opposition and 330 *Dáil Debates*, col. 1360, Minister for Posts and Telegraphs, Patrick Cooney, November 5, 1981.
42. 96 *Seanad Debates*, col. 440, October 29, 1981.
43. John Stanley in "Privatisation: Just Political Posturing", *The Irish Times*, October 19, 1981.
44. M. Godet & O. Ruyssan, *The Old World and the New Technologies*, European Communities, Commission, Luxembourg, 1981, p.12
45. See *Report of Posts and Telegraphs Review Group 1978-1979* presented to the Minister for Posts and Telegraphs, May 1979, Dublin, Stationery Office, (Prl. 7883).
46. A.N. Holcombe, *Public Ownership of Telephones on the Continent of Europe*, London, Constable & Co. Ltd, Houghton Mifflin Company, 1911.
47. *Ibid.*, p. 444.
48. *Report of Public Services Organisation Review Group 1966-1969*, Stationery Office, 1969. Chairman: Liam St. John Devlin.
49. 269 *Dáil Debates*, col. 880, December 4, 1973, on Second Stage of *Telephone Capital Bill, 1973*.
50. *Report of Posts and Telegraphs Review Group 1978-1979*, presented to the Minister for Posts and Telegraphs, May 1979, Stationery Office, (Prl 7883), p.6.
51. *Ibid.*, p.1.
52. *Ibid.*, p.2.
53. *Ibid.*, p.4.
54. *Reorganisation of Postal and Telecommunications Services*, laid by the Government before each House of the Oireachtas, May 1980, Dublin, Stationery Office (Prl 8809).
55. *Reorganisation of Postal and Telecommunications Services*, laid by the Government before each House of the Oireachtas, May, 1981, Dublin,

Stationery Office, (Prl 9805).

56. Department of Tourism, transport and Communications, *Telecom Inquiry*, Dublin, Stationery Office, 1991.

57. John A. Glackin, *Chestvale Properties Limited and Hoddle Investments Limited*, Interim Report, July 1992 (Pl. 9061) and Final Report, July 1993 (Pl. 9989), Dublin, Stationery Office.

58. *Ibid.*

10: *Wireless Telegraphy*

1.   See E. Larsen, *Telecommunications, A History*, F. Mullan Ltd, London 1977; wireless telegraphy facilitated communication from afar without the aid of wires.

2.   *AG v Edison Telephone Co* (1880) 6 QBD 244, 249.

3.   *Wireless Telegraphy Acts, 1926-1988* and *Broadcasting Authority Acts, 1960-1993*.

4.   4 Edw 7, ch 24.

5.   *Ibid.*, ss 1 and 2.

6.   *Ibid.*, s. 1(3).

7.   *Ibid.*, s. 1(4).

8.   The 1904 Act was only to be in force until the July 31, 1906, but by virtue of the *Wireless Telegraphy Act, 1906* (6 Edw 7 Ch. 13) and a succession of *Expiring Laws Continuance Acts*, the 1904 Act continued in force until repealed by the *Wireless Telegraphy Act, 1926*.

9.   The First Lord of the Admiralty (The Earl of Selborne) on Second Reading of the *Wireless Telegraphy Bill, 1904*, 140 *Parliamentary Debates*, Lords, cols. 512-513, August 13, 1904.

10. See *Larsen*, n. 1 p.48.

11. See n. 8, *supra*.

12. See document no 117 in Postmaster General's file, published in Appendix 1 of *Special Committee on Wireless Broadcasting*, ordered to be printed February 27, 1924, Dublin.

13. *Ibid.*

14. 4 Edw. 7 ch. 24.

15. Memorandum dated November 9, 1923 in File S.3394, D/T, "*Post Office; Wireless Licences for Ships Registered in Saorstat Éireann*", National Archives, Dublin.

16. *Ibid.*, memorandum dated November 11, 1924.

17. *Ibid.*

18. File S. 3669, D/T, "Wireless Stations in Saorstát Éireann", National Archives, Dublin.

19. File S. 3669, loc. cit and Departmental File T. 33736/46, Posts and Telegraphs.

20. *Ibid.*

21. S.R. & O. 1922, No. 315.

22. Opinion dated November 6, 1924, Files S.3669 and T.33736/46, *loc. cit.*
23. Files S. 3669 and T. 33736/46, *loc. cit.*
24. Memorandum dated October 27, 1928, *ibid.*
25. File S. 3157, D/T, "Disconnection of certain transatlantic cables", National Archives, Dublin.
26. Memorandum dated December 17, 1930: see Files S.3669 and T.33736/46 *loc. cit.*
27. *Ibid.*
28. Memorandum dated May 21, 1947 in Files S.3669 and T.33736/46, *loc. cit.*
29. Memorandum dated June 11, 1947, Files S.3669 and T.33736/46, *loc. cit.*
30. From File TW. 8348, vol. 2, D/T "Wireless Telegraphy Act 1904: Adequacy or otherwise of powers; semi-official correspondence with British P.O.", National Archives, Dublin.
31. See Notice of Motion, May 5, 1925, (1636 No. 6). A short Act was passed entitled the *Wireless Telegraphy (Explanation) Act, 1925,* (15 & 16 Geo 5 ch. 67) — which was intended to "resolve any doubt as to the validity of the existing licence system".
32. File S.4717, D/T, "Wireless Telegraphy Act, 1926", National Archives, Dublin.
33. S. 3(6) of the 1926 Act was amended by substitution by s. 11(c) of the *Wireless Telegraphy Act, 1972.*
34. Reply dated January 31, 1928 in File S.4717, *loc. cit.*, National Archives, Dublin.
35. Amended by substitution by s. 11(c) of the *Wireless Telegraphy Act, 1972.*
36. See n. 34.
37. See n. 32 *supra.*
38. Section 6(2A) of *Wireless Telegraphy Act, 1926* as inserted by s. 17(2) of the *Broadcasting Act, 1990.*
39. The 1926 Act was amended by the *Wireless Telegraphy Act, 1956,* the *Broadcasting Authority Act, 1960,* the *Wireless Telegraphy Act, 1972* the *Broadcasting and Wireless Telegraphy Act, 1988,* and the *Broadcasting Act, 1990.* The collective citation of *Wireless Telegraphy Acts 1926 to 1988* was authorised by s. 21 (3)(b) of the *Broadcasting and Wireless Telegraphy Act, 1988.*
40. S. 2 of the *Wireless Telegraphy Act, 1926.* S. 2 was amended by s. 18 of the *Broadcasting Authority (Amendment) Act, 1976* and s. 2(8) of the *Broadcasting and Wireless Telegraphy Act, 1988.*
41. Ibid; and s. 2(a) of the 1988 Act.
42. S. 6 of the *Wireless Telegraphy Act, 1926* empowers the Minister for Communications to make regulations in regard to licences.
43. *Broadcasting (Receiving Licences) Regulations, 1961 to 1986.*
44. *Wireless Telegraphy (Experimenter's Licence) Regulations 1937 to 1986.*
45. *Wireless Telegraphy (Business Radio Licence) Regulations 1949 to 1986* and

Wireless Telegraphy (Radio Link Licence) Regulations 1992 (S.I. No. 319 of 1992).

46.   Wireless Telegraphy (Wired Broadcast Relay Licences) Regulations 1974 to 1988; Wireless Telegraphy Act, 1926 (Section 3) (Exemption of Certain Wirelesss Broadcast Relay Stations) Order, (S.I. No. 200 of 1976).

47.   Wireless Telegraphy (Personal Radio Licence) Regulation 1982 (S.I. No. 8 of 1982). See also Wireless Telegraphy (Control of Sale, Letting on Hire or Manufacture and Importation of Radio Transceivers) Order, 1981 (S.I. No. 400 of 1981).

48.   Wireless Telegraphy (Television Programme Retransmission) Regulations, 1989 (S.I. No. 39 of 1989).

49.   See Statutory Instruments Nos 113 of 1960, 108 of 1963, 223 of 1963, 331 of 1973, 258 of 1976, 170 of 1979, 171 of 1979, 339 of 1983, 340 of 1983, 290 of 1990 and 291 of 1990.

50.   Wireless Telegraphy (Community Repeater Licence) Regulations, 1988 (S.I. No. 83 of 1988).

51.   S.I. No. 45 of 1926.

52.   S. 5 of the Wireless Telegraphy Act, 1926, as amended by s. 2 of the Wireless Telegraphy Act, 1956 and s. 17 of Broadcasting Act, 1990.

53.   S. 3 of the Wireless Telegraphy Act, 1926 as amended by s. 12 of the Broadcasting and Wireless Telegraphy Act, 1988 (possession etc. of apparatus for wireless telegraphy without a licence); section 11 of the Wireless Telegraphy Act, 1926 (prohibition on certain classes of messages); s. 12 of Wireless Telegraphy Act, 1926 (restriction on user of apparatus for wireless telegraphy).

54.   Ibid. s.10.

55.   S. 2 of the 1956 Act amended s. 5 of the 1926 Act. A person had thus to license apparatus for wireless telegraphy for a place other than a premises (eg. radio in a car) although such a person had a relevant licence for apparatus kept at a particular premises. The requirement to license sound broadcasting receivers was abolished from September 1, 1972 by an order entitled, Wireless Telegraphy Act, 1926 (Section 3) (Exemption of Sound Broadcasting Receivers) Order, 1972 (S.I. No. 211 of 1972).

56.   High Court, Divisional Court, January 19, 1956, (Haugh, McLoughlin and Murnaghan JJ), unreported.

57.   Ibid.

58.   S.I. No. 261 of 1937.

59.   See Memorandum for Government from Minister for Posts and Telegraphs dated February 9, 1956 in File S. 15984, D/T, National Archives, Dublin.

60.   259 Dáil Debates, col. 1226, March 8, 1972.

61.   Brigid Hogan O'Higgins TD, ibid., col. 1233. She also noted in the same sentence that "when one's bank account can be inspected, one can hardly call his soul his own".

62.   S. 2 of the Wireless Telegraphy Act, 1972.

63. *Ibid.*, ss. 3,4 and 6.
64. S. 7, *ibid.*, as amended by s. 17 of the *Broadcasting and Wireless Telegraphy Act, 1988.*
65. S. 9 of the *Wireless Telegraphy Act, 1972.*
66. S. 10 of the *Wireless Telegraphy Act, 1972* created offences in connection with the following matters:— registration of television dealers under s. 2 of the 1972 Act; notification and recording of sales and payments relating to television sets under ss. 3 and 4 of the 1972 Act; notification concerning apparatus or equipment capable of radiating certain radio frequency power under s. 6 of the *Wireless Telegraphy Act, 1972;* restriction of manufacturing or importation of certain wireless telegraphy apparatus; cancellation or failure to comply with special conditions under s. 8 of the *Wireless Telegraphy Act, 1972* for the purpose of conservation of the radio frequency spectrum and avoidance of undue interference with wireless telegraphy.
67. Departmental File, "Wireless Telegraphy & Signalling Bill", TW 8348(8), National Archives, Dublin.
68. *Ibid.*
69. *Ibid.*, memorandum of January 11, 1926.
70. *Ibid.*
71. S. 12 of the *Broadcasting and Wireless Telegraphy Act, 1988.*

11: *State Broadcasting: Regulation by the Government and Ministers for Post and Telegraphs, 1926-1953*

1. *The Irish Times*, January 10, 1924.
2. See documents numbered 56, 57 and 58 in Postmaster General's file, Appendix 1 of *Final Report of Dáil Special Committee on Wireless Broadcasting*, Dublin, 1924.
3. *The White Paper on Wireless Broadcasting*, Post Office, signed by Seamus Breathnach, Aire an Phoist, November 1923, reproduced as document No. 303 in Appendix 1 of *Final Report of Dáil Special Committee on Broadcasting*, Dublin 1924.
4. *Ibid.*
5. 52 *Seanad Debates*, cols. 6-7, January 20, 1960.
6. White Paper on *Wireless Broadcasting, loc. cit.*
7. The UK Postmaster-General had made a similar announcement in the House of Commons on May 4, 1922. The UK Postmaster-General had accepted the recommendations of the *Wireless Sub-Committee of the Imperial Communications Committee presided over by Sir Henry Norman.*
8. *Broadcasting Committee* (Sykes Report, 1923) [Cmnd. 1951].
9. *Ibid.*
10. Order of the Dáil dated December 14, 1923. The Committee was directed that it report back to the Dáil not later than January 16, 1924.
11. *First Interim Report* dated January 15, 1924; *Second Interim Report* dated January 31, 1924; *Third Interim Report* dated March 31, 1924 — all set

out in *Reports of Special Committee on Wireless Broadcasting*, Dublin, ordered to be printed February 27, 1924.

12. Para 6 of Final Report *ibid.*
13. *Ibid.*, para 5.
14. *Ibid.*, para 408 of minutes.
15. *Ibid.*, para 408 of minutes.
16. Memorandum dated December 18, 1924, File S. 3532A, D/T, *"Wireless Broadcasting in Ireland — Establishment and Organisation of"*, National Archives, Dublin.
17. *Ibid.*
18. 6 *Dáil Debates*, cols. 2866-2868, April 3, 1924. See also memorandum of the Minister for Finance dated December 15, 1924 to the Executive Council in File S. 3532A, D/T, *loc. cit.*
19. 6 *Dáil Debates*, cols. 2878-79, April 3, 1924.
20. 6 *Dáil Debates*, cols. 2876-2877, April 3, 1924.
21. 7 *Dáil Debates*, cols. 384-390, May 7, 1924.
22. S. 2 of 1926 Act.
23. S. 19 of Radio and Television Act, 1988.
24. S. 2 of 1926 Act as amended by s. 34(c) of the *Broadcasting Authority Act, 1960*.
25. File S.4717, D/T, "Wireless Telegraphy Act, 1926", National Archives, Dublin.
26. *State (Lynch) v Cooney* [1982] IR 337; *Nova Media Services Ltd v Minister for Posts and Telegraphs* [1984] ILRM 16.
27. File S. 4717, *loc. cit.* National Archives, Dublin.
28. *Ibid.*
29. M. Gorham, *Forty Years of Irish Broadcasting*, The Talbot Press, 1967.
30. See generally Rex Cathcart, *The Most Contrary Region; The BBC in Northern Ireland 1924-1984*, The Blackstaff Press, 1984, chapter 4, "The War Years and After".
31. Directive from the Empire Division of Ministry of Information, memorandum dated May 17, 1940, BBC Written Archives Centre, Caversham.
32. J.M. Andrews to F.W. Ogilvie, Director-General, BBC, dated July 10, 1941 in File "Policy-Éire, 1930-43", BBC Archives Centre, *loc. cit.*
33. *Ibid.*
34. F.W. Ogilvie to J.M. Andrews, August 2, 1941 in BBC Archives Centre, *loc. cit.*
35. J.M. Andrews to F.W. Ogilvie, August 6, 1941, BBC Archives Centre, *loc. cit.*
36. See memorandum to George Marshall dated March 17, 1942 BBC Archives Centre, *loc. cit.*
37. Cathcart, *op. cit.* p. 124.
38. *Ibid.*, p. 125
39. *Ibid.*, p. 127.
40. *Ibid.*, p. 128.

41. See the start of this chapter.
42. Memorandum dated April 4, 1934 entitled "Advertising (Sponsored) Programmes — Question of future policy in regard to", in File S. 9520A, D/T, "Sponsored Broadcasting", National Archives, Dublin.
43. *Ibid*.
44. *Ibid*.
45. *Ibid*.
46. Cabinet Minutes, April 13, 1934 in File S. 9520A, *ibid*.
47. See memorandum dated September 21, 1938 submitted by the Minister for Posts and Telegraphs for consideration by the Government on the subject of commercial advertising for radio stations in Éire in File S. 9520A, D/T, "Sponsored Broadcasting", National Archives, Dublin.
48. Letter dated February 20, 1934 in File S. 2726A, D/T, "Broadcasting — High Power Station in Cork", National Archives, Dublin.
49. *Ibid*.
50. Memorandum entitled "Double Chain Service for the Irish Free State" in File S. 2726A, *loc. cit*.
51. Letter dated August 18, 1934 in File S. 9520A, D/T, *loc. cit*.
52. *Ibid*.
53. *Ibid*.
54. Article in *The Irish Times*, September 29, 1983, "1930s Campaign for Private Radio".
55. Memorandum dated September 28, 1934, "Proposal to lease the Cork Broadcasting Station to a Private Company for Commercial broadcasting", File S. 2726A, D/T, "Broadcasting — High Power Station in Cork", National Archives, Dublin.
56. *Ibid*.
57. Cabinet Minutes, October 10, 1934, File S. 2726A, *loc. cit*.
58. Memorandum on commercial advertising from radio stations in Éire dated September 21, 1938, File S. 9520A, D/T, "Sponsored Broadcasting", Cabinet Files, National Archives, Dublin.
59. *Ibid*.
60. Cabinet Minutes, November 4, 1938, File S. 9520A, *loc. cit*.
61. Memorandum dated August 21, 1939 entitled "International Commercial Advertising for Radio Stations in Éire, Principal objections to", in File S. 9520A, D/T, "Sponsored Broadcasting", Cabinet Files, National Archives, Dublin.
62. Memorandum dated January 3, 1944, "Proposal of Farndale Pictures Ltd, London to lease 24 hours weekly from Radio Éireann for sponsored programmes", in File S. 9520A, *loc. cit*.
63. *Ibid*.
64. Cabinet Minutes, January 4, 1944 in File S. 9520A, *loc. cit*.
65. Cabinet Minutes, May 5/6 1949 in File S. 9520B, *loc. cit*.
66. Memorandum dated April 3, 1950.
67. Cabinet Minutes April 14, 1950 in File S. 2726B, D/T, "Broadcasting

— High Power Station in Cork", Cabinet Files, National Archives, Dublin.

68. Letter to Taoiseach dated November 27, 1945 in File S. 13773A, D/T, "National Culture, Proposed Permanent Council, Proposed Cultural Minister", National Archives, Dublin.

69. Memorandum from the Minister for Posts and Telegraphs submitted to the Taoiseach on January 22, 1946 in File S. 13773A, *loc. cit.*

70. *Ibid.*

71. Memorandum from the Minister for Posts and Telegraphs submitted to the Taoiseach on November 27, 1945 in File S. 13773A, *loc. cit.*

72. File S. 13773A, *loc. cit.*

73. *Ibid.*

74. See letter of Minister for Posts and Telegraphs to the Taoiseach dated October 30, 1945 in File S. 13756, D/T, "Irish Language broadcasting", National Archives, Dublin.

75. *Ibid.*

76. Concluded at Geneva on September 23, 1936. The Irish Instrument of Accession was deposited with the League of Nations on May 25, 1938. See Treaty Series No. 4 of 1938.

77. Letter dated February 6, 1952 to M. Yaroslav Stetzko written on the instructions of the Taoiseach, Eamon de Valera, in File S. 10436B, D/T, "Broadcasting in the Cause of Peace: International Convention", National Archives, Dublin.

78. Note on Memorandum to the President of the Executive Council dated September 26, 1936 in File S. 9092A, D/T, "Shortwave Broadcasting Station", National Archives, Dublin.

79. Letter dated November 19, 1949 in File S.9092C, *loc. cit.*

80. Letter dated January 27, 1949 in File S. 9092C, *loc. cit.*

81. Memorandum dated May 16, 1949 in File S.9092C, *loc. cit.*

82. *Ibid.*

83. *Ibid.*

84. Extract from Cabinet Minutes dated May 17, 1949 in File S. 9092C, *loc. cit.*

85. File S. 9092C, D/T, *loc. cit.*

86. *Ibid.*

87. Memorandum dated October 18, 1949 in File S.9092C. *loc. cit.*

88. *Ibid.*

89. See File S. 9092D, D/T, "Shortwave Broadcasting Stations, 2 July 1951 to 15 May 1956", National Archives, Dublin.

90. *Ibid.*

91. M. Gorham, *Forty Years of Irish Broadcasting*, The Talbot Press, 1967, p. 161.

92. Memorandum for the Government, "Wireless Broadcasting — Appointment of Director", dated January 8, 1947 in File S.7480B, D/T, "Director of Broadcasting", National Archives, Dublin.

93. 112 *Dáil Debates*, col. 814 at col. 822, July 20, 1948.

94. *Ibid.*, cols. 822-823.
95. See memorandum of León Ó Broin, Secretary of Department of Posts and Telegraphs, dated July 27, 1954 in File H.6225/54, vol 1, D/Comm, (R & B), "Statutory Board for Broadcasting", National Archives, Dublin.
96. Memorandum for the Government, "Broadcasting Control and Operation" dated May 15, 1952 in File S. 3532B, D/T, "Wireless Broadcasting in Ireland, Establishment and Organisation of", National Archives, Dublin.
97. *Ibid.*
98. *Ibid.*
99. Memorandum for the Government "Observations of the Minister for Finance on the Memorandum on Broadcasting Control and Operation submitted by the Minister for Posts and Telegraphs", dated May 29, 1952 in File S. 3532B, *loc. cit.*
100. *Ibid.*
101. *Ibid.*
102. Memorandum dated May 15, 1952, *ibid.*
103. *Ibid.*
104. Memorandum dated May 29, 1952 *loc. cit.*
105. *Ibid.*
106. Cabinet Minutes dated July 18, 1952, "Broadcasting: Control and Operation" in File S. 3532B, *loc. cit.*
107. Memorandum for the Government dated October 13, 1955 in File S. 3532C, D/T, "Wireless Broadcasting in Ireland: establishment and organisation", National Archives, Dublin.
108. *The Leader*, August 30, 1952.
109. *Ibid.*
110. *Ibid.*, and editorial of *Irish Press*, September 2, 1952. However, *The Leader* on August 30, 1952, conscious of the inevitable tensions inherent in a broadcasting service operated under the direct control of the State, warned the Minister that "corroded hatchets [were] already being unearthed and testy pedants [were] rubbing their grimy hands with anticipatory glee".
111. *The Irish Times*, October 25, 1945.
112. Communication of the Clerk of the Dáil dated March 23, 1926 to D. O'Hegarty, Secretary of Executive Council, in File S. 7321 "Broadcasting Dáil Proceedings", National Archives, Dublin.
113. Executive Council Minutes, March 25, 1926 in File S. 7321, *loc. cit.*
114. Memorandum for consideration by the Executive Council, "General Election-Political Broadcasts" dated May 28, 1937 in File S. 9908A, D/T, "Broadcasting, Political", National Archives, Dublin.
115. Cabinet Minutes in File S. 9908A, *loc. cit.*
116. Amended by substitution by s. 16 of the *Broadcasting Authority (Amendment) Act, 1976.*
117. Memorandum for the Government, "Broadcast of political matter

from Radio Éireann", dated July 31, 1951, and minutes of meetings of Dáil Committee on Procedure and Privileges dated May 13, and June 3, 1948 in File S. 9908 B/1, D/T, "Broadcasts — Political", National Archives, Dublin.

118. Minutes of May, 13, 1948 in File S. 9908 B/1, *loc. cit.*
119. Minutes of June 3, 1948, *loc. cit.*
120. *Ibid.*
121. 112 *Dáil Debates*, col. 823, Minister for Posts and Telegraphs, James Everett, July 20, 1948.
122. *Ibid.*, col. 824.
123. Memorandum for the Government, "Broadcast of political matter from Radio Éireann", in File S. 9908 B/1, *loc. cit.*
124. *Ibid.*
125. *Ibid.*
126. Cabinet Minutes, August 8, 1951 in File S.9908 B/1, *loc. cit.*
127. *Ibid.*
128. *Ibid.*
129. *Ibid.*
130. *Ibid.*
131. *Ibid.*
132. Memorandum dated July 13, 1957 in File S.9908, B/2, D/T "Radio and Television: political broadcasts", National Archives, Dublin.
133. *Ibid.*
134. Cabinet Minutes, November 5, 1951 in File S. 9908, B/1, D/T, *loc. cit.*
135. 143 *Dáil Debates*, cols. 1363-1364, December 2, 1953.
136. *Ibid.*
137. *Ibid.*
138. Cabinet Minutes, August 8, 1951 in File S.9908 B/1, *loc. cit.*
139. Draft communication to the Ceann Comhairle, "Political Broadcasting associated with Memorandum for the Government, Political Broadcasting", dated February 20, 1952 in File S. 9908, D/T. *loc. cit.*
140. *Ibid.*
141. Communication from the Secretary of the Government to the Private Secretary of the Minister for Posts and Telegraphs dated April 5, 1952 in File S. 9908 B/1, *loc. cit.*
142. Letter of C.J. Brennan to An Taoiseach dated May 4, 1953 in File S. 9908 B/1, *loc. cit.*
143. *Forty Years of Irish Broadcasting*, Talbot Press Ltd, 1967, p. 249.
144. For a discussion on these issues, see G.W. Hogan, "Federal Republic of Germany, Ireland and the United Kindgom: Three European Approaches to Political Campaign Regulation", 21 *Capital University Law Review*, 1 (1992).

12: *Broadcasting Regulation 1953-1993*

1. Memorandum prepared for first meeting of Television Commission, April 9, 1958 in File TW. 3756, vol. 8, D/Comm, (R & B), "T.V. Commission; First Meeting, 9 April 1958", National Archives, Dublin.
2. See chapter 11.
3. *Report of Television Committee*, dated September 4, 1953 in File S. 14996A, D/T "Television: General", National Archives, Dublin.
4. *Ibid.* s. 6(iii).
5. *Ibid.* s. 6(i).
6. Memorandum for the Government dated October 12, 1955 in File S. 3532C, D/T, "Wireless Broadcasting in Ireland; establishment and organisation", National Archives, Dublin.
7. *Ibid.*
8. *Ibid.*
9. Cabinet Minutes, October 21, 1955 in File S.3532B, D/T, *loc. cit.*
10. First Supplementary Report on Television, dated March 13, 1956, in File S. 14996A, D/T, *loc. cit.*
11. *Ibid.*
12. Address by His Holiness Pope Pius XII to delegates of the European Broadcasting Union in October 1955 reproduced in Appendix II to 1956 Television Report, *loc. cit.*
13. *Ibid.*
14. Memorandum dated June 13, 1956 entitled "Government Policy in regard to Television" in File S. 14996A, *loc. cit.*
15. *Ibid.*
16. Cabinet Minutes dated July 6, 1956 in File S. 14996A, D/T, National Archives, Dublin.
17. See File TW.894, vol. 3, D/Comm, (R & B), "Television: Memorandum To Government etc.", National Archives, Dublin.
18. See Memorandum of León Ó Broin to Minister dated June 28, 1957, in File TW.894, vol. 3, *ibid.*
19. *Ibid.*
20. See draft memorandum for Government "1. International Commercial Broadcasting. 2. Television", dated July 20, 1957, in File TW.894 vol. 3, *ibid.*
21. European Broadcasting Convention, Copenhagen, 1948 (under the auspices of the International Telecommunications Union) ratified by Ireland on July 17, 1950.
22. Memorandum dated July 26, 1957 in File TW.894, vol. 3, *loc. cit.*
23. File TW. 894, vol 3, *loc. cit.*
24. Letter dated July 25, 1957 in File TW.394, vol. 3, *loc. cit.*
25. *Ibid.*
26. *Ibid.*
27. See draft reply dated July 29, 1957 in File TW.894, vol. 3, *loc. cit.*
28. Draft reply dated July 29, 1957 and (separately) copy reply as signed

by the Minister for Posts and Telegraphs, Neil Blaney, dated July 30, 1957 in File TW.894, vol. 3, *loc. cit.*

29. See memorandum of discussion in Department of Finance dated July 29, 1957, in File TW. 894, vol. 3, *loc. cit.*

30. *Ibid.*

31. *Ibid.*

32. Memorandum dated September 17, 1957, in File 894, vol 3, D. Comm (R & B), "Television: Memorandum to Government etc.", National Archives, Dublin.

33. Address by His Holiness, Pope Pius XII, to delegates of the European Broadcasting Union in October 1955, Appendix II to the Posts and Telegraphs, *First Supplementary Report on Television* in File S. 14996A, D/T, *loc. cit.*

34. Memorandum dated September 17, 1957 in File 894, vol 3, *loc. cit.*

35. See *supra*.

36. Memorandum of Secretary of the Government dated October 25, 1957, in File S. 3532C, D/T, "Wireless Broadcasting in Ireland, establishment and organisation", National Archives, Dublin.

37. Memorandum for the Government dated January 10, 1958 in File S.14996 B, D/T, "Television General", National Archives, Dublin.

38. Memorandum to Minister dated January 3, 1957, in File TW.894, vol. 3, *loc. cit.*

39. *Ibid.*

40. Letter of Tánaiste to Minister for Posts and Telegraphs dated January 6, 1958 in File TW.894, vol. 3, *loc. cit.*

41. *Ibid.*

42. "Post Office Observations", memorandum for the Goverment dated January 10, 1958 in File S.14996B, D/T, *loc. cit.*

43. *Ibid.*

44. *Ibid.*

45. See memoranda dated February 24, 1958 and March 3, 1958 in File TW.894, vol. 3, *loc. cit.*

46. The warrant of appointment was given under the seal of the Minister for Posts and Telegraphs on March 26, 1958. The terms of reference are set down at page 5 of *Report of the Television Commission, 1959* published by the Stationery Office. The Chairman was Hon. Mr. Justice G.D. Murnaghan.

47. Memorandum dated January 29, 1959 in File S.14996C, "Television: General", National Archives, Dublin.

48. *Ibid.*

49. *Ibid.*

50. *Ibid.*

51. File S. 14996B, D/T, "Television General", National Archives, Dublin.

52. See *Report of the Television Commission 1959*, Dublin, Stationery Office.

53. See letter of Seán MacEntee to the Taoiseach dated July 21, 1958 in File S. 14996B, D/T, *loc. cit.*

54. *Ibid.*
55. Note dated July 24, 1958 in File S. 14996B, D/T, *loc. cit.*
56. Minority Report (Appendix B) (International Commercial Sound Broadcasting) of Television Commission, unpublished. See File TW 894 vol 2, D/Comm, (R & B), "Report of Television Commission: Preliminary Submission to Government", National Archives, Dublin.
57. The printed proposals are contained in File S. 14996B, D/T, *loc. cit.*
58. See memorandum marked "secret and confidential" addressed to the Secretary, Department of External Affairs, Dublin, dated September 11, 1958 from the Ambassador to the Holy See in File 14996B, D/T, *loc. cit.*
59. Minority Report, see n. 56 *supra.*
60. *Interim report of Television Commission*, dated December 23, 1958 in File TW 3756, vol. 5, D/Comm. (R & B), "Television Commission: Interim Report", National Archives, Dublin.
61. *The Interim Minority Report of the Television Commission,* dated December 18, 1958 and signed by Roger McHugh, Síle Ní Chinnéide (with agreement in part by Colleen Stafford) in File TW 3756, vol. 5, *ibid.*
62. Memorandum dated January 7, 1959 to the Secretary, Department Posts and Telegraphs in File TW. 3756, vol. 3, D/Comm (R & B).
63. Memorandum by Secretary of the Government to the Private Secretary, Minister for Posts and Telegraphs, dated March 24, 1959 in File TW.3756, vol. 3, *ibid.*
64. First Ad Interim *Report of Coimisiún um Athbheochan Na Gaeilge* dated March 20, 1959 (English version) in File 3756, vol. 4, D/Comm, (R & B), "Television Commission: copy of main Memorandum to Government", National Archives, Dublin.
65. Observations of the Minister for Posts and Telegraphs on the First Ad Interim *Report of An Coimisiún um Athbheochan Na Gaeilge* dated May 1959 in File TW.3756, vol. 4, *ibid.*
66. *Ibid.*
67. Memorandum for the Government "Report of the Television Commission", dated July 14, 1959 in File TW.3756, vol 4, *ibid.*
68. *Ibid.*
69. Para. 155 of Report, *ibid.*
70. Memorandum for Government dated July 14, 1959 in File TW.3756, vol. 4, *loc. cit.*
71. Para. 94 of Report, *loc. cit.*
72. Para. 61 of chapter VI of Commission Report, *loc. cit.*; Memorandum for Government dated July 14, 1959 in File TW. 3756, vol. 4, *loc. cit.*
73. Memorandum for Government dated July 14, 1959, *loc. cit.*
74. See para. 24 of Memorandum for Government dated July 14, 1959, *loc. cit.*
75. Memorandum of meeting with León Ó Broin and others dated June 30, 1959 in File TW 894, vol. 6, D/Comm. (R & B) "Report of Television

Commission; Memorandum for Government, 1959", National Archives, Dublin.

76. Memorandum for Government dated July 14, 1959 in File TW. 894, vol. 6, *loc. cit.*
77. Memorandum dated July 21, 1959 in File TW.894, vol. 6, D/Comm (R & B), *loc. cit.*
78. Memorandum of Secretary of Government dated July 31, 1959 in File TW.894, vol. 6, D/Comm (R & B), *loc. cit.*
79. S. 3 of *Broadcasting Authority (Amendment) Act, 1966.*
80. Section 16 of 1960 Act was later amended by s. 5 of the *Broadcasting Authority (Amendment) Act, 1966*, s. 12 of the *Broadcasting Authority (Amendment) Act, 1976* and s. 3 of the *Broadcasting Authority (Amendment) Act 1979.*
81. Ss. 2, 3 and 4 of 1968 Act.
82. S. 2(1) *ibid.*
83. Ss. 5 and 6 of 1968 Act.
84. See later in this chapter.
85. 234 *Dáil Debates*, col. 1272, May 9, 1968.
86. See *Broadcasting Review Committee Report 1974*, (Prl. 3827), Stationery Office, Dublin.
87. *Ibid.*, chapter 3, para 3.4.
88. *Ibid.*, para 3.4.2.
89. *Ibid.*, para 3.4.3.
90. *Ibid.*, para 4.4.
91. *Ibid.*, paras 4.11 and 4.15
92. *Ibid.*, para 24.10.
93. See chapter 17.
94. *Loc. cit.*
95. Dr. Conor Cruise O'Brien, Minister for Posts and Telegraphs, at Second Stage of *Broadcasting Authority (Amendment) Bill, 1975*, 79 *Dáil Debates*, col.763, March 12, 1975.
96. S. 16 of 1976 Act which amended s. 31 of the *Broadcasting Authority Act, 1960* by the substitution of a new subsection for s. 31(1) of the 1960 Act.
97. S. 4 of the 1976 Act which inserted ss. 18A, 18B and 18C after s. 18 of the *Broadcasting Authority Act, 1960.*
98. S. 2 of 1976 Act.
99. S. 6 of 1960 Act and repealed by s. 21 of 1976 Act.
100. 79 *Seanad Debates*, col. 772, March 12, 1975.
101. Sen. Mary Robinson, 79 *Seanad Debates*, col.942, March 19, 1975; Sen. Alexis FitzGerald, 81 *Seanad Debates*, col. 1369.
102. 285 *Dáil Debates*, col. 653, October 30, 1975 on Second Stage of *Broadcasting Authority (Amendment) Bill, 1975*
103. *Ibid.*
104. See speech of Minister for Posts and Telegraphs, Dr. Conor Cruise O'Brien on Second Stage of *Broadcasting Authority (Amendment) Bill*

1975, 285 *Seanad Debates*, cols. 382-383, October 28, 1975.
105. *Ibid.*
106. 343 *Dáil Debates*, col. 960, June 8, 1983, Minister of State at the Department of Posts and Telegraphs.
107. 376 *Dáil Debates*, cols. 1188-89, December 8, 1987, Minister for Communications, Ray Burke.
108. *Ibid.*
109. *Ibid.* col. 1190.
110. 120 *Seanad Debates*, cols. 779-780, June 21, 1988.
111. 120 *Seanad Debates*, col. 780, June 21, 1988.
112. *Radio and Television Act, 1988 (Establishment Day Order), 1988* (S.I. No.269 of 1988).
113. See, for example, Ronan Foster, "Century's Stars Fail to Shine", *The Irish Times*, May 22, 1990.
114. *Ibid.*
115. See, for example, *Irish Independent*, June 6, 1990, pages 1 and 10.
116. *Ibid.* p. 1.
117. *The Irish Times*, June 29, 1990.
118. 399 *Dáil Debates*, col. 1573, Minister for Communications, Ray Burke, on Second Stage of *Broadcasting Bill, 1990*.
119. *Ibid.*
120. S. 9(1)(c) of *Radio and Television Act, 1988*.
121. 399 *Dáil Debates*, col. 1587, Jim Mitchell, June 7, 1990.
122. 401 *Dáil Debates*, col. 1411, July 11, 1990 Report and Final Stages of *Broadcasting Bill, 1990*.
123. *Ibid.*
124. S.4 of the *Broadcasting Authority (Amendment) Act, 1993*.
125. *Ibid.*
126. Eilish Pearce, "Beyond Burke's Law", *Sunday Press*, July 8, 1990.

13: *Cable Television*

1. North [and East] of line from Sligo to Dublin and along a coastal strip from Dublin to Wexford. See, generally, chapter 13 of *Broadcasting Review Committee Report 1974* (Prl 3827), Dublin, Stationery Office.
2. See, generally, *Report of the Cable System Committee, Dublin, Stationery Office* (Pl. 2937), submitted to the Minister for Posts and Telegraphs, December 1984 and the Home Office, *Report of the Inquiry into Cable Expansion and Broadcasting Policy*, HMSO, Cmnd 8679 (presented to UK Parliament in October 1982).
3. See definition in chapter 8.
4. See definition in chapter 10.
5. This summary of the main stages in the development of cable television in Ireland is based on information supplied to the Broadcasting Review Committee and summarised in chapter 13 the *Broadcasting*

Review Committee Report 1974 (Prl. 3827), Dublin, Stationery Office. See also *Monthly Report No. 96* National Prices Commission, June 1980, Stationery Office, (Prl. 9000); *Report of the Cable Systems Committee, 1984* (Pl. 2937) and *Report of Study Into Cable Television Systems in the Greater Dublin Area, 1986,* Stationery Office (Pl. 4295).

6.   The Minister for Posts and Telegraphs had objected to allowing cable television in Ballymun; the final decision was taken by the Government. See remarks of Joseph Brennan (former Minister for Posts and Telegraphs) on Second Stage of *Broadcasting Authority (Amendment) Bill, 1975* in 285 *Dáil Debates,* cols. 667-668. The Department of Posts and Telegraphs was influenced by the desire to maintain Radio Éireann's revenue from commercial advertising.

7.   The corporate name "Radio Éireann" was changed to "Radio Telefis Éireann" by s. 3 of the *Broadcasting Authority (Amendment) Act, 1966.*

8.   In addition to the information contained in the *Broadcasting Review Committee Report 1974, loc. cit.,* the Minister for Posts and Telegraphs, Gerard Collins, summarised legal developments relating to cable relay systems on the Committee stage of the *Wireless Telegraphy Bill, 1972, 72 Seanad Debates,* cols. 718-719, March 22, 1972.

9.   The second Interim Report was not published — but its recommendations are summarised in para. 13.29 of the *Broadcasting Review Committee Report, 1974 loc. cit.*

10.   *Wireless Telegraphy (Wired Broadcast Relay Licence) Regulations 1974* (S.I. No. 67 of 1974).

11.   Dr. Conor Cruise O'Brien, 285 *Dáil Debates,* col. 395, 1975 on Second Stage of *Broadcasting Authority (Amendment) Bill, 1975.*

12.   S. 3A(6) of the *Wireless Telegraphy Act, 1926* as amended by section 17 of the *Broadcasting Authority (Amendment) Act, 1976.*

13.   S. 17 of the 1976 Act which inserted s. 3A after s. 3 in the *Wireless Telegraphy Act, 1926.*

14.   See *Report of the Cable Systems Committee submitted to the Minister for Communications in December 1984,* Stationery Office, Dublin, (Pl.2937) para 55, chaired by Mrs. Margaret Downes.

15.   *Ibid.,* para 53.

16.   *Ibid.,* para 55.

17.   *Ibid.,* para 107.

18.   *Ibid.,* paras 95 to 102. See chapter 20 in relation to the current fee.

19.   *Ibid.,* para 55.

20.   *Report of Study into Cable Television Systems in the Greater Dublin Area, 1986,* Dublin, Stationery Office, (Pl. 4295) para. 61, p. 33.

21.   *Ibid.*

22.   *Ibid.*

23.   Ithiel de Sola Pool in *Technologies of Freedom,* The Belnap Press of Harvard University Press, 1983, p. 151. See also Thomas W. Hazlett, "Cabling America: Economic Forces in a Political World" in Cento Veljanovski, (ed.), *Freedom of Broadcasting,* Institute of Economic

Affairs, UK, 1989, pp. 208-223, where this issue and other related issues are discussed in the US context.

24. *Report of the Study into Cable Television in the Greater Dublin Area*, 1986, Dublin, Stationery Office, (Pl. 4295), para 4.6, p. 23 and para 6.15 p. 40.

25. *Ibid.*

26. *Ibid.*

27. *Ibid.*, paras 4.6 and 6.15.

28. *Ibid.*, para 6.13(vii) p. 39.

29. *Cabinet Committee on Cable Communications — Report to the President* (Washington, D.C. Government Printing Office, 1974). See also Mark Nadel, "A Unified Theory of the Fourth Amendment: Divorcing the Medium From the Message", *Fordham Law Journal*, February 1983.

30. *Report of Study into Cable Television Systems in the Greater Dublin Area*, *loc. cit.* para 6. 13(iii), p. 38.

PART IV: TELECOMMUNICATION PRIVILEGES, POWERS AND DUTIES

14: *Introduction*

1. See Holdsworth, *History of English Law* (1924), vol 4, p. 344; vol 6 p. 327.

2. *Darcy v Allein* 11 Co. Rep. 84; Moore K.B. 671, Noy 173, 77 Eng. Rep. 1260 (1602): *Holdsworth, op. cit.*, vol. 4 p. 344. Parliament enacted the *Statute of Monopolies* (21 Jac.1.c.3) that gave legislative effect to Lord Coke's judicial interpretation. See n. 40.

3. *Holdsworth, op. cit.*, vol. 4 p. 321.

4. 3 Coke's Inst. 181 c. 85.

5. The words of Mr. Justice Story in *Charles River Bridge v Warren Bridge et al*: 11 Peters 420, 607; 9 L Ed, 773, 848 (1837).

6. *Principles of Political Economy*, p. 143.

7. Farrer, *The State in Relation to Trade* (1902); Henry C. Adams, *Relation of the State to Industrial Action* (1887).

8. See generally W.J. Baumol, "On the proper cost tests for natural monopoly in a multi-product industry", *American Economic Review*, Vol 67, No. 5, December 1977, p. 180.

9. Richard Posner, "Natural Monopoly and its Regulation", 21 *Stan L Rev, 548* (1969).

10. S. 4 of *Telegraph Act, 1868* (32 & 33 Vict. 73) as amended by s. 8 of the *PTS Act, 1983*.

11. S. 87(1) of *PTS Act, 1983* as amended by reg. 3 of *EC (Telecommunications Services) Regulations 1992* (S.I. No. 45 of 1992).

12. S. 87(3) of 1983 Act.

13. *Council Directive of 28 June 1990 (Open Network Provision)*

(90/387/EEC) OJEC No. L1921/1, 24.7.90 and *Commission Directive of 28 June 1990 (Telecommunications Services)* (90/388/EEC) No. L. 192/10, implemented in Ireland by the *European Communities (Tele-communications Services) Regulations, 1992* (S.I. No. 45 of 1992).

14.   See *ibid*.
15.   Ss. 87(1) and 111 of the 1983 Act.
16.   See reg. 3 of 1992 Regulations, *loc. cit*. The expression "public tele-communications network" and "voice telephony services" are defined in reg. 2 of the 1992 Regulations.
17.   See, for example, the prohibition on simple third party resale of data transmission capacity on leased lines in *Licence under Section III of the Postal and Telecommunications Services Act, 1983 to Provide Public Tele-communications Services* issued by the Department of Communications. Other conditions are also specified but are not relevant to the present definition of value-added telecommunications services.
18.   See *Licence, ibid*.
19.   *Ibid*.
20.   See, for example, the *PTS Acts, 1983 and 1984, Broadcasting Authority Acts 1960 to 1993, Radio and Television Act, 1988* and *Broadcasting Act, 1990*, and the *Wireless Telegraphy Acts 1926 to 1988*.
21.   Schemes in the form of statutory instruments are made pursuant to section 90 of the *PTS Act, 1983*. See *Telecommunications Schemes, 1992 and 1993*.
22.   See the *Radio and Television Act, 1988*.

15: *Privileges, Powers and Duties of the Government, Minister for Communications and Minister for Arts and Culture*

1.   S. 1(ix) and Eighth Part of the Schedule of the 1924 Act.
2.   See s. 7 and Fourth Schedule of *PTS Act, 1983*.
3.   *Postal and Telecommunications Services Act, 1983 (Bord Telecom Éireann) Vesting Day Order, 1983* (S.I. 408 of 1983).
4.   S. 3(b) of 1983 Act.
5.   *Tourism, Transport and Communications (Alteration of Name of Department and Title of Minister) Order, 1993* (S.I. No. 17 of 1993).
6.   *Broadcasting (Transfer of Departmental Administration and Ministerial Functions) Order, 1993* (S.I. No. 13 of 1993); *Gaeltacht (Alteration of Name of Department and Title of Minister) Order, 1993* (S.I. No. 22 of 1993).
7.   32 & 33 Vict. c.73.
8.   S. 8 and Fourth Schedule, Part 1, of *PTS Act, 1983* and *Ministers and Secretaries (Amendment) Act, 1983*.
9.   *Telegraph Act, 1863* (26 & 27 Vict. c.112), s. 3; *Telegraph Act, 1869* (32 & 33 Vict. c.73) s. 3.
10.   *Attorney General v Edison Telephone Company of London* (1880) 6 QBD 244.

11. See *Re Regulation and Control of Radio Communication in Canada* [1932] AC 304, PC, at 316.
12. See, also, *EC (Telecommunication Services) Regulations, 1992* (S.I. No. 45 of 1992) where these issues are further regulated.
13. S. 34(a).
14. S. 5 of the *Telegraph Act, 1869* (32 & 33 Vict. c.73) repealed by S.7 of *PTS Act, 1983*; s. 5 of *Wireless Telegraphy Act, 1926*.
15. S. 87(1) of 1983 Act as amended by reg. 3 of the *EC (Telecommunications Services) Regulations 1992* (S.I. No. 45 of 1992).
16. As set out in s. 87(3) of *PTS Act, 1983*.
17. Ss. 89 and 111 (1)(a) of *PTS Act, 1983*.
18. S. 111(2) *PTS Act, 1983*.
19. See, for example, *Postal and Telecommunications Services Act, 1983 (Section 111(1)) Order 1989* (S.I. No. 77 of 1989), which enabled the granting of a licence to An Post to provide a public national tele-communication service within the exclusive privilege of Telecom Éireann. See also *EC (Telecommunications Services) Regulations 1992* (S.I. No. 45 of 1992) which facilitated the granting of tele-communication value-added network service licences to persons to compete with Telecom Éireann. Many licences have been granted by the Minister to suppliers of telecommunication equipment.
20. See n.5 above.
21. S. 110(1)(a) of *PTS Act, 1983*.
22. S. 110(1)(b), *ibid*.
23. S. 110(5), *ibid*.
24. S. 111(1)(a), *ibid*.
25. *Ibid*.
26. *Ibid*.
27. *Ibid*.
28. S. 111(2) *ibid*.
29. Pursuant to S. 111(1) of the *PTS Act, 1983*.
30. *Postal and Telecommunications Services Act, 1983 (Section 111(1)) Order, 1989* (S.I. No. 77 of 1989) in relation to a limited national tele-communication service and a licence pursuant to S. 111(2) of the *PTS Act, 1983* in relation to the public international telecommunication mail service.
31. *EC (Telecommunications Services) Regulations 1992* (S.I. No. 45 of 1992).
32. S. 17 of *PTS Act, 1983* and clauses 2(10) and 5 of Memorandum of Association of Telecom Éireann. A similar clause was at issue in *Hennessy v National Agricultural and Development Association* [1947] IR 159 where the memorandum contained a prohibition on the alteration of the articles of association without the previous approval of the Minister for Industry and Commerce. Purported alterations without the previous approval of the Minister were held to be null and void.
33. S. 10(3)(d) *PTS Act, 1983*. See also clause 5 of Memorandum of Association of Telecom Éireann.

34.   Ss 18 and 22 *ibid*.
35.   S. 23 *ibid*.
36.   S. 27(1)(a) *ibid*.
37.   S. 27(2) *ibid*.
38.   S. 28(1) *ibid*.
39.   S. 32(1) *ibid*.
40.   S. 32(2) *ibid*.
41.   S. 33(1) *ibid*.
42.   S. 33(2) *ibid*.
43.   Ss. 34 and 35 of, and Part 1 of the First Schedule to, the *PTS Act, 1983* were repealed by s. 26 of the *Worker Participation (State Enterprises) Act, 1988*.
44.   Ss. 40(3) and 41(2) of *PTS Act, 1983*.
45.   *Ibid*. See *Maher v AG* [1973] IR 140 where the conclusivity of a medical certificate was held unconstitutional.
46.   S. 44 and Second Schedule *ibid*.
47.   *Ibid*.
48.   S. 46 *ibid*.
49.   S. 51 *ibid*.
50.   S. 42 *ibid*.
51.   S. 89(1) *ibid*.
52.   S. 89(2) *ibid*.
53.   S. 90(2) *ibid*.
54.   S. 95 *ibid*.
55.   S. 98(3)(a) *ibid*.
56.   Article 39 of *Articles of Association of Telecom Éireann*.
57.   Article 38 *Ibid*.
58.   Article 42 *ibid*.
59.   Article 46(2) *ibid*.
60.   Article 16 *ibid*.
61.   S. 16(2)(f) of *PTS Act, 1983* and Article 55 of *Articles of Association of Telecom Éireann*.
62.   Article 69 *ibid*.
63.   Article 85 *ibid*.
64.   Article 89 *ibid*.
65.   See definition in s. 2 of *Wireless Telegraphy Act, 1926*, as amended by s. 18 of the *Broadcasting Authority (Amendment) Act, 1976* and s. 2 of Broadcasting and *Wireless Telegraphy Act, 1988*.
66.   See n. 6 above.
67.   *Ibid*.
68.   S. 5 of 1926 Act as amended by s. 34 of *Broadcasting Authority Act, 1960*.
69.   See, for example, *Minister for Posts and Telegraphs v Campbell* [1966] IR 69 for a consideration of the term "keeping and possession".
70.   S. 3(3) of *Wireless Telegraphy Act, 1926* as amended by s. 11(b) of *Wireless Telegraphy Act, 1972* and s. 12 of the *Broadcasting and Wireless Telegraphy Act, 1988*.

71. S.8 of the *Wireless Telegraphy Act, 1926* as amended by s. 17 of the *Broadcasting and Wireless Telegrapy Act, 1988.*
73. S. 76(1) of the *PTS Act, 1993* and *Postal and Telecommunications Services Act, 1983 (Wireless Telegraphy) (No.1) Order, 1983* (S.I. No. 419 of 1983).
74. S. 76(4) of the *PTS Act, 1983* and *Postal and Telecommunication Services Act, 1983 (Wireless Telegraphy) (No. 3) Order, 1983* (S.I. No. 423 of 1983).
75. S. 76(3) of *PTS Act, 1983* and *Postal and Telecommunication Services Act, 1983 (Wireless Telegraphy) (No.2) Order, 1983* (S.I. No. 420 of 1983).
76. S. 77 of *PTS Act, 1983.*
77. S. 34(3) of *Broadcasting Authority Act, 1960* as amended by s. 7(1) of *Broadcasting Authority Act, 1966.*
78. See n.6 above.
79. *Broadcasting (Receiving) Licence Regulations 1961 to 1986.*
80. *Wireless Telegraphy (Experimenter's Licence) Regulations 1937 to 1986.*
81. *Wireless Telegraphy (Business Radio Licence) Regulations 1949 to 1992* and *Wireless Telegraphy (Radio Link Licence) Regulations 1992* (S.I. No. 319 of 1992).
82. *Wireless Telegraphy (Wired Broadcast Relay Licence) Regulations 1974* (S.I. No. 67 of 1974) and 1988 (S.I. No. 82 of 1988).
83. *Wireless Telegraphy (Personal Radio Licence) Regulations, 1982* (S.I. No. 8 of 1982).
84. *Wireless Telegraphy (Television Programme Retransmission) Regulations 1989* (S.I. No. 39 of 1989).
85. S. 6(3) of *Wireless Telegraphy Act, 1926.*
86. S. 7 of *Wireless Telegraphy Act, 1926* as amended by s. 17 of *Broadcasting and Wireless Telegraphy Act, 1988.* In relation to the Minister for Arts and Culture, see n.6 above.
87. See for example, reg. 13(1) of *Broadcasting (Receiving Licences) Regulations 1961* (S.I. No. 279 of 1961) and reg. 15(1) of *Wireless Telegraphy (Personal Radio Licence) Regulations 1982* (S.I. No. 8 of 1982).
88. See for example reg. 13(2)(b) of 1961 Regulations, *ibid* and reg. 15(2) of the 1982 Regulations, *ibid.*
89. S. 9 of *Wireless Telegraphy Act, 1926.*
90. S. 12A (2) of *Wireless Telegraphy Act, 1926* inserted by s. 34(f) of the *Broadcasting Authority Act, 1960.*
91. S. 12A(4) *ibid.*
92. S. 12A(6) *ibid.*
93. S. 12(A) of 1926 Act creates several offences.
94. S. 12A(9) of 1926 Act as inserted by s. 34(f) of *Broadcasting Authority Act, 1960* and amended by substitution by s. 19 of the *Broadcasting Authority (Amendment) Act, 1976.*
95. S. 12A(9)(b) *ibid.*
96. S. 12A(9)(b)(i) and (ii) and s. 12A(9A) *ibid.*
97. S. 12A(14) of *Wireless Telegraphy Act, 1926* as inserted by s. 19 of *Broadcasting Authority (Amendment) Act, 1976.*
98. S. 12A(11)(a) of *Wireless Telegraphy Act, 1926* as inserted by s. 34(b) of

Broadcasting Authority Act, 1960.
99. S. 12 of the 1926 Act.
100. *Wireless Telegraphy (Control of Interference from Electric Motors) Regulations, 1963* (S.I. No. 108 of 1963); *Wireless Telegraphy (Control of Interference from Ignition Apparatus) Regulations, 1963* (S.I. No. 223 of 1963).
101. S. 12A(13) of *Wireless Telegraphy Act, 1926* as inserted by s. 34(f) of *Broadcasting Authority Act, 1960. See Broadcasting Authority (Control of Interference) Orders, 1960 and 1963.*
102. S. 5 of *Wireless Telegraphy Act, 1972*. See n. 6 above in relation to the Minister for Arts and Culture.
103. S. 7(2) of *Wireless Telegraphy Act, 1972.*
104. S. 10(2) *ibid.* as amended by s. 12 of the *Broadcasting and Wireless Telegraphy Act, 1988.*
105. S. 7(3) of *Wireless Telegraphy Act, 1972.*
106. *Wireless Telegraphy (Control of Sale, Letting On Hire or Manufacture, and Importation of Radio Transceivers) Order, 1981* (S.I. No. 400 of 1981).
107. S. 8 of *Wireless Telegraphy Act, 1972*. See n.6 at the start of this chapter in relation to the Minister for Arts and Culture.
108. *Ibid.*
109. S. 3 of *Wireless Telegraphy Act, 1972* and n.6 at the start of this chapter.
110. S. 76(3) of *PTS Act, 1983* and *Postal and Telecommunications Services Act 1983 (Wireless Telegraphy) (No. 2) Order, 1983* (S.I. No. 420 of 1983).
111. S. 2 of *Wireless Telegraphy Act, 1972* as amended by s. 19 of the *Broadcasting and Wireless Telegraphy Act, 1988.*
112. S. 3 and Part 1 of Schedule to *Wireless Telegraphy Act, 1972*; s. 76(3) of *PTS Act, 1983* and *Postal and Telecommunications Services Act, 1983 (Wireless Telegraphy) (No. 2) Order, 1983* (S.I. 420 of 1983).
113. The section is headed "Unlicensed Broadcasting".
114. S. 4(1) of *Broadcasting Authority Act, 1960* and s. 2 of *Broadcasting Authority (Amendment) Act, 1976.*
115. S. 4(2) of 1960 Act.
116. S. 5(2) of *Broadcasting Authority Act, 1960.*
117. S. 7(2) *ibid.*
118. S. 13(4) *ibid.*
119. S. 15(5) *ibid.*
120. S. 15(6) *Ibid.*
121. S. 16(3) *ibid.*
122. S. 16(3)(c) of 1960 Act.
123. S. 19 of the *Broadcasting Authority Act, 1960* as amended by substitution by s. 14(1) of the *Broadcasting Authority (Amendment) Act, 1976.*
124. S. 2 of *Broadcasting Authority (Amendment) Act, 1993.* See chapter 12 for a consideration of the *Broadcasting Act, 1990.*
125. S. 21(1) of the *Broadcasting Authority Act, 1960* as amended by substitution by s. 5 of the *Broadcasting Authority (Amendment) Act, 1976.*

126. Memorandum entitled "Advisory Committee" dated January 4, 1960 in File S.16748A, "Broadcasting Authority Legislation 1959", National Archives, Dublin.
127. *Ibid.*
128. *Ibid.*
129. S. 21 of *Broadcasting Authority Act, 1960.*
130. S. 5 of *Broadcasting Authority (Amendment) Act, 1976.*
131. S. 23 of the *Broadcasting Authority Act, 1960.* The limit on repayable advances is increased from time to time. Current advances may not exceed twenty five million pounds in the aggregate by virtue of s. 2 of the *Broadcasting Authority (Amendment) Act, 1979* which substituted a new paragraph for paragraph (6) of s. 23(2) of 1960 Act inserted by the *Broadcasting Authority (Amendment) Act, 1976.*
132. S. 8 of *Broadcasting Authority (Amendment) Act, 1976.*
133. Memorandum for the Government dated December 3, 1959 in File S. 16748A, "Broadcasting Authority Legislation 1959", National Archives, Dublin.
134. S. 25(1) of *Broadcasting Authority Act, 1960.*
135. Ss. 27 & 28 of 1960 Act.
136. S. 26(3) *ibid.*
137. S. 31(1) of the 1960 Act (as amended by substitution by s. 16 of the *Broadcasting Authority (Amendment) 1976)* and s. 31(2) of the 1960 Act.
138. Para 2(1) of Schedule to *Radio and Television Act, 1988.*
139. Para 1(1) *ibid.*
140. Para 3 *ibid.*
141. See Schedule to *Radio and Television Act, 1988.*
142. S. 5(1) *ibid.*
143. Ss. 17 and 18 *ibid.*
144. S. 5(2) *ibid.*
145. S. 17 ibid and s. 6 of *Broadcasting Act, 1990.*
146. S. 5(3) of *Radio and Television Act, 1988.*
147. S. 5(4) *ibid.*
148. S. 7(2)(a) *ibid.*
149. S. 7(2)(b) *ibid.*
150. S. 7(2) and 9(c) *ibid.*
151. S. 7(2)(d) *ibid.*
152. S. 7(2)(e) *ibid.*
153. S. 7(2)(f) *ibid.*
154. S. 7(3)(a) *Ibid.*
155. 381 *Dáil Debates,* cols. 1224-1225, June 1, 1989.
156. *Ibid.*
157. See E.G. Hall and P.J.C. McGovern, *Annotation to Broadcasting and Wireless Telegraphy Act, 1988* in *Irish Current Law Statutes Annotated,* Sweet and Maxwell.
158. S. 3 of the *Broadcasting and Wireless Telegraphy Act, 1988.*
159. S. 4 *ibid.*

160. The High Court, unreported, No. 1978, 1805R, *ex tempore* judgment of Hamilton J, March 23, 1978. See *The Irish Times* of March 24/25, 1978.
161. *Ibid.*
162. [1984] ILRM 161.
163. [1984] ILRM 170.
164. See cases above.
165. February 6, 1989, *The Irish Times Law Report*, February 20, 1989, Supreme Court.
166. Barron J, February 1, 1989, unreported.

16: *Censorship of the Broadcasting Media including Section 31 of the Broadcasting Authority Act, 1960*

1.   For a UK perspective, see Colin R. Munro, *Television Censorship and the Law*, Saxon House, 1978.
2.   Dispatch dated January 5, 1927 in File S. 5234, D/T, "Wireless Broadcasting: Restrictions in the Irish Free State (1926-1927)", National Archives, Dublin.
3.   *Ibid.*
4.   Letter dated November 25, 1941 in File 82/56, vol. 3 D/Comm, (R & B), "Proposals re Broadcast of Religious Services", National Archives, Dublin.
5.   *Ibid.*
6.   See correspondence dated December 1, 1941 and memorandum from the Director of Broadcasting dated December 10, 1941 in File 82/56, vol 3, *ibid.*
7.   Letter dated December 2, 1941 in File 82/56, vol 3, *ibid.*
8.   File 82/56, vol. 3, *ibid.*
9.   Letter dated September 19, 1947 in File 82/56, vol. 3, *ibid.*
10. *Ibid.*
11. Letter dated September 21, 1947 to Minister for Posts and Telegraphs in File 82/56, vol. 3 *ibid.*
12. *Ibid.*
13. See memorandum of Secretary of the Minister dated September 26, 1947 in File 82/56, vol. 3, *ibid.*
14. Memorandum dated January 28, 1955 in File H.6225, vol 14, D/Comm, (R & B), "Proposals for Establishment of Statutory Board," National Archives, Dublin.
15. 224 *Dáil Debates*, cols. 1045-1046, October 12, 1966.
16. See Official Notice of Military Censorship of Newspapers and Publications of July 2, 1922 and Official Notice of Military Censorship of Reports of Military Operations of July 2, 1922. (Vol. 1 of bound SRO p. 67).
17. Article 2A of 1922 Constitution which had been inserted by the *Constitution (Amendment No. 17) Act, 1931* was repealed in 1937 with the rest of the 1922 Constitution.

18. Paper dated January 23, 1940 in File S. 11586A *ibid*.
19. *Ibid*.
20. Memorandum dated February 6, 1940, "Memorandum Regarding Censorship" in File S. 11586A, *ibid*.
21. *Ibid*.
22. In File S. 11586A *Ibid*.
23. *Ibid*.
24. Article 2(1), (S.I. No. 20 of 1941).
25. *Emergency Powers (No. 151) Order, 1942* (S.I. No. 45 of 1942).
26. Memorandum from the Office of the Controller of Censorship dated January 1942 in File S. 11586B, "Censorship of Publications (including newspapers and periodicals)", National Archives, Dublin.
27. *Emergency Powers (No. 359) Order 1945* (S.R.& O No. 119 of 1945).
28. S. 2 of the *Offences Against the State Act, 1939* as amended by s. 5 of the *Offences Against the State (Amendment) Act, 1972*.
29. S. 2 of *Offences Against the State Act, 1939*.
30. *Ibid*.
31. *Ibid*.
32. S. 18(1A) of *Broadcasting Authority Act, 1960* as amended by substitution by s. 3 of the *Broadcasting Authority (Amendment) Act, 1976*.
33. S. 11(1)(b) of the *Wireless Telegraphy Act, 1926* has been amended by substitution by s. 12(f) of the Broadcasting and *Wireless Telegraphy Act, 1988*.
34. S. 31(1A) of the 1960 Act as amended by substitution by s. 16 of the *Broadcasting Authority (Amendment) Act, 1976*.
35. S. 31(1B) *ibid*.
36. 180 *Dáil Debates*, col. 728.
37. 179 *Dáil Debates*, col. 761, February 24, 1960.
38. *Ibid*.
39. 52 *Seanad Debates*, cols. 529-530, February 10, 1960.
40. See File TW 6049, vol 10, D/Comm, (R & B), "Broadcasting Authority Bill, 1959, Minister's Speech in Dáil, Brief etc.", National Archives, Dublin.
41. *Ibid*.
42. *Ibid*.
43. 52 *Seanad Debates*, col. 528, February 10, 1960.
44. *Ibid*., col. 531.
45. *Ibid*.
46. See File S. 516748B, "Broadcasting Authority Legislation 1959", National Archives, Dublin.
47. Letter dated February 8, 1960 in File S. 16748B, *ibid*.
48. Letter dated February 8, 1960 in File S. 16748B, *ibid*.
49. *The Irish Times*, January 13, 1961.
50. [1982] IR 337.
51. In oral arguments from writer's own note of the High Court proceedings.

52. [1982] IR 337 at 354.
53. Memorandum from the Taoiseach to the Secretary of his Department
     dated March 30, 1960 in File S. 14996D, "Television General", National
     Archives, Dublin.
54. *Ibid.*
55. S. 17 of the *Broadcasting Authority Act, 1960* later amended by
     substitution by s. 13 of the *Broadcasting Authority (Amendment) Act,
     1976.*
56. Memorandum of Secretary of the Government to Taoiseach, dated
     April 4, 1960 in File S. 14996D, *loc. cit.*
57. S. 4 of the *Broadcasting Authority Act, 1960.*
58. S. 6 of the 1960 Act later repealed by s. 21 of the 1976 Act but replaced
     with additional safeguards by s. 2 of the 1976 Act.
59. S. 7 of the 1960 Act.
60. Memorandum from Taoiseach to Secretary of the Government dated
     April 5, 1960 in File S. 14996D D/T, *loc. cit.*
61. *Ibid.*
62. See File S. 14996D, *loc. cit.*, which also contains the text of the address
     of the Minister for Posts and Telegraphs at the first meeting of the
     Broadcasting Authority.
63. Article 1.
64. Address, *loc. cit.*
65. *Ibid.*
66. *Ibid.*
67. *Ibid.*
68. *Ibid.*
69. Meeting of December 8, 1960. See Memorandum for the Government
     dated January 11, 1960 in File S. 16772A, "Television Films:
     Censorship", National Archives, Dublin.
70. *Ibid.*
71. See address in File S. 14996D, *loc. cit.*
72. *Ibid.*
73. See 227 *Dáil Debates*, cols. 1662-1664, April 13, 1967 and cols.
     2154-2160, April 20, 1967.
74. Letter of Director General, Edward J. Roth, to Taoiseach, Seán Lemass,
     dated September 1, 1961 in File S. 9908 C/61, D/T "Radio and
     Television: Political Broadcasting", National Archives, Dublin.
75. Memorandum of Attorney General, Amdreas O'Keeffe, dated
     September 5, 1961 in File S. 9908, C/61 *loc. cit.*
76. Letter of September 5, 1961 in File S. 9908, C/61 *loc. cit.*
77. *Ibid.*
78. Letter quoted in report of *Irish Independent* of September 22, 1961 in
     File S. 9908, C/61, D/T *loc. cit.*
79. Letter dated July 13, 1970 from the then Minister for Justice, Desmond
     O'Malley, to the Minister for Posts and Telegraphs, Gerard Collins,
     read out by Dr. Cruise O'Brien on Committee Stage of the *Broadcasting*

Authority (Amendment) Act, 1976, 288 *Dáil Debates,* cols. 995-998, March 2, 1976. In 1976, Gerard Collins, TD, then in opposition, considered that the Minister for Posts and Telegraphs, Dr. Conor Cruise O'Brien was wrong to read out confidential letters between one Minister and another in Government, 288 *Dáil Debates,* col. 1003, March 2, 1976.

80. *Ibid.,* col. 997.
81. *Ibid.,* col. 998.
82. Letter dated July 17, 1970 read by the Minister for Posts and Telegraphs, Dr. Cruise O'Brien, cols. 998-1000, *loc. cit.*
83. *Ibid.,* col. 999.
84. *Ibid.,* cols. 999-1000.
85. S. 31(1) of the 1960 Act, later amended by substitution by s. 16 of the *Broadcasting Authority (Amendment) Act, 1976.*
86. 256 *Dáil Debates,* col. 2453, November 18, 1971.
87. 257 *Dáil Debates,* col. 323, November 24, 1971.
88. *Ibid.,* col. 324.
89. 261 *Dáil Debates,* cols. 1288-1293, June 8, 1972.
90. *Ibid.,* cols. 1288-1289.
91. See earlier section of this chapter.
92. 263 *Dáil Debates,* col. 2460, November 23, 1972.
93. *Ibid.,* col. 2460.
94. See generally Kieran Woodman, *Media Control in Ireland 1923-1983,* Officina Typographica, Galway University Press, 1985, chapter entitled "The Politics of Censorship"; León Ó Broin, "The dismissal of the Irish Broadcasting Authority", in *European Broadcasting Review,* March 1973, p. 24; Paul O'Higgins, "The Irish TV Sackings" in *Index on Censorship,* vol. 3 pt. 1 (1973) p. 24; 264 *Dáil Debates,* cols. 54 et seq. November 28, 1972 and Peter Feeney, "Censorship and RTE" in *The Crane Bag,* vol. 8, No. 2, 1984.
95. In *Re Kevin O'Kelly* (1974) 108 ILTR 97.
96. The letter of the Minister for Posts and Telegraphs dated November 21, 1972 is set out in 264 *Dáil Debates,* col. 1717, December 14, 1972.
97. 264 *Dáil Debates,* col. 1371, December 13, 1972.
98. *Ibid.,* cols. 1365-1366.
99. 79 *Seanad Debates,* col. 769, March 12, 1975.
100. *Report of the Broadcasting Review Committee 1974* (Prl. 3827), Stationery Office, Dublin. See observations of Minister for Posts and Telegraphs, Dr. Conor Cruise O'Brien, on Second Stage of *Broadcasting Authority (Amendment) Bill 1975,* 79 *Seanad Debates* col. 769, March 12, 1975.
101. *Ibid.*
102. 79 *Seanad Debates,* col. 784, March 12, 1975.
103. *Ibid.,* col. 785.
104. See *The Irish Times,* March 29, 1979.
105. "Are our broadcasting structures out of date?", *Irish Broadcasting Review,* Summer 1978, p. 6.
106. 18th Report, RTE, (Prl. 9945, May 7, 1981) Stationery Office, Dublin.

107. *Ibid.*, Evidence Question 329.
108. *Ibid.*, Evidence Question 330.
109. *Ibid.*, para 129.
110. *Ibid.*, para 129.
111. *Broadcasting Authority Act, 1960 (Section 31) Order 1993* (S.I. No. 1 of 1993).
112. Pursuant to s. 12 of the *Radio and Television Act, 1988*.
113. *Broadcasting Guidelines for RTE Personnel*, RTE, 1989, p. 60 as amended in September 1993. See also *O'Toole v RTE* [1993] ILRM 458 considered in chapters 26 and 30.
114. See definition of "document" in s. 2 of the *Offences Against the State Act, 1939* as amended by s. 5 of the *Offences Against the State (Amendment) Act, 1972*.
115. S. 10(1) of 1939 Act, *ibid.*
116. *O'Toole v RTE* [1993] ILRM 458.
117. [1982] IR 337. The order involved was the *Broadcasting Authority Act, 1960 (Section 31) (No. 2) Order 1982* (S.I. No. 21 of 1982).
118. [1982] IR 337 at 356.
119. *Ibid.* at 361.
120. Writer's personal notes of proceedings in court.
121. Application No. 15404/89, decision of April 16, 1991.
122. S.I. No. 3 of 1989.
123. *Muller and Others*, judgment of the Eur. Court H.R. of 24 May 1988, Series A No. 133 p. 20, para 29 with further references.
124. *Sunday Times Case*, judgment of the Eur. Court H.R. of 26 April 1979, Series A, No. 30, p. 29 para 45.
125. [1982] IR 337 at 381.
126. See *Muller and Others*, *loc. cit.*
127. For example, see *The Sunday Times Case*, *loc. cit.*
128. See chapters 26 and 27.
129. See *The Irish Times*, March 16, 1988.
130. *Ibid.*
131. *The Irish Times*, March 21, 1988.
132. *Ibid.*
133. See *Eleventh Annual Report of the Broadcasting Complaints Commission* (1989).
134. *Broadcasting Authority Act, 1960 (Section 31) Order, 1987*, (S.I. No. 13 of 1987).
135. S.18(1)(b) of the *Broadcasting Authority Act, 1960* as amended by substitution by s.3 of the *Broadcasting Authority (Amendment) Act, 1976*.
136. Unreported, High Court, July 31, 1992 per O'Hanlon J; [1993] ILRM 458, Supreme Court.
137. The current order is the *Broadcasting Authority Act, 1960 (Section 31) Order, 1993* (S.I. No. 1 of 1993).
138. S. 31 of the *Broadcasting Authority Act, 1960* as amended by substitution by s.16 of the *Broadcasting Authority (Amendment) Act, 1976*.

139. S. 18(1) of the *Broadcasting Authority Act, 1960* as amended by substitution by s.3 of the *Broadcasting Authority (Amendment) Act, 1976*.
140. See n.136 above.
141. *Brandon Books Ltd v RTE*, unreported, July 16, 1993 (HCt).
142. *Broadcasting Authority Act, 1960 (Section 31) Order, 1992*, (S.I. No. 4 of 1992).
143. *O'Toole v RTE* [1993] ILRM 458.
144. *The Irish Times*, May 26, 1993.
145. Decision awaited.
146. See Mark Bonham-Carter, "Whose Service?" in *Index on Censorship*, vol. 17 No. 8, September 1988.
147. 138 House of Commons *Official Report* (6th Series) col. 885; 500 House of Lords *Official Report* (5th series) cols. 1139-1140.
148. These four factors were outlined in the affidavit of Mr. Scoble, assistant Under-Secretary of State in the Home Office and head of the broadcasting department. See opinion of Lord Ackner in *Brind v Secretary of State* [1991] 1 All ER 720.
149. Set out in opinion of Lord Ackner in *Brind, loc. cit.*, at 727-728.
150. *Ibid.*
151. *Ibid.*
152. *Ibid.*
153. [1991] 1 All ER 720
154. *Ibid.* See also D. Kinley, "Legislation, Discretionary Authority and the European Convention on Human Rights," 13 *Statute Law Review*, 63 (1992).
155. S. 16(3)(b) of *Broadcasting Authority Act, 1960*.
156. S. 4(11) of *Radio and Television Act, 1988*.
157. S. 52 of the *Telegraph Act, 1863* as amended by s.8 of the *PTS Act, 1983*.

17: Privilege, Powers and Duties of Telecom Éireann

1. See s. 87 of *PTS Act, 1983*.
2. S. 87 of *PTS Act, 1983* as amended by Reg. 3 of the *European Communities (Telecommunications Services) Regulations, 1992* (S.I. No. 45 of 1992).
3. *Council Directive No. 90/387/EEC of 28 June 1990; Commission Directive No. 90/388/EEC of 28 June 1990*.
4. Reg. 3 of *European Communities (Telecommunications Services) Regulations, 1992* (S.I. No. 45 of 1992). The expression "public telecommunications network" and "voice telephony service" are defined in Reg. 2 of the 1992 Regulations.
5. Reg. 3(2), *ibid*.
6. S. 4 of the *Telegraph Act, 1869* subsequently amended by s. 8 of *PTS Act, 1983*.
7. S. 87(2) of *PTS Act, 1983*.
8. *Ibid.*

9.   S. 111 *ibid.*
10.   See n. 3 *supra.*
11.   S. 111(2) of *PTS Act, 1983.*
12.   *Postal and Telecommunications Services Act, 1983 (Section 111(1)) Order 1989* (S.I. No. 77 of 1989).
13.   Pursuant to S.111(2) of *PTS Act, 1983.*
14.   *Commission Directive of 16 May 1988 on Competition in the Markets in Telecommunications Terminal Equipment* (OJ L 131/73, 27.5.88).
15.   Notice dated October 1992 published in national newspapers on October 30, 1992.
16.   *Ibid.*
17.   The conditions are set out in the *Telegraph Act, 1863* (26 & 27 vict. c. 112), the *Telegraph Act, 1868* (31 & 32 vict. c. 110), the *Telegraph Act, 1869* (32 & 33 vict. c. 73), the *Telegraph Act, 1878* (41 & 42 Vict. c. 76), the *Telegraph Act, 1892* (55 & 56 Vict. c. 59), the *Telegraph (Construction) Act, 1908* (8 Edw. 7, c.33), the *Telegraph (Arbitration) Act, 1909* (9 Edw. 7 c 20), the *Telegraph (Construction) Act, 1911* (1 & 2 Geo. 5. c. 39), the *Telegraph (Construction) Act, 1916* (6 & 7 Geo. 5. c. 27), the *PTS Act, 1983* and the *Telecommunications Scheme, 1992* (S.I. No. 19 of 1992).
18.   S. 6(1) and (2) of the *Telegraph Act, 1863* (26 & 27 Vict. c. 112).
19.   *Ibid.* s. 6(3).
20.   *Ibid.* s.6(4).
21.   See n. 17 *supra.*
22.   Laid by the Government before each House of the Oireachtas, May 1981 (Prl.9805) Stationery Office, para 4.6.
23.   Para 3.12 *ibid.*
24.   S. 3(4) of the *Telecommunications Act, 1981* which was subsequently repealed by the UK *Telecommunications Act, 1984.*
25.   Unreported February 29, 1979; see report of the *ex tempore* judgment in *The Irish Times,* March 1, 1979.
26.   See *Telecommunications Schemes, 1992 and 1993* including the limitations on liability in Articles 48 and 49 of the 1992 Scheme and individual subscriber contracts. See also *McCord v ESB* [1980] ILRM 153.
27.   *AT & T Annual Report,* 22-23, 1907; T. Vail, "Public Utilities and Public Policy" 3 *Atlantic Monthly,* 307, 315, March 1913.
28.   47 U.S.C. ss. 151 *et seq.*
29.   S. 3(1)(a) of UK *Telecommunications Act, 1984.*
30.   S. 3(2)(a) *ibid.*
31.   *AG v Paperlink Ltd* [1984] ILRM 373.
32.   S.I. No. 45 of 1992. See also above.
33.   These services are considered in chapter 18.
34.   Reg. 4(1)(b)(ii) of the *European Communities (Telecommunication Services) Regulations, 1992* (S.I. No. 45 of 1992).
35.   S. 87(1) of the *PTS Act, 1983* as amended by Reg 3 of the 1992 Regulations, *ibid.*

36. Reg. 4(1)(a) and (b)(i) of the 1992 Regulations, *loc. cit.*
37. Reg. 4(1)(a) of the 1992 Regulations, *loc. cit.*
38. S.I. No. 45 of 1992.
39. S. 15(2) of the *PTS Act, 1983.*
40. *1992 Review of the Situation in the Telecommunications Services Sector, Communication from the Commission,* Brussels, 21 October 1992.
41. *Ibid.*
42. Press Release 7280/93, *Resolution of Council of the European Communities, June 16, 1993.*
43. *Council Directive of 17 December 1990 on Procurement Procedures of Entities operating in the Water, Energy, Transport and Telecommunications Sectors (90/531/EEC,* OJ L 297/1, 29/10/90f. See P. Lee, *Current EC Legal Developments: Public Procurement,* Butterworths, 1992.
44. *European Communities (Award of Contracts by Entities Operating in the Water, Transport and Telecommunications Sectors) Regulations 1993* (S.I. No. 103 of 1993); *European Communities (Review Procedures for the Award of Contracts by Entities operating in the Water, Energy, Transport and Telecommunications Sectors) Regulations, 1993* (S.I. No. 104 of 1993).
45. *Council Directive 93/38 EEC,* OJEC No. L 199/84, August 9, 1993.

18: *The Privileges and Duties of Other Providers of Carrier-Related Telecommunication Services*

1. The exceptions are set out in s. 5 of the *Telegraph Act, 1869,* (32 & 33 Vict. c.73) repealed by s.7 of the *PTS Act, 1983;* the *de jure* monopoly was established by s. 4 of the *Telegraph Act, 1869* (32 & 33 Vict. c. 73) later amended by s. 8 of the *PTS Act, 1983.*
2. EC Directives Nos. 88/301/EEC, 90/387/EEC and 90/388/EEC.
3. See *Report of Post and Telegraphs Review Group 1978-1979* (Dublin, Stationery Office, Prl 7883) (chaired by Dr. Michael J. Dargan); the White Paper entitled *Reorganisation of Postal and Telecommunications Services;* Dublin, Stationery Office, (Prl 9805) and speech of Minister for Communications, John Wilson, on Second Stage of *PTS Bill, 1982,* 334 *Dáil Debates,* cols. 1589 *et seq.* May 19, 1982.
4. 334 *Dáil Debates,* col. 1593, May 19, 1982.
5. 334 *Dáil Debates,* col. 1967, July 6, 1983.
6. See chapter 17.
7. *Commission Directive No. 88/301/EEC of May 16 1988 (Terminal Equipment)* in particular.
8. Notice from Department of Communications published in the national press on January 29, 1990.
9. Notice from the Department of Communications published in the national press on October 30, 1992.
10. S.I. No. 45 of 1992.
11. See n. 2 *supra.*
12. Reg. 8(1) of the *European Communities (Telecomunications Services)*

Regulations, 1992 (S.I. No. 45 of 1992). This had been a feature of telecommunication law since 1983. See s.8 and the Fourth Schedule, Part II of the *PTS Act, 1983* which amended Reg. 26(1) of the *Telephone Regulations 1980* (S.I. No. 195 of 1980).

13. Reg. 8(5) of 1992 Regulations, *loc. cit.*
14. Reg. 9 of the 1992 Regulations, *loc. cit.*
15. *Use of Recording Devices*, 11 FCC, 1033 (1947).
16. *Hush-a-Phone Corp v United States*, 238 F. 2d 266, 269 at No. 10 (D.C. Cir. 1956).
17. *Carterfone Device*, 13 F.C.C. 2d 420, 14 F.C.C. 2d 571, (1968). See also *AT&T Foreign Attachment Revisions*, 15 F.C.C. 605 (1968), 18 F.C.C. 2d 781 (1969).
18. *Ibid.*
19. *Mebane Home Telephone Co.* 53 F.C.C. 2d 473, 476 (1975) See generally Fuhr, "Competition in the Terminal Equipment Market After Carterfone", 28 *Antitr Bull* 699 (1983).
20. See *Registration Program*, 56 F.C.C. 2d 593 (1975), 58 F.C.C. 2d 736 (1976). See also *North Carolina Util Comm'n v FCC*, 537 F. 2d 787 (4th Cir. 1976). See generally Note, "Competition in the Telephone Equipment Industry: Beyond Telerent", 86 *Yale L.J.* 538 (1977).
21. *Second Computer Inquiry*, 77 F.C.C. 2d. 384, reconsid., 84 F.C.C 2d. 50, (1981), further reconsid., 88 F.C.C 2d 512 (1981), aff'd *sub. nom Computer & Communications Indus. Assoc v. FCC*, 693 F. 2d 198 (D.C. Cir. 1982).
22. *United States v AT&T Co*, 552 F. Supp 131 (DDC 1982), Modification of Final Judgment Opinion.
23. *Ibid.*, p. 163 n. 137.
24. S.I. No. 45 of 1992.
25. Licence issued under s. 111 of the *PTS Act*, 1983, as amended by the 1992 Regulations, *loc. cit.*
26. *Ibid.*

19: *Privilege, Powers and Duties of Radio Telefís Éireann (RTE)*

1. S. 17(1) of 1926 Act.
2. S. 17(2) *ibid.*
3. S. 3 of 1960 Act; s. 3 of *Broadcasting Authority (Amendment) Act, 1966* changed the corporate name of the Authority from "Radio Éireann" to "Radio Telefís Éireann".
4. S. 34(6) of 1960 Act.
5. S. 16(2)(a) of 1960 Act.
6. S. 16(3)(a) of 1960 Act.
7. [1982] IR 337 at 343.
8. S. 16(3)(a) of *Broadcasting Authority Act, 1960*.
9. S. 16 of *Broadcasting Authority Act, 1960* as amended by ss. 5 and 7(2)

of the *Broadcasting Authority (Amendment) Act, 1966* and s.12 of *Broadcasting Authority (Amendment) Act, 1976.*

10. S. 16(2)(b) of the 1960 Act as amended by substitution by s. 12 of the *Broadcasting Authority (Amendment) Act, 1976.*

11. S. 17 of 1960 Act.

12. 79 *Seanad Debates*, col. 764, March 12, 1975, Second Stage of the 1975 Bill.

13. *Broadcasting Review Committee Report 1974* (Prl. 3827), Stationery Office, Dublin p.20, section 3.4.3(iii).

14. S. 17 of *Broadcasting Authority Act, 1960* as amended by substitution by s. 13 of the *Broadcasting Authority (Amendment) Act, 1976.*

15. 79 *Seanad Debates*, col. 764, March 12, 1975.

16. S. 18(3) of *Radio and Television Act, 1988.*

17. Memorandum for the Government dated December 3, 1959 in File S. 16748A, "Broadcasting Authority: Legislation 1959", National Archives, Dublin.

18. See Chapter IX, "National Outlook, Culture and Language" in *Report of the Television Commission, 1959*, Stationery Office, Dublin.

19. See Memorandum for the Government dated December 3, 1959 in File S.16748A, "*Broadcasting Authority: Legislation 1959*", National Archives, Dublin.

20. Supreme Court, unreported, July 16, 1976.

21. *Ibid.*

22. S. 18 1(a) of *Broadcasting Authority Act, 1960* as amended by substitution by s.3 of the *Broadcasting Authority (Amendment) Act, 1976.*

23. 81 *Seanad Debates*, col. 471, June 4, 1975.

24. *Ibid.*

25. S. 18(1) of *Broadcasting Authority Act, 1960* as amended by substitution by s. 3 of the *Broadcasting Authority (Amendment) Act, 1976.*

26. Para 4.2 (p.52) of *Broadcasting Guidelines for RTE Personnel*, RTE, 1989.

27. Para 4.3 (p.52) *ibid.*

28. Para 5.5 (p.53) *ibid.*

29. S. 18(1A) of *Broadcasting Authority Act, 1960* as amended by substitution by s. 3 of *Broadcasting Authority (Amendment) Act, 1976.*

30. 289 *Dáil Debates*, cols. 699-700, Committee Stage of *Broadcasting Authority (Amendment) Bill, 1975*, March 31, 1976.

31. *Ibid.*

32. *Council Directive 89/552/EEC Regarding Broadcasting Activities.*

33. Reg. 7 of the *European Communities (Television Broadcasting) Regulations, 1991* (S.I. No. 251 of 1991). See also "Standards of Taste and Decency in relation to the Portrayal of Violence or Sex on Television and Radio", *Broadcasting Guidelines for RTE Personnel*, RTE, 1989.

34. Reg. 7(2) *Ibid.*

35. Reg. 7(3) *ibid.*

36. S. 18(1B) of *Broadcasting Authority Act, 1960* as amended by substitution by s. 3 of the *Broadcasting Authority (Amendment) Act, 1976*.
     For a consideration of privacy in the Irish context see F. O'Hannrachain, "Privacy and Broadcasting" 10 *ILTSJ* 267 (1971); B. Walsh,
     "The Judicial Power and the Right to Privacy", (1977) 3 *DULJ* 3; E.
     O'Dell, "Does Defamation Value Free Expression?" (1990) 12 *DULJ*
     (ns) 50, 70-75; R. Clark, *Data Protection Law in Ireland*, Dublin, The
     Round Hall Press, 1991, ch. 1; B. McMahon and W. Binchy, *The Irish
     Law of Torts*, 2nd ed., Dublin, Butterworths, 1992; G. Quinn, "Duties
     of the 'Right' and the 'Good' and the Judicial Evolution of the Right
     to Privacy in the US and the Republic of Ireland", a paper delivered
     to the Law and Philosophy Meeting in Trinity College on February
     28, 1992. See also the *Calcutt Report on Privacy and Related Matters*,
     HMSO (Cm 1102), 1990 and the *Calcutt Review of Press Self-Regulation*,
     HMSO (Cm 2135), 1993.
37. See, for example, *Cosgrave v Ireland* [1982] ILRM 48.
38. S. 18B-1(d) of *Broadcasting Authority Act, 1960* as amended by
     substitution by s. 4 of *Broadcasting Authority (Amendment) Act, 1976*.
39. Senator John Horgan on Committee Stage of *Broadcasting Authority
     (Amendment) Bill 1975*, 81 *Seanad Debates*, cols. 523-525.
40. *Broadcasting Guidelines for RTE Personnel*, RTE, 1989, p. 32.
41. *Ibid*.
42. S. 3 of *Wireless Telegraphy Act, 1926* as amended by s. 12 of the
     Broadcasting and Wireless Telegraphy Act, 1988.
43. *Council Directive 89/552/EEC regarding Broadcasting Activities*.
44. Reg. 3(1) of *European Communities (Television Broadcasting) Regulations
     1991* (S.I. No. 251 of 1991).
45. Reg. 3(2) *ibid*.
46. *Ibid*.
47. Reg. 3(3) *ibid*.
48. Article 6 of the *EC Council Directive 89/552/EEC*.
49. Reg. 4 of the 1991 Regulations, *ibid*.
50. S. 24 of *Broadcasting Authority Act, 1960*.
51. S. 7 of *Broadcasting Act, 1990*.
52. S. 26 of 1960 Act.
53. S. 27 of 1960 Act as amended by s. 10 of the *Broadcasting Authority
     (Amendment) Act, 1976*.
54. S. 20 of *Broadcasting Authority Act, 1960*. S. 20(3) of the 1960 Act was
     amended by substitution by s. 14(3) of the *Broadcasting Authority
     (Amendment) Act, 1976*, and was later repealed by s. 19 of the
     Broadcasting Act, 1990 but replaced by s. 3 of the *Broadcasting Act, 1990*.
     S. 20(5) was repealed by *European Communities (Broadcasting Authority
     Act, 1960) Regulations 1983* (S.I. No. 187 of 1983).
55. See chapter 15.
56. S. 30 of the 1960 Act and First Schedule of Act.
57. S. 6 of *Broadcasting Authority (Amendment) Act, 1976*.

58. Reg. 6 of the *European Communities (Television Broadcasting) Regulations, 1991* (S.I. No. 251 of 1991).
59. See chapter 27, n. 17.
60. 224 *Dáil Debates*, cols. 1045-46, October 12, 1966. Mr. Lemass's statement was prompted by allegations that the Minister for Agriculture, Mr. C.J. Haughey, had somehow censored news details on RTE.
61. "Censorship and RTE", *The Crane Bag*, vol 2, 1984. p. 63.
62. 356 *Dáil Debates*, col. 1803, March 7, 1985.
63. *Ibid.* cols. 1803-04.
64. See chapter 16 where, *inter alia*, the dismissal of the RTE Authority in 1972, is considered.
65. "RTE seems sadly lacking in self-respect", *Irish Independent*, September 30, 1989.
66. "II Thou shalt not annoy thy Minister", *Sunday Independent*, October 1, 1989.
67. S. 2 of *Broadcasting Authority (Amendment) Act, 1976*.

20: *Cable Television and Multi-Point Distribution Systems (MMDS) Providers*

1. *Broadcasting Review Committee,* Second Interim Report. This report was never published but its recommendations are summarised at para 13.29 of the *Broadcasting Review Committee Report, 1974; Report of the Cable Systems Committee,* (chaired by Mrs. Margaret Downes), December 1984, Dublin, Stationery Office, (Pl. 2937); *Restrictive Practices Commission, Report of Study into Cable Television Systems in the Greater Dublin Area;* Dublin, Stationery Office (Pl. 4295).
2. S. 2 of *Wireless Telegraphy Act, 1926* as amended by S. 19(b) of the *Broadcasting Authority (Amendment) Act, 1976*.
3. *Telegraph Act, 1863* (26 & 27 Vict. c. 112) s. 3 and *Telegraph Act, 1869* (32 & 33 Vict. c. 73) s.3.
4. *Wireless Telegraphy (Wired Broadcast Relay Licence) Regulations 1974* (S.I. No. 67 of 1974) and the *Wireless Telegraphy (Wired Broadcast Relay Licence) (Amendment) Regulations, 1988* (S.I. No. 82 of 1988).
5. The *Wireless Telegraphy Act, 1926 (Section 3) (Exemption of Certain Wired Broadcast Relay Stations) Order 1976* (S.I. No. 200 of 1976) provided for abolition of the requirement to license cable systems when the number of service points did not exceed 100.
6. The form of the licence is set out in the schedule to the 1974 Regulations, *loc. cit.*
7. Defined in the Regulations as "a station".
8. See *State (Westward Cables Ltd) v Minister for Posts and Telegraphs* (1983 No. 693 SS) unreported, High Court. See report in *Irish Independent*, May 15, 1984; the Minister for Communications (the successor to the Minister for Posts and Telegraphs) was reported as having given an

undertaking in the High Court to Westward Cables Ltd (a licensee to provide cable television service) that he would take all feasible steps to enforce the *Wireless Telegraphy Acts*. See also *State (Connaught Multi-Channel TV Ltd) v Minister for Communications* (1983, No. 743.SS) Keane J, July 23, 1984, High Court, unreported and *Cork Communications v Minister for Communications*, unreported, High Court, *The Irish Times*, August 24, 1989.

9.   See previous note for reference.
10. See Reg. 3 of the *1974 Regulations* as amended by Reg. 4 of the *1988 Regulations*.
11. See Second Schedule to *1974 Regulations* as amended by the *1988 Regulations*.
12. *Ibid*. n. 10.
13. Reg. 9(2)(a) of the *1974 Regulations* as amended by substitution by Reg. 4 of the *1988 Regulations*.
14. Reg. 9(4)(f)(a) of the *1974 Regulations* as amended by substitution by Reg. 4 of the *1988 Regulations*.
15. Reg. 12(b) of the *1974 Regulations, loc. cit.*
16. See Article 3 in *Wired Broadcast Relay Licence in Schedule to 1974 Regulations, loc. cit.* as amended by substitution by reg. 4 of the *1988 Regulations loc. cit.*
17. *Wireless Telegraphy (Television Programme Restransmission and Relay) Regulations, 1991* (S.I. No. 252 of 1991). The earlier regulations are the 1974, 1988 and 1989 regulations referred to in the notes to this chapter.
18. Article 7 of licence, *ibid*.
19. Reg. 12(e) of *1974 Regulations, loc. cit.*
20. Reg. 10 of *1974 Regulations, loc. cit.*
21. Reg. 12(c) of *1974 Regulations, loc. cit.*
22. *Wireless Telegraphy (Television Programme Retransmission) Regulations 1989* (S.I. No. 39 of 1989).
23. Reg. 9(j) of *1989 Regulations, loc. cit.*
24. Reg. 8 of *1989 Regulations.*
25. Reg. 6(3) of *1989 Regulations.*
26. Reg. 6(2) of *1989 Regulations.*
27. Reg. 9(c) and Article 3 of licence set out in Schedule to *1989 Regulations, loc. cit.* But see n. 17 above together with the text in relation to cable television.
28. Reg. 11 of *1989 Regulations.*
29. Art. 7 of licence, set out at Schedule to *1989 Regulations.*
30. S.9(4) of the *Broadcasting Act, 1990.*
31. See annotation of the *Broadcasting Act 1990* by David Barniville in *Irish Current Law Statutes Annotated 1990*, London, Sweet & Maxwell.

21: *The Powers and Duties of the Independent Radio and Television Commission and Private Broadcasting Service Providers*

1. 381 *Dáil Debates*, cols. 882 et seq. 1988.
2. Para 5 of Schedule to *Radio and Television Act, 1988*.
3. *Ibid.*
4. Para 13 *ibid.*
5. The Independent Radio and Television Commission has been subject to review by the High Court and Supreme Court. See *Dublin and County Broadcasting v IRTC*, unreported, High Court, per Murphy J May 12, 1989 and *TV 3 v IRTC*, unreported, Supreme Court, October 26, 1993. These cases may be compared with *R v ITC ex p TSW, The Times*, Law Report, March 30, 1992, House of Lords.
6. See chapter 15.
7. S. 4(7) of 1988 Act.
8. See chapter 12.
9. See chapter 15.
10. S.17 of *Radio and Television Act, 1988*. See also *Wireless Telegraphy (Wired Broadcast Relay Licence) Regulations, 1974* (S.I. No. 67 of 1974), *Wireless Telegraphy (Wired Broadcast Relay Licence) (Amendment) Regulations 1988* (S.I. No. 82 of 1988) and the *Wireless Telegraphy (Television Programme Retransmission) Regulations, 1989* (S.I. No. 39 of 1989).
11. S. 9(2) of *Radio and Television Act, 1988*.
12. S. 18(2) of 1988 Act.
13. 521 *HL Debates*, col. 364, July 11, 1990.
14. [1973] QB 629; [1973] 1 All ER 689, CA.
15. See also *R v Independent Broadcasting Authority ex parte Whitehouse, The Times*, April 14, 1984 D.C.
16. [1988] ILRM 472.
17. 4 *Harvard Law Review*, 193 (with Samuel D. Warren). See privacy references in chapter 19 n. 36.
18. S. 9(4) of *Radio and Television Act, 1988*.
19. 120 *Seanad Debates*, col. 800, June 21, 1988.
20. S. 10 of *Radio and Television Act, 1988* and s. 4 of the *Broadcasting Act, 1990*.
21. S. 10(5) *Radio and Television Act, 1988*.
22. S. 10(3) *ibid*. See chapter 31 where this issue is considered.
23. S. 10(4) *ibid.*
24. S. 11(1) *ibid.*
25. S. 11(2) *ibid.*
26. *Radio and Television (Complaints by Members of the Public) Regulations, 1992* (S.I. No. 329 of 1992).
27. S. 12 of 1988 Act, *ibid.*
28. Individual contracts between the Commission and the broadcasting contractor are available from the Independent Radio and Television

Commission on payment of a fee. The details referred to in the text
were based on typical standard terms.

29.   Copies of existing individual licences may be obtained from the
       Independent Radio and Television Commission on payment of a fee.
       The text here is based on standard terms and conditions.

30.   The current Constitution and Convention are comprised in the *Final
       Acts of the Plenipotentiary Conference,* Geneva 1992 ITU, Geneva, 1993.

31.   See, for example, the *dicta* of Henchy J. in *McCord v ESB* [1980] ILRM
       153 at 161.

22: *Powers and Functions of the Broadcasting Complaints Commission*

1.   See *Report of Broadcasting Complaints Commission for the year 1977,*
       Broadcasting Complaints Commission, Dublin. [The Hon. Mr. Justice
       T.C. Kingsmill-Moore was chairman of the Broadcasting Complaints
       Committee and the first chairman of the Broadcating Complaints
       Commission until his death in January 1979.]

2.   S. 18A-(2) of *Broadcasting Authority Act, 1960,* as amended by sub-
       stitution by s. 4 of *Broadcasting Authority (Amendment) Act, 1976.*

3.   S. 18A-(8) *ibid.*

4.   Minister for Posts and Telegraphs, Dr. Conor Cruise O'Brien on
       Committee Stage of the *Broadcasting Authority (Amendment) Bill, 1975,*
       290 *Dáil Debates,* col. 703, May 5, 1976.

5.   See, for example, Deputy Lawlor, *ibid,* col. 703, who argued about the
       Commission being on the same level as the judiciary which would
       probably be unconstitutional. Dr. Conor Cruise O'Brien's reply is at
       290 *Dáil Debates,* col. 703 May 5, 1976.

6.   S.18A of the *Broadcasting Authority Act, 1960* as inserted by s.4 of the
       Broadcasting Authority (Amendment) Act, 1976 in relation to RTE;
       s.11(3) of the *Radio and Television Act, 1988* and the *Radio and Television
       (Complaints by Members of the Public) Regulations 1992,* (S.I. 329 of 1992)
       in relation to non-RTE broadcasting services.

7.   S. 18B(1)(a) of *Broadcasting Authority Act, 1960* as amended by
       insertion of s.4 of *Broadcasting Authority (Amendment) Act, 1976;* s. 18(1)
       of 1960 Act as inserted by s. 3 of the 1976 Act, in relation to RTE. See
       previous note in relation to non-RTE broadcasting services and ss.
       9(1)(b) and 18(1) of the *Radio and Television Act, 1988.*

8.   S. 18B(1)(b) *ibid.* and s.11(4)(iii) of the *Radio and Television Act, 1988.*

9.   S. 18B(1)(b) of the 1960 Act as amended by the 1976 Act, s. 18(1) of
       1960 Act as amended by the 1976 Act and S.11(4)(iii) of the *Radio and
       Television Act, 1988.*

10.   S. 18(1A) of the 1960 Act as amended and s. 9 of the *Radio and Television
       Act, 1988.*

11.   S. 18B(1)(c) of the 1960 Act as amended by the 1976 Act; s.31(1) of
       Broadcasting Authority Act, 1960 as amended by insertion by s. 16 of

the *Broadcasting Authority (Amendment) Act, 1976* and ss. 11 and 12 of the *Radio and Television Act, 1988.*

12. S. 18B(1)(d) and s.18(1B) of the 1960 Act as amended by the 1976 Act; ss. 9(1)(e) and 11 of the *Radio and Television Act, 1988.*

13. S. 18B(1)(e) of the 1960 as amended by the 1976 Act; s. 11(4)(iv) of the *Radio and Television Act, 1988.*

14. S. 18B(1)(f) *ibid.*

15. S. 18B(1)(g) of 1960 Act as inserted by s.8(1) of the *Broadcasting Act, 1990.*

16. Council Directive of October 3, 1989, (89/552/EEC), Official Journal of the European Communities, No. L. 298/23, 17.10.89.

17. The Convention was opened for signature in May 1989.

18. S. 18B(2) of 1960 Act as amended by insertion by s.4 of the 1976 Act.

19. S. 18B(2)(a) of the 1960 Act as amended by the 1976 Act; s.11 of the *Radio and Television Act, 1988.*

20. S. 18B(4) of the 1960 Act as amended by the 1976 Act.

21. S. 18B(10) *ibid.*

22. S. 18B(12) *ibid.*

23. 285 *Dáil Debates*, col. 385, October 28, 1975, on Second Stage of *Broadcasting Authority (Amendment) Bill, 1975.*

24. *Ibid.,* col. 386.

25. 290 *Dáil Debates*, col. 629, Committee Stage of *Broadcasting Authority (Amendment) Bill, 1975, May 5, 1976.*

26. *Ibid.,* cols. 640–641.

27. *Ibid.,* col. 641.

28. *Ibid.*

29. S. 18B(11) of the 1960 Act as amended by the 1976 Act.

30. S.18B(11) *ibid* and s.11(4)(a)(i) of the *Radio and Television Act, 1988.*

31. See above.

32. S. 18B (11A) of 1960 Act as amended by insertion by s. 8(2) of *Broadcasting Act, 1990.*

33. See 18C(1) of 1960 Act as amended by insertion by S. 4 of 1976 Act.

34. *Ibid.*

35. *Ibid.*

36. S. 18C(2) *ibid.*

37. See, for example, *Annual Report of the Broadcasting Complaints Commission 1979-80*, Broadcasting Complaints Commission, Dublin. See also subsequent reports.

38. *Eighth Report of the Broadcasting Complaints Commission*, Broadcasting Complaints Commission, Dublin.

39. Decision of Commission, May 1983.

40. The details are set out in the *Seventh Annual Report of the Broadcasting Complaints Commission for Year ending 30 March 1985.* Broadcasting Complaints Commission, Dublin.

41. S. 18(1)(b) of *Broadcasting Authority Act, 1960* as amended by substitution by s. 3 of the *Broadcasting Authority (Amendment) Act, 1976.*

42. See *Seventh Annual Report of Broadcasting Complaints Commission for year ended March 1985*, Broadcasting Complaints Commission, Dublin.

43. *Ibid.*

44. S. 18(b) of *Broadcasting Authority Act 1960* as amended by substitution by s. 3 of the *Broadcasting Authority (Amendment) Act, 1976*.

45. 12 BVerfGE 205, 1961.

46. S. 18(1B) of *Broadcasting Authority Act, 1960* as amended by insertion by s. 3 of the *Broadcasting Authority (Amendment) Act, 1976*.

47. See *Ninth Annual Report of the Broadcasting Complaints Commission for Year ending March 1987*, Broadcasting Complaints Commission, Dublin.

48. *Ibid.*

49. S.18(1A) of *Broadcasting Authority Act, 1960* as amended by insertion by s. 3 of the *Broadcasting Authority (Amendment) Act, 1976*.

50. See *Tenth Report of the Broadcasting Complaints Commission for Year ending March 1988*, Broadcasting Complaints Commission, Dublin.

51. *AG (SPUC) v Open Door Counselling* [1987] ILRM 477.

52. As amended by insertion by S. 3 of the *Broadcasting Authority (Amendment) Act, 1976*.

53. See *Tenth Report of Commission, loc. cit.*

54. See *Twelfth Annual Report of the Broadcasting Complaints Commission for Year ending March 1990*, Broadcasting Complaints Commission, Dublin. See also complaint of Alan Dukes T.D. in the same Report.

55. *Ibid.*

56. *Ibid.* The approach of the Commission may be compared with the decision of the US Supreme Court in *New York Times Co v Sullivan*, 376, US 254 (1964) where the Court held that the State's common law of libel was constitutionally deficient in failing to provide safeguards for freedom of speech and press in libel actions brought by public officials against critics of their official conduct. See E. O'Dell, "Does Defamation Value Free Expression? The Possible Influence of *New York Times v Sullivan* on Irish Law", (1990) 12 *DULJ* (ns) 50.

57. "The Broadcasting Complaints Commission", (1983) *Public Law*, 37 at 39.

58. *Ibid.*

59. S. 18(1)(g) of *Broadcasting Authority Act, 1960* as inserted by s. 8(1) of the *Broadcasting Act, 1990*.

60. Stationery Office, Dublin, Prl. 9945, May 7, 1981.

62. See Andrea Millwood Hargrare, *Taste and Decency in Broadcasting*, Broadcasting Standards Council with John Libbey. See also A.M. Hargrave (ed.), *A Matter of Manners: The Limits of Broadcasting Language*. Broadcasting Standards Council with John Libbey, 1991.

PART V: THE REGULATION OF TELECOMMUNICATION: GENERAL ANALYSIS AND CONCLUSIONS

23: *General Analysis of Development of Telecommunication Law in Ireland*

1. February 3, 1776 related in Boswell's *Life of Johnson*. Incidentally, Johnson added in the same sentence: "[I]t is but accidental that [laws] last longer than their causes". This observation is applicable to certain telecommunication legislation.
2. S. 4 of the *Telegraph Act, 1869* as amended by s. 8 of *PTS Act, 1983*.
3. See chapter 11.
4. *Telegraph Act, 1869 (32 & 33 Vict. c.73) s. 5.*
5. *Postmaster General v National Telephone Co Ltd* [1909] AC 269, 274.
6. *Ibid.*
7. S. 87 of the 1983 Act.
8. 336 *Dáil Debates*, col. 1132, June 22, 1982.
9. Chapter 11.
10. Chapter 10.
11. Chapter 10.
12. 2 & 3 Eliz. 2 c.55.
13. S. 13 of UK *Telecommunication Act, 1981* (c.38).
14. *Competition and Choice: Telecommunications Policy for the 1990s* (White Paper) (Cm. 1461), London, HMSO.
15. *Ibid.*, para 3.6.
16. Foreword to White Paper, *ibid.*
17. *White Paper, loc. cit.*, para 3.16.
18. *Ibid.*, para 4.4.
19. *Ibid.*, para 5.7.
20. *Ibid.*, para 5.19.
21. *Ibid.*, para 7.12.
22. S. 111 of the *PTS Act, 1983* as amended by the *European Communities (Telecommunication Services) Regulations, 1992* (S.I. No. 45 of 1992). See, however, *Meagher v Minister for Agriculture*, High Court, unreported, April 1, 1993, now on appeal to the Supreme Court and N. Travers, "Necessity and Chaos: How Constitutionally to Implement an EC Directive into Irish Law", 87 *Gazette*, ILSI 258 (1993).
23. S. 180 of the UK *Broadcasting Act, 1990*
24. See, for example, s.76(1) of the UK *Broadcasting Act, 1990* in relation to certain local broadcasting delivery services.
25. A.C. Hutchinson in "The Rise and Ruse of Administrative Law and Scholarship" in (1986) 48 *MLR* 293, n.3, considers that for many persons "ideology" is a disturbing and subversive word. He adopted the word in his paper as meaning a reference to the consolidation of ideas, beliefs and assumptions which comprise a certain way of thinking about law at any given time.

26. C.R. Perry, *The Victorian Post Office*, Suffolk, The Boydell Press, 1992, p. 262.
27. *Report of Posts and Telegraphs Review Group 1978-1979*, presented to the Minister for Posts and Telegraphs, 1979, Dublin, Stationery Office, (Prl.7883).
28. *Ibid.*, p.1.
29. *Ibid.*, p.2.
30. See generally Madsen Pirie, *Privatisation in Theory and Practice*, London, Adam Smith Institute, 1985. The manifesto of the Conservative Government, elected in 1979 and re-elected in 1983, 1987 and 1992, contained a policy of moving State operations towards the private sector. Dr. Pirie at p. 21 argues that the Conservative Governments of 1979 and 1983, through privatisation programmes, have achieved "the largest transfer of property since the dissolution of the monasteries under Henry VIII — a transfer from the State to its citizens".
31. *United States v American Tel & Tel Co*, 552 F Supp 131, 145 (D.D.C. 1982); aff'd *sub nom. Maryland v United States*, 460 U.S. 1001 (1983).
32. See speech of Dick Spring, TD, for the Labour Party, 336 *Dáil Debates*, col. 1202, June 22, 1982.
33. 101 *Seanad Debates*, col. 306, June 29, 1983.
34. 101 *Seanad Debates*, col. 560, July 5, 1983.
35. Ss. 89 and 111 of *PTS Act, 1983* as amended by the *European Communities (Telecommunication Services) Regulations, 1992* (S.I. No. 45 of 1992).
36. See chapter 11.
37. See chapter 11.
38. 6 *Dáil Debates*, col. 2877, April 3, 1924.
39. *Ibid.*
40. See chapter 11.
41. Dr. Ronan Fanning in *The Irish Department of Finance*, IPA, Dublin, 1978, p. 112.
42. *Report of the Television Commission*, Dublin, Stationery Office, 1959, p 23.
43. See speech of Minister for Posts and Telegraphs on Second Stage of *Broadcasting Authority Bill 1959*, 52 *Seanad Debates*, cols. 10-13, January 20, 1960.
44. Presented to the Dáil, June 27, 1985.
45. Minister for Posts and Telegraphs on the Second Stage of *Local Radio Bill, 1985*, 360 *Dáil Debates*, col. 765, July 5, 1985.
46. S. 16 of 1985 Bill.
47. 360 *Dáil Debates*, cols. 774-775, July 5, 1985.
48. 360 *Dáil Debates*, col. 843, Frank Cluskey, July 5, 1985.
49. Deputy O'Sullivan, 377 *Dáil Debates*, col. 1663, February 10, 1988.
50. Deputy M. Higgins, 377 *Dáil Debates*, col. 1713, February 10, 1988.
51. 52 *Seanad Debates*, col. 9, January 20, 1960, Second Stage of *Broadcasting*

Authority Bill, 1959.

52.   A non-statutory executive body set up by the Minister for Posts and Telegraphs to run the broadcasting service.

53.   BBC archives EI/957, BBC Archives Centre, Caversham.

54.   Letter dated February 10, 1958 in File S. 14996B, D/T, "Television General", National Archives, Dublin.

55.   Letter dated February 11, 1958 in File S. 14996B, D/T, *ibid.*

56.   *Ibid.*

57.   Note dated February 12, 1958 in File S. 14996B, D/T, *ibid.*

58.   *Canada, Royal Commission on Broadcasting Report, 1957.*

59.   Can. Stat., c. 22 (1958) s.10.

60.   Can. Rev. Stat. C.B-11, s. 3(b) (1970).

61.   S. 17 of the *Broadcasting Authority Act, 1960* as amended by substitution by s. 13 of the *Broadcasting Authority (Amendment) Act 1976.*

62.   Jacob and Teune, "The Integrative Process: Guidelines for Analysis of the Bases of Political Community;" *The Integration of Political Communities,* 1964 at 26 (P. Jacob and J.V. Toscano, eds).

63.   Peter W. Johansen, "The Canadian Radio — Television Commission and the Canadianization of Broadcasting", 26 *Fed Comm BJ* 183, 205 (1973).

64.   *Public Service Idea in British Broadcasting,* Broadcasting Research Unit, UK.

65.   *Ibid.*

66.   See *European Communities (Telecommunications Services) Regulations, 1992* (S.I. No. 45 of 1992).

67.   *Report of Study into Cable Television in Greater Dublin Area,* 1986, Dublin, Stationery Office, (Pl 4295) paras 4.10, 5.9 and 7.8.

68.   Article 6, OJEC, No. 131/73, 27.5 1988.

69.   Speech entitled "Telecommunications — The Government Policy Perspective", Government Information Services, September 16, 1993.

70.   Nicholas Johnson, "The Public Interest and Private Broadcasting: Looking at Communications as a Whole", Address to the Resource for the Future and the Brookings Institution Conference on the Use and Regulation of the Radio Spectrum, Airlie House, Warrenton, Virgina, September 1967, p. 10.

71.   *Ibid.*

24: *The Case For and Against Regulation*

1.   See generally Fowler and Brennan, "A Marketplace approach to Broadcast Regulation", 60 *Tex L Rev* 207 (1982); T.J. Brennan, "Economic Efficiency and Broadcast Content Regulation", 35 *Fed. Comm. L.J.* 117 (1983), and remarks of Mark Fowler before the Thomas Jefferson Award Dinner, February 19, 1982 in 10 *Hastings Comm/Ent, LJ* 435 at 436.

2.   *Ibid.*

3. *Ibid.*, 10 *Hastings Comm/Ent LJ*, 435-437 at 437.
4. R.H. Coase, "The Federal Communications Commission", 2 *JL & Econ*, 1, 17 (1959) and D.W. Webbink, "Radio Licenses and Frequency Spectrum Use Property Rights", *Comm L*, June 1987, at 3-4, 25-26.
5. 32 & 33 Vict c.73 as amended by s.8 of *PTS Act, 1983*.
6. The term "natural resources" has been considered by Walsh J in *Webb v Ireland* [1988] IR 353 at 390 to 394.
7. See chapter 15.
8. *Columbia Broadcasting System Inc v Democratic Nat'l Comm* 412 US 94, 173-74 (1973).
9. 47 U.S.C. s. 301 (1970).
10. *Electricity (Supply) Acts 1927 to 1985.*
11. S. 35 of *Electricity (Supply) Act, 1927*.
12. See, for example, *Tormey v Ireland* [1985] IR 289; [1985] ILRM 375.
13. See chapter 14.
14. Case 155/73 *Sacchi* [1974] ECR 409.
15. The Court of Justice did not incorporate any portion of this Commission argument in its final opinion but the Court did not challenge these assumptions as it did those of the German and Italian Governments regarding the exempt status of national broadcast monopolies.
16. See chapter 14.
17. Press Release of Department of Communications published on January 29, 1990. This issue is considered in chapter 18.
18. *European Communities (Telecommunications Services) Regulations, 1992* (S.I. No. 45 of 1992).
19. The concept of universal telecommunication services is considered further in chapter 17.

25: *The Jurisprudence of the Courts and International Influences*

1. (1880) 6 QBD 244.
2. See definitions of "telegraph" and "telegram" in chapter 2.
3. P. S. Atiyah in the Chorley Lecture 1984 published in (1985) 48 *MLR* 19.
4. [1932] AC 304.
5. S. 3 of *Telegraph Act, 1863* and s.3 of *Telegraph Act, 1869*.
6. *Ibid.*
7. (1880) 6 QBD 244, 254.
8. 198 *Hansard*, col. 764, July 26, 1869.
9. See generally discussion of "consequentialism" in Alan Paterson, *The Law Lords*, London, Macmillan, 1982 at pp.167, 177-9 and 207.
10. [1909] AC 269.
11. Earl of Halsbury and Lords Macnaghten, Collins and Gorell.
12. [1909] AC 269, 272.
13. See definition in chapter 8.

14. High Court, King's Bench Division, unreported, June 28 1909; Divisional Court, King's Bench Division, Gibson, Madden and Kenny JJ, unreported, January 31, 1910. The case is noted for the quality of its legal representation. The Attorney General and the Solicitor General appeared for the Postmaster General. The Attorney General, R. Cherry, KC, MP, was later to become a Lord Justice of Appeal; the Solicitor General, Redmond Barry, KC, MP, was later to become Lord Chancellor of Ireland. Among the counsel for the Great Southern and Western Railway were James H. Campbell, KC, MP, who subsequently became Lord Chancellor and Stephen Ronan KC, who later became a Lord Justice of Appeal.
15. *Ibid.*
16. *Ibid.*
17. *Ibid.*
18. *Ibid.*
19. *Ibid.*
20. *Ibid.*
21. [1984] ILRM 161; writer present in court.
22. 32 & 33 Vict. c.73.
23. [1932] AC 304.
24. *British North America Act, 1867* (30 & 31 Vict. c.3), s. 92, head 10(a).
25. [1932] AC 315, 316.
26. *Ibid.*
27. *Ibid.* at 317.
28. *Ibid.*
29. [1965] IR 294.
30. For the right to communicate, see *AG v Paperlink Ltd* [1984] ILRM 373 and in relation to privacy of telephone conversations, see *Kennedy v Ireland* [1987] IR 587.
31. The High Court, unreported, 1978/1805 *ex tempore* judgment of Hamilton J, March 23, 1978.
32. [1984] ILRM 161; [1984] ILRM 170.
33. IR£50 maximum for a first conviction, IR£100 maximum on a second conviction pursuant to s. 3(3) of the *Wireless Telegraphy Act, 1926* as amended by s. 11(b) of the *Wireless Telegraphy Act, 1972.*
34. [1984] ILRM 373.
35. Ss. 14 and 87 of the *PTS Act, 1983.*
36. J. O'Reilly and M. Redmond, *Cases and Materials on the Irish Constitution,* Law Society of Ireland, 1980, p. xii.
37. See *United States v Von's Grocery Co.,* 384, US 270, (1966).
38. See *Commonwealth v Dyer,* 243 Mass. 472, cert denied 262 U.S. 751; *Louisville Gas Co. v Citizens' Gas-Light Co.,* 115 US 683; *Indianapolis Cable Street R. Co. v Citizens Street R. Co.,* 127 Ind. 369.
39. [1974] ECR 409.
40. [1980] ECR 833, [1981] 2 CMLR 362.
41. *Case C-260/89 ERT* [1993] 2 CEC 167.

42. *Case 41/83*, reported in Fifteenth Competition Report (1985), points 95
     to 101 and [1985] 2 CMLR 368.
43. *Case C-18/88 RTT (Belgium) v S.A. "GB-Inno-BM,"* December 13, 1991.
44. Bull EC-2-1985, point 2.1.10 (Germany); Bull. EC 12 1985, point 2.1.79
     (France).
45. Case C-202/88 judgment 19 March 1991, [1991] ECR 1, 1223, [1992] 5
     CMLR 552.
46. Directive 88/301, under Articles 90(3) 37, 3(f), 5 and 86(b) and (d).
47. Directive 90/388/EEC, OJ 1990, 192/10.
48. Joined cases C-271, 281 and 289/90, judgment November 17, 1992.
49. C-320/91, judgment 19 May 1993. The Commission's stance on
     liberalisation has been vindicated generally in the following cases: the
     Cordless Telephone case reported in the Fifteenth Competition Report
     (EC) (1985); the *Modem case*, reported in Fifteenth Competition Report
     (EC) (1985); the IBM undertaking on SNA interfaces, Bull. EC 10-1984,
     point 3.4.1; Case 311/84 *Centre Belge d'Etudés de Marche —
     Telemarketing SA v Compagnie Luxembourgeoise de Telediffusion SA*
     [1986] 2 CMLR 558.
50. *Green Paper on the Development of the Common Market for
     Telecommunications Services and Equipment*, COM (87), 290 final, 1987;
     *Green Paper on a Common Approach in the field of Satellite Communications
     in the European Community*, COM (90), 490 final, 20 November 1990.
51. Resolution of Council of the European Communities, June 16, 1993,
     OJEC No. C 213/1, August 6, 1993.
52. *European Communities (Telecommunication Services) 1992* (S.I. No. 45 of
     1992) which, inter alia, amended s. 87 of the *PTS Act, 1983; Council
     Directive No. 90/387/EEC of 28 June 1990 (Open Network Provision)* OJ
     No. L192 of 24 July 1990; *Commission Directive No. 90/388 EEC of 28
     June 1990 (Competition Directive)* OJ No. L.192 of 24 July 1990.
53. *Ibid.*, 1992 Regulations.
54. *Ibid.*
55. See Notices of Department of Communications published in national
     press of January 29, 1990 and October 30, 1992.
56. See reference at n. 50 above.
57. *Ibid.*
58. *Guidelines on the Application of EEC Competition Rules in the
     Telecommunication Sector* (91C/233/02) OJEC 6.9.91.
59. *Commission Decision of 18 October 1991 relating to a proceeding pursuant
     to Art. 85 of the EEC Treaty (IV/32.737 Eirpage)*, OJEC No.L. 306/22,
     7.11.91.
60. *Ibid.*
61. Title XII, Trans-European Networks, Articles 129b and 129c of the
     Treaty on European Union (Maastricht) 1992.
62. *Ibid.*
63. *Review of the Situation in the Telecommunications Sector*, Communi-
     cation by the Commision, Brussels, 21 October, 1992.

64. See EC Green Paper, *Television Without Frontiers*, COM (84) 300, 14 June 1984; *Council Directive (EEC) 89/522 of 3 October 1989 on the pursuit of television broadcasting activities.*

65. See recitals to *Council Directive 89/522/EEC of 3 October 1989.* See *European Communities (Television Broadcasting) Regulations 1991* (S.I. No. 251 of 1991) which gave effect to provisions of *Council Directive 89/552/EEC.* See also chapter 19.

66. There also are treaties, agreements, recommendations of the Parliamentary Assembly and Recommendations of the Committee of Ministers.

67. *Groppera Radio AG v Switzerland* (1990) 12 EHRR 321.

68. *Sacchi v Italy*, 5 European Commission of Human Rights Decisions and Reports, p. 43.

69. See n. 67 *supra.*

70. *Autronic AG v Switzerland* (1990) 12 EHRR 485.

71. *Ibid.*

72. *In Re Ó Laighléis* [1960] IR 93.

73. *Desmond v Glackin* [1992] ILRM 490. Henchy J expressed the view in the *State (Walsh) v DPP* [1981] IR 412 at 440 that there was a presumption that the law of contempt of court in Ireland was in conformity with the European Convention on Human Rights, particularly Articles 5 and 10(2). In *Derbyshire Co. Council v Times Newspapers Ltd* [1993] 1 All E 1011 some judges expressed the opinion that Article 10 of the Convention may be resorted to in order to help resolve some uncertainty or ambiguity in municipal law. See also Lord Ackner in *Brind v Secretary of State for the Home Department* [1991] 1 All ER 720.

74. See Eric Barendt, "The Influence of the German and Italian Constitutional Courts on their National Broadcasting Systems", *Public Law* [1991] 93-115.

75. *Third Television case*, 57 BVerfGE 295, (1981).

76. 73 BVerfGE 118 (1986).

77. See Eric Barendt, loc. cit., p. 104.

78. Case No 1 *BvF* 1/85, 1/88 published in Media Perspektiven Dokumentation 1 (1991) 1 to 48.

79. Decision 826/1988, *Gazetta Ufficiale*, July 20, 1988, p. 67.

80. 73 BVerfGE 118, (1986).

81. Decision 826/1988, *Gazetta Ufficiale*, July 20, 1988 p. 67.

82. *United States v American Tel & Tel. Co.*, 552 F. Supp. 13, 145 (D.D.C. 1982); aff'd sub nom. *Maryland v United States*, 460 US 1001 (1983).

83. See R.B. McKenna and R.L. Sylter, "The Modification of Final Judgment: An Exercise in Judicial Overkill", 9 *Comm/Ent LJ* 13. (1986).

84. *Sherman Antitrust Act, 1890.*

85. See *American Tel & Tel Co.*, *loc. cit.*

86. *Ibid.*

87. *Ibid.*

88. See generally L.B. Schwartz, "Forum and Substance: Introduction to

the Symposium on the Divestiture of American Telephone and Telegraph Company", 9 *Comm/Ent LJ* 1 (1986); R.B. McKenna and R.L. Slyter, "The Modification of Final Judgment: An Exercise in Judicial Overkill" 9 *Comm/Ent LJ* 9 (1986); J.R. Worthington, "The Case for Continued Judicial Enforcement of the AT&T Decree", 9 *Comm/Ent LJ* 75 (1986) and J.P. Denvir, "The Dole Bill: Freeing the Telephone Company Seven", 9 *Comm/Ent LJ* 113, (1986).

89.   See *Schwartz, loc. cit.*

90.   There is also the power of the Minister for Enterprise and Employment in relation to an abuse of a dominant position including the power to direct a sale of assets; see s.14 of the *Competition Act, 1991.*

26: *Freedom of Expression*

1.   See the debate between Eoin O'Dell and the Law Reform Commission in E. O'Dell, "Reflections on a Revolution in Libel", Part 1 (1991) 9 *ILT* (ns) 181; Part 2 (1991) 9 *ILT* (ns) 214; E O'Dell, "Does Defamation Value Free Expression?" (1990) 12 *DULJ* (ns) 50; *Law Reform Commission, Report on the Civil Law of Defamation* (1991) pp. 110-124.

2.   See *ibid., AG v Paperlink Ltd* [1984] ILRM 373 and Keane J in *Oblique Financial Services Ltd v The Promise Production Co Ltd & Ors*, High Court, unreported, February 24, 1993.

3.   In *State (Lynch) v Cooney* [1982] IR 337 at 361, Chief Justice O'Higgins for the Supreme Court stated that the organs of public opinion specified in Article 40.6.1.i of the Constitution "must be held to include television as well as radio".

4.   *Red Lion Broadcasting v Federal Communications Commission*, 395 US 367 (1969) per White J, US Supreme Court.

5.   S. 96(d) of the *PTS Act, 1983.*

6.   S. 13(1)(a) of the *Post Office (Amendment) Act, 1951* as amended by substitution by s. 8 of the *PTS Act, 1983.*

7.   S. 13(1)(b) *ibid.* See also generally article 25 of the *Telecommunications Scheme 1992* (S.I. No. 19 of 1992).

8.   Section 4(e) of *PTS Act, 1983.*

9.   S. 11 of the *Wireless Telegraphy Act, 1926* as amended by s. 12 of the *Broadcasting and Wireless Telegraphy Act, 1988.*

10.   S. 10 of the *Wireless Telegraphy Act, 1926* in relation to radio communication generally; s. 16(3)(b) of *Broadcasting Authority Act, 1960*, in relation to RTE; s.4(ii) of the *Radio and Television Act, 1988* in relation to the private broadcasting service and s. 110(2) of the *PTS Acts 1983 and 1984* in relation to Telecom Éireann.

11.   See chapter 16.

12.   S. 18(1) of the *Broadcasting Authority Act, 1960* as amended by s. 3 of the *Broadcasting Authority (Amendment) Act 1976*; s. 9 of the *Radio and Television Act, 1988*

13.   S. 18(1A) of the 1960 Act *loc. cit.*; s. 9(1)(a) of the 1988 Act, *loc. cit.*

14.   London, Hunter & Stevens (1819).

15. J.S. Mill, *Utilitarianism, Liberty and Representative Government*.
16. 250 US 627 at 630.
17. Oxford University Press, 1988, p. 161.
18. John Wigmore, "Abrams v US: Freedom of Speech and Freedom of Thuggery in War-Time and Peace-Time", 14 *Illinois Law Review* 539 (1920).
19. *Ibid.*, at 559.
20. S. Ingber, "The Marketplace of Ideas: A Legitimising Myth", 1984 *Duke Law Journal*, 1, 25.
21. E. Baker, "Scope of the First Amendment Freedom of Speech", 25 *University of California in Los Angeles Law Review*, 964 at 965-981, (1978); B. Duval, "Free Communication of Ideas and the Quest for Truth: Towards a Technological Approach to First Amendment Adjudication", 41 *George Washington Law Review*, 161, 191-94 (1972). See also Kent Greenawalt, *Speech, Crime and the Uses of Language*, New York, Oxford University Press, 1989, chapter 2, "Rationales for Freedom of Speech" for a perceptive discussion of this and other related issues.
22. *Schenck v United States*, 249 US 47, 52 (1919).
23. *Ibid.*
24. *Ibid.*
25. Nimmer, "Is Freedom of the Press a Redundancy: What Does it Add to Freedom of Speech?" 26 *Hast LJ* 639 (1975) at 653 construing *Whitney v California*, 274 US 357, 372 (1927).
26. See Alexander Meiklejohn, "The First Amendment is an Absolute", (1961) *Sup Ct Rev 245*, 253-263.
27. 274 US 357, 375-8, (1927).
28. 468 US 364 (1984).
29. Quoting *NAACP v Claiborne Hardware Co*, 458 US 886 (1982), *Carey v Brown*, 447 US 455, 467 (1980).
30. As amended by substitution by s. 16 of the *Broadcasting Authority (Amendment) Act, 1976*.
31. 468 US 364 (1984) quoting *Thornhill v Alabama*, 310 US 88, 101-102 (1940).
32. 376 US 254 (1964). See O'Dell, (1990) 12 *DULJ* (ns) 50.
33. *Ibid.*, at 270.
34. S. Shriffin, "Defamatory Non-media Speech and First Amendment Methodology", 25 *University of California in Los Angeles Law Review*, 915, 932 (1978).
35. 79 *Seanad Debates*, col. 782, March 12, 1975.
36. *Ibid.*
37. 79 *Seanad Debates*, cols. 784-785, March 12, 1975.
38. *Ibid.*
39. [1982] IR 337 at 361.
40. 67 *Dáil Debates*, cols. 1634-5, 1937.
41. Walter Bagehot, *The Work And Life of Walter Bagehot*, 1915.
42. *AG v X* [1992] ILRM 401.

43.   Adopted by Justice Holmes in *Schenck v United States*, 249 US 47 at 52 (1919).
44.   [1982] IR 337.
45.   *Ibid.*
46.   *Ibid.*
47.   *Broadcasting Authority Act, 1960 (Section 31) Order, 1993* (S.I. No. 1 of 1993).
48.   S. 17 of *Broadcasting Authority Act, 1960* as amended by substitution by s. 13 of *Broadcasting Authority (Amendment) Act, 1976.*
49.   S.11(1)(b) of *Wireless Telegraphy Act, 1926.*
50.   S.11(3) of the *Wireless Telegraphy Act, 1926* as amended by substitution by s. 12(f) of the *Broadcasting and Wireless Telegraphy Act, 1988.*
51.   Application No. 15404/89, April 16, 1991.
52.   (1992) 14 EHRR 153.
53.   *Broadcasting Authority Act, 1960 (Section 31) Order, 1993* (S.I. No. 1 of 1993).
54.   *State (Lynch) v Cooney* [1982] IR 337.
55.   395 US 444 (1969).
56.   See eg. *Dennis v United States*, 341 US 494 (1951).
57.   249 US 47 (1919).
58.   *Noto v United States*, 367 US 290 (1961). See also *Herndon v Lowry*, 301 US 242 (1937) and *Bond v Floyd*, 385 US 116 (1966).
59.   *Ibid.* The Court referred to *Yates v United States* 354 US 298 (1957), *DeJonge v Oregon* 299 US 353 (1937) and *Stromberg v Califorinia* 283 US 359 (1931).
60.   *Broadcasting Authority Act, 1960 (Section 31) Order, 1993,* (S.I. No. 1 of 1993).
61.   *Abrams v United States*, 250 US 616 (1919).
62.   *Ibid.* at 630-631.
63.   See n. 60 *supra.*
64.   450 US 518 (1972).
65.   244 F 535 (1917).
66.   Ibid at 543.
67.   Words paraphrasing s. 31(1) of the *Broadcasting Authority Act, 1960* as amended by substitution by s. 16 of the *Broadcasting Authority (Amendment) Act, 1976* which were in turn based on the constitutional prohibition expressed in Article 40.6.1.i of the Constitution.
68.   S. 31 of *Broadcasting Authority Act, 1960* as amended by substitution by s. 16 of the *Broadcasting Authority (Amendment) Act, 1976.*
69.   *The Irish Times*, August 3, 1992. See also Dr. Conor Cruise O'Brien, "The Section 31 Debate: No Grounds for an Appeal in O'Toole Case". *Sunday Independent*, August 2, 1992; Professor Ronan Fanning, "The Section 31 Debate: Political Weapons of the Future", *Sunday Independent*, August 2, 1992; Professor J.A. Murphy, "The Section 31 Debate: Expose the Bankruptcy of Their Violent Views", *Sunday Independent*, August 2, 1992; Marie McGonagle, "[O'Toole] Judgment

Might Return Section 31 To Its Rightful Place" *The Irish Times*, August 3, 1992.

70. 319 US 190 at 226 (1943).
71. 395 US 367 (1969).
72. 47 USCA s. 301.
73. 104 SCt 3106 (1984).
74. *Ibid.*, at 3116 n.11.
75. 376 *Dáil Debates*, col. 1190, December 8, 1987.
76. 476 US 488 (1986), aff'd on narrower grounds, 754 F.2d 1396 (9th Cir. 1985) on retrial 67 R.R. 2d 366 (1990).
77. *Ibid.*, at 494
78. 694 F.2d 119 (7 Cir. 1982)
79. *Ibid.*, at 126.
80. R. Posner, *Economic Analysis of Law*, 361-362 (3rd ed. 1986).
81. *Ibid.*
82. The Belnap Press of Harvard University Press, Cambridge, Mass., 1983.
83. *Ibid.*, pp. 224-5.
84. *Chronicle of International Communications, July*, 1983.
85. R. Coase, "The Federal Communications Commission", 2 *J Law & Econ* (1959).
86. S. 18(1) of *Broadcasting Authority Act, 1960* as amended by substitution by s.3 of the *Broadcasting Authority (Amendment) Act 1976* in relation to RTE; s. 9(1(a) and (b) of the *Radio and Television Act, 1988* in relation to the private broadcasting services.
87. First Amendment freedoms.
88. *Mayflower Broadcasting Corp*, 8 FCC 333 (1940).
89. *Ibid.*, at 340.
90. *Editorialising by Broadcast Licensees*, 13 FCC 1246 at 1253 (1949).
91. *Ibid.*, at 1253-54.
92. 47 USC s. 399(A) 1970.
93. Congressman William Springer, Hearings on H.R. 6746 and s. 1160 before the House Comm. on Interstate and Foreign Commerce, 90th Cong. 1st Sess. 42 at 641 (1967).
94. *Federal Communications Commission v League of Women Voters of California*, 468 US 364 (1984).
95. *Columbia Broadcasting System Inc v FCC*, 453 US 367, 395 (1981) quoting *Columbia Broadcasting System Inc. v Democratic National Committee*, 412 US 94, 110, (1973) See also *FCC v Midwest Video Corp*, 440 US 689, 703 (1979).
96. 468 US 364 quoting *New York Times v Sullivan*, 376 US 254, 270 (1964).
97. 381 *Dáil Debates*, cols. 1155-1156, June 1, 1988.
98. *Ibid.*
99. *Ibid.*
100. S. 18(1) of the *Broadcasting Act, 1960* as amended by substitution by section 3 of the *Broadcasting Authority (Amendment) Act, 1976*.

101. S. 9(1)(a) and (b) of the *Radio and Television Act, 1988*.
102. For arguments in relation to the presumption against constitutionality in the context of prior restraint on expression in the United States, see *Bantam Books Inc v Sullivan*, 372 US 58, 70 (1963); *Near v Minnesota*, 283 US 697 (1931); *New York Times Co v United States*, 403 US 713 (1971).
103. *Federal Communications Commission v League of Women Voters of California*, 468 US 364 (1984).
104. See for example ss.6 and 90 of the UK *Broadcasting Act, 1990*, c.42.
105. 47 C.F.R. S. 73.1930 (1981).
106. S. 18(1) of the *Broadcasting Authority Act, 1960* as amended by substitution by s. 3 of the *Broadcasting Authority (Amendment) Act, 1976* in relation to RTE; S. 9 of *Radio and Television Act, 1988* in relation to the private broadcasting services.
107. 418 US 241 (1974).
108. Official Journal of the European Communities, No. L 298/23.
109. *Ibid.*, article 23.5.
110. Unreported, High Court, July 31, 1992; *O'Toole v RTE (No. 2)* [1993] ILRM 458 (SCt).
111. S.18(1) of the *Broadcasting Authority Act, 1960* as amended by substitution by s.3 of the *Broadcasting Authority (Amendment) Act, 1976*.
112. Chapter 20.
113. Reg. 8 of *Wireless Telegraphy (Television Programmes (Retransmission) Regulations, 1989* (S.I. No. 39 of 1989).
114. Reg. 6(4) of 1989 Regulations, supra.
115. Reg. 9(2) of *Wireless Telegraphy (Wired Broadcast Relay Licence) Regulations 1974* (S.I. No. 67 of 1974) as amended by substitution by Reg. 4 of *Wireless Telegraphy (Wired Broadcast Relay Licence) (Amendment) Regulations, 1988* (S.I. No. 82 of 1988).
116. 460 US 575 (1983).
117. 106 S Ct 2034 (1986) at 2037.
118. *Ibid.*
119. Chapter 20.
120. Regulation 10 and Article 3 of licence in *Wireless Telegraphy (Wired Broadcast Relay Licence) Regulations, 1974* (S.I. No. 67 of 1974) in relation to cable television; Reg. 9(c) and Art. 3 of licence set out in *Wireless Telgraphy (Television Programme Retransmission) Regulations, 1989* (S.I. No. 39 of 1989) in relation to MMDS.
121. 768 F. 2d 1434 (D.C. Cir. 1985) cert. denied, sub nom. *National Association of Broadcasters v Quincy Cable TV Inc*, 106 S.Ct. 2889, L. Ed 2d 977 (1986).
122. 768 F. 2d at 1451-52 (1985).
123. 418 US 241, 94 S.Ct. 2831, 41 L. Ed 2d 730 (1974).
124. *United States v O'Brien*, 391 US 367, 88 SCt 1673, 20 L Ed 2d 672 (1968).
125. *Ibid.*

126. FCC Public Notice, "Commission Will Not Appeal Quincy Cable TV" released August 5, 1985.
127. S. 9(c) of *Radio and Television Act, 1988.*
128. S.15, *ibid.*
129. Ray Burke, 120 *Seanad Debates,* col. 790, June 21, 1988.
130. Ray Burke, 376 *Dáil Debates,* col. 1192, December 8, 1987.
131. *McCann v An Taoiseach,* unreported, High Court hearing of June 15, 1992. Carney J refused relief on June 16, 1992. See also *Wilson v IBA* 1979 SLT 279; *Wilson v IBA (No. 2)* 1988 SLT 276; *R. v BBC ex p. Owen* [1985] QB 1153 and *Lynch v BBC* [1983] NI 193.
132. *McKenna v An Taoiseach,* unreported, High Court, June 8, 1992 per Costello J.
133. Gerard Quinn "The Systems-Maintenance of Constitutional Rights and the Case of Government Speech", (1989) 7 *ILT (ns)* 8.

27: *The Right to Communicate*

1. [1984] ILRM 373.
2. [1986] IR 597; [1987] ILRM 52. See also *McKenna v An Taoiseach,* unreported, High Court, June 8, 1992, a case that involved allegations of a lack of impartiality on the part of the Government in relation to its information campaign in the referendum in the Maastrict Treaty. In *McKenna,* Costello J did not accept that the plaintiff's right to communicate was at issue.
3. [1987] ILRM 135.
4. *Ibid.* at 138.
5. R. Byrne and W. Binchy, *Annual Review of Irish Law, 1987,* The Round Hall Press, Dublin, p. 89.
6. [1984] ILRM 373.
7. *Ibid.* at 381.
8. *Ibid.*
9. Le Duc in L.S. Harms, J. Richstad and K.A. Kie (eds.), *Right to Communicate; Collected Papers,* Honolulu Social Sciences and Linguistics Institute, University of Hawaii at Manoa, 1977, p. 165.
10. [1984] ILRM 373 at 381.
11. See a further consideration of the right to communicate in *Kearney v Minister for Justice* [1986] IR 116; [1987] ILRM 52.
12. UNESCO Right to Communicate Working Group, Ottawa, 1980 quoted by D. Fisher in *The Right to Communicate, A Status Report,* UNESCO, Paris, 1982, p.54.
13. Report of the Canadian Telecommission, entitled *Instant World,* Information Canada, Ottawa p.3.
14. Henry Hindley in "A Right to Communicate? A Canadian Approach" in L.S. Harms and J.Richstad (eds.), *Evolving Perspectives on the Right to Communicate,* Honolulu: East-West Center, East-West Communication Institute, 1977, p.119-127.

15. *Leander Case* (1987), 9 EHRR 433; *Gaskin v UK* judgment of July 7, 1989 (Eur. Ct. of HR), Series A, No. 160.

16. *Lamont v Postmaster General*, 381 US 301 at 308 (1965).

17. *RTE v Magill (No. 1)* [1988] IR 97; RTE v *Magill (No. 2)* [1989] IR 554; *Commission Decision 89/205* of 21 Dec. 1988 (OJ 1989 L 78/43) — Magill TV Guide/ITP/BBC and RTE; *RTE v EC Commission* [1991] 4 CMLR 586 and companion cases, *BBC v EC Commission* [1991] 4 CMLR 669 and *ITP v EC Commission* [1991] 4 CMLR 749. The EC Commission cases were on appeal to the Court of Justice in October 1993.

18. *Many Voices, One World*, Report of the International Commission for the study of Communication Problems, UNESCO, Paris, 1980. pp. 172-3.

19. See communiqué issued by the International Association for Mass Communication Research (IAMCR) June, 1993.

20. *Ibid.*

21. See Article 40.3.1 of the Constitution, *Ryan v AG* [1965] IR 294 and *AG v Paperlink* [1984] ILRM 373.

22. *AG v Paperlink* [1984] ILRM 373 at 384, *per* Costello J.

23. 397 US 728, 736-37 (1970).

24. Article 40.6.1.i of the Constitution.

25. *Ibid.*

26. See File TW 6049, D/Comm (R&B) "Broadcasting Authority Bill 1959, Minister's Speech in Dáil, Brief etc.", National Archives, Dublin.

27. See definition of "wireless telegraphy" in chapter 10.

28. S. 11 of the *Wireless Telegraphy Act, 1926* as amended by s. 12(1)(f) of the *Broadcasting and Wireless Telegraphy Act, 1988*.

29. *Ibid.*

30. S. 9(1)(d) of the *Radio and Television Act, 1988*.

31. S. 96(d) of the *PTS Act, 1983*.

32. S. 13(1)(a) of the *Post Office (Amendment) Act, 1951* as amended by substitution by s. 8 of the *PTS Act, 1983*. Penalties range up IR£50,000 and 5 years imprisonment on indictment.

33. Article 25 of the *Telecommunications Scheme, 1992* (S.I. No. 19 of 1992). See also Telephone Information Service Information Dealer Agreement (Telecom Éireann) and Telecom Éireann's *Code of Practice for Telephone Information Services*.

34. Reg. 6 of *Inland Post Warrant, 1939* (S.R. & O.1939, No. 202).

35. *Dillon v Minister for Posts and Telegraphs*, unreported, June 3, 1981, Supreme Court. A significant extract of Henchy J's judgment is set out in R. Byrne, *Cases and Comment on Irish Commercial Law and Legal Technique*, Dublin, Round Hall Press, 2nd Edition, 1988, pp. 47-9.

36. *R v Webb*, 2 C & K 938 (1848).

37. *R v Stanley* [1965] 2 QB 32.

38. S. 22(1)(b) of the UK *Post Office Act, 1953*.

39. In *R v Anderson* [1971] 3 All ER 1152, the word "obscene" in its context as an alternative to "indecent" was held to have its ordinary meaning

(or dictionary meaning) which included matters which were shocking or lewd.

40. The *Shorter Oxford English Dictionary*, London, 3rd edition. See also *People (AG) v Simpson*, 93 ILTR 33 a criminal prosecution concerning an indecent performance.
41. *Ibid.*
42. 109 S Ct 2829 (1989).
43. S. 223(b) of the US *Communications Act of 1934*, 47 USC, (as amended in 1988).
44. *Butler v Michigan*, 352 US 380 (1957).
45. *Ibid.*
46. Pursuant to s. 13(1)(a) of the *Post Office (Amendment) Act, 1951* as amended by s. 8 of the *PTS Act, 1983*.

28: Interception of Telecommunication

1. See s. 98(5) of the *PTS Act, 1983*, as amended by substitution by s. 13(3) of the *Interception of Postal Packets and Telecommunications Messages (Regulation) Act, 1993 (the Interception Act, 1993)*, and s. 1 of the *Interception Act, 1993*.
2. 258 *Dáil Debates*, col. 2139, February 17, 1972 by the Minister for Justice, Desmond O'Malley.
3. Explanatory Memorandum of *Interception Bill, 1992*.
4. 18 *Dáil Debates*, cols. 502-503, February 15, 1927.
5. 18 *Dáil Debates*, col. 507, February 15, 1927.
6. *Ibid.*
7. 23 *Dáil Debates*, cols. 462-463, April 26, 1928.
8. *Ibid.*, col. 463, Mr. Heffernan, Parliamentary Secretary to the Minister for Posts and Telegraphs.
9. 118 *Dáil Debates*, col. 2380, December 15, 1949, Mr. Corish.
10. 164 *Dáil Debates*, cols. 711-712, November 20, 1957, Oscar Traynor.
11. *Ibid. Post Office Act, 1908*, (8 Edw 7 ch. 48).
12. *Ibid.*
13. 246 *Dáil Debates*, col. 1332, May 9, 1970.
14. *Ibid.*
15. 164 *Dáil Debates*, cols. 711-713, November 20, 1957, Oscar Traynor, Minister for Justice.
16. 258 *Dáil Debates*, col. 2140, February 17, 1972, Desmond O'Malley, Minister for Justice.
17. 341 *Dáil Debates*, cols. 1752-1755, April 26, 1983, Jim Mitchell, Minister for Justice.
18. 209 *Dáil Debates*, col. 402, April 23, 1964.
19. 8 Edw 7 ch. 48.
20. S. 7 of *PTS Act, 1983*.
21. S. 89 of the *Post Office Act, 1908* (8 Edw 7. ch. 48).
22. See s. 11(2) of the *Adaptation of Enactments Act, 1922*.

23.   See definition of "intercept" in s. 98(5) of the *PTS Act, 1983* as amended by substitution by s. 13(3) of the *Interception Act, 1993*.
24.   S. 98(2)(a)(iii) of *PTS Act, 1983*.
25.   132 *Seanad Debates*, col. 755, May 6, 1992, Second Stage of *Interception Bill, 1992*.
26.   S. 18 of the *Official Secrets Act, 1963* (No. 1 of 1963) repealed by s. 14 of the *Interception Act 1993*.
27.   See generally *Webb v Ireland* [1988] IR 353.
28.   See generally *Entick v Carrington*, 19 State Trials 1030 (1765) and *Congreve v Home Office* [1976] QB 629.
29.   *Ibid.*
30.   *Ibid.*
31.   *Klass and Others*, judgment of September 6, 1978, (Eur. Court H.R.) (Series A, No. 28); *Malone*, judgment of August 2, 1984, (Eur. Court H.R.) (Series A, No. 82); *Kruslin v France* (1990) 12 EHRR 547; *Huvig v France* (1990) 12 EHRR 528; *Ludi v Switzerland*, judgment of June 15, 1992, (Eur. Court H.R.) *The Times*, August 13, 1992.
32.   *Ibid.*
33.   *Ibid.*
34.   *Ibid.*
35.   *Ibid.*
36.   [1987] IR 587
37.   *Ibid.*
38.   S. 2(1) of the *Interception Act, 1993*.
39.   S. 1 of the *Interception Act, 1993*.
40.   See n. 31.
41.   S. 8 of the *Interception Act, 1993*.
42.   See n. 31.
43.   S. 9 of the *Interception Act, 1993*.
44.   *Katz v United States*, 389 US 347 (1967).
45.   See *Lynham v Butler (No. 2)* [1933] IR 74, *McDonald v Bord na gCon* [1965] IR 217 and *State (Shanahan) v AG*, [1964] IR 239.
46.   Mr Justice Brian Walsh, "The Irish Constitution and Fundamental Freedoms — 50 Years On", Lecture to the Irish Association of Law Teachers, December 4, 1987, University College, Dublin. (No official script is available; the writer relies on his own notes of the lecture.)
47.   Title III of the *Omnibus Crime Control and Safe Streets Act of 1968*, 18 U.S.C. ss. 2510-20, (1982).
48.   S. 4(1) of the *PTS Act, 1983*.
49.   S. 98(5) of the *PTS Act, 1983* as amended by substitution by s. 13(3) of the *Interception Act, 1993*.
50.   S. 98(2) of the *PTS Act, 1983*.
51.   As amended by s. 7 of the *PTS Act, 1983*.
52.   S.98(2)(b) of the *PTS Act, 1983*.
53.   S. 98(2)(a)(ii) of the 1983 Act.
54.   S. 98(2)(a)(iii) of the 1983 Act.

55. *Criminal Code R.S.C 1970 c. C.-34*, Part IV-1 as enacted by the *Protection of Privacy Act (1973-74)*, Can. c. 50.
56. *Wireless Telegraphy Acts 1926 to 1988*.
57. Section 3(3) of the *Wireless Telegraphy Act, 1926* as amended by substitution by s. 12(1) of the *Broadcasting and Wireless Telegraphy Act 1988*.
58. S. 3(2) of the *Wireless Telegraphy Act, 1926* as amended by s. 11 of the *Wireless Telegraphy Act, 1972*.
59. S.(2)(b) of the *Wireless Telegraphy Act, 1926* as amended by substitution by s. 2(1) of the *Broadcasting and Wireless Telegraphy Act, 1988*.
60. S. 11(2) of the *Wireless Telegraphy Act, 1926*.
61. See, for example, reg. 12(c) of the *Broadcasting (Receiving Licences) Regulations, 1961* (S.I. No. 279 of 1961).
62. S. 98(5) of the *PTS Act, 1983* as amended by s. 13(3) of the *Interception Act, 1993*; s. 1 of the *Interception Act, 1993*.
63. S. 4(1) of the *PTS Act, 1983*.
64. S. 2(2) of the 1985 Act (ch. 56) which amended s. 45 of the *UK Telecommunications Act, 1984*.
65. 431 *Dáil Debates*, col. 60-64, Report Stage of *Interception Bill, 1992*, May 19, 1993.
66. Ss. 98(2B) and (2C) of the *PTS Act, 1983* as inserted by s.13(2) of the *Interception Act, 1993*.
67. *Kennedy v Ireland* [1987] IR 587.
68. 442 US 735, (1979).
69. 666 P. 2d 135 (Colo. 1983). See Comment, "On Privacy, Pen Registers and State Constitutions: The Colorado Supreme Court Rejects *Smith v Maryland*", 15 U Tol L Rev 1467 (1984).

29: *The Pervasiveness Rationale*

1. Quoted by J. Attali and Y. Stourdze, "The Birth of the Telephone and Economic Crisis: The Slow Death of Monologue in French Society", I de Sola Pool (ed,), *The Social Impact of the Telephone*, The MIT Press, 1977, p. 99.
2. Quoted by A. Aspinall, *Politics and the Press 1780-1850*, Home and Van Thal, 1949, p.1.
3. *Ibid.*
4. *Ibid.*
5. See File S. 5111/3, "Messages from Radio Stations: Broadcasting in President's name", National Archives, Dublin.
6. 52 *Seanad Debates*, cols. 11-12, January 20, 1960.
7. *The Irish Times*, January 1, 1962, p.3. The full text is published in M. McLoone and J. MacMahon (eds.), *Television and Irish Society*, RTE/IFI, 1984, Appendix 1, p. 149.
8. AGB TAM for RTE (1992).

9.   *Broadcasting/Cablecasting Yearbook 1989*, Washington DC, Broadcasting Publications, 1989.
10.   Joint Committee on State-Sponsored Bodies, 18th Report, *Radio Telefís Éireann* (Prl. 9945), May 1981.
11.   *1981 Report*, loc. cit., para 114.
12.   *Ibid.*, para 115.
13.   *Ibid.*
14.   *1981 Report, ibid*, Evidence, Question 287.
15.   *Ibid.*, para 118.
16.   Minister for Posts and Telegraphs on Second Stage of *Broadcasting Authority (Amendment) Bill, 1975, 79 Seanad Debates*, col. 78, March 12, 1975.
17.   See chapter 16.
18.   Application No. 15404/89, *Purcell v Ireland*, European Commission of Human Rights, April 16, 1991.
19.   *Ibid.*
20.   120 *Seanad Debates*, col. 776, June 21, 1988.
21.   *Banzhaf v F.C.C.*, 405 F. 2d. 1082, 1100 (D.C. Cir. 1968), Cert. denied, 396 US 842, (1969).
22.   412 US 94, 127-28 (1973).
23.   438 US 726; 98 S Ct 3026, (1978).
24.   *Ibid.*, Stephens J delivering the opinion of the Supreme Court.
25.   *Ibid.*
26.   *Ibid.*, at 3048-49 (Brennan J, dissenting).
27.   *Ibid.*, Stephens J delivering the opinion of the Supreme Court.
28.   D. Pearl, L. Bouthilet and J. Lazar, *Television and Behaviour: Ten years of scientific progress and implications for the Eighties* (vols. 1 & 2) U.S. Government Printing Office, Washington D.C. 1982.
29.   See for example, J.L. Freedman, "Effect of television violence on aggressiveness", *Psychological Bulletin, 96*, 227, 246.
30.   F.S. Andison, "TV violence and viewer aggression: A cumulation of study results 1956-1976", *Public Opinion Quarterly*, 41, 314-331, 1977; L. Friedrich-Cofer and A.C. Huston, "Television violence and aggression: The debate continues", *Psychological Bulletin* 100, 364-371, 1986. See also B.J. Wilson, D. Linz and B. Randall, "Applying Social Science Research to Film Ratings: A Shift from Offensiveness to Harmful Effects", paper presented to the Mass Communication Division at the International Communication Association Convention, Trinity College, Dublin, 1990.
31.   L.R. Huesmann, "Psychological processes promoting the relation between exposure to media violence and aggressive behaviour by the viewer", *Journal of Social Issues*, 42, 125-139.
32.   480 F. Supp. 199 (S.D. Fla). (1979).
33.   *Ibid.* at 200.
34.   *Ibid.*
35.   *Ibid.* at 206.

36. *Ibid* at 205. See also *Olivia N. v National Broadcasting Co.,* 123 Cal App 3d 488, 178 Cal Rptr, 888 (1981), cert. denied, 458 US 1108 (1982). See also the decision of the Georgia US Supreme Court in *Walt Disney Production v Shannon* 247 Ga. 402; 276 SE 2d 580 (1981). See generally John L. Diamond and James L. Primm, "Re-discovering Traditional Tort Typologies to Determine Media Liability for Personal Injuries: From the Mickey Mouse Club to Hustler Magazine", 10 *Comm/Ent LJ* 969-997, (1988).
37. See Patricia J. Williams, "*Metro Broadcasting, Inc v FCC*: Regrouping in Singular Times", 104 *Harvard Law Review,* 525-546.
38. 110 SCt 2997 (1990).
39. Patricia J. Williams, *loc. cit.,* n. 36 at 537.
40. See the decision of the German Constitutional Court in the *Third Television Case,* 57 BVerfGe 295 (1981).

30: *The Statutory Duties of Objectivity and Impartiality in Broadcasting Services*

1. The obligation of impartiality has been a feature of UK regulation of over-the-air broadcasting since the *Television Act 1954.*
2. S. 18(1) of the *Broadcasting Authority Act, 1960,* as amended by substitution by s. 3 of the *Broadcasting Authority (Amendment) Act, 1976.*
3. See *Report of Tribunal appointed by An Taoiseach on December 22, 1969,* dated August 5, 1970, Dublin, Stationery Office, Prl. 1363.
4. The legal representation before the Tribunal is set out in chapter 1 of *Report of Tribunal, ibid.* The Tribunal is noted, *inter alia,* for the distinguished quality of the 32 barristers who appeared before it, many of whom have since attained judicial rank.
5. *Report of Tribunal, ibid,* para 136.
6. *Ibid.,* para 15.18.
7. "Censorship and RTE", *The Crane Bag,* vol. 8, no. 2, 1984, p. 63.
8. Letter dated July 13, 1970 from the Minister for Posts and Telegraphs read in full by Dr. Conor Cruise O'Brien, Minister for Posts and Telegraphs on Committee Stage of the *Broadcasting Authority (Amendment) Bill 1975,* 288 *Dáil Debates,* cols. 995- 998, March 2, 1976.
9. Letter dated July 17, 1970, read by Dr. Conor Cruise O'Brien at 288 *Dáil Debates,* cols. 998-1000.
10. *Ibid.,* col. 1000.
11. *Ibid.*
12. *Ibid.,* col. 1000. In 1976, Gerard Collins, TD, then in opposition considered that the then Minister for Posts and Telegraphs, Dr. Conor Cruise O'Brien, was wrong to read out confidential letters between one Minister and another in Government, 288 *Dáil Debates,* col. 1003, March 2, 1976.
13. *1974 Report, loc. cit.,* para 15.4.
14. *Ibid.,* para 15.9.

15. *Ibid.*, para 15.11.
16. S. 18(1) of *Broadcasting Authority Act, 1960* as amended by substitution by s. 3 of the 1976 Act.
17. S. 18(1)(c) *ibid.*
18. *Ibid.*, s. 18(1).
19. Ss. 9(1) and 18(1) of the *Radio and Television Act, 1988.*
20. See n. 16 supra.
21. Unreported, High Court, July 31, 1992, per O'Hanlon J, See *The Irish Times,* August 1, 1992; [1993] ILRM 458, (Supreme Court).
22. *Broadcasting Authority Act, 1960 (Section 31) Orders, 1990,* (S.I. No. 11 of 1990) and 1991 (S.I. No. 6 of 1991) which were in existence at the relevant time.
23. *Ibid.* n. 21.
24. *O'Toole v RTE* [1993] ILRM (Supreme Court) *per* the Chief Justice.
25. Majid Tehranian, *Technologies of Power: Information Machines and Democratic Prospects,* Ablex Publishing Company, Norwood, NJ (1990) p. 237.
26. *Ibid.*
27. S. 18(1) of the *Broadcasting Authority Act, 1960* as amended by substitution by s. 3 of the *Broadcasting Authority (Amendment) Act, 1976;* s. 9(1)(a) and (b) of *Radio and Television Act, 1988.*
28. S. 18(1A) of *Broadcasting Authority Act, 1960* as amended by substitution by s. 3 of the *Broadcasting Authority (Amendment) Act, 1976;* s. 9 (1)(d) of *Radio and Television Act, 1988.*
29. S. 17(b) of *Broadcasting Authority Act, 1960* as amended by substitution by s. 13 of the *Broadcasting Authority (Amendment) Act, 1976;* s. 18(3)(b) of *Radio and Television Act, 1988.*
30. S. 18 of the *Broadcasting Authority Act, 1960* as amended by substitution by s. 3 of the *Broadcasting Authority (Amendment) Act, 1976.*
31. 18th Report (Prl. 9945) May 7, 1981, Stationery Office, Dublin.
32. 1981 Report, loc. cit, para 119.
33. *Broadcasting Guidelines for RTE,* 1989, p. 51.
34. 1981 Report, loc. cit. para 120. However, s. 18(1) of the *Broadcasting Act, 1960* as amended by s. 3 of the *Broadcasting Authority (Amendment) Act, 1976* provides that should it prove impractical in a single programme to apply impartiality, two or more related broadcasts may be considered as a whole, provided that the broadcasts are transmitted within a reasonable period.
35. See s. 18(1) of 1960 Act, *loc. cit.*
36. 1981 Report, *loc. cit.*, paras 122, 123 and 126.
37. *Ibid.*, para 129.
38. *Ibid.*, Evidence, Question 362.
39. *Ibid.*, Evidence, Question 363.
40. Dr. Conor Cruise O'Brien, "Why We Must Call Murder "Murder"; *Irish Independent,* April 3, 1993; Dr. C. Cruise O'Brien, "Avoiding Terrorists", *Irish Independent,* April 9/10 1993; statement of Frances

Fitzgerald, TD, under the heading of "RTE is Accused of 'Falsifying Reality'", April 3, 1993 and Dr. C. Cruise O'Brien, "The Selective Historical Tradition and the Terrorists", *Irish Independent*, April 17, 1993.

41. *Ibid.*
42. S. 18(1) of the *Broadcasting Authority Act, 1960* as amended by s.3 of the *Broadcasting Authority (Amendment) Act, 1976*, in relation to RTE; ss 9(1) and 18(1) of Radio and Television Act, 1988 in relation to the private commercial broadcasting services.
43. S. 9(2) of *Radio and Television Act, 1988*.
44. 47 U.S.C. s. 315.
45. 26 FCC 715, R.R. 701 (1959); *Daly v United States*, 286 F 2d. 146, (7th Cir. 1961). The Court stated the FCC letters that had formed the basis of the fairness rulings were interpretative opinions of the Commission and were to be regarded as formal orders of the Commission from which appeals could be taken.
46. 47 U.S.C. s.315 (1959).
47. S. 18B-1 of the *Broadcasting Authority Act, 1960* as amended by insertion by s.4 of the *Broadcasting Authority (Amendment) Act, 1976*. See chapter 22.
48. S. 18B(11A) of the *Broadcasting Authority Act, 1960* as amended by insertion by s.8 of the *Broadcasting Act, 1990*.
49. *AG v Paperlink Ltd* [1984] ILRM 373; *AG ex rel McWhirter v Independent Broadcasting Authority* [1973] 1 QB 629.
50. *Scots Law Times*, November 16, 1979, p. 279. In *Lynch v BBC* [1983] NI, 193 Hutton J considered that the was no legal duty enforceable by the courts on the BBC to act with impartiality as between political parties. It should be noted that the primary instruments of regulation of the BBC are a Royal Charter and a licence granted by the Home Secretary. See also *Marshall v BBC* [1979] 1 WLR 1071 C.A. and *McAliskey v BBC* [1980] NI 44, ChD In *R v Horseferry Magistrates Court* [1986] 2 All ER 666, Lloyd LJ considered in relation to an alleged breach of statutory duty by the IBA (section 4(3) of the UK *Broadcasting Act, 1981* that the doctrine of contempt of statute did not apply to that statutory provision. A private individual had issued a summons against the IBA claiming contempt of statute on the basis of breach of statutory duty.
51. C. 19.
52. See, for example, *O'Mahony v RTE*, High Court (per Barron J) unreported *The Irish Times*, September 14, 1985; *Century Radio v RTE*, High Court, (per Murphy J.) unreported, *Irish Independent*, February 23rd, 1990, and *[X] v RTE*, Supreme Court, unreported, *The Irish Times*, March 29, 1990, where the Supreme Court refused to grant the plaintiff an injunction restraining RTE from naming him as a person who allegedly had been in the Birmingham bombings in 1974 in a television programme to be broadcast that evening. The case, however, related to alleged defamation; the reasoning of the Supreme

Court has been criticised in R. Byrne and W. Binchy, *Annual Review of Irish Law 1990*, Dublin, Round Hall Press, p. 535.

53. *O'Toole v RTE*, unreported, High Court, July 31, 1992, per O'Hanlon J [1993] ILRM 458, Supreme Court only.

54. See reference supra.

55. See *[X] v RTE* and other cases in note 52.

56. The precise authority for the FCC's Fairness Doctrine is uncertain but s. 315(a) of the *Federal Communications Act of 1934*, 47 U.S.C. referred, inter alia, in a non-directive sense to the obligation on broadcasters in connection with the presentation of newscasts, news interviews, news documentaries, and on-the-spot coverage of news events "to operate in the public interest and to afford reasonable opportunity for the discussion of conflicting views on issues of public importance".

57. 412 US 94 (1973).

58. *Ibid.*, 110-111.

59. *Syracuse Peace Council*, 2 FCC. Rcd. 5043, 5057 (1987).

60. *Ibid.*, at pp. 5048-58.

61. The FCC, *ibid*, relied here on *FCC v League of Women Voters*, 468 US 364 (1984) where the US Supreme Court indicated a basis for reconsidering its application of the First Amendment to the electronic media because of the transformation of the telecommunication marketplace by the new technology.

62. See Jerome A. Barron, "What Does the Fairness Doctrine Controversy Really Mean?" 12 *COMM/ENT* (Winter 1989) 205-244.

63. *Syracuse Peace Council*, 867 F 2d at 669 (DC Cir 1989).

64. *National Broadcasting Co v FCC*, 516 F 2d 1101, 1192-11 (1974).

65. *CBS v Democratic National Committee*, 412 US 94, 117 (1973) (Burger CJ concurring).

66. Foreword to J. O'Reilly and M. Redmond, *Cases and Materials on the Irish Constitution*, Incorporated Law Society of Ireland, 1980, p. xii.

67. *Bridges v California*, 314 US 252 (1941).

68. *Ibid.* at 282. This balancing of First Amendment interests was embraced by a majority of the US Supreme Court in *American Communications Association v Douds*, 339 US 382 (1950).

69. *Red Lion Broadcasting Co. v FCC*, 395 US 367, 392 (1969).

70. *Ibid.*, at 392.

71. *Editorialising by Broadcast Licensees*, 13 FCC 1249 (1949).

72. *United States v Associated Press*, 52 F Supp 362, 372. (SDNY 1943)

73. Judge Learned Hand, "A Plea for the Open Mind and Free Discussion", in *The Spirit of Liberty*, New York, Alfred A. Knopf, 1953, p. 284.

74. *Abrams v United States*, 250 US 616, 630 (1919) (dissenting opinion of Justice Holmes).

75. *Associated Press v United States*, 236 US 20. (1945).

76. Jerome A. Barron, "Access to the Press — A New First Amendment Right", 80 *Harvard Law Review* (1967); J.A. Barron, *Freedom of the Press*

for Whom? The Right of Access to Mass Media, Bloomington, Indiana University Press, 1974; J. A. Barron, "What Does the Fairness Doctrine Controversy Really Mean?", 12 *Comm/Ent LJ*, 205-244 (1989).

77. Justice White delivering the opinion of the US Supreme Court in *Red Lion Broadcasting Co. v FCC*, 395 US 367 (1969).
78. S. 18(1) of the *Broadcasting Authority Act, 1960* as amended by substitution by s. 3 of the *Broadcasting Authority (Amendment) Act, 1976*.
79. The concept of "due accuracy and impartiality" is enshrined in UK legislation. See s. 6(1)(c) of the *Broadcasting Act, 1990* (c. 42).
80. S. 9(1)(b) of the *Radio and Television Act, 1988*.
81. See, for example, the debates in the House of Lords on the UK *Broadcasting Bill, 1990*, 521 *Hansard* (Lords) cols. 10-1767 and 522 *Hansard* (Lords) 154-1903.
82. S. 6(1)(d) of the UK *Broadcasting Act, 1990* (c.42).

31: Prohibitions on Advertising on the Broadcast Media

1. S. 20(4) of the *Broadcasting Authority Act, 1960* and s. 10(3) of the *Radio and Television Act, 1988*.
2. 7 & 8 Geo. 5 c. 21.
3. "The RTE Code of Standards for Broadcast Advertising" is set out in *Broadcasting Guidelines for RTE Personnel*, RTE, 1989. The code published by the Independent Radio and Television Commission is entitled *Codes of Standards, Practice and Prohibitions in Advertising and other Forms of Commercial Promotion in Broadcasting Services*.
4. Report of the *Television Commission 1959*, Dublin, Stationery Office, para 111.
5. 52 *Seanad Debates*, cols. 475-475, February 10, 1960.
6. *Ibid.*, col. 476.
7. *Ibid.*
8. *Ibid.*
9. Para 6 of Second Schedule to *Television Act, 1954* (c.55).
10. Dublin, Stationery Office, 1974 Prl. 3827, para 8.4.
11. *Ibid.*, para 8.14.
12. *Ibid.*, para 8.6.
13. *Report of the Committee on the Future of Broadcasting*, London, HMSO, Cmnd 6753, p. 163.
14. *Loc. cit.*, para 8.7.
15. *Ibid.*, para 8.15.
16. 120 *Seanad Debates*, cols. 1064-1065, June 22, 1988.
17. S. 6(1)(d) of the UK *Broadcasting Act, 1990*.
18. *Ibid.*, s. 7(1)(b).
19. 120 *Seanad Debates*, cols. 1064-1065, June 22, 1988. See similar provisions in the UK *Broadcasting Act, 1990*, ss. 8 and 9 in relation to television and ss. 92 and 93 in relation to radio.
20. Council Directive of 3 October 1989 on the co-ordination of certain

provisions laid down by law, regulation or administrative action in Member States concerning the pursuit of broadcasting activities 89/552/EEC.

21. See Bibliography at end of book.
22. See *Pittsburgh Press Co v Pittsburgh Comm'n on Human Relations*, 413 US 376, 385 (1973).
23. See *Central Hudson Gas & Elec Corp v Public Service Comm'n*, 447 US 557, 561 (1980).
24. In *Virginia State Board of Pharmacy v Virginia Citizens Consumer Council*, 425 US 748 (1975), the US Supreme Court held that commercial speech did in fact deserve constitutional protection, but that the State could regulate such speech in certain circumstances. See also *Dun and Bradstreet v Greenmoss*, 472 U.S. 749, 758 n.5 (1985); *Central Hudson Gas & Elec Corp v Public Service Comm'n on Human Rights*, 413 US 376, 385 (1973); *Ohralik v Ohio Bar Association*, 436 US 447 (1978).
25. S. 20(4) of the *Broadcasting Authority Act, 1960* and s. 10(3) of the *Radio and Television Act, 1988*.
26. See the words expressed in s. 6(d) of the UK *Broadcasting Act, 1990* (c.42). For a US perspective, see Note, "Televangelism and the Federal Communications Commission: To regulate or Retreat", 91 *Dick L Rev* 553 (1986).
27. See n. 25 above.

32: *Whither Now?*

1. Delivered at the Massachusetts Institute of Technology in October 1990.
2. *Ibid.*
3. See chapter 30.
4. See chapter 26.
5. See chapter 31.
6. [1987] IR 587, 593.
7. *United States v White*, 401 US 745, 786 (1971).
8. 277 US 438.
9. *Ibid.*
10. *Katz v United States*, 389 US 351 (1967).
11. The idea of a constitutional amendment in the context of the US Constitution has also been suggested by Professor Laurence H. Tribe, Tyler Professor of Constitutional Law, Harvard Law School. See "US: The Consequences of Digital Electronics and the Constitution", *Inter Media*, May-June 1991, vol. 19, No. 3.

Table of Cases

Table of Pre-Union British Statutes, British Statutes up to 1922, Statutes of Saorstát Éireann and Public General Acts of the Oireachtas of Ireland

Table of Other Statutes

Table of Statutory Instruments

Table of Constitutions, Treaties, Declarations, Conventions, and European Communities Legislation

League of Nations

United States

Bibliography

Adams, M., *Censorship: The Irish Experience*, Alabama, University of Alabama Press, 1968.

Allen, C., *Telegraph Cases Decided in the Courts of America, Great Britain and Ireland*, New York, Hurd and Houghton; Cambridge: The Riverside Press, 1873.

Allen, T., "The National Television Radio Link Network", in *Technical Journal*, Spring 1987, Dublin, Telecom Éireann.

Andison, F.S., "TV Violence and Viewer Aggression: A Cumulation of Study Results 1956-1976", *Public Opinion Quarterly*, 41, 314-331, 1977.

Ang, P.H., "A Proposed Free Speech Model for the Computer Bulletin Board", a paper presented to the International Communications Association Annual Conference, Trinity College, Dublin, June, 1990.

Article 19, *No Comment (Censorship, Secrecy and the Irish Troubles)* Article 19, (The International Centre on Censorship), London, 1989.

Aspinall, A., *Politics and the Press 1780-1850*, Home and Van Thal, 1949.

Atkin, D. "Indecency Regulation in the Wake of Sable: Implications for Telecommunication Media", a paper presented to the International Communication Association Annual Conference, Trinity College, Dublin 1990.

Atiyah, P.S., "Common Law and Statute Law", (1985), 48 *MLR* 1.

Bagehot, W., *The Work and Life of Walter Bagehot*, 1915.

Baker, E., "Scope of the First Amendment Freedom of Speech", 25 *University of California in Los Angeles Law Review*, 964 (1978).

Baldwin R and McCrudden, C., *Regulation and Public Law*, London, Weidenfield and Nicolson, 1987.

Barendt, E., *Freedom of Speech*, Oxford, Clarendon Press, 1985.

_____, "The Influence of the German and Italian Constitutional Courts on their National Broadcasting Systems", [1991] *Public Law*, 1991, 93-115.

Barron, J.A., "Access to the Press — A New First Amendment Right", 80 *Harvard Law Review*, 1967.

_____, *Freedom of the Press for Whom? The Right of Access to Mass Media*, Bloomington, Indiana University Press, 1974.

_____, "What does the Fairness Doctrine Controversy Really Mean?" 12 *Comm/Ent L.J.* (Hastings Communications and Entertainment Law Journal), 1989, 205-244.

Bate, S de B., *Television by Satellite — Legal Aspects*, Oxford ESC Publicity Ltd, 1987.

Batelle-Geneva Center for Applied Economics, *Competition vs Monopoly in Telecommunications: The Case of Enhanced Services and Customer Premises Equipment: A Note on the Debate in Europe*, Geneva, 1985.

Baumol, W.J., "On the Proper Cost Tests for National Monopoly in a Multi-Product Industry", *American Economic Review*, vol 67, no. 51 December 1977.

Berger, V., *Case Law of the European Court of Human Rights*, vol. 1 (1959 to 1987) and vol 2, (1988-1990), Dublin, The Round Hall Press.

Besley, M. and Laidlaw, B., *The Future of Telecommunications (An Assessment of the Role of Competition in UK Policy)*, London, Institute of Economic Affairs, 1989.

Bollinger, L., *The Tolerant Society*, Oxford University Press, 1988.

Bonham-Carter, M, "Whose Service", 17 *Index on Censorship*, September, 1988.

Boswell, J., *Life of Samuel Johnson*, London, 1791, (many subsequent editions).

Brennan, T.J., "Economic Efficiency and Broadcast Content Regulation", 35 *Fed. Comm. L.J.*, 117, (1983).

Briggs, A., *The BBC (The First Fifty Years)*, Oxford, Oxford University Press, 1985.

Bright C., *Submarine Telegraphs*, London, 1896.

British Broadcasting Corporation, Written Archives, Archives Centre, Caversham, UK.

British Parliamentary Papers.

Broadcasting Complaints Commission, *Reports of the Broadcasting Complaints Commission 1977 to date*, Broadcasting Complaints Commission, Dublin.

Broadcasting Research Unit, *The Public Service Idea in British Broadcasting*, London.

Brooks J., *Telephone: The First Hundred Years*, New York, Harper & Row, 1975.

Brown, R., *Telecommunications*, London, Aldus Books, 1969.

Bruce, R., (and others), *The Telecom Mosaic (Assembling The New International Structures)*, London, International Institute of Communications, Butterworths, 1988.

_____, *From Telecommunications to Electronic Services, (Report of the Study of Telecommunications Structures)*, London, International Institute of Communications, Butterworths, 1986.

Byrne, G., *To Whom it Concerns, Ten Years of the Late Late Show*, Dublin, Torc Books, 1972.

Byrne R., and Binchy, W., *Annual Review of Irish Law*, 1987 to 1992, Dublin, The Round Hall Press.

Carnegie Commission Report on the Future of Public Broadcasting, *A Public Trust*, New York, 1979.

Carr, J.G., *The Law of Electronic Surveillance*, Second Edition, New York, Clark Boardman, 1986, with annual releases.

Carmichael, E.G.M., *The Law Relating to the Telegraph, Telephone and Submarine Cable*, London, Knight & Co., 1904.

Cathcart, R., *The Most Contrary Region (History of the BBC in Northern Ireland)*, Belfast, The Blackstaff Press, 1984.

Christus Rex (Journal of Sociology), *The Media of Social Communication*, Christus Rex, vol. XIX, No. 1, Maynooth, 1965.

Clark, D.G. and Hutchison, E.R., *Mass Media and the Law: Freedom and Restraint*, New York, Wiley — Interscience, 1970.

Clark, R., *Data Protection Law in Ireland*, Dublin, Round Hall Press, 1991.

Clarke, A.C., *1984 Spring (A Choice of Futures)*, London, Granada Publishing Ltd, 1984.

Coase, R.H., "The Federal Communication Commission", 2 *J.L & Econ*, 1, 17 (1959).

Codding, Jr., G.A., and Rutkowski, A.M., *The International Telecommunications Union in a Changing World*, Washington, Artech House, 1982.

Cogan, D., de, (University of East Anglia, Norwich, England), "Dr. E.O.W. Whitehouse and the 1858 Transatlantic Cable", 10 *History of Technology*, 1985, 1-15.

_____, "From Technical Wonder to Profitable Investment: The Economics of 19th Century North Atlantic Telegraphy", paper presented to the American Historical Association, Fall Meeting, October 1986, (not published).

_____, paper entitled "Cable Landings In and Around Newfoundland", (not published).

_____, paper entitled "The Early History of British Empire Communications", (not published).

_____, "James Graves and the Valentia Telegraph Station", *Electronics and Power*, July, 1984.

_____, paper entitled "An Introduction to the Technology of the Valentia Cable Station", 1986, not published.

_____, "The Commercial Cable Co. and their Waterville Station", IEE History of Technology Weekend, Trinity College, Dublin, July, 1987.

_____, paper entitled, "The Bewleys and their Contribution to Transatlantic Telegraphy, a Preliminary Report", IEE History of Technology Weekend, Trinity College, Dublin, July 1987.

_____, paper entitled "Development of the Distributed Sea Earth in Transatlantic Telegraphy", *IEE Proceedings*, vol. 134, Pt. A. No. 7, July 1987.

_____, "Ireland and the Physics of Submarine Telegraphy", Science in Ireland 1800-1980, Tradition and Reform, Trinity College, Dublin, 1988.

Coke's Inst. 3. 181 c. 85.

Collins, A.M., "Commercial Speech and Free Movement of Goods and

Services at Community Law", in J. O'Reilly, (ed), *Human Rights and Constitutional Law, Essays in Honour of Brian Walsh*, Dublin, The Round Hall Press, 1992.

Comment, "On Privacy, Pen Registers and State Constitutions: The Colorado Court Rejects Smith v Maryland", 15 *U. Tol. L. Rev.* 1467 (1984).

Comm/Ent Law Journal (since 1987 designated as Hastings Comm/Ent L.J.) a journal of communications and entertainment law, Hastings College of Law, University of California, 1978 to date.

Communications and the Law (legal periodical) Westpoint, (USA) and London, Meckler Publishing, 1979 to date.

Cooley, T., (Judge), *Cooley on Torts*, (U.S.) 2nd edition, 1888.

Crump, D., (and others) *Cases and Materials on Constitutional Law*, New York, Matthew Bender, 1989, with supplement.

Curran, J., (and others), (eds), *Mass Communication and Society*, London, Edward Arnold, 1977.

Curran, J., and Seaton, J., *Power Without Responsibility (The Press and Broadcasting in Britain)*, 3rd ed, London, Routledge, 1988.

Dáil Debates, Dublin, Stationery Office.

Denvir, J.P., "The Dole Bill: Freeing the Telephone Company Seven", 9 *Comm/Ent L.J.* 113, (1986).

Diamond, J.L., and Primm, J.L., "Re-discovering Traditional Tort Typologies to Determine Liability for Personal Injuries: From the Mickey Mouse Club to Hustler Magazine", 10 *Comm/Ent L.J.* 969-997.

Dibner, B., *The Atlantic Cable*, New York, Blaisdell Publications, 1964.

Dowling, J., and Doolan, L., *Sit Down and Be Counted*, Dublin, Wellington Publishers Ltd, 1969.

Dunlap, O.E., *Communications in Space*, New York, Harper & Row, 1962.

Duval, B., "Free Communication of Ideas and the Quest for Truth: Towards a Technological Approach to First Amendment Adjudication", 41 *George Washington Law Review*, 161 (1972).

Dwyer, J.M., "The Role of Satellite Communications in the Development of the Irish Telecommunications Network 1984/1986", Dublin, Department of Posts and Telegraphs, 1983.

_____, "Communications via Satellite" in *Engineering in Telecom Éireann*, Dublin, Telecom Éireann, 1984.

Electric and International Telegraph Company, *Government and Telegraphs, Statement of the case of the Electric and International Telegraph Company against the Government Bill for Acquiring Telegraphs*, May, 1868 (pamphlet).

Fanning, R., *The Irish Department of Finance*, 1922-1958, IPA, 1978.

_____, "II Thou shalt not annoy thy Minister", *Sunday Independent*, October 1, 1989.

_____, "The Section 31 Debate: Political Weapons of the Future", *Sunday Independent*, August 2, 1992.

Farrell B., (ed.), *Communications and Community in Ireland*, Cork, Mercier Press in collaboration with RTE, 1984.

Farrer, *The State in Relation to Trade*, 1902.

Fawcett, H., "Modern Socialism" in *Essays and Lectures*, London, 1872.

Fawcett, J., *Outer Space, New Challenge to Law and Policy*, Oxford University Press, 1984.

Federal Communications Law Journal, (legal periodical) School of Law, University of California, Los Angeles, 1937 to date.

Feeney, P., "Censorship and RTE", *The Crane Bag*, vol 8 No. 2, 1984, 19.

Fennelly, N. "The Irish Constitution and Freedom of Expression", in D. Curtin and D. O'Keeffe, (eds.), *Constitutional Adjudication in European Community and National Law*, Dublin, Butterworths, 1992.

Ferguson, M., (ed.), *New Communication Technologies and the Public Interest*, London, Sage, 1986.

Field, H.M., *History of the Atlantic Telegraph*, New York, 1865.

Fisher, D., *Broadcasting in Ireland*, London, Routledge and Kegan Paul, 1978.

Fisher, D., and Harms, L.S., *The Right to Communicate: A New Human Right*, Dublin, Boole Press, 1982.

Flynn, L., "Locating the Missing Link: Postal Communication Monopolies in Ireland and EC Law", 10 *ILT* (ns) (1992) 233 and 247.

Foster, R., "Century's Stars Fail to Shine", *The Irish Times*, May 22, 1990.

Fowler, M., and Brennan, T.J., "A Marketplace approach to Broadcast Regulation", 60 *Tex. L. Rev.*, 207 (1982).

Fowler, M., *Remarks before the Thomas Jefferson Award Dinner*, February 19, 1982, 10 *Comm/Ent LJ*, 435.

Franklin, M.A., *Cases and Materials on Mass Media Law* (2nd ed.) New York, The Freeman Foundation Press, 1982 with 1985 supplement.

Freedman, J.L., "Effect of Television Violence on Aggressiveness", *Psychological Bulletin*, 96, 227.

Friedrich-Cofer, L., and Huston, A.C., "Television Violence and Aggression: The Debate Continues", *Psychological Bulletin*, 100, 364-371, 1986.

Fuhr, "Competition in the Terminal Equipment Market After Carterfone", 28 *Antitr Bull*, 699, (1983).

Garvey, L.M., "The Elfordstown Earth Station", *Technical Journal*, Spring 1987, Dublin, Telecom Éireann.

Geller, H., "The FCC under Mark Fowler; a Mixed Bag", 10 *Comm/Ent L.J.* 521, (1987-88).

Gellhorn, E., and Pierce, R.J., *Regulated Industries*, St. Paul, Minnesota, West Publishing Co., 1982.

Gibbons, L., "From Megalith to Megastore Broadcasting and Irish Culture", in Bartlett, T., (ed), *Irish Studies*, Dublin, Gill and Macmillan.

Gibbons, T., *Regulating the Media*, London, Sweet & Maxwell, 1991.

Ginsburg, D.H., *Regulation of Broadcasting* (American Casebook Series), St. Paul, Minnesota, West Publishing Co. 1979 with 1983 Supplement.

Godet, M., & Ruyssan, O., *The Old World and the New Technologies*, Luxembourg, Commission of the European Communities, 1981.

Gorham M., *40 years of Irish Broadcasting*, Dublin, RTE, Talbot Press Limited, 1967.

Graves J., (First Superintendent at Valentia Telegraph Station), *Thirty Six Years in the Telegraph Service*, unpublished technical autobiography, The original manuscript is in the possession of the Graves family.

Greenawalt, K., *Speech, Crime and the Uses of Language*, New York, Oxford University Press, 1989.

Haiman, F.S., *Freedom of Speech*, Skokie, Illinois, National Textbook Co., 1978.

Hall, E.G. and McGovern, P.J.C., *Irish Report, Europe and the Media*, F.I.D.E. and Nederlandse Vereniging voor Europees Recht, 1984.

Hall, E.G., and McGovern, P.J.C., "Regulation of the Media: Irish and European Community Dimensions", (1986) 8 *DULJ* (ns).

Hall, E.G., and McGovern, P.J.C., Annotation to Broadcasting and Wireless Telegraphy Act, 1988, *Irish Current Law Statutes Annotated*, London, Sweet & Maxwell.

Hall, E.G., and McGovern, P.J.C., Annotation to the Radio and Television Act, 1988, *Irish Current Law Statutes Annotated*, London, Sweet & Maxwell.

Hand, L., *The Spirit of Liberty*, New York, Alfred A. Knopf, 1953.

Handell S., *The Electronic Revolution*, Penguin, 1967.

Harms, L.S., Richstad, J., and Kie, K.A., (eds.), *The Right to Communicate; Collected Papers*, Honolulu Social Sciences and Linguistics Institute, University of Hawaii at Manoa, 1977.

Harms, L.S., and Richstad J., (eds.), *Evolving Perspectives on the Right to Communicate*, Honolulu: East-West Center, East-West Communication Institute, 1977.

Hogan, G.W., and D. Morgan, *Administrative Law*, (2nd ed.), London, Sweet & Maxwell, 1991.

Hogan, G.W. "Constitutional Interpretation", in the special issue of F. Litton (ed.), *Administration*, vol. 35 no. 4, 1987 entitled, *The Constitution of Ireland 1937-1987*, pp. 173-191.

_____, "Federal Republic of Germany, Ireland and the United Kingdom: Three European Approaches to Political Campaign Regulation", 21 *Capital University Law Review*, 1.

Holcombe, A.N., *Public Ownership of Telephones on the Continent of Europe*, London, Constable & Co. Ltd, Houghton Mifflin Company, 1911.

Holdsworth, W., *A History of English Law*, 1903 (subsequent editions).

Horgan, J., "1930s Campaign for Private Radio", *The Irish Times*, September 29, 1983.

Horwitz, R.B., *The Irony of Regulatory Reform: The Deregulation of American Telecommunications*, New York, Oxford, Oxford University Press, 1989.

Huesmann, L.R., "Psychological Processes Promoting the Relation Between Exposure to Media Violence and Aggressive Behaviour by the Viewer", *Journal of Social Issues*, 42, 125-139.

Huffman, J.L., and D.M. Trauth, "Dial-A-Porn and the Conservative Rehnquist Court: The Sable Decision as an Example of Judicial Restraint", a paper presented to the International Communication Association Annual Conference, Trinity College Dublin, June 1990.

Hutchinson, A.C., "The Rise and Ruse of Administrative Law and Scholarship", 48 *Modern Law Review*, 293, (1986).

Independent Radio and Television Commission, *Codes of Standards, Practice and Prohibitions in Advertising and Other Forms of Commercial Promotion in Broadcasting Services*, Dublin.

Ingber, S., "The Marketplace of Ideas: A Legitimising Myth", (1984) 25 *Duke Law Journal*, 1.

International Commission for the Study of Communication Problems (chaired by Sean MacBride), *Many Voices, One World*, London, Kogan Pages Ltd; New York, Unipub; Paris, UNESCO, 1980.

International Institute of Communications (11C), *Reforming the Global Network*, London, IIC, 1989.

_____, "U.S: The Consequences of Digital Electronics and the Constitution", *Intermedia*, May-June 1991.

International Telecommunication Union, *From Semaphore to Satellite*, ITU, Geneva, 1965.

_____, *Great Discoveries: Telecommunications*, Geneva, ITU, 1991.

Irish Communications Review, 1991- , Dublin, Institute of Technology, College of Commerce, Rathmines, Dublin.

Irish Broadcasting Review, (1978-1983) RTE, Dublin.

Jacob, P., and Toscano, J.V., (eds.), *The Integration of Political Communities*, 1964.

Johansen, P.W., "The Canadian Radio — Television Commission and the Canadianisation of Broadcasting", 26 *Fed. Comm. L.J.* 183 (1973).

Johnston, N., *The Public Interest and Private Broadcasting: Looking at Communications as a Whole*, Warrenton, Virgina, USA, Airlie House, 1967.

Johnston T., "Expert Systems and Public Policy" *Inter Media*, Journal of the International Institute of Communications, July-September 1984, vol. 12, p.43.

Jowell, J., "Broadcasting and Terrorism, Human Rights and Proportionality", [1990] *Public Law*, 149.

Justice, *Freedom of Expression and the Law*, London, Justice, 1990.

Kalven, H.(Jr), *A Worthy Tradition: Freedom of Speech in America*, New York, Harper & Roe, 1988.

Kieve J., *The Electric Telegraph, A Social and Economic History*, David & Charles, Newton Abbot, 1973.

Kelly, J.M., *Fundamental Rights in Irish Law and Constitution*, 2nd edition, 1968.

_____, "Are our Broadcasting Structures Out of Date?", *Irish Broadcasting Review*, Summer 1978, p.6.

Kelly, J.M., with G.W. Hogan and G. Whyte, *The Irish Constitution*, 2nd edition with supplement, Jurist Publishing Co., 1987.

Kingsford-Smith, D., and Oliver, D., (eds.), *Economical with the Truth: The Law and Media in a Democratic Society*, Oxford, ESC Publishing, 1990.

Kitner, E.W., *An Antitrust Primer*, 2nd ed., New York, Macmillan, 1973.

Kommers, D.P., *The Constitutional Jurisprudence of the Federal Republic of Germany*, Duke University Press, Durham and London, 1989.

Lambert, R.S., *Ariel and All His Equality — an Impression of the BBC from Within*, London, Gollancz, 1940.

Larsen, E., *Telecommunications, A History*, London, F. Mullen Ltd, 1977.

Lee, P., *Current EC Legal Developments: Public Procurement*, Butterworths, 1992.

Lester, A., and Pannick, D., *Advertising and Freedom of Expression in Europe*, London, International Chamber of Commerce, 1984.

Litton, A.J., "The Growth and Development of the Irish Telephone System", *Journal of the Statistical and Social Inquiry Society of Ireland*, 1961-1962.

Lundstedt, S.B., *Telecommunications Values and the Public Interest*, New Jersey, Ablex Publishing Corp. 1990.

McGonagle, M., "[O'Toole] Judgment Might Return Section 31 To Its Rightful Place", *The Irish Times*, August 3, 1992.

McKenna, R.B., and Sylter, R.L., "The Modification of Final Judgment: An Exercise in Judicial Overkill", 9 *Comm/Ent L.J.* 13. (1986).

McLoone, M., and MacMahon, J., (eds.), *Television and Irish Society*, RTE/IFI, 1984.

McLuhan, M., *Understanding Media*, The Extensions of Man, London, Routledge and Kegan Paul, 1964.

McMahon, B., and W. Binchy, *The Irish Law of Torts*, 2nd ed., Dublin, Butterworths, 1992.

McRedmond, L., *Written on the Wind*, (Personal Memories of Irish Radio 1926/1976), Dublin, RTE, Gill and Macmillan, 1976.

McWhinney, E., (ed.), *The International Law of Communications*, New York, Oceana, 1971.

Meiklejohn, A., "The First Amendment is an Absolute", 1961 *Sup. Ct. Rev.* 245,253-263.

Merrett, J., *Three Miles Deep*, London, Hamish Hamilton, 1958.

Mill, J.S. *Principles of Political Economy*, London, 1848, (many subsequent editions).

_____, *On Liberty*, London, 1859, (many subsequent editions).

_____, *Utilitarianism, Liberty and Representative Government*, London, 1861 (many subsequent editions).

Milton, J., *Areopagitica*, London, (1644), (many subsequent editions).

Mullen, A., "The Development of Telecommunications Technology in the Irish Post Office", paper read to the Institute of Engineers in Ireland, April 5, 1973.

Mulryan, P., *Radio Radio (The Story of Independent Local Community and Pirate Radio in Ireland)*, Dublin, Borderline Publications, 1988.

Munro, C.R., *Television Censorship and the Law*, Saxon House, 1978.

_____, "The Broadcasting Complaints Commission", [1983] *Public Law*, 37.

Murphy, J.A. "The Section 31 Debate: Expose the Bankruptcy of their Violent Views", *Sunday Independent*, August 2, 1992.

Nadel, M., "A unified Theory of the Fourth Amendment: Divorcing the Medium From The Message", *Fordham Law Journal*, February 1983.

Noam, E., Ithiel de Sola Pool Memorial Lecture 1990, Massachusetts Institute of Technology, 1990.

Nimmer, "Is Freedom of the Press a Redundancy: What does it Add to Freedom of Speech", 26 *Hast. L.J.* 639 (1975).

Note, Competition in the Telephone Equipment Industry: Beyond Telerent", 86 *Yale L.J.* 538 (1977).

Note "Televangelism and the Federal Communications Commission: To Regulate or Retreat", 91 *Dick L. Rev.* 553 (1986).

O'Brien, C. Cruise., "RTE Seems Sadly Lacking in Self-respect", *Irish Independent*, September 30, 1989.

_____, "The Section 31 Debate: No Grounds for an Appeal in O'Toole Case", *Sunday Independent*, August 2, 1992.

_____, "Why We Must Call Murder 'Murder'", *Irish Independent*, April 3, 1993.

_____, "Avoiding Terrorists", *Irish Independent*, April 9/10, 1993.

_____, "This Selective 'Historical Tradition' and the Terrorists", *Irish Independent*, April 17, 1993.

Ó Broin, A.P.G., "Cable Television Networks at Limerick and Shannon", *Technical Journal*, Spring 1987, Dublin, Telecom Éireann.

Ó Broin L., "The Dismissal of the Irish Broadcasting Authority", *European Broadcasting Review*, March 1973, p. 24.

_____, "Just Like Yesterday: An Autobiography", Dublin, Gill and Macmillan, 1986.

O'Dell, E., "Does Defamation Value Free Expression?" (1990) 12 *DULJ*, (n.s) 50.

_____, "Reflections on a Revolution in Libel", Part 1, 9 ILT, (n.s) 181, (1991); Part 2, 9 *ILT* (n.s.) 214 (1991).

_____, "Speech In A Cold Climate: The 'Chilling Effect' of the Contempt Jurisdiction", in Heffernan (ed.), *Perspectives on Human Rights in Ireland and Europe*, Dublin, The Round Hall Press, 1993 (forthcoming).

Ó hAllmhuráin, S., (ed.), *Aviation Communications Service, 1936-1986*, Dublin, 1986.

O'Hannrachain, F., "Privacy and Broadcasting", 10 *ILTSJ* 267 (1971).

O'Higgins P., "The Irish T.V. sackings", *Index on Censorship*, vol. 3 pt. 1 (1973) p. 24.

_____, *Cases and Materials on Civil Liberties*, London, Sweet & Maxwell, 1980.

O'Neill, J.W., "Telecommunications in Ireland during the First Half of the Twentieth Century", The Institute of Electrical Engineers, Irish Branch, paper read in Trinity College Dublin on February 15, 1951.

O'Reilly, J., and Redmond, M., *Cases and Materials on the Irish Constitution*, Dublin, Law Society of Ireland, 1980.

Parris, H., *Constitutional Bureaucracy*, Allen and Unwin, London, 1969.

Pastore, J.O., *The Story of Communications: From Beacon to Telstar*, New York, 1964.

Paterson, A., *The Law Lords*, London, Macmillan, 1982.

Pearl, D., Bouthilet, L., and Lazar, J., *Television and Behaviour: Ten Years of Scientific Progress and Implications for the Eighties* (vols. 1 & 2) U.S. Government Printing Office, Washington D.C. 1982.

Pearse, E., "Beyond Burke's Law", *Sunday Press*, July 8, 1990.

Perry, C.R., *The Victorian Post Office*, Suffolk, The Boydell Press, 1992.

Pirie, M., *Privatisation in Theory and Practice*, London, Adam Smith Institute, 1985.

Pitt, D.C., *The Telecommunications Function in the British Post Office* (A case Study of Bureaucratic Adaptation), London, Saxon House, 1980.

Ploman, E., *International Law Governing Communications and Information: A Collection of Basic Documents*, Frances Pinter (Publishers) Ltd, 1982.

Pool, I de Sola, (ed.), *The Social Impact of the Telephone*, The MIT Press, 1977.

_____, *Technologies of Freedom*, The Belnap Press of Harvard University Press, 1983.

_____, *Technologies Without Boundaries*, (edited by E.M. Noam) Cambridge Mass, Harvard University Press, 1990.

Posner, R., "Natural Monopoly and Its Regulation", 21 *Stan L Rev*, 548, (1969).

_____, *Economic Analysis of Law*, U.S. (3d ed. 1986). Post Office Central Archives, Post Office HQ., St. Martin Le Grand, London.

Postman, N., *Amusing Ourselves to Death*, London, Methuen, 1987.

Quinn, G., "The Systems Maintenance Function of Constitutional Rights and the Case of Government Speech", (1989) *ILT* (ns) 8.

_____, "The Right of Lawyers to Advertise in the Market for Legal Services: A Comparative American, European and Irish Perspective", 20 *Anglo-American Law Review*, 403, (1991).

_____ ",Theories of the 'Right' and the 'Good' and the Judicial Evolution of the Right to Privacy in the US and the Republic of Ireland", A paper delivered to a Law and Philosophy Meeting, Trinity College, Dublin, February 28, 1992.

Railway Times, Third Series, April 18, 1868, pp. 428-9 on the Nationalisation of the then telegraph business.

Rao, G., "The Italian Mass Media and the Role of the Judicial System", Paper presented to the 40th International Communication Association Annual Conference, Dublin, 1990.

Reith, J., *Into the Wind*, London, Hodder and Stoughton, 1949.

Robertson, G., *Freedom, the Individual and the Law*, London, Penguin Books, 1989.

Robertson, J.H., *The Story of the Telephone: A History of the Telecommunications Industry of Britain*, London, Pitman & Sun, 1947.

Robinson, M., "Paying Lip-Service to Freedom of Speech", *The Independent*, June 2, 1989, p.13.

Rosenthal, R. (ed), *McLuhan, Pro & Con*, Pelican Books, 1969.

Ryan, J., "Field Trial with Integrated Serviced Digital Nework (ISDN) in Telecom Éireann", *Technical Journal*, winter 1989/1990, Dublin, Telecom Éireann.

RTE, (Radio Telefís Éireann), *Annual Reports*.

RTE Working Party on Women in Broadcasting: Report to the RTE Authority, Dublin, RTE, April 1981.

RTE, *Broadcasting Guidelines for RTE Personnel*, RTE, 1989.

Savage (Jr), *The Origin of Irish Radio*, unpublished M.A., thesis, Department of Modern Irish History, UCD, 1982.

Scherer, J., "European Telecommunications Law: The Framework of the Treaty", *European Law Review*, October, 1987.

Schwartz, L.B., "Forum and Substance: Introduction to the Symposium on the Divestiture of American Telephone and Telegraph Company", 9 *Comm/Ent L.J.* 1 (1986).

Schwartz, I.E., "Broadcasting and the EEC Treaty", 1986, 11 *European Law Review*, 7-60.

Sheehan, H., *Irish Television Drama: A Society and Its Stories*, Dublin, RTE, 1987.

Shriffin, S., "Defamatory Non-media Speech and First Amendment Methodology", 25 *University of California in Los Angeles Law Review*, 915, 932 (1978).

Smith, A., *The Shadow in the Cave (The Broadcaster, the Audience and the State)*, London, Allen & Unwin, 1973.

_____, *The Politics of Information*, London, Macmillan, 1978.

_____, (ed.), *Television and Political Life (Studies in Six European Countries)*, London, Macmillian, 1979.

Studies, *What's The News*, vol. LXXIII, Autumn 1984, no. 291, Dublin, 1984.

Sussman, L.R., *Power, the Press and the Technology of Freedom (The Coming Age of ISDN)*, New York, Freedom House, 1989.

Tegg, W., *Posts and Telegraphs, Past and Present with an Account on the Telephone and Phonograph*, London, W. Tegg & Co., 1878.

Tehranian M., *Technologies of Power: Information Machines and Democratic Prospects*, Ablex Publishing Company, Norwood, N.J. (1990).

Telecom Éireann, *Annual Reports*, 1983.

_____, *Technical Journal*, a periodical journal, Spring 1986 to date.

Thomas, L., and R. LaRose, "I See You Calling But You Can't Come In: Telecommunications Privacy Policy and User Responses to Calling Party Information", a paper presented to the International Communication Association Annual Conference, Trinity College, Dublin, June 1990.

Thompson, B., "Broadcasting and Terrorism", [1989] *Public Law*, 527.

_____, "Broadcasting and Terrorism in the House of Lords", [1991] *Public Law*, 346-353.

Toffler, A., *Future Shock*, London, Pan Books, 1970.

_____, *The Third Wave*, Pan Books, 1981.

_____, *Previews and Premises*, Pan Books, 1984.

Travers, N., "Necessity and Chaos: How Constitutionally to Implement an EC Directive into Irish Law", 87 *Gazette ILSI*, 258 (1993).

Tribe, L.H., *American Constitutional Law*, 2nd ed, Mineola, The Foundation Press, 1978.

Tunstall, J., *Communications Deregulation: The Unlesahing of America's Communications Industry*, London, Basil Blackwell, 1986.

Ungerer, H., *Telecommunications in Europe*, Brussels, Commission of the European Communities, Revised edition, 1990.

Vail, T., "Public Utilities and Public Policy", 3 *Atlantic Monthly*, 307, March 1913.

Veljanovski, G.G., (ed), *Freedom of Broadcasting*, London, Institute of Economic Affairs, 1989.

Veljanovski, G.G., and Bishop, W.D., *Cable by Choice*, London, Institute of Economic Affairs, 1983.

Wadegaonkar, D., *The Orbit of Space Law*, London, Stevens and Sons, 1984.

Walsh, B., (Judge), "The Judicial Power and the Protection of the Right to Privacy", (1977) *DULJ* 3.

_____ ",The Irish Constitution and Fundamental Freedoms - 50 Years On", Lecture to the Irish Association of Law Teachers, December 4, 1987, University College, Dublin.

Warren, S.D., and Brandeis, L.D., "The Right to Privacy", 4 *Harvard Law Review*, 193 (1890).

Watt, D., *Law of Electronic Surveillance in Canada*, Toronto, Carswell Company, 1979, with supplements.

Webb, H.L., *The Development of the Telephone in Europe*, Electrical Press Ltd, London, 1911.

Webbink, D.W., "Radio Licenses and Frequency Spectrum Use Property Rights", *Comm.L.*, June 1987.

Wentam, B., *The Third Age of Broadcasting*, London, Faber and Faber, 1982.

Whale, J., *The Half-Shut Eye (Television and Politics in Britain and America)*, London, Macmillan, 1970.

_____, *The Politics of the Media*, London, Fontana, 1977.

Westin, A.F., *Privacy and Freedom*, London, The Bodley Head, 1970.

Wigmore, J., "Abrams v. US: Freedom of Speech and Freedom of Thuggery in War-Time and Peace-Time", 14 *Illinois Law Review*, 539 (1920).

Williams, P.J., "Metro Broadcasting Inc v FCC: Regrouping in Singular Times", 104 *Harvard Law Review*, 525-546.

Williams, R., *Television: Technology and Cultural Form*, Fontana, 1974.

Wilson, B.J., Linz, D., and Randall B, "Applying Social Science Research to Film Ratings: A Shift from Offensiveness to Harmful Effects", paper presented to the Mass Communication Division at the International Communication Association Convention, Trinity College, Dublin, 1990.

Woodman, K., *Media Control in Ireland 1923/1983*, Galway, Officina Typographica, Galway University Press, 1985.

Worthington, J.R., "The Case for Continued Judicial Enforcement of the AT&T Decree", 9 *Comm/Ent L.J.* 75 (1986).

Zuckman, H.L., *Mass Communications Law* (3rd ed.) St. Paul, Minnesota, West, 1988.

Official Publications

IRELAND

Dáil Reports.

Seanad Reports.

Reports of the Dáil Special Committee on Wireless Broadcasting, First Interim Report, Dáil Report, sgd. January 1924; Second Report, Dáil Report, Dáil Report 1 of 1924 sgd January 1924; Third Interim Report, Dáil Report 4 of 1924, sgd January 1924; Final Report, Dáil Report 6 of 1924, sgd. March 1924.

Report of the Television Commission, 1959, Dublin, Stationery Office. (The chairman was The Hon. Mr. Justice G.D. Murnaghan.)

Report of Public Services Organisation Review Group 1966-1969, Dublin, Stationery Office, 1969.

Report of Tribunal appointed by An Taoiseach on December 22, 1969, (Money-Lending Tribunal) dated August 5, 1970, Dublin, Stationery Office, (Prl. 1363).

National Prices Commission, (A Study by Kader Asmal), Consumer Councils in Public Enterprise, Dublin, Stationery Office, (Prl. 2506) 1972.

Broadcasting Review Committee Report 1974, (Prl. 3827), Dublin, Stationery Office, (Prl 3827) under the chairmanship of Mr. Justice G.D. Murnaghan.

National Prices Commission, Monthly Report No. 53 (July 1976), which, inter alia, sets out a summary of main conclusions reached by consultants into RTE, Dublin, Stationery Office, (Prl. 5634), 1976.

Report of Posts and Telegraphs Review Group 1978-1979, Dublin, Stationery Office (Prl. 7883), 1979.

Reorganisation of Postal and Telecommunications Services (Green Paper) laid by the Government before each House of the Oireachtas, May 1980, Dublin, Stationery Office, (Prl. 8809).

Reorganisation of Postal and Telecommunications Services, (White Paper) laid by the Government before each House of the Oireachtas, May, 1981, Dublin, Stationery Office, (Prl. 9905).

Investment Plan 1981, laid by the Government before each House of the Oireachtas, January 1981, Dublin, Stationery Office, (Prl. 9471).

Joint Oireachtas Committee on State-sponsored Bodies, 18th Report, RTE,

Dublin, Stationery Office, (Prl. 9945) May 7, 1981.

Report of the Cable Systems Committee, Dublin, Stationery Office, (Pl. 2937), 1984.

Houses of the Oireachtas, Joint Committee on Legislation, Proposals for Legislation: Local Radio Authority, (Hearing of Oral Submissions: Minutes of Evidence) December 7, 13, 20, 1983, 10, 17, January 1984, February 14, 1984, Dublin, Stationery Office.

Review of Radio Telefís Éireann (Report to the Minister for Communications by Stokes, Kennedy Crowley), Dublin, Stationery Office, (Pl. 3494), 1985.

Restrictive Practices Commission, Report of Study Into Cable Television Systems in the Greater Dublin Area, 1986, Dublin, Stationery Office, (Pl. 4295), 1986.

Houses of the Oireachtas, Joint Committee on Commercial State-Sponsored Bodies, Seventh Report, Bord Telecom Éireann, (Pl. 4718) 1987.

Department of Tourism, Transport and Communications, Telecom Inquiry, Dublin, Stationery Office, 1991.

Glackin, J.A., Chestvale Properties Limited and Hoddle Investments Limited, Interim Report, July 1992 (Pl. 9061) and Final Report, July 1993 (Pl. 9989) Dublin, Stationery Office.

Law Reform Commission (Ireland)

Consultation Paper on the Civil Law of Defamation, Dublin, March, 1991.

Report on the Civil Law of Defamation, Dublin, December, 1991.

Report on the Crime of Libel, Dublin, December 1991.

European Communities

Green Paper on Television, Television Without Frontiers, COM (84) 300, 14 June 1984.

Towards a Dynamic Economy: Green Paper on the Development of the Common Market for Telecommunications Services and equipment, COM (87) 290.

Towards a Europe-wide Systems and Services; Green Paper on a Common Approach in the Field of Satellite Communications in the European Community, COM (90) 490, 20 November 1990.

Guidelines on the Application of EEC Competition Rules in the Telecommunications Sector (91C/233/02) OJEC, 6 September 1991.

1992 Review of the Situation in the Telecommunications Services Sector, Communication by the Commission, Brussels, 21 October 1992.

United Kingdom Reports

Hansard Debates, Lords and Commons.

British Parliamentary Papers.

Report from the Select Committee on Railway Communications, July 1840, SCR 1840.

Report from the Select Committee on Telephones together with the Proceedings of the Committee, Minutes of Evidence and Appendix ordered by the House of Commons to be printed August 9, 1898, London, HMSO.

The Post Office - A Historical Summary, HMSO, London, 1911.

Broadcasting Committee Report (Cmnd. 1951), 1923 (The Sykes Report).

Report of the Broadcasting Committee, 1925, (Cmnd 2599), 926 (The Crawford Report).

Report of the Committee on the Future of Broadcasting, (The Annan Report), London, HMSO, (Cmnd. 6753) 1977.

Broadcasting, London, Home Office, (Cmnd 7294) 1978.

Liberalisation of the Use of British Telecommunications Network, Department of Industry, (Michael E. Beesley Study) London, HMSO, 1981.

Report of the Inquiry into Cable Expansion and Broadcasting Policy, (Chairman: Lord Hunt) London, HMSO, (Cmnd 8679), 1982.

Report of the Independent Review of the Radio Spectrum (30-960 MHz) (Chairman Dr. J.H.H. Merriman) London, HMSO, (Cmnd 9000), 1983.

Davies, E., Telecommunications, A Technology for Change, London, HMSO, 1983.

House of Lords Select Committee on the European Communities, Television Without Frontiers, London, HMSO, (HL 43), 1985.

Deregulation of the Radio Spectrum in the UK, Department of Trade and Industry (CSP International Study), London, HMSO, 1987.

Radio: Choices and Opportunities (A Consultative Document), London, HMSO, (Cm 92), 1987.

Home Office, Broadcasting in the '90s: Competition, Choice and Quality, (The Government's Plans for Broadcasting Legislation), London, HMSO, (Cm 517) 1988.

Calcutt Report on Privacy and Related Matters, London, HMSO, (Cm 1102).

Competition and Choice, Telecommunications Policy for the 1990s, London, HMSO, (CM. 1461), 1991.

Calcutt Review of Press Self-Regulation, London, HMSO (Cm 2135, 1993).

Canada

Royal Commission on Broadcasting Report, 1957.

Instant World, Telecommunications Report, Ottawa, Information Canada.

Inter American Court of Human Rights

To License A Journalist? Perspectives on Freedom, New York, Freedom House, 1976.

Organisation for Economic Co-operation and Development (OECD)

Trends of Change in Telecommunications Policy, OECD, Paris 1987. An Explanation of Legal Issues in Information and Communication Technologies, OECD, Paris, 1987.

United States

US Government

Cabinet Committee on Cable Communications — Report to the President, Washington, D.C., Government Printing Office, 1974.

US House of Representatives, Telecommunications in Transition: (The Status of Competition in the Telecommunications Industry), Washington, US Government Printing Office, 1981.

NTIA Telecom 2000, Charting the Course for a New Century, National Telecommunications and Information Administration, US Department of Commerce, Washington, D.C., 1988.

Federal Communications Commission (FCC)

FCC, Mayflower Broadcasting Corp., 8 FCC 333 (1940).

FCC, Use of Recording Devices, 11 FCC, 1033, (1947).

The Fairness Doctrine: In the Matter of Editorialising by Broadcast Licensees, 13 FCC 1246, June 1, 1949.

FCC, Lar Daly, Decision 26 FCC 715, R.R. 701 (1959).

FCC Procedures on Transfer and Assignment Applications, Report and Order, 32 FCC 2d 689, (1962).

FCC, Carterfone Device, 13 FCC 2d 420, 14 FCC 2d 571, (1968).

Registration Program , 56 FCC, 2d 593 (1975), 58 FCC 2d 736 (1976).

Second Computer Inquiry, 77 FCC 2d. 384, reconsid., 84 FCC 2d. 50, (1981), further reconsid., 88 FCC 2d 512 (1981), aff'd sub. nom Computer & Communications Indus. Assoc v FCC, 693 F. 2d 198 (D.C. Cir. 1982).

FCC Public Notice, "Commission Will Not Appeal Quincy Cable T.V.", released August 5, 1985.

FCC Syracuse Peace Council, 2 FCC. Rcd. 5043, (1987).

Sources from the National Archives, Dublin

File S.1933, D/T, "Posts and Telegraphs, Proposed Termination of Ministry, 1922".

File S.5111/3 Messages from Radio Stations: Broadcasting in President's Name".

File S.4174, "P.O. Proposed Transfer of P.O. Services in Six Counties to Belfast Government".

File S.3394, D/T, "Post Office; Wireless Licences for Ships Registered in Saorstát Éireann".

File S. 3669, D/T, "Wireless Stations in Saorstát Éireann".

File S.3157, D/T, "Disconnection of Certain Trans-Atlantic Cables".

File TW.8348, D/C, vol. 2, "Wireless Telegraphy Act 1904: Adequacy or Otherwise of Powers: Semi-Official Correspondence with British P.O".

File S.4717, D/T, "Wireless Telegraphy Act, 1926".

File S. 5234, D/T, "Wireless Broadcasting: Restrictions in the Irish Free State (1926-1927)".

File S. 3532A, D/T, "Wireless Broadcasting in Ireland - Establishment and Organisation of".

File S. 9520A, D/T, "Sponsored Broadcasting".

File S. 2726A, D/T, "Broadcasting - High Power Station in Cork".

File S. 3532B, D/T, "Wireless Broadcasting in Ireland, Establishment and Organisation Of".

File S. 5111/11, "President's Speech at Opening of Athlone Broadcasting Station" (February 6, 1933).

File S. 11992 "Communications - External and Internal, Emergency Measures in the Event of Invasion or Internal Attack".

File S.3532C, D/T, "Wireless Broadcasting in Ireland: Establishment and Organisation".

File S. 7321 "Broadcasting Dáil Proceedings".

File S. 9908A, D/T, "Broadcasting, Political".

File S. 9908 B/1, B/2, D/T, "Radio and Television: Political Broadcasts".

File S.13773A, D/T, "National Culture, Proposed Permanent Council, Proposed Cultural Minister".

File S.13756, D/T, "Irish Language Broadcasting".

File S.10436B, D/T, "Broadcasting in the Cause of Peace: International Convention".

File S.9092D, D/T, "Shortwave Broadcasting Stations, 2 July 1951 to 15 May 1956".

File S.7480B, D/T, "Director of Broadcasting".

File H.6225/54, vol 1, D/Comm, (R & B), "Statutory Board for Broadcasting".

File 82/56, vol. 3, D/Comm, (R & B), "Proposals re Broadcast of Religious Services".

File H.6225, vol. 14, D/Comm, (R & B) "Proposals for Establishment of Statutory Board".

File S. 11586A "Censorship of Publications (including newspapers and periodicals)".

File S. 14946 A2, D/T, "Post Rates: General, Telegraph Bill 1953".

File TW.3756, vol. 8, D/Comm, (R & B), "T.V. Commission, First Meeting, 9 April 1958".

File TW 3756, vol. 5, D/Comm. (R & B), "Television Commission: Interim Report".

File S. 14996A and B, D/T "Television: General".

File TW.894, vols 2 and 3, D/Comm, (R & B), "Television: Memorandum to Government etc".

File 3755, vol. 4, D/Comm, (R & B) "Television Commission: copy of main Memorandum to Government," (which contains the First Ad Interim Report of Coimisiún um Athbheochan na Gaeilge dated March 20, 1959 (English version).

File TW 894, vol. 6, D/Comm, (R & B) "Report of Television Commission; Memorandum for Government, 1959".

File TW 6049, vol 10, D/Comm, (R & B), "Broadcasting Authority Bill, 1959, Minister's Speech in Dáil, Brief etc".

File S. 516748B, "Broadcasting Authority Legislation 1959".

File S. 16772A, D/T, "Television Films: Censorship".

File S.16748A, D/T, "Broadcasting Authority Legislation 1959".

File S. 9908, C/61, D/T "Radio and Television: Political Broadcasts".

Index